# Economics, values, and organization

In this path-breaking book, economists and scholars from other disciplines use standard economic tools to investigate the formation and evolution of normative preferences. The collection's premise is that an adequate understanding of how an economy and society are organized and function cannot be reached without an understanding of the formation and mutation of values and preferences that determine how we interact with others. Its chapters explore the two-way interaction between economic arrangements or institutions and preferences, including those regarding social status, the well-being of others, and ethical principles. Contributions have been written especially for this volume and are designed to address a wide readership in economics and other disciplines. The contributors are leading scholars who draw on such diverse fields as game theory, economic history, the economics of institutions, and experimental economics, as well as political philosophy, sociology, and psychology, to establish and explore their arguments.

# Economics, values, and organization

Edited by

**AVNER BEN-NER**
*University of Minnesota*

**LOUIS PUTTERMAN**
*Brown University*

CAMBRIDGE UNIVERSITY PRESS
Cambridge, New York, Melbourne, Madrid, Cape Town, Singapore,
São Paulo, Delhi, Dubai, Tokyo, Mexico City

Cambridge University Press
32 Avenue of the Americas, New York, NY 10013-2473, USA

www.cambridge.org
Information on this title: www.cambridge.org/9780521774116

First published 1998
Reprinted 1999
First paperback edition 1999

A catalog record for this publication is available from the British Library

ISBN 978-0-521-58087-8 Hardback
ISBN 978-0-521-77411-6 Paperback

# Contents

# Foreword

*Amartya Sen*

In Shakespeare's *King John*, the Bastard ridicules the narrowly self-interested behavior of his fellow royalty: "Since kings break faith upon commodity, / Gain, be my lord, for I will worship thee."[1] Shakespeare evidently thought that people *could* behave in other – nicer – ways, and many of his characters (indeed most of them) give evidence of having a variety of norms and values.

In contrast, many economic models tend to proceed as if the assumption of universal pursuit of self-interest is the only motivation that can be legitimately presumed in serious economic analysis. In this imagined world, the *homo economicus* has, it would appear, not only taken over from the Neanderthals, but has turned everyone, in the Bastard's words, into "smooth-faced gentlemen, tickling commodity."

Why the near-ubiquity of this assumption? Are economists not aware of other motivations, other concerns that human beings have? The editors of this illuminating and innovative collection of papers (Avner Ben-Ner and Louis Putterman) argue that we economists know more than we betray in our formal writings. In motivating the project, the editors mention that they had been struck by the fact that "norms, values, and the effects on these of historical processes are frequently mentioned" by academic economists in informal discussions (for example, "in casual conversations over meals"). But Ben-Ner and Putterman are also struck by the recognition that these issues tend to be "absent from the formal analyses" of economists. It is not that economists do not know about – or take an interest in – matters of values and norms. They do. But something holds us back, they argue, from paying attention to these "moral sentiments" in our formal economic work.

Ben-Ner and Putterman speculate that "economics disregards these

[1] William Shakespeare, *The Life and Death of King John*, act 2, scene 2, 598–99.

vii

issues because they do not arise logically from the fundamental premise that underlies most economic research, that of *homo economicus.*" The world is made to fit this momentous assumption, rather than the assumption being made to fit the world. The analytical discipline that confines itself to such constricted behavioral regularity is, by now, very extensively developed, with many technical achievements to its credit. This has tended to make the limiting assumption seem robust and natural. The analytical tools and the tradition of exacting and rigorous analysis associated with formal economics also militate against departures that may appear to be mushy and soft. The exclusion of moral sentiments is, thus, hard to alter in mainstream economics.

### The program and the project

The editors, however, argue – this time more cheerfully – that the "time may have arrived" by now "when the questions of values and institutions can begin to be attacked using available and emerging analytical tools, without loss of rigor, but with much gain in relevance and generality." The basic task, thus, which the editors' program involves, is one of *adaptation*: how to make fuller use of contemporary economic analysis both (1) to take more note of the *influence* of norms and values, and (2) to have more investigation of the *formation* of values and norms. The book is the result of an initial project – and a conference – within this general program.

The editors have been particularly keen on extending modern economic analysis beyond standard limits – to address issues of moral, social, and indeed economic sophistication. They have been particularly keen on exploring "the possibilities for a research agenda that treats values as partly endogenous to the economic system, and economic systems and their performances as partly functions of people's values." The conference and the essays resulted from this attempt.

I shall not try to describe the main findings. The chapters are not only interesting and often innovative, they are also extremely accessible and easy to read. They are arranged in five substantial parts, followed by a characteristically insightful and stimulating essay, in the form of an Epilogue, by Douglass North (an economist who has consistently tried hard to broaden the reach of contemporary economics). The five parts deal respectively with "The Formation and Evolution of Social Norms and Values" (Robert Sugden, Ken Binmore, Chaim Fershtman and Yoram Weiss, and Jane Mansbridge); "The Generation and Transmission of Values in Families and Communities" (Nancy Folbre and Tom Weisskopf, Samuel Bowles and Herbert Gintis, Timur Kuran, and John

Michael Montias); "Social Norms and Culture" (Robert Frank, Susan Rose-Ackerman, and Viviana Zelizer); "The Organization of Work, Trust, and Incentives" (Ernst Fehr and Simon Gächter, Andrew Schotter, Jonathan Baron, and Russell Hardin); and "Markets, Values, and Welfare" (Bruno Frey and Robert Lane). The editors provide a useful guide to the volume in their Preface, and discuss in their own chapter (Chapter 1: "Values and Institutions in Economic Analysis") the background and the framework of their project and the way the findings presented here can be best interpreted and understood.

### Three complementarities

While I shall refrain from trying to comment individually on the wide-ranging chapters – theoretical and applied – included in this collection of studies, I would like to take this opportunity to make a few general comments on three significant distinctions relevant to accommodating values and norms in economic analysis. The distinctions are, I believe, important to seize in order to interpret and understand the literature, and even to appreciate the tasks which the contributors to this volume have undertaken. The comments deal with general principles rather than specific applications.

In particular, I would argue that what may appear to be "either–or" dichotomies are not in fact so, and that it is especially important to examine the *complementarities* between apparently exclusive choices in each of the three divergences to be considered.

(1)     *Complementarity between reflective selection and evolutionary selection*

Norms and values are subjected to reflection and rational selection, as Immanuel Kant and Adam Smith both emphasized.[2] Kantian principles of "categorical imperative" and Smithian discipline of "the impartial spectator" are among the prominent procedures that have been suggested with respect to the ways we can – and do – reason about what norms to accept and act on. The selection here is conscious, critical, and can be intensely volitional. In contrast, in modern "evolutionary" theory, social choice emerges through survival, and this process of natural selection works through ex post consequences in the world at large rather

---

[2] Immanuel Kant, *Critique of Practical Reason* (1788), trans. L. W. Beck (New York: Bobbs-Merrill, 1956); Adam Smith, *The Theory of Moral Sentiments* (1970), republished, eds. D. D. Raphael and A. L. Macfie (Oxford: Clarendon Press, 1975).

than through ex ante reflections in the mind of each person. The organizational and institutional alternatives are simultaneously selected along with valuational regularities.

There is no question whatsoever that the recent work on evolutionary theory, including the study of evolutionary games, has thrown much light on the way behavioral norms and values may get socially selected and manage to survive and flourish.[3] The question that arises is not the need for taking note of evolutionary selection, which is clearly important. But, once evolutionary survival is taken into account, must the burden of selection fall *entirely* on that process (with conscious selection reduced to simple endorsement of natural selection)? Why can't the two means of selection be both actively at work? Since human beings are reflective creatures who take their values and critical powers seriously, the role of conscious and scrutinized selection will not be obliterated merely because evolutionary selection is also going on. Critical reflection does not give immunity from evolutionary selection, but nor does evolutionary selection convert reflective beings into thoughtless automatons.

Similarly, the process of transmission of values need not take the form of selection by nonreflective survival only. Norms and mores are propagated and dispersed through a variety of processes, in which the influence of education as well as public debates and private discussions (inside and outside the family) can play significant parts. Even the imitation of standard behavior can extend the reach of reflection through making choices of different people interdependent. As Adam Smith noted, "Many men behave very decently, and through the whole of their lives avoid any considerable degree of blame, who yet, perhaps, never felt the sentiment upon the propriety of which we found our approbation of their conduct, but acted merely from a regard to what they saw were the established rules of behaviour."[4] The "approbation of conduct" associated with reflection has a reach that is not confined to each person separately.

The high reliance on reflective selection in the tradition of moral philosophy often irritates the evolutionary theorist. For example, Ken Binmore's elegantly irate attempt (in his book *Playing Fair*) at "deKanting" not merely Kant himself but also such contemporary moral thinkers as John Rawls can be seen as a significant critique of moral

---

[3] This acknowledgment does not eliminate the reasonableness of Robert Sugden's pointer, in this volume, to the possibility that even the *sustained* expectations and behavior patterns may not be invariably "socially beneficial."

[4] Smith, *The Theory of Moral Sentiments* (1976 ed.), p. 162.

philosophy's tendency to neglect consequential reasoning and to ignore the discipline of evolutionary selection.[5] But that critique should really suggest the need not so much to "deKant" anything, as to complement reflective selection by evolutionary analysis. The rules that we live by cannot be untouched by our critical reasoning, just as they cannot be uninfluenced by evolutionary selection. Acknowledgment of one influence does not eliminate the other.[6]

## (2)    *Complementarity between direct and indirect valuation*

In acting according to norms and values, we may be interested in their indirect and non-immediate effects, in addition to their immediate results (including direct moral satisfaction, or their contiguous prudential merits such as the pleasure at being well thought of by others). For example, we may refrain from grabbing the most comfortable chair at a party either because we think that such restraint is the right way to behave (based on a direct moral argument), or because we do not like the way people would look at us if we were to run to the comfortable chair to grab it before others (an immediate prudential concern). But in addition to these direct arguments, we may have indirect reasons for the same abstinence, such as avoiding the long-run consequences of our *reputation* as self-indulgent and weird chair-grabbers (a prudential concern involving the future).[7] The relevance and reach of indirect consequences (reputation effects, benefit from having and enjoying trust, reciprocal gains from gifts, etc.) have been well brought out by recent work in this area (including some presented here).

However, these findings should not serve as the basis for ignoring the direct arguments – moral as well as prudential. Even if the answer to the question (to borrow from Chaim Fershtman's and Yoram Weiss's chapter in this volume) "why do we care what others think about us?" can be given in terms of the material gains we make from being favorably viewed by others, this would not dismiss the reasonableness of worrying directly about what others think of us (it is indeed comforting to be well thought of, and may even give us some moral confidence that we are not behaving badly). Indirect effects complement rather than supplant direct concerns.

---

[5] Ken Binmore, *Playing Fair* (Cambridge, Mass.: MIT Press, 1994).

[6] I have tried to illustrate the two-way relationship in "Maximization and the Act of Choice," *Econometrica* 65 (July 1997).

[7] The example and the rich variety of the consequences involved are discussed in my "Maximization and the Act of Choice."

(3)     *Complementarity between ethics and prudence*

Many ethical rules can be extensively explained by their prudential role, for example, the fact that good moral reputation can be a great money maker. Recent work on the personal advantage from socially oriented norms and conduct has certainly thrown much light on non-moral ways of explaining moral behavior.[8]

The question that arises is whether this indicates that moral reasoning is redundant. This would be a complete non sequitur. Consider that we fully accept a demonstration that *even if* people were totally amoral (as far as deliberate thinking goes), moral rules of behavior would still emerge (through indirect effects, natural selection, etc.). This would be an important recognition, but this would not be the same as establishing that people *are in fact* amoral in their thinking and choice. A hypothetical exercise cannot establish an empirical regularity.

In fact, the two processes can each work separately and they can even work together. It is important to see how and why the prudential process can operate with or without moral reasoning, but this does not eliminate the actual role of moral reasoning itself.

### Concluding remarks

I end with two final remarks. First, in acknowledging the possibility of prudential explanation of apparently moral conduct, we should not fall into the trap of presuming that the assumption of pure self-interest is, in any sense, more "elementary" than assuming other values. Moral or social concerns can be just as basic and elementary. If someone asks you the way to the railway station, the elementary reason for giving the right answer (if you know it) is that you have been asked for a help which you can readily provide at little cost and that helping a person is reason enough in itself. This basic recognition is not disestablished by a demonstration that such conduct may be evolutionarily stable and in the long run prudentially beneficial even to you.

The prudential and the moral, the evolutionary and the reflective, and the indirect and the direct routes all have legitimacy of their own. The point is to enrich the possibilities of explanation and then to examine

---

[8] Jane Mansbridge, in her essay in this volume, gives reasons to think that norms cannot be grounded *solely* in self-interest. I shall not pursue this issue here, but for the purpose at hand, it is important to note that even if that is the case, the fact that a good deal of moral behavior can have prudential explanation is not a negligible achievement of the recent work on the reach of prudential concerns (Mansbridge need not, of course, deny this).

which combination may work best. There is no particular reason for an *a priori* bias in favoring one direction or the other.

Second, the complementarities I have tried to discuss in this Foreword are, I believe, particularly central for the general program of which this book of essays is an impressive outcome. Studying endogeneity of values and use of ultimately amoral, economic reasoning to explain and assess norms and principled conduct enriches our understanding of valued behavior. But there is no need, in this program, to lose the insights and understandings we have received from Kant, Smith, Bentham, Mill, and others (and from contemporary moral and social analysts). The essays included here do, in fact, show a variety of inclinations in the balancing of (1) direct and indirect reasoning, (2) reflective and evolutionary analyses, and (3) moral and prudential concerns. This makes the overall outcome of the book less neat, but I believe ultimately more rich as a result. We have much reason to be grateful to the editors as well as the authors.

# Preface

A few years ago, we participated in a conference in which core issues in the economics of institutions and organizations were discussed by academic economists (see the June 1993 issue of the *Journal of Comparative Economics*). We were struck then by the fact that norms, values, and the effects on these of historical processes were frequently mentioned during the paper sessions, yet were largely absent from the formal analyses of the papers. We noticed too that in casual conversations over meals, we found ourselves talking about problems such as crime, drug abuse, our declining sense of community, family instability, and the moral culture confronting our children, problems that seemed to be of great importance to our lives but that had little intersection with our economic analyses, though these purported to deal with the most basic institutional structures of society. Surely, we thought, how society organizes its economic life must have far-reaching consequences for such problems through its influence both on people's economic opportunities and incentives, and also on their normative attitudes and preferences. For instance, how much we invest in personal relationships may depend in part upon whether they promise dimensions of economic and physical security that are unavailable from the market and the state. But such investment decisions may also depend on how much we value the relationships in their own right, and on whether we believe that we can identify others who likewise do so. Both economic changes and changes in valuations and trust could alter our calculations, and one type of change may well impact upon the other. To take another example, whether corporations treat their employees in a manner designed to engender loyalty and consummate performance or rather as disposable inputs to production that can be moved or terminated in response to small changes in market

We thank several contributors for their comments on earlier versions.

conditions may depend substantially on the intensity of product market competition and financial market discipline facing firms, but it may also depend on what norms of employment are current, on whether employees are inclined to reciprocate loyalty, and on other value-related factors that could in turn be influenced by those more narrowly economic ones.

Why had economists not been addressing such issues in their research? Part of the answer is given by the disciplinary division of labor, whereby social issues of the kinds just mentioned are not the ordinary preoccupation of most economists, who focus instead on prices, productivity, costs, and revenues, leaving the treatment of values and related issues to other disciplines. But more important, perhaps, is the possibility that economics disregards these issues because they do not arise logically from the fundamental premise that underlies most economic research, that of *homo economicus*. Being, by assumption, bereft of concern for friend and foe as well as for right and wrong, and caring only about his own well-being, *homo economicus* cannot, by construction, be at the center of a meaningful theory of how and when behavior is influenced by ethics, values, concern for others, and other preferences that depart from those of standard economic models. While such an oversight might simply be accepted as a regrettable cost of intellectual specialization, the problem may be more serious, for the "human nature" that lies at the heart of most economic analyses may fail to describe accurately and usefully either the actual persons who are the subject of economic analysis or the potential persons that may develop as a result of their interaction with institutions and organizations that are under the control of economic decision makers.

Attempts have been made in the past to investigate the issues that concern this volume from an economic perspective, but the mainstream of economic scholarship has not been significantly affected by them. The time may have arrived, however – that this is indeed the case is a point argued in our discussion in Chapter 1 – when the questions of values and institutions can begin to be attacked using available and emerging analytical tools, without loss of rigor, but with much gain in relevance and generality.

We broached the question of the usefulness and timeliness of starting a discussion of values and institutions with a number of well-known economists and were greatly encouraged by their replies that a conference on these issues would be desirable and worthy of their moral support. With that support, we were able to secure the necessary financial and institutional backing to permit us to invite leading scholars in economics and other disciplines to participate in a conference on economics, values, and organization. Its broad theme, and that of the present volume, was the two-way interaction between (on the one hand) the values that help to shape people's behaviors as social actors and (on the other) the arrangements by way of which economic and social life are organized. Its premises were that the institutional structure of an economy and society are influenced by our values, which cause alternative arrangements to be differentially successful; and that the values that influence people's behaviors are in turn affected by the nature of the institutional environments within which they are socialized and in which they operate throughout their lives. Our aim has been *to explore the possibilities for a research agenda that treats values as partly endogenous to the economic system, and economic systems and their performances as partly functions of people's values.* These very general themes are raised at a time when many proclaim the fabric of modern society to be under stress due to a crisis of values.

The Conference on Economics, Values, and Organization took place at Yale University on April 19–21, 1996. It was an intense and exciting weekend, with about sixty scholars from economics and other disciplines and a small number of graduate students and journalists in attendance. Most of the chapters that make up the present volume are revised versions of papers presented at the conference.

The body of the book begins with our introductory chapter, "Values and institutions in economic analysis," which attempts to meet two objectives. First, we try to provide a more complete exposition of this volume's themes as we view them – a task begun only cursorily in this Preface. We do this, inter alia, by suggesting motivations for studying these topics, and by situating the project in the context of both contemporary economic analysis and current social discourse. The chapter's second aim is to offer some views about how human preferences and values might be modeled, and on the relationship between values and institutions. We argue that an understanding of this two-way relationship requires a more comprehensive characterization of human motivation than that which lies at the core of standard economic models, and that such a characterization may be arrived at without inviting methodological chaos if we are guided by empirically corroborated theories of genetic and cultural evolution. The chapter concludes with illustrative applications of our conceptual framework to the institutions of the family, the workplace, and social insurance mechanisms.

Part I, which follows, consists of four chapters on the formation and evolution of social norms and values. They explore, in turn, the questions of how norms evolve, of what the evolutionary underpinnings of justice and empathy are, and of why people care about how they are regarded by others. In "Normative expectations: the simultaneous evolution of institutions and norms," Robert Sugden lays the groundwork for a theory of normative expectations in which people are motivated in part by a desire to avoid the disapproval that, as a result of normal human psychology, is aimed at those who act contrary to the expectations and interests of others. He suggests that these desires and expectations sometimes deter people from acting in their strict self-interest, and thus have the "motivating force" to affect behavioral outcomes. However, Sugden rejects the idea that the normative expectations that arise and are sustained are primarily those that are "socially functional." If the conventions that norms support "are unintended consequences of self-interested behavior," he argues, "we seem to have no general warrant for assuming them to be socially beneficial."

In "A utilitarian theory of political legitimacy," Ken Binmore attempts to provide a "naturalistic" defense of utilitarianism as a normative foundation for social policy. Binmore offers a new evolutionary explanation for the intuitive appeal of the "veil of ignorance" (Rawls 1974; Harsanyi 1977) as a device for assessing the fairness of resource allocations. He argues that evolution invented the veil of ignorance as an equilibrium selection device for the game of life, and that the device was rendered feasible by the endowment of human beings with capacities to imagine themselves not only in their fellows' shows, but also with their fellows' preferences. The chapter studies conditions under which the use of the coordinating mechanism made possible by such empathy leads to the implementation of a weighted utilitarian outcome.

Perhaps the most important check on narrowly selfish behavior is the concern that the typical person has for how he or she is regarded by others (or the avoidance of disapproval, in the formulation of Robert Sugden). In "Why do we care what others think about us?" Chaim Fershtman and Yoram Weiss ask how such a concern could be viable in a world in which only the fit survive. They show that even though fitness may be determined only by monetary rewards, players who care about the social status that is conferred by behaving cooperatively relative to the average in society may earn higher average payoffs than do those who, not caring about status, routinely choose the uncooperative behavior in a prisoner's dilemma type of game.

Against the contention that human values can be derived ultimately only from self-interest, Jane Mansbridge argues for including in that derivation innate emotions, innate cognitive capacities and limitations, and the internal logic of a norm. In her "Starting with nothing: on the impossibility of grounding norms solely in self-interest," Mansbridge suggests that societies will need to invest less effort in creating an effective norm if they build on innate emotional proclivities, innate cognitive capacities, and the characteristic internal structure of existing master norms. Concern or love for others is innate; commitment to what one ought to do, or duty, is a primordial response to human interaction; and acquiescence to an embedded logic may function as an external constraint. None of these processes is adequately captured by "self-interest" as commonly understood.

Part II consists of four chapters on questions of values, families, and communities, which help to shift the analysis from the more general societal level marking Part I to social units intermediate between individual and society. The papers also highlight ways in which values, value-perpetuating institutions, or value changes may entail mixes of desirable and undesirable consequences. In "Did Father know best? Families, markets, and the supply of caring labor," Nancy Folbre and Tom Weisskopf discuss changes in the provision of care for children, the aged, and others. They argue that the growth of the market, including increased female labor force participation, has led to increased reliance on self-interested rather than other-interested motivations for the supply of care services, with contradictory effects. On the positive side there has been a reduction in the level of coercion imposed on women as caregivers, which is likely to have improved the quality of care services. On the negative side the increased role of self-interested motivations in the supply of care services has arguably reduced the quality of those services. Moreover, in a competitive market, altruistic caregivers are penalized in ways that discourage the formation of other-regarding norms and values. To address this problem, the authors call for social policies to enforce both male and female responsibilities for the provision of care services.

In "How communities govern: the structural basis of prosocial norms," Samuel Bowles and Herbert Gintis provide a model capturing the premise that certain kinds of cooperation may be sustainable only in groups small enough to be marked by repeated interaction among pairs of individuals, and by an ability to recognize who belongs to the group and shares in its cooperative norms. Such an arrangement is argued to have its negative side in the form of noncooperative or exploitative behaviors toward out-group members. They argue that community-like social structures have survived the growth of modern markets and states not because of social inertia or nostalgia, but because they meet real and present needs. Those who are concerned either to perpetuate or to eliminate the existence and characteristics of communities need first to understand them better, they suggest.

Timur Kuran proposes that moral values differ from other preferences, including moral preferences, in that individuals treat them as absolute requirements rather than as objectives subject to trade-offs and bound by opportunities. In "Moral overload and its alleviation," he suggests that societies commonly inculcate in their members values that they cannot satisfy, leaving them in a state of "moral overload." The resulting "moral dissonance" then stimulates collective efforts to alleviate that overload through means ranging from redemption opportunities to moral compartmentalization and moral reconstruction. Kuran ends his essay by observing that the *policy* of promoting multiculturalism will generate moral overload insofar as it makes people adopt values impossible to satisfy within existing physical and financial constraints. He predicts, on this basis, that the current American ideal of multiculturalism is unsustainable.

John Michael Montias's "Moral diversity and specialized values: some observations" discusses instances in which ethnic minorities might be seen as having constituted "moral" subgroups within larger economic and social systems. He considers the specialized division of labor that can arise in such circumstances, with both its mutual benefits and its potential dangers. The chapter raises the question of whether this particular form of "communalism" and "moral diversity" is on balance advantageous or disadvantageous to aggregate economic progress.

Economists are used to thinking of markets either as self-regulating or as subject to the regulation of the state, but such a conception overlooks the ways in which norms and social sanctions may circumscribe exchange relationships with or without state intervention. The three chapters constituting Part III look at selected aspects of social and cultural norms governing competition and exchange. Their themes include the social regulation of undesirable competition and the social distinctions between approved and disapproved exchanges, and between commercial exchange and gift giving. In "Social norms as positional arms control agreements," Robert Frank argues that some norms exist to attenuate competitive excesses that might otherwise be generated by "winner-take-all" competitions. He demonstrates that such contests can induce socially inefficient effort levels, so that there may be a common interest in moderating their intensity. He argues that while adherence to the norms which achieve such moderation can be collectively beneficial, such norms will tend to break down when enforcement via small-scale social networks is undermined by geographic mobility and other social or technological factors.

In "Bribes and gifts," Susan Rose-Ackerman discusses the distinctions between ordinary exchange, gift giving, and bribery. She interprets bribes as payments by third parties to induce an agent to disregard the interests of his principal and suggests that society outlaws such payments so as to improve the functioning of agency relationships, notwithstanding the fact that the briber's willingness to pay appears to signal a valuable alternative use for the resources in question. When social changes such as those associated with the modernization of a feudalistic economy cause previously acceptable patron–client interactions to be reclassified as bribery, she points out, the delineation of boundaries between gifts and bribes in the legal code may be at variance with that in the popular culture or in the private moral codes of key actors, and growing pains will accordingly be experienced by the economy and the state.

Using the example of a monetary transfer from a man to a woman, Viviana Zelizer argues that it is impossible to draw legal and ethical distinctions of the sort discussed by Rose-Ackerman without considering details of the relationship between the parties. In her "How do we know whether a monetary transaction is a gift, an entitlement, or compensation?" Zelizer suggests that three major variants of monetary transfers – gifts, entitlements, and payments for service – can be distinguished with reference to the emotional content and the duration of the relationship to which they are attached. The fashion in which the monetary transfer is executed, and its timing, vary across cultures.

The themes of Part IV are trust, reciprocity, commitment, and incentives in organizations. Its chapters provide new experimental evidence on the roles of trust and reciprocity in work organizations, review relevant literature from a more general standpoint, and examine the roles of individual and institutional commitment in organizations. In "How effective are trust- and reciprocity-based incentives?" Ernst Fehr and Simon Gächter report the results of a series of laboratory market experiments in which "firms" and "workers" were offered opportunities to engage in "reciprocal altruism" and "punishment." These opportunities, easily shown to be irrelevant if all agents behaved neoclassically, are capable of engendering Pareto superior outcomes when agents evince reciprocity-based behavior and expect other agents to do the same. Fehr and Gächter's agents exhibit such behaviors, offering costly rewards and "efforts" without enforceable promises of compensation, engaging in costly punishments of breaches of trust despite the impossibility of reputational benefits because of the one-shot nature of the interactions, and seeming in many instances to anticipate that such breaches will be punished, despite the lack of benefit to the punisher.

Andrew Schotter's chapter, "Worker trust, system vulnerability, and the performance of work groups," is also based on experimental evidence about employment settings, but this time ones in which compensation is based on the effort levels of *groups* of workers. A first-stage experiment is conducted using two distinct games, one designed to facilitate cooperative outcomes, the other to make them more difficult to achieve. The focus of the chapter is on the second stage, in which each group plays the same game. The author–experimenter's interest is in whether a group's experience in the first stage influences its second-stage behavior. The result suggests that a background of expectations conducive to the formation of trust among economic agents – such as that generated by playing the first-stage game – can indeed increase the attainment of cooperative outcomes in a subsequent setting.

Jonathan Baron, in his "Trust: beliefs and morality," argues that trust is important in many settings, in addition to the workplace emphasized in both of the previous chapters. Baron reviews a large body of literature from psychology and experimental economics that finds that trust is, in part, a belief about others, and also a behavioral disposition that can be learned, taught, and experientially accumulated.

The traditional political question Who is the custodian of the custodians? is often answered, The more virtuous. In his "Institutional commitment: values or incentives?" Russell Hardin argues that political leaders and bureaucrats do not have to be morally motivated in order for them to be good public servants. The behavior of self-interested individuals may be directed to the pursuit of organizational goals, in Hardin's view, through the maintenance of organizational norms (institutional commitments) that deter harmful collective action.

Part V deals with relationships between market incentives, values, and well-being. Its chapters suggest that the types of incentives that form the backbone of the market economy can have negative effects on preferences, either by weakening socially valuable intrinsic motivations or by leading people to a mistaken appraisal of their true interests. In "Institutions and morale: the crowding-out effect," Bruno S. Frey argues that there are important situations in which economic incentives act in a perverse fashion as a result of the crowding out of "intrinsic motivation." He provides evidence, in particular, that offering residents financial compensation for the siting of an environmentally risky project in their community seems to lower, rather than raise, their willingness to accept that siting – a willingness that is conceivably based on some sort of civic virtue or on reasoning that "someone must bear this cost." His other principal example concerns tax avoidance, which he finds to be statistically unrelated to the expectation of penalties, but significantly negatively related to the extent to which institutions of direct democracy are developed.

In "The joyless market economy," Robert Lane revisits Tibor

Scitovsky's (1977) inquiry into why increased economic well-being does not seem to translate into increased happiness. He reviews evidence from psychological research suggesting an increase in "dysphoria" and depression over a forty-five-year period in the United States and a concomitant decline in several components of self-reported "happiness." He argues that the market economy has been successful in raising the quantity and technical quality of the goods and gadgets that we consume but has induced preferences and behaviors that reduce, rather than increase, our happiness. The linkages among our economic institutions, our preferences, and our sense of well-being that are suggested by Lane are distinctly disquieting.

The book concludes with Douglass North's "Where have we been and where are we going?" The chapter, which expands upon North's conference keynote address, places the investigation of institutions and values in a historical evolutionary perspective. North points to the brevity of the era of modern economic development within the larger panorama of human social evolution and argues that institutional arrangements lie at the heart of any explanation of the phenomenon of economic change. He also argues that there is a need to understand human behavior in terms of the conceptions of the developing paradigms of cognitive and evolutionary psychology.

The chapters in this volume are bound together by several common assumptions and themes. First, all of them start their investigations with the individual and his or her decision making. Second, they recognize the centrality of self-interest but go on to ask whether there are other factors, or types of preferences, that give rise to behavior that differs from that characterized by self-interest only. Third, many of the chapters seek to ground their assumptions about individual motivation in scientific evidence, whether that associated with evolutionary theory, psychological studies, or experimental findings from economics. Fourth, they focus on interactions among individuals – be they coworkers, employers, neighbors, or members of their ethnic group. Fifth, they are concerned with ways in which the behaviors of individuals merge into social behaviors and institutions, and with the ways in which social norms and institutional arrangements feed back, in turn, upon the calculations and preferences of individuals. Sixth, most of the chapters consider the evolution over time of both individuals' preferences and their environments, a process that is ultimately recognized to involve a two-way interaction. Finally, all chapters cut across disciplinary lines, enriching economic discourse with insights from psychology, sociology, political science, philosophy, and even biology.

The subject of norms, values, and preference formation is increasingly attracting the attention of economists, as evidenced not only by the work presented in this volume but also by the recent surge in related work (much of it unpublished at the time of this writing). Yet this field of inquiry, now in its initial stages, still lacks a unified analytical framework and, as the contributors to this volume make clear, a common set of conclusions. In particular, there is little empirical evidence to support or refute various theoretical claims made in this volume. What difference does it make, in terms of concern for others or respect for norms, whether we live and work in a small versus a large community? Does the moral behavior of an employer affect employees' dispositions at work and after hours? Does education of one type or another affect moral preferences and behavior in economic and other settings? These and other questions, so easily disposed of on the pages of newspapers and in political speeches, continue to elude theoretical understanding and to await empirical resolution. This book suggests, however, that research on such topics may be quite productive, and that economists, in dialogue with scholars from other disciplines, may be ready to begin generating useful answers.

In a sense, the work presented here is the joint product of a collaborative community of scholars. In particular, the content of this book has been shaped not only by its authors, but also by the contributions made by all conference attendees, whether acting as formal discussants (identified by asterisks in the following) or making comments from the floor or outside formal sessions. Attendees at the conference, other than the authors, included the economists Kaushik Basu* (Cornell University), John Broome* (Bristol University), Catherine Eckel (Virginia Polytechnic and State University), Duncan Foley (Barnard College), Avner Greif* (Stanford University), Joel Guttman (Bar-Ilan University), Albert Hirschman (Institute for Advanced Studies), Bentley MacLeod (Boston College), Michael McPherson* (Macalester College), Alanson Minkler (University of Connecticut), Barry Nalebuff* (Yale University), Julie Nelson* (University of California, Davis), Mancur Olson* (University of Maryland), Talbot Page (Brown University), Jean-Philippe Platteau (University of Namur), Robert Pollak (Washington University), John Roemer* (University of California, Davis), Alvin Roth* (University of Pittsburgh), Ariel Rubinstein* (Tel-Aviv University), Ekkehart Schlicht* (University of Munich), Robert Shiller* (Yale University), Burton Weisbrod* (Northwestern University), Martin Weitzman (Harvard University), and Peyton Young* (Johns Hopkins University).

The exchanges at the conference were also enriched and enlivened by the active participation of scholars from other disciplines, including

Bruce Ackerman (Yale University Law School), Martin Daly (Psychology, McMaster University), Paul DiMaggio* (Sociology, Princeton University), Baruch Fischhoff* (Decision and Social Sciences, Carnegie-Mellon University), Shelly Kagan* (Philosophy, Yale University), David Kiron (Philosophy, Tufts University), Douglas MacLean* (Philosophy, University of Maryland, Baltimore), Theodore Marmor* (School of Organization and Management, Yale University), David Messick* (Kellogg School, Northwestern University), Charles Perrow* (Sociology, Yale University), and Ian Shapiro* (Political Science, Yale University), Robert Putnam (Government, Harvard University), who made a thought-provoking dinner presentation, and journalists Robert Kuttner (*The American Prospect*), Rick Perlstein (*Lingua Franca*), and David Warsh (*Boston Globe*).

A panel of distinguished scholars closed the conference with thoughts about the issues raised and the manner in which they had been addressed. The members of this panel, Allan Gibbard (Philosophy, University of Michigan), Daniel Kahneman (Psychology, Princeton University), Harrison White (Sociology, Columbia University), and Margo Wilson (Psychology, McMaster University), offered perspectives from moral philosophy, experimental psychology, organizational sociology, and evolutionary psychology. Their contributions underscored the necessity and feasibility of an interdisciplinary approach to the study of values and institutions, and the need to base our understanding of human nature on the full spectrum of available scientific evidence.

As editors we extend our thanks especially to the authors of the chapters collected here. To a person, they showed exceptional discipline in keeping to the deadlines of the conference and volume, so that the work could be brought out with as short as possible a lapse of time. We offer our sincere thanks for their cooperation and trust. Cambridge University Press's readers, who made comments at various stages of this project, also helped to improve individual chapters and the entire volume.

We extend our thanks to Amartya Sen not only for his thoughtful Foreword, but also for his early support of our project. For such support, we are likewise grateful to Kaushik Basu, Jon Elster, Daniel Hausman, Douglass North, Mancur Olson, John Roemer, Ariel Rubinstein, and Ekkehart Schlicht.

Finally, we would like to thank Ian Shapiro, Director of Yale's Program on Ethics, Politics and Economics, which hosted our conference, and Amrit Singh, who coordinated preparations for it. We also thank the Olmsted Fund in the Program on Ethics, Politics and Economics, Yale's Kempf Fund and Institution for Social and Policy Studies, and the

MacArthur Foundation, for the financial support that made this project possible. And we thank Samar Barakat, who assisted in preparing this volume, and our editor, Scott Parris, and the others at Cambridge University Press who provided valuable suggestions and without whose help this volume could not have been published so expeditiously.

REFERENCES

Harsanyi, John (1977). *Rational Behavior and Bargaining Equilibrium in Games and Social Situations*. Cambridge: Cambridge University Press.
Rawls, John (1971). *A Theory of Justice*. Cambridge, Mass.: Harvard University Press.
Scitovsky, Tibor (1977). *The Joyless Economy: An Inquiry into Human Satisfaction and Consumer Dissatisfaction*. New York: Oxford University Press.

# Contributors

**Jonathan Baron** is Professor of Psychology and has been at the University of Pennsylvania since 1974. His research concerns two questions: How can we measure subjective utilities accurately? What intuitions stand in the way of maximizing utility socially or individually? Examples of such intuitions are those that distinguish omission and commission. His books include *Thinking and Deciding* (1994), *Morality and Rational Choice* (1993), *Psychological Perspectives on Justice* (co-edited with Barbara Mellers, 1993), and *Personal Intuition, Public Failure* (forthcoming).

**Avner Ben-Ner** is Professor and Director of the Industrial Relations Center, Carlson School of Management, University of Minnesota, and has previously taught at the State University of New York at Stony Brook, the University of California at Davis, the University of Tel Aviv, and Yale University. His research focuses on the determinants and consequences of the organization of different types of firms, the structure of economic systems, and the evolution of preferences. He is the coauthor of *Comparative Economics* (1994) and coeditor of *The Nonprofit Sector in the Mixed Economy* (1993), and has published articles in a number of anthologies and journals including the *Journal of Comparative Economics*, the *American Economic Review*, and the *Yale Law Journal*.

**Ken Binmore**'s career as an economist began after his appointment to the Chair of Mathematics at the London School of Economics in 1976. His early nonmathematical work was in bargaining theory. He then turned to the foundations of game theory and experimental economics. Currently he works on evolutionary game theory and political philosophy as Director of the Center for Economic Learning and Social Evolution at University College London. He is the author of some fifty published papers and ten books. His ambition is to be taken seriously as a philosopher by the philosophy profession.

**Samuel Bowles** teaches economics at the University of Massachusetts. He received his doctorate from Harvard University in 1965 and taught there until 1972. With Herbert Gintis he wrote *Schooling in Capitalist America* and *Democracy and Capitalism: Community, Property and the Contradictions of Modern Social Thought*, as well as scholarly articles on the economics of education, microeconomic theory, political philosophy, sociology, and Marxian economics. His current research concerns the evolution of preferences and norms and the economic sources of social inequality.

**Ernst Fehr** earned a Ph.D. in economics at the University of Vienna. Until 1994, he taught at the Technical University of Vienna and wrote numerous articles on labor market theory, in particular on the theory of involuntary equilibrium unemployment. Since 1991, he has worked in the field of experimental labor economics. Currently, his research is focused on reciprocity and coalition formation in competitive markets, the formation and enforcement of social norms, the regularities of boundedly rational behavior in intertemporal choice sitautions, and the extent and causes of nominal inertia in wage and price setting. He has published papers in a number of periodicals including *American Economic Review*, *Econometrica*, *Economic Journal*, and *Quarterly Journal of Economics*. Since 1994 he has been Professor at the University of Zurich, Switzerland.

**Chaim Fershtman** is Professor at the Eitan Berglass School of Economics at Tel Aviv University. He obtained his B.Sc. in mathematics from Hebrew University in 1977 and his Ph.D. in economics from the same institution in 1983. His research fields include industrial organization and economic theory. He has held visiting positions at Northwestern University and Yale University. His papers appear in various periodicals, including *American Economic Review*, *Economic Journal*, and *Journal of Political Economy*.

**Nancy Folbre**, Professor of Economics at the University of Massachusetts at Amherst, has done extensive research on the relationship between gender inequality and economic development. In addition to articles published in academic journals, she is the author of *Who Pays for the Kids?: Gender and the Structures of Constraint* (Routledge, 1994), and the coauthor of the *New Field Guide to the U.S. Economy* (The New Press, 1995). She is currently at work on an intellectual history of the dialogue between feminist theory and political economy and is an Associate Editor of the new journal *Feminist Economics*.

**Robert H. Frank** is the Goldwin Smith Professor of Economics, Ethics and Public Policy at Cornell University. Educated at Georgia Tech and UC Berkeley, he was a Peace Corps volunteer in Nepal. His books include *Choosing the Right Pond, Passions within Reason, Microeconomics and Behavior*, and (with Philip Cook) *The Winner Take All Society*. He is also the author of articles in *American Economic Review, Journal of Economic Perspectives*, and other periodicals.

**Bruno S. Frey** earned his Ph.D. in economics at Basel in 1965. He became Associate Professor of Economics at the University of Basel in 1969, was Professor of Economics at the University of Constance from 1970 to 1977, and has been Professor of Economics at the University of Zurich since 1977. He has been Managing Editor of the journal *Kyklos* since 1969. His research activities include the application of economics to politics, international political economy, the environment, family, conflict, history, art, and the theory of economic policy. More recently, he has researched the connection between economics and psychology. He has published over 270 articles in professional journals in economics and is the author of seven books, including *Economics as a Science of Human Behavior* (1992) and *Not Just for the Money: An Economic Theory of Personal Motivation* (1997).

**Simon Gächter**, born in 1965, studied economics and philosophy as an undergraduate. He studied economics at the University of Vienna and the Institute for Advanced Studies, Vienna, Austria, where he earned his Ph.D. in 1994. Since 1994, he has been Assistant Professor at the University of Zurich, Switzerland. His main research interests are market organization, coordination problems in social dilemma (public good) games, and in particular, the impact of social norms on (labor) markets and social dilemma situations.

**Herbert Gintis** is Professor of Economics at the University of Massachusetts at Amherst. He has also taught at Harvard University and the University of Paris and has been a Fellow of the Institute for Advanced Study, Princeton. He is the coauthor or coeditor of five books, three of these with Samuel Bowles, and the author of numerous journal articles. He is coeditor of the journal *Metroeconomica* and cochair of the MacArthur Foundation research project on economic environments and the evolution of norms and preferences.

**Russell Hardin** earned B.A. and B.S. degrees from the University of Texas, a B.A. from Oxford University, and a Ph.D. in political science from M.I.T. (1971). He is currently Professor and Chair of the Department of Politics at New York University. He is the author of *One for All* (1995), *Morality within the Limits of Reason* (1988), and *Collective Action* (1982). He was for many years the Editor of *Ethics*. His *Liberalism, Constitutionalism, and Democracy* is forthcoming from Oxford University Press.

**Timur Kuran** received an A.B. from Princeton University in 1977 and a Ph.D. from Stanford University in 1982. He is Professor of Economics and King Faisal Professor of Islamic Thought and Culture at the University of Southern California. His essay in this book was completed while he was John Olin Visiting Professor at the Graduate School of Business, University of Chicago. His research explores, on the one hand, the evolution of preferences, values, and institutions, and on the other, linkages between religion and economics. His recent publications include essays on the unpredictability of revolutions, the effects of public discourse on the transmission of knowledge, the social construction of ethnic identity, Islamic economic thought, and the economic impact of Islam. He is the author of *Private Truths, Public Lies: The Social Consequences of Preference Falsification* (1995). He edits the interdisciplinary Economics, Cognition, and Society series for the University of Michigan Press.

**Robert E. Lane** is Eugene Meyer Professor of Political Science Emeritus at Yale University, a Research Associate at the Yale Institution of Social and Policy Studies, and a member of the senior common room at Nuffield College, Oxford. He is a past president of the American Political Science Association and of the International Society of Political Psychology. His most recent book is *The Market Experience* (1991); his forthcoming book is tentatively entitled *Democracy's Distress and Market Misery: Maximizing Well-Being in Market Democracies.*

**Jane Mansbridge** is Professor of Public Policy at the John F. Kennedy School of Government at Harvard University. She is the author of *Beyond Adversary Democracy* and *Why We Lost the ERA* (corecipient of the American Political Science Association's Kammerer Award in 1987 and Schuck Award in 1988), editor of *Beyond Self Interest*, and author of several articles on the role of non-self-interested motivations in political action.

**John Michael Montias** is Professor Emeritus of Economics and the Institution of Social and Policy Studies at Yale University. His articles and books have dealt with the theory of economic systems, the economies of

Eastern Europe, and the economics of the arts. He is Founding Editor of *Journal of Comparative Economics* and past President of the Association for Comparative Economics Studies. He has taught and done research at the Center for Advanced Study in Social Sciences, the Wissenschaftskolleg in Berlin, and other institutions. His current research focuses on the economics of the arts.

**Douglass C. North** earned his Ph.D. in economics at the University of California (Berkeley) in 1952. From 1951 to 1983, he taught at the University of Washington in Seattle, and since 1983, he has been Luce Professor of Law and Liberty and Director of the Center of Political Economy at Washington University in St. Louis. His numerous books and articles include *The Rise of the Western World* (1971, with Robert Thomas), *Structure and Change in Economic History* (1981), and *Institutions, Institutional Change, and Economic Performance* (1990). In 1993, he was awarded the Nobel Memorial Prize in Economic Science for having renewed research in economic history and for demonstrating the role of organizational change in generating economic growth.

**Louis Putterman** studied at Columbia University and Yale University before commencing his career of teaching and research at Brown University, where he is currently Professor of Economics. His work touches on a number of topics, including incentives, property rights, and the organization of production at firm and farm level; labor-managed firms and collective farms; rural development in Tanzania; agriculture and industrial reform in mainland China; and the theory of market socialism. He is the author of numerous scholarly articles and author, coauthor, editor, or coeditor of seven books, including *Division of Labor and Welfare: An Introduction to Economics Systems* (1990) and *The Economic Nature of the Firm: A Reader* (2nd ed., 1996).

**Susan Rose-Ackerman** is Henry Luce Professor of Law and Political Science at Yale University. She holds a Ph.D. in economics from Yale University. Among her publications are *Corruption: A Study in Political Economy* (1978), *Rethinking the Progressive Agenda: The Reform of the American Regulatory State* (1992), and *Controlling Environmental Policy: The Limits of Public Law in Germany and the United States* (1995). She is editor of *The Economics of Non Profit Institutions* (1986).

**Andrew Schotter** received his Ph.D. from New York University in 1974. He is currently Professor of Economics at that university, where he has also served as the Co-Chairman of the C. V. Starr Center for Applied Economics and as Chair of the Department of Economics. He has worked in the areas of applied game theory, experimental economics, and the economics of social institutions. He is the author of *The Economic Theory of Social Institutions* (1981), *Free Market Economics: A Critical Appraisal* (1990), and *Microeconomics: A Modern Approach* (1992).

**Robert Sugden** was born in 1949. He studied history and economics at the Universities of York and Newcastle upon Tyne before taking up his current post as Professor of Economics at the University of East Anglia. His research has been a series of investigations into the scope and limitations of rational choice models. This has led to many publications in welfare economics, social choice theory, choice under uncertainty, and experimental economics, and at the interface of philosophy and economics. His *Economics of Rights, Cooperation and Welfare* (1986) pioneered the use of evolutionary game theory to explain the emergence of conventions and norms.

**Yoram Weiss** earned B.A. and M.A. degrees at the Hebrew University of Jerusalem before obtaining his Ph.D. in economics from Stanford University in 1968. He is currently D. Ross Professor of Labor Economics, Tel Aviv University, and has also taught at Stanford, the University of Chicago, the University of California at San Diego, and U.C.L.A. His research contributions include work on the analysis of labor supply, occupational choice and investments in human capital, the pricing of firms during inflation, and the analysis of divorce and divorce settlements. His papers have appeared in numerous periodicals including the *International Economic Review*, *Journal of Political Economy*, and *Review of Economic Studies*, and he has been Editor of the *Journal of Labor Economics*.

**Thomas E. Weisskopf** (Ph.D. Economics, M.I.T., 1966) taught at the Indian Statistical Institute and at Harvard University before joining the faculty of the University of Michigan, where he is Professor of Economics. At Michigan he has worked in the Economics Department and the Social Science Program of the Residential College; he was appointed Director of the College in July 1996. He has coauthored a half dozen books (most recently *After the Waste Land: Democratic Economics for the Year 2000*, with Samuel Bowles and David Gordon, 1991) and has published articles in the fields of economic development, macroeconomics, comparative economic systems, and political economy in a wide range of journals. He is currently working on a collaborative project to develop a textbook on "economics in context" for use in Russia.

**Viviana Zelizer** is Professor and Chair of the Department of Sociology at Princeton University. She is the author of *Morals and Markets: The Development of Life Insurance in the United States* (1979), *Pricing the Priceless Child: The Changing Social Value of Children* (1985), and *The Social Meaning of Money* (1994). She is currently working on the connection between social relations and forms of payment in a variety of economic settings.

# INTRODUCTION

# CHAPTER 1

# Values and institutions in economic analysis

*Avner Ben-Ner and Louis Putterman*

## Introduction

The subject of values was once considered to lie beyond the purview of economic science. Preferences, taken as given to the agent and society, were seen as being about goods, dates of consumption, and states of the world, not about means (how to behave), or about beneficiaries other than the self. But as industrial civilization ends a turbulent century with rising anxiety over its social health and cohesion, the subject of values has begun seeping into economic discourse.

That neoclassical economics viewed values as an alien issue may have been natural given the positivistic spirit of its proponents. Robbins (1932) defined economics as a science of means–ends relationships, with the choice of ends (preferences) being of no account. And when Adam Smith's "Invisible Hand" revealed itself in the theory of general equilibrium, its manifestation was that of a vector of prices supporting an optimal allocation of resources, with preferences, technologies, endowments, and even the structure of property rights and institutions taken as givens. "De gustibus non disputandum est" and, a fortiori, "de moribus," since economics was becoming a science of prediction and testing, whereas value statements are inherently not amenable to falsification. Assuming behavior based on self-interest, exploring where that led using deductive reasoning and mathematics, and testing the resulting conclusions using data on observable choices: These became the methodological Tao of the economics profession.

But as research in the neoclassical tradition expanded, it became clear that the economics of the midtwentieth century had not really been as self-consistent as had been hoped. Assuming profit-maximizing firms and

We thank Ken Binmore, Timur Kuran, Margo Wilson, and participants at the Conference on Economics, Values, and Organization, for helpful comments.

utility-maximizing households possessing full information on their environments, the standard theory could indeed show how a competitive economy would simply "run itself." But once the institutions of the economy were themselves to be explained, benign and "well-behaved" equilibria seemed far less assured. When, instead of firms, one looked at individual possessors of skills, funds, and so forth, each maneuvering for their own advantages, then the emergence of entities having well-defined organizational objectives became anything but a certainty. When, instead of traders in the marketplace exchanging homogeneous goods and money of costlessly verifiable quality, one looked at agents trading in the face of monitoring costs and asymmetric information, the presumption that the trader would faithfully fulfill his part in an agreed exchange could no longer be maintained. And when the very institution of property was considered not as a given but rather as an outcome of predatory struggles and of collective rule making, the view of economic life as a matter of producing and trading from given endowments took on a distinctly quaint appearance.

Taking self-interest to be as thoroughgoing as neoclassicism has heretofore presumed, and thus letting no institution be taken for granted but instead insisting that all be explained on grounds of self-interested action by rational individuals, raises the puzzle of how the Invisible Hand gets on with its work. Are people constantly looking for opportunities to steal from and cheat one another, and do they desist from such acts, where and when they do, only to avoid expected penalties exceeding expected gains, or in the expectation of gaining through repeated interactions? Beyond the realm of the narrowly economic, is such a representation of behavior equally true of participants in public life, of soldiers on the battlefield, of clergy at the pulpit, of child-care providers beside their tender charges, of academics purportedly seeking scientific truths? Or might self-interest, rather, be less thoroughgoing or universal, or be broader in nature, with some people identifying themselves with others or feeling better off when acting according to values other than the maximization of their consumption and the avoidance of effort? And could the mix of interests, or the weights placed on selfish, altruistic, and moral considerations, not be determined in part by the environment facing the individual?

At one time, such questions seem to have led to an impasse. One could adopt the model of thoroughgoing economic man, but at the cost of ignoring realistic complexities in human behavior and psychology. Or one could call for a broader and, we think, more realistic economics, but at the seeming expense of formal rigor, and thus condemning one's work to the margins of the discipline's discourse. However, recent signs suggest that economists stand poised, today, to crack the nut of complex preferences. In models of the family and of savings behavior, assumed interdependencies of welfare have played increasingly important roles. In the theory of games and other branches of microeconomics, the idea that players or agents may be of particular "types" – more or less rational or opportunistic, for example – has gained a firm foothold, and the endogenous determination of these types has begun to be explored. As the process proceeds, economists, usually an imperialistic lot ever eager to invade the territory of other disciplines, have shown more openness to using ideas from without. Evolutionary biology has provided the model of evolutionary game theory, psychology has introduced the concepts of norms and framing, and sociology has offered notions of reciprocity and reference group.

Because trade and competition boost prosperity and because universal honesty would reduce the cost of trade, it is easy to see why one might wish for a world in which people are motivated by self-interest in those choices where this proves collectively beneficial but are internally deterred from acting self-interestedly in situations in which opportunism is collectively harmful. While real societies fall short of this ideal, at least some do so, arguably, by less wide a margin than economists sometimes presume. This raises the question, What determines where along the spectrum from "moral" optimum to moral worst case a given society comes to reside? And the further question: Are any of the relevant variables within the scope of human control?

In this essay, we argue that there is no scientific basis for the assumption that own well-being or command over resources is the exclusive and immutable concern of human individuals. The natural sciences, evolutionary biology in particular, and other social and behavioral sciences, especially the evolutionary approaches that have been emerging in psychology and other fields, suggest that individual human beings may be genetically inclined toward concern not only with their own success in acquiring the resources necessary for thriving and reproducing, but also with the success of offspring and other kin. They suggest, further, that we will be inclined, conditionally, toward cooperation with others, toward concern with how we are viewed by others, toward hostility to those who fail to reciprocate our cooperation, and toward receptivity to moral reasoning that is consistent with these and other propensities. Like all genetic inheritances, such propensities do not directly dictate characteristics, but rather they are shaped into characteristics – in this case, preferences – under the influences of the environment in which the genes achieve their expression, with cultural, social, and economic factors being among the most important of these influences upon human behavioral predispositions or preferences. Real, evolved human beings are therefore capable of cooperation, of coordinated social behavior, and of responsiveness to concerns about process, but to degrees that differ with the experiences, cues, and incentives to which they are exposed.

These last points, however, anticipate the approach to studying the genesis of values and their relationship to institutions that we will argue for later in this essay. Before developing that approach and our arguments for it at greater length, we first offer further motivation for the more general project of studying the relationship of values to institutions, which is the theme of this volume as a whole. This is done in part 1 of our chapter, where we elaborate upon our reasons for believing that economists must understand values. In part 2, we draw on recent literature and on our perspectives as students of economic institutions and organization[1] to discuss conceptual and methodological issues concerning the endogenization of values in economic analysis. We also develop there our ideas concerning evolved receptivities to preference patterns, the influence upon these of environmental cues, and the simultaneous evolution of institutions and of preferences, including values. In part 3, we explore the endogenization of value formation and the values/institutions nexus by way of illustration. A brief conclusion follows.

## 1    Why values matter in economics

Numerous lines of argument lead to the common conclusion that values matter for economics, and that the two-way interaction between economic arrangements and values merits serious attention. To motivate the rest of our essay and the study of the relationship between values and economic arrangements more broadly, we sketch three such lines here: First, we argue that the stock of values helps determine the cost of operating the economy, and even the economic transactions that take place. Second, we point out that value considerations are likely to be crucial to the solution of impasses in the theory of strategic interactions – that is, of games. Third, we consider the evidence that contemporary society is suffering from a "crisis of values."

As elaborated further in part 2, the individual may be viewed as being endowed with preferences that are usefully (although in some respects

---

[1] See, for example, Putterman (1990) and Ben-Ner, Montias, and Neuberger (1993).

arbitrarily) grouped as *self-regarding*, *other-regarding*, and *process-regarding*. Self-regarding preferences concern the individual's own consumption and other outcomes, other-regarding preferences concern the consumption and outcomes of others, and process-regarding preferences concern the manner in which the individual in question and others behave, including the ways in which they attain outcomes of interest. We shall refer to process-regarding preferences mainly as values, but sometimes also as codes of behavior, mores, ethics, and by other terms, depending mostly on the context. We thus think of values as arguments of the utility function.[2] And we shall maintain the standard distinction between preferences and behavior, distinguishing between values and ethics on the one hand and values-based and ethical behavior on the other hand, and emphasizing the point that behavior that might be judged as moral may stem from amoral or even immoral attitudes.

## 1.1    *Values and transactions*

Almost every economist is familiar with Adam Smith's dictum "It is not from the benevolence of the butcher, the brewer, or the baker that we expect our dinner, but from their regard to their own interest." A standard interpretation of this idea is that benevolence is simply too scarce a resource to serve as the foundation for a prosperous economy, whereas self-interestedness is in plentiful supply and nearly universal. A more subtle interpretation is that even if benevolence were widespread, it is not clear how the specialization and exchange that sustain prosperity could be supported by it, since there may be no effective mechanism to solve the information and coordination problems confronting a legion of altruistic citizens looking to engage in collectively beneficial activities, whereas such a mechanism is fortuitously found to arise – in the form of the price system – when individuals have regard for their private con-

---

[2] Our definition of values is different, and perhaps narrower, than other definitions offered for the term. Hechter (1993, p. 3), for example, noting that there is no consensual definition of the term, defines values as relatively general and durable internal criteria for evaluation, distinguishing them from preferences, which he views as more labile. Like Hechter and others, we will reserve the term "norm" for something "external to actors" or resulting from the interaction of a number of actors – a usage that still permits us to say that the desire to adhere to a norm may be one of the individual's values or process-regarding preferences. Another definition takes values to be "principles, or criteria, for selecting what is good (or better, or best) among objects, actions, ways of life, and social and political institutions and structures" (Schwartz 1993a). Rabin (1995) models values as constraints rather than arguments in the utility function. We return to this issue in part 2.

cerns. However widespread benevolence is, therefore, self-interest might be the sine qua non of a prosperous economy.

However, the argument appears capable of going only so far before confronting an important dilemma. While self-interest can lead butchers, brewers, and bakers into mutually advantageous exchanges under idealized conditions of full information, once information becomes incomplete, it is less clear that unalloyed self-interest is what is required. In particular, producing and supplying other parties with goods of desired quality now become only one possible avenue to one's own well-being, competing with options such as theft of others' property, engaging in cost-reducing but concealable adulteration of the products one sells, failing to honor one's side of exchange agreements, and so forth. For given probabilities of success of each of the latter strategies, it may be the case that the more thoroughgoing the self-interest upon which economic agents act, or the less checked by considerations of "morality," the more likely they are to choose such actions over value-generating production and exchange. While the actions in question may be primarily redistributive in intent, they are typically value-reducing in consequence because (1) they attract effort away from productive activity; (2) they lead to monitoring, contract writing, theft deterrence, enforcement, and other costly activities; and (3) they reduce trading and increase otherwise inefficient self-provision activities that substitute for it.

The listed value-reducing actions might be thwarted, for example, by threatening thieves with having their hands cut off, throwing contract defaulters into prison, or privately punishing product adulterators and defaulters by nonrenewal of trade. As just suggested, however, detection consumes resources, and each of these deterrents has its costs. Prisons use up real resources, chopped off hands represent lost productive potential, and there is the dilemma of statistical errors: To avoid punishing the falsely accused (letting the guilty go free), society must allow more actual perpetrators to get away (punish some who commit no crime). To operate the nonrenewal strategy, traders need to hold out the prospect of long-term interaction, which puts a check on mobility and the search for better trading matches. They may also have to offer one another "continuation rents," which means that markets will not clear (see Bowles and Gintis 1993). The upshot is that the more thoroughgoing or less circumscribed the self-interestedness of trading partners, the more recourse must be had to costly deterrents and the more otherwise beneficial trades will be forgone, and thus the smaller will be the net gains from trade. All of this means that if society can somehow mold individuals who produce and trade honorably with the gusto of self-interest, but who refrain from theft and cheating out of adherence to a social code or norm, all might be better off. A mixture of self-interest and normative constraint, not self-interest alone, is what now appears to be required in order to achieve maximum Smithian prosperity.[3]

Norm-based behavior seems desirable not only in the market, but also in such contexts as group production settings, where cooperative behavior is often jointly beneficial to those engaged in team production. A large literature now starts from the proposition that employers and employees have potentially opposed interests, since the employer wants to elicit maximum effort for minimum compensation, whereas the employee wishes exactly the opposite. With full information, their conflict can be resolved at the bargaining stage, with a handshake sealing an agreement that both parties know will be carried out (threatened penalties will follow noncompliance and thus need not be invoked). With imperfect information, however, the worker may attempt to minimize effort at the contract implementation stage, forcing the employer to undertake costly supervision, to offer job rents, and to implement threats of firing the occasional violator even when doing so is irrational, but for reputation effects. Groups of producers (for example, in a profit-sharing team or partnership) might similarly work together for mutual productivity and joint earnings gains, but self-interest could lead them toward collectively inferior outcomes, in which all shirk their duties as the privately rational solution of the prisoner's dilemma in which they find themselves. The capacity to refrain from opportunism once the employment handshake takes place or to act cooperatively so long as others are seen as doing so can be beneficial to all parties. While the literature discusses "forcing contracts" (e.g., Holmstrom 1982) and co-operation enforced by "trigger strategies" in repeated games (e.g., MacLeod 1987; Putterman and Skillman 1992), where neither costly monitoring nor moral commitment is invoked, these approaches run into problems including those of moral hazard (see Eswaran and Kotwal 1984; MacLeod 1987), multiplicity of equilibria and sensitivity to renegotiation, boundedness of rationality, and the need for trust (see Schotter, this volume). A meaningful capacity to engage in mutually fruitful cooperation may thus in many cases depend upon the presence of an ability to adhere to norms which deviate from simpler forms of self-interest.

---

[3] That Adam Smith himself appreciated this point (especially in his 1759 book) has been emphasized by Sen (1987, 1993), among others. That cooperative behavior might be fostered by institutions other than or supplemental to markets is argued by Bowles and Gintis (this volume); a parallel point is made by Greif (1994).

## 1.2    *Values, game theory, and experimental economics*

The need to incorporate values in economic analysis has become manifest in an area of economics that has been dominated by the *homo economicus* model in its purest form, game theory. Predictions of game-theoretic models predicated on players behaving in strictly self-interested and rational ways do not conform well with many observers' intuitions about how interactions among players are concluded in the real world and with findings of experiments. In recent years, an increasing number of attempts have been made to reconcile theoretical predictions with empirical findings and observation, primarily by modifying the concept of the rationality of the individual. This has amounted to placing various bounds on how individuals reason about their opponents' moves, how many future potential moves they can anticipate, how much information they have at their disposal, how they process information, how they learn from past experiences, or how they deal with uncertainty. Work on bounded rationality has helped to provide a more realistic understanding of human behavior without discarding the essential and very useful framework supplied by game theory.[4]

However, tweaking with rationality alone has proved insufficient; some consideration of the rules of the game and the institutions that give rise to them, and of motivations of players beyond self-interest, has also been found necessary. Working partly under the influence of psychologists like Kahneman and his colleagues (e.g., Kahneman, Knetsch, and Thaler 1986), game theorists have sought to incorporate into their models also concepts such as the sense of fairness individuals bring to bear on their interactions (see, for example, Rabin 1993). The rules of the game – when players are allowed to move, what moves are permissible, for how long a game is played, and so on – are found to have great impact on the outcome of games. Many equilibria are quite sensitive to the specification of these rules, and therefore a quest to understand them (rather than just assume them) has taken game theorists to the analysis of the formation of institutions.

Some of the key issues can be illustrated with the ultimatum game, which represents one of the simplest games of interaction, however minimal, between individuals. (We return to this game in more detail in part 2). One player, designated as the proposer, is given the opportunity to propose a division of a certain sum (a gift) between herself and another player, designated as the responder. If the latter accepts the

---

[4] For a few examples, see Abreu and Rubinstein (1988) and Vega-Redondo (1994); for a general discussion, see Kreps (1990, chap. 6).

proposal, the division is carried out; if he rejects it, neither player receives anything. This game has a unique equilibrium in which rational, self-interested proposers who have no concern for the other player and no regard for fairness as commonly understood offer a token sum to respondents with similar attributes, who accept the proposal (from which they have something, even if little, to gain) rather than reject it, in which case they gain nothing.

But this outcome almost never materializes in experiments, for token proposals are rarely made, and even more rarely are they accepted. A sizable literature in game theory and experimental economics has emerged to try to make sense of these findings. The upshot of this literature (summarized by Camerer and Thaler 1995) is that a great many proposers and respondents seem not to understand what is going on in the game (or proposers think that of respondents), that players care about each other, that they don't want to feel or be regarded as "dupes" who accept low proposals, or that they just play by certain rules or adhere to certain principles regardless of the opportunities afforded by the specific game. Since there is no question that some players do not quite understand the setup of the ultimatum game, simple as it is, the question is whether there are other important factors that also affect the outcome. There is ample evidence that factors other than bounded rationality do affect outcomes. For example, subjects' gender, familiarity with each other, and cultural and educational background have clear effects on proposals and responses (Eckel and Grossman 1994; Hoffman, McCabe, and Smith 1996; Roth et al. 1991; Frank, Gilovich, and Regan 1993).[5] Although some of these factors are likely correlated with the nature and degree of bounded rationality, it is extremely unlikely that they *are not* strongly related to how much players care about each other, how they think of themselves and each other, and what they regard as acceptable or desirable behavior in the circumstances that arise in these games. In other words, the extant evidence strongly suggests that behavior in ultimatum game experiments is affected by other- and process-regarding preferences, in addition to self-regarding preferences.

Critics of one-shot-game experiments (such as the ultimatum game) claim that such experiments can never test what they purport to test: how a proposer would make her offers knowing that the respondent has no way to punish a stingy offer or reward a generous one. The reason is that

---

[5] The relationship between background variables and behavior remains to be investigated. In particular, it is not clear whether culture or education operates through individuals' values or their degree and nature of bounded rationality.

a one-time experiment is in fact part of a long string of encounters with others, albeit with different individuals over time. Individuals cannot extract themselves from their experience of continuous human interactions in order to hide in the fold of time provided by the experiment. In truth, critics say, proposers and respondents act rationally and self-interestedly in the repeated game of life (see, for example, Aumann 1990).

Although this argument is offered by defenders of the *homo economicus* model against attribution of non-self-interested motivation to players in one-shot ultimatum games, it is clearly inconsistent with the most demanding concepts of rationality. Why would a fully rational individual $A$ adopt the same behavior toward $B$, in a non-repeating interaction, as she does in her repeated interactions with $C$? Certainly, it is possible that $A$ does so because she is only boundedly rational. But it is also possible that $A$ carries over to one-time encounters standards of behavior that suit repeated interactions because she treats these as guidelines for how individuals *should* interact ($A$ has process-regarding preferences).[6] Nor can we rule out that $A$ may act as she does out of concern about $B$ (other-regarding preferences).

The game-theoretic literature focuses on the adoption of standards of behavior or strategies (and rarely, explicitly on preferences) and suggests that their emergence depends on the institutions available in a society. These institutions include anything and everything that helps individuals learn about what others do, from customs, norms, and laws to common frames of reference and focal points. Strategies are embedded in routines, codes of conduct, rules of thumb, social instincts and proclivities, and so on. Many game theorists have adapted the evolutionary framework, especially models originating with the biologist John Maynard Smith (1982). In biology, genes are viewed as the carriers of strategies, and they are transmitted to offspring; success is measured in the number of the offspring carrying particular genes. In evolutionary game-theoretic models, genetic reproduction is usually replaced by imitation and enculturation.[7] But in nearly all models preferences matter, either

---

[6] Kreps (1990) discusses this issue, which he terms retrospection, as a variant of bounded rationality. At some level, the disagreement is only about terminology, whether we should characterize behavior as generated by self-interest, moderated by bounded rationality and retrospection, or governed by self-interest along with other- and process-regarding preferences. But the carry-over effect can be reduced to behavior consistent with the simple *homo economicus* assumption only at the risk of emptying that assumption of the content ascribed to it by most users.

[7] The question of what is being maximized – payoffs or fitness – remains unsettled and the two concepts are often conflated.

through a selection process that affects the mix of individuals with fixed but different preferences or through an adaptation of preferences that are determined endogenously in the process of maximizing fitness (reproductive success).[8]

All of this means that it is difficult, in the theoretical and experimental study of games, to avoid the invocation of some notion of concern for others, values, and/or norms. Put differently, it takes extraordinary intellectual contortions to construct explanations of observed real-life or experimentally induced phenomena that are based on a value-free *homo economicus*; these explanations strain credulity. This seems to have led some game theorists, such as Binmore and Samuelson (1994), to reject the model of *homo ludens* (game theory's version of *homo economicus*, who has only self-regarding preferences) as often absurdly unrealistic, in favor of a *homo sociologicus*, who behaves as though he were optimizing, or stated differently, in favor of *homo economicus*, who, when optimizing, behaves as though he were employing a social norm.

One difficulty with incorporating bounded rationality and values in economic models has been the excessive degrees of freedom these concepts allow the modeler, since it is possible to obtain virtually any result by invoking suitable definitions of these concepts. With so much fluidity and so little ability to restrict its range, this route to explaining behavior is understandably regarded as dangerously ad hoc. But carefully designed experiments coupled with original theorizing are increasingly helping to distinguish among bounded rationality, values, and other preferences, and to define their meaning. We present some thoughts about how economics might (when necessary) take leave of *homo economicus* without plunging into chaos, in part 2.

## 1.3    *The contemporary context: Does society face an ethical crisis?*

The nineteenth century had seen numerous social movements and philosophies arise to contend against the inequalities, inhumanities, and socially atomizing tendencies of industrial capitalism. The twentieth century in its turn became the stage for an immense experiment in nonmarket economics, and for a global contest between the states embracing and those opposing that experiment. With the collapse of Soviet-style socialism at the end of the 1980s, that contest had more or less run

---

[8] See, for example, articles in the special issue on evolutionary game theory of *Journal of Economic Theory* (vol. 8, no. 2, August 1992) and Weibull (1996). Guth and Yaari (1992) and Guth (1995) model the endogenous evolution of preferences; see also Fershtman and Weiss (this volume).

its course. The system whose defenders proclaimed it better adapted to "human nature as we know it,"[9] the system that took self-interest as given and permitted it an extensive sphere of action, the system that as well had evinced relative hospitality toward political democracy and individual freedoms emerged victorious, with leading public, civic, and intellectual figures throughout the world concurring in the belief that desired prosperity and liberty can best be achieved through its institutions of free exchange and private property.

Yet, even as this victory and strengthened ideological consensus around liberalism were being celebrated, the viability of the prevailing order was coming increasingly into question, for the internal discontents of industrial market societies appeared to loom as large as ever. Typical listings of these problems have included high levels of crime and violence, family instability, racial tensions and xenophobia, seemingly intractable poverty and unemployment, self-destructive behaviors including substance abuse and suicide, social unconnectedness and depression, and widespread alienation among the young. While it is beyond the scope of this essay to assess whether such problems are in some global sense more severe today than was the case fifty or one hundred years ago, the alarm on these issues that has spread from one end to the other of the contemporary political spectrum, and their constant discussion in news and opinion media as well as among politicians of all stripes, are sufficient to suggest to us that the concerns involved have real bases.[10]

When we look at the state of the family as an institution, for instance, several contemporary phenomena that arguably bear important relation to either the inculcation or the playing out of values come particularly clearly to the fore. First, statistics show degrees of fragility of marriages and numbers of births to unmarried mothers that have no recent precedent.[11] Second, there has been a large increase, of late, in the number of

---

[9] Knight (1957, p. 270); also cited by Williamson (1985, p. 3).

[10] We adduce later some, mostly indirect, evidence about changes in values, behavior, and institutions. Evidence is lacking, in part, because of problems in measurement of values (Hechter 1993; Fischhoff 1993). An equally great difficulty stems from an identification problem: The behavior and institutions we observe in reality tend to reflect equilibrium outcomes, so that moral or immoral behaviors are not determined only by individuals' preferences, including values, and the economic constraints they face, but also by the measures taken to limit their undesirable effects or enhance their desirable effects. For example, actual theft in department stores cannot be taken as a measure of the values held by the populace regarding the treatment of others' property, both because extensive antitheft measures are available in stores, and because the extent of "moral" behavior is also determined by factors working through self-interest, so that the frequency of theft may also be affected by economic cycles that produce more or fewer needy people.

[11] Data from Vital Statistics of the United States, which show that the proportion of children born out of wedlock rose from 3 percent to 18 percent among white and from

households composed of single parents with children.[12] Third, there has been a rapid movement of women out of full-time household roles and into the external labor force, and a corresponding movement of young children to day care outside family settings. Fourth, these changes have been accompanied by changes in income patterns, including the relative impoverishment of both divorced and unmarried women with children, and by changes in the time that parents have available to spend with their children (Schor 1991).

While on the one side, many would hold that some of these trends, such as declining marital stability, reflect at least in part changes in widely held values, on the other side many fear that the combined effect of these trends will be to undermine families' effectiveness as inculcators of positive values, thus contributing to a decline in society's moral capital stock. Some, indeed, have sought to link some of these changes to changes in behavior; for example, the propensity to violence and other forms of social and economic distress such as crime, drug abuse, and poverty seems to be greater in children of poor, unwed parents.[13]

Those who see signs of more generalized decay in the moral underpinnings of society are hardly forced to direct their gaze at families only. Behavior in the company boardroom, in political life, in advertising, and in other spheres of life shows signs of operating with lessened reference to moral values, they may claim. A recent *Boston Globe* column, for instance, lamented the fact that a local businessman who responded to the humanitarian needs of his employees and their families and who promised to rebuild his factory after a devastating fire rather than move from the region to one with lower labor costs had been treated as a hero in the local and national presses. While the individual in question was certainly deserving of praise, the author argued, his actions were precisely those that most business owners would have claimed to be normal

24 percent to 64 percent among black mothers, between 1965 and 1990 (cited by Akerlof, Yellen, and Katz 1996).

[12] Census Bureau data show that in 1991, married couples with children accounted for only 26 percent of U.S. households, and that of households including children, 25 percent did not include a married couple. The proportion of households in the "married with children" category was over 40 percent as recently as 1979.

[13] See Akerlof et al. (1996), Palermo and Simpson (1994), Anderson (1990), Kotlowitz (1991), Lemann (1991), Massey and Denton (1993), Wacquant (1993), and Wilson (1987). Of course, changes in the family institution need not all be for the worse. Shifts toward gender equality are still applauded by most, those toward more choice in sexual matters are approved by many, and the ability to leave a bad marriage must also not be unappreciated. Also, strong families may emphasize self-interest, or a narrow concept of altruism, thus failing to impart values of mutual responsibility and actually *contributing* to the further tilting of value systems toward unalloyed self-interest or narrow group-oriented interest.

only a generation ago.[14] Amoral businesses and the profit motive stand accused today – even by traditional defenders of free enterprise – of everything from buying their way to favorable government legislation (including measures that compromise the environment and consumer or worker health and safety) to polluting the minds of children with glamorous depictions of violence and dehumanized depictions of sex in television, films, pop music lyrics, and electronic games.[15] Yet Easterlin and Crimmins find that in recent decades "support grew for capitalist institutions such as profit making and advertising" (1991, p. 499). Moreover, those authors find a broad range of value changes suggesting that the market ethos has continued to make inroads in the culture of the day. Thus, during the same period, the authors assert, "[j]obs offering money and status became more preferred relative to those with opportunities for self-fulfillment or public service." A drop in the importance attached to "developing a meaningful philosophy of life" and "helping others" and a corresponding rise in the desire to "become well off financially" are also found by those authors in comparisons of responses to surveys conducted between the late 1960s and the early 1990s.[16]

The moral values of the young are argued to have changed for the worse in a number of studies. Bovasso et al. (1991) attempt to track the moral judgments made by college students from 1929 to 1988, in four categories: misrepresentation, violation of religious norms, selfishness, and crime. Although many of the changes are small, self-reported tolerance of misrepresentation, crime, and selfish behaviors (such as habitually failing to keep promises and not giving to charity when able to) has increased since 1958. "The college youth of the 1980s have retained the hedonistic orientation of the 1960s," they conclude, "but the severity of their judgment of selfishness and misrepresentation for financial gain has decreased since the 1960s" (1991, pp. 476–77). Cheating in schools and dishonesty in other settings may likewise be on the rise. In a survey administered to over one thousand U.S. high school students in 1969, 34 percent of respondents reported having used a "cheat sheet"; in 1989 the figure was double that; in 1969, 34 percent agreed that "sometimes it is necessary to be dishonest," whereas 67 percent did so in 1989; the per-

---

[14] See Goodman (1995). Essentially the same points were made about this case in remarks by former U.S. Labor Secretary Robert Reich on February 13, 1996.

[15] The director of psychological services at Swarthmore College, for example, recently argued that "increases in violent crime, weapon carrying, drug dependency, eating disorders, and youth suicide rates in recent decades are both reflected by and promoted by commercial interests. Addiction cultivation, whether to cigarettes, alcohol or other drugs, diets, or violence per se is extremely profitable for its purveyors" (Whitaker 1993).

[16] See Easterlin and Crimmins (1991, p. 499); see also Conger (1988).

centage of students who said they would turn in a twenty-dollar bill they found at school dropped from 81 percent to 32 percent; and the percentage answering yes to the question, "Are most people in the U.S.A. today honest?" fell from 49 percent to 24 percent (Schab 1991); interestingly, "over 80 percent were convinced that the poor were more honest than the rich" (p. 841).

Some value changes may have long-term and others shorter-term causes. Some of these causes may be narrowly economic in nature, others less so;[17] some may be lasting, others cyclical;[18] and some negative value changes may be associated with additional but desirable changes. Be that as it may, at least some of the problems that we have enumerated are real ones, and any headway that social science may make in addressing them would be widely welcomed. With economic forces playing such a large part in explaining such decisions as those regarding marriage, divorce, childbearing, and the undertaking of criminal acts, our discipline might be expected to contribute to improving understanding of these phenomena and to helping devise corrective policies. Unfortunately, economists have made little progress in analyzing these and other pressing issues – a fact that Henry Aaron (1994) has recently attributed precisely to the exclusion of values from economic analysis. We concur with Aaron's assessment and hope that by breaking old disciplinary taboos and marrying the rational-choice perspective of economics with analysis of the formation and mutation of values, the chapters collected in this volume will help to overcome that deficiency.[19]

## 2     Some theory

### 2.1    *Preferences*

The standard depiction of human motivation and behavior in economic theory is parsimonious. *Homo economicus* cares about his own well-being; sometimes modelers allow him to care about the welfare of others,

---

[17] An instance of the short term, economic variety, is provided by Easterlin and Crimmins's (1991) argument that the increasing importance of private materialism during the 1970s and 1980s found in their study, as just cited, was "caused by a growing feeling of economic deprivation in the post-1973 period as real wages declined." A similar observation is made by Yankelovitch (1994).

[18] For instance, Bovasso et al. (1991) show that tolerance of "vices" was nearly as high in the 1920s as in the 1980s, and swings between "materialism" and other concerns may likewise show an alternating pattern over long periods. Similar swings and cycles in the family institution and behavior have been observed (Coontz 1992).

[19] Concern about values has strengthened in other social sciences as well. See, for example, Aaron, Mann, and Taylor (1994); Hechter (1993); Bellah et al. (1991); and Etzioni (1996).

too, but this is often regarded as a way to address "minor" phenomena (such as voluntary donations) and is also viewed by many as a regrettable departure from the desired goal of explaining behavior on the basis of pure self-interest. *Homo economicus* refrains from actions that most people regard as morally reprehensible only if her valuable reputation would be damaged, or if the expected punishments inflicted on her would outweigh her expected gains. *Homo economicus* has no moral compunction, does not engage in actions just because some abstract social norms require doing so; nor does she have feelings of guilt (e.g., for violating a norm), pride (e.g., from being praised), or self-esteem (e.g., for having overcome a temptation to cheat and having acted honestly instead). In short, *homo economicus* is not someone with whom most people would like to be compared.[20]

As we mentioned earlier, the "resort" to other- and process-regarding preferences has been viewed quite negatively by some economists, who consider the essence of their trade to be explaining as much as possible of human behavior from the starting point of "rational economic man." That the *homo economicus* paradigm is indeed a powerful one is easily illustrated by some simple analytics of "morality." For instance, "moral behavior" is insightfully viewed as a public good that it would benefit all to see upheld, but that the individual may find profitable to forgo when the private gain of a single "immoral" act exceeds the actor's share of the resulting social costs ("breakdown of morality"). Such reasoning yields the useful prediction that, ceteris paribus, it will be easier to obtain adherence to a moral code in a small group, in which each individual's share of the costs is significant, than in a large one, in which it is negligible. It suggests, too, that "moral" dealings are more likely between pairs of individuals who know one another's identity and expect to interact repeatedly. It permits linking "moral behavior" to the severity and probability of sanctions. And it suggests why belief in an omnipotent and omniscient God who may deal out infinite punishment with perhaps small but unknown probability may act to deter much "immorality," and why declining belief either in the existence or in the sternness of such a being may lead to a decline in the average level of "moral" behavior.[21]

---

[20] Not all economists have dealt with human motivation and behavior in accordance with *homo economicus* assumptions. In particular, Akerlof (1980, 1982); Basu, Jones, and Schlicht (1987); Frank (1988); Rotemberg (1994); Kandel and Lazear (1992); Hirschmann (1985); Rabin (1993); and even Adam Smith (1971 [1759]), as noted earlier, along with others, have contributed much to alternative views of motivation and behavior.

[21] See McKenzie (1977), who draws heavily on Buchanan (1965) and on Olson (1971). See also Guttman et al. (1992). Psychologist Donald Campbell uses similar reasoning, argu-

However, important elements remain absent from such an account, as well, even if we leave aside the questions of the rationality of such beliefs, and of how moral codes come about. Few mothers seem to require either the fear of God or social sanctions to devote caring attention to their children. People make the effort to vote in elections despite negligible tangible benefit. And the fact that families, schools, and opinion leaders devote resources to inculcating normative beliefs suggests that most people believe that human beings can be made to act according to certain norms even when they are not afraid of external penalties and hoping for extrinsic rewards. Indeed, the large investments we make in socialization suggest that either (1) this belief in normative receptivity has some basis or (2) the belief that human beings are fairly rational has none. Neglecting the way in which process- and other-regarding norms change not only with the size of relevant groups and the probability of repeated interactions, but also with changes in the prevalence and efficacy of socializing agents and institutions, would leave some of the most important sources of value transmission unaccounted for.

In this section we seek to describe preferences and behavior in a way that not only allows individuals to recognize themselves, but, more importantly, holds promise of allowing us to integrate the interactions between values and institutions into our analysis. We do so while staying close to the otherwise fruitful and rigor-imposing tenets of economic methodology. Our object is to characterize individual preferences and behavior richly enough to conform with commonsense observations and with the findings of social-scientific research (including psychology and the social research of biologists), and parsimoniously enough to be useful for systematic inquiry into the ways in which institutions and organizations affect the behavior of individuals through altering their preferences.

As is standard in economics, we think of the individual as being endowed with preferences regarding her own consumption and other outcomes. While a great deal can be explained by such (self-regarding) preferences, and we have no intention of denying their centrality, we think further progress is made possible by acknowledging that the individual may also have preferences with respect to both the consumption and outcomes of others (other-regarding preferences) and the process through which these outcomes are attained (process-regarding

ing that "for larger social units the precarious establishment of cooperative social units has been accompanied by fantastic transcendental belief systems, with rewarding and punishing reincarnations and afterlives promising individuals a net hedonic gain optimized over a longer period than their immediate lives." He goes on to posit a naturally selected proclivity toward "awed indoctrination" (Campbell 1986, 177); see also Burkert (1996).

preferences). To begin tracing the steps we think necessary for going beyond approaches conventional in the past, it seems helpful initially to elaborate on relevant "nonstandard" preferences in something like the following manner:

*Self-regarding preferences* are the essence of *homo economicus.*[22] *Other-regarding preferences* reflect concern either for the overall well-being or for certain of the activities or outcomes of other individuals. They have both altruistic or benevolent and envious or malevolent varieties. The individual who is other-regarding or altruistic to the degree that she derives satisfaction from the well-being of each and all of her fellows equal to that which she derives from her own private welfare is improbable; the individual who, conversely, enjoys equally the pains of all others, is pathological. Most individuals care about themselves, and then to varying – but lesser, and perhaps declining – degrees they care about some outcomes that affect their relatives, friends, coworkers, neighbors, countrymen, and so on.

Individuals care about the manner in which they themselves and others behave, including the ways in which they attain outcomes of interest.[23] These are *process-regarding preferences* (a term which we use, a bit loosely, interchangeably with "values," "ethics," "codes of behavior," and similar terms). Uncommon is the individual who is strictly indifferent about whether he has achieved his income through honest work or blind luck, whether he has cheated others or treated them fairly, whether his gain was achieved by helping or by harming others. Likewise, individuals care about how others comport themselves.[24]

---

[22] The difference between the characterization of preferences advocated here and that of the neoclassical tradition should not be exaggerated. We do think self-regarding preferences to be so important that the standard economic model which assumes a strict *homo economicus* will give a good account of behavior in a wide variety of situations. The salience of self-interest is also underscored by our observation, in section 2.2, that the inculcation and elicitation of other-regarding and process-regarding preferences often rely on appeals to self-regarding preferences. It might be noted, finally, that the evolutionary perspective on preferences which we propose beginning in section 2.3 suggests that the grouping of preferences under separate categories of the sort we use here is artificial, however useful it may be for taking our first steps beyond the conventional approach.

[23] As noted by Ariel Rubinstein at the Conference on Economics, Values, and Organization, there is a potential difficulty in applying maximization approaches when the method of maximization is said to be of concern but is not among the outcomes over which the maximand is defined. Clearly, what we have in mind is that some aspects of method may be included formally in the function to be maximized, or as constraints to maximization. In the former case, it may be better to think of the process as being among the outcomes that concern the actor.

[24] Campbell (1983, 1986) argues that ethics correspond to the way we would like *others* to behave, and that we accept the same strictures for ourselves at most as a necessary cost

As in the case of outcome-regarding preferences, process-regarding preferences vary in intensity across individuals and, for given individuals, across processes. Values and codes of behavior that guide actions are internalized to varying degrees by different people. One individual may rank types of behavior in terms of their acceptability to him: Never murder, cause bodily harm only in extreme cases, cheat only in certain situations, lie only if the gain is very large, withhold useful effort whenever a minimal threshold of benefit is attained, and so on. Another individual's rankings or intensities may be quite different. And process norms and their relative intensities can also vary across groups.

Like the category of other-regarding preferences, that of process-regarding preferences (or values) is an inclusive one that is not restricted to values of which moral authorities might approve. For instance, the desire to act according to the codes of conduct of a juvenile or criminal gang also fits comfortably within the rubric of process-regarding preferences, although it may not meet most standards of prosociality or virtue. Adherence to the process constraints inherent in the norms of behavior of some families, communities, or ethnic groups may entail discrimination or even violence against outsiders, as noted by Bowles and Gintis (this volume). Some values may be dysfunctional for economic performance, as argued by Kuran and by Montias (this volume). And there is much room for disagreement about which values are good or bad. The upshot of all this is that while many references to values in our essay are implicitly about ones widely approved of, it is not analytically necessary to restrict the concept of process-regarding preferences to that subclass only.

Our distinction between other-regarding preferences and process-regarding preferences is comparable with the distinction between altruism and manners suggested by Camerer and Thaler (1995); see also McCloskey (1994). These ideas may be formalized also by seemingly retaining an objective function defined solely over personal outcomes, introducing concern for others and for process as constraints. This is the formalization suggested by Rabin (1995), who shows that the two alternative formulations are not entirely equivalent (see also Kuran, this volume). Another approach, attributable to Sen (1987), is to permit individuals to have possibly normative metapreferences over their potential preference functions, with an ability to distinguish between those preferences they might act on selfishly, and those which they would

of getting them to do so. One reason we might accept this cost is that, insofar as we care how others regard us, we prefer to think of ourselves as moral individuals. Indeed, we may be inclined to suppress from consciousness any indications to the contrary (Wright 1994). Our interest for the moment, however, is with the primitive fact of moral concerns, with theoretical explanations of their origins to be discussed later, in section 2.3.

morally prefer themselves to have.[25] Still other formulations allow for both the other- and process-regarding preferences suggested here but make no distinction between them. Finally, a concern for process is often identified with a desire to meet the expectations of others, or to be regarded well by them. Thus, Sugden (this volume) suggests that individuals' desires to act in accord with other people's expectations can be "treated as an additional motivating factor, not included in the payoffs." Likewise, Fershtman and Weiss (this volume) model behavior as being motivated by concern for social status – how other people regard one's behavior – in addition to self-interest.

## 2.2     *Preferences and behavior*

Economists distinguish between preferences and behavior. A given set of preferences may lead to different behaviors in the face of different constraints; different sets of preferences may lead to the same behaviors under different constraints. The distinction between preferences and behavior is equally useful in the context of values and other-regarding preferences and the behaviors induced by them. For example, an honest person resists the temptation to steal because of her beliefs in right and wrong.[26] An individual holding no such value may well behave honestly (refrain from stealing or committing even more minor infractions) for totally self-regarding reasons.[27] And many people may be weakly honest

[25] Mansbridge (this volume) notes Sen's emphasis on the importance of "counter-preferential choice" and goes on to argue that "both love and duty contrast with self-interest, and cannot be reduced to it." Our own suggestion of viewing human behavioral predispositions as inclusive of all three of these categories, somewhat more broadly construed as other-regarding, process-regarding, and self-regarding preferences, may differ methodologically but is not substantively in conflict with her position.

[26] Several dozen passengers on a vehicle caught in a flood in India in 1973 are reported to have drowned rather than escape by means of a rescue rope that had been used by passengers of a different caste (McKean 1974, cited by McKenzie 1977, p. 213). Orthodox Muslims and Jews would incur great costs to avoid eating pork or eating at all on particular days. "Progressive-minded" individuals will avoid voicing opinions that they deem politically unconscionable. Other examples are provided by Darwin 1871, pp. 99–100.

[27] He may respond to the possibility of punishment if caught behaving dishonestly or may seek, given the prospect of repeated interactions over time with the same group of economic actors, to build a profitable reputation for being honest (which may outweigh in his case the occasional benefits of dishonest behavior), and so forth. The following excerpt from a work of fiction illustrates the point well. Says Mr. Lander, the shipowner: "This business may not look very good on the front side. But on the back it is full of what they call ethics. And the two most important rules are: You don't cheat a customer. And you never cheat a fellow shipowner. . . . You screw the state and the authorities if an opportunity presents itself. . . . But you don't cheat a customer. Because you need cus-

in the sense that they prefer to be honest but choose not to be when the cost is high enough. Such sensitivity of process-regarding behavior to relative prices means that the framework proposed here is amenable to the same kind of analysis as is the familiar neoclassical framework; for example, if process-regarding preferences reflect adherence to a norm, then such adherence can be analyzed in much the same manner as purchase of a tangible good (see Rabin 1995; Kuran, this volume).

But the influence of preferences on behavior should not be underestimated. An honest mechanic will not perform unnecessary work or charge for fictitious repairs. A conscientious worker will not shirk if he thinks he is treated well. A trustworthy manager will not break a promise made to an employee or superior. A reliable business partner is good for his word. As we shall argue later, the strength and distribution of preferences in society are neither uniform nor fixed, and many such reputational differences may reflect no more than the long-term outlooks of selfish persons in situations where it makes sense to invest in them. Nonetheless, the burden of our argument is that behavior can in fact be affected by affecting preferences, in addition to standard variables more conventionally considered in economic analysis.

Along with preferences, cognitive abilities and habits, and in particular the ways and degrees in which rationality is bounded, are important to consider as determinants of behavior. People vary in their ability to calculate the course of action that is best given their preferences and constraints. They also vary in their inclinations to expend mental energy or time on calculations. While the *inclination* to calculate is readily conceived of as a process-regarding preference, the *ability* to do so is an endowment that determines how well one can pursue her preferences. But since practice may improve proficiency, over time calculativeness (the preference) may also engender sharper calculating abilities. This is an example of the manifold interactions between cognitive abilities and preferences.

To see how both preferences of all types and cognitive characteristics determine an individual's behavior under a given set of economic constraints, consider again the example of the ultimatum game. There are $x$ dollars to be divided between $A$ and $B$. $A$ makes a proposal for a division; if $B$ accepts the proposal, it is implemented, but if $B$ rejects it, the $x$ dollars are withdrawn and neither gets anything. A fully rational and

tomers to come back. And above all, you never cheat a broker. We shipping folks stick together. The way it works is, I have a customer who has a ship and you have a customer who has a cargo, and we bring them together. Next time it's the other way around. A ship broker lives off other ship brokers, who live off other ship brokers" (Peter Hoeg, *Smilla's Sense of Snow* [New York: Farrar, Straus & Giroux, 1993], pp. 200–201).

self-interested individual $A$ who knows with certainty that $B$ is equally rational and self-interested will propose a division that gives next to nothing to $B$, knowing that it will be accepted. The same proposer will make a more generous offer if she believes that $B$ is either boundedly rational in the sense that he does not understand that he cannot affect the division in his favor by refusing a very small offer in a one-shot game or if she believes that $B$ subscribes to an inviolable concept of fairness that would lead him to reject an offer of less than a certain amount or percentage. Thus $A$ may make more or less generous offers, depending on her assumptions about $B$'s cognitive abilities, ethical positions, and other-regarding preferences.

The proposer's own preferences and abilities will likewise affect the offers she makes (but, unlike the reverse case, not the likelihood of their acceptance in a one-shot game). A somewhat other-regarding proposer may offer, for example, a 60–40 division, taking advantage of her position as first mover, but not exhausting that advantage (assuming she believes she could do so) because of her concern for $B$. Alternatively, with little or no other-regarding feelings, $A$ could still adhere to a process-oriented notion of fairness that holds, for example, that all rewards should be meted out according to contribution only, with windfalls being distributed equally to those involved in the event; she would therefore propose a 50–50 allocation.[28]

Many other possibilities, based on combinations of different types and degrees of the three categories of preferences as well as the nature and degree of bounded rationality, can be constructed (and matched with outcomes of the kind that have been found in experiments with the ultimatum game). Thus what many may consider as ethical behavior – sharing a windfall with one's fellow – indeed may stem from the sharer's (proposer's) ethical attitude, but may also be the consequence of the other person's (responder's) ethical attitude or the result of the expectation that third-party observers of the interaction may approve of sharing;[29] bounded rationality (as noted), altruism, and the proposer's attitude toward the risk that the respondent may be refusal-prone, will

---

[28] This does not suggest that $A$ must be a universal altruist to act in the way suggested in the text. The participation in the game puts $A$ in a partnership of sorts with $B$, since $A$'s fate is linked to $B$'s fate via $B$'s ability to block any rewards to $A$. Hence $A$ may well believe that $B$, as her partner, should receive a reward according to the principle cited in the text; yet in the absence of a partner, she may decide to keep the entire amount $x$ to herself. This may account for the finding that proposers act more selfishly in the "dictator game," where $A$ decides how much to give to $B$, who is entirely passive (Hoffman, McCabe, and Smith 1996).

[29] Kreps (1990, pp. 116–20) examined the consequences of another process-regarding preference – of not wanting to be taken advantage of (being a "dupe") – for possible outcomes of the ultimatum game. His discussion suggests that it is not easy to deduce

affect her proposals, too. Finally, the absolute size of the windfall may affect the offers made and accepted, as may its size relative to the wealth of the individuals concerned (a wealthier individual may be able to act more easily on her ethical concerns than a poorer one).[30]

The example of the ultimatum game suggests a number of general (not necessarily new) lessons for economic theorists. First, the behavior of individuals can be affected by their own other- and process-regarding preferences. Second, the perceived or imputed preferences of other actors may matter just as much to the behavior of an individual as his own preferences so that, in a static framework with stable preferences, it is sufficient that only *part* of the population be guided by moral considerations for the rest of the population to find it utility-maximizing to act in a manner that resembles moral behavior.[31] Third, while the foregoing raises the possibility of saving *homo economicus* by attributing virtuous or caring (or, for that matter, vicious or callous) behavior only to a few exogenous *others*,[32] such an approach remains timid and incomplete. If, as we argue later, the inculcation of other- and process-regarding preferences is to a considerable degree a result of rational calculations, and if the maintenance of such preferences depends upon interactions with others in predictable ways, then we can go much further by embracing and endogenizing such preferences within a broader economic calculus, rather than merely acknowledging them as unexplained oddities. Indeed, the framework of stable preferences is clearly unsatisfactory, for many an individual who holds fairness or other-regarding preferences dear will not continue to sustain them if she gathers sufficient evidence that they are violated or not reciprocated by others: hence the need to consider the evolution of preferences in situations in which individuals accumulate experience with both the behavior of others and the preferences which they impute to them.[33]

---

from one's behavior whether she is an ethical person or just one who wants to make the point that she is not a dupe.

[30] Generally, anonymity of both $A$ and $B$ tends to generate outcomes that come closest to the situation in which $A$ and $B$ are self-interested rational actors, although substantial positive offers are nonetheless the norm. Face-to-face interactions among players familiar with each other represent the other extreme, in which outcomes result most often in a near 50–50 division. Variations in these conditions are likely to be associated with differences in the relative intensities of the three categories of preferences discussed here.

[31] For an early statement of this point, see Becker (1976).

[32] This prospect has not been missed by theorists of orthodox inclination; an even more neoclassical strategy is seen in models which generate seemingly unselfish behaviors by simply introducing a small doubt about whether some other agents may be of an unselfish or irrational type. See, e.g., Aumann (1990), and Kreps et al. (1982).

[33] To be sure, the number of "moral" actors may remain small after the endogenous inculcation of values has been modeled. For instance, Guttman (1996b) provides a

Economists who have accepted the need for an "extended" model of preferences[34] have moved cautiously. Attempting to begin from familiar ground, some have attacked questions of altruism and conscience by asking whether "economic man," whose real concerns are with maximizing a conventional function of wealth and leisure, might *choose* to have an altruistic or moral utility function, or to work to endow his offspring with one, because this would lead to better outcomes in terms of that narrower set of preferences.[35] Such an approach yields interesting results, showing that broadened utility functions might indeed be rationally chosen on the basis of narrow ones, but it also has some drawbacks. It is unclear, for instance, which set of preferences are the real preferences of the agent: Are they those with which the preferences governing behavior are selected, or the latter preferences themselves? If the players of a game that looks like a prisoner's dilemma to *homo economicus* have willed themselves into finding cheating others distasteful only because such an attitude is useful to them as economic men and women, how can we be sure that the real tastes governing their choice of attitude won't reassert themselves once the playing is under way? We believe, however, that there is a more important reason for making a cleaner departure from the neoclassical *homo economicus* model. It is that once we permit plasticity of the utility function, there is no satisfactory theoretical rationale for proceeding from a presumption of individual self-interest and nothing more. On the contrary, that body of extant scientific theory which does offer a real foundation for a scientific theory of preferences – the theory of natural selection which we discuss presently – suggests that *homo economicus* is a virtual impossibility.[36]

theoretical model in which it pays for parents to invest in a moral taste in their children, even when the probability of success is low. The existence of some genuinely or unalterably moral individuals makes feigning such tastes profitable for the rest of the population. While this outcome has a ring of authenticity, we believe that a more realistic model would also allow for intermediate outcomes, with some children becoming somewhat moral, and with adults thus varying widely in their degrees of internalized versus opportunistic "virtue."

[34] We borrow the term "extended preference" from Paul Romer (personal communication).

[35] See, for example, Frank (1988), Rotemberg (1994), Bernheim and Stark (1988), and Weisbrod (1977). Models such as that of Guttman (1996b) and of Fershtman and Weiss (this volume), in which a parent selects a desirable utility function for the offspring based on narrower utility grounds, are similar in this respect.

[36] Darwin was probably the most articulate proponent of the naturalist view of human tendencies, and as willing as anyone else to ground these tendencies in as few "primitives" as possible. However, even he found the description of all behavior as selfishly motivated to be unsatisfactory. After discussing self-sacrifice, he concludes that we cannot explain "the most noble part of our nature" by recourse to "the base principle of

## 2.3    *Genes and the origin of preferences*

While the *homo economicus* approach has remained firmly entrenched in economics since the midnineteenth century, its depiction of motivation is scarcely in line with modern behavioral science, a fact that led Gunnar Myrdal to complain as early as 1929 that economics was basing itself on "a dinosaur psychology." It is not just that human behavior is sometimes at variance with predictions of models based on the *homo economicus* assumption; more importantly, science provides no reason to expect that it could be otherwise. In his book *Darwin's Dangerous Idea*, Daniel Dennett (1995) argues that many philosophers, humanists, and even cognitive scientists continue, more than a century after Darwin, to resist the idea that *homo sapiens* could have been produced entirely by evolution, with no helping hand from on high. He might have extended his tarring brush equally to economists, whose *homo economicus* seems to have been created by some invisible "manus ex machina." Human beings, after all, did not spring fully grown from the head of some Enlightenment philosopher. Rather, they have evolved along an eons-long path of organic mutation and selection. To the extent that human beings have predictable behavioral propensities, these would have emerged initially from the organic evolutionary process, undergoing further modification by cultural processes that were themselves shaped by biologically given capabilities.[37]

selfishness . . . unless indeed the satisfaction which every animal feels when it follows its proper instincts, and the dissatisfaction felt when prevented, be called selfish" (Darwin 1871, pp. 98–99). The claim, often made today, that reducing every voluntary action to selfishness is tantamount to a tautology, seems to have resonated well with Darwin. This is not to say that consideration of self-interest alone is always an inferior point of departure for certain analytic purposes or that it is always necessary to work with a full-fledged model of evolved human beings. But it is necessary to acknowledge which simplifications are made, why, and how they may affect the outcomes of a particular analysis.

[37] While arguing for the theory of evolution is probably unnecessary and beyond the scope of this chapter, we may briefly paraphrase Buss (1995), who, in a review of the literature of evolutionary psychology, suggests that only three causal processes are thought capable of producing complex physiological and psychological mechanisms: evolution by natural selection, creation by a supernatural being, and seeding by extraterrestrial organisms. Buss argues that while creationism is unfalsifiable and seeding theory pushes the required explanation to a different level, "[e]volution by natural selection, in contrast, is a powerful and well-articulated theory that has successfully organized and explained thousands of diverse facts in a principled way" (1995, p. 20). The evolutionary approach to behavior is thus "unlikely to be supplanted by another unless some radically new causal process . . . is discovered to account for the complex adaptations that characterize humans and other species" (1995, p. 26).

Where do preferences, indeed human nature, come from? Evolutionary biological theory and evolutionary psychology, the human-specific theory derived from it, argue that "there is a universal human nature, but that this universality exists primarily at the level of evolved psychological mechanisms, not of expressed cultural behaviors" (Cosmides, Tooby, and Barkow 1995, p. 5). While evolution leads to universal human traits, there are differences in expressed behaviors due to variations across individuals in exact genetic blueprints (male vs. female, blue eyes vs. brown, and perhaps differences in temperamental and related predispositions) and due to the shaping of behaviors, not only by genes but also by environmental stimuli ranging from facts of birth order, child rearing, and childhood nutrition to broader differences in cultural and institutional environments. The complex functional design that constitutes human nature represents adaptations which have been produced by a process of natural selection over a geological time scale and most recently genetically adapted to the way of life of our Pleistocene hunter–gatherer ancestors (but almost certainly not to current circumstances).[38]

Cosmides, Tooby, and Barkow (1992, p. 9) explain this process as follows:

> Imagine that a new design feature arises in one or a few members of a species, entirely by chance mutation. . . . Let's say that this new design feature solves an adaptive problem better than designs that already exist in that species: . . . [for example, a] new learning mechanism [that] allows one to find food more efficiently. By so doing, the new design feature causes individuals who have it to produce more offspring, on average, than offspring who have alternative designs. If offspring can inherit the new design feature from their parents, then it will increase in frequency in the population. Individuals who have the new design will tend to have more offspring than those who lack it, those of their offspring who inherit the new design will have more offspring, and so on, until, after enough generations, every member of the species will have the new design feature. Eventually . . . the more reliable learning mechanism will become universal in that species, typically found in every member of it.

The unit of natural selection is not the individual organism (as one might falsely infer from the preceding excerpt), but the gene. The organism – the individual person – is the vehicle (host, bearer) through which the gene replicates itself (Dawkins 1989). It is the rationality of the gene,

---

[38] This is because the number of generations since the industrial, and probably even the agricultural, revolution is simply too short to have permitted much natural selection to occur (see also the comparison of postagricultural and overall human history in Douglass North's chapter, this volume).

so to speak, that is considered to be the driving force of evolution. The rationality of the gene means that genes that procreate at the fastest rate can be regarded as if carrying out a cost–benefit analysis in comparison of alternative strategies, where a strategy is a trait (such as caring for offspring) that affects the behavior of the gene's vehicle (a microbe, a daffodil, an aardvark, a woman, or a man).[39]

Thus whereas economists posit that the individual acts so as to maximize his or her utility, biological theory hypothesizes that traits are selected for according as they maximize the proliferation of organisms bearing the associated genes.[40] Traits that increase the inclination or ability of organisms to experience psychic well-being (or to have access to more resources, or to have increased personal longevity) can survive, of course, and pleasure (resources) and genetic survival are associated. But the correlation between pleasure or wealth seeking and genetic fitness is far from total.[41]

Consider the fact that human (and many animal) mothers will sacrifice

[39] It is only figuratively, of course, that one should think of genes as optimizing. As Maynard Smith (1982, p. 5) put it (in seeking to provide an analogy that allows using the terminology of intentionality in explaining evolution), "When calculating the path of a ray of light between two points, $A$ and $B$, after reflection or refraction, it is sometimes convenient to make use of the fact that the light follows the path which minimises the time taken to reach $B$. It is a simple consequence of the laws of physics that this should be so; no-one supposes that the ray of light setting out from $A$ calculates the quickest route to $B$."

[40] While the main contours of evolutionary theory are uncontroversial, many details are contested by theorists of various persuasions. However, differences among different versions of evolutionary theory have only a limited effect on our story of the evolution of preferences.

[41] Utilitarian theory was developed mostly before evolutionary theory (Bentham wrote in 1789, much before Darwin). Although J. S. Mill published his *Utilitarianism* in 1861 (in *Fraser's Magazine*), two years after Darwin's *On the Origins of Species by Means of Natural Selection*, Mill showed no awareness of Darwin's work. However, Darwin, writing *The Descent of Man, and Selection in Relation to Sex*, in 1871, discussed Mill's ideas favorably, although he thought them not sufficiently informed by evolutionary theory. Darwin thought that there is no evolutionary basis for the "Greatest Happiness Principle" (see Darwin 1871, chap. III), yet he argued that "the social instincts . . . no doubt were acquired by man, as by the lower animals, for the good of the [narrow] community" (Darwin 1871, p. 103). This weak version of the "group selection" theory is now viewed as erroneous by many evolutionary theorists. Darwin held mostly an organism-centered theory (the concept of genes was unknown to him) and had difficulty going beyond a warriorlike characterization of humans, yet he believed that there are traits like altruism that persist, and their existence baffled him scientifically. It has been conjectured that it was Darwin's difficulty (like that of many other scientists, until Hamilton [1964]) in explaining acts of sacrifice by an organism whose survival depends on its own, not others', success that led to his occasional recourse to the idea of group selection. See Cronin (1992) for a detailed discussion.

nourishment, rest, and sexual contact while caring for newborn offspring. These tendencies have been selected for in the course of our evolution because they enhanced the prospects that offspring would survive to procreate. A gene for nurturing, the removal of which causes mothers to ignore their offspring, who then die within days, may recently have even been discovered in mice (Brown et al. 1996). Mutations causing neglect of offspring (or absence of genes causing attention to them) need not arise exclusively in laboratories but may also occur accidentally in nature. Yet they are obviously not viable, simply because the vehicles carrying the altered gene (the mice) cannot transmit these genes to viable mice, so that there is no mechanism for passing the mutation from generation to generation.[42]

Not only is the pleasure, consumption, or resource accumulation of the individual or her proclivity to pursue these single-mindedly *not* what is selected for through the process of evolution, but even his or her physical survival is not central to evolution. If the chances of survival of a gene are increased by having its bearers sacrifice themselves to save enough others of its bearers to make benefit exceed cost for the gene (in the sense of multiplying itself at the fastest feasible pace), such behavior would be selected for. This principle of *inclusive fitness* means that genes that inclined their bearers to be solicitous toward their siblings would have been selected for in our past.[43] Solicitous behavior probably works through feelings of empathy and concern, as well as through tendencies of parents to help cultivate such behavior and of offspring to be receptive of parental messages.[44]

But cooperative tendencies may not be confined to one's relations with relatives. Favorable attitudes toward one's relatives based on the reproduction of the same genes seem to be complemented by at least

---

[42] It might be supposed that the parent makes present sacrifices for the offspring mainly because of the anticipation of a future personal return. Bergstrom (1996) reviews the evidence on this and concludes that both theory and empirical research suggest that it is not generally true – calculated rates of return to parents are extremely low or negative.

[43] Let $r$ be the degree of relatedness among two organisms, and assume $r = 1/2$ among parent and child, sibling and sibling; $r = 1/4$ among half-siblings, nieces, nephews, aunts, and uncles; $r = 1/8$ among first cousins. Then the logic of natural selection under inclusive fitness would favor propensities to sacrifice oneself for two or more siblings, for eight or more cousins, and so on, with appropriate adjustments for the remaining procreative and nurturing potential of those involved.

[44] See Hamilton (1964) and Bergstrom (1995) on "kin altruism"; see also discussions in Dawkins (1989), Cronin (1992), and Wright (1994). In Hanson and Stuart (1990), natural selection of preferences over offspring's consumption is modeled as the solution to a problem of maximizing steady-state per capita consumption, which is there equivalent to genetic fitness.

conditionally favorable attitudes toward members of the group with which ancestral individuals had to cooperate in order to survive and allow their genes to reproduce. Some sociobiologists and evolutionary psychologists have argued that genes favoring the playing of tit-for-tat-type strategies in settings resembling the prisoner's dilemma would have been favored because they would have advanced the survival and reproductive success of those bearing them under conditions of nonanonymous repeated play. In a small community of the sort our ancestors probably lived in during the course of human genetic evolution, each individual could remember whether a given other had behaved cooperatively ("fairly") or not (had "cheated") in previous interactions. Cooperators would have been favored as partners – the tendency to do so itself selected for by its evolutionary fitness – and would accordingly have thrived. Thus a built-in inclination to cooperate, and to feel moral outrage at those who do not, may have been selected for in the course of evolution.[45] Desires for approval by others, and inclinations to emulate the behaviors and apparent attitudes of others in the absence of strong

---

[45] Hirshleifer and Martinez Coll (1988) rightly caution against drawing overly strong inferences from Axelrod's (1984) much celebrated work on the evolution of cooperation, pointing out that varying payoff structures and assumptions about the selection process among strategies can generate different strategy choices, or populations of mixed player types. Yet the indeterminacy of theoretical models and computer simulations needs to be viewed alongside accumulating evidence from psychological experiments and neuroscience, which seem broadly supportive of reciprocity theory. Although the exact mechanism remains unknown, for instance, an important element of cooperation appears to be the ability to recognize partners to past interactions, thus a memory for faces and actions associated with those faces. The human brain apparently has a capacity for such specific memory lodged in specific places, "the underside of both occipital lobes, extending forward to the inner surface of the temporal lobes. This localization of cause, and specificity of effect, indicates that the recognition of individual faces has been an important enough task for a significant portion of the brain's resources to be devoted to it" (Axelrod and Hamilton 1981, p. 1395). Hence it is likely that an inclination to cooperate with known others has been hard-wired in us, as has a suspicion of strangers. Note the suggestion, however, that it is a desire *to be perceived as* a cooperator that will have been selected for, since a tendency to cheat and thereby conserve one's resources for oneself and one's kin when one is sure to get away with it would in principle have been a favored trait. Cosmides (1989) argues that perhaps natural selection endowed us with an ability to search for cheaters through a procedure that detects violations of social rules and finds experimental support for her hypothesis. For a readable discussion of the issue of reciprocal altruism, see Wright (1994, chap. 9); see also Guth and Yaari (1992), which analyzes a game-theoretic model of the evolution of reciprocal altruism. We note, finally, that the importance of resentment as a marker of normative assessment, stressed by Daniel Kahnemann and Allan Gibbard in their separate remarks at the Conference on Economics, Values, and Organization, fits well with the basic argument about genetic selection of such propensities toward behavior among nonkin.

reasons to do otherwise, may have been favored for roughly the same reasons.

Among the interesting implications of the theory of reciprocal altruism is that because they evolved in situations of relatively small numbers and high individual identifiability, today's human beings might be more prone to cooperation than is currently individually rational.[46] At the same time, modern men and women, moving among others whom they do not recognize as either cooperators or defectors, are likely to be less cooperative and more suspicious of one another than would be the case were the same partners to interact on a more regular basis (see Bowles and Gintis, this volume).

The foregoing should make it clear enough that while the organism that is the result of human evolution has some innate empathy and an inclination toward reciprocity, she can be quite as devious as *homo economicus* in pursuit of her interests.[47] The picture of relations between the sexes and of the associated status rivalry that emerges from considering the strategic interest of the genes of males and females is also hardly comely.[48] The "selfishness" of the genes translates not only into consideration for kin and known persons with whom one might cooperate, but also into a struggle to assure that a gene's bearer – a person – thrives, reproduces, and (where possible) sees its offspring through to reproduction as well. This means that the role of self-regarding preferences remains central.

Actual, evolved persons are also somewhat less rational than *homo economicus*, since instead of being endowed with perfect calculating

[46] In other words, the large-numbers problems identified by Buchanan (1965) and Olson (1971) might partly be avoided by the "hard-wiring" of traits acquired in a small-numbers environment. Compare also Bowles (1990) and Guttman (1996a). Like other economists, we note that the term "reciprocal altruism," favored by some biologists, is something of a misnomer, for the logic behind it favors no sacrifice except in the anticipation of at least equal future gains for oneself, in this respect contrasting with kin altruism, which may dictate genuine "self-sacrifice."

[47] There is incomplete agreement about the deviousness of *homo economicus*; for instance, Hirshleifer (1994) claims that her "dark side" has not been adequately explored. This reading of received economics is consistent with Williamson's inclination (1975, 1985) to *add* "opportunism" to the usual assumptions about human behavior, as well as with Bowles and Gintis's (1993) argument that a more thoroughgoingly self-seeking *homo economicus* will have its revenge on promoters of its more genteel textbook cousin by changing problems once assumed solved by markets into ongoing "contested exchange" relationships.

[48] On the other hand, we differ with Schwartz's (1993b) view that sociobiology, and by extension evolutionary psychology, simply provides a further instance of the primacy of the idea that human beings are selfish. The "selfishness" of the gene and the selfishness of the person are quite different matters.

machines, they have complex cognitive and emotional equipment built piggyback on the more primitive nervous systems of reptilian and early mammalian ancestors, mixing emotive and rational elements in the process of cognition (Goleman, 1995; de Sousa 1987; MacLeod 1996) and permitting the individual to deceive his or her own self when it is evolutionarily functional to do so.

## 2.4    *Culture and co-evolution*

It is implausible to explain behavior in too fine a degree of detail on a genetic evolutionary basis alone. For one thing, selection of purely random modifications of genetically embedded behavioral propensities could have been fine-tuned to a limited degree only over the course of a mere fifty thousand generations or so.[49] Moreover, cultural change can in principle occur far more rapidly than genetic because to some degree its adaptations are *designed*, and because its means of proliferation include asexual copying as well as imposition (e.g., of behavioral standards). Of course, culture is a product of gene-based organisms, in the sense that it is built upon physically evolved mental and emotional machinery. Furthermore, the human capacity for culture can only have evolved if it showed evolutionary fitness from the standpoint of the usual genetic criteria. While this suggests that humans will not have developed social propensities or psychological traits that were counterproductive to their fitness in the environment in which they evolved, it is worth noting that cultural variability remains possible, so that behavior may not be uniquely linked to genes.

Biologists distinguish between the characteristics of the developed organism, including realized behavioral propensities, denoted the phe-

---

[49] Great caution is surely called for before proclaiming traits maladaptive, for a hidden source of fitness may await discovery. In our present ignorance it seems noteworthy, though, that genetic evolution has left us with imperfectly adapted backs, unneeded but frequently dangerous tonsils and appendixes, and such seemingly anomalous and presumably nonadaptive propensities as those toward homosexuality or schizophrenia, as well as suicidal impulses. A problem with some of the argumentation in evolutionary theory (the extreme "adaptationist" or "reductionist" position), it seems to us, is that it leaps from arguing that a certain mutation would have been beneficial to concluding that the mutation must have occurred. This reminds us of the joke about the economist who discounts a friend's report that there is a twenty dollar bill lying before him on the sidewalk, insisting that had there been one there, it would have already been picked up by somebody. There is at best some probability that a hypothetically beneficial mutation (twenty dollar bill) will have occurred (been picked up) given a certain frequency of mutations (passers-by) and a certain period of time. See Gould (1993, 1997) for a critical evaluation of the adaptationist position.

notype, and the underlying genetic makeup, or genotype (see, for example, the discussion of Tooby and Cosmides [1990]). An organism's phenotype is determined by both its genotype and its environment. For instance, the mouse gene mentioned earlier is apparently necessary for the evolution of nurturing behavior, but it is not the only factor contributing to such behavior. Brown et al. (1996), like others before them, found that mice possessing the "nurturing gene" learn how to nurture from observing other mice engaging in such behavior. More generally, psychological traits may well occur in bundles of expressed behavior that are not decomposable. If this is so, then while a particular bundle may have fitness value, not all its components will necessarily have this property, and certainly not under all conditions that may arise in different places and times. For example, Burkert (1996) argues for the existence of a biological basis for humans' religious beliefs, while pointing out some of the unavoidable correlates of religions (such as warfare) which may not have fitness value. In the past million years or so, cultural change and genetic change may also have interacted; for instance, changes in brain structures that enhanced linguistic capacity may have had greater fitness value after primitive language use had begun to evolve, so the appearance of language may have accelerated the evolution of language-capable brain structure (Lumsden and Wilson 1983).

Dual theories of inheritance, which give weight to both genetic and cultural factors, treat culture as an aspect of human phenotypes, and as a system for the transmission and selection of traits in its own right (Cavalli-Sforza and Feldman 1981; Boyd and Richerson 1985; Durham 1991). The theories vary with regard to the autonomy of culture. Dawkins (1989) suggested that the "meme," a proposed analogue to genes operating in cultural transmission, is propagated from brain to brain by forces having little to do with genetic survival; Lumsden and Wilson (1983) use the image of genes holding culture on a leash; Durham (1991) proposes a positive correlation between genetic and cultural evolutionary fitness; and Cavalli-Sforza and Feldman (1981) lean toward a tight fit between the two. One example of interaction between the genetic and cultural evolutionary processes may be that pertaining to the aforementioned problem of cooperation among nonrelatives, where the logic of parent–child and sibling–sibling altruism no longer appears to hold. The evolution of *cultural* constructs conforming to the basic ethos of first cooperating with a member of one's group, then punishing him if deceived, may not only have been favored by a genetic process of the sort referred to, but also may have reinforced and accelerated that process in the later stages of its development. Cultural constructs include institutions, values, and norms, and their evolution over time and in different places was determined in part by local and temporal circumstance and happenstance.[50]

The role played by emotions that are little if at all consciously controlled by those subject to them is also of great importance to, and might help to explain, the peculiar tendency to seek revenge on someone who has wronged us even when the further cost to us cannot be rationally justified. But again, notions of justice, reciprocity, and the like, may have evolved in culture in a fashion complementary to, and possibly more refined than, these genetic predispositions. Thus, there could be the physiological basis of an "ethics module" in our nervous system, but its detailed contents and the extent of its development could be determined by our general culture and by our individual socialization experiences.[51] An interesting example of the effect of socialization on ethical attitudes, and perhaps on an ethics module, is the effect on personality of the order of an individual's birth in the family. Sulloway (1996) regards the family not simply as a shared environment, but as a set of niches that provide different siblings with different outlooks. He argues that competition over family resources, especially parental attention and affection, creates rivalries among siblings, and the order of birth confers distinct advantages and disadvantages that come to shape personalities. For instance, eldest children tend to identify with parents and authority and support the status quo, whereas later borns rebel against it. These differences appear to manifest themselves in different preferences, such as greater sympathy for others exhibited by later borns. Thus children are born without a specific gene for firstborn or later born, yet develop preferences based on the order of birth on the basis of broad genetic propensities, illustrating the phenotype–genotype dynamic. Competition over resources exists outside the family, too, and its effect on the evolution of the preferences of individuals in the course of their personal lives and in response to their personal experiences, within the confines of the inherited genetic makeup, should also be considered.

---

[50] See the discussion by Durham (1991), who argues that cultural selection operates primarily through the mediation of what he calls "secondary values," which are standards or criteria that were in their own turn selected for by the biological evolutionary process acting on the usual criterion of inclusive fitness. It is the biological–evolutionary selectedness of the secondary values which, according to Durham, causes most of our choices among cultural alternatives to be made in a fitness-enhancing manner. On the role of culture in the evolution of cooperation, see Boyd and Richerson (1985, chap. 7).

[51] On the ethics module, see Dennett (1995, chap. 16). The propensity to anger at being "wronged" by others, while itself "irrational," may also be seized upon by the rational self, which may calculate which threats to issue on the basis of largely rational criteria, although the credibility of the threats depends upon an "irrational" inclination to carry them out when they are ex post "irrational" (see Frank 1988).

The respective roles of culture and of genes in determining the characteristics of individual persons bears some similarity to the roles of prices and tastes in the theory of Stigler and Becker (1977). There, people are endowed with a common set of basic tastes, but what particular goods they eventually favor as means of satisfying those tastes is determined by a taste-acquisition process, in which relative prices and incomes play key roles. However, it is not necessarily only the details of taste (whether one prefers pizza or apple pie) in a narrow sense that are affected by environment and prices, as in the Stigler–Becker theory, but also perhaps such fundamentals as the relative weights placed on self-, other-, and process-regarding preferences.[52] Thus, our environments, including institutions created by people themselves, may affect our preferences in ways that then have important impacts on social behavior and outcomes, both by affecting the relative costs and benefits of different forms of behavior, and by offering different role models and messages of acculturation.

In sum, evolutionary theory provides a scientific framework for predicting the type of preferences we are likely to be endowed with.[53] If we pose to it the question of whether we human beings are red in tooth and claw or kindhearted and harmless, what it tells us is that our genes have been tested and tested again for reproductive success and that while this demands of the individual organism a degree of what is commonly seen as selfishness, we evolved human beings are also inclined to help our fellow gene bearers and to cooperate with less closely related conspecifics where collectively higher payoffs are likely to result. At the same time, our phenotypic behaviors are not determined by our genes alone. While receptivity to environmental influences is broadly circumscribed by genetic propensities, our environments, including culture, also importantly influence our moral propensities. The longer "leash" humans enjoy as compared to all other animal species stems from the

---

[52] For example, the proportion of "collectivists" versus "individualists" seems to vary significantly across countries (Hofstede 1980). As the cross-national experiment by Roth et al. (1991) shows, "generous" offers in ultimatum games are proposed and accepted in different proportions in different countries. Evolutionary models with multiple equilibria, and of course with different equilibria when the environmental parameters (e.g., the payoff functions) differ, have also been derived. See, for instance, the hawks–doves model (e.g., Maynard Smith 1982; Mailath 1992).

[53] As Campbell (1986, p. 172) puts it: "Rationality in economic theory is primarily a rationality of the means whereby individuals . . . maximize utilities. Especially where the behavior of persons is at issue, the content of the utilities is left open, unspecified by theory. . . . [E]volutionary biology offers the promise of theoretical grounds for predicting such contents, that is, predicting what sort of interests the products of biological evolution would be apt to have."

disproportionately large brain with which they ended up in the evolution process.

Reference to the length of the leash on which our genetic propensities hold us brings us to a brief, but, from a normative standpoint, rather important remark, with which we will conclude this portion of the discussion. Although our essay is not primarily concerned with the strictly normative question of what our values *ought* to be (our interest lies in the question of what our values are, how they evolve, and how they are and might be affected by the arrangement of our social and economic life), we want to emphasize that our insistence upon the importance of evolutionary explanations for human traits should not be understood as an endorsement of the view that "the good" is that which is good for the genes. On the contrary, we would seek a thorough knowledge of the implications of evolution the better to rebel against what is frequently the amoral tyranny of the genes, unthinking machines that happen to have a knack for replicating. Of course, a belief in a freedom so to rebel implies a belief in a degree of autonomy between culture and/or individual, and genes, of just the type that we have advanced here. And a belief that moral choice is a meaningful possibility may require openness to a domain of genuine moral reasoning (Hausman and McPherson 1996), which our discussion by no means rules out. Human nature is neither strictly selfish nor strictly innate, but rather includes dispositions toward altruism and openness to moral sensibilities which are shaped over time by environmental stimuli. The plasticity of preferences provides some scope for actions aimed at shaping them, at least within the constraints imposed by our natures.[54]

## 2.5    *Institutions, organizations, and changes in preferences*

We will use the term "institutions" to refer to rules, laws, norms, and customs, and the term "organizations" to refer to the social settings within which activities such as production, learning, and consumption take place. Institutions include the legal or accepted ways of carrying out various activities, such as the rules and laws governing market exchange, jurisprudence, and politics, and also widely held normative notions such as those regarding fairness and reciprocity. Organizations include firms,

---

[54] Campbell (1986, p. 177) writes: "We probably have an innate ambivalence (facultative polymorphism) . . . an available repertoire of cooperative group solidarity and another one of individual optimization at the expense of the group." It is just such an ambivalence that opens to us a space for moral reasoning and that makes efforts at moral education (and other attempts to influence preferences) both explicable and potentially efficacious.

families, schools, media, government agencies, and courts. There is interplay between the categories: For instance, norms of family interaction shape behavior in actual families; legal norms and procedures govern activity in specific courts.

Institutions and organizations come into being for a variety of reasons and in a variety of ways. Our sketch of human evolution implies that some institutions and associated organizations may rest importantly on innate impulses, and that all must to some degree be consonant with innate predispositions, cognitive mechanisms, etc. But the concept of culture implies human invention, a degree of freedom from direct genetic determination. Institutions may arise simply from the cumulative effect of the uncoordinated actions of individuals. Satisfactory conventions may be hit upon accidentally and then may be replicated over time and space by intergenerational transmission, by horizontal copying within and among groups, and by imposition by one group upon another. The time it takes to reach an equilibrium (e.g., to attain a convention) may be shortened if people or organizations with authority impose a solution that belongs to the set of potential equilibria or if "moral entrepreneurs" intervene in suggesting an institution or help create the conditions that facilitate reaching an equilibrium, for instance, by suggesting coordination around a preexisting focal point or similar transaction-cost-reducing moves.

There is indeed a (probably quite large) set of institutions and organizations that have come into existence through imposition, the results of which sometimes benefited primarily those who labored to impose their solutions, and at other times benefited much larger groups, or at least were accepted by broader groups.[55] Moreover, an institution may turn out to be universally harmful but be adopted anyway, if the costs become clear only long after it entrenches itself.[56] And once interests are formed around the existence of a particular institution and its legitimacy has been established through various means, its survivability increases, other considerations notwithstanding.

Moral entrepreneurs are individuals – in early societies, shamans, elders, and chiefs; in later ones, philosophers, social theorists and activ-

---

[55] Durham (1991, p. 430) lists imposition of cultural choices on some actors by others as one of the fundamental forces of cultural evolution. Slavery and serfdom, and rules governing which side of the road to drive on, are a few out of numerous examples of institutions that were imposed by a few upon many to benefit few and many, respectively.

[56] Durham (1991) terms "opposition" the survival of a cultural trend despite its negative contribution to genetic fitness and asserts that such exceptions to the general rule of cultural evolution are in fact observed in certain instances.

ists, preachers, and others – who both participate in shaping and articulating moral codes (and other conventions) and help to establish vehicles, including beliefs, ceremonies, and pedagogical practices, that serve to insert those codes into the cultures of their society. Their actions constitute a common event[57] which affects the expectations of individuals aware of it, thus opening the road to the emergence of new institutions and organizations.

Whether an institution or organization actually will come into existence and how long it will survive depend on the actions of individuals. Individuals decide whether to participate or not, whether to abide by a norm or not, on the basis of their perception of the costs and benefits, including strictly selfish but in many cases also other- and process-regarding considerations. Since the strength of an institution depends upon the proportion of persons who adhere to it, the outcomes of such calculations will – sometimes glacially, sometimes precipitously – affect the perpetuation of that institution. Likewise, the fate of an individual organization, and of the genre of organization to which it belongs, depends on these sorts of calculations. Many institutions rise and fall in part on the strength of individuals' empathy for one another; on their mutual respect or fear; on their willingness to abide by rules; their readiness, on the contrary, to free ride; and so on – that is, on the full sets of self-, other-, and process-regarding preferences that were shaped by prior forces of inclusive genetic fitness, cultural evolution, and individual experience.[58] Organizations and social arrangements must thus function at any given moment with the raw material of preferences that happen to be at hand. Accordingly, the matching of preferences to institutions is a determinant of institutional outcomes and viability. For instance, if the butcher, baker, and brewer are hardworking and care about their households but not about yours, you may find that you eat better in a market system than in a commune, and if most people place great store in eating, communes may become few and economies consisting of private firms serving customers in markets may flourish.

The chapters in this volume suggest numerous examples of how values

---

[57] Young (1996b) suggests the following examples of common events: a news item (Rosa Parks refuses to sit in the back of a bus), a speech ("I Have a Dream"), or a new theory (*Das Kapital*).

[58] For various perspectives on the evolution of institutions, see Schotter (1981), Ullmann-Margalit (1977), North (1990), Schlicht (1995), Sugden (this volume), and Young (1996a, 1996b). On organizations, see Alchian (1950), DiMaggio and Powell (1983), and Nelson and Winter (1982). For analysis of organizations that emphasize the dependence of organizational survival on individual calculations, which in turn are determined by individual values, see Ben-Ner (1987, 1988) and Hansmann (1996).

affect institutions. Certain forms of trust may be prerequisites for doing business (North) or for reaching high payoff outcomes in organizations (Schotter). Inclinations to reciprocate and punish may raise payoffs to employer and employee (Fehr and Gächter; see also Fehr and Tyran, 1996). The presence of an appropriate norm may smooth the flow of traffic over a bridge (Sugden). The waning of female acquiescence to patriarchal values with respect to who cares for the young or elderly may push "caring" activities into the market, altering their quality and emotional benefits (Folbre and Weisskopf). The strength or weakness of norms of honesty may help to determine the effectiveness of a government bureaucracy or judiciary (Rose-Ackerman), with important impacts on countries' abilities to achieve economic growth. Overly stringent morals may impede the development of competitive markets (Montias) or reduce the ability to focus on productive activities (Kuran).

With such examples in mind, we can also go on to look at the relationship between institutions and values as a two-way street. Individuals' preferences help to determine which organizations and institutions are perpetuated, but organizations and institutions in turn affect preferences. For instance, exposure of the young to certain ideas or practices may lead to their favorable disposition toward them, to a preference for following them, and to behavior intended to satisfy those preferences. Attempts to affect family structures, school curricula, and television programming or their viewing indicate the common belief in such exposure-value links, since their aims are to affect the values of today's youth and their behavior today and tomorrow. An institution may thus provide for its replication by instilling the preference that it be maintained. The remainder of this section explores some of the principal methods of shaping preferences, and the institutions and organizations that play key roles in that process. (We return to the issue of the mutuality of effects of institutions upon values and of values upon institutions in the next section.)

The view that institutions affect values is of course not new; Aristotle and Plato articulated such ideas and were followed by a long string of philosophers, politicians, and others. Those who could, sought to shape various institutions to protect and advance the preferences they preferred *others* to hold.[59] Owners of slaves, feudal privileges, or wealth, for instance, promoted belief in the sanctity of the property from which they

---

[59] Campbell (1983), as noted earlier, suggests viewing morality as the set of rules to which one wants others to subscribe, and which one will accept for oneself also if *their* doing so requires it. Marx depicted morality as the rules that the ruling class prescribed for the ruled, to be followed by rulers only at their own convenience.

benefited where doing so saved on the costs of guards and private armies. Other-regarding preferences have also inspired value promotion, in some instances by those with a genius for identifying a widely shared common interest – the "moral entrepreneurs" mentioned earlier. Selfish and collectivist motives may also have mixed, as when Abraham adopted a moral code with the understanding that his "seed would be as numerous as the stars." God, it would seem, understands incentives (and inclusive fitness).

There are several methods of shaping the preferences of individuals, and there exist diverse institutions and organizations through which these methods can be applied. The combined effectiveness of methods with institutions and organizations depends, of course, on the target individuals' receptivity, the degree to which their true preferences are known to others, the observability of their actions, and so on. Here, we suggest a few general ideas about the effects of institutions and organizations on preferences, discussing briefly several methods of shaping preferences, from inculcation by preaching to practice of desirable behavior and role modeling, and several institutions and organizations, from schools and families to social networks and the media. In this discussion, we focus mainly on a modern, Western context.

One common method for shaping preferences is to inculcate them directly, generally during the so-called impressionable years of childhood. Teachers tell children over and over again what is right and wrong, as do parents and other adults, and signs proclaiming virtues and denouncing vices in classrooms and other institutions are just one, visible example of the multichannel barrage of moral messages.[60] Teaching values is also done through the retelling of fables, myths, and religious stories in which the virtuous are rewarded and the sinful suffer – note well the appeal to self-regarding preferences of the message receivers (more on this later). While recourse to inculcation resembles simple brainwashing – what is repeated often enough becomes directly fixed in the brain – its efficacy seems also to depend on emotional associations with the messenger, such as a trusted parent or role model; on acceptance of his or her authority (as with a parent or elder); and perhaps even on the content of the message (viz. the perhaps innate receptivity to urgings to help siblings or to notions of fairness and due punishment). Trusting parents and authority figures is probably a human genetic predisposition, which is further shaped by the operative social environment.

---

[60] In a recent decision, the Tennessee legislature recommended that the "ten commandments" be posted in schools and state agencies; in communist countries, moral exhortations were displayed in various media.

Preferences can also be shaped through appeals to reason, through attempts to teach that society cannot function without respect and caring for others and without voluntary submission to certain rules of behavior or civility. Schools, media, political persuasion, and other institutions and organizations that address more mature individuals, or organizations in which such individuals participate, are the common executors of this method. In comparison with inculcation, this method requires less paternalism by preference shapers toward learners and more rationality on their parts, but both methods share the belief that individuals' preferences can be affected through discourse.[61]

Exposure of individuals to behaviors reflecting certain preferences is yet another way of transmitting such preferences. Observation teaches "how things are done here," which is the essence of socialization.[62] Children observe how adults behave, and the tendency to learn through emulation causes them to internalize some of the values that guide adults' behavior. Observation also allows the observer, child and adult, to infer what kinds of behavior, and therefore preferences, are rewarded and sanctioned, and therefore what it is in one's self-interest to learn. This method is largely grounded in the human proclivity to reciprocate behavior with like behavior, and therefore it can be carried out most effectively in settings that foster repeated interactions.[63]

Incentives that appeal directly to self-regarding preferences are often employed to shape other- and process-regarding ones. Prizes are offered for being a virtuous person (a monetary prize for returning a lost item); praise (which is almost universally craved – see again Fershtman and Weiss, this volume) goes to those who seem to behave in desirable other- or process-regarding ways (a plaque naming the donor of a university or hospital building); and punishment may result from seeming to act on

---

[61] The effects of institutions and organizations on the preferences of adults are seldom discussed, reflecting the assumption that past their (early) youth, individuals are too old to learn or unlearn anything in the realm of values. More often, the implicit assumption is that adults hold the desirable values, and the only problem is to induce them to belong to traditional families to transmit these values to their offspring. It is unclear that either assumption is correct.

[62] The effectiveness of observation as a source of change in preferences is suggested by the finding of Bunn et al. (1992), that "those students who saw others cheat had an increase in the probability of having cheated in college of .41 ... [and] ... a 10 percentage point increase in one's expectation about what proportion of other students are cheating was associated with an increase in the probability of having cheated in college of .10." Unfortunately, self-reported cheating, and self-reported observations and expectations about others cheating, are not externally verified in this study, so correlations due to desires for moral self-justification cannot be ruled out.

[63] Axelrod (1986, p. 1105) writes, "The actions of others provide information about what is proper for us, even if we do not know the reasons."

wrong preferences. By changing the costs and benefits of holding particular preferences, as judged by the preferences one already holds (for praise and rewards, and for avoidance of punishment), such prizes and punishments help to shape "pro-social" preferences, building a specific behavioral phenotype from genetic stuff shapable in a multitude of possible directions. Repeated or transparent appeals to self-interest, especially by those unable to signal virtue on their own parts, may by contrast foster the kind of calculativeness that allows only the opportunistic feigning of other- and process-regarding preferences.[64]

The effectiveness of institutions and organizations at shaping preferences depends on a number of properties, including the frequency and continuity of interactions among individuals, the types and transparency of actions in which individuals may engage, and the ability to store and produce information about individual and group behaviors and outcomes. Particularly relevant to our discussion, for instance, is the fact that institutions may provide more or fewer opportunities for practicing virtuous behavior. Thus, interactions within families and small groups may permit desirable other- and process-regarding preferences to be rewarded more reliably than they can be in large-group and anonymous interactions. If within-group attitudes are not built on negative feelings toward outsiders, then habituation to other-regarding or virtuous behavior in the small-group setting may help build "moral muscle" and predispose individuals to behave similarly in situations involving outsiders, as a result of processes of cognitive carry-over or dissonance avoidance.[65]

Organizations such as firms – in part, perhaps, because of our innate cognitive biases – take on some of the attributes of persons in their interactions with us. A typical individual has many fewer interactions with other individuals in social or business relations than does a typical organization, such as a firm of moderate size, which may interact daily

---

[64] The currencies of self-interest and of altruism or virtue may not be smoothly interchangeable, as when reliance on incentives that appeal to self-regarding preferences seems to crowd out behavior based on other- and process-regarding ones (Hirschman 1985; Frey 1993; Frey, this volume). However, this crowding-out phenomenon with stable preferences does not conflict with the possibility of inducing preference *change* toward desirable other- and process-regarding preferences by appealing to self-interest.

[65] Bowles and Gintis, and Montias (this volume) consider cases involving communities of larger size in which much the opposite occurs. Campbell (1983, p. 35) considers "a double standard of preaching, an altruistic morality for exhortation to others, a self-serving one for own offspring," but he conjectures that "in the long run such a system would not work to produce complex social coordination, even though it would end up with the altruistic preachings heard by the offspring generation being many times more numerous than the selfish ones."

with hundreds or thousands of employees and customers. As with individuals, those controlling an organization may choose to have it behave in a manner that reflects more narrowly selfish interests or in one that seems also to put weight on certain virtues and on the well-being of others. Because organizations are much fewer than individuals and perhaps for that reason more easily accessed by promoters of social change, because their objectives and behavior are designed, and because they have frequent and sustained interactions with many individuals, the effects of moral attitudes and behavior by organizations may be relatively influential in engendering similar and reciprocal attitudes and behavior by individuals with whom they come in regular contact.

Institutions that help screen individuals according to their preferences or that help individuals to signal their preferences may also induce changes in preferences. If it is relatively easy to identify individuals' preferences, then individuals possessing desirable preferences can be rewarded, promoting the processes of learning and habituation described earlier. By contrast, if individuals are entirely anonymous and their preferences are totally unknown, it is only their behavior or its consequences that can be judged and rewarded.[66] This is done primarily by permitting reputations to be built through repeated interactions. Institutions that use long-term relationships to foster familiarity, affection, and consistency in the interpretation of signals can assist in the screening and signaling of individuals' types or characters. Stable social networks, such as firms and voluntary organizations, thus become stores of information about the individuals that populate them.

Institutions and economic arrangements can also affect preferences as an unintended by-product of their primary function. Television programming, intended by the supplier as a means of earning advertising revenue and by the viewer as a means of entertainment, may have unintended effects on values. Firms are operated to produce some products, but through their incentive schemes they may induce certain preferences in their employees. And schools are run primarily to impart skills and knowledge, but at the same time they can be used as a vehicle for "molding values." More abstract institutional arrangements, such as market coordination of economic life or conventions with respect to property rights, may also affect preferences. Typically seen as being embraced by a society for their benefits to material prosperity and their consistency with individual freedoms, markets may at the same time help

---

[66] Guth (1995) finds that when there is a lot of uncertainty about the types of individuals with whom one interacts, the evolutionarily stable strategy may fail to support beneficial reciprocal behavior.

mold values like competitiveness and individualism, may strengthen work ethics or concerns with reputation, or, by reducing both the demand for and the feasibility of reciprocity, they may lower the preference for engaging in it. Although the feedback of such effects on institutional viability and individual welfare can be expected to affect an institution's persistence at least in the long run, if key decisions governing the evolution of institutions and economic arrangements are guided mostly by other considerations, then their effects on the evolution of preferences may have the character of unrecognized externalities.

An important question concerning the influences that organizations and institutions have on preferences is whether their effect is permanent or transitory. The answer may depend in part upon the timing and consistency of these influences: Cultural norms communicated consistently through many channels in childhood may be extremely durable, especially if congruent with innate predisposition; the impact of values communicated by some but not other agents at later points in life may be comparatively fragile. In most intermediate cases, there may be a degree of inertia in preferences and behavior that ensures some continuity even when the operation of particular methods of shaping preferences is discontinued. However, the strengths of induced preferences may tend to weaken with time when the stimuli which encourage or sustain them are no longer present.[67]

### 2.6    *The two-way interaction between institutions and preferences*

A full understanding of the effects of preferences on institutions, and of institutions on preferences, requires a view of their relationship as operating in two directions at once. But researching such a two-way relationship rigorously presents serious methodological challenges. If both institutions and values are endogenous, what can be the starting point for one's analysis?

As usual, what can be treated as exogenous and what as endogenous depends upon the problem at hand. If we are studying the evolution of multicelled organisms from earlier forms of life, such basics as the origins of sexual reproduction need to be explained, perhaps by reference to

---

[67] The Hutterite colonies in Canada have succeeded in the transmission of preferences differing considerably from those of the surrounding society through cultural channels for more than four hundred years through organizational design and isolation. The inculcation of other-regarding preferences (selflessness, solidarity) is emphasized in various Hutterite practices, presumably because in the absence of such practices Hutterite children would be more selfish than what is regarded as necessary to ensure the continuity of the colonies in the desired form. See Wilson and Sober (1994).

success in thwarting fatal predation by parasites (Tooby and Cosmides 1990). If we are studying family formation in human beings, sexual reproduction and physiological specialization among the sexes, basic facts of brain structure and chemical processes, and nutritional requirements can be taken as givens, but details of the social relations between the sexes and within family or corresponding social units may not be. If we are studying the rise of divorce and of out-of-wedlock childbirth in the late twentieth century, both basic biological drives and a backlog of social norms concerning gender roles and sexual behavior can be taken as given, and other factors, such as changing economic opportunities and demands, the structure of public assistance programs, and broad cultural trends, may be the relevant exogenous variables (Akerlof, Yellen, and Katz 1996).

In some instances, it may be possible to conduct full-blown general equilibrium analyses, in which both institutions and values are determined simultaneously by such exogenous factors as initial genetic and cultural endowments, resources, and technologies. In general, tractability will require that such studies focus on only a few variables at a time, so researchers need to be alert to the sensitivity of their conclusions to their choice of modeling and empirical research strategy. At other times, it may be worth trading the simultaneity and self-contained character of general equilibrium analysis for the greater modeling richness that might be obtained by having recourse to more partial equilibrium and recursive-type structures, in which one set of variables (values or institutions) is taken as an initial given, and its effects on the other set (institutions or values) is then analyzed. The impact of this round of effects on the first set of variables may then be looked at, and so on.

Illustrating system properties by way of simulation will be a useful technique in both general equilibrium and partial equilibrium or recursive models, if closed-form solutions are unattainable without excessive sacrifice of complexity. Insights into directions of change may be invaluable even when they come without identification of an overall equilibrium, for in situations in which change is slow and unpredictable exogenous disruptions are likely, both the existence and the nature of equilibrium may be irrelevant for practical purposes.

The approach advocated in this essay is one that would generally take genetic receptivities toward preference patterns as a given. For the classes of problems touched upon in this essay and book, these genotypic patterns will differ from those of *homo economicus* insofar as the typical person pursues objectives other than maximization of wealth, pleasure, or longevity of the individual – as has been suggested will be the case because of the nature of the inclusive fitness criterion and the incremental character of the evolutionary process. Behavioral phenotype is then determined, at a second level of analysis, both by genetic inheritance and by environment, which includes both general cultural elements and details like birth order, family size and economic situation, and parental experience. Whereas genetic propensities vary perhaps modestly and more or less uniformly across all of humanity, general culture is shared within groups of varying sizes, some very large, while the final set of factors, the details of the individual's environment, vary widely within populations.

At the level of analysis which is likely to characterize most applied research, one takes as given a particular moment in cultural evolution and a certain set of demographic structures and organizational forms. One then looks at the effects of particular changes or sets of changes – intensified competition in international markets, increasing participation of women in labor markets, waning of certain sexual taboos – upon the shaping of preferences and the further evolution of economic and social arrangements. We provide brief and informal illustrations of this last type of analysis in part 3 of this essay, but first we close this section with some remarks taking a longer evolutionary view and attempting to reconnect with some of the broader issues of our essay.

Institutions and values have evolved in tandem over the ages. At the time when primate societies were gradually shading into human, culture as such may have been minimal, but social norms, feelings of concern, jealousy, and so on, toward others, and senses of right and fairness already may have manifested recognizably human qualities.[68] Our early ancestors would have developed vocabularies to describe and guide such feelings and moral senses, with details differing with the terrain and with some culling of more versus less successful adaptations through the effects of differential survival.

As societies shifted from the hunting and gathering that characterized human life for all but the most recent millennia on to pastoral and agricultural systems and then to still more complex orders marked by social stratification, writing, taxation, formal religion, and cities, it is increasing technical mastery of environments, permitting greater population densities and the support of first small and then larger portions of the population at above-subsistence levels, that appears to be the key factor explaining social and economic evolution. Yet scientific and technical knowledge is itself an aspect of culture, and change was brought about not by new tools alone, but by the combination of new tools and

---

[68] Trivers (1983) and de Waal (1996) discuss cooperative tendencies in baboons, chimpanzees, dolphins, and whales.

know-how with new and increasingly complex social divisions of labor, organized in accordance with normative, legal, and belief systems that at most times meshed with current techniques and at some times also permitted the groundwork to be laid for further technical and social changes.

The technological and organizational developments characteristic of capitalism, for example, may at least initially have been associated with evolving notions of private property, of personal liberties, of a domain for states, of correct settings for reproductive and child-rearing activities, and so forth. The evolution of institutions such as labor and capital markets involved not only organizational and technical innovations, but also changes in moral notions such as the construction of norms governing employment relationships out of elements of earlier master–servant and master–apprentice precedents and the relaxation of prohibitions on so-called usury.

A hallmark of cultural, just like biological, evolution is that because adaptations can build upon accumulations of prior know-how using the principle of modularity, change tends to accelerate with time. Estimates suggest that it took two billion years for the first life forms to evolve to the eukaryotic stage (in which cells contain membrane-bound nuclei), 0.7 billion years for eukaryotes to become multicellular, and ever shorter spans to the appearance of complex land animals, and so forth, on to the first human beings. In much the same way, humans spent upward of a million years in their prehistoric "twilight" but no more than a few thousand years from the birth of irrigated agriculture to the apogee of literature and philosophy in ancient China, India, and Greece and less than two more millennia to Copernicus, Newton, and the early merchant states of Europe. From there, it was but a few generations more to Darwin, Einstein, and the beginnings of modern industry and medicine, and mere decades thence to modern quantum physics and genetic engineering, the global marketplace, the birth-control pill, and the Internet.

Numerous scholars have taken note of the changes in norms and values that have accompanied social transitions such as the birth and demise of feudalism or the rise of modern capitalism. Yet, while there is undoubtedly some validity in the notion that the moral "superstructure" of a society (to use Marx's phrase) is adapted to its sociotechnical or economic "substructure," there are also reasons for doubting that the accelerating pace of technical and organizational change has been matched by equally rapid and appropriate adaptations in accompanying normative and acculturation systems. We continue to teach the ethics of the Bible and other ancient texts centuries after the societies that gave birth to them changed beyond recognition. There may be good reasons for doing so in a world without contemporary moral compass, but the differential speeds of organizational and technical versus moral change may also give cause for concern. "Moral evolution" may move slowly because the foundations of our moral systems, which seem partly inherited through our genes and partly handed down from millennia of culture, are only in smaller part supported by our powers of reason and have thus far remained understudied by science. Campbell, who argues that market mechanisms and legal systems may have worked well in the past because of a "residue of awed indoctrination," suggests that "[i]f indeed the process Weber described as *die Entzauberung der Welt* [loss of the enchanted worldview] still proceeds apace, we must look to alternative means to protect collective goods" (1986, p. 177).

Today's industrialized societies have seen a transition over but a few generations from a state in which most individuals spent their lives in a single locality, produced many of their own necessities, and interacted with small numbers of known others within a fairly rigid socioeconomic structure to one in which people depend for their livelihood on selling commodities or labor for cash, work for a series of employers and live in a number of localities during their lifetime, and are able to purchase an extraordinary variety of goods from large numbers of sellers, with many employers and sellers being large, bureaucratic entities whose local personnel are short-term hires. Not only are people interacting less personally, and with less opportunity to benefit from reciprocity through repeat interaction, in their production and trading activities; they are also interacting less with one another because of the increasing cost of time, the availability of economic alternatives to investing in relationships with others, and the attractiveness and accessibility of amusements (e.g., television) that do not require social interaction. With less interplay and less clear interdependence, people may develop fewer loyalties and affections and may thus feel less regard for others (Putnam 1995).

An interesting example that may illustrate the points made in the previous two paragraphs might be found in a comparison of the contemporary worlds of the Western countries and East Asia. It has often been remarked that the vigorous performance of Japanese industry in the post–World War II period may be attributable in part to patterns of loyalty between employee and firm, to trust between trading partners, and to a work ethic, that are products of a culture emphasizing family ties, hard work, honesty, thrift, and rule obedience. Two related and complementary explanations may be offered for the origins of that culture. First, in its recent past as a firmly ordered feudal agrarian society, Japan consisted of tight-knit social and economic networks that fostered loyalty, obligation, and mutual "monitoring" in a wide array of activities due to the transparency of individual actions in these networks, and the adherence to a corresponding set of widely shared values which made this possible. These factors tend to engender stronger other-regarding and process-regarding preferences than do the corresponding aspects of a more loosely knit society.

Second, this social structure has allowed for deliberate, top-down institutional design through borrowing, adaptation, and innovation by moral entrepreneurs. One aspect of the Japanese institutional landscape (often neglected in Western discourse about things Japanese) is that firms are said, including by their top executives, to be run primarily in the interests of their core employees, secondarily for the benefit of customers, and only lastly for the benefit of shareholders (Aoki 1990; Miyazaki 1993). If this is indeed so, the implication is that those Japanese who are covered by this system have most of their encounters outside the family with institutions that act as if they have beneficent other- and process-regarding preferences. As we argued earlier, this would tend to engender similar preferences in individuals.

As the greater recency of Japan's transformation into an industrial market society as compared with Western industrial counterparts wanes, and as the pressure for freer international and domestic trade (as well as for institutional change within Japan) mounts, the possibility rises that Japan's differences with Western counterparts in the late twentieth century will dwindle, and that many of the same social complaints heard in Europe and North America today will become mainstays in Japan as it moves into the next century. This suggests that business dealings based on trust will become more difficult in Japan, as they are now in the West; that engendering loyalty within family-style employment relations will be less and less easy; and that hard work will need, more and more, to be purchased with complex incentive and supervision systems.[69]

An interpretation of the "crisis of values" viewpoint, in light of the foregoing, is that contemporary individuals possess a stock of civility,

---

[69] At least some of the hard work of employees in large Japanese firms might be explained by the fact that a large part of their compensation takes the form of bonuses (Freeman and Weitzman 1987; Aoki 1990). But repeated-game models of self-interested behavior show that the high-effort outcome of profit sharing is only one of a multiplicity of possible equilibria. Since an equilibrium represents a set of endogenously developed norms (as Axelrod [1986] argued), cultural and normative factors can still be assigned a role in selecting just how efficacious such profit sharing really is (Weitzman and Kruse 1990; Weitzman and Xu 1994).

fairness, and other preferences which have been partly handed down from past societies. Although Bowles and Gintis (this volume) are probably right to suggest that institutions are unlikely to survive even as vestiges unless they serve some useful role in the current context, the principal institutions and organizations transmitting the values in question – families, communities, churches, and so on – may today be weakening, even as the institutional settings in which the values are reinforced – small towns, repeated relationship-specific trade – are replaced by less reinforcing forms of organization. Families and other primary value transmitters may be weakening under the influences of still-expanding personal choice and mobility, and of the skeptical or nihilistic cultural order spawned by a variety of factors, including the shocks that Copernicus, Darwin, and others caused to earlier worldviews. Calls for moral regeneration, family values, and religious revival are quite understandable in this context, even if a literal return to the past is neither possible nor desirable. The premise of our research agenda is that understanding our problems – in this case, those of the moral basis of a society we would want to live in – is the first step to effectively addressing them.

## 3 Applications

We have argued that human behavior is governed by preferences, of both inherited and experiential origin, that include preferences with respect to one's self but also ones with respect to process and to the well-being of others. And we have argued that preferences both are influenced by the institutions and organizations of societies and help to determine the selection and the performance of those institutions and organizations. In this part, we illustrate these propositions in a manner suggestive of their relevance to those who design and run organizations, to policymakers, and to social scientists who would advise them. The present discussion concerns three examples – the family, the workplace, and national social insurance – although limits of space and expertise mean that even for these examples we can offer only broad hints of the promise of our framework. The applications are organized around the key questions that the framework of the previous part helps us to address: What are the determinants of individuals' behavior (a question we address with an emphasis on the role of preferences)? What environmental factors mold these preferences? How are these factors embedded in institutions and organizations? And how can the decisions of managers, policymakers, and others, affect institutions, values, and behavior in socially desired ways?

### 3.1    *Values in three institutional examples*

The institution of the *family*, already much remarked on in our essay, offers an attractive subject for illustrative analysis. Families are arguably the foremost of the social settings in which preferences, including values, are shaped. Certain moral inclinations either are instilled or fail to be instilled at a young age, and if the presence of these inclinations is critical to the smooth functioning of society in civic, commercial, and other respects, then the socialization with which families provide their children as a means of equipping them for success in the wider world creates a positive (or negative) externality to society as a whole. Families are also important economically, playing prominent roles as direct providers of labor and as consumers. Family structures are influenced by economic forces, such as changes in the costs of raising children. Understanding how families affect values and how values affect families could contribute to addressing concerns about family instability and the contribution of families to society's moral capital stock.

In modern societies, most families are formed and either maintained or discontinued as the result of choices by adult male and female partners. The main motivators of family formation include the desire for sexual relations and the desire for procreation. Core features of these drives are almost certainly hard-wired into us as in other species. For the individual, sustained intimacy and emotional security may be other benefits sought in marriage. Family formation is also desired as an assurance of financial support from one's offspring and of care in the event of sickness. Both the drive to leave offspring beyond a single generation and the desire for care in one's own time of need may motivate investment not only in the immediate physical welfare of children, but also in their "moral upbringing." Success in that enterprise can increase children's future fitness if others select for signs of such morality in those with whom they interact, and it can also increase the likelihood of their providing the required care to their parents when the time comes (solving what would otherwise be from an economic viewpoint a time inconsistency problem in intergenerational reciprocity).

A second institution which intrigues us is the *workplace*, or, more specifically, the relationship between employer and employee, about which we have also commented in this essay. Whereas family and school are central institutions where values are shaped in one's youth, the workplace reaffirms and strengthens or invalidates and weakens values held by employees. Since employment relationships are critical to productivity, to households' economic security, and to living standards, the interactions between values and the structure of employment relationships are potentially of great significance.

The biblical observation that man must eat "by the sweat of his brow" rightly implies that it is necessity that is the first motivator of productive effort, and in standard economic models, its instrumental role in augmenting wealth or consumable resources is the only motivator of work. It is unreasonable, however, to suppose that workers check their extended preferences at the door of the factory or office, and more sensible to suppose that they enter as human beings, and that as Akerlof (1982) suggests, they relate as such to both employer and fellow employees. For example, jealousy, resentment, gratitude, concern for coworkers, and loyalty may complement the desire for personal gain as sources of their behavior, and cooperation may be selected as the outcome of an effort-choice game when propensities toward reciprocity are appropriately reinforced. Here, too, society may inherit a stock of moral capital, including for instance a work ethic, pride in craftsmanship, professionalism, loyalty, and solidarity. These may be sustained or depleted by an employer's practice of incentive schemes that may either build on such moral capital or instead strengthen employees' self-regarding preferences and erode their concern for fairness and for the well-being, or the favorable regard, of others.

For the third illustration, consider an institution that operates at the societal level: *national social insurance schemes*. Such schemes, highly developed and fiscally significant in today's industrialized nations, have potentially important implications from the standpoint of social justice, efficiency, and order. To be sure, the shaping of preferences has little or nothing to do with what social insurance schemes were designed to do, and how their operation depends upon and affects preferences might easily be overlooked. Yet even the relatively nonaltruistic explanation of these systems as mechanisms of societal insurance which each individual would favor from behind a "veil of ignorance" (before knowing her actual economic status) is consistent with the idea that ex post support for them depends in part upon a certain "moral attitude." For those who believe that the provision of certain basic guarantees is a requirement of a civilized society, the question is, How can such guarantees be put in place in such a manner as to impose the least feasible burden on, and to maintain the most support from, those who must pay for them. Preference and value questions arise on both sides of the issue, because they can affect the levels of abuse of social insurance programs by beneficiaries and providers, which can in turn affect program costs and the support of contributors (taxpayers). To the extent that program design can itself influence value-related behaviors and preferences, these effects may therefore be critical to program viability.

Both the desire for personal insurance and certain shared moral principles may explain support for social insurance programs in developed economies. Consider, however, the motivation of recipients. Their own positions make them candidates for morally hazardous behaviors such as the fabrication of claims for benefits and failure to make good faith efforts to find employment. Thus, the less are these potential recipients constrained by "moral" preferences, the more abuse of such programs we can expect to see, and the more costly will the programs be to operate. Abuse by beneficiaries may directly reduce the level of benefits available to the genuinely needy, and it may lead also to further reductions through its impact upon the preferences of the taxpayers, who may take a less charitable view of such programs the more that they believe they are being abused. The honesty and efficiency of the personnel of government agencies and nonprofit organizations that act as agents of the public in providing social services may also be affected by moral factors and may in turn affect public willingness to pay.

## 3.2    *Policy interventions and the values–institutions nexus*

Suppose now that we ourselves are moral onlookers who wish to help society to strengthen families in which emotionally and morally healthy children can be raised, to improve the design of workplaces so that both productivity and satisfaction are enhanced, and to provide humane levels of social insurance at the lowest feasible cost. We would approach these tasks very differently depending upon the model that we believe best describes human behavioral propensities. For example, let us first, as a thought experiment, erase our earlier priors and assume that self-interest is after all the only effective motivator, and universally so. On this assumption, families may well be a lost cause, for the motivation to form and to remain in families would appear to be waning rapidly as the stigma of divorce and of sex outside marriage have declined, as the availability of alternative forms of insurance has increased, and as the likelihood of support from family members shrinks with their increased mobility and individualism. Employment relations may have some hope of being effectively engineered for economic men, using piece rates where hard-to-monitor quality and equipment care issues are unimportant, setting up competitive tournaments for promotion which ease monitoring demands by requiring relative ranking only, and relying on reputational mechanisms to dissuade employers from reneging on their end of employment contracts. But with severe asymmetric information in the workplace and with external markets for reputation working only imperfectly, one would expect to see a very different world of organizations, assuming a population of economic persons – one in which productivity would fall below already observed potentials and where the imperatives of motivation would preclude making work anything other than an unmitigated (if necessary) evil.

Under the same assumptions, social insurance programs might have to be limited to the benefits that are in the private ex post interests of the majority of the taxpayers, to employ tough rules of eligibility, to build in abuse-deterring costs such as the requirement of working for one's benefits, and to enforce draconian penalties for beneficiaries and providers found to be abusing them. Indeed, the market economy as a whole could be expected to function rather restrictedly, in a world of economic persons, on the behavioral assumption of pursuit of self-interest unmitigated by concern for others or for process, as each agent would always be certain of being cheated by every other agent whenever it was in his interest to do so, and the deterrence value of prospective penalties could only exist to the extent that it could be made to be in someone's self-interest to monitor misdeeds (including self-serving accusations). Under such conditions, much potentially beneficial trade would be forgone in the interest of maintenance of long-term dyadic relationships or the security of outright self-sufficiency.

However, if behavioral propensities are of the more complex variety that we have argued them to be, far more fruitful approaches might be available, the best of which would take into account the receptivity of human beings to the influence of their experiences, the mixes of preferences that may be sustainable, and the ways in which institutions can influence the preferences on which behaviors are based. The recent intensification of discourse about "family values" is suggestive of forces set in motion in reaction to the past generation's swing of the social pendulum. While that pendulum never returns to the same status quo ante, these reactions may promote the evolution of families and similar support networks in directions more consistent not only with the contemporary environment, but also with the more durable moral fundamentals of civilized society and with contemporary extensions of those fundamentals such as equality of the sexes (Folbre and Weisskopf, this volume). Although some of these changes may, as it were, "well up" from below, the modification of tax and transfer systems to encourage parental responsibility is a policy response that uses economic inducements to strengthen an institution having such beneficial moral, emotional, and insurance effects – in the last instance helping to alleviate pressures on the social insurance schemes we have also discussed here.

Policy thinking should be directed, as well, to strengthening other institutions which may buttress, supplement, or provide alternatives to the family's role in the socialization of children, for instance, improving preschool programs and the value-related components of schooling.

In the workplace, complex, extended preferences do not unseat pecuniary quid pro quo from its center stage position (although a recognition of self-regarding intrinsic motivation may sometimes be of first-order importance). Reciprocity and loyalty are now possibilities, but opportunism and attempts to free ride on or take advantage of the naivete of others are no less so. Outcomes depend on the experiences with which workers enter the employment relationship, the mix of workers and their individual proclivities, the nature and history of their relationship with the specific employer, and the possibilities inherent in the relevant production processes and technologies. It may be profitable for an employer to commit to a long-term relationship with employees, structuring an environment rewarding reciprocity and nourishing inclinations toward loyalty on both sides. Narrowing pay differentials even when good indicators of individual productivity are available could induce goodwill and corresponding effort from a work group whose members are inclined to view one another with sympathy, as in Akerlof's (1982) example; or that may fail to happen, for instance if potential work group members are steeped in an ethos of individualism of the sort that may have strengthened since the observations about which Akerlof theorized were recorded. Self-employment and forgoing of some scale economies will prove superior for incentive reasons, in some instances; in others, group production with profit sharing. While the potential impact of effort elicitation problems on macroeconomic outcomes is already well known from the efficiency–wage literature, it may also be worth considering the external effects of the strategies of individual firms by way of their influence on the receptivity of workers who change positions to the incentive environments of their new firms (see Schotter, this volume).[70] As in the efficiency–wage case, this could be the basis of certain policy prescriptions perhaps resembling, for instance, the U.S. Department of Labor's recent proposals to award favorable tax treatment to firms that engage in certain relationship-enhancing labor practices.

---

[70] Another negative externality of (perhaps privately optimizing) employers who deplete, rather than invest in, employees' moral capital is that society at large may be harmed by the negative attitudes that employees develop toward other people and toward civic behavior in general (see the comments made by interviewees in *The New York Times*'s series of front-page articles "The Downsizing of America" that appeared daily between March 2 and March 9, 1996).

Perhaps one of the most important points to be made with regard to social insurance is that "virtuous behavior" of potential beneficiaries – not applying for or accepting assistance where it is unneeded or where the relevant qualifications are not in truth met – is unlikely to be an "all or nothing" proposition. Part of the motivation for avoiding such acts may be the desire to avoid feelings of shame. When individuals have not completely internalized the norm in question, the level of shame felt by them with respect to these acts may be an increasing function of the likelihood which they attach to their being discovered, and of the importance to them of the individuals likely to learn of them. It is, on the other hand, likely to be decreasing with the proportion of others who are believed to engage in the disapproved act. The first linkage suggests that insurance may be more difficult to provide at the level of the society than at that of the family, where discovery by others who matter to one is more likely. The second suggests a reason why societies may find their ability to provide such insurance declining over time: Values of self-reliance, which may have been firmly implanted in most individuals when families were their principal support systems, begin to erode as the option of using the more impersonal insurance of the state is exercised by both some deserving and some undeserving recipients. By reducing the shame of others, the perception that some are cheating can lead to a spiraling epidemic of fraud – which, again, will reduce both the capacity to help the truly needy and the amount of funding that taxpayers are willing to provide.[71] Such observations may point in the direction of putting greater effort into the discouragement and detection of abuses, into considering methods to reduce the anonymity of applicants or at least abusers, and into avoiding too complete a shift away from reliance upon the resources of the family and other small groups. However, too blatantly treating each potential recipient as a suspected cheater could further deplete the remaining reservoir of civic virtue for reasons of the sort discussed by Frey (this volume), and eliminating or cutting back social insurance too severely could impact negatively on overall acceptance of the social order by certain groups of individuals, with ultimately higher cost to society. Thus, our remarks here, as with our other examples, are only meant to illustrate the potential value of taking into account the effects of program design on values and the effects of values on program viability, and not to lay out any specific set of policy recommendations.

---

[71] See Lindbeck (1995). Similar points can be made with respect to nonpayment of taxes and other socially disapproved acts.

## Conclusions

Economists take pride in the rigorous manner with which their models of constrained maximization of self-interested objective functions permit them to analyze problems of exchange under given institutions, and in some cases also the choice of institutions themselves. At the beginning of this essay we offered three reasons why it may be necessary to go beyond such models. First, the institutions of a market economy could become prohibitively costly to operate were all norms of fair dealing and reciprocity to be displaced by selfish calculation. Second, it is difficult to reconcile some game-theoretic predictions with observed behaviors unless models of preferences are extended to include elements conventionally excluded from them. Third, some of the most pressing social problems of the day may reflect stresses on society's normative fabric, and such stresses both affect and are affected by the functioning of institutions, including families, firms, and states. Putting the strengths of economic science to work on the task of addressing these problems, we have argued, may be impossible, in many instances, without explicit recognition of value–institution linkages.

Exactly how best to do this is a matter that can hardly be prescribed to the satisfaction of all researchers; which approaches prove the most promising will be known only as the types of analysis illustrated in this volume are further criticized, tested, and developed. Our own general comments have boiled down to suggesting that models of individuals solving constrained maximization problems, often in complex interaction with one another, should remain at the center of economic methodology (with due allowance for limits to rationality) but that the objectives individuals are assumed to pursue should be permitted to include what we have called other- and process-regarding concerns. Those concerns are not to be called upon ad hoc to explain what is otherwise inexplicable. Rather, they would be modeled as outcomes of the environments in which individuals develop and live, within boundaries set by genetic predispositions. Both the parameters of those predispositions and the selection of institutions and norms are in principle amenable to analysis using deductively generated evolutionary models that, if based on properly specified fitness criteria and tested for empirical corroboration, can provide guidance for making the paradigmatic transition from *homo economicus* to real existing man and woman in a nonarbitrary fashion.

A society's economic arrangements arise to meet a variety of needs. In prehistoric environments means of survival, social norms, and even the cognitive and emotional equipment supporting behavior and social interaction would have evolved in congruent ways given the workings of processes of selection. By contrast, modern technical and institutional changes occur on time scales in which certainly genetic predispositions, and to some degree also a heritage of normative orientations, are essentially givens. And institutional change is often driven by factors that make congruence with the needs of norm reinforcement at most a secondary consideration. While patterns of small-group socialization and repeated economic interaction may be more favorable for inculcating values and for providing the ongoing rewards and benefits that support their long-term maintenance, the productivity advantages of large organizations, complex divisions of labor, individual mobility, and anonymous exchanges may become driving forces behind change in economic arrangements, weakening the reproduction of socially beneficial norms. But a decline in the stock of desirable values may eat into the benefits of economic complexity. While recognition of such tendencies could lead to checks on excessive economic atomization, socially appropriate responses may not be forthcoming if individuals react to these trends according to private, rather than social, rationality. Unless some individuals – be they religious figures, political leaders, philanthropists, or social scientists – consider the interest of society as a whole and identify ways of making productively and allocatively superior arrangements consistent with a virtuous moral equilibrium, the system as a whole may be unsustainable or may demand unacceptable trade-offs between life quality and material gain.

In truth, we are skeptical of claims that the temple of moral civilization is collapsing on our, and only our, generation. Alarm over moral decline may be as old as civilization itself. The metaphor of collapse may be a bit too dramatic. Yet our times are marked by levels of change in technology, attitudes, and life-style that are unusual for their sweep and speed, and that give such alarm a definite cogency. At the very least, we think that social scientists would not be earning their keep were they to treat such problems as simple fantasy or as the responsibility of other disciplines and professions. Some economists, in particular, may feel tempted to see these problems as best left to psychologists, sociologists, or moral philosophers, supposing that it is the social, rather than the economic institutions that require attention. We would argue that there can be no true understanding of social organization without a clear understanding of economic arrangements; that there is no clean separability of institutions into economic and noneconomic; and that institutions, including firms and markets, both affect and are affected by values. This, and the manifest potential of economic analysis, lead us to believe that the study of problems having both economic and moral dimensions can benefit not only from the economic approach in general, but also from uses of that approach which explicitly incorporate value endogeneity and the mutual influences of values upon institutions and of institutions upon values.

## REFERENCES

Aaron, Henry (1994). "Public Policy, Values, and Consciousness," *Journal of Economic Perspectives* 8: 3–21.
Aaron, Henry, Thomas Mann, and Timothy Taylor, eds. (1994). *Values and Public Policy*. Washington, D.C.: The Brookings Institution.
Abreu, Dilip, and Ariel Rubinstein (1988). "The Structure of Nash Equilibrium in Repeated Games with Finite Automata," *Econometrica* 56(6): 1259–81.
Akerlof, George (1980). "A Theory of Social Custom, of Which Unemployment May Be One Consequence," *Quarterly Journal of Economics* 90: 749–75.
———(1982). "Labor Contracts as Partial Gift Exchange," *Quarterly Journal of Economics* 97(4): 543–69.
Akerlof, George, and Janet Yellen (1990). "The Fair Wage–Effort Hypothesis and Unemployment," *Quarterly Journal of Economics* 105: 255–83.
Akerlof, George, Janet Yellen, and Michael Katz (1996). "An Analysis of Out-of-Wedlock Childbearing in the United States," *Quarterly Journal of Economics* 111(2): 277–317.
Alchian, Armen, A. (1950). "Uncertainty, Evolution and Economic Theory," *Journal of Political Economy* 58: 211–21.
Alchian, Armen A., and Demsetz, Harold (1972). "Production, Information Costs, and Economic Organization," *American Economic Review* 62(5): 77–95.
Anderson, Elijah (1990). *StreetWise*. Chicago: University of Chicago Press.
Aoki, Masahiko (1990). "Towards an Economic Model of the Japanese Firm," *Journal of Economic Literature* 28: 1–27.
Aumann, Robert J. (1990). "Irrationality in Game Theory," in Partha Dasgupta et al., eds., *Economic Analysis of Markets and Games: Essays in Honor of Frank Hahn*, pp. 214–27. Cambridge and London: MIT Press.
Axelrod, Robert (1984). *The Evolution of Cooperation*. New York: Basic Books.
———(1986). "An Evolutionary Approach to Norms," *American Political Science Review* 80(4): 1095–111.
Axelrod, Robert, and William D. Hamilton (1981). "The Evolution of Cooperation," *Science* 211(27): 1390–96.
Barkow, Jerome H., Leda Cosmides, and John Tooby, eds. (1992). *The Adapted Mind: Evolutionary Psychology and the Generation of Culture*. New York: Oxford University Press.
Basu, Kaushik, Eric Jones, and Ekkehart Schlicht (1987). "The Growth and Decay of Custom: The Role of the New Institutional Economics in Economic History," *Explorations in Economic History* 24: 1–21.

Becker, Gary (1976). "Altruism, Egoism, and Genetic Fitness: Economics and Sociobiology," *Journal of Economic Literature* 14(3): 817–26.

Bellah N. Robert, Richard Madsen, William M. Sullivan, Ann Swidler, and Steven M. Tipton (1991). *The Good Society*. New York: Vintage Books.

Ben-Ner, Avner (1987). "Preferences in a Communal Economic System," *Economica* 57: 207–21.

——— (1988). "The Life Cycle of Worker-Owned Firms in Market Economies: A Theoretical Analysis," *Journal of Economic Behavior and Organization* 10: 287–313.

Ben-Ner, Avner, John Michael Montias, and Egon Neuberger (1993). "Basic Issues in Organizations," *Journal of Comparative Economics* 17: 207–42.

Ben-Porat, Yoram (1980). "The F-Connection: Families, Friends, and Firms and the Organization of Exchange," *Population and Development Review* 6(1): 1–30.

Bergstrom, Theodore (1995). "On the Evolution of Altruistic Ethical Rules for Siblings," *American Economic Review* 85(1): 58–81.

——— (1996). "Economics in a Family Way," *Journal of Economic Literature* 34(4): 1903–34.

Bernheim, Douglas B., and Oded Stark (1988). "Altruism Within the Family Reconsidered: Do Nice Guys Finish Last?" *American Economic Review* 78: 1034–45.

Binmore, Ken, and Larry Samuelson (1994). "An Economist's Perspective on Evolution of Norms," *Journal of Institutional and Theoretical Economics* 150: 45–63.

Bovasso, Gregory, John Jacobs, and Salomon Rettig (1991). "Changes in Moral Values over Three Decades, 1958–1988," *Youth and Society* 22: 468–81.

Bowles, Samuel (1985). "The Production Process in a Competitive Economy: Walrasian, Neo-Hobbesian, and Marxian Models," *American Economic Review* 75: 16–36.

——— (1990). "Mandeville's Mistake: The Moral Autonomy of the Self-Regulating Market Reconsidered." Unpublished paper, University of Massachusetts, Amherst.

Bowles, Samuel, and Herbert Gintis (1993). "The Revenge of Homo Economicus: Contested Exchange and the Revival of Political Economy," *Journal of Economic Perspectives* 7(1): 83–102.

Boyd, Robert, and Peter Richerson (1985). *Culture and the Evolutionary Process*. Chicago: University of Chicago Press.

Brennan, Geoffrey, and Alan Hamlin (1995). "Economizing on Virtue," *Constitutional Political Economy* 6 (Winter): 35–56.

Brown, Jennifer, Hong Ye, Roderick Bronson, Pieter Dikkes, and Michael Greenberg (1996). "A Defect in Nurturing in Mice Lacking the Immediate Early Gene *fosB*," *Cell* 86 (July 26): 297–309.

Buchanan, James M. (1965). "Ethical Rules, Expected Values, and Large Numbers," *Ethics* 76: 1–13.

Bunn, Douglas, Steven Caudill, and Daniel Gropper (1992). "Crime in the Classroom: An Economic Analysis of Undergraduate Student Cheating Behavior," *Journal of Economic Education* 23: 197–207.

Burkert, Walter (1996). *The Creation of the Sacred: Tracks of Biology in Early Religions*. Cambridge, Mass.: Harvard University Press.

Buss, David M. (1995). "Evolutionary Psychology: A New Paradigm for Psychological Science," *Psychological Inquiry* 6(1): 1–30.

Camerer, Colin, and Richard H. Thaler (1995). "Ultimatums, Dictators and Manners," *Journal of Economic Perspectives* 9(2): 209–19.

Campbell, Donald T. (1983). "The Two Distinct Routes Beyond Kin Selection to Ultrasociality: Implications for the Humanities and the Social Sciences," in Diane Bridgeman, ed., *The Nature of Prosocial Development: Interdisciplinary Theories and Strategies*, pp. 12–41. New York: Academic Press.

——— (1986). "Rationality and Utility from the Standpoint of Evolutionary Biology," in Robin M. Hogarth and Melvin W. Reder, eds., *Rational Choice: The Contrast Between Economics and Psychology*, pp. 171–180. Chicago and London: University of Chicago Press.

Cavalli-Sforza, L. Luca (1993). "How Are Values Transmitted," in Michael Hechter, Lynn Nadel, and Richard E. Michod, eds., *The Origin of Values*, pp. 305–18. New York: Aldine de Gruyter.

Cavalli-Sforza, L. Luca, and Marcus Feldman (1981). *Cultural Transmission and Evolution: A Quantitative Approach*. Princeton, N.J.: Princeton University Press.

Conger, John (1988). "Hostages to Fortune: Youth, Values, and the Public Interest," *American Psychologist* 43: 291–300.

Coontz, Stephanie (1992). *The Way We Never Were*. New York: Basic Books.

Cosmides, Leda (1989). "The Logic of Social Exchange: Has Natural Selection Shaped How Humans Reason? Studies with the Wason Selection Task," *Cognition* 31: 187–276.

Cosmides, Leda, John Tooby, and Jerome H. Barkow (1992). "Introduction: Evolutionary Psychology and Conceptual Integration," in J. H. Barkow, L. Cosmides, and J. Tooby, eds., *The Adapted Mind: Evolutionary Psychology and the Generation of Culture*, pp. 3–18. New York: Oxford University Press.

Craig, Ben, and John Pencavel (1992). "The Behavior of Worker Cooperatives: The Plywood Companies of the Pacific Northwest." *American Economic Review* 82: 1083–105.

Craig, Ben, and John Pencavel (1995). "Participation and Productivity: A Comparison of Worker Cooperatives and Conventional Firms in the Plywood Industry," *Brookings Papers on Economic Activity: Microeconomics* 121–74.

Crimmins, Eileen, Richard Easterlin, and Yasushiko Saito (1991). "Preference Changes among American Youth: Family, Work, and Goods Aspirations 1976–86," *Population and Development Review* 17: 115–33.

Cronin, Helen (1992). *The Ant and the Peacock*. Cambridge: Cambridge University Press.

Dahl, Robert (1985). *A Preface to Economic Democracy*. Berkeley: University of California Press.

Daly, Martin, and Margo Wilson (1983). *Sex, Evolution, and Behavior*. Boston: Willard Grant.

Darwin, Charles (1871). *The Descent of Man, and Selection in Relation to Sex*. Princeton, N.J.: Princeton University Press (photo reproduction of the original edition published by J. Murray, London).

Dawkins, Richard (1989). *The Selfish Gene*, new ed. Oxford: Oxford University Press.

De Sousa, Ronald (1987). *The Rationality of Emotion*. Cambridge, Mass.: MIT Press.

Dennett, Daniel C. (1995). *Darwin's Dangerous Idea*. New York: Simon & Schuster.

DiMaggio, Paul J., and Walter W. Powell (1983). "The Iron Cage Revisited: Institutional Isomorphism and Collective Rationality in Organizational Fields" *American Sociological Review* 47: 147–60.

Durham, W. H. (1991). *Coevolution: Genes, Culture, and Human Diversity*. Stanford, Calif.: Stanford University Press.

Easterlin, Richard, and Eileen Crimmins (1991). "Private Materialism, Personal Self-Fulfillment, Family Life, and Public Interest: The Nature, Effects, and Causes of Recent Changes in the Values of American Youth," *Public Opinion Quarterly* 55: 499–533.

Eckel, Catherine C., and Philip Grossman (1994). "Chivalry and Solidarity in Ultimatum Games." Working paper, Department of Economics, Virginia Polytechnic and State University.

Eswaran, Mukesh, and Ashok Kotwal (1984). "The Moral Hazard of Budget-Breaking," *Rand Journal of Economics* 15(4): 578–81.

Etzioni, Amitai (1988). *The Moral Dimension*. New York: Free Press.

——— (1996). *The Golden Rule: Community and Morality in a Democratic Society*. New York: Basic Books.

Fehr, Ernst, G. Kirchsteiger, and A. Riedl (1993). "Does Fairness Prevent Market Clearing? An Experimental Investigation," *Quarterly Journal of Economics* 108(2): 437–60.

Fehr, Ernst, and Jean-Robert Tyran (1996). "Institutions and Reciprocal Fairness," *Nordic Journal of Political Economy* 23(2): 133–44.

Fischhoff, Baruch (1993). "Value Elicitation: Is There Anything in There?" in Michael Hechter, Lynn Nadel, and Richard E. Michod, eds., *The Origin of Values*, pp. 187–214. New York: Aldine de Gruyter.

Frank, Robert (1988). *Passions Within Reason*. New York: W. W. Norton.

Frank, Robert, Thomas Gilovich, and Dennis Regan (1993). "Does Studying Economics Inhibit Cooperation?" *Journal of Economic Perspectives* 7: 159–71.

Frank, Robert, Thomas Gilovich, and Dennis Regan (1996). "Do Economists Make Bad Citizens?" *Journal of Economic Perspectives* 10: 187–92.

Freeman, Richard, and Martin Weitzman (1987). "Bonuses and Employment in Japan," *Journal of the Japanese and International Economies* 1(2): 168–94.

Frey, Bruno (1993). "Does Monitoring Increase Work Effort? The Rivalry with Trust and Loyalty," *Economic Inquiry* 31(4): 663–70.

Goleman, Daniel (1995). *Emotional Intelligence*. New York: Bantam Books.

Goodman, Ellen (1995). "What a Sorry Message: That a *Mensch* Is So Rare," *Boston Globe*, December 21.

Gould, Stephen Jay (1993). *The Book of Life*. New York: Norton.

——— (1997). "Evolution: The Pleasures of Pluralism," *New York Review of Books*, June 26, 47–52.

Granovetter, Mark (1985). "Economic Action and Social Structure: The Problem of Embeddedness," *American Journal of Sociology* 91: 481–510.

Greif, Avner (1994). "Cultural Beliefs and the Organization of Society: A Historical and Theoretical Reflection on Collectivist and Individualist Societies," *Journal of Political Economy* 102: 912–50.

Guth, Werner (1995). "An Evolutionary Approach to Explaining Cooperative Behavior by Reciprocal Incentives," *International Journal of Game Theory* 24: 323–44.

Guth, Werner, and Menachem Yaari (1992). "Explaining Reciprocal Behavior in Simple Strategic Games: An Evolutionary Approach," in Ulrich Witt, ed., *Explaining Process and Change: Approaches to Evolutionary Economics*, pp. 23–34. Ann Arbor: University of Michigan Press.

Guttman, Joel M. (1996a). "Rational Actors, Tit-for-Tat Types, and the Evolution of Cooperation," *Journal of Economic Behavior and Organization* 29: 27–56.

——— (1996b). "On the Stability of Cooperative Social Norms among Rational Agents." Unpublished paper, Bar-Ilan University.

Guttman, Joel, Shmuel Nitzan, and Uriel Spiegel (1992). "Rent Seeking and Social Investment in Taste Change," *Economics and Politics* 4: 31–42.

Hamilton, William D. (1964). "The Genetical Theory of Social Behavior, Parts I and II," *Journal of Theoretical Biology* 7: 1–16, 17–32.

Hansmann, Henry (1996). *The Ownership of Enterprise*. Cambridge, Mass.: Belknap Press of Harvard University Press.

Hansson, Ingemar, and Charles Stuart (1990). "Malthusian Selection of Preferences," *American Economic Review* 80: 529–44.

Harsanyi, John (1982). "Morality and the Theory of Rational Behavior," in Amartya Sen and Bernard Williams, eds., *Utilitarianism and Beyond*. Cambridge: Cambridge University Press.

Hausman, Daniel M., and Michael S. McPherson (1996). *Economic Analysis and Moral Philosophy*. New York: Cambridge University Press.

Hechter, Michael (1993). "Values Research in the Social and Behavioral Sciences," in Michael Hechter, Lynn Nadel, and Richard E. Michod, eds., *The Origin of Values*, pp. 1–30. New York: Aldine de Gruyter.

Hechter, Michael, Lynn Nadel, and Richard E. Michod, eds. (1993). *The Origin of Values*. New York: Aldine de Gruyter.

Hirschman, Albert O. (1985). "Against Parsimony," *Economics and Philosophy* 1: 7–21.

Hirshleifer, Jack (1994). "The Dark Side of the Force," *Economic Inquiry* 32: 1–10.

Hirshleifer, Jack, and Juan Carlos Martinez Coll (1988). "What Strategies Can Support the Evolutionary Emergence of Cooperation?" *Journal of Conflict Resolution* 32: 367–98.

Hoffman, Elizabeth, Kevin McCabe, and Vernon Smith (1995). "Ultimatum and Dictator Games (Reply to Camerer and Thaler)," *Journal of Economic Perspectives* 9(4): 236–39.

Hoffman, Elizabeth, Kevin McCabe, and Vernon Smith (1996). "Social Distance and Other-Regarding Behavior in Dictator Games," *American Economic Review* 86(3): 653–60.

Hofstede, Geert H. (1980). *Culture's Consequences: International Differences in Work-Related Values*. Beverly Hills, Calif.: Sage Publications.

Holmstrom, Bengt (1982). "Moral Hazard in Teams," *Bell Journal of Economics* 13: 324–40.

Holmstrom, Bengt, and Paul Milgrom (1991). "Multitask Principal-Agent Analyses: Incentive Contracts, Asset Ownership, and Job Design," *Journal of Law, Economics, and Organization* 7: 24–52.

Kahneman, Daniel, Jack L. Knetsch, and Richard Thaler (1986). "Fairness as a Constraint on Profit Seeking: Entitlements in the Market," *American Economic Review* 76: 728–41.

Kandel, Eugene, and Edward Lazear (1992). "Peer Pressure and Partnerships," *Journal of Political Economy* 100: 801–17.

Knight, Frank (1957). *Risk, Uncertainty and Profit*. New York: Kelley & Millman.

Kolm, Serge-Christophe (1996). "Moral Public Choice," *Public Choice* 87: 117–41.

Kotlowitz, Alex (1991). *There Are No Children Here*. New York: Doubleday.

Kreps, David (1990). *Game Theory and Economic Modelling*. New York: Oxford University Press.

Kreps, David, Paul Milgrom, John Roberts, and Robert Wilson (1982). "Rational Cooperation in the Finitely Repeated Prisoner's Dilemma," *Journal of Economic Theory* 27: 245–52.

Lazear, Edward (1989). "Pay Equality and Industrial Politics," *Journal of Political Economy* 97: 561–80.

Lemann, Nicholas (1991). *The Promised Land*. New York: Alfred Knopf.

Lindbeck, Assar (1995). "Hazardous Welfare-State Dynamics," *American Economic Review* (Papers and Proceedings) 85: 9–15.

Lumsden, Charles, and Edward O. Wilson (1983). *Promethean Fire: Reflections on the Origin of Mind*. Cambridge: Harvard University Press.

Lundberg, Shelly, and Robert A. Pollak (1993). "Separate Sphere Bargaining and the Marriage Market," *Journal of Political Economy* 100(6): 988–1010.

MacLeod, Bentley (1987). "Behavior and the Organization of the Firm," *Journal of Comparative Economics* 11: 207–20.

————(1988). "Equity, Efficiency, and Incentives in Cooperative Teams," in Derek Jones and Jan Svejnar, eds., *Advances in the Economic Analysis of Participatory and Labor-Managed Firms.* Greenwich: JAI Press.

————(1996). "Decision, Contract and Emotion: Some Economics for a Complex and Confusing World." Paper Prepared for the Harold Innis Memorial Lecture, Canadian Economics Association Meetings, St. Catherine, Ontario, May.

McCloskey, Donald (1994). "Bourgeois Virtue," *American Scholar* 63(2): 177–91.

McKenzie, Richard B. (1977). "The Economic Dimensions of Ethical Behavior," *Ethics* 87(3): 208–21.

Mailath, George J. (1992). "Introduction: Symposium on Evolutionary Game Theory," *Journal of Economic Theory* 57: 259–77.

Malcomson, James (1984). "Work Incentives, Hierarchy, and Internal Labor Markets," *Journal of Political Economy* 92: 486–507.

Massey, Douglas, and Nancy Denton (1993). *American Apartheid: Segregation and the Making of the Underclass.* Cambridge: Harvard University Press.

Maynard Smith, John (1982). *Evolution and the Theory of Games.* Cambridge: Cambridge University Press.

Michod, Richard E. (1993). "Biology and the Origin of Values," in Michael Hechter, Lynn Nadel, and Richard E. Michod, eds., *The Origin of Values,* pp. 261–72. New York: Aldine de Gruyter.

Mill, John Stuart (1936). *Principles of Political Economy.* London: Longmans, Green.

Miyazaki, Hajime (1993). "Employeeism, Corporate Governance, and the J-Firm," *Journal of Comparative Economics* 17(2): 443–69.

Moffitt, Robert (1983). "An Economic Model of Welfare Stigma," *American Economic Review* 73: 1023–35.

Myrdal, Gunnar (1953 [1929]). *The Political Element in the Development of Economic Theory.* Trans. Paul Streeten. Cambridge, Mass.: Harvard University Press.

Nelson, Richard R., and Sidney Winter (1982). *An Evolutionary Theory of Economic Change.* Cambridge, Mass.: Belknap Press of Harvard University Press.

North, Douglass (1990). *Institutions, Institutional Change and Economic Performance.* Cambridge: Cambridge University Press.

Olson, Mancur (1971). *The Logic of Collective Action: Public Goods and the Theory of Groups.* Cambridge, Mass.: Harvard University Press.

Palermo, George, and Douglas Simpson (1994). "At the Roots of Violence: The Progressive Decline and Dissolution of the Family," *International Journal of Offender Therapy and Cognitive Criminology* 38: 105–16.

Putnam, Robert D. (1995). "Tuning In, Tuning Out: The Strange Disappearance of Social Capital in America," *Political Science and Politics* 28(4): 664–83.

Putterman, Louis (1990). *Division of Labor and Welfare: An Introduction to Economic Systems.* Oxford: Oxford University Press.

——— (1993). "Ownership and the Nature of the Firm," *Journal of Comparative Economics* 17: 243–63.

Putterman, Louis, and Gilbert Skillman (1992). "The Role of Exit Costs in the Theory of Cooperative Teams," *Journal of Comparative Economics* 16: 596–618.

Rabin, Matthew (1993). "Incorporating Fairness into Game Theory and Economics," *American Economic Review* 83(5): 1282–1302.

——— (1995). "Moral Preferences, Moral Constraints, and Self-Serving Bias." Working Paper, Department of Economics, University of California, Berkeley, August.

Rawls, John (1971). *A Theory of Justice.* Cambridge, Mass.: Harvard University Press.

Robbins, Lionel (1932). *An Essay on The Nature and Significance of Economic Science.* London: Macmillan.

Romer, David (1984). "The Theory of Social Custom: A Modification and Some Extensions," *Quarterly Journal of Economics* 99: 717–27.

Rotemberg, Julio (1994). "Human Relations in the Workplace," *Journal of Political Economy* 102: 684–717.

Roth, Alvin, Vesna Prasnikar, Masahiro Okuno-Fuhiwara, and Shmuel Zamir (1991). "Bargaining and Market Behavior in Jerusalem, Ljubljana, and Tokyo: An Experimental Study," *American Economic Review* 81: 1068–95.

Rowe, David C. (1994). *The Limits of Family Influence: Genes, Experience, and Behavior.* New York and London: Guilford Press.

Schab, Fred (1991). "Schooling without Learning: Thirty Years of Cheating in High School," *Adolescence* 26: 839–47.

Schlicht, Ekkehart (1995). "On Custom," *Journal of Institutional and Theoretical Economics* 149(1): 178–203.

Schor, Juliet B. (1991). *The Overworked American: The Unexpected Decline of Leisure.* New York: Basic Books.

Schotter, Andrew (1981). *The Economic Theory of Social Institutions.* Cambridge: Cambridge University Press.

Schwartz, Barry (1993a). "On the Creation of Value," in Michael Hechter, Lynn Nadel, and Richard E. Michod, eds., *The Origin of Values*, pp. 153–86. New York: Aldine de Gruyter.

——— (1993b). "Why Altruism Is Impossible . . . and Ubiquitous," *Social Service Review* 67(3): 314–43.

Sen, Amartya (1974). "Choice, Orderings and Morality," in Stephan Körner, ed., *Practical Reason*, pp. 55–82. New Haven: Yale University Press.

——— (1987). *On Ethics and Economics.* Oxford: Blackwell.

——— (1993). "Moral Codes and Economic Success." Suntory-Toyota International Centre for Economics and Related Disciplines Development Economic Research Programme Paper No. 49.

Shapiro, Carl, and Joseph Stiglitz (1984). "Equilibrium Unemployment as a Worker Discipline Device," *American Economic Review* 74: 433–44.

Shepher, Joseph, and Lionel Tiger (1975). *Women in the Kibbutz*. New York: Harcourt Brace Jovanovich.

Smith, Adam (1904 [1776]). *The Wealth of Nations*. London: Methuen & Co.

———(1971 [1759]). *Theory of Moral Sentiments*. New York: Garland.

Stigler, George J., and Gary S. Becker (1977). "De Gustibus Non Est Disputandum," *American Economic Review* 67(2): 76–90.

Sulloway, Frank J. (1996). *Born to Rebel: Birth Order, Family Dynamics, and Creative Lives*. New York: Pantheon Books.

Tooby, John, and Leda Cosmides (1990). "On the Universality of Human Nature and the Uniqueness of the Individual: The Role of Genetics and Adaptation," *Journal of Personality* 58(1): 17–67.

Trivers, Robert (1983). "The Evolution of Cooperation," in Diane Bridgeman, ed., *The Nature of Prosocial Development: Interdisciplinary Theories and Strategies*, pp. 43–60. New York: Academic Press.

Ullmann-Margalit, Edna (1977). *The Emergence of Norms*. Oxford: Clarendon Press.

Vega-Redondo, Fernando (1994). "Bayesian Boundedly Rational Agents Play the Finitely Repeated Prisoner's Dilemma," *Theory and Decision* 36(2): 187–206.

de Waal, Frans (1996). *Good Natured: The Origins of Right and Wrong in Humans and Other Animals*. Cambridge: Harvard University Press.

Wacquant, Loic (1993). "Dangerous Places: Violence and Isolation in Chicago's Ghetto and the Parisian 'Banlieue,'" in W. J. Wilson, ed., *Urban Poverty and Family Life in the Inner City*. Oxford: Oxford University Press.

Weibull, Jurgen (1996). *Evolutionary Game Theory*. Cambridge: M.I.T. Press.

Weisbrod, Burton (1977). "Comparing Utility Functions in Efficiency Terms or, What Kind of Utility Functions Do We Want?" *American Economic Review* 67: 991–95.

Weitzman, Martin, and Douglas Kruse (1990). "Profit Sharing," in Alan Blinder, ed., *Paying for Productivity: A Look at the Evidence*. Washington, D.C.: Brookings Institution.

Weitzman, Martin, and Chenggang Xu (1994). "Chinese Township-Village Enterprises as Vaguely Defined Cooperatives," *Journal of Comparative Economics* 18: 121–45.

Whitaker, Leighton (1993). "Violence Is Golden: Commercially Motivated Training in Impulsive Cognitive Style and Mindless Violence," *Journal of College Student Psychotherapy* 8: 45–69.

White, Harrison C. (1993). "Values Come in Styles, Which Mate to Change," in Michael Hechter, Lynn Nadel, and Richard E. Michod, eds., *The Origin of Values*, pp. 63–92. New York: Aldine de Gruyter.

Williamson, Oliver (1975). *Markets and Hierarchies: Analysis and Anti-Trust Implications*. New York: Free Press.

———(1985). *The Economic Institutions of Capitalism*. New York: Free Press.

Wilson, David Sloan, and Elliot Sober (1994). "Re-introducing Group Selection to the Human Behavioral Sciences," *Behavioral and Brain Sciences* 17: 585–608.

Wilson, William J. (1987). *The Truly Disadvantaged*. Chicago: University of Chicago Press.

Wright, Robert (1994). *The Moral Animal: Why We Are the Way We Are: The New Science of Evolutionary Psychology*. New York: Pantheon Books.

Yankelovitch, Daniel (1994). "How Changes in the Economy Are Reshaping Values," in Aaron, Henry, Thomas Mann, and Timothy Taylor, eds., *Values and Public Policy*, pp. 16–53. Washington, D.C.: Brookings Institution.

Yezer, Anthony M., Robert S. Goldfarb, and Paul J. Poppen (1996). "Does Studying Economics Inhibit Cooperation? Watch What We Do, Not What We Say or How We Play," *Journal of Economic Perspectives* 10: 177–86.

Young, H. Peyton (1996). "The Economics of Convention," *Journal of Economic Perspectives* 10: 105–22.

——(1996). "Social Coordination and Social Change." Working paper, Department of Economics, Johns Hopkins University.

PART I

THE FORMATION AND EVOLUTION OF
SOCIAL NORMS AND VALUES

CHAPTER 2

# Normative expectations: the simultaneous evolution of institutions and norms

*Robert Sugden*

On the road I use on my journey to work, there is a narrow bridge over a river, not wide enough to allow two vehicles to pass. Although the road is quite heavily used, the highway authority has not followed the common practice of putting up signs to give priority to traffic traveling in a particular direction. But there is no need for any signs: Everyone who uses the bridge seems to follow a clear set of rules. Once one vehicle is crossing the bridge, any number of others behind it will follow, and those going the other way have to wait until there is a gap in the traffic flowing against them. So at busy times there are long periods in which all the traffic flows one way. What is more interesting is what happens when traffic is lighter, and two vehicles approach the bridge from opposite directions, with clear road in between. Then the one which is nearer to the bridge maintains speed and the other slows down and gives way. I shall call this convention the *first-on* rule. How is it enforced? Principally, I think, by the fact that if two vehicles meet in the middle of the bridge, both drivers suffer, whichever one of them eventually backs up. So if, approaching the bridge, you expect the other driver to maintain speed, you do best by giving way, while if you expect the other to give way, you do best to maintain speed. So the "rule" is a system of mutual expectations which is self-reinforcing: Each person, acting on her own expectations about the others, is led to act in a way that confirms the others' expectations about her.

It is extremely rare for two drivers to meet in the middle of the bridge – so rare that, although I have used the bridge almost every weekday for ten years, I do not have enough experience to generalize about what

An earlier version of this chapter was presented at the Conference on Economics, Values, and Organization, Yale University, April 1996. I am grateful for the comments I received from many participants at that conference, and in particular from my two discussants, Jane Mansbridge and Ariel Rubinstein.

happens in this event. But one recent incident suggests that this case, too, may be resolved by mutually consistent expectations. I was approaching the bridge from one direction, another driver from the other. I judged that I was slightly closer to the bridge than the other driver. He speeded up. Seeing him do this, I speeded up too. I got on to the bridge before he did by a few seconds. We both stopped. Almost immediately, he backed up and let me through. And this is what I expected him to do. I expected this, not only in the empirical sense of "expect" (this is what I thought *would* happen) but also in the normative sense: I felt that this is what *ought* to happen; I was in the right and he was in the wrong.

In this example, normative expectations may seem to do little work. The first-on rule appears to be an equilibrium in which each driver acts in his self-interest, given his empirical expectations; if this is the case, then we can explain the stability of the rule without invoking norms. But it is probably not true that it is in *every* driver's self-interest to follow the rule – just in most drivers' interests, most of the time. Suppose I am driving a fast car with good brakes and am late for work, and the first-on rule favors a cyclist coming the other way. Neither of us wants an accident, but the cyclist has much more to lose. I may think that if I ignore the rule, he will get out of my way before I have to brake. Cases like this may be exceptional, but there is a danger that they will undermine the mutual expectations which support the rule in the nonexceptional cases. If impatient car drivers do not give way to cyclists, then cautious cyclists (who cannot tell whether the approaching car driver is impatient or not) may find it pays them to give way to car drivers in general. And then less impatient car drivers will find that it pays to ignore the rule when they meet cyclists; and so on. Thus, it is possible that the first-on rule is stable only if, in exceptional cases, individuals act on that rule even though doing so is contrary to self-interest. And perhaps the reason why they do so is that they feel the force of a system of normative expectations.

In this chapter, I shall present a sketch of a theory of normative expectations. I shall show how conventional practices can generate normative expectations, and how such expectations can be significant for the stability of conventions.

## 1    Values

My analysis of normative expectations is intended as a contribution to the much larger enterprise described by Avner Ben-Ner and Louis Putterman (this volume) – the enterprise of understanding the role of values in economic behavior. I agree with Ben-Ner and Putterman that, if we are to explain the existence and survival of some of the fundamental institutions of a market economy, we need a richer model of human beings than is provided by the rational, self-interested agent of neoclassical theory. Minor revisions to the neoclassical model, such as allowing bounded rationality or allowing each individual to have altruistic preferences about other people's consumption, will not be enough. We need a theory in which individuals can be motivated by considerations other than self-regarding or other-regarding preferences: In Ben-Ner and Putterman's terms, we need a theory in which individuals can be motivated by *values*.

If a theory of values is to be useful for economics, what properties should it have? I suggest that we should look for theories that have *explanatory power*, that make values *endogenous*, and that are *naturalistic*.

The first two of these properties are closely related. In neoclassical theory, behavior is determined by preferences, and preferences are exogenous. The strategy of taking preferences as given, rather than trying to explain them, clearly limits the explanatory power of economics. However, most neoclassical economics is based on very restrictive assumptions about the nature of preferences. Each individual is assumed to have preferences only over her own consumption of a clearly defined set of goods, and these preferences are assumed to satisfy certain general restrictions, such as completeness, transitivity, and convexity. Thus, the range in which preferences are allowed to vary is quite limited. Because of this feature, neoclassical theory can have considerable explanatory power, even though preferences are exogenous.

The limitations imposed by taking preferences as given become much more serious as soon as we start to relax these general restrictions. There is a real danger that a theory which treats values simply as a kind of preference will be empty: Invoking "preferences for acting morally" can become an ad hoc strategy which insulates economic theory from falsification by eliminating its predictive power.

David Kreps, Paul Milgrom, John Roberts, and Robert Wilson's (1982) classic analysis of the finitely repeated Prisoner's Dilemma is a good example of a theory which is open to this criticism. Kreps et al. prove the following result: A very small probability that each of the players will follow the Tit-for-Tat strategy can be sufficient to generate an equilibrium in which there is cooperation for almost the whole length of the game. But, of course, a rational player with standard Prisoner's Dilemma payoffs would not play Tit-for-Tat for the whole game, since it always pays to defect in the last round. It is therefore necessary to treat the Tit-for-Tat player as a distinct "type," defined by having nonstandard preferences. One interpretation of these preferences is that they represent a moral commitment to reciprocity. On this interpretation, Kreps and associates' result tells us that a small probability of morally motivated action can be sufficient to induce everyone to cooperate almost all of the time. Notice, however, that in this model, the normative element (the probability that players may have a taste for reciprocity) is an unexplained assumption about preferences. Game-theoretic analysis shows how players' beliefs that their opponents might have a taste for reciprocity can generate expectations that their opponents will *in fact* act as if they had that taste (even though it is highly probable that they do not have it). But if we fed in different assumptions about the moral tastes of nonstandard players, we would presumably derive correspondingly different conclusions about the behavior of standardly rational ones.

A theory of values is much less likely to be ad hoc if it provides an explanation of the formation of values. Further, as Ben-Ner and Putterman (this volume) argue, it is only by making values endogenous that we can hope to explain how institutions impact on values.

My list of desirable properties for a theory of values ends with the property of naturalism. By this, I mean that the theory should not appeal to propositions about what "really" is good or bad, right or wrong. Of course, people's moral reasoning may be part of the subject matter of the theory. When we reason as moral agents, we often *feel* that there are moral facts that we can sense in some way. Nevertheless, the nature of such supposed facts is far too shadowy to provide the basis for social theory. If, as social theorists, we have to explain how people arrive at this moral sense, we must do so without assuming the existence of moral facts.

To economists, trained in a positivist tradition, this may seem obvious. But it is easy to slip between statements about people's moral beliefs and substantive moral statements. It is particularly difficult to avoid the temptation of thinking that the subject matter of a theory of values consists of dispositions to act in ways that "really" are morally praiseworthy. But if we take a naturalistic approach, the set of morally praiseworthy actions is an illegitimate construct. Nor is there any reason to suppose that the set of actions that we (the theorists) regard as morally praiseworthy constitutes a useful theoretical category. Compare consumer theory: I happen to dislike chewing gum and to like chocolate, but as a microeconomist, I recognize that both belong to the category of consumption goods, and that the demand for each of those goods can be explained by a common theory.

Thus, the first essential for a theory of values is a naturalistic delimitation of its subject matter. The approach that I shall follow derives from David Hume's *Treatise of Human Nature* (1978). For Hume, there are no moral facts, only moral sentiments. Or, more accurately, the only moral facts are facts of psychology, concerning the causes of certain kinds of sentiment. Thus, the distinguishing feature of what we call virtue is that it gives rise to the sentiments of approval and admiration, while the distinguishing feature of what we call vice is that it gives rise to the sentiments of disapproval and blame:

> Take any action allow'd to be vicious: Wilful murder, for instance. . . . The vice entirely escapes you, as long as you consider the object. You never can find it, till you turn your reflexion into your own breast, and find a sentiment of disapprobation, which arises in you, towards this action. Here is a matter of fact; but 'tis the object of feeling, not of reason. It lies in yourself, not in the object. So that when you pronounce any action or character to be vicious, you mean nothing, but that from the constitution of your nature you have a feeling or sentiment of blame from the contemplation of it. (pp. 468–69)

However, Hume's account of moral sentiments makes them more than mere personal likes and dislikes. It is a convention of language that moral judgments are made from "*steady* and *general* points of view" (pp. 581–82), just as judgments of relative size are corrected for the effects of perspective. A murder that I read about in the newspaper may generate a less intense sensation of disapproval in me than the stealing of my own wallet, but because in general, murders tend to evoke in me stronger sensations of disapproval than do incidents of pickpocketing, my moral condemnation of murder is stronger. Moral sentiments, then, are sentiments of approval or disapproval that apply to general classes of actions. I propose that we should treat the class of such sentiments, and the causes of these sentiments, as the subject matter of the theory of values.

Normative expectations constitute a subclass of moral sentiments. I shall give a more formal definition of normative expectations later in the chapter; for the present, it is sufficient to say that, on my definition, normative expectations are tied to conventional practices; they exist when people expect each other to follow some convention and disapprove of breaches of it. I shall present a theory in which normative expectations are endogenous: The theory is intended to explain both how a conventional practice can generate normative expectations, and how those expectations can affect the stability of the practice.

## 2     Normative expectations

The concept of normative expectations can be traced back to Hume (1978, pp. 484–513). It is useful to begin by looking at Hume's analysis: The issues that it deals with are ones that have to be faced by any theory of normative expectations.

Hume argues that justice (essentially, the existence of rules of property that are generally respected) "establishes itself by a kind of convention or agreement; that is, by a sense of interest, suppos'd to be common to all, and where every single act is perform'd in expectation that others are to perform the like" (p. 498). Explaining the claim that property rights are, at root, conventions, Hume writes:

> I observe, that it will be for my interest to leave another in the possession of his goods, *provided* he will act in the same manner with regard to me. He is sensible of a like interest in the regulation of his conduct. When this common sense of interest is mutually express'd, and is known to both, it produces a suitable resolution and behaviour. (p. 490)

Thus, on Hume's account, rules of justice originate as regularities in behavior in relation to human interaction. The regularities which are relevant for justice have the special property that it is in each individual's interest to conform to them, provided others can be expected to conform too. Further, for a given class of interactions, there is more than one potential regularity which has that property. Thus, it is *only* when there is a general expectation of conformity to a particular regularity that everyone has an interest in conforming to it. I shall follow Hume in calling such regularities "conventions."

For Hume, individual interest explains how the rules of justice become established, and (at least in simple societies) it provides each person with his motivation for acting on those rules: This is "the *natural* obligation to justice, *viz.* interest." But for Hume there is a further and quite distinct question to answer: "Why we annex the idea of virtue to justice, and of vice to injustice" (p. 498). Although the establishment of the rules of justice is explained by self-interest, those rules have normative force for us. Hume recognizes that, from the viewpoint of "reason and public interest," many of the specific rules which determine property rights are arbitrary; they are often based merely on imaginative analogies (p. 506). But nevertheless, we come to regard it as virtuous to act on those rules.

Hume offers a naturalistic account, based on the psychology of sympathy, of how the conventions of justice become norms. I shall use the word "norm" to refer to any regularity in behavior within a given community which is generally expected, not only in the empirical sense, but also in the normative sense. That is, conformity with the regularity elicits sentiments of approval while failure to conform elicits disapproval.

On Hume's account, human nature is such that we tend to derive a kind of satisfaction from other people's satisfaction, and a kind of uneasiness from other people's uneasiness. The intensity of natural sympathy depends on time and place and relationship, but such variations of viewpoint do not affect moral judgments, which apply to general classes of actions (recall section 1). Thus, Hume argues, we tend to give moral approval to institutions which work for the general good. Despite their arbitrariness at the level of detail, the rules of justice are such institutions. And so, although "self-interest is the original motive to the *establishment* of justice," "a sympathy with public interest is the source of the *moral approbation*, which attends that virtue" (pp. 499–500). The rules of justice, once established, become norms.

I am not sure how important Hume thinks these moral sentiments are in ensuring the *stability* of justice. At some points in the *Treatise*, Hume seems to suggest that the rules of justice evolve in small societies, and that in such societies, self-interest is sufficient to make those rules stable. As societies grow, a free-rider problem becomes increasingly significant, but this is counterbalanced by the emergence of moral sentiments:

> To the imposition then, and observance of these rules, both in general, and in every particular instance, [men] are at first mov'd only by a regard to interest; and this motive, on the first formation of society, is sufficiently strong and forcible. But when society has encreas'd to a tribe or nation, this interest is more remote; nor do men so readily perceive, that disorder and confusion follow upon every breach of these rules, as in a more narrow and contracted society. But tho' in our own actions we may frequently lose sight of that interest, which we have in maintaining order, and may follow a lesser and more present interest, we never fail to observe the prejudice we receive, either mediately or immediately, from the injustice of others; as not being in that case either blinded by passion, or byass'd by any contrary temptation. Nay when the injustice is so distant from us, as no way to affect our interest, it still displeases us; because we consider it as prejudicial to human society. . . . And tho' this sense, in the present case, be deriv'd only from contemplating the actions of others, yet we fail not to extend it even to our own actions. The *general rule* reaches beyond those instances, from which it arose; while at the same time we naturally *sympathize* with others in the sentiments they entertain of us. (p. 499)

Here, the idea seems to be that in large societies, individuals are motivated by a desire for the moral approval of others, and this motivation is important for the stability of justice. In other places, however, Hume is more skeptical about the motivating power of morality: Interest is a "passion," while morality is only a "taste." For example, when discussing sympathy, Hume says:

> My sympathy with another may give me the sentiment of pain and disapprobation, when any object is presented, that has a tendency to give him uneasiness; tho' I may not be willing to sacrifice any thing of my own interest, or cross any of my passions, for his satisfaction. . . . Sentiments must touch the heart, to make them controul our passions: But they need not extend beyond the imagination, to make them influence our taste. (p. 586)

In these passages, Hume seems to be grappling with two problems. The first problem is that self-interest seems incapable of fully explaining why, in large societies, individuals comply with the rules of justice. But those rules do not work for the general good unless they are generally followed. Thus, the emergence of a convention must precede the emergence of the corresponding moral sentiment: Sympathy with the public interest could not motivate anyone to be the first person to follow any particular rule of justice. And so the explanation of how a convention first comes into existence has to rely on self-interest. But if self-interest cannot explain the stability of justice, how is it to explain the emergence of justice?

The second problem is to provide a naturalistic account of how individuals can be motivated to act contrary to self-interest. If our natural sympathies are partial, how do we come to take an impartial view of the general good? By treating impartiality as a convention of language, Hume may be able to explain how a *discourse* of morality can evolve, but when conclusions are reached within that discourse, why do they, rather than the original natural sympathies, motivate action?

David Lewis (1969) presents a modern variant of Hume's argument. Lewis defines "convention" rather narrowly, in terms of what he calls coordination problems. A coordination problem is a game with the following two properties: First, it has two or more *coordination equilibria*. A coordination equilibrium is a list of strategies, one strategy $s_i$ for each player $i = 1, \ldots, n$, such that for each player $i$, (1) $s_i$ is a best reply to the other players' strategies (that is, the list of strategies is a *Nash equilibrium*), and (2) given that $i$ plays $s_i$, he most prefers that each other player $j$ should play $s_j$. Second, the players are indifferent (or almost indifferent) between the coordination equilibria. (This condition rules out games like Chicken and Battle of the Sexes in which there are conflicts of interest between the players; it also rules out games in which one equilibrium is better than another for all players.) If the players have a common expectation that one of the coordination equilibria will come about, and hence are led to play in such a way that it does come about, then that equilibrium is a convention in Lewis's sense. (It is also a convention by my broader definition.)

Lewis offers an explanation of how conventions emerge. This explanation does not require anyone to act contrary to self-interest. And clearly, once a convention (as defined by Lewis) has become established, it is in each player's interest to follow it. However, Lewis makes the additional claim that conventions tend to become norms:

> So if [other people] see me fail to conform [to a convention], not only have I gone against their expectations; they will probably be in a position to infer that I have knowingly acted contrary to my own preferences, and contrary to their preferences and their reasonable expectations. They will be surprised, and they will tend to explain my conduct discreditably. The poor opinions they form of me, and their reproaches, punishment and distrust are the unfavorable responses I have evoked by my failure to conform to the convention. (p. 99)

In this account, norms are a special kind of expectation. Each person $i$ has an empirical expectation that other people (such as $j$) will behave in a particular way; $i$ acts on this expectation; having so acted, $i$ wants the others to act as he has expected them to; and if $j$ fails to act as expected, $i$ regards $j$ as having acted discreditably.

In Lewis's model, norms are merely the by-products of conventions. Although a desire to avoid disapproval might provide an additional motivation for individuals to follow conventions, we can explain conventions without invoking that motivation. Thus Lewis does not need to tackle the problems which confronted Hume's argument. However, by adapting and extending Lewis's analysis, we may be able to explain how individuals can sometimes be motivated to act contrary to self-interest.

In my book, *The Economics of Rights, Co-operation and Welfare* (1986, pp. 145–77) and in Sugden (1989), I suggest that it is part of normal human psychology for us to feel resentment against individuals whose acts are both contrary to our expectations and contrary to our interests – particularly if we believe that those individuals knew their acts would have those properties. In addition, it is part of human nature for us to feel unease at being the focus of another person's resentment. Among the factors that can motivate individuals' actions is the desire to avoid this kind of resentment. So far, the argument is very similar to Lewis's.

Now suppose that in some society there is some regularity $R$ in behavior, such that (1) if an individual conforms to $R$, it is in his interest that others conform to $R$; (2) in most (but not necessarily all) cases, if an individual expects others to conform to $R$, it is in his interest to conform to $R$; and (3) most people in the society expect most other people to conform to $R$. Then those people who conform to $R$ will feel resentment against those who do not. Further, each person will tend to feel some desire (not necessarily strong enough to overcome other competing desires) to avoid this resentment by conforming to $R$. In such a case, I shall say that the general expectation of conformity to $R$ is a *normative expectation*.

This characterization of normative expectations can be expanded to include cases in which $R$ prescribes actions by some individuals which are contrary to the interests of others. For example, consider the case of the two drivers meeting in the middle of the narrow bridge, and suppose that $R$ is a well-established rule that the driver who reached the bridge second backs up. This rule clearly satisfies (2) and, by virtue of its being well established, (3). However, (1) may be satisfied only partially. It is in the interest of first-on drivers that second-on drivers conform to $R$, but the converse may not hold. In this case, I suggest, first-on drivers who conform to $R$ will resent second-on drivers who fail to conform, even if there is no resentment against first-on drivers who are unconventionally submissive.

To encompass cases like this, let $R'$ be any subset of the actions which make up $R$. (In the example, $R$ prescribes that first-on drivers stay put and that second-on drivers back up; $R'$ prescribes only that second-on drivers back up.) I shall say that there is a normative expectation of $R'$ if the following conditions are met: (1) if an individual conforms to $R$, it is in his interest that others conform to $R'$; (2) in most (but not necessarily all) cases, if an individual expects others to conform to $R$, it is in his interest to conform to $R$; (3) most people in the society expect most other people to conform to $R$.

The class of cases covered by my definition of a normative expectation includes the cases considered by Lewis but is broader in two respects. First, I do not require that it is always in a person's interest to conform to the regularity $R$. In the cases which Lewis considers, the person whose action is "explained discreditably" appears to have acted contrary to his own preferences, as well as contrary to other people's preferences and expectations; among the reasons why the action reflects discredit on the actor is that it appears to be irrational. But, I suggest, we can explain why such an action is resented without making use of the assumption that it was contrary to the self-interest of the actor. By not requiring that self-interest always dictates conformity to the convention, my analysis allows us to consider cases in which normative expectations and self-interest pull in opposite directions; if normative expectations have some motivating force, then there can be cases in which individuals follow conventions even though this is contrary to self-interest.

The second difference between my analysis and Lewis's is that, unlike Lewis, I do not require that the relevant interaction is a coordination game. For example, it could have the structure of a Battle of the Sexes game, in which the equilibrium $R$ which has become established favors some members of society (say, men) relative to others (say, women). In such a game, it is in each woman's interest to conform to $R$ if she expects most men to conform; and given that a woman does conform to $R$, it is in her interest that men conform too. Thus, isolated cases in which men fail to conform may be resented by women, just as isolated failures of women to conform may be resented by men. Alternatively, the interaction might take the form of a game in which there are two Nash equilibria, one of which Pareto dominates the other. (Consider two different rules for assigning priority on the narrow bridge – say, the first-on rule and a rule that gives priority to traffic in one particular direction. Each rule is a Nash equilibrium, but one of them may be better for all drivers in the long run.) For some games of this type, a Pareto-dominated equilibrium, once established, satisfies my conditions for the existence of normative expectations: Even though the convention is inefficient, breaches of it are resented.

These conclusions may seem surprising. Commentators on my work have often objected that conventions that clearly favor one group of people at the expense of another, or that clearly do not work for the general good, will not generate genuinely *normative* expectations. The objection runs like this: Such conventions, once established, clearly generate *empirical* expectations of conformity. When one person breaches such a convention, those who are harmed by that action may feel some negative emotion – perhaps anger – toward the nonconformer, but this is not a *moral* response. Conversely, in those cases in which breaches of conventions are subject to genuine moral disapproval, that disapproval rests on something more than the emotion that I have called "resentment": There must be some prior belief that the convention is socially beneficial or fair, so that what is being resented is not just a harm but also a wrong.

In considering this objection, it is important to recognize the conventional nature of normative expectations: Each individual's belief that each individual ought to conform to a regularity $R$ is conditional on $R$'s being generally followed. Approval and disapproval are not directed at $R$

itself: They are directed at individual acts of conformity and nonconformity, given that conformity is the general practice. One may disapprove of breaches of an established convention without approving of the convention itself.

A more fundamental response to the objection is that it fails fully to appreciate what is required for a naturalistic analysis of values. In such an analysis, the definition of a moral sentiment has to be naturalistic; one cannot then object that some of the sentiments allowed by the definition are not "really" moral. Following Hume, I have defined a moral sentiment as a sentiment of approval or disapproval which applies to a general class of actions (see section 1). I submit that my definition of normative expectations identifies a set of cases in which, given normal human psychology, we can expect to find sentiments of approval and disapproval associated with general classes of action – namely, those actions which conform to, and those which do not conform to, the relevant regularity $R$.

By now it will be clear that my analysis of normative expectations is very different from Ben-Ner and Putterman's (this volume) picture of norms as solutions to "problems" and "challenges" faced by communities. Ben-Ner and Putterman seem to see norms primarily as rules that are socially functional, and that are consciously adopted because people recognize the value of those functions. When considering mechanisms for the transmission of norms, Ben-Ner and Putterman focus on deliberate transmission by parents, teachers, politicians, and religious leaders. In contrast, normative expectations as I have analyzed them are the unintended consequences of initially self-interested behavior. Whether such norms are socially functional depends on whether the conventions they support are functional, and if those conventions are the products of social evolution – if they too are unintended consequences of self-interested behavior – we seem to have no general warrant for assuming them to be socially beneficial. (For further argument against the presumption that social evolution favors efficient conventions, see Sugden [1986, 1995] and Ellison [1993].) Of course, these approaches to the study of values are not mutually exclusive: One may recognize the significance of normative expectations without denying the importance of other kinds of values.

In one respect, the picture of normative expectations as unintended consequences suggests that such norms are quite robust. A common conservative theme in public debate is the fear that social order is threatened by the supposed decay of traditional moral codes, such as those taught by the Christian churches; the implication that is often drawn is that the government should do more to promote traditional moral education. If I am right, however, normative expectations do not depend on general moral precepts such as the Golden Rule or Kant's categorical imperative, or on universal moral theories. In some cases, normative expectations may be *consistent with* general moral theories, but the connection is incidental.

For example, suppose I am traveling on a crowded train without a seat. I see someone leave her (unreserved) seat to go to the toilet, leaving her coat on the seat as a marker. The thought of taking her seat is tempting, but I also have the sense that I ought not to take it. With sufficient ingenuity, no doubt, we could construct moral arguments to show that taking the seat is contrary to the prescriptions of, say, rule utilitarianism or Christianity or Lockean libertarianism. But does any of these sophisticated lines of reasoning provide the correct explanation of my sense of unease about taking the seat? I think not. What really matters, I suggest, is my knowledge that most people do not take other people's seats in this sort of situation, that the passenger who has left the seat knows this, that she has left the seat in the expectation that it will not be taken, that she does not want me to take it and would resent my taking it. Further, the other passengers on the train know this. They often act as she has, relying on the same expectations. So they will be inclined to take her side, sympathizing with her resentment of me. I feel unease at the prospect of exposing myself to other people's ill will. In cases like this, the stability of norms depends on some degree of social awareness: People must be capable of recognizing the patterns of behavior that are generally followed and generally expected, they must be able to sense other people's ill will toward them when it exists, and they must have a desire to avoid such ill will. But that is all that is needed.

In another respect, however, normative expectations may be fragile. They are self-reinforcing: The expectation that $R$ will be followed induces $R$-following behavior, and the observation of $R$-following behavior induces the expectation that $R$ will be followed. This causal loop can work to protect a set of expectations by restoring equilibrium after a shock, but only if the equilibrium is stable and the shock not too great. The opposite possibility is that, as a result of random variation or of small changes in underlying parameters, expectations or behavior may move out of the basin of attraction of the original equilibrium (that is, they may change in such a way that there is no tendency to return to that equilibrium). The well-known "broken window effect," in which an unoccupied building can remain intact for a long period, but as soon as one window has been broken is repeatedly vandalized, may be an example. Some police forces regard this effect as significant enough to justify a "zero tolerance" policy of targeting petty crime.

In the rest of this chapter, I shall investigate the stability or instability of conventions, and the ways in which normative expectations can help to stabilize conventions that might otherwise break down. I shall do this within the framework of a simple and familiar model of conflict between two individuals: the Hawk–Dove (or Chicken) game. It is convenient to begin by analyzing some variants of this game on the conventional assumption that normative expectations have no motivating force. This is the subject of section 3. Normative expectations will be considered in section 4.

### 3    Two versions of the Hawk–Dove game

The Hawk–Dove game involves two players, one occupying role 1 and the other role 2. Each player chooses one of two strategies, Dove or Hawk. As is usual in evolutionary game theory, I assume a very large population of individuals, from which pairs of players are repeatedly drawn at random to play the game; one is randomly assigned role 1 and the other role 2. Individuals are identical, and so the utility payoffs of every individual, conditional on the role she plays, can be represented in a single matrix. This is shown as Table 1.

I shall assume a tendency for individuals to gravitate toward strategies that maximize expected utility, given the role that they are playing and given the frequencies with which the alternative strategies are played by their potential opponents. By imposing the restriction that $a_{21} > a_{11}$ and $b_{21} > b_{11}$, I am making Hawk the best reply to Dove. It would be normal to require also that Dove is the best reply to Hawk, that is, that $a_{12} > a_{22}$ and $b_{12} > b_{22}$. My reason for not imposing this latter restriction is that I want to allow the possibility that in some exceptional circumstances, Hawk is a dominant strategy. For reasons which will emerge shortly, the restrictions that $a_{21} - a_{11} + a_{12} - a_{22} > 0$ and $b_{21} - b_{11} + b_{12} - b_{22} > 0$ are convenient in that they allow me to use a simplified notation, but nothing of substance hangs on them. Roughly, these restrictions prevent Hawk from being "too good" a reply to Hawk, while not ruling out the case in which Hawk is a dominant strategy. The additional requirement that $a_{21} > a_{22}$ and $b_{21} > b_{22}$ ensures that if a player chooses Hawk, he prefers that his opponent choose Dove. I leave open the possibility that a Dove might prefer his opponent to be a Hawk (as may be true for the narrow bridge: If you slow down to let the other driver through, you want her to cross as quickly as possible).

The narrow bridge problem is an example of the class of interactions for which the Hawk–Dove game can be used as a model. Interpret role 1 as "first arrival," role 2 as "second arrival," Dove as the strategy of

Table 1. *The Hawk–Dove game*

|  |  | Role 2 | |
|---|---|---|---|
|  |  | Dove | Hawk |
| Role 1 | Dove | $a_{11}, b_{11}$ | $a_{12}, b_{21}$ |
|  | Hawk | $a_{21}, b_{12}$ | $a_{22}, b_{22}$ |

$a_{21} > a_{11}, \quad b_{21} > b_{11}$

$a_{21} - a_{11} + a_{12} - a_{22} > 0, \quad b_{21} - b_{11} + b_{12} - b_{22} > 0$

$a_{21} > a_{22}, \quad b_{21} > b_{22}$

giving way, and Hawk as the strategy of maintaining speed. Hawk is always the best reply to Dove, and apart from a few exceptional cases like that of the impatient car driver and the cyclist, Dove is the best reply to Hawk.

The narrow bridge is itself no more than a model. The fundamental problem that it represents is that of conflict over scarce resources. Consider any situation in which two individuals are aware that there is some resource that they both want, but only one can have, and in which each individual has some power to harm the other. Think of the Hawk strategy as an attempt to take the resource, backed by a readiness to hurt the other and to risk being hurt in the process. And think of the Dove strategy as allowing the other individual to take the resource, at least if he shows any inclination to fight. When a Dove meets a Dove, either the resource is divided between them or who gets it is determined randomly. The asymmetry between role 1 and role 2 might represent the distinction between the individual who is in possession of the resource and the individual who is not. With this kind of interpretation, the Hawk–Dove game has been used to model conflicts over resources between animals of the same species (Maynard Smith and Price 1973; Maynard Smith and Parker 1976). There seems no reason not to apply it to humans.

In human conflicts, a shared expectation that one role will play Hawk and the other Dove can be interpreted as a de facto property right, awarding the resource to the Hawk. Thus the Hawk–Dove game might serve as a model of the evolution of property – the most fundamental institution in economics. We do not have to locate that evolutionary process in a mythical state of nature or in the distant past. The emergence of de facto property rights is a continuing process. Markets may work more smoothly when property rights are defined by formal laws and enforced by the state, but they can come into existence and persist without any such external support: Think of black markets in Eastern

Europe before the collapse of communism, or of trade in gambling, alcohol, and narcotic drugs under regimes of prohibition. These markets depend on there being common recognition of de facto property rights and commonly recognized forms of contract. Thus, it may be fruitful to think of the fundamental institutions of a market economy as a spontaneous order, which the written law codifies rather than creates. The Hawk–Dove game offers a possible starting point for an analysis of that spontaneous order.

To provide a benchmark for what follows, I begin by analyzing a particularly simple version of the Hawk–Dove game. This analysis is adapted from Sugden (1986, chap. 4), which in turn was based on Maynard Smith and Parker (1976).

It is useful to begin by defining indices of the players' *strengths*, $s_1$ and $s_2$:

$$s_1 = \frac{\left(a_{21} - a_{11}\right)}{\left[\left(a_{21} - a_{11}\right) + \left(a_{12} - a_{22}\right)\right]} \tag{1a}$$

$$s_2 = \frac{\left(b_{21} - b_{11}\right)}{\left[\left(b_{21} - b_{11}\right) + \left(b_{12} - b_{22}\right)\right]} \tag{1b}$$

These two indices summarize the significant features of the game's payoffs. The restrictions I have already imposed imply that $s_1$ and $s_2$ are positive and finite. Let $p_i$, $p_j$ be the probabilities with which players in roles $i, j$ play Hawk. (Here and throughout the paper, $\{i, j\} = \{1, 2\}$.) Then it is easy to verify that Hawk is expected utility maximizing for player $i$ if and only if $p_j \leq s_i$. The higher is $s_i$, then, the higher the probability can be that $j$ plays Hawk, before it is in $i$'s interest to play Dove. In the standard case, with $a_{21} > a_{11}$ and $b_{21} > b_{11}$, we have $s_i < 1$ for each role $i$; in the exceptional case in which Hawk is a dominant strategy for role $i$, we have $s_i \geq 1$. For the present, I shall assume the standard case.

The game has three Nash equilibria: (1) $p_1 = 1$, $p_2 = 0$; (2) $p_1 = 0$, $p_2 = 1$; and (3) $p_1 = s_2$, $p_2 = s_1$. In the context of an evolutionary analysis, a Nash equilibrium is a state in which there is no tendency for the frequencies $p_1$, $p_2$ to change. With any plausible model of the dynamic process, (1) and (2) are stable but (3) is not (see, for example, Sugden [1986, chap. 4]). Thus, the system can be expected to gravitate toward one or the other of the first two equilibria. Each of these stationary points may be interpreted as an assignment of de facto property rights – to role 1 in the first equilibrium, to role 2 in the second. Each assignment is conventional in the sense that, in order to explain why individuals respect this particular assignment rather than some other, we have to appeal to their expectation that others will respect it.

Notice that the asymmetry between roles need not be linked to any asymmetry in strength. All that matters is that there is some distinction between roles which the players recognize. In the case of the narrow bridge, for example, role 1 might be "approaching from the north" and role 2 "approaching from the south"; in terms of payoffs, the game might be completely symmetrical as between these roles. Nevertheless, the implication of the analysis is that one of the two possible conventions will become established.

If there is a difference in strength between the roles, the convention which favors the stronger role (that is, equilibrium [1] if $s_1 > s_2$, equilibrium [2] if $s_2 > s_1$) will be called *intuitive*; the one which favors the weaker role will be called *counterintuitive*. In the language of game theory, the intuitive convention is *risk dominant* (Harsanyi and Selten 1988, 82–89). Even if there is such a difference in strengths, either convention, once established, is stable. Self-interest is sufficient to induce conformity to the convention.

To show how a de facto assignment of property rights might not be sustainable by self-interest, I shall now introduce some uncertainty into the model. It is a common feature of game-theoretic modeling that conclusions can be changed radically by the introduction of small amounts of uncertainty. John Nash's (1950, 1953) analysis of bargaining is a classic example. Nash's Demand Game is a simple and appealing model of a bargaining problem. If the payoffs of the game are common knowledge, then every Pareto-efficient combination of strategies is a Nash equilibrium, but if a small amount of uncertainty is introduced, there is a unique equilibrium. Similarly, Hans Carlsson and Eric Van Damme (1993) present a class of $2 \times 2$ games in which the payoffs differ along a continuum. In almost all of these games, considered in isolation, there is more than one equilibrium, but crucially, there are some extreme cases in which there is a dominant strategy solution. It turns out that if the players are even slightly uncertain about where on the continuum their game is located, there is a unique equilibrium solution for the class of games as a whole, and this corresponds with the risk-dominant equilibrium in each game. It is as if the whole class of games is infected by the extreme cases. In the light of examples like these, we have to be very cautious in drawing implications for real-world interactions from games in which there is no uncertainty and more than one equilibrium.

To investigate whether the conventional solutions to the Hawk–Dove game are robust to uncertainty about the payoffs, I relax the assumption that the payoff matrix is the same for all games and is known to the players. Instead, I assume that for each individual, the payoffs from playing a given role can vary from game to game; in any specific game, an individual knows her own payoffs but not those of her opponent.

I model this idea in the following way: As before, each game is between a player in role 1 and a player in role 2, each player knowing his own role. However, I now assume that for each role $i$, $s_i$ is an independent random variable whose value lies in an interval $[0, m_i]$; $m_i$ is strictly positive and finite; the density function for $s_i$, which is the same for all individuals, is continuous and has strictly positive values over $(0, m_i)$. Notice that I do not impose the restriction that $m_i < 1$; thus, I leave open the possibility that Hawk might be a dominant strategy for one or both of the players. In every game, each player knows her own strength, but not the strength of her opponent. Thus a strategy for an $i$ player must specify whether that player will choose Hawk or Dove, conditional on each possible value of $s_i$.

Given the assumption that $s_i$ and $s_j$ are independent, the probability that the $j$ player in any specific game will choose Hawk is independent of the $i$ player's strength. So if, for a given frequency distribution of strategies for role $j$, it is optimal for an $i$ player to play Hawk when his strength is $s_i'$, it must be uniquely optimal for him to play Hawk when his strength is $s_i'' > s_i$. Thus, whatever the pattern of play by $j$ players, it is optimal for $i$ players to follow a strategy with a *threshold* strength: That is, there is some value $v_i$ such that an $i$ player chooses Hawk if $s_i > v_i$ and Dove if $s_i < v_i$. Since players are identical except for random variations in strength, the optimal threshold is the same for all $i$ players. Notice that low values of $v_i$ indicate "toughness": The lower the threshold for role $i$, the greater the range of cases in which $i$ players choose the Hawk strategy.

For each role $i$, we may define a function $g_i$ from $[0, m_j]$ to $[0, m_i]$, such that if all $j$ players use the threshold $v_j$, the optimal threshold for $i$ players is $g_i(v_j)$. Clearly

$$pr[j \text{ plays Hawk}] = pr[s_j > v_j] \qquad (2)$$

Since $g_i(v_j)$ is the optimal threshold for $i$ players, and since the strength distributions have been assumed to be continuous, $i$ players must be indifferent between Hawk and Dove when $s_i = g_i(v_j)$; thus

$$pr[j \text{ plays Hawk}] = g_i(v_j) \qquad (3)$$

Hence

$$pr[s_j > v_j] = g_i(v_j) \qquad (4)$$

There are two equations (4), one with $i = 1$, $j = 2$, the other with $i = 2$, $j = 1$. Any solution to these two equations is a Nash equilibrium. Since

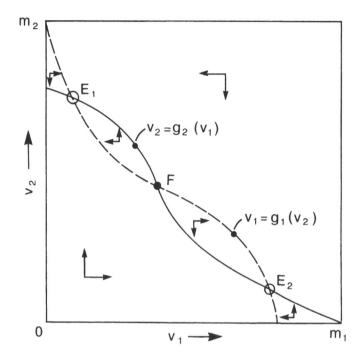

Figure 1

$pr[s_j > 0] = 1$ and $pr[s_j > 1] \geq 0$, we have $g_i(0) = 1$ and $g_i(1) \geq 0$. Notice that the continuity of the distribution of $s_j$ implies the continuity of $g_i(.)$. If the $g_i(.)$ functions are continuous, there must be at least one equilibrium. Figure 1 shows a possible configuration; $E_1$, $E_2$, and $F$ are equilibria.

A full dynamic analysis (for example, using replicator dynamics) would be complicated, because the set of possible strategies is a continuum. But an intuitive analysis of stability can be given by imagining that at any time, all players in a given role use the same threshold (not necessarily the optimal one), and that this threshold tends to change in the direction which leads to local increases in individuals' expected utility. Notice that the graph of $g_2(v_1)$ is the locus of $(v_1, v_2)$ combinations at which $v_2$ is optimal; at points above this graph, $v_2$ is too high to be optimal, while at points below the graph it is too low to be optimal. Similarly, the graph of $g_1(v_2)$ is the locus of $(v_1, v_2)$ combinations at which $v_1$ is optimal; at points to the right of this graph, $v_1$ is too high to be optimal, while at points to the left it is too low. Figure 1 shows one possible configuration of $g_1(.)$ and $g_2(.)$, with the associated dynamics. In

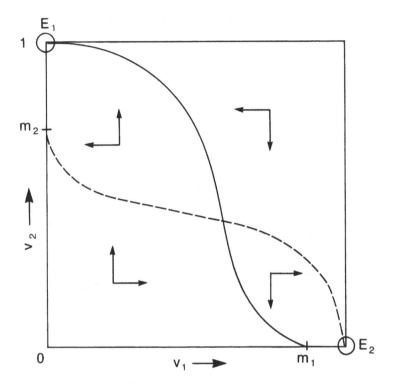

Figure 2

this and subsequent diagrams, the locus of points at which $v_2$ is optimal is represented by a solid curve, while the locus of points at which $v_1$ is optimal is represented by a broken curve. Stable equilibria are denoted by circles. Of the three equilibria in Figure 1, $E_1$ and $E_2$ are stable while $F$ is unstable.

Figure 2 shows a case which, despite the existence of uncertainty, is quite similar to the original Hawk–Dove game. This case has two significant features. First, $m_1, m_2 \leqslant 1$: The probability that Hawk is a dominant strategy for either role is zero. Second, the frequency distributions of $s_1$, $s_2$ are unimodal, so that the graphs of $g_1(.)$ and $g_2(.)$ have the S-shaped forms shown in the figure. Under these conditions, there are two stable equilibria $(v_1^*, v_2^*)$: These are $(0, 1)$ and $(1, 0)$, marked as $E_1$ and $E_2$ in the diagram. They may be interpreted as conventions which assign de facto property rights to one of the roles – to role 1 in the case of $(0, 1)$, to role 2 in the case of $(1, 0)$. As in the original Hawk–Dove game, conventions may be intuitive or counterintuitive. If the distribution of $s_i$ stochastically

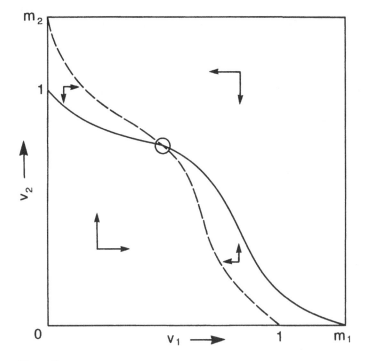

Figure 3

dominates that of $s_j$, we can say that role $i$ is *stronger* than role $j$. Figure 2 has been drawn so that role 1 is the stronger role. In this case, $(0, 1)$ is the intuitive convention and $(1, 0)$ is the counterintuitive one.

Figure 3 shows a contrasting case. Here, $m_1$, $m_2 > 0$, with the implication that neither $(0, 1)$ nor $(1, 0)$ can be an equilibrium. The distributions of $s_1$ and $s_2$ are such that there is only one stable equilibrium $E$; in equilibrium, there is little difference between the thresholds used by the two roles. In other words, the asymmetry between role 1 and role 2, although recognized by the players, is not used to resolve conflict. Strong players of both roles play Hawk while weaker ones play Dove; when two strong players meet, there is a Hawk–Hawk fight. While the conventions of Figure 2 might be interpreted as examples of spontaneous order, the equilibrium of Figure 3 is more like a Hobbesian state of nature.

Figure 1 can now be seen to represent a case intermediate between Figures 2 and 3. In each of the stable equilibria $E_1$ and $E_2$, one role uses a much lower threshold than the other and consequently is much more likely to play Hawk. To this extent, the asymmetry between roles is used to resolve conflict. However, not all conflicts are resolved peacefully. For example, equilibrium $E_1$ favors role 1: In most games, the 1 player chooses Hawk and the 2 player chooses Dove. But in this equilibrium, if a 2 player is particularly strong, he chooses Hawk, and if a 1 player is particularly weak, she chooses Dove.

A comparison of Figures 1, 2, and 3 is enough to show that how far de facto property rights evolve depends critically on the configuration of $g_1(.)$ and $g_2(.)$. It seems that an analysis which ignores uncertainty may produce overoptimistic conclusions about the likelihood and robustness of spontaneous order. This suggests that there might be cases in which putative conventions are stable only if they are supported by normative expectations.

## 4      Modeling normative expectations

Consider either version of the Hawk–Dove game. Suppose a stable equilibrium is reached in which all or most interactions are resolved by convention – say the convention "role 1 plays Hawk; role 2 plays Dove." If we are considering the original version of the game, with no uncertainty, all players will be following the convention. If we are considering the version in which payoffs vary and players do not know their opponents' strengths, then the supposition is that the equilibrium is like $E_1$ in Figure 1 or in Figure 2, that is, an equilibrium with $v_1$ close to 0 and $v_2$ close to 1. On either interpretation, such a convention can be expected to generate normative expectations.

To see why, let $R$ stand for the regularity "role 1 plays Hawk; role 2 plays Dove," and let $R'$ stand for "role 2 plays Dove." Then we have (1) if an individual conforms to $R$, it is in his interest that others conform to $R'$; (2) in most cases, if an individual expects others to conform to $R$, it is in his interest to conform to $R$; and (3) most people in the society expect most other people to conform to $R$. Thus there will be a normative expectation that players in role 2 choose Dove (see section 2).

Having shown that normative expectations can be generated in the Hawk–Dove game, I now consider how the analysis of the game is affected if normative expectations have motivating force.

The idea that normative expectations have motivating force cannot be expressed easily in game-theoretic terms. It is a commonplace of game theory that everything that matters to a player is included in the utility payoffs; thus, once the payoffs have been specified, there can be no other motivating factors to be considered: Players simply maximize expected utility. But notice one implication of this position: given the payoffs of the game, and leaving aside cases of indifference, each player's choice of strategy is fully determined by the probabilities attached to the strategy choices of the other players. For example, in the Hawk–Dove game, any given set of payoffs for a player $i$ imply an index of "strength" $s_i$ such that whether $i$ chooses Hawk or Dove depends on whether $p_j$, the probability that the other player chooses Hawk, is less than or greater than $s_i$ (see section 3). Thus, a player's payoffs tell us how she responds to the different beliefs which she might hold about her opponent's strategy choices, and, at least as far as behavior is concerned, they can tell us nothing more than this. But these are not the only beliefs which the player holds about the game and which are endogenous in the model. What if a player's strategy choice is influenced by some of those other beliefs? The simple answer is that such influences cannot be represented through the payoffs. If it is an axiom of game theory that all motivating factors are incorporated in the payoffs, then the theory has to deny that any of those other beliefs can influence behavior.

The problem is that the motivating force of normative expectations works through some of the beliefs that game theory has deemed to be irrelevant to behavior. On my account, one player can be motivated to conform to some regularity in behavior because (among other things) she believes that the other player believes that she will conform to it. In other words, behavior is influenced by beliefs about *beliefs about* strategy choices.

The task of constructing a new form of game theory, in which beliefs about beliefs can influence behavior, is beyond the scope of this chapter. All I can offer here is a speculative account of how, in such a theory, normative expectations might affect behavior in the Hawk–Dove game. I shall focus on the second version of that game, in which players do not know their opponents' payoffs.

Clearly, "payoffs" can no longer be interpreted in the standard sense, as von Neumann–Morgenstern utility indices which incorporate all motivating factors. Instead I shall interpret them as measures of self-interest; the desire to act in accordance with other people's expectations will be treated as an *additional* motivating factor, not included in the payoffs. To simplify the analysis, I shall continue to use "strength," as defined in section 3, as an index of a player's payoffs, and I shall assume that players condition their strategy choices on their own strength. Thus, other considerations being equal, stronger players are more likely to choose Hawk than are weaker players. I shall continue to assume that all players are identical, except for random variations in strength between games. Thus, in equilibrium, there will be a threshold value $v_i$ for each role $i$, such that every player in that role chooses Hawk if her strength is greater than $v_i$ and Dove if it is less.

Now consider any player in a given role $i$. Let $v_i$ be a threshold which is being used by every other $i$ player, and let $v_j$ be a threshold which all $j$ players are using. At this stage, there is no assumption that either $v_i$ or $v_j$ is optimal. Given any pair of values $v_i$, $v_j$, we can ask what threshold $v_{<i}^{\#}>$ our player would wish to use. As $v_j$ increases, with $v_i$ constant, the probability that an opponent plays Hawk falls, and so, for the normal self-interested reasons considered in section 3, the optimal threshold for any $i$ player stays constant or falls. As $v_i$ increases, with $v_j$ constant, the probability that *other* $i$ players choose Dove increases. If $j$ players' expectations reflect actual frequencies, their beliefs that their $i$-playing opponents will choose Dove must rise. If the original $i$ player recognizes this, then the higher the value of $v_i$, the stronger is her belief that her opponent expects her to play Dove. Thus, given the hypothesis about the motivating force of normative expectations, an increase in $v_i$ will increase (or at least, not decrease) our player's optimal threshold, making her less likely to choose Hawk. The implication of all this is that we can define two functions $f_1$ and $f_2$, such that

$$v_i^{\#} = f_i(v_i, v_j) \tag{5}$$

Each function is nondecreasing in its first argument and nonincreasing in its second.

The model is in equilibrium when each player's threshold is optimal, given the thresholds used by everyone else. This is the analogue in the present framework of Nash equilibrium in conventional game theory. Formally, an equilibrium is a pair of thresholds $(v_1^*, v_2^*)$ such that $v_1 = f_1(v_1^*, v_2^*)$ and $v_2 = f_2(v_2^*, v_1^*)$.

To investigate the dynamics of this model, we may consider two loci in $(v_1, v_2)$ space, analogous with the $g_i(v_j)$ functions used in section 3. For concreteness, consider a particular one of these loci, namely, the set of $(v_1, v_2)$ combinations such that, if all 1 players use the threshold $v_1$, and all 2 players except one use the threshold $v_2$, the optimal threshold for the remaining 2 player is $v_2$. This, then, is the set of $(v_1, v_2)$ combinations at which 2 players do not wish to change their thresholds; I shall denote this locus by $L_2$. What is the shape of this locus? Recall that for any given value of $v_2$ (interpreted as the threshold used by all 2 players except the one whose choices we are considering), increases in $v_1$ imply decreases in $v_2^{\#}$, the optimal threshold for our 2 player. In other words: The less Hawkish 1 players are, the more Hawkish 2 players wish to be. It follows from this that, for any given value of $v_2$, there can be no more than one $v_1$ value on the locus $L_2$. In contrast, for any given value of $v_1$, increases in $v_2$ imply *increases* in $v_2^{\#}$: The more Dovish other 2 players are, the more Dovish each 2 player wishes to be. Thus, for a given $v_1$, there can be more

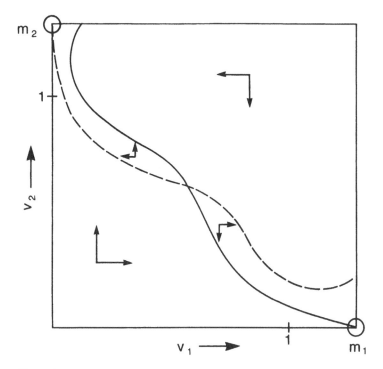

Figure 4

than one $v_2$ on the locus. For example, if normative expectations in favor of Dove playing are particularly powerful when the probability of Dove playing is close to unity, the locus may have a backward-bending region at high values of $v_2$. The solid curve in Figure 4 is an example of such a locus. To the right of any locus $L_2$, $(v_1, v_2)$ combinations are such that, given the behavior of the other players, each 2 player wishes to reduce his threshold. The opposite applies at points to the left of this locus.

The other locus $L_1$, which denotes the set of $(v_1, v_2)$ combinations at which no 1 player wishes to change her strategy, can be constructed in a similar way. The broken curve in Figure 4 is an example of such a locus. Above any locus $L_1$, each 1 player wishes to reduce her threshold; below it, the opposite is true. The intersections of $L_1$ and $L_2$ are equilibria. Figure 4 shows one possible configuration, with the associated dynamics.

The main difference from the analysis in section 3 is that it is now possible (as in Figure 4) to have equilibria in which one or other of the thresholds $v_1$, $v_2$ is greater than unity. Recall that to use a threshold greater than unity is to be willing to play Dove in at least some cases in

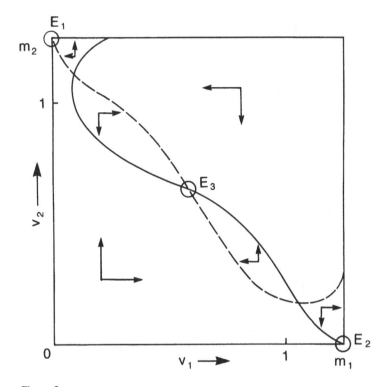

Figure 5

which, measured in terms of self-interest, Hawk is the dominant strategy. Clearly, no purely self-interested player would behave in this way, but a player who was partly motivated by normative expectations might do so, if the cost in terms of self-interest were not too great and if his opponents had a sufficiently strong expectation of such behavior.

Figure 5 shows another possible configuration. Here there are three stable equilibria, $E_1$, $E_2$, and $E_3$. Compare $E_1$ and $E_3$ (a similar comparison can be made between $E_2$ and $E_3$). $E_1$ is a regime of fully respected de facto property rights, while $E_3$ is a Hobbesian regime in which property rights are not recognized. Notice that $E_1$ is close to the edge of the basin of attraction of $E_3$. Thus, were $E_1$ to have become established, a relatively small perturbation might be enough to dislodge this equilibrium, setting off a process of changes in expectations leading to $E_3$. Since $E_3$ is stable with respect to much larger perturbations, this switch might prove irreversible. This "tipping" from one equilibrium to another seems similar to the broken window effect. We might think of $E_1$ as a rather fragile convention whose stability depends on normative expectations.

## 5    Conclusions

The main purpose of this chapter has been to develop the outlines of a theory of normative expectations, in which people are to some degree motivated by a desire to meet other people's expectations about them. In this theory, conventions and norms evolve together, with the result that people come to believe that they ought to act according to those conventions that have become established. Although people's underlying propensity to form normative expectations is taken as given, the content of the norms to be found in a society is not: Thus, the evolution of certain kinds of norms is in principle capable of being explained in much the same way that evolutionary game theory explains the emergence of conventions.

It would be foolish to suggest that the formal models I have presented in sections 3 and 4 are *directly* capable of explaining the processes by which norms develop and are sustained in real societies. In developing these models, my aim has been more exploratory. It has been to test whether the concept of normative expectations, which up to now has usually been discussed in rather philosophical ways, can be incorporated into the kinds of formal theory that economists can use. I hope I have shown that it can be – provided that we are willing to jettison some of the dogma of game theory.

REFERENCES

Carlsson, Hans, and Eric Van Damme (1993). "Global Games and Equilibrium Selection," *Econometrica* 61: 989–1018.

Ellison, Glenn (1993). "Learning, Local Interaction, and Coordination," *Econometrica* 61: 1047–71.

Harsanyi, John C., and Reinhard Selten (1988). *A General Theory of Equilibrium Selection in Games*. Cambridge, Mass.: MIT Press.

Hume, David (1978). *A Treatise of Human Nature*. Oxford: Clarendon Press (first published 1740).

Kreps, David M., Paul Milgrom, John Roberts, and Robert Wilson (1982). "Rational Cooperation in the Finitely Repeated Prisoner's Dilemma," *Journal of Economic Theory* 27: 245–52.

Lewis, David (1969). *Convention: A Philosophical Study*. Cambridge, Mass.: Harvard University Press.

Maynard Smith, John, and G. A. Parker (1976). "The Logic of Asymmetric Contests," *Animal Behavior* 24: 159–75.

Maynard Smith, John, and G. R. Price (1973). "The Logic of Animal Conflicts," *Nature* 246: 15–18.

Nash, John F. (1950). "The Bargaining Problem," *Econometrica* 18: 155–62.

———(1953). "Two-Person Cooperative Games," *Econometrica* 21: 128–40.

Sugden, Robert (1986). *The Economics of Rights, Co-operation and Welfare.* Oxford: Blackwell.

—— (1989). "Spontaneous Order," *Journal of Economic Perspectives* 3: 85–97.

—— (1995). "The Coexistence of Conventions," *Journal of Economic Behavior and Organization* 28: 241–56.

CHAPTER 3

# A utilitarian theory of political legitimacy

*Ken Binmore*

> He who would understand *baboon* would do more towards metaphysics than John Locke.
>
> Charles Darwin

## 1    Introduction

Although the burgeoning discipline of welfare economics is based on essentially utilitarian principles, the foundations of utilitarianism have received little attention in recent years. This chapter seeks to reopen the debate by drawing a distinction between Harsanyi's (1977) two defenses of utilitarianism, which are referred to, respectively, as his teleological and nonteleological theories.[1] It is argued that the modern consensus on political legitimacy requires a theory of the second type.

The organizational role of the state is seen as being to enforce laws that the people make for themselves under ideally fair circumstances. Harsanyi's nonteleological argument employs Rawls's devices of the original position to determine the nature of the ideally fair compromise and finds the result to be utilitarian. However, the Kantian principles to which both Harsanyi and Rawls appeal leave the vital question of how utilities are to be compared unresolved. This difficulty is seen as being symptomatic of a much deeper malaise in adopting a Kantian or metaphysical approach to the original position. This chapter therefore attempts to outline a new defense of the original position based on Humean or naturalistic considerations.

The original position is taken to be a stylized version of a fairness

[1] I am grateful to the Economic and Social Research Council and to the Leverhulme Foundation for funding this reseach through the Centre for Economic Learning and Social Evolution at University College London.

101

norm that evolved along with the human race. The empathetic preferences that are necessary as inputs when the device is employed are seen as being shaped by the forces of social evolution. These forces will tend to equip everyone with the same empathetic preferences, which then provide a standard for making interpersonal comparisons of utility. A government that enforces the rules that people would make for themselves in such an original position will then employ a weighted utilitarian welfare function in which the weights are derived from this common standard.

This very brief outline typifies the telegraphic nature of the chapter, which has been telescoped from chapter 2 of a draft book, "Just Playing." When complete, this will be the second volume of *Game Theory and the Social Contract*, the first volume of which has been published by M.I.T. Press with the subtitle *Playing Fair*.

## 2     Naturalism

I find that the chief obstacle in gaining understanding for the reinterpretation of Harsanyi's ideas offered in this paper is the naturalism on which it is based. Moral philosophers typically hold that the purpose of their discipline is to uncover universal principles that we all ought to follow when interacting with our fellows. A naturalist denies that such principles exist. He may well wish that society would adopt his own pet schemes for reform, but his allegiance to naturalism prevents his claiming any special authority for his views, since he knows that he would be advocating different reforms if he had been brought up in a different culture. As Xenophanes put it, "The gods of the Ethiopians are black and flat-nosed, and the gods of the Thracians are red-haired and blue-eyed."

A naturalist sees himself as a scientist, exploring the biological and social facts on which our moral intuitions are based. Such facts are contingent. They would have been otherwise if biological and social history had taken a different course. Moral behavior in chimpanzees and baboons differs from moral behavior in humans because their biological history differs from ours. Moral behavior in other human societies differs from moral behavior in our society because their social history differs from ours.

Such frank relativism is too much for many to swallow. As always, David Hume faced up squarely to the issue, but Adam Smith was the first of many to seek to have it both ways. However, those who wish to enter the pulpit to preach that one society is better than another are not entitled to appeal to naturalistic theories of ethics. Even the wishy-washy liberal doctrine that all societies are equally meritorious receives no support from naturalism. There is no culture-free Archimedean standpoint from which to apply a moral lever to the world. If we could liberate ourselves from all cultural prejudices, we would find that morality no longer had any meaning for us.

When advocating reform, the temptation for a naturalist to claim authority for his goals when disputing with a traditionalist is hard to resist. But naturalism offers authority only when means are discussed. A naturalist may criticize the feasibility of the reforms proposed by a traditionalist or point out that they will not achieve the objectives for which they are intended. He may suggest that the social tools with which evolution has equipped a society may be used to achieve other ends than those for which they are currently employed. But when it comes to the determination of ends, a traditionalist has no reason to regard the expertise of a naturalist as any more relevant than his own experience of life. Nor has a naturalist any reason to respect a traditionalist's claims for any noncontingent Moral Facts he may imagine he can demonstrate by metaphysical means. Still less need a naturalist be defensive should he be accused of being unable to justify any Moral Facts of his own. In brief, values do not predate the social contract a society operates – our choice of social contract creates our values.

Seeking to read this chapter as an unconditional justification of utilitarianism can therefore only lead to confusion. To a naturalist, all moral imperatives are hypothetical. The chapter claims only that those who feel that the modern consensus on political legitimacy requires that the fairness norm modeled by the device of the original position should be used on a large scale are arguing for utilitarianism.

## 3    Utilitarian theories

Francis Hutcheson (1755) argued that we should seek the greatest happiness for the greatest number (Scott 1966). In an unguarded moment, Bentham[2] repeated this formula, and hence provided the enemies of utilitarianism with a stick with which its advocates have been beaten ever since. However, unambiguous definitions are easily supplied in the case of a society of fixed size.

I define a utilitarian narrowly to be a consequentialist who has an additively separable common good function. He therefore adds together his estimate of the well-being of each citizen to obtain his measure of the

---

[2] I am grateful to my colleague Fred Rosen for pointing out that Bentham probably derived the formula neither from Hutcheson nor from Leibniz, but from Beccaria's *Crimes and Punishments* (Shackleton 1972).

welfare of society as a whole. Even within such a narrow definition, it is necessary to distinguish among a number of different types of utilitarian.

### 3.1    *Ipsedixists*

Sen (1976) denies that Harsanyi (1977) is properly to be counted as a utilitarian at all, because his theories are very firmly based on what people want rather than on what they would want if only they knew what was good for them. But how do we know what people ought to want? The literature is full of interminable lists of criteria that must somehow be distilled into the one and only true summum bonum, but these lists reflect only too obviously the cultural and class prejudices of their compilers. History provides many examples. The Spanish Inquisition tortured and burned heretics "for their own good." Until comparatively recently, helpless invalids were bled "for their own good." Victorian do-gooders manufactured purpose-built antimasturbation harnesses into which pubescent children were strapped at night "for their own good."

Will modern do-gooders be judged any less harshly by future generations? My guess is that a particularly bad press awaits those who believe that life is always an unmitigated good, and hence must be inflicted even on those whose suffering is so great that they beg for an easy death. Those who sabotage birth control initiatives for similar reasons have even less prospect of being remembered kindly. In brief, modern do-gooders may be less barbaric than their predecessors, but the source of their inspiration is no more reliable. Mill (1962) doubtless overstates the case when he says that all errors that an individual is likely to commit "are far outweighed by the evil of allowing others to constrain him to what they deem his good," but it cannot be denied that history has little positive to say about paternalists who ignore the wishes of those within their power. Bentham called them ipsedixists – those who offer their own moral prejudices in the guise of moral imperatives.

### 3.2    *Ideal observers*

An ipsedixist sees no reason why he should not seek to impose on others whatever conception of the Good is built into his own personal preferences. For example, Rousseau (1913a) insists that the "general will" is not to be confused with the "will of all." As Rousseau (1913b) explains, the former is known only to those of "sublime virtue" and so its objectives must be achieved by "bringing all the particular wills into conformity with it."

However, utilitarians belonging to the more mainstream line take for granted that the standard for a common good should be *impersonal.* Instead of offering some dressed-up version of their own prejudices as the standard for a society to follow, they therefore propose that the preferences of some invented ideal observer should determine the goals toward which all members of a society ought to strive in common.

If an ideal observer is entirely free of personal prejudices, then his preferences must somehow be obtained by aggregating the preferences of all the citizens in the society being studied. He then serves as an embodiment of Rousseau's "will of all." Utilitarians argue that the utility of the ideal observer for a given state should be obtained by simply adding the utilities of each citizen in the state.

Such a view leaves three questions open:

- What constitutes utility?
- Why should individual utilities be added?
- Why should I maximize the sum of utilities rather than my own?

Early utilitarians like Bentham and John Stuart Mill had little to offer in answer to any of these questions. With characteristic frankness, Bentham (1962) says, "That which is used to prove everything, cannot itself be proved." As for the additivity of happiness, this is quaintly described as a "fictitious postulatum."[3]

Mill (1962) sometimes endorses this position but also offers a half-hearted attempt at providing a proof of utilitarianism. The proof consists of a chapter devoted to the claim that what people desire is happiness. Having established this proposition to his own satisfaction, he then rests on his laurels – apparently not feeling the need to tackle the second or third question.[4] Modern moral philosophers writing in the utilitarian tradition seem largely to have lost interest in foundational questions altogether.

Fortunately, Harsanyi (1977) is an exception to this rule, along with such followers as Broome (1991) and Hammond (1988, 1992). Although Harsanyi does not himself make this distinction, I believe that he is best seen as wearing two hats when writing on utilitarian subjects: a teleological hat and a nonteleological hat.

In his teleological hat, he offers some foundations for the ideal observer approach to utilitarianism. He then answers the first of the three

---

[3] "This addibility of happiness, however when considered rigorously it may appear fictitious, is a postulatum without the allowance of which all political reasonings are at a stand" Bentham (1962).

[4] All we are offered on the second question is the observation "Each person's happiness is a good to that person, and the general happiness is therefore a good to the aggregate of all persons."

questions posed earlier by interpreting utility in the sense of Von Neumann and Morgenstern. The players' utilities then simply serve to describe their preferences. The second question is answered by appealing to the intuitions we supposedly have about the nature of the Good, which is conceived of as some preexisting platonic form. Like Euclid, with his idealized points and lines, Harsanyi encapsulates his intuitions on this subject in a set of axioms. The axioms include the requirement that the ideal observer, whose individual good is to be identified with the common good, should be as rational as each individual citizen. If his expected utility for any lottery depends only on the expected utilities assigned to the lottery by the citizens in the society he serves, the Von Neumann and Morgenstern rationality then guarantees that his utility function can be expressed as a weighted sum of the utilities of all the citizens in society (Binmore 1994).

However, Harsanyi has nothing substantive to say when asked the third question. The existence of a common good whose advancement somehow takes priority over our own individual concerns is simply taken for granted. Once we have deduced the properties of this common good from his axioms, Harsanyi sees his task as being over. Nor do other teleological champions of the Good have anything on offer that might conceivably plug this large gap in their armor. They simply assert that we have a moral duty to carry out whatever actions are moral according to whatever theory is being defended.

Personally, I think it a major error for utilitarians to fudge the issue of why citizens should pursue the aims of some ideal observer rather than furthering their own individual interests. The question that needs to be decided is whether utilitarianism is a moral system to be employed by *individuals* in regulating their interactions with others, or whether it is a set of tenets to be followed by a *government* that has the power to enforce its decrees. It is understandable that utilitarians are reluctant to argue that their doctrine should be forced down the throats of people who find it hard to swallow. They prefer to imagine a world in which their thoughts are embraced with open arms by all the citizens of a utilitarian state. As with Marxists, there is sometimes talk of the state withering away when the word has finally reached every heart. On the other hand, most utilitarians see the practical necessity of compulsion. As Mill (1962) puts it, "For such actions as are prejudicial to the interests of others, the individual is accountable, and may be subjected to social or legal punishment."

My own view is that utilitarians would be wise to settle for the public policy option, which Hardin (1988) refers to as "institutional utilitarianism." If those in power are inclined to personify the role of the government of which they form a part, then they may be open to the suggestion that its actions should be rational in the same sense that an individual is rational. In a society with egalitarian traditions, Bentham's (1987) "everyone to count for one, nobody to count for more than one" will also be attractive. If the powerful are persuaded by such propaganda, then Harsanyi's (1977) teleological argument will require that the government act as though it had the preferences of a utilitarian ideal observer.

Old-fashioned whigs like me will remain unpersuaded, but not because we are repelled by the idea that citizens need to be coerced into compliance. As long as someone is guarding the guardians, we see coercion as a practical necessity in a large modern state. Who would pay their taxes on time and in full unless compelled to do so? Even Hayek (1960) creates no difficulties on this score. Provided laws are framed impersonally, he is willing to say, "When we obey the laws . . . we are not subject to another man's will and are therefore free."

## 3.3    *Philosopher–king*

Having considered two forms of *teleological* utilitarianism, we now consider the framework within which this paper reinterprets Harsanyi's (1977) *nonteleological* approach. In contrast to the axiomatic theory reviewed previously, Harsanyi's nonteleological theory does not take the existence of an a priori common Good for granted. Instead, the *process* used by the citizens of a polity to agree on a common policy is given priority. Harsanyi joins Rawls (1972) in employing the device of the original position to model the case when the process used for this purpose is socially just.

In the both the teleological forms of utilitarianism studied, an agency outside the system enforces an exogenously determined conception of the Good on those inside the system. The second differs from the first in insisting that the Good be determined in an impersonal manner. In a nonteleological version of utilitarianism, the agency's notion of the good is endogenously determined. I model such an agency as an impartial philosopher–king, who acts only on the basis of a mandate he receives from the citizens he rules.

In seeking to model such an impartial philosopher–king, let us suppose him to be all-powerful but entirely benign. Let us also assume that he has no largesse of his own to distribute, all the productive potential of the state being vested in the hands of his subjects. His role then becomes entirely organizational. First he receives a mandate from the people to pursue certain ends, and then he insists that each person take whatever action is necessary to achieve these ends. In real life, people are only too ready to vote for an end but against the means for attaining it. However, in a rational society, people will accept that working together toward an ambitious goal may require some surrender of their personal freedom. Without a philosopher–king to police their efforts at self-discipline, the citizens would have no choice but to rely on their own feeble powers of commitment to prevent any free-riding. The ends that they could jointly achieve would then be severely restricted. But with a philosopher–king to enforce the laws that they make for themselves, the citizens of a society will have a much larger feasible set open for them to exploit.

*Political legitimacy:* The preceding account of the function of a philosopher–king bears a close resemblance to the theory used by modern political parties with liberal pretensions to justify the actions they take when in power.

Edmund Burke, the Whig credited with being the founder of modern conservatism, did not see matters this way. In a famous speech to the voters of Bristol, he expounded his version of the *ipsedixist* doctrine that someone voted into power is justified in pursuing his own personal view of what is best for his constituents even if it conflicts with theirs. The Marxist doctrine of the dictatorship of the proletariat is an extreme *ideal observer* theory. The dictator is the ideal observer and the requirement of impersonality ensures that any aggregation of preferences will make him look like a proletarian in societies in which the proletariat is in a large majority. In modern times, neither of these extremes is at all popular. It is perhaps not even controversial to suggest that we are all social democrats now, paying lip service to a theory of power which is essentially that of the *philosopher–king*.

I therefore think it of some importance that this chapter shows that applying Harsanyi's (1977) nonteleological ideas to the theory of the philosopher–king leads no less inexorably to utilitarianism than applying his teleological ideas to the ideal observer theory.

## 4     Empathetic preferences

The previous section distinguished three questions for a utilitarian to answer: What constitutes utility? Why should individual utilities be added? Why should I maximize the sum of utilities rather than my own?

When passing from the ideal-observer theory to that of the philosopher–king, attention centered on the third of these questions. It was unnecessary to renew consideration of the first question, because utility is to be interpreted in the sense of Von Neumann and Morgenstern in both types of theory. However, the second question was mentioned only in passing when discussing the ideal-observer theory and not at all when discussing the philosopher–king theory. But it is important to recognize that Harsanyi's answer to the second question in an ideal-observer context will not suffice in a philosopher–king context.

To make this point, it is necessary to review Harsanyi's use of the idea of an empathetic preference. Empathetic preferences are identical to the extended sympathy preferences developed by Suppes (1966), Arrow (1978), Sen (1970), and Harsanyi (1977). Adam is expressing a personal preference when he says that he would rather have a fig leaf to wear than an apple to eat. On the other hand, if someone says that he would rather be Adam wearing a fig leaf than Eve eating an apple, then he is expressing an empathetic preference.

Modeling an individual's empathetic preferences using a Von Neumann and Morgenstern utility function $v_i$ is easy, provided one bears in mind that his empathetic utility function is quite distinct from his personal utility function $u_i$. Let $C$ be the set of possible consequences or prizes. Let $\{A, E\}$ be the set consisting of Adam $(A)$ and Eve $(E)$. A personal utility function $u_i$ assigns a real number $u_i(C)$ to each $C$ in the set $C$. By contrast, an empathetic utility function $v_i$ assigns a real number $v_i(C, j)$ to each pair $(C, j)$ in the set $C \times \{A, E\}$. The number $u_i(C)$ is the utility the individual will get if $C$ occurs. The number $u_i(\mathcal{D}, E)$ is the utility he would derive *if he were Eve* and $\mathcal{D}$ occurs. To write $u_i\ (C) > u_i(\mathcal{D})$ means that the individual prefers $C$ to $\mathcal{D}$. To write $v_i(C, A) > v_i(\mathcal{D}, E)$ means that he would rather be Adam when $C$ occurs than Eve when $\mathcal{D}$ occurs.

*Empathetic preferences in the original position:* If I am Adam seeking to coordinate with Eve using the device of the original position, I must make decisions as though I do not know whether I am Adam or Eve. I agree with Harsanyi (1977) in believing that such a veil of ignorance creates exactly the type of decision problem for which Von Neumann and Morgenstern utility functions were designed. However, for reasons that will be discussed in section 9, Rawls (1972) feels quite differently about the matter.

The zero and the unit on Von Neumann and Morgenstern utility scales can be chosen at will, but then our freedom for maneuver is exhausted. To keep matters simple while juggling with utility scales, assume that everybody at least agrees that there is a worst outcome $\mathcal{L}$ and a best outcome $\mathcal{W}$ in the set $C$ of feasible social contracts. Perhaps $\mathcal{L}$ is the event that everybody goes to hell and $W$ is the event that everybody goes to heaven. We may then take $u_A(\mathcal{L}) = u_E(\mathcal{L}) = 0$ and $u_A(\mathcal{W}) = u_E(\mathcal{W}) = 1$.

Such an arbitrary choice of utility scales is surprisingly often proposed as a means of making interpersonal comparsions of utility. But it is not the method employed by Harsanyi (1977). He argues that if an individual is totally successful in empathizing with Adam, then the preferences he will express when imagining himself in Adam's shoes will be identical to Adam's personal preferences. However, the Von Neumann and Morgenstern theory of expected utility tells us that two Von Neumann and Morgenstern utility scales which represent the same preferences can only differ in the location of their zeros and units. It follows that

$$v_i(C,A) = \tilde{u}_A(C) = \alpha u_A(C) + \gamma \tag{1}$$

where $\alpha > 0$ and $\gamma$ are constant. Similarly, for suitable constants $\beta > 0$ and $\delta$,

$$v_i(C,E) = \tilde{u}_E(C) = \beta u_E(C) + \delta \tag{2}$$

Although the zeros and units on Adam and Eve's personal scales have been fixed, the zero and unit on the observer's empathetic utility scale remain undetermined. Somewhat arbitrarily, I shall therefore fix this scale so that $v_i(\mathcal{L}, A) = 0$ and $v_i(\mathcal{W}, E) = 1$. We are then not free to meddle anymore with the observer's empathetic utility scale. It follows that the two constants $U_i > 0$ and $V_i > 0$ defined by

$$U_i = v_i(\mathcal{W}, A) \text{ and } 1 - V_i = v_i(\mathcal{L}, E) \tag{3}$$

tell us something substantive about his empathetic preferences. Indeed, these two parameters characterize the observer's empathetic preferences. To see this, substitute the four value $v_i(\mathcal{L}, A) = 0$, $v_i(\mathcal{W}, E) = 1$, $v_i(\mathcal{W}, A) = U_i$, and $v_i(\mathcal{L}, E) = 1 - V_i$ into equations (1) and (2). The result will be four equations in the four unknowns $\alpha$, $\beta$, $\gamma$, and $\delta$. Solve these equations and substitute the resulting values for $\alpha$, $\beta$, $\gamma$, and $\delta$ back into (1) and (2). We then find that my empathetic utility function $v_i$ can be expressed entirely in terms of the two parameters $U_i$ and $V_i$:

$$v_i(C, A) = U_i u_A(C)$$
$$v_i(C, E) = 1 - V_i\{1 - u_E(C)\} \tag{4}$$

These equations imply that $U_i$ of Eve's utils are equivalent to $V_i$ of Adam's utils. This standard for comparing utils is *intrapersonal* rather than *interpersonal*. It is the observer's own idiosyncratic standard and need not be shared by anyone else. But it does not help very much that we should each have our own private intrapersonal standards for comparing utils if we are unable to agree on a common interpersonal standard to be applied when joint decisons are made. Nor is social choice theory very encouraging about the possibility of aggregating our intrapersonal standards. Hylland (1991) has shown that a version of Arrow's paradox applies, and so the only aggregation methods that meet the usual criteria of social choice theory are essentially dictatorial.[5] Such a procedure fits comfortably into an ipsedixist philosophy. The ideal observer approach can also be accommodated if the ideal observer is treated as an imaginary citizen. But this chapter is devoted to exploring the notion of a philosopher–king, who must derive *all* his standards from the people.

## 5     The original position

Rawls (1972) and Harsanyi (1977) propose the device of the original position as a means of determining a fair system of rules for a society to adopt. To employ the device, each citizen is asked to envisage the social contract to which he would agree *if* his current and future role in society were concealed from him behind a veil of ignorance. In considering the social contract on which to agree under such hypothetical circumstances, each person will pay close attention to the plight of those who end up at the bottom of the social heap. Devil take the hindmost is not such an attractive principle when you yourself may be at the back of the pack. As Rawls argues, the social contract negotiated in the original position is therefore likely to generate outcomes that the underprivileged might reasonably regard as fair.

In modeling the use of the original position in later sections, attention is restricted to the case of two players, Adam and Eve. When they enter the original position, they forget their identities. Adam will then be referred to as player I and Eve as player II. Behind the veil of ignorance, each player believes that there is half a chance that he will turn out to be Adam and half a chance that he will turn out to be Eve. It is important to recognize that they cannot evaluate their plight in this situation unless they are able to quantify their empathetic preferences as described in section 3.

I agree with Harsanyi and Rawls on the virtues of the original position, but I differ with both on two important counts. In the first place, I think their view that citizens are somehow committed, morally or other-

---

[5] Arrow's theorem is irrelevant in the later part of the chapter, since the condition of unrestricted domain does not apply.

wise, to whatever compromise would be reached behind the veil of ignorance is mere wishful thinking. Without a philosopher–king to enforce the compromise reached in the original position, it would be necessary to restrict the feasible social contracts to those that are self-policing. In game-theoretic terms, such contracts would need to be equilibria in the game of life (Binmore 1996, chaps. 3 and 4).

Second and more importantly, I am unable to understand the reverence accorded to Immanuel Kant's moral philosophy, and hence remain unmoved by the appeals that Harsanyi and Rawls both make to his authority in their respective defenses of the original position. For example, Rawls (1972) argues that the original position provides a "procedural interpretation of Kant's concept of autonomy and the categorical imperative."

My own view, which is defended at much greater length in Binmore (1994), is that the interest of the original position lies in the fact that it represents a stylized version of do-as-you-would-be-done-by principles that are *already* firmly entenched as joint decision-making criteria within the system of commonly understood conventions that bind society together. It is distinguished from other versions by its power to answer objections like, Don't do unto others as you would have then do unto you – they may have different tastes from yours. To advocate the use of a device like the original position is therefore not to call upon people to do something that is foreign to their nature or that lies outside their experience as social animals. All that is being suggested is that a familiar social tool be recognized as such, and then that it be adapted for use on a wider scale. The proposal is entirely pragmatic. If our evolutionary history had tabled some rival to the original position as a fairness norm, I would be proposing this rival norm instead.

Taking such a naturalistic line on the nature of the original position creates opportunities for investigating the problem of interpersonal comparison of utility that Harsanyi's (1977) Kantian approach finesses away. He postulates a very thick veil of ignorance behind which people forget the empathetic preferences they have in real life and so find it necessary to adopt new empathetic preferences. He then appeals to a principle that has become known as the Harsanyi doctrine. In its extended form, the doctrine asserts that rational individuals placed in identical situations will necessarily respond identically. The empathetic preferences that Adam and Eve adopt in the original position will therefore be the same, and the problem of interpersonal comparison is solved. Since both players will be led to the same standard for comparing utils, no difficulties can arise in taking this as their common standard.

Binmore (1994) criticizes the use of the Harsanyi doctrine in such a context at length. However, even if its use could be adequately defended, how would poor mortals like us be able to predict the empathetic preferences that the super-rational players of game theory would adopt behind the thick veil of ignorance envisaged by Harsanyi? Even if we could, why should we substitute these empathetic preferences for those we already have?

My own approach to this question is radically different from Harsanyi's. I think that we have empathetic preferences at all only because we need them as inputs when using rough-and-ready versions of the device of the original position to make fairness judgments in real life. Insofar as people from similar cultural backgounds have similar empathetic preferences, it is because the use of the original position in this way creates evolutionary pressures that favor some empathetic preferences at the expense of others. In the meduim run, the result is that everybody tends to have the same set of empathetic preferences.

## 6    Empathy and fairness

Chapter 2 of Binmore (1996) sketches a possible evolutionary history for the device of the original position as a fairness norm. Very briefly, it is argued that the origins of the device are to be found in primitive food-sharing agreements. If player I is lucky enough to have an excess of food this week, then it makes sense for him to share with player II in the expectation that she will be similarly generous when she is lucky in the future.

To see the similarity between bargaining over mutual insurance pacts and bargaining behind the veil of ignorance, think of players I and II as not knowing whether tomorrow will find them occupying the role of Mr. Lucky or Ms. Unlucky. It then becomes clear that a move to the device of the original position requires only that the players put themselves in the shoes of somebody else – either Adam or Eve – rather than in the shoes of one of their own possible future selves. The same distinction separates Buchanan and Tullock's (1962) "veil of uncertainty" from Rawls's (1972) veil of ignorance. Dworkin (1981) similarly distinguishes between "brute luck" and "opportunity luck."

But what of the origins of the capacity to empathize with a fellow man rather than a possible future self? On this subject, one has to look no further than the relationships that hold within families. In accordance with Hamilton's (1963, 1964) rule for games played within families, each player's payoff consists of a weighted sum of the fitnesses of him and his kinfolk, with each weight equal to his degree of relationship to the relative concerned. For example, the weight that Adam will attach to the fitness of a first cousin is 1/4, because they share this fraction of their genes. To express empathetic preferences outside the family, Adam has therefore only to adapt the mechanisms that evolved within the family to a new purpose.

However, a problem remains. The weights we use when discounting the fitnesses of our partners in a family game are somehow obtained from estimating our degree of relationship to our kinfolk from the general dynamics of the family and our place in it. But where do we get the weights to be used when discounting Adam and Eve's personal utils when constructing an empathetic utility function?

I see the empathetic preferences held by the individuals in a particular society as an artefact of their upbringing. As children mature, they are assimilated to the culture in which they grow up largely as a consequence of their natural disposition to imitate those around them. One of the social phenomena they will observe is the use of the device of the original position in achieving fair compromises. They are, of course, no more likely to recognize the device of the original position for what it is than we are when we use it in deciding such matters as who should wash how many dishes. Instead, they simply copy the behavior patterns of those they see using the device. An internal algorithm then distills this behavior into a preference-belief model against which they then test alternative patterns of behavior. The preferences in this model will be empathetic preferences – the inputs required when the device of the original position is employed.

I plan to short-circuit the complexities of the actual transmission mechanism by simply thinking of a set of empathetic preferences as being packaged in a social signal or meme – which is Dawkins's (1976) name for the social equivalent of a gene. The imitative process is seen as a means of propagating such memes in much the same way that the common cold virus finds its way from one head to another. As always, I keep matters simple by assuming that all games to be played are games of complete information, which means that the rules of the game and the preferences of the players are taken to be common knowledge. In particular, it is assumed that the hypothetical bargaining game played behind the veil of ignorance has complete information. The empathetic preferences with which the players evaluate their predicament in the original position are therefore taken to be common knowledge. Along with a set of empathetic preferences, a meme will also carry a recommendation about which bargaining strategy to use in the original position. Only when the stability of the system is threatened by the appearance of a "mutant" meme will they have reason to deviate from this normal bargaining strategy.

To explore the issue of evolutionary stability, imagine that all players are currently controlled by a normal meme $N$. A mutant meme $M$ now appears. Will it be able to expand from its initial foothold in the population? If so, then the normal population is not evolutionarily stable.

Only one of the two standard conditions for evolutionary stability is needed here – namely, the condition that $(N, N)$ should be a *symmetric* Nash equilibrium of the underlying game in which $M$ and $N$ are strategies (Binmore 1992). In brief, $N$ must be a best reply to itself.

To interpret this condition, imagine that player I has been infected with the mutant meme $M$ while player II remains in thrall to the normal meme $N$. Both players will test their recommended bargaining strategy against the empathetic preferences they find themselves holding and adjust their behavior until they reach a Nash equilibrium of their bargaining game. I shall be assuming that this Nash equilibrium implements a suitable version of the Nash bargaining solution of the game. As a consequence, player I and player II will each now receive some share of the benefits and burdens in dispute.

The imitation mechanism that determines when it is appropriate to copy the memes we observe others using will take account of who gets what. Onlookers will almost all currently be subject to the normal meme $N$ and so will evaluate the shares they see player I and II receiving in terms of the empathetic preferences embedded in $N$. If player I's payoff exceeds player II's then I assume that onlookers who are vulnerable to infection are more likely to be taken over by the meme $M$ controlling player I than by the meme $N$ controlling player II. But then $M$ will be a better reply to $N$ than $N$ is to itself.

A necessary condition for the evolutionary stability of a normal population is therefore that the empathetic preferences originally held by players I and II constitute what I call a symmetric *empathy equilibrium.* In order to test whether a pair of empathetic preferences constitutes an empathy equilibrium each player should be asked the following question:

> Suppose that you could deceive everybody into believing that your empathetic preferences are whatever you find it expedient to claim them to be. Would such an act of deceit seem worthwhile to you *in the original position* relative to the empathetic preferences that *you actually hold?*

The right answer for an empathy equilibrium is *no.*

The tautological appearance of the argument leading to this criterion is misleading, since two substantive assumptions are concealed in the woodwork. In the simple two-person case with which we commonly work, player I is actually Adam and player II is actually Eve. However, players I and II are envisaged as being ignorant of their identities. Each acts as though he or she may turn out to be Adam or Eve with probability 1/2. In this state of imagined uncertainty, they evaluate their prospects using their *empathetic* preferences. Someone who imitates player II in the preceding argument therefore joins player II in pretending that he doesn't know that player II is Eve. The imitator therefore doesn't evaluate player II's payoff in terms of Eve's *personal* utils, as he might well do if he were looking on from outside the players' society without empathizing with what was passing through Eve's mind. He joins Eve in adopting player II's point of view and so interprets payoffs as player II interprets them. In the definition of an empathy equilibrium, this requirement appears as the condition that a player only considers whether an act of deceit would be worthwhile to him *in the original position*.

This assumption is entirely natural in the case of prehistoric insurance contracts. It would then be stupid to wait until after the uncertainty was resolved to evaluate the decisions made before it was known who would be the lucky hunter. I know that people very commonly do make such stupid evaluations – arguing that it was a mistake to bet on Punter's Folly because Gambler's Ruin actually won the race. The equivalent prehistoric mistake would be to judge that the lucky hunter went wrong in negotiating an insurance contract with his unlucky colleague, because he then had to part with some of his food without receiving anything in return. But tribes that implicitly internalized such reasoning would eventually lose the evolutionary race.

The second substantive assumption hidden in the woodwork concerns the *symmetry* of the empathy equilibria to which attention will be confined. For the argument supporting symmetry to make sense, it is essential that everyone learn from everyone. If men only imitate men and women only imitate women, there is no reason why Adam and Eve's empathetic preferences should be the same. An essential precondition for confining attention to symmetric empathy equilibria is therefore that all the citizens of a society share in a common culture.

## 7    Nonteleological utilitarianism

Section 3 argued that the modern consensus on political legitimacy is most closely matched by a philosopher–king theory. This section seeks to generate foundations for a philosopher–king version of utilitarianism by adapting Harsanyi's (1977) nonteleological approach to the purpose.

The theory depends on distinguishing between short-run and medium-run phenomena. The short run corresponds to economic time –

the time required for a market to adjust to an unanticipated piece of news. I assume that preferences are fixed in the short run. The medium run corresponds to social time – the time needed for cultural norms or social conventions to adjust to a change in the underlying environment. I assume that personal preferences are fixed in the medium run, but that enough time is available in the medium run for empathetic preferences to adjust until they reach an empathy equilibrium. If we had occasion to refer to the long run in this chapter, it would correspond to biological time, and all preferences would be variable.

## 7.1    *The short run*

In the fable to be told, an impartial philosopher–king represents a benign and enlightened government that exists solely to enforce the laws that the people make for themselves. The state is simplified to the Garden of Eden, where the only citizens are Adam and Eve. Their problem is to negotiate a suitable marriage contract.

It is important to keep in mind that this is to be an old-style marriage, in that the philosopher–king will ensure that Adam and Eve remain bound by their marriage vows even though one or the other may beg for release after the gilt has worn off the gingerbread. He does not, of course, bind them against their will at the time of their marriage. On their wedding day, they *want* their vows to bind, because they know that they will be tempted to go astray in the future. Nor does he impose the form of the contract upon them. He accepts that they will determine their marriage contract using the device of the original position.

All that will matter about a contract $C$ in the analysis that follows is the fact that it generates a payoff pair $x = (u_A(C), u_E(C))$. Figure 1(a) shows the feasible set of all such contracts. The set $X$ is assumed to be closed, bounded above, and comprehensive for the usual reasons. The asymmetries of the set $X$ register the ineradicable inequalities between Adam and Eve for which the device of the original position provides redress.

Behind the veil of ignorance, the players face an uncertain situation. They do not know which of two events, $AE$ or $EA$, will be revealed after their negotiations are concluded. Because we chose the notation, we know they will actually observe event $AE$, in which player I is Adam and player II is Eve. But the protagonists themselves must also take account of the event $EA$ in which player I turns out to be Eve and player II to be Adam. Unlike Harsanyi (1977), I allow Adam and Eve to come to an arrangement that makes the social contract contingent on who turns out to occupy which role. That is to say, they are assumed free to

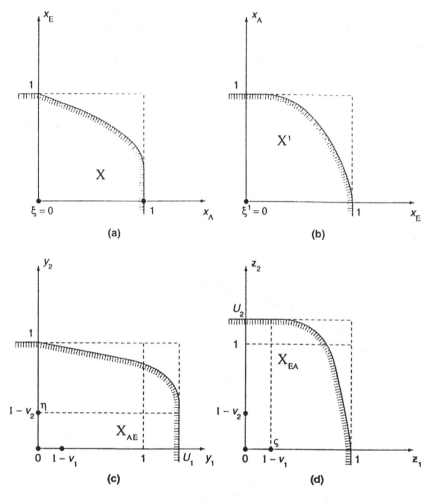

Figure 1. Various transformations of the set $X$

agree to operate one social contract $C$ if event $AE$ occurs and another social contract $\mathcal{D}$ if event $EA$ occurs. This contingent social contract will be denoted by $(C, \mathcal{D})$.

Suppose that player I's preferences are given by his empathetic Von Neumann and Morgenstern utility function $\upsilon_1$. His expected utility for the contingent social contract $(C, \mathcal{D})$ is then

$$w_1(C, \mathcal{D}) = \frac{1}{2}\upsilon_1(C, A) + \frac{1}{2}\upsilon_1(\mathcal{D}, E) \tag{5}$$

In this expression, $\upsilon_1(C, A)$ is the utility player I derives if the social contrat $C$ is operated with him in Adam's role. Similarly, $\upsilon_1(\mathcal{D}, E)$ is the utility he derives if the social contract $\mathcal{D}$ is operated with him in Eve's role.

We have seen that the empathetic utility function of a person who empathizes fully with both Adam and Eve can be expressed in terms of their personal utility functions $u_A$ and $u_E$. Writing $w_1(C, \mathcal{D})$ of (5) and the corresponding formula for $w_2(C, \mathcal{D})$ in terms of Adam and Eve's *personal* preferences, we obtain that

$$w_1(C, \mathcal{D}) = \frac{1}{2} U_1 u_A(C) + \frac{1}{2}\left\{1 - V_1\left(1 - u_E(\mathcal{D})\right)\right\} \tag{6}$$

$$w_2(C, \mathcal{D}) = \frac{1}{2}\left\{1 - V_2\left(1 - u_E(C)\right)\right\} + \frac{1}{2} U_2 u_A(\mathcal{D}) \tag{7}$$

*An aside on Harsanyi's approach:* The considerations that lead to (6) and (7) are more complicated than Harsanyi (1977) requires for his own nonteleological defense of utilitarianism. To reduce them to something recognizable in Harsanyi's work, begin by suppressing the irrelevant constants $\frac{1}{2}(1 - V_1)$ and $\frac{1}{2}(1 - V_2)$. Observe next that Harsanyi does not admit contingent social contracts and so (6) and (7) can be simplified by writing $C = \mathcal{D}$. Finally, recall that Harsanyi assumes that Adam and Eve will have the *same* empathetic preferences behind the veil of ignorance, with the result that $U_1 = U_2 = U$ and $V_1 = V_2 = V$. When these simplifications are incorporated into (6) and (7), the bargaining problem faced by players I and II in the original position becomes trivial, since each player then wants to maximize the *same* utility function. They will therefore simply agree on the social contract $C$ that maximizes the utilitarian social welfare function:

$$w(C) = \frac{1}{2} U u_A(C) + \frac{1}{2} V u_E(C)$$

My difficulty with this version of Harsanyi's nonteleological defense of utilitarianism lies in the argument he deploys to ensure that $U_1 = U_2 = U$ and $V_1 = V_2 = V$. In order to guarantee that players I and II both agree in the original position that $V$ of Adam's utils are worth $U$ of Eve's, he proposes that the veil of ignorance should be assumed so thick that Adam and Eve forget their empathetic preferences along with their personal preferences. Each must therefore formulate new empathetic preferences in the original position. An appeal to the Harsanyi doctrine – which says that rational folk in identical circumstances will be led to identical conclusions – then guarantees that the empathetic preferences they construct are identical. However, Harsanyi offers no insight into the considerations to which players I and II would appeal in determining the weights $U$ and $V$ that characterize their new empathetic preferences.

My own approach is based on how it seems to me that the device of the original position is actually used in real life. If practice is to be our guide, then we must not follow Harsanyi and Rawls in postulating a thick veil of ignorance. On the contrary, the veil of ignorance needs to be taken to be as thin as possible. Adam and Eve must certainly still forget their personal preferences along with their identities, but it is essential that they do not forget the *empathetic* preferences with which their culture has equipped them. To isolate Adam and Eve in a Kantian void from the cultural data summarized in their empathetic preferences and then to ask them to make interpersonal comparisons seems to me like inviting someone to participate in pole-vault competition without a pole.

*The bargaining problem behind the veil of ignorance:* Since I am not willing to apply the Harsanyi doctrine in the original position, it is necessary to return to the asymmetric equations (6) and (7). These will be interpreted geometrically before applying Nash's bargaining theory.

The simplest type of bargaining problem can be formulated as a pair $(T, \tau)$, where $T$ consists of all payoff pairs on which the two players can agree and $\tau$ is the payoff pair that will result if there is a disagreement. Our first problem is therefore to determine the set $T$ of feasible payoff pairs for players I and II in the original position.

Figure 1(a) shows the set $X$ of feasible personal payoffs pairs that Adam and Eve can achieve by coordinating on a suitable social contract. Behind the veil of ignorance, players I and II attach probability $1/2$ to both events $AE$ and $EA$. Since they evaluate an uncertain prospect by calculating its expected utility, they regard a contingent social contract that leads to the payoff pair $y$ when $AE$ occurs and $z$ when $EA$ occurs as equivalent to the pair

$$t = \frac{1}{2}y + \frac{1}{2}z \tag{8}$$

which is simply a compressed version of (6) and (7).

The payoff pair $t$ is shown in Figure 2(a). It lies halfway along the line segment joining the payoff pairs $y$ and $z$. The pair $y$ lies in the set $X_{AE}$ consisting of all payoff pairs that players I and II regard as attainable should $AE$ occur. The set $X_{AE}$ has a similar shape to $X$ but needs to be rescaled in order to reflect the relative worth that player I places on Adam's utils and player II places on Eve's utils. From (4), we know that

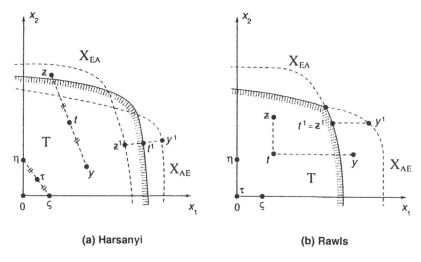

(a) Harsanyi    (b) Rawls

Figure 2. Constructing the set $T$

player I regards a payoff of $x_A$ to Adam as being worth $y_1 = U_1 x_A$. Similarly, player II regards a payoff of $x_E$ to Eve as being worth $y_2 = 1 - V_2(1 - x_E)$. To obtain $X_{AE}$ from the set $X$, we must therefore replace each payoff pair $x = (x_A, x_E)$ in $X$ by the rescaled pair $y = (y_1, y_2) = (U_1 x_A, 1 - V_2(1 - x_E))$. The resulting set $X_{AE}$ is shown in Figure 1(c).

To obtain $X_{EA}$ from the set $X$ is slightly more complicated because player I will become Eve if $EA$ occurs. However, his payoffs are measured on the horizontal axis while hers are measured on the vertical axis. As shown in Figure 1(b), it is therefore necessary to begin by swapping over Adam and Eve's axes to obtain the set $X'$ (which is simply the reflection of $X$ in the line $x_A = x_E$). After this transformation, player I's payoffs and Eve's payoffs are both measured on the horizontal axis, and so we can proceed as before. The set $X_{EA}$ has a similar shape to $X'$ but needs to be rescaled in order to reflect the relative worth that player I places on Eve's utils and player II places on Adam's utils. To obtain $X_{EA}$ from $X'$, replace each payoff pair $x = (x_E, x_A)$ in $X'$ by the rescaled pair $z = (z_1, z_2) = (1 - V_1(1 - x_E), U_2 x_A)$. The set $X_{EA}$ is shown in Figure 1(d).

The preceding discussion of how $X_{AE}$ and $X_{EA}$ are constructed from $X$ is a necessary preliminary to drawing the set $T$ of all payoff pairs that are feasible for players I and II in the original position. As Figure 2(a) illustrates, $T$ is the set of all $t = \frac{1}{2} y + \frac{1}{2} z$, with $y$ in $X_{AE}$ and $z$ in $X_{EA}$. (The Pareto frontier of $T$ can be characterized as the set of all $t = \frac{1}{2} y + \frac{1}{2} z$ with the property that the tangent to the Pareto frontier of $X_{AE}$ at $y$ has the same slope as the tangent to the Pareto frontier of $X_{EA}$ at $z$.)

Having tied down the set $T$, the next step in specifying the bargaining problem $(T, \tau)$ is to determine the status quo $\tau$. Chapter 2 of Binmore (1996) describes how Nash's variable threats theory can be used in principle to determine $\tau$. But such considerations are short-circuited here by simply assuming that Adam and Eve's alternative to signing a marriage contract is that they revert to the preceding status quo represented in Figure 1(a) as the payoff pair $\xi = (\xi_A, \xi_E)$. This is mirrored in Figure 1(b) by the payoff pair $\eta = (\xi_E, \xi_A)$. Behind the veil of ignorance, players I and II therefore evaluate the consequences of a disagreement as being equivalent to the payoff pair $\tau = \frac{1}{2}\xi + \frac{1}{2}\eta$ illustarted in Figure 2(a).

*Solving the bargaining problem:* The bargaining problem faced by players I and II in the original position has been formulated as the pair $(T, \tau)$ shown in Figure 2(a). It is easy to describe the solution to this bargaining problem in geometric terms. As illustrated in Figure 3(a), Nash's theory of bargaining with commitment predicts that the bargaining outcome will be the symmetric Nash bargaining solution $\sigma$ for the bargaining problem $(T, \tau)$.

Before discussing what this solution implies for Adam and Eve's personal payoffs, it is as well to emphasize the strong informational assumptions required by the argument leading to the payoff pair $\sigma$ in Figure 3(a). In the original position, players I and II forget whether they are Adam or Eve. Since their own empathetic preferences are common knowledge, it follows that they must also forget which empathetic preference derives from Adam and which from Eve. But everything else is assumed to be common knowledge between players I and II. This assumption is essential in the case of *all* the data used to construct the bargaining problem $(T, \tau)$. Players I and II therefore know the rules of the game of life, and hence which potential social contracts are feasible. Each also knows Adam and Eve's personal preferences and his own empathetic preferences together with those of his bargaining partner.

All this is a great deal to know and so it is worth observing that a more general approach that does not depend on making such strong epistemological assumptions is possible. However, without strong informational assumptions, it is necessary to appeal to Harsanyi's (1967) theory of games of incomplete information, with the result that the technical problems would become much harder. But there are no conceptual obstacles to an advance in this direction.[6]

---

[6] The Nash bargaining solution must be generalized as in Harsanyi and Selten (1972). A corresponding generalization of Nash's threat theory appears in Binmore (1987).

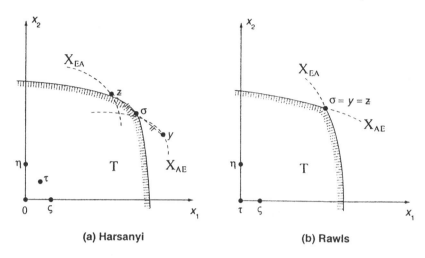

Figure 3. Applying the Nash bargaining solution to $(T, \tau)$

Returning to the question of how an agreement on $\sigma$ in the original position translates into personal payoffs to Adam and Eve, it is necessary to recall that for $\sigma$ to be admissible as a member of the set $T$, it must be of the form $\sigma = \frac{1}{2}y + \frac{1}{2}z$, where $y$ is in $X_{AE}$ and $z$ is in $X_{EA}$. One must also remember that the bargaining that supposedly takes place behind the veil of ignorance is only hypothetical. Adam and Eve only pretend to forget their identities when using the device of the original position to compute a fair social contract. In fact, player I is actually Adam and player II is actually Eve. Of the two events $AE$ and $EA$, it is therefore the former that actually obtains.

It follows that the social contract $C$ which will actually be operated corresponds to the payoff pair $y = (y_1, y_2)$ in $X_{AE}$ illustrated in Figure 3(a). In terms of Adam and Eve's original personal utility scales, the social contract $C$ yields the payoff pair $h = (h_A, h_E)$ defined by $y_1 = U_1 h_A$ and $y_2 = 1 - V_2(1 - h_E)$. As far as I know, there is no neat way to summarize the payoff pair $h$ in terms of the set $X$ and the underlying game of life. However, matters become more promising in the symmetric case illustrated in Figure 4(a).

When $U_1 = U_2 = U$ and $V_1 = V_2 = V$, Figure 3(a) translates into the symmetric Figure 4(a). In particular, the bargaining problem $(T, \tau)$ becomes symmetric, and so the outcome

$$N = \frac{1}{2}H + \frac{1}{2}K \qquad (9)$$

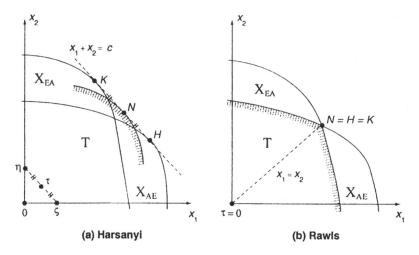

Figure 4. The symmetric case: $U_1 = U_2 = U$ and $V_1 = V_2 = V$

obtained by using the symmetric Nash bargaining solution is symmetric as well.

The symmetry ensures that the payoff pair $N$ can be achieved using the same social contract $C$ whether $AE$ or $EA$ occurs. However, the event that actually obtains is $AE$, and so the personal payoff pair $h = (h_A, h_E)$ that Adam and Eve actually experience when $C$ is implemented is given by $H_1 = Uh_A$ and $H_2 = 1 - V(1 - h_E)$.

In the asymmetric case, it proved difficult to characterize the payoff pair $h$ as a point of $X$. But here it is easily identified as the point $x$ in $X$ at which the weighted utilitarian social welfare function

$$W_h\left(x\right) = Ux_A + Vx_E$$

is maximized. To see this, observe that $H$ and $K$ in Figure 4(a) lie on a common tangent $x_1 + x_2 = c$ to the Pareto frontiers of $X_{AE}$ and $X_{EA}$. It follows that $H$ is the point in $X_{AE}$ at which the social welfare function $W_H(x) = x_1 + x_2$ is maximized. But the function defined by $x_1 = Ux_A$ and $x_2 = 1 - V(1 - x_E)$ that maps $X_{AE}$ to $X$ transforms $x_1 + x_2$ into $Ux_A + 1 - V(1 - x_E)$. The constant $1 - V$ is irrelevant to the maximization, and so maximizing $W_H$ on $X_{AE}$ is the same as maximizing $W_h$ on $X$.

Figure 5(a) shows the location of $h$ as the point $x$ in $X$ at which $W_h$ is maximized. Recall that such utilitarian bargaining solutions are independent of the status quo. This fact signals that, although it is never

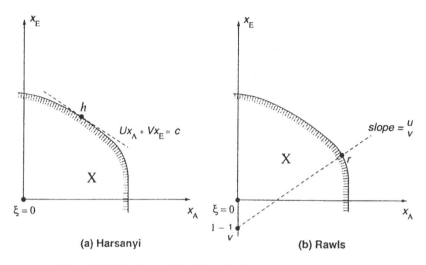

Figure 5. Utilitarian and Rawlsian solutions

possible to forget what would happen if there were a disagreement in a bargaining discussion, the precise location of $\tau$ proves irrelevant to the final utilitarian conclusion when $U$ and $V$ are given.

Provided that one is willing to swallow the assumption that $U_1 = U_2 = U$ and $V_1 = V_2 = V$, the argument leading to $h$ in Figure 5(a) extends Harsanyi's nonteleological defense of utilitarianism to the case of contingent social contracts. In itself, such an achievement would not be worth the effort. But we need the apparatus developed along the way to tackle the question of how the parameters $U_1$, $U_2$, $V_1$, and $V_2$ are determined in the medium run.

## 7.2    The medium run

The preceding discussion is a short-run analysis in which all preferences are fixed. We now turn to the medium run, in which personal preferences are fixed but social evolution has the chance to mold empathetic preferences. The aim is to study the effect of the forces of social evolution on the values of $U_1$, $U_2$, $V_1$, and $V_2$ that determine the shape of the sets $X_{AE}$ and $X_{EA}$ in Figure 3(a).

As section 7.1 recalls, Harsanyi (1977) makes a Kantian appeal to the Harsanyi doctrine in order to argue that $U_1 = U_2 = U$ and $V_1 = V_2 = V$. The same result is achieved equally cheaply here by restricting attention to symmetric empathy equilibria. The argument of section 7.1 is then adequate to demonstrate that Adam and Eve will can upon the philosopher–king to maximize the utilitarian welfare function

$$W_h = Ux_A + Vx_E$$

It is therefore entirely painless to translate Harsanyi's (1977) non-teleological defense of utilitarianism into my naturalistic terms.

However, Harsanyi's appeal to his doctrine leaves us with no clue as to how the all-important ratio $U/V$ is determined. If we were unconcerned about why the players think it appropriate to treat $V$ of Adam's utils as being worth the same as $U$ of Eve's, then Harsanyi's silence on this subject would create no problem. But the question of how interpersonal comparisons are made seems to me too important to be shrugged aside.

Although the relevant mathematics are suppressed in this chapter, I believe that the fact that insight can be obtained into this question using the concept of an empathy equilibrium is one of the major advantages of my approach. Chapter 2 of Binmore (1996) demonstrates that, even for asymmetric empathy equilibria, the personal payoffs Adam and Eve receive as a result of bargaining as though behind the veil of ignorance are precisely the same as they would have received if they had solved the bargaining problem $(X, \xi)$ directly using the symmetric Nash bargaining solution. When allowed to operate in the medium run, the effect of social evolution is therefore to leach out all moral content from the device of the original position.

## 8     Morality as a short-run phenomenon

We have just seen that the result of social evolution operating in the medium run is that Adam and Eve will get precisely the same personal payoffs if they play fair by using the device of the original position as they would if they were to bargain face-to-face with no holds barred. So what use is a fairness norm if it serves only to conceal the iron fist in a velvet glove? The answer is that the type of morality with which we are concerned has its bite in the *short run*.

To understand how I see fairness norms operating in practice, one must begin by imagining that groups of people assembled in different places at different times for various purposes find themselves continually facing the need to coordinate on Pareto-efficient solutions to new problems. Such minisocieties are simplified in my treatment to pairs of men and women seeking some modus vivendi that I refer to as a marriage contract. In our Garden of Eden fable, Adam is therefore a representative man and Eve is a representative woman.

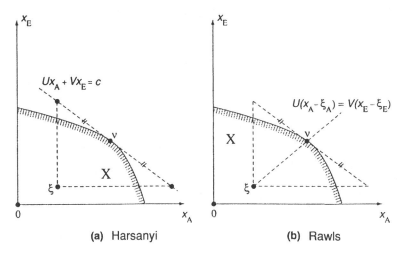

(a) Harsanyi          (b) Rawls

Figure 6. Interpersonal comparison

To keep matters simple, it will be assumed that all pairs always face the *same* set $X$ of feasible social contracts, and the same state of nature $\xi$. Each Adam and Eve choose a social contract using the device of the original position. It will also be assumed that social evolution operates in the medium run to shape the manner in which Adam and Eve make interpersonal comparisons of utility. Eventually, everybody will therefore use the same weights $U$ and $V$ when comparing Adam's utils with Eve's. In the presence of a philosopher–king with the power and the inclination to enforce any social contract that Adam and Eve may write for themselves, the weights $U$ and $V$ can then be computed as shown in Figure 6(a). The rules for this computation are as follows:

(1)   Find the symmetric Nash bargaining solution v of the bargaining problem $(X, \xi)$.
(2)   Choose the weights $U$ and $V$ to make the weighted utilitarian solution for $(X, \xi)$ coincide with v.

Note the influence of the state-of-nature point $\xi$. Although its location is irrelevant to the weighted utilitarian solution v when $U$ and $V$ are given, it is *not* irrelevant to how $U$ and $V$ are determined in the medium run.

But what does it matter what $U$ and $V$ are, since we can determine the Nash bargaining solution $v$ of $(X, \xi)$ without their aid? The answer is that the values of $U$ and $V$ are relevant *in the short run* after some change in the underlying environment alters the set of feasible contracts. Perhaps the result of some innovation is that the set of available social

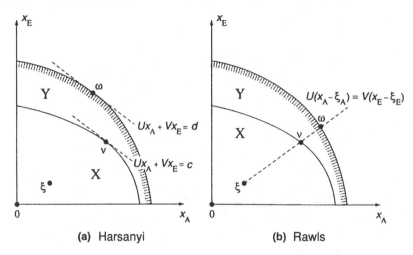

Figure 7. Morality in the short run

contracts expands from $X$ to $Y$, as illustrated in Figure 7(a). The fairness norm being operated now has a chance of fulfill the function for which it originally evolved – to shift its minisociety to a new Pareto-efficient social contract $\omega$ without damaging internal conflict. In the short run, $U$ and $V$ remain fixed, and so the new social contract $\omega$ is located as shown in Figure 7(a). In short:

(3)   The new social contract is the weighted utilitarian solution $\omega$ for the bargaining problem $(Y, \xi)$, computed with the weights $U$ and $V$ that evolved for the problem $(X, \xi)$.

Of course, if the representative problem faced by Adam and Eve continues to be $(Y, \xi)$ for long enough, then the standard for making interpersonal comparisons will adjust to the new situation and so the moral content of the social contract will again be eroded away. But it would be wrong to deduce that morality has only a small and ephemeral role to play in regulating the conduct of our affairs. If matters seem otherwise, it is because we mislead ourselves by thinking of morality as something to be taken out of its glass case only when grand and difficult problems need to be addressed. The real truth is that we use our innate sense of justice all the time in resolving the innumerable short-run coordination problems that continually arise as we try to get along with those around us. Such coordinating problems are usually so mundane and we solve them so effortlessly that we do not even think of them as problems – let alone moral problems. Like Molière's Monsieur Jourdain, who was delighted to discover that he had been speaking prose all his life, we are moral without knowing that we are moral.

Although I find few takers for the claim, I think the observation that morality works so smoothly much of the time that we don't even notice it working is of considerable significance. Just as we only take note of a thumb when it is sore, so moral philosophers tend to notice moral rules only when attempts are made to apply them in situations for which they are ill adapted. As an analogy, consider Konrad Lorenz's observations of a totally inexperienced baby jackdaw going through all the motions of taking a bath when placed on a marble-topped table. By triggering such instinctive behavior under abnormal circumstances, he learned a great deal about what is instinctive and what is not when a bird takes a bath. But this vital information is gained only by avoiding the mistake of supposing that bath-taking behavior confers some evolutionary advantage on birds placed on marble-topped tables. Similarly, one can learn a great deal about the mechanics of moral algorithms by triggering them under pathological circumstances – but only if one does not make the mistake of supposing that the moral rules have been designed to cope with pathological problems.

Finally, I doff my shabby naturalistic or descriptive hat and optimistically don a prescriptive hat of the type worn by Harsanyi (1977) or Rawls (1972). As section 2 insists, the descriptive arguments offered in this chapter do not *justify* these or any other prescriptive recommendations. I simply observe that a useful social tool has been washed up on the beach by the tide of evolution and invite others with cultural prejudices similar to mine to join in using it to advance our common cause.

We do not need to confine the device of the original position to the small-scale problems for which it evolved. We can deliberately seek to expand its circle of application by trying to apply this familiar social tool on a larger scale. That is to say, we can try to achieve Pareto-improving solutions to large-scale coordinating problems by appealing to the same fairness criteria that we use to solve small-scale coordinating problems. But such an enterprise will not work unless we put aside the temptation to romanticize our fairness intuitions. In particular, people make interpersonal comparisons of utility as they do – not as we would wish them to.

If my descriptive theory is anywhere near correct, appeals to fairness that ignore the realities of power are doomed, because the underlying balance of power is what ultimately shapes the interpersonal comparisons necessary for fairness judgments to be meangingful. Philosophers with utopian ambitions for the human race tell me that such conclusions are unacceptable. But I think this is just another example of an argument being rejected because it has unwelcome implications. In particular, the fact that fairness norms do not work as utopian thinkers would like them to work should not discourage us from trying to use them in the manner in which they actually do work. Others are free to toy with grandiose plans to convert our planet into a new Jerusalem, but we old-fashioned whigs are content to aim at finding workable ways of making life just a little bit more bearable for everyone.

## 9     Retelling the Rawlsian story

This section briefly follows through the consequences of replacing Harsanyi's (1977) use of Bayesian decision theory by the maximin principle favored by Rawls (1972).

Section 7 must therefore be replayed with the assumption that a player in the original position proceeds as though whichever of the two events $AE$ and $EA$ he dislikes more were certain to occur. Matters then proceed as in the reconstruction of Harsanyi's theory until equation (8) is reached. At this point, it is necessary to diverge from Harsanyi's argument because we are no longer to make the Bayesian assumption that player $i$ seeks to maximize $t_i = \frac{1}{2}y_i + \frac{1}{2}z_i$. Instead, we must take the most pessimistic of all possible views and assume that player $i$ seeks to maximize

$$t_i = \min\{y_i, z_i\} \tag{10}$$

The payoff pair $t = (t_1, t_2)$ defined by (10) is shown in Figure 2(b).

The set $T$ is easier to describe than in Harsanyi's case since it is simply the set of all payoff pairs that lie in both $X_{AE}$ and $X_{EA}$. That is to say, $T = X_{AE} \cap X_{EA}$. Figure 3(b) shows how to compute the symmetric Nash bargaining solution $\sigma$ in this new case. When the situation is not too far from being symmetric, $\sigma$ lies at the point where the Pareto frontiers of $X_{AE}$ and $X_{EA}$ cross. Figure 4(b) illustrates the fully symmetric case when $U_1 = U_2 = U$ and $V_1 = V_2 = V$.

The personal payoff pair $r = (r_A, r_E)$ shown in Figure 5(b) tells us how Adam and Eve evaluate the social contract $C$ after emerging from behind the veil of ignorance to discover that $AE$ actually obtains. It is determined by the requirement that

$$Ur_A = 1 - V(1 - r_E)$$

One may characterize $r$ as the proportional bargaining solution with weights $U$ and $V$ for the bargaining problem $(X, \alpha)$, in which the status quo $\alpha$ is $(0, 1 - 1/V)$.

Having replayed section 7.1 in a Rawlsian style, it is natural to seek to do the same for section 7.2. But the attempt fails, since it turns out that symmetric empathy equilibria do not exist. This disappointing conclusion should come as no surprise. The meaningless location of the status quo in Figure 5(b) already signals that something is awry – and the reason is not hard to find. One cannot expect meaningful conclusions if one grafts the maximin principle onto a utility theory for which only the maximization of expected utility makes any sense.

However, I do not think that the appropriate response is to lose faith in utility theory and to return to Rawls's (1972) concept of primary goods. I believe that Harsanyi's (1977) analysis of what players will agree on behind the veil of ignorance is correct when a philosopher–king is available to enforce the rules that they make for themselves. But the interesting case for constitutional questions seems to me to arise when no philosopher–king is available. Agreements made in the original position must then be self-enforcing. Under such conditions, chapter 4 of my forthcoming book puts what I hope is a strong case for a Rawlsian form of egalitarianism (Binmore [1997]).

REFERENCES

Arrow, K. (1978). "Extended Sympathy and the Problem of Social Choice," *Philosophia* 7: 233–237.
Bentham, J. (1962). *Bentham MSS, University College London Catalogue of the Manuscripts of Jeremy Bentham.* London. (Edited by A. Milne; second edition).
——— (1987). "An Introduction to the Principles of Morals and Legislation," in *Utilitarianism and Other Essays.* Harmondsworth, England: Penguin Books. (Essay first published 1789).
Binmore, K. (1987). "Nash Bargaining Theory II," in K. Binmore and P. Dasgupta, eds., *Economics of Bargaining.* Cambridge: Cambridge University Press.
——— (1992). *Fun and Games.* Lexington, Mass.: D. C. Heath.
——— (1994). *Playing Fair: Game Theory and the Social Contract I.* Cambridge, Mass.: MIT Press.
——— (1997, forthcoming). *Just Playing: Game Theory and the Social Contract II.* Cambridge, Mass: MIT Press.
Broome, J. (1991). *Weighing Goods.* Oxford: Basil Blackwell.
Buchanan, J., and G. Tullock (1962). *The Calculus of Consent: Logical Foundations of Constitutional Democracy.* Ann Arbor: University of Michigan Press.
Dawkins, R. (1976). *The Selfish Gene.* Oxford: Oxford University Press.
Dworkin, R. (1981). "What Is Equality? Parts I and II," *Philosophy and Public Affairs* 10: 185–345.

Hamilton, W. (1963). "The Evolution of Altruistic Behavior," *American Naturalist* 97: 354–56.

———(1964). "The Genetic Evolution of Social Behavor, Parts I and II," *Journal of Theoretical Biology* 7: 1–52.

Hammond, P. (1988). "Consequentialist Foundations for Expected Utility," *Theory and Decision* 25: 25–78.

———(1992). "Harsanyi's Utilitarian Theorem: A Simpler Proof and Some Ethical Connotations," in R. Selten, ed., *Rational Interaction: Essays in Honor of John Harsanyi*. Berlin: Springer-Verlag.

Hardin, R. (1988). *Morality within the Limits of Reason*. Chicago: University of Chicago Press.

Harsanyi, J. (1967). "Games with Incomplete Information Played by 'Bayesian' Players, Parts I–III," *Management Science* 14: 159–82.

———(1977). *Rational Behavior and Bargaining Equilibrium in Games and Social Situations*. Cambridge: Cambridge University Press.

Harsanyi, J., and R. Selten (1972). "A Generalized Nash Solution for Two-Person Bargaining Games with Incomplete Information," *Management Science* 18: 80–106.

Hayek, F. (1960). *The Constitution of Liberty*. Chicago: University of Chicago Press.

Hutcheson, F. (1755). *System of Moral Philosophy*. London.

Hylland, A. (1991). "Subjective Interpersonal Comparisons," in J. Elster and J. Roemer, eds., *Interpersonal Comparisons of Well-Being*. London: Cambridge University Press.

Mill, J. S. (1962). "On Liberty," in M. Warnock, ed. *Utilitarianism*. London: Collins. (Essay first published 1859).

———(1987). "Utilitarianism," In *Utilitarianism and Other Essays*. Harmondsworth, England: Penguin Books. (Essay first published 1863).

Rawls, J. (1972). *A Theory of Justice*. Oxford: Oxford University Press.

Rousseau, J.-J. (1913a). "A Discourse on Political Economy," in G. Cole, ed., *Rousseau's Social Contract and Discourses*, pp. 249–87. London: J. M. Dent. (First published 1755).

———(1913b). "The Social Contract," in G. Cole, ed., *Rousseau's Social Contract and Discourses*, pp. 5–123. London: J. M. Dent. (First published 1762).

Scott, W. (1966). *Francis Hutcheson*. Cambridge: Cambridge University Press. (First published 1900).

Sen, A. (1970). *Collective Choice and Social Welfare*. San Francisco: Holden Day.

———(1976). "Welfare Inequalities and Rawlsian Axiomatics," *Theory and Decision* 7: 243–62.

Shackleton, R. (1972). "The Greatest Happiness of the Greatest Number: The History of Bentham's Phrase," *Studies on Voltaire and the Eighteenth Century* 90: 1461–82.

Suppes, P. (1966). "Some Formal Models of Grading Principles," *Synthèse* 6: 284–306.

CHAPTER 4

# Why do we care what others think about us?

*Chaim Fershtman and Yoram Weiss*

*A social instinct is implanted in all men by nature.*
Aristotle, *Politics*, Bk. I: Ch. 2

*Honour is the prize of virtue. . . . It is chiefly with honours and dishonours that the proud man is concerned. . . . Therefore, the truly proud man must be good.*
Aristotle, *Ethics*, Bk. IV: Ch. 3

## 1    Introduction

Social reward mechanisms are often used to resolve externality problems and to induce cooperation. Such mechanisms can be effective only if people care about social status: that is, they care about what other people think about them. It may be argued that caring about the opinion of others is wired into all human beings and characterizes us as "social animals." This observation led many researchers to extend individual preferences beyond pure selfishness, adding considerations such as altruism, social status, and peer effects, and to examine the economic and social implications of such extended preferences.[1] However, we cannot expect all individuals to care equally about the opinion of others. Some individuals may be more motivated by economic considerations

This chapter was originally prepared for the Conference on Economics, Values, and Organization, April 19–21, 1996, Yale University. We would like to thank Eddie Dekel, Martin Dufwenberg, Paul DiMaggio, David Frankel, Ariel Rubinstein, John Roemer, Avner Shaked, and Martin Weitzman and the participants of the seminars at Chicago, the London School of Economics, Northwestern, Tilburg, and Tel Aviv universities for valuable comments and discussion.

[1] Examples for this line of research are Frank (1987), Bernheim (1994), Bagwell and Bernheim (1996), Corneo and Jeanne (1995a, 1995b), Fershtman and Weiss (1993), Fershtman, Murphy, and Weiss (1996), Robson (1992), and Okuno-Fujiwara and Postlewaite (1995).

(money), others by social considerations (status). The relative importance that the "average" person gives to these two considerations is a subject of debate between economists and sociologists. We would like to contribute to this debate by examining the question whether preferences that put substantial weight on "what other people think" can survive under the forces of economic competition.

The purpose of this chapter is to characterize the circumstances under which socially minded preferences survive in the long run. We adopt an evolutionary approach, where the preference profile in society is determined endogenously by a process of economic selection. The surviving preferences are those that generate economically viable behavior. In such a framework, the exogenously given preferences are replaced by an exogenous "fitness" criterion which determines the number of individuals with given preferences. In contrast with most evolutionary models, we consider the evolution of preferences, rather than the evolution of strategies.[2]

We consider a simple model in which individuals are randomly matched and are involved in a two-person interaction, playing some variation of the prisoner's dilemma game. We assume that the social status of an individual is determined by his own action, compared with the actions of other members of society. The marginal social reward for individual action (effort in our model) is assumed to be positive. High (low) social status is awarded to individuals who exert above (below) average effort. Individuals, however, can differ in the importance that they assign to social rewards. Some may care about the opinion of others; others may not. We do not assume any given profile of types but look for the one that emerges as an outcome of an evolutionary process.

A basic assumption of our analysis is that social status does not contribute directly to fitness. The survival of a particular type depends exclusively on its economic success. It would seem, therefore, that individuals influenced by social considerations cannot survive in the long run. This is not necessarily the case, however, because socially minded individuals can induce others to act in a way that is beneficial for their fitness. In particular, if two socially minded individuals meet, and each knows the preferences of his opponent, both might select higher effort levels, increasing the fitness of both.

In this chapter we identify the circumstances under which preference for social status is an effective means for escaping the prisoner's di-

---

[2] For evolutionary models that endogenize preferences, see Basu (1995), Bester and Guth (1994), Dekel and Scotchmer (1994), Fershtman and Weiss (1996), Hirshleifer (1980), Robson (1996), and Rogers (1994).

lemma. First, the marginal social reward must be nonnegligible and not excessive. If the marginal social reward is too small, it will not affect behavior. If it is too large, the socially minded exert effort irrespective of whom they meet. Asocial individuals may take advantage of such behavior and obtain higher fitness. It is only in the intermediate region, where socially minded individuals discriminate between opponents, exerting effort only when matched with their own type, that socially minded preferences can survive in the long run.

A social reward mechanism requires that individuals' actions are observable to other members of society. It is also required that, in each match, the equilibrium outcome is determined by the true types of the two individuals. Otherwise, the socially minded individuals cannot gain fitness. Throughout our analysis, we assume that, in each match, the players act as if their types are observable. This assumption can be justified by a setup in which, following a match, the two players are involved in a (finitely) repeated game in which they learn to play the Nash equilibrium and that the learning period is short compared to the period in which they play the game.

The particular specification of the preference for status influences its effectiveness as social reward. As noted by Coleman (1990, p. 130), "Status is complex, for although it constitutes a general medium of exchange, it does not have a single denomination that is independent of the particular awarder–recipient pair." Generally, it is not obvious which is the relevant reference group for an individual and which opinions he cares about. In this chapter, individuals vary in only one respect, their preference for status, and we examine two alternative specifications: In the first specification, a socially minded individual cares about the opinion of all members of society. In the second specification, socially minded individuals care only about the opinion of other socially minded individuals. In the first case, only one type of individual survives in the long run, depending on the level of social rewards. In the second case, the two types can coexist, but their proportion depends on the level of social rewards.

The effectiveness of social rewards also depends on the specification of the economic environment and the available choices. In this chapter, we consider two modifications of the basic model, allowing individuals to invest in schooling and migrate across societies with different reward structures. We show that investment options can enhance the effectiveness of social status. The option of immigration restricts the social rewards structure and eliminates societies where such rewards are too low or too high.

## 2    The model

Consider a society in which there is a large number of identical individuals, who live for one period (generation). A constant population is maintained through a process of birth and death. In each period, individuals are randomly matched into pairs and play a prisoner's dilemma game. When individuals $i$ and $j$ meet, each player chooses an effort level $e_i$ and $e_j$ from the set $\{0,1\}$. That is, each player can choose whether or not to exert effort.

Let us denote the monetary returns of individual $i$ which he obtains in economic interaction when matched with individual $j$ by

$$m_i = P_i(e_i, e_j) \tag{1}$$

The values of $P_i(.,.)$ are given in this payoff matrix:

player $j$

|  | | 0 | 1 |
|---|---|---|---|
| player $i$ | 0 | $\alpha, \alpha$ | $\beta, \delta$ |
|  | 1 | $\delta, \beta$ | $\gamma, \gamma$ |

where $\beta > \gamma > \alpha > \delta$. We further assume that the efforts of the two players are complementary, that is, $\alpha - \delta > \beta - \gamma$.[3] Thus, the efficient outcome is for both players to exert effort, but the equilibrium outcome is that no player exerts effort. Into this familiar prisoner's dilemma framework we introduce the notion that, besides monetary considerations, players are motivated by social rewards, such as social status.

Sociologists emphasize the importance of social status in motivating individual behavior. As Coleman writes, "The awarding of status appears to be the most widespread functional substitute for money in social and political systems. Although it can bring various benefits, social status, or recognition by others, has long been recognized by psychologists as a primary source of satisfaction to the self. That is, an interest in status can be regarded as being held by every person" (Coleman 1990, 130).

In our model, there are only two possible variables that distinguish between individuals: their choice of effort and their payoffs. If social status depends only on monetary payoffs, then there is no effect of social

---

[3] We use the usual terminology, defining actions as strategic complements if increased effort by player $j$ implies an increase of the marginal payoff of player $i$. Thus, when player $j$ increases his effort from 0 to 1, the marginal payoff for player $i$ increases from $\delta - \alpha$ to $\gamma - \beta$.

status on our analysis and the equilibrium is the same as in the standard prisoner's dilemma. We thus assume that the individual's actions determine his social status. Specifically, we assume that social status depends on the individual's choice of effort compared with the average effort in society. That is,

$$s_i = \sigma\left(e_i - e^a\right) \tag{2}$$

where $s_i$ represents the social status of individual $i$, $\sigma$ is a positive parameter representing the marginal increase in social status associated with higher levels of individual effort, and $e^a$ is the average level of effort in the population.

The utility function of an individual combines both monetary payoffs and social status and is assumed to take the following additive form:

$$u_i = m_i + \xi_i s_i \tag{3}$$

where $\xi_i$ is a preference parameter describing the importance individual $i$ gives to social rewards. This preference parameter may vary across individuals. We allow individuals to be of two types: those with $\xi = 1$ who care what other individuals think about them and those with $\xi = 0$ who do not care what other individuals think. We shall denote these types as 1 and 0, and refer to the individuals of each type as socially minded and asocial, respectively.

For social rewards to be effective, it is required that individual actions are publicly known. It is also required that the outcome of the game between any two matched players depends on their *true* types. Rather than assuming that each player immediately recognizes the type of his rival, we shall assume that each pair of players plays many (but finite) rounds of the game and that learning takes place. The simplest learning process is the one in which each player myopically plays the best response against his rival's action in the previous round. With only two actions for each player, this process converges quickly (at most in three rounds) to a Nash equilibrium of the game with observed types. Therefore, the Nash equilibrium payoffs are good approximations of the average payoffs of the repeated game. The restriction that players act myopically is in the spirit of evolutionary models that often rely on bounded rationality.

Since there is a large number of players, each player views $e^a$ as given. In particular, the choices that he and his opponent make have a negligible effect on $e^a$. The additive form of utility function (3), combined with the linearity of the status function (2), simplifies the analysis as it implies that the equilibrium strategies in each match are independent of $e^a$.

When two players of type 0 meet, they play the prisoner's dilemma game. In equilibrium, the players exert no effort and their payoffs are ($\alpha$, $\alpha$). However, in matches where at least one of the players is of type 1, the game changes. The equilibrium effort and payoffs for such pairs depend on the social environment, which is represented by the size of the social status coefficient, $\sigma$. We shall now describe the equilibrium outcomes, as a function of the preferences of the two players and the level of $\sigma$.

When type 1 plays with type 0 the payoff matrix is converted to the following matrix:

type 0

|          |   | 0 | 1 |
|----------|---|------|------|
| type 1   | 0 | $\alpha, \alpha$ | $\beta, \delta$ |
|          | 1 | $\delta + \sigma, \beta$ | $\gamma + \sigma, \gamma$ |

Note that the matrix does not fully describe the payoffs of the type 1 player. We need to subtract from his payoff at each strategy combination the amount of $\sigma e^a$, but this has no effect on the equilibrium strategy. As seen from the matrix, type 0 still exerts no effort, since this is a dominant strategy for him. However, the type 1 player may now choose to exert effort, depending on the marginal social rewards, $\sigma$.

For $\sigma < \alpha - \delta$, the pair remains locked in a prisoner's dilemma; both players choose zero effort and their monetary payoffs are ($\alpha$, $\alpha$).

For $\sigma > \alpha - \delta$, the equilibrium is such that the type 1 player exerts effort, the type 0 player exerts no effort, and their monetary payoffs are ($\delta$, $\beta$).

When two players of type 1 are matched, the payoff matrix becomes

type 1

|          |   | 0 | 1 |
|----------|---|------|------|
| type 1   | 0 | $\alpha, \alpha$ | $\beta, \delta + \sigma$ |
|          | 1 | $\delta + \sigma, \beta$ | $\gamma + \sigma, \gamma + \sigma$ |

where, again, we ignore the constant $\sigma e^a$, which needs to be subtracted from the payoffs of each player at any strategy combination.

Examining the possible equilibria at different values of $\sigma$, we obtain the following:

For $\sigma < \beta - \gamma$, the game is still a prisoner's dilemma and the unique equilibrium is that both players exert no effort and their monetary payoffs are ($\alpha$, $\alpha$).

For $\alpha - \delta > \sigma > \beta - \gamma$, there are two equilibria (in pure strategies): Either both players play 0 and get $(\alpha, \alpha)$ or they both play 1 and get $(\gamma, \gamma)$, as monetary payoffs. We assume that with some given probability $\lambda$, $0 \le \lambda \le 1$, the players play the high effort equilibrium and with the complementary probability they play the low effort equilibrium. We do not make any assumption on the probability $\lambda$, except that it is strictly positive. That is, in some matches between two players of type 1, the players will actually play the high effort equilibrium.[4] Alternatively, we may allow the players to mix their strategies and consider the (unique) mixed-strategy equilibrium.[5]

For $\sigma > \alpha - \delta$, both players put great emphasis on social status and their dominant strategy is to exert effort, yielding the monetary payoffs $(\gamma, \gamma)$.

## 3    The evolution of preferences

Why would anyone care about the opinion of others? To answer this question, we consider the evolutionary formation of preferences. While most of the evolutionary game theory literature discusses the players' choice of strategy and tries to justify certain notions of equilibria, in this chapter we consider the *evolution of preferences* rather than the *evolution of strategies*. That is, we assume that players play the Nash equilibrium strategies and analyze the formation of their preferences.

We follow the biological models of evolution and assume that the proportion of individuals of a given type in the population increases if their expected monetary payoff exceeds the average payoff in the population.[6] We thus define the fitness of a particular type in terms of his *monetary* payoffs, rather than his utility, which also takes into account social rewards. The underlying assumption is that even when people care about social rewards, their fitness is determined by their economic success.

---

[4] Given our assumption that the players behave myopically, the equilibrium selection is determined by the first action of the player who moves first. The assumption is that some known random mechanism determines the first mover and his first move. One can also use the Pareto selection and say that $\lambda$ is equal to 1. That is, in every match between two type 1 players, they will play the equilibrium strategies that yield the highest payoffs.

[5] In the mixed-strategy equilibrium, each player chooses high effort with probability

$$p = \frac{(\alpha - \delta) - \sigma}{(\alpha - \delta) - (\beta - \gamma)}$$

[6] See Maynard Smith (1982) for the biological foundation and the surveys of economic applications by Hammerstein and Selten (1994) and Weibull (1995).

Consider a society with a given status function $\sigma(e_i - e^a)$. Let $q$ be the proportion of individuals of type 1 in the society. Let $M(i, j)$ be the expected monetary payoffs of a type $i$ player when matched with a type $j$ player. Note that given our assumptions, $M(i, j)$ does not depend on $q$. The expected equilibrium payoff of each type, however, does depend on $q$. Let

$$W^1(q) = qM(1, 1) + (1 - q)M(1, 0) \tag{4}$$

and

$$W^0(q) = qM(0, 1) + (1 - q)M(0, 0) \tag{5}$$

be the expected equilibrium payoffs of types 1 and 0, respectively. Let

$$\overline{W}(q) = qW^1(q) + (1 - q)W^0(q) \tag{6}$$

be the average payoff in the population. The difference $W^i(q) - \overline{W}(q)$ is a measure of the (relative) *fitness* of type $i$. By assumption, the (relative) reproduction rate of type $i$ is increasing in his (relative) fitness. If the changes in the proportions of types are not too great, the intergenerational transmission of preferences can be approximated by the continuous time process[7]

$$q = \frac{dq}{dt} = q\big(W^1(q) - \overline{W}(q)\big) = q(1 - q)\big(W^1(q) - W^0(q)\big) \tag{7}$$

A population of type $k \in \{0,1\}$ is evolutionarily stable if it yields a rest point of (7), and when almost all members of the population are of this type, then the fitness of these typical members is greater than that of any member of the atypical type (see Maynard Smith 1982, p. 14). That is, given the "replicator dynamics" assumed in (7), the proportion of atypical individuals in the population must decline. Thus, a population consisting of only type 1 players is evolutionarily stable if $W^1(q) > W^0(q)$ for every $q$ close to 1. Similarly, a population consisting of only type 0 is evolutionarily stable if $W^1(q) < W^0(q)$ for every $q$ close to 0. For brevity, we shall say that a particular type is evolutionarily stable if a population consisting only of this type is evolutionarily stable.

While we allow the composition of individual preferences to vary over time, we hold the social status function constant. That is, a society is characterized by a given fixed value of $\sigma$. Using the results in section 2 on the equilibrium actions and payoffs in each match, we can calculate the fitness of different types in a given society to determine the sustainable preference profiles that are induced by alternative values of $\sigma$.

---

[7] See Maynard Smith (1982, pp. 183–88).

*Proposition 1:* (i) For low values of the marginal social reward σ, i.e., σ < β − γ, any combination of types is evolutionarily unstable but the behavior of the two types is indistinguishable.

(ii) For intermediate values of σ, i.e., β − γ < σ < α − δ, a society in which all individuals are socially minded is evolutionarily stable, while a society consisting of asocial individuals is evolutionarily unstable.

(iii) For high values of the marginal social reward σ, i.e., σ > α − δ, a society in which all individuals are asocial is evolutionarily stable, while a society consisting of only socially minded individuals is evolutionarily unstable.

*Proof:* (i) Given our previous analysis, for σ < β − γ, in every match the equilibrium effort is (0, 0) and the monetary payoffs are (α, α), irrespective of the types of the matched players. Thus, for any $q$, we get that $dq/dt = 0$ and, therefore, any profile of types is evolutionarily unstable.

(ii) When β − γ < σ < α − δ, then, using the equilibrium effort levels specified in section 2, the expected fitness of a type 0 player is

$$W^0(q) = q\alpha + (1-q)\alpha \tag{8}$$

and the expected fitness of a type 1 player is

$$W^1(q) = q[\lambda\gamma + (1-\lambda)\alpha] + (1-q)\alpha \tag{9}$$

Since γ > α and, by assumption, λ > 0, we obtain that $W^1(q) > W^0(q)$ for every $q$, which means that for β − γ < σ < α − δ, only type 1 is evolutionarily stable.

(iii) When σ > α − δ then the fitness of the type 0 player is

$$W^0(q) = q\beta + (1-q)\alpha \tag{10}$$

The fitness of the type 1 player is

$$W^1(q) = q\gamma + (1-q)\delta \tag{11}$$

Since β > γ and α > δ, we obtain that $W^0(q) > W^1(q)$ for every $q$. Thus, only type 0 is evolutionarily stable. ∎

The main result in Proposition 1 is that when the marginal effect of status is neither too high nor too low, a population consisting only of socially minded individuals is evolutionarily stable. This result implies that, in such a case, individuals who maximize fitness end up, in equilibrium, with lower fitness than those who maximize another objective.[8] Such a phenomenon occurs because when a type 1 player is matched with a type 0 player, they play the original equilibrium strategies (0, 0), but when two players of type 1 are matched, they sometimes play the cooperative strategies (1, 1). Thus, a socially minded individual exerts effort only if he meets his own type. When the marginal effect of social status is too high, socially minded individuals exert effort irrespective of the type of player whom they meet. Players of type 0 take advantage of such indiscriminate behavior and gain fitness relative to type 1 players (recall that $\beta > \gamma$). Therefore, in this case, socially minded individuals are eventually replaced by asocial individuals. When the marginal value of status is too low it does not change the behavior of the players and the outcome of the game.

The observation that it is possible to have evolutionarily stable preferences that differ from the maximization of fitness is also made by Bester and Guth (1997). They examine altruistic preferences, such that each player cares about his rival's payoff in pairwise interactions, and demonstrate that strategic complementarity is required for this kind of altruism to be evolutionarily stable. Although we discuss only complementary actions, Proposition 1, with proper redefinition of the three ranges, also holds for actions that are strategic substitutes.[9]

## 4    Do the socially minded care about the opinion of asocial individuals?

Can someone who does not care about respect respect someone else? Alternatively, will a person be equally motivated by the respect of all individuals in society, or does he care only about what socially minded individuals think about him? The answer to these questions is not at all obvious. To the extent that status entails some subsequent transfer of monetary rewards it is probably not important how a person attains status.[10] But as noted by Coleman (1990, p. 130), "Status is not like

---

[8] For a similar result in the analysis of strategic delegation see, for example, Fershtman and Judd (1987).

[9] For strategic substitutes, the lower, intermediate, and upper ranges are $\sigma < \alpha - \delta$, $\alpha - \delta < \sigma < \beta - \gamma$, and $\sigma > \beta - \gamma$, respectively.

[10] The possibility that status entails economic rewards is inconsistent with our (implicit) assumption that conferring status is costless to the provider. Social rewards are an operative mechanism for resolving externalities only if the provision of status is relatively cheap or unavoidable. Otherwise, giving respect becomes a strategic decision and it is difficult to avoid the free rider problem.

money, but has properties peculiar to itself. For an individual, status in the eyes of one individual may mean little, but status in the eyes of another means much." To incorporate such considerations in a simple way, imagine that individuals move in two separate spheres. In the economic sphere, they meet and engage in economic activities that become public information. In the social sphere, they meet and engage in transfer of prestige. Meetings in each sphere are random and independent.[11] In this case, if only socially minded individuals are willing to confer prestige, or if one cares only about the opinion of socially minded individuals, the utility functions may be rewritten as

$$u_i = m_i + \xi_i q\sigma\left(e_i - e^a\right) \tag{12}$$

The marginal social reward, as seen by a socially minded individual with $\xi = 1$, is now given by $q\sigma$. That is, the importance of status in motivating effort is increasing with the proportion of socially minded individuals in the population, $q$. Such a reformulation affects our results in the following manner: For $\sigma < \beta - \gamma$, it is still true that in every match the equilibrium effort is $(0, 0)$ and the monetary payoffs are $(\alpha, \alpha)$, irrespective of the types of the matched players. For $\beta - \gamma < \sigma < \alpha - \delta$, it is still true that the only evolutionarily stable equilibrium is with $q = 1$. However, for $\sigma > \alpha - \delta$, the only stable equilibrium is at $q = (\alpha - \delta)/\sigma$. That is, at high levels of $\sigma$, the population includes, in the steady state, individuals of both types. Type 0 players gain fitness whenever $q$ is high and type 1 players exert effort indiscriminately. However, type 1 players are not driven away, because they reduce their effort as their proportion declines and then gain fitness.[12] Finally, for any $\sigma$, there is a sufficiently low $q$ that the society may be trapped for a while in a low effort equilibrium.[13] This is because when $q$ is small, $q\sigma$ will be sufficiently small to retain the basic prisoner's dilemma structure of the game, as in part (i) of Proposition 1.

The reason for the different predictions of the two formulations is easy to identify. Under one formulation status is provided by the whole society independently of the distribution of types in the society. That is, even if almost all individuals in society are asocial and do not care about

---

[11] In practice, the social and economic spheres are not separate in this sense, as exemplified by the professions.

[12] Because of discontinuities, $dq/dt$ is not defined at $q = (\alpha - \delta)/\sigma$. However, local stability is maintained by the fact that $dq/dt$ is negative (positive) at slightly higher (lower) values of $q$.

[13] Strictly speaking, this is not an evolutionarily stable equilibrium, because no $q$ in this region is locally stable. Therefore, a sequence of shocks, where in each shock the number of socially minded individuals rises slightly, can pull the economy out of this region.

their own status, still, for those few who care, the marginal social reward remains the same, and their choice of effort is not affected. (The level of utility is influenced by the distribution of types through its effect on average effort, but this has no impact on choices.) Under the alternative formulation, the distribution of types in society affects the social rewards function and influences the choice of effort by the socially minded individuals.

## 5    Education, effort, and status

It is well established that education is closely associated with status. Educated individuals and members of occupations with a large proportion of educated individuals enjoy high prestige. To understand these links fully, one must allow workers to differ in ability, and occupations to differ in the demand for educated workers (see Fershtman, Murphy, and Weiss 1996). However, even in the confines of our simple framework, where individuals differ only in their preference for status, we can explain how workers are sorted into different occupations (schooling groups) on the basis of their demand for status.

We now modify the simple model of section 2, assuming that, before being matched, each person can decide whether to obtain education or not. Education is viewed here as a costly action that enhances the individual's own productivity. Matched individuals engage in the same game as before, except that, if they obtain education, their monetary payoffs are given by $\mu P_i(e_i, e_j)$, where $\mu > 1$. The cost of acquiring education is denoted by $c$. The salient feature is that the expected returns to schooling depend on the efforts exerted by the two players in prospective matches. In order to make the problem interesting we assume that $(\mu - 1)\gamma > c > (\mu - 1)\alpha$, so that schooling will be acquired in a population where all players exert effort but will not be undertaken if all players exert no effort. Under this assumption, the incentives to invest in schooling depend on the preference profile in society, represented by $q$.

We are interested in the correlation between preferences and education. In particular, can the demand for status induce investment in schooling? One can always generate such a correlation, simply by adding to this model the feature that education directly provides social status. Casual observation suggests that this is indeed the case. The point that we wish to make, however, is that such a direct social reward for schooling is not necessary to obtain a correlation between status-oriented preferences and investment in education. It is sufficient for effort to be socially rewarded to create such a correlation, because effort and investment decisions interact.

Following our previous analysis of the three possible ranges of the marginal social reward for effort, let us examine, first, the case in which $\sigma$ is relatively small, i.e., $\sigma < \beta - \gamma$. In such a case, any matching between two individuals, regardless of their type, will yield an equilibrium in which both players exert no effort and obtain the payoffs $(\alpha, \alpha)$. If an individual of type 0 invests in education, his expected returns are $\mu\alpha - c$, while without education he gets $\alpha$. Since we assume that $c > (\mu - 1)\alpha$, such an individual is better off not investing in education. For $\sigma < \beta - \gamma$, the considerations of a type 1 individual are the same and he, too, will not acquire education.

Consider, next, the intermediate range of $\sigma$, where $\beta - \gamma < \sigma < \alpha - \delta$. In such a case, a type 0 individual will get $\alpha$ in any possible matching and, as explained, will not acquire education. An individual of type 1 will acquire education if

$$(\mu - 1)\big[q\lambda\gamma + (1 - q\lambda)\alpha\big] > c \tag{13}$$

The education decision depends on $q\lambda$, that is, on the percentage of type 1 individuals in the society and on the probability of getting the cooperative outcome when two type 1 players are matched. If both of these probabilities are sufficiently high, then a positive correlation between education and preferences for social status arises. Type 1 individuals invest in education, while type 0 individuals do not. An interesting implication of this separation is that the relative fitness of type 1 individuals is higher than in the case without investment options. On the basis of our previous analysis, we can conclude that, in the range $\beta - \gamma < \sigma < \alpha - \delta$, the only evolutionarily stable population is one in which all individuals are socially minded, i.e., $q = 1$.

When $\sigma > \alpha - \delta$, the equilibrium fitness of an asocial individual is always higher than that of a socially minded individual, and, therefore, he has greater incentive to invest in education. Both types will obtain education if $(\mu - 1)[q\gamma + (1 - q)\delta] > c$; only type 0 individuals get education if $(\mu - 1)[q\beta + (1 - q)\alpha] > c > (\mu - 1)[q\gamma + (1 - q)\delta]$; and both types will not obtain education if $(\mu - 1)[q\beta + (1 - q)\alpha] < c$. Since, for $\sigma > \alpha - \delta$, the only evolutionarily stable situation is that all individuals are of type 0, i.e., $q = 0$, in the long run no one invests in education.

## 6    On the formation of social status functions

The main concern in this chapter has been the possibility of having an evolutionarily stable society in which individuals care about what other people think about them and act in a cooperative manner. Thus far, we have assumed a given social status function and investigated its implications. In particular, we have shown that if the marginal social rewards are sufficiently high, but not excessive, then an equilibrium in which individuals cooperate is evolutionarily stable. But how does a social status function which satisfies these requirements emerge?

The evolution of social norms, which are represented here by the marginal social reward $\sigma$, is influenced by two distinct forces: the voluntary adoption by individuals of different norms of behavior and the relative success of individuals who adopt such norms. This chapter has been concerned only with the second force; we now wish to discuss the first force briefly.

The voluntary adaptation of modes of behavior or cultural traits may occur by imitation within a society or by migration among societies. As economists, we can probably say more on the process of migration. Having determined the implications of a given social status function for an isolated society, we can calculate the expected utility for each type in different societies and predict the direction of the migration flows. We model migration as a voluntary individual decision, based on the expected *utility*, which takes into account status considerations, in addition to economic costs and benefits.[14] However, the reproduction rate of each type within each society is determined by (relative) economic fitness.

In this exposition we shall mainly be concerned with the case where migration is much faster than evolution. In such a world, a society cannot survive if there is another society where individuals of both types enjoy higher utility. In addition, a steady state must have the property that, in each society, the net migration flow and net reproduction rate must be *both* zero. Let us now examine which kind of societies (that is, which values of $\sigma$) can coexist in a steady state. For this analysis, it is convenient to assume that status depends on the number of socially minded individuals (as in section 4) and that mixed strategies are allowed.

Consider, first, two societies $a$ and $b$, with different values of $\sigma$, such that $\sigma_a < \sigma_b$ and $\beta - \gamma < \sigma_i < \alpha - \delta$, for $i = a, b$. Assuming that both societies are in an evolutionarily stable equilibrium, we know that $q_a = q_b = 1$. If players are allowed to play mixed strategies, then type 1 players in society $i$, $i = a, b$, will choose, in equilibrium, to exert effort with probability

$$p_i = \frac{(\alpha - \delta) - \sigma_1}{(\alpha - \delta) - (\beta - \gamma)} \tag{14}$$

[14] See Young (1996) for a model of evolutionary formation of norms. Migration has been introduced in a related context by Bowles and Gintis (1996), who consider societies which differ in the cost of identifying cooperative behavior.

and enjoy the expected utility

$$u_i^1 = p_i\big[p_i\gamma + (1 - p_i)\delta\big] + (1 - p_i)\big[p_i\beta + (1 - p_i)\alpha\big] \quad (15)$$

Note that, in equilibrium, utility coincides with fitness because all individuals in each society are identical (i.e., type 1). The expected utility of type 1 players, $u_i^1$, is a convex function of the probability of choosing high effort, $p_i$, attaining a maximum at $p_i = 1$. As seen in (14), in a mixed-strategy equilibrium, $p_i$ is *decreasing* in $\sigma_i$ (otherwise, the players will not mix the two actions). Thus, for every $\sigma_b$ there is a $\sigma_a$ sufficiently close to $\beta - \gamma$ that $u_a^1 > u_b^1$. Therefore, socially minded individuals will prefer to migrate to the society with lower $\sigma$. Thus, in the intermediate region, only a society with the lowest marginal reward, i.e., $\sigma = \beta - \gamma$, can survive.[15]

Consider, next, two societies $a$ and $b$, with different values of $\sigma$, such that $\sigma_a < \sigma_b$ and $\sigma_i > \alpha - \delta$, for i = $a$, $b$. Assuming that both societies are in an evolutionarily stable equilibrium, we have $q_i = (\alpha - \delta)/\sigma_i$. Evaluating the utilities of the two types in steady state, we obtain

$$u_i^1 = q_i\gamma + (1 - q_i)\delta + \sigma_i q_i(1 - q_i) = q_i\gamma + (1 - q_i)\alpha \quad (16)$$

and

$$u_i^0 = q_i\beta + (1 - q_i)\alpha \quad (17)$$

It is seen that the utility levels of both types increase in $q_i$ and, therefore, decline in $\sigma_i$. It follows that all individuals, irrespective of type, will migrate to the society with the lower $\sigma$. Thus, in the upper region, only the society with the lower marginal reward, $\sigma = \alpha - \delta$, can survive.[16]

Consider, finally, two societies $a$ and $b$, such that $\sigma_a < \beta - \gamma$ and $\sigma_b > \alpha - \delta$. Assuming that society $b$ is in an evolutionarily stable equilibrium, the expected utilities of the two types, given by (16) and (17), exceed $\alpha$. Society $a$ is evolutionarily unstable, in the sense that $q_a$ is undetermined, but for any $q_a$ both types have an expected utility of only $\alpha$. Therefore, individuals of both types in society $a$ will migrate to society $b$. Thus, a society in which status is negligible cannot survive in the long run.

It remains to compare the societies $a$ and $b$ such that $\sigma_a = \beta - \gamma$ and $\sigma_b = \alpha - \delta$. In this case, $q_a = q_b = 1$ and $u_a^1 = u_b^1 = \gamma$. Thus, socially minded individuals, who are the only prevailing type, are indifferent between the two societies. Further analysis suggests that this situation is locally stable and both societies can coexist. Imagine that, for some reason, there is an

---

[15] Observe that the condition $\sigma = \beta - \gamma$ implies that a socially minded individual is indifferent between effort and no effort if his rival exerts effort.

[16] Observe that the condition $\sigma = \alpha - \gamma$ implies that a socially minded individual is indifferent between effort and no effort if his rival exerts no effort.

injection of a small number of asocial individuals into society $a$. Holding $\sigma_a$ and $\sigma_b$ constant, individuals of type 1 in society $a$ will stop to exert effort and can expect a utility of only $\alpha$. Some type 1 players will, therefore, migrate to society $b$, where they expect to obtain $\gamma$. The type 0 players will also migrate to society $b$, where they expect a payoff of $\beta$. After this migration, type 1 players in society $b$ will start discriminating against type 0 players. Therefore, the number of type 0 players will start to decline. Alternatively, consider an injection of asocial individuals into society $b$. These new players have no incentive to move to society $a$, where they expect a payoff of only $\alpha$. However, socially minded individuals will now migrate from $b$ to $a$. Again, the changing mix in society $b$ will cause type 1 players to discriminate against type 0 players, and the number of asocial individuals will decline. We thus see that a small injection of asocial players in any society causes the socially minded individuals to migrate. The implied reduction in the fitness of the asocial players restores the original equilibrium. We conclude the following:

*Proposition 2:* If socially minded individuals care only about the opinion of other socially minded individuals and if migration is free, then the only societies which may survive in the long run are such that status is neither too high nor too low, yielding higher fitness to the socially minded individuals.

## 7    Concluding remarks

The effectiveness of social rewards requires that at least some individuals in society care about the opinions of their fellow individuals. The problem, however, is that socially minded individuals who care about social status may have lower fitness than asocial individuals who selfishly maximize their fitness and, therefore, will be eventually driven out by evolutionary forces. In this chapter, we identified a potential evolutionary advantage for the socially minded individuals, derived from an impact on the behavior of other individuals whom they meet and with whom they engage in economic interaction.

In our model, the only way a person who cares about status can gain fitness is by inducing his rivals in economic interactions to select actions that are beneficial to his fitness. This idea is quite distinct from a possible *direct* effect of status on fitness, based on *economic benefits* that high social status may entail. Clearly, if social status directly influences fitness, then social rewards are much more effective, but in such a case one escapes the prisoner's dilemma only by falling into the jaws of the free rider problem. We have therefore maintained the assumption that providing prestige to others does not detract economic resources from the giver nor directly provide resources to the receiver.

The main conclusion of this chapter is that social status *can* serve as a social reward mechanism. However, the simple examples analyzed in this chapter illustrate that considerations of economic fitness (and competition) severely limit the effectiveness of social status as a social reward mechanism. In particular, socially minded preferences are evolutionarily stable only if social rewards are neither excessive nor negligible. If individuals can move freely across societies with different status functions, then only societies with social rewards in the intermediate range survive.

REFERENCES

Bagwell, L. S., and B. D. Bernheim (1996). "Veblen Effects in a Theory of Conspicuous Consumption," *American Economic Review* 86(3): 349–73.

Basu, K. (1995). "Civil Institutions and Evolution: Concepts, Critique and Models," *Journal of Development Economics* 46(1): 19–33.

Bernheim, B. D. (1994). "A Theory of Conformity," *Journal of Political Economy* 102(5): 841–77.

Bester, H., and W. Guth (1997, forthcoming). "Is Altruism Evolutionarily Stable?" *Journal of Economic Behavior and Organization*.

Bowles S., and H. Gintis (1996). "Optimal Parochialism." Mimeo, University of Massachusetts.

Dekel, E., and S. Scotchmer (1994). "On the Evolution of Attitudes Towards Risk in Winner-Take-All Games." Mimeo.

Coleman, S. J. (1990). *Foundations of Social Theory*. Cambridge, Mass.: Harvard University Press.

Corneo, G., and O. Jeanne (1995a). "Adam Smith's Second Invisible Hand." Discussion Paper No. A-492, University of Bonn.

Corneo, G., and O. Jeanne (1995b). "Status-Seeking Can Generate Long Run Growth in the Solow Cass Model." Discussion Paper No. A-497, University of Bonn.

Fershtman, C., and K. Judd, (1987). "Equilibrium Incentives in Oligopoly," *American Economic Review* 77(5): 927–40.

Fershtman, C., K. M. Murphy, and Y. Weiss (1996). "Social Status, Education and Growth," *Journal of Political Economy* 104(1): 108–32.

Fershtman, C., and Y. Weiss (1993). "Social Status, Culture and Economic Performance," *Economic Journal* 103: 946–59.

Fershtman, C., and Y. Weiss (1996). "Social Rewards, Externalities and Stable Preferences." Working Paper No. 17–96, Tel Aviv University.

Frank, R. H. (1987). "If Homo Economicus Could Choose His Own Utility Function, Would He Want One with a Conscience?" *American Economic Review* 77(4): 593–604.

Hammerstein, P., and R. Selten (1994). "Game Theory and Evolutionary Biology," in R. J. Aumann and S. Hart, eds., *Handbook of Game Theory with Economic Applications*, Vol. 2, 929–93. Amsterdam: Elsevier.

Hirshleifer, J. (1980). "Privacy: Its Origin, Function, and Future," *Journal of Legal Studies* 9: 649–64.

Maynard Smith, J. (1982). *Evolution and the Theory of Games*. Cambridge: Cambridge University Press.

Okuno-Fujiwara, M., and A. Postlewaite (1995). "Social Norms in Random Matching Games," *Games and Economic Behavior* 9: 79–109.

Robson, J. A. (1992). "Status, the Distribution of Wealth, Private and Social Attitudes to Risk," *Econometrica* 60(4): 837–57.

———(1996). "A Biological Basis for Expected and Non-expected Utility," *Journal of Economic Theory* 68(2): 397–424.

Rogers, A. R. (1994). "Evolution of Time Preference by Natural Selection," *American Economic Review* 84(3): 460–81.

Weibull, J. W. (1995). *Evolutionary Game Theory*. Cambridge Mass.: MIT Press.

Young, H. P. (1996). "Social Coordination and Social Change." Mimeo. Johns Hopkins University.

CHAPTER 5

# Starting with nothing: on the impossibility of grounding norms solely in self-interest

*Jane Mansbridge*

> To examine the process whereby norms are internalized is to enter waters that
> are treacherous for a theory grounded on rational choice.
>
> James Coleman 1990, p. 292

Two trends within the discipline of economics have produced a recent focus on values, in contrast to self-interest. The first trend takes seriously the role of institutions (e.g., the firm) in shaping economic behavior. The second applies economic forms of analysis to traditionally noneconomic venues. Both trends have revealed that predicting behavior in firms, political systems, and families requires, even more strongly than in the market, taking account of values other than self-interest. Yet for scholars trained in economics or game theory, the temptation is to derive values themselves from self-interest. The goal is to "start with nothing" – that is, nothing but self-interest and rationality.

This enterprise is as old as the beginning of written philosophy. If, as some speculate, this kind of theorizing in ancient Athens was particularly characteristic of the democrats, it may have been less likely to be preserved in the aristocrats' private libraries. Whatever the reason, today we have only fragments of pre-Socratic thinking. We must try to reconstruct what the various pre-Socratic schools believed primarily through the refutations of their opponents, Plato, Aristotle, and Xenophon. We can be fairly sure, however, that some of the pre-Socratic theorists tried to base morality primarily (or totally) on self-interest, and politics on a social contract of self-interested individuals.[1]

---

[1] For social contract thinking, see Aristotle, *Politics* iii.1280b10 and 1280b29; for hints of a moral theory based on self-interest, see Glaucon and Thrasymachus in Plato's *Republic* 358E–359B. 359–61. 338C ff. The suggestion that these ideas are intimately connected with democratic thinking derives from Havelock (1957/1964) and is highly speculative. The tradition of grounding morality in self-interest continued with the Roman

Against this long-standing contention that human values can be derived ultimately only from self-interest, I will outline the evidence for including in our analyses of the evolution of norms[2] the three components of innate emotions, innate cognitive capacities and limitations, and the internal logic of a norm. I conclude that societies will need to invest less effort in creating an effective norm if they build on innate emotional proclivities, innate cognitive capacities, and the characteristic internal structure of existing master norms. I then suggest that concern, or love, for others is innate to the human animal and that commitment to what one ought to do, or duty, is a primordial human response to human interaction. Neither the reaction to concern for another that results in helping the other nor the reaction to the promptings of duty that results in self-sacrifice can adequately be captured by the word "self-interest."

### Building blocks for norms

As yet we know little about the innate character of those human emotions that can be pressed into service for the creation and policing of social norms. Robert Frank (1988) has argued persuasively that certain emotions, which may either be directly innate or result from innate capacities to form deeply ingrained habits, produce behavior patterns that are not easily susceptible to rational control. These emotions send signals (often costly signals) on which others can rely in predicting behavior. These emotions also prompt the people who experience them to act in ways that in a less emotional state they conclude was not good for them. Among these emotions, Frank considers particularly useful for creating and policing social norms the desire for revenge, strong emotional commitments to the norms of fairness, and concern for other human beings.

Most research on the innate character of such emotions has focused on concern for other human beings. Hoffman (1981, pp. 129–130), for example, provides evidence that newborn infants cry more frequently in response to hearing the cries of other newborns than to hearing equally loud and noxious sounds, including computer-simulated infant cries. By

Greek Epictetus in the first century and flourished in Western Europe from the seventeenth century to the present. For brief histories of the interpretation of human action according to self-interest alone, see Mansbridge (1990a), Batson (1991), and Monroe (1996).

[2] Because I will be analyzing the process of internalizing norms, I will use the word "norm," often reserved for a social convention (external to the individual actor), interchangeably with the word "value," often reserved for a normative commitment (internal to an actor).

the time children are two, they respond to distress in others by trying to comfort the distressed, often in consequentially inappropriate ways. A child will pat a crying baby on the head or offer him a toy (Radke-Yarrow and Zahn-Wexler 1984). Mothers in turn seem to be equipped with hormones that, particularly in the first days after a child's birth, make them particularly protective of that child.

If we set out to explain how norms develop, it makes sense to build into that analysis whatever innate tendencies to help or hurt others we can identify, on the grounds that these capacities and tendencies are resources on which social institutions can draw, just as economies draw on the natural resources of a geographical region. Yet James Coleman (1990, pp. 296 ff.), for example, tries to map out the processes that produce internalized norms by simply comparing the costs to the norm creator of producing the punishments and rewards that establish the internalization of a norm to the benefits to that norm creator of having the norm internalized. One would expect the accuracy of his predictions to be diminished by not including in the predictive equation any factors other than the costs to the norm creator of trying to get the other to internalize the norm.

Among our internalized norms are norms of patriotism, team spirit, familial responsibility, and friendship that rest in part on an affective decision that the good of others will count in one's utility as much as, or more than, one's own material welfare. Accuracy in predicting the emergence of such norms (see Coleman 1990, pp. 158–62, 518–20, on "affine agency") is likely to be diminished if we cannot consider possibly innate factors such as kinship (including the sharing of genes), perceived likeness between self and others, and perceived threat to one's group by others perceived as unlike. Empirical studies of the innate human tendency to make the good of others our own are in their infancy, but we may expect experimental and developmental psychology, neuroscience, and evolutionary biology to produce more evidence on this score in the near future.[3] In the meantime, we should not neglect the possibility that

---

[3] For primate behavior, e.g., chimpanzees helping nonkin with food and rescue in situations unlikely to be reciprocated, see Wilson (1970/1979, p. 30) and Goodall (1986, p. 378). This behavior might derive from an overgeneralization of reciprocal altruism (Alexander 1987). For brain studies see Panksepp (1989). For a comparison of identical and fraternal twins on questionnaire reports of altruism, suggesting that from 56 to 72 percent of the variance might be of genetic origin, see Rushton (1986). For possible genetic tendencies to favor like individuals, see Rushton (1989) with critics. Batson (1991) (discussed later) demonstrates that helping behavior derives from many different sources. For this reason, among others, we would expect the behaviors typed as altruistic on a questionnaire (e.g., Rushton 1986) to derive from different sources as well; one would not expect a single "altruism gene," but rather a repertory of genetic capacities on

societies may draw upon such innate tendencies as important building blocks in constructing their norms.

Similarly, human agents engaged in constructing norms have at their disposal a variety of innate human cognitive capacities and deficiencies. For example, innate cognitive capacities dispose human beings to see some things more easily than others. If we are "hard-wired" to notice deviations from the usual (a capacity perhaps developed as a protection against danger) or to distinguish subtle features of human physiognomy (allowing considerable differential recognition), one would expect societies to make use of these capacities in constructing in-group and out-group norms. As the relevant human sciences begin to delineate human cognitive capacities and limitations, it makes sense to begin to integrate their findings into our understanding of how societies construct norms.

Finally, some of our ways of thinking have an internal logic that "commands" assent. Once a human group has created an elaborated number system (as opposed to systems that allocate only into the four categories "one," "two," "three," and "many"), the statement "two plus two equals four" commands assent. The norm of justice may have a similar internal logic.

Isaiah Berlin (1955–56) has pointed out that the very concept of a rule requires equality among the units within the categories of that rule. If a rule specifies that first sons inherit the property of the father, and if I am a first son who does not inherit that property or if the property goes to someone who is not a first son, I can rightly claim unfairness. In both cases, I can claim that the rule has not been properly applied, and that claim will rightly command assent. It is inherent to the meaning of a "rule" that within its categories units are to be treated equally.

A rule has this logical structure in largely particularistic societies as well as in more universalistic societies. If the norm is that no women can milk cows and no men can prepare skins (Murdoch and Provost 1973, table 8), the embedded rule treats all women equally except when a relevant reason can be given for the exception. As a consequence, arguments regarding a rule will be about whether the rule applies in particular circumstances, whether a given individual is accurately described by the categories of the rule, and what the reasons are for establishing the

which cultural processes can draw. Heritability can also be indirect, causing an environment which then causes the behavior. If adults in a given culture were particularly nurturant to red-haired, blue-eyed children with symmetric features, and if nurturant adult behavior fostered altruistic behavior in a child, then one would expect altruistic behavior to be passed on "via" the genes for red hair. See Ben-Ner and Putterman (this volume) for possible relations between genes and culture.

categories. Implicitly, the burden of proof is on those who would estab-lish the category boundaries. As soon as the rationale for the category boundaries falls, equality reigns within the new, larger category. Equal-ity, Berlin argues, is the conceptual default position in any rule.

Another candidate for an internal normative logic might be the proce-dural justice inherent in the device, applicable only among free and equal individuals, of letting one individual cut a cake and the other choose. Wherever individuals are normatively held to be free and equal, the fairness of such a procedure may well command assent (cf. Rawls 1971). Its internal logic may follow what Binsmore (this volume) labels "our inbuilt sense of justice." There might also be an internal logic to the practice of speech, involving the assumption that on some level the participants are trying to reach understanding (Habermas 1974/1979).

When a proposition – such as that within categories of a rule units are to be treated equally – commands assent, societies will find it easier to establish social norms congruent with that internal logic than to establish norms incongruent with it.

## Love and duty as primordial and distinct from "self-interest"

Among the emotional and cognitive resources available to the human psyche, two have particular relevance to the study of the relation be-tween values and institutions. The first is the capacity, indeed perhaps the compulsion, to make another's good one's own, which I will call "love."[4] The second is the capacity to act against one's preferences on the grounds that one ought so to act, which I will call "duty."[5] Together these form the primary prosocial nonegoistic motives.

Some writers (e.g., Smith 1759/1984; Dawes, van de Kragt, and Orbell 1990) claim that love is the only truly nonegoistic motive. They consider duty, or following one's conscience, no more than placating a "socially instilled" inner desire. Other writers (e.g., Kant 1785/1949, pp. 15–16; Sen 1978/1990) claim, to the contrary, that duty is the only truly nonegoistic motive. They consider love, or making another's good one's own, a case in which a person's "sense of well-being is psychologically dependent on someone else's welfare," whereas "commitment [duty] does involve, in a very real sense, counterpreferential choice" (Sen 1978/

---

[4] I have borrowed the term from Jon Elster (1990). Others give this faculty the name "affection" (Hume), "sympathy" (Sen 1978/1990), "empathy" (Jencks 1990), "we-feeling" (Dawes, van de Kragt, and Orbell 1990), or "affine agency" (Coleman 1990).

[5] Again I borrow the term from Elster (1990). Others have called this capacity "principle" (Hume), "commitment" (Sen 1978/1990), "morality" (Jencks 1990), or "conscience" (Dawes, van de Kragt, and Orbell 1990).

1990, pp. 32, 33). Finally, some writers claim that neither love nor duty is truly nonegoistic. I will argue against all three of these positions that both love and duty contrast with self-interest and cannot be reduced to it.

One form of the reduction of duty and love to self-interest is tautological, defining "choice" as any "attempt to select an alternative that will enhance one's welfare." Any action one chooses then by definition advances one's welfare and is hence in one's self-interest (Kennett 1980). One can treat this reduction of love and duty to self-interest as no more than a semantic move, albeit one with pernicious consequences.[6] A semantic move prompts a semantic response, pointing out that if we call all behavior "self-interested," we lose the meaningful distinction, important for moral praise and blame, between "selfish" and "unselfish" behavior. To prevent this loss, we must distinguish between "selfish self-interest" (or "narrow self-interest") and "unselfish self-interest," a cumbersome pair of locutions that begs linguistically for the kind of canceling we do on fractions, reducing for simplicity the mouthful of words involved in "selfish self-interest" and "unselfish self-interest" to the simple denominators "self-interest" and "unselfishness."

Another form of the claim is more substantive, claiming that although many actions seem altruistically motivated, those actions are actually motivated by desires for status, recognition, reciprocity, or avoiding others' resentment. As theorists with training in game theoretic or economic modeling expand the project of basing value systems on self-interest alone (e.g., Coleman 1990; Sugden, this volume), their work heightens the importance of making a substantive, as well as a semantic, case against reduction to self-interest. I make this substantive case here by arguing that in the creation of norms, altruistic impulses, commitments to duty, and agreement to the logic of a moral argument have an effect independent of desires for status, reciprocity, or the effects – long and short run – on avoiding others' resentment.

In regard to love, or we-feeling, we already have, as indicated earlier, some evidence for the innate attachment of human beings to others of their species and particularly to their children. Psychologists may also someday find evidence for an innate tendency to cathect onto a group of which one finds oneself a part. At the moment we know that in England, the United States, and a few other countries in which the experiments have been run, individuals tend to favor their group against others even

---

[6] Why pernicious? Human beings are more likely to act unselfishly after being exposed to models of unselfish behavior. Interpreting all nonegoistic behavior as egoistic reduces the degree to which the readers of those interpretations are exposed to unselfish behavior. Therefore, interpreting nonegoistic behavior as egoistic diminishes a powerful incentive to unselfish behavior. This in turn reduces the likelihood of human cooperation. See Mansbridge (1990b).

when the "group" of which they are a member has been created by no more than a toss of a coin. In the "minimal group experiments" that demonstrate this tendency (Brewer and Kramer 1986), individuals usually distribute goods unequally to favor their group rather than distribute equally, even though an equal distribution would increase the total to be distributed. The suggestion that the group favoritism displayed in these experiments might be innate derives from the minimality of the stimulus (including the toss of a coin, chosen for its culturally symbolic depiction of pure randomness) creating the group (such as "the heads group" or "the tails group") that triggers the group-favoring reaction. Perceptions of likeness leading to greater cooperation can also be triggered by such trivial events as sharing a birthday (Miller, Downs, and Prentice forthcoming). Norms prescribing self-sacrifice or loyalty to one's group undoubtedly draw in part upon the character of such impulses.

It is notoriously difficult to explain the emergence and survival of self-sacrifice when individuals sacrifice their interests for the good of others who have little or no genetic relation to them.[7] We may require a theory in which an innate tendency to make one's own the good of others perceived as like is coupled in some way with traits that favor reproduction (cf. Boyd and Richerson 1990 on dual evolution). Robert Frank (1988, 1990) shows how people motivated by altruistic impulses can be, if observably different from others, more attractive as partners in voluntary ventures that require trustworthy commitment. Observable differences allow potential cooperators to choose to interact selectively with one another, reaping the rewards of cooperation and depriving more narrowly self-interested individuals of those rewards. Altruistic behavior stemming from innate impulses might be protected from extinction by the dynamic Frank describes. Innate impulses to empathy and love (even on a collective scale) seem to exist; the mystery is to explain their emergence and survival.[8] That these impulses often produce praise and help generate social norms is not so hard to understand.

---

[7] Darwin pointed out more than one hundred years ago that "the bravest men, who were always willing to come to the front in war, and who freely risked their lives for others, would on an average perish in larger numbers than other men" (1871, i, p. 163, cited in Cronin 1991, p. 327).

[8] Batson (1991, pp. 210–11) suggests that the impulse to altruism can cross species, as when a dog risks his life to save a human being in contexts where reciprocity, or the preservation of future sources of food and care, seems a highly unlikely motivation. See Frank (1988), Mansbridge (1990b), Ben-Ner and Putterman (this volume), and Bowles and Gintis (this volume) for the ancestral settings and current institutional arrangements that might promote the survival and reproductive success of cooperators. In comments at the conference from which the chapters in this volume derived, Charles Perrow added to Bowles and Gintis's optimal parochialism the consideration that networks of small units

The psychologist Daniel Batson has done the most persuasive work on love, or "altruism," which he defines as "a motivational state with the ultimate goal of increasing another's welfare" (Batson 1991, p. 6).[9] He explicitly distinguishes this state from (1) helping behavior, (2) helping in order to gain external and internal rewards or avoid external and internal punishment (for example, guilt), and (3) helping in order to "reduce aversive arousal caused by witnessing another's suffering" (pp. 44–45). He postulates that in true altruism, "attachment" (otherwise called "love, caring, feeling close, we-feeling, or bonding" [p. 85]) leads to adopting the other's perspective, which is a precondition for arousing empathetic emotion, which in turn produces helping behavior if helping is (1) possible, (2) perceived to be positive for the recipient, and (3) perceived to be more positive than having someone else help.

In a series of cleverly designed experiments, Batson has gone a long way toward disproving the contention that all "altruistic" behavior can be explained by the desires to avoid unpleasant feelings or self-punishment or to gain social approval, a sense of efficacy, or shared pleasure. He first eliminated the aversive-arousal reduction hypothesis by making it easy in one condition of the different experiments for subjects to escape from the situation, then showing that when escape was easy those feeling high empathy for a person in need tended to help that person, whereas those with low empathy tended to choose escape. He eliminated the social approval hypothesis by showing that high empathy subjects helped no less even when no one else would know how they acted, whereas those with low empathy helped more when others would know of their action than when others would not. He eliminated the self-punishment hypothesis by showing that high empathy subjects helped even when they had information justifying not helping, whereas those with low empathy helped primarily when no such information was provided. He eliminated the personal efficacy hypothesis by showing that

---

might provide the most efficient institutional protection, because networks have low information costs but the potential for greater amassed wealth and power. Paul Di Maggio added that altruists might benefit from relatively impermeable enclave boundaries, because social sanctions are most effective in bounded situations that are costly to escape. Bowles made the point that social incentives work not only directly but also through mimicking, because people who are well thought of are more likely to be copied. David Messick pointed out that patterns of reciprocity among vampire bats depend on the bats' ability to recognize those individuals who had benefited them in the past.

[9] Monroe (1996, p. 8) adds the condition that "the act must carry some possibility of diminution in my own welfare." This condition is much disputed in the literature.

high empathy subjects had much more positive mood changes when the victim received relief provided by others than when the victim received only relief provided by the subjects themselves. Finally, he eliminated the hypothesis that empathetic altruists want to share in the joy of the one helped by showing that high empathy subjects, but not low empathy subjects, maintained their levels of helping even when they knew they would not learn the results of their efforts. (Low empathy subjects also helped more the more they thought the welfare of those they were helping would improve, whereas high empathy subjects helped at high rates no matter what the likelihood of improvement.)[10]

In non-experimental field research Kristen Monroe (1996) also provides some evidence that altruistic acts cannot be explained fully by social rewards, feelings of efficacy, or even what she rightly calls the "frustratingly tautological" concept of psychic goods. In interviews with an exceptionally altruistic sample, of five Carnegie Heroes and ten rescuers of Jews during the Holocaust, she asked her interlocutors consciously to scrutinize the motivations for their acts. Their answers showed remarkable similarities. They also showed remarkable differences from the motivations given in her interviews with five philanthropists as well as with five millionaires who had almost all given some money and time to charitable works. Whereas the motivations for helping of the philanthropists and millionaires could be fairly easily characterized as having to do primarily with the desire for social rewards, feelings of efficacy ("participation altruism," or taking pleasure in causing another's good fortune), and psychic gratification (indicated in part by giving to causes when they could "see the payoff" [p. 144]), the heroes and rescuers seemed to have acted primarily from what Monroe characterizes as "canonical expectations" (settled expectations about what human behavior is right and proper) and a specific sense of self in relation to others. The most salient canonical expectation emerged in some version of saying that one had "no choice" about helping another human being in extreme need.[11] The

---

[10] Batson also moved toward eliminating the complicated hypothesis that empathetic altruists want to relieve (through an action of helping) the vicarious suffering they expect to continue to feel even after escaping from the situation. In two carefully designed experiments he was able to show that high empathy subjects gave statistically significantly as much help when they expected a subsequent external mood enhancement as when they did not (Batson 1991, table 10.11).

[11] Monroe defines a canonical expectation as the expectation of a "coherent sequence of actions and events in a given situation," involving both cognition and affect, stored in the actor's memory as scripts and schemas to guide behavior, thus explaining the "habitual

most salient component of identity was having a self-image in which the individual felt, in some sense, a part of all humanity.[12] These features cropped up repeatedly among the heroes and rescuers whom Monroe interviewed, less among the philanthropists, and far less among the entrepreneurs.

Like Batson, Monroe scrutinized at length competing explanations, specifically from economic theory, evolutionary biology, and psychology. She pressed her interviewees about their motivations, explicitly raising the possibility of social rewards, feelings of efficacy, and psychic goods. Far more than the answers of the philanthropists and millionaires, those of the heroes and rescuers suggested that such considerations may not have been particularly relevant to their actions. The spontaneity with which they made their decisions to act, their frequent sacrifice of the good of their families as well as themselves, the risks to their lives, the social condemnation they often faced by those (particularly other members of their families) who learned what they were doing, their frequent refusal of honors or even public mention for their actions, and their repeated insistence that what they had done was "Nothing special. No big deal" (1991, p. 145) and only "what anyone would have done," makes it hard to explain their motives in terms of social rewards, efficacy, or even "psychic gratification."[13]

---

altruism that is nonconscious or reflexive in origin, such as automatically helping the weak" (Monroe 1996, p. 13).

[12] Monroe (1996, pp. 202ff.). Monroe combines canonical expectations and identity into the concept of "perspective" (pp. 14–15, 198ff.).

[13] Monroe also explored one reward or sanction that Batson and some others would consider nonaltruistic – the feeling of guilt that might have accompanied nonaction. This motive seems less likely among the heroes, who often acted immediately and without reflection, than among the rescuers, who even if they began their commitments impulsively usually had time to think over their actions later and decide for or against future acts. With some rescuers, potential guilt at not living up to inner standards could have played a dispositive role in leading them to take extraordinary risks. Monroe attempted to explore this motivation by asking about guilt "for past wrongs," finding that "not one person in the sample said they acted to alleviate past guilt," and that the only person to whom the guilt explanation rang at all true was a philanthropist whose psychiatrist had told him he "suffered from a ghetto conscience" (1996, p. 149). This investigation would probably not have uncovered the guilt or lowered self-esteem people might feel for not having lived up to their own "canonical expectations," even if they seemed to feel no heightened self-esteem for having lived up to those expectations. Most convincing is her interview with Margot, a rescuer, to whom Monroe said that some people say "they didn't think they could live with themselves if they'd not helped Jews. Is that true for you?" Margot answered, "It has nothing to do with it. . . . You don't think about these things. You can't think about these things. It happened so quickly." The spontaneity of many rescuers' actions and this explicit rejection of the socially approved

Duty is, if anything, even harder to parse out than love. In addition to their capacities for empathy and love, all human beings seem to have a capacity for duty, that is, for willing themselves to do what they do not want but believe they ought to do. In every society we know, parents and the larger society teach their offspring what it means to fulfill their duty. Duties are not voluntarily acquired,[14] and individual identity is constituted partly through one's given duties (Sandel 1982).[15] In human history the duties one has to one's ancestors, one's gods, one's people, and one's family come first; more elaborated religions come second. Although one's duty can accord with feelings of love, the two can also conflict – as in the story of Abraham and Isaac in the Bible or of Arguna in the Bhagavadgita. Even Thomas Hobbes, who derived the content of natural laws from self-interest, recognized that logically, in the form in which he derived them, those laws were only the recommendations of prudence. To become duties, or "commands," they had to issue from the mouth of God (Hobbes 1651/1947; Warrender 1957).[16]

We have far fewer studies of duty than of love, perhaps because psychologists, who do the experimental work, have tended to define this motive as activity aimed at gaining "internal rewards" (Batson 1991, p. 44).[17] The idea that one's duty is external to the individual, a conceptualization central to the way most societies have described duties and most individuals have experienced them, does not often figure in these psychologically oriented ways of thinking.[18] Nor does the idea of

motivation of "not being able to live with myself" support Batson's rejection of the self-punishment hypothesis. In their more extensive quantitative study of rescuers, Oliner and Oliner (1988) also distinguish the two motives of sympathy and duty.

[14] Philosophers in the Anglo-American tradition have used the slight difference in the ordinary language connotations of the two words "duty" and "obligation" to make duty denote involuntary bonds and obligation voluntary ones (cf. Rawls 1971, p. 113 and accompanying notes).

[15] In many societies one's individual name conjures up dutiful relationships, as when members of a family have the same surname or when their surname specifies a familial relation (e.g., "Lavransdatter" or "Ben-Ner").

[16] See Kuran (this volume) for the point that even genetically based values, developed to address distinct problems, can conflict.

[17] Duties are also defined as "situation-specific behavioral expectations generated from one's own internalized values, backed by self-administered sanctions and rewards" (Schwartz and Howard 1982, p. 329, cited in Batson 1991, p. 45).

[18] At the end of his discussion of altruism, however, Batson (1991, pp. 198–99) devotes three important paragraphs to what he calls "an alternative interpretation: upholding moral principles" as ends in themselves, not as means to alleviate feelings of guilt. He categorizes this form of motivation as "neither egoistic nor altruistic: it is of a third, impersonal type," and points out that the reasons for helping Jews offered by rescuers refer often to the desire to uphold moral principles. Batson calls for further research on this motivation.

duty as constitutive of identity. Because even Anglo-American philosophy has tended to neglect duty in favor of voluntary obligation, an adequate study of duty might require collaboration among psychologists, philosophers, and scholars versed in non-Western thinking. Whether the particular cognitive capacities of human beings to perceive and act upon their sense of duty affects the evolution of norms is an area that has not yet been explored.

Most human beings, I conjecture, act from a complex combination of love and duty, as well as from self-interest, at almost every moment. The welfare mother who turns a trick to get the wherewithal to support her children is engaged in a complex negotiation of duty, love, and self-interest. So am I, as I write an article I hope will do others some good but at the same time brings me credit. Usually only in psychological experiments or extreme situations can one find the motivations in a relatively pure form. Deeply internalized norms that become part of one's own self-concept – norms to care for one's children, to do useful work, or to rescue vulnerable others – seem in most cases to have derived from complex mixtures of affective impulses and cognitive commitments. These deeply internalized norms are probably influenced not only by the evolution of social expectations but also by innate emotional proclivities, cognitive capacities, and even the internal logic of the norms themselves.

### The internal logic of justice in shaping moral norms

Regarding issues of justice, the analysis of values and institutions can usefully distinguish between merely social norms, the breach of which normally produces only irritation, and norms of justice or morality, the breach of which normally produces resentment. This distinction raises problems for Sugden (this volume), who argues for the evolution of moral norms from social conventions if the following conditions hold: (1) If one individual conforms to a convention, then it is in his/her interest that others conform to the same convention; (2) if one individual expects others to conform to a convention it is, in most cases, in his/her interest to conform to it, and (3) most people in the society expect most other people to conform to the convention. In these conditions, Sugden argues, those who conform to the convention will feel resentment against those who do not, and each person will "tend" to feel some desire to avoid that resentment (p. 82). In these kinds of cases, conventional practices will generate normative expectations, which will then evolve into "moral" norms.

Sugden's case relies heavily on the costs to an actor of the resentment of others. It goes beyond the standard utility-maximization approach not by adding avoidance of the sanctions of others, which is a standard move, but by assuming that those sanctions will flow automatically from the breaking of a convention when (1) there is a widespread expectation that people will conform to that convention and (2) there is a cost to "me" when "you" do not conform. The rationality of obeying the norm rests on avoiding the sanctions of those who will resent its being broken. Sugden's innovation lies in the assertion that those who experience the broken norm and incur a cost will impose sanctions automatically through their resentment.

But will I always feel resentment whenever there is a widespread expectation that people will conform to a convention and there is a cost to me when they do not conform? I think not. Resentment, as opposed to irritation, will occur only when, along with a social norm's being broken, that social norm contains some "moral" content. As Rawls (1970, p. 533) points out, "[R]esentment is a moral feeling. If we resent . . . it must be . . . the result of unjust institutions, or [morally] wrongful conduct." I am irritated at a cost to me, but I am resentful at that cost to me when I attribute to the action that produced the cost some (perhaps small) degree of unfairness.

Coleman (1990, p. 242) has described norms as specifying "what actions are regarded by a set of persons as proper or correct, or improper or incorrect." This language encompasses the full range of meaning of the term "norm," as Durkheim intended it. That is, it encompasses table manners and the color of socks among teenagers at a particular school. Moral norms are a subset of social norms. Any statement of approval or disapproval which applies to a general class of actions should thus be taken to be only a normative statement, not a moral statement. Within the larger class of normative statements, *moral* norms apply to matters of ethical rightness and *social* norms to matters of societal propriety.

Imagine that I am a new student at a high school. I notice on my first day at school that everyone is wearing white socks when I have black ones. I go home, throw out all my old black socks and buy myself ten pairs of white. I come back the next day wearing a pair of my new socks, only to find that the person at the next desk is wearing black socks exactly like the many pairs I just threw out. All of Sugden's conditions hold (because I have paid money for white socks and thrown out my black ones it is now in my interest that others conform to the same convention; if I expect others to conform to it, it is in most cases in my interest to conform to it; and most people in the society expect others to conform to it). But I am unlikely to feel resentment at my convention-breaking neighbor. I am more likely to feel irritation.

Consider, in contrast, the first-to-the-bridge example that Sugden raises. My reaction of resentment, rather than irritation, results from the fact that certain justice-based norms underlie the seemingly arbitrary convention of first-to-the-bridge. The first of these norms involves reciprocity: In the usual course of events, I will get to the bridge first this time, but you will get to it first the next time or at another random time. The reciprocity is, in turn, based on a version of the norm of equality. This is a first-come, first-served norm, which treats all drivers equally. In this case, the two cars are in a condition of equality; each can successfully block the other if both enter the bridge, and the reigning social system accords neither driver the legitimate social, political, or economic sanctions to force the other off.

One can imagine, for example, a host of other possible norms, such as that the car of the higher person in a hierarchy takes precedence, or that the right of continuous first passage is auctioned off to the highest bidder. But in our society, under the first-come, first-served norm that governs access to the bridge lie justice-based norms of equality and reciprocity that fuel the resentment experienced by whoever finds this particular version of the first-come, first-served norm violated to her cost. Another's breaking a social convention to one's cost creates irritation; breaking a convention perceived as *moral* or *fair* creates resentment.[19]

It is true that people can come to believe that what is expected is also intrinsically just. This process can develop in two ways. First, one's society can subscribe to a cosmology in which for most of the received universe whatever is is just. Certain traditional societies seem to have had world views with this characteristic, and in less traditional societies the concatenation of the "natural" and the "just" persists in many instances. Second, one can come to base one's behavior and investments on a set of expectations, the upsetting of which for no reasonable cause will accurately be perceived as unjust. The common law dubs such a situation "detrimental reliance" and often provides damages for its breach. In both cases of cosmology and detrimental reliance, however, arguments that the traditional ways are not in fact just and that reliance ought not to have been so heavily placed upon a particular expectation can reduce or even eliminate the conviction that justice inhered in an expectation. The reduction or elimination of the conviction of injustice then reduces or eliminates the likelihood of feeling resentment, rather than anger or irritation, at the act that upset one's expectation.

[19] In Sugden's example of the woman who leaves her seat with her coat on it, the same kind of first-come, first-served egalitarian rule also applies, just as with the bridge. That norm could have been, again, that whoever placed higher in a hierarchy could take the seat or that the seats would be at the disposition of the highest bidder.

Further research may reveal innate components of the impulse to express resentment, thereby inflicting a social sanction, or even innate components of the impulse actively to punish a transgressor perceived as having acted unjustly. Frank (1988) reports among late-twentieth-century Americans an ample willingness to sacrifice money, time, and emotional well-being in order to punish those who are perceived as acting unjustly, even in such trivial matters as selling beer on a beach at above what is perceived as the "just" price.

If we add justice-based considerations to mere expectation, we can see how conventions come under challenge when their underlying fairness comes under challenge. The Quakers, influenced by their strong religious belief that all were equal in God's eyes, refused to doff their caps to the king. Women, becoming conscious of the unequal distribution of the costs of familial altruism, began to challenge the conventional norm that females should provide most care. Much of the force of contemporary cultural and social criticism comes from uncovering the asymmetric beneficiaries of large numbers of social conventions, such as the convention that the "gender-neutral" pronoun be the word "his." Revealing that these social norms are not in fact neutral but violate the moral norm of equality is perceived by many as a prima facie reason for changing the existing social norms.

Distinguishing between social norms, which do not rest on any perception of justice and injustice, and moral norms, which do involve these deeper considerations, suggests that if an inefficient, Pareto-dominated equlibrium were generally perceived as not only inefficient but unjust, breaches of the norm supporting that equilibrium might *not* automatically generate resentment. If a norm were perceived as unjust, the challenge to it would presumably provoke a contest, in which some, while granting the justice of a different pattern, would feel anger or irritation at the change – presumably because of their own path-dependent costs – but others would encourage that change for justice-based reasons. A departure from an unjust norm, even if unsuccessful, might generate instead of resentment a wistful approval of the brave (if futile) gesture aimed at overturning the existing norm in favor of one more just.

If we move beyond the first level of breaking an expectation and the irritation among those whose expectations are deceived, and ask why some expectations become *moral* norms, imbued with an aura of justice, and others do not, we return to the very thicket from which Sugden would have us escape. How does a social norm become a moral norm? Sympathetic identification with the public interest (not desire for the moral approval of others), the very aspect of Hume's model that Sugden rejects, could help distinguish between the instances in which one would expect resentment and those in which one would not. So may long-run processes of social learning that stretch back to hunter–gatherer times, or even genetic predispositions, as Avner Ben-Ner and Louis Putterman (this volume) suggest.

An earlier section of this chapter raised one further possibility: that some moral norms are embedded in our conceptual apparatus. So the first abstract contender for justice may be equality, as in the ancient Athenian proverb "Justice *is* equality." An equally powerful contender may be, as Sugden suggests, what has always been done. Detrimental departure from established expectations can then produce resentment. But in modern times "what has always been done" does not serve as a criterion for justice as well as it has in the past. From monarchy to patriarchy, existing institutions previously considered just on traditional grounds are now being asked to provide substantive rationales. And in this process, equality – as Isaiah Berlin contended – is the default position.

## Conclusion

The burgeoning recent research on innate emotions, on cognitive capacities and limitations, and on the kinds of propositions that "command" assent suggests that beginning with nothing but self-interest and rationality will not produce accuracy in describing and predicting human action, although it can provide a provocative and useful heuristic exercise. As we begin to explore the relation between values and institutions, it will be well to consider not only the evolution of social expectations, and not only the costs and benefits to different social actors of establishing particular value systems within particular institutions, but also the proximate and ultimate resources on which actors can draw to establish those value systems. The proximate resources will always be context-dependent and path-dependent. The ultimate resources depend on our innate emotive and cognitive capacities, as well as on the structure of normative thinking itself.

REFERENCES

Alexander, Richard D. (1987). *The Biology of Moral Systems*. New York: De Gruyter.
Batson, C. Daniel (1991). *The Altruism Question: Toward a Social-Psychological Answer*. Hillsdale, N.J.: Lawrence Erlbaum Associates.
Berlin, Isaiah (1955–56). "Equality," *Proceedings of the Aristotelian Society* 56: 301–26.

Binmore, Ken (1992). *Fun and Games*. Lexington, Mass.: D. C. Heath.

Brewer, Marilyn B., and Roderick M. Kramer (1986). "Choice Behavior in Social Dilemmas: Effects of Social Identity, Group Size, and Decision Framing," *Journal of Personality and Social Psychology* 50: 543–49.

Coleman, James (1990). *Foundations of Social Theory*. Cambridge, Mass.: Harvard University Press.

Cronin, Helena (1991). *The Ant and the Peacock*. Cambridge: Cambridge University Press.

Dawes, Robyn M., Alphons J. C. van de Kragt, and John M. Orbell (1990). "Cooperation for the Benefit of Us – Not Me, or My Conscience," in Jane Mansbridge, ed., *Beyond Self-Interest*. Chicago: University of Chicago Press.

Elster, Jon (1990). "Selfishness and Altruism," in Jane Mansbridge, ed., *Beyond Self-Interest*. Chicago: University of Chicago Press.

Frank, Robert H (1988). *Passions within Reason: The Strategic Role of the Emotions*. New York: W. W. Norton.

———(1990). "A Theory of Moral Sentiments," in Jane Mansbridge, ed., *Beyond Self-Interest*. Chicago: University of Chicago Press.

Goodall, Jane (1986). *The Chimpanzees of Gombe*. Cambridge: Harvard University Press.

Habermas, Jürgen ([1974] 1979). *Communication and the Evolution of Society*. Trans. Thomas McCarthy. Boston: Beacon Press.

Havelock, Eric A. ([1957] 1964). *The Liberal Temper in Greek Politics*. New Haven, Conn.: Yale University Press.

Hobbes, Thomas ([1651] 1947). *Leviathan*. London: J. M. Dent & Sons.

Hoffman, Martin L. (1981). "Is Altruism Part of Human Nature?" *Journal of Personality and Social Psychology* 40: 121–37.

Jencks, Christopher (1990). "Varieties of Altruism," in Jane Mansbridge, ed., *Beyond Self-Interest*. Chicago: University of Chicago Press.

Kant, Immanuel ([1785] 1949). *Fundamental Principles of the Metaphysic of Morals*. Trans. Thomas K. Abbott. Indianapolis: Bobbs-Merrill.

Kennett, David A. (1980). "Altruism and Economic Behavior, I," *American Journal of Economics and Sociology* 39: 183–98.

Mansbridge, Jane (1990a). "The Rise and Fall of Self-Interest in the Explanation of Political Life," in Jane Mansbridge, ed., *Beyond Self-Interest*. Chicago: University of Chicago Press.

———(1990b). "On the Relation between Altruism and Self-Interest," in Jane Mansbridge, ed., *Beyond Self-Interest*. Chicago: University of Chicago Press.

Miller, Dale, Julie Downs, and Deborah Prentice (forthcoming). "Minimal Conditions for the Creation of the Unit Relationship: The Social Bond Between Birthday Mates," *European Journal of Social Psychology*.

Monroe, Kristen Renwick (1996). *The Heart of Altruism*. Princeton, N.J.: Princeton University Press.

Murdoch, George P., and Caterina Provost (1973). "Factors in the Division of Labor by Sex: A Cross-Cultural Analysis," *Ethnology* 12: 203–25.

Oliner, Samuel P., and Pearl M. Oliner (1988). *The Altruistic Personality*. New York: Free Press.

Panksepp, J. (1989). "Psychobiology of Prosocial Behaviors," in Carolyn Zahn-Waxler, E. M. Cummings, and R. Iannotti, eds., *Altruism and Aggression: Biological and Social Origins*. New York: Cambridge University Press.

Radke-Yarrow, Marian, and Carolyn Zahn-Waxler (1984). "Roots, Motive, and Patterns in Patterns in Children's Prosocial Behavior," in Ervin Staub et al., *Development and Maintenance of Prosocial Behavior*. New York: Plenum.

Rawls, John (1971). *A Theory of Justice*. Cambridge, Mass.: Harvard University Press.

Rushton, J. Philippe (1989). "Genetic Similarity, Human Altruism, and Group Selection," *Behavioral and Brain Sciences* 12: 503–18.

Rushton, J. Philippe, et al. (1986). "Altruism and Aggression: The Heritability of Individual Differences," *Journal of Personality and Social Psychology* 50: 1192–98.

Sandel, Michael J. (1982). *Liberalism and the Limits of Justice*. Cambridge: Cambridge University Press.

Sen, Amartya ([1978] 1990). "Rational Fools," in Jane Mansbridge, ed., *Beyond Self-Interest*. Chicago: University of Chicago Press.

Smith, Adam ([1759] 1984). *The Theory of Moral Sentiments*. Indianapolis: Liberty Press.

Warrender, Howard (1957). *The Political Philosophy of Hobbes*. Oxford: Oxford University Press.

Wilson, Edward O. ([1970] 1979). *On Human Nature*. New York: Bantam.

PART II

THE GENERATION AND TRANSMISSION OF

VALUES IN FAMILIES AND COMMUNITIES

CHAPTER 6

# Did Father know best? Families, markets, and the supply of caring labor

*Nancy Folbre and Thomas E. Weisskopf*

Even economists, the most cold-blooded of all social scientists, are beginning to worry that our economy cannot rely entirely on the individual pursuit of self-interest. Altruism, trust, and solutions to coordination problems are now important topics of research. Why this rather surprising loss of confidence in rational economic man? Perhaps he is running into problems because his rational economic wife is no longer taking such good care of him. Women are now much less likely than they once were to devote themselves entirely to their families. Increases in women's independence are widely perceived as a threat to social integration. Many conservatives blame feminism, abortion, out-of-wedlock births, and affirmative action for our most serious social woes.

In this chapter, we agree that there is cause for concern about a possible decline in the quality of care services. But we reject the conservative argument that women are to blame and insist on the need for state policies that would promote norms, values, and preferences for caring among both men and women. The first section characterizes the motives underlying the provision of care services, offering several reasons why a shift toward more self-interested, pecuniary motives may have negative implications for social welfare. The second section explores the possibility that such a shift is taking place. We argue that the expansion of markets has contradictory effects, weakening patriarchal coercion, but also rewarding purely self-interested behavior.

Patriarchal forms of coercion had some positive indirect effects on the supply of caring services but were neither sustainable nor fair.

This chapter was prepared for presentation at the Conference on Economics, Values, and Organization, held at Yale University in New Haven, Connecticut, April 19–21, 1996. We are grateful to Paula England, Gil Skillman, Julie Nelson, Nancy Tuana, and conference participants for helpful discussions of the arguments developed in this chapter; Elissa Braunstein provided valuable research assistance.

171

Unfortunately, their legacy remains influential: Values, norms, and preferences continue to assign women more responsibility for caring than men. We should not long for the return of the old "Father knows best" family. Rather, we should devise ways of rewarding caring labor that promote affection and reciprocity among citizens while preserving the salutary effects of markets – respect for individual choice and challenges to traditional gender roles.

# 1     For love or money?

## 1.1     *Caring labor*

We generally think of a person who cares as one who is concerned about the welfare of other people and will act on the basis of that concern. One could, of course, care only about oneself, but a "caring person" is someone who is attentive and responsive to the needs and wants of others. Within the discourse of left political economy, caring is closely associated with solidarity. Within the discourse of neoclassical economics, it is closely associated with altruism. Whatever the theoretical context, the concept of care challenges the assumptions of methodological individualism because it suggests that the boundaries of the self cannot always be neatly defined (England and Kilbourne 1990).

When the term "care" is applied to work, it often describes the product of the work – the provision of care services – and not the attitude or the motives for doing the work. The most obvious examples of care services are infant care and nursing, but many other activities within the scope of the "helping professions," such as teaching and social work, include a high care services component. Care service labor involves the expenditure of time and energy in personal contact with persons being cared for. Such labor may be undertaken for a variety of motives, not specific to any particular institutional context; it may be given away, traded among family members or friends, or sold in the labor market.

We believe that the motives underlying the supply of care service labor have important implications for the quality of the services provided. In particular, we believe it is useful to distinguish motives reflecting a caring attitude from motives which do not. Therefore, we use the term "caring labor" to denote labor that is both objectively and subjectively caring, i.e., labor that is involved in the provision of care services *and* is motivated by caring attitudes. Specifically, we restrict the term "caring labor" to care service work performed out of a sense of affection or concern for others rather than out of narrow self-interest.

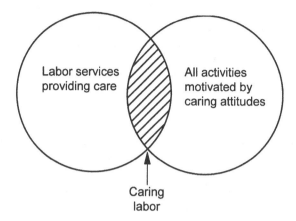

Diagram 1

The affection or concern underlying caring labor may be contrasted with the motivation for work characteristic of *homo economicus* ("rational economic man"), who is conventionally presumed to face a labor/leisure trade-off and to compare the additional utility to be gained from extra income against the disutility of additional labor. Most self-interested labor undertaken in our society is market labor, with the reward to labor taking the form of monetary compensation. But narrowly self-interested labor can also take place outside the labor market, with nonmonetary rather than monetary rewards. And caring labor may sometimes be remunerated, even if it is provided for largely non-self-interested reasons. The distinction between caring motives and non-caring motives, in other words, is not the same as the distinction between nonmarket and market activities, though the two dichotomies are related.

Nor is caring labor the only way in which caring attitudes can be expressed. Out of affection or concern, one could make a gift in money or in kind to another person, or one could provide another with a continuing income or continuing access to some purchased service. One could express one's care by taking another person to a fabulous restaurant, as well as by cooking and serving that person a special dinner. Indeed, a dinner out may be more appreciated by the recipient – depending on his/her tastes as well as on the cooking abilities of the dinner provider. However, what we will call "caring provision" – the supplying of money or resources for the acquisition of care services from a third party – is rarely a perfect substitute for the actual performance of caring labor.

These conceptual distinctions are illustrated in Diagram 1. One circle in the diagram describes all work activities involving the provision of care services, regardless of motivation. Another circle contains all activities motivated by affection or concern, whether or not they involve working to provide care services. The intersection of these two circles describes caring labor: the provision of care services by means of labor that is motivated by caring attitudes. The diagram suggests that a reduction in caring labor does not necessarily imply an overall reduction in caring, and that a decrease in the provision of care services does not necessarily imply a decrease in those that were genuinely motivated by care. However, it suggests the need to explore the substitutability between different forms of expressing care (purchasing things for people versus doing things for them) and between different motives for supplying care services (self-interest versus care).

### 1.2    *Caring motives*

What does it mean to perform a task out of a sense of "affection or concern for others, rather than out of narrow self-interest"? We can shed light on the nature of caring labor by distinguishing first a broad range of motives for care service labor ranged along a continuum from the most caring to the least caring.[1] Of course any given care service work may be done for a combination of the following motives, but it is analytically useful to consider each separately.

1. *Altruism.* People are prepared to do a great deal of work in providing care services to those whom they love or for whom they feel affection. A genuine relationship of love or affection is completely voluntary, unburdened by any element of coercion. Examples include the love between two adults in a successful intimate relationship and the affection of most parents for their children. Altruism is the term most commonly used to describe satisfaction derived from enhancing the well-being of another person. In a formal neoclassical framework, altruism is modeled in terms of positively interdependent utilities.

Care service labor motivated by altruism does not necessarily require any reward or quid pro quo, other than evidence that the cared-for person benefits from it. It may even be undertaken completely independently of the response of the cared-for person (a case we think of as

---

[1] Our continuum of motives for care service labor is similar, but not identical to a continuum running from the most "other-regarding" to the most "self-regarding," in the sense in which these terms are used by Ben-Ner and Putterman (this volume).

saintliness). But altruistic preferences may be somewhat endogenous, because if they remain entirely unappreciated they often dissipate over time. Parents take loving care of their children for many years, but after a certain point, they expect their care to be reciprocated to some extent. If this expectation is completely disappointed, their preferences may change. Similarly, a spouse or partner may provide one-sided care out of genuine affection. In the long run, however, lack of reciprocity often dampens the willingness to continue doing so.

2. *A sense of responsibility.* Most people recognize certain duties or obligations that they perform even though they derive no direct pleasure from them. One could argue, of course, that they derive pleasure from fulfilling their duty, but moral categories cannot always be reduced to a utilitarian calculus (Sen 1987). Therefore, it is important to consider the possibility that moral values central to a person's character and identity motivate caring labor. Examples include care of a senile or comatose relative or care of a delinquent child "with an attitude."

Care service labor undertaken out of a sense of responsibility does not require direct reciprocity between the care provider and the care receiver. However, responsibilities are socially constructed, and they are often based on some generalized reciprocity. If many people fail to conform to social norms of responsibility, the norms themselves tend to weaken. Thus, an individual's willingness to fulfill caring responsibilities may depend, to some extent, on his or her perception of how seriously others take such responsibilities.

3. *Intrinsic enjoyment.* People may take care of others simply because they enjoy it; caring can be its own reward. A good example would be a parent's helping a child learn to talk or to walk. Participating in this process can be a satisfying and enjoyable experience. The capacity to derive such intrinsic enjoyment is a preference of the kind posited as exogenous by neoclassical economics. That women are generally considered to exhibit this preference to a greater extent than men suggests that it is not randomly distributed, and that it is influenced by cultural norms as well as perhaps by biological factors (Fuchs 1988).

Whatever its source, intrinsic enjoyment usually entails at least some affection for the person being cared for and often requires some show of reciprocity from the cared-for person.

4. *Expectation of an informal quid pro quo.* Care service labor is sometimes done in the expectation that the care recipient will return the favor, sooner or later, by giving care (or something else of value) to the caregiver. For instance, two people who live together may take turns preparing meals for one another, or two friends may take turns

caring for one another during illnesses. The quid pro quo need not itself involve care services; for example, one person in a family may stay home and nurture the family while the other earns a wage and provides the financial resources for the household.

Clearly this motive for care service labor is highly contingent on reciprocity; if the care recipient does not ultimately reciprocate in some way, the caregiver will cease to do the work. The caregiver, however, has no guarantee of a quid pro quo, and no recourse to adjudication if it is not forthcoming. Moreover, it is often difficult to spell out the precise terms of the exchange or to determine whether or not a given exchange is in some sense fair. Such calculations are indeed irrelevant, because what is called for is much more of a gift exchange than a market trade (Akerlof 1982).

People's willingness to provide care service labor in exchange for some future quid pro quo, in spite of the noncontractual and nonenforceable nature of the exchange, suggests that there is more at work here than a narrowly self-interested calculus. Certainly there is a significant element of self-interest: I am willing to do something for you because I expect that, as a result, you will do something for me. But I am more likely to enter into this kind of imprecise and unenforceable exchange if (1) I can live with the possibility that you will not reciprocate soon or (2) I can trust you ultimately to reciprocate.

The first condition would hold if I derive some satisfaction from doing the care service labor for you, whether or not you reciprocate; this means that I am probably supplying some caring labor. The second condition would hold if I believe that you are trustworthy enough to reciprocate in the future – even if at that time it is no longer in your narrow self-interest to do so. This latter case does not directly imply that I care for you, but, in having confidence in your trustworthiness, I am showing respect for you, which is likely at least to be correlated with care for you. In entering into an exchange with you based on an informal quid pro quo, rather than an enforceable contract, I am therefore expressing some mixture of care and respect for you, rather than treating you simply as instrumental to the achievement of a personal goal.

The self-interested element of reciprocity can be modeled in terms of a prisoner's dilemma (PD) supergame. The caregiver and the care receiver repeatedly play a PD game in which the giver has the choice of providing care (cooperating) or not (defecting), and the receiver has the choice of meeting the giver's expectations of a quid pro quo (cooperating) or not (defecting). As has been well analyzed, self-interested persons in this situation will find it optimal to follow a tit-for-tat strategy in which they cooperate as long as the other party is observed to do the same (Taylor 1987).[2] But, to the extent that the reciprocity is not narrowly self-interested, continuation of the reciprocal exchanges (cooperation) may be possible in spite of lapses from full reciprocity (defection).

5. *A well-defined and contracted-for reward.* Much of the care service labor undertaken in our society is done not in the general expectation of some informal quid pro quo, but in the virtual certainty of a precisely defined reward. This is clearly the case with care service labor supplied in the labor market in exchange for an agreed upon wage (whose payment is subject to judicial enforcement). It is also the case when the labor is supplied in exchange for some kind of nonmonetary compensation instead of a wage payment; what matters is that there is an explicit, contracted-for reward for care service work done. Here the element of self-interest clearly looms large.

At first blush it would appear that most care service labor in modern societies is motivated by contractual reward, for we know that there are legions of hospital workers, schoolteachers, social workers, day care workers, and others, providing care services in exchange for a wage or salary. For many of these workers, however, other motives come into play: Some are altruistic or feel responsible for those for whom they are caring, derive intrinsic enjoyment from it, or expect informal reciprocity. The extent to which care service labor is motivated by contractual reward is therefore overstated by the ratio of the number of care service workers who receive such a reward to the number who do not, for many of the former are likely to have multiple motives.

The range of possible motives has important implications for the care service labor market. First, the more that care service workers are motivated by motives 1–4 in our taxonomy, ceteris paribus, the less they will demand in contractual reward for doing care service labor – i.e., the lower will be their reservation wage for doing the work. Second, the level of the actual wage (or the actual contractual reward) of care service workers will tend to be lower, ceteris paribus, the greater the relative importance of such nonpecuniary motives. These implications are analyzed in more detail in Appendix A.

6. *Coercion.* A final possible motive for care service labor is that people may be forced or obliged to do it. What this really means is that, instead of being offered a positive reward for doing the work, a person

---

[2] In private correspondence, Paula England has pointed out that a modified tit-for-tat strategy, involving "loose accounting" in which people give one another the benefit of the doubt even after an isolated defection, can and often does sustain more cooperative outcomes than would be predicted from more strictly self-interested behavior in PD supergames.

Table 1. *Typology of motives for care service labor*

| Motives | Consequences of (a) doing and (b) not doing the work |
|---------|-------------------------------------------------------|
| 1. Altruism | (a) I gain the satisfaction of helping someone I care about. |
| | (b) I forgo the satisfaction of helping someone I care about. |
| 2. A sense of responsibility | (a) I feel good about having helped someone in a way that I expect decent people to do. |
| | (b) I feel guilty about having let someone down by failing to do what I expect decent people to do. |
| 3. Intrinsic enjoyment | (a) I gain enjoyment while helping someone. |
| | (b) I forgo a chance to gain enjoyment while helping someone. |
| 4. Expectation of an informal quid pro quo | (a) I am likely to get something back from another person. |
| | (b) I risk not getting something back from another person. |
| 5. A well-defined and contracted-for reward | (a) I get paid, or otherwise compensated. |
| | (b) I miss an opportunity to earn money, or some other reward. |
| 6. Coercion | (a) I avoid a penalty or punishment. |
| | (b) I incur a penalty or punishment |

faces a negative sanction for failing to do it. In the most extreme case the sanction could involve physical harm, injury or death. More commonly it involves some lesser deprivation. For example, the wife in a traditional patriarchal family may do housework, raise children, and provide other services to her husband because failing to do so would expose her to the likelihood of ridicule and possibly social ostracism from the community, even if she were not threatened with physical harm by her husband.

We use the term "coercion" to describe this motive for care service labor, because the labor is being provided under duress. As in the case of the reward motive, the coercion motive involves a situation in which it is in a person's self-interest to do the care service work rather than not, so the choice to do it is in that limited sense "voluntary." But in the case of coercion the terms of the choice are much less favorable to the chooser.

Our taxonomy of motives for care service labor is summarized in Table 1, where each motive is listed together with a brief indication of the corresponding consequences of doing or not doing the work. Which of these motives are associated with caring labor? In other words, which of them involve care service labor provided out of a sense of "affection or concern for others, rather than out of narrow self-interest"?

The first and second motives for care service labor, altruism and a sense of responsibility, most clearly qualify as caring, according to our definition. The third and fourth motives, enjoyment and informal quid pro quo, are likely to contain some elements of caring. The remaining two motives, contractual reward and coercion, do not involve caring labor as we have defined it. A person performing care service labor only for these motives is doing so out of regard for her or his own welfare, in a way that is analytically separable from the welfare of the recipient.

As we have noted in discussing them, the first four motives all reflect preferences that may be partially endogenous, and they tend to be difficult to sustain in the long run without some degree of reciprocity. Therefore, we would expect the supply of caring labor to be affected by values and norms which help to overcome the kind of coordination problems that can undermine long-run reciprocity.

In practice, care service labor is likely to be motivated by a combination of several of the motives described. In particular, a person may perform care service labor out of a mixture of caring and narrowly self-interested motives. For instance, workers may not be able to meet the costs of their own subsistence through the provision of purely caring labor and may therefore choose a paying job that also affords them an opportunity to express care. In doing this they may have to forgo higher pay and absorb a negative compensating differential for the opportunity to express care.[3] The extent to which people take relatively low-paid caring jobs, as well as the extent to which people devote unpaid labor to social and family needs, will clearly depend on the strength of caring motives.

### 1.3    *Caring changes*

What if the supply of caring labor is declining faster than the demand for it? The demand for caring labor is likely to be affected by the demographic structure of the population. Since children consume a great deal of caring labor, a decline in the number of children relative to the number of adults probably entails a decline in demand. This decline may be countervailed, however, by an increase in the number of dependent

---

[3] Whether or not such workers actually absorb a negative compensating differential depends on the overall demand for care service labor (see Appendix A). The relatively low salaries of child care workers and hospital nurses in the United States, however, suggest that the demand for care services is often insufficient to relieve care service workers of negative compensating differentials.

elderly. A decline in the supply of caring labor per dependent person could be cause for concern.

A decline in caring labor need not imply a decline in overall care service provision, since that can be provided by self-interested labor. Humans probably have an intrinsic need to be cared for by others, but a decline in caring labor need not imply a decline in overall caring, for it can instead take the form of caring provision (e.g., buying things for people rather than performing care services for them). The question for economists is whether a decline in caring labor is likely to be accompanied by an increase in other ways of providing the same benefits at no greater cost. We explore several reasons why it may not be.

First of all, caring labor satisfies an apparent basic human need to be and to feel valued by others in a way that cannot be satisfied by the receipt of care services from self-interested labor. Caring labor differs from self-interested labor not only in the motivation of the caregiver, but also in one of its "joint products": confirmation to the care recipients that someone cares about them. They may wonder whether the caregiver is motivated by altruism, responsibility, enjoyment, or an informal quid pro quo, but they can be confident that the care they receive is not contingent upon narrow self-interest. Being cared for in this way surely contributes to one's sense of self-worth and thereby to one's well-being.

The purchase of goods or services for other people through what we have called caring provision may also provide a sense of security and self-worth. But there are limits to the extent to which purchases can substitute for the actual expenditure of a person's time and energy. Without the latter, something essential is missing. Providing an intangible service via one's own labor conveys a degree and kind of care that cannot be reduced to monetary terms.

Caring labor is necessarily provided in close personal contact with the recipient. It encompasses not just activities such as preparing meals or changing a bedpan, but services that require person-specific knowledge and skills, such as the informal counseling involved in talking things over. Caring labor is particularly crucial to what the philosopher Ann Ferguson calls "sex-affective" production, meeting another person's sexual and emotional needs (Ferguson 1989). Exchanging valuable rings is a sign of affection, but one that has little credibility unless combined with a more profound commitment to spend time directly meeting one another's needs.

The importance of motivation and the fact that caring labor generates a joint product of "caring" along with the service itself suggest that the substitution of self-interested care service labor (CSL) for caring CSL could have several adverse consequences. A standard welfare analysis detailed in Appendix A shows that the sum of consumer and producer surplus in the CSL market is reduced if the values or circumstances of CSL suppliers change so as to lead them to offer more self-interested CSL and less caring CSL. Moreover, there is a further loss in social welfare sustained by those who were previously uncoerced and uncompensated for their supply of CSL and who now require some compensation. They lose what we call the "warm glow," the positive satisfaction they had derived from performing caring labor.

The caring that is the joint product of caring labor has intrinsic value. When it accompanies care service, the recipient is better off than when there is no caring. Thus the substitution of self-interested CSL for caring CSL has a direct adverse effect on social welfare by reducing the extent of caring. A relative reduction in caring motives can also indirectly impose some costs by exacerbating the informational asymmetry and agency problems that arise when quality is difficult to measure, as is often the case with care services (Titmuss 1970). Thus, the cost of monitoring self-interested labor can be quite high, particularly when the care service provider is engaged by a third party rather than by the care service recipient.

We conclude that a relative decline in the supply of caring labor in a society would indeed constitute a significant social problem. Moreover, this problem would not be solved automatically by market forces. Increasing the wage offered for care service provision could have several positive effects, eliciting higher levels of skill, reducing levels of worker turnover, and enhancing opportunities for workers to develop a genuine caring relationship with clients. On the other hand, higher wages increase the opportunity cost of work that is not motivated by pecuniary concerns. A higher price cannot, by definition, elicit a greater supply of labor motivated by altruism, responsibility, enjoyment, or an informal quid pro quo. Indeed, a higher price may even have a crowding out effect by eroding the kind of values which underlie the motivation for caring labor (Frey, this volume; Stark 1995).

## 2 The supply of caring labor

Both conservative concerns about the decline of the family and liberal concerns about the deterioration of community imply fears of a possible reduction in the supply of caring labor. Any tendency to romanticize the good old days, however, must face the feminist criticism that traditional families and communities often subordinated women. The implications of this subordination can be explained in terms of the analysis outlined previously. Patriarchal control over women imposes direct coercion on the supply of caring services, which reduces their quality. It also imposes indirect coercion: Values and norms assign women more responsibility for care and encourage them to develop more altruistic preferences than men. The expansion of labor markets tends to undermine direct and indirect patriarchal coercion. As women enter wage employment, they often gain a new economic independence that allows them to escape forced responsibilities for providing caring services, with positive implications for the quality of care. Women also begin to challenge the indirect coercion of traditional gender-biased values, norms, and preferences, with more ambiguous consequences. It proves much easier for women to reduce their own supply of caring labor than to persuade men to offer more.

## 2.1    *Patriarchal coercion*

The notion that the traditional patriarchal family was a reliable source of caring labor is implicit in much liberal as well as conservative discourse. A television comedy series produced in the United States in the 1950s, "Father Knows Best," provided a particularly disarming cultural expression of this point of view. It seems, however, that at least some of the happiness and stability of the traditional family rested on coercive practices that limited women's potential for individual autonomy and enforced cultural values and norms that associated femininity with altruism and masculinity with self-interest (Folbre and Hartmann 1988). The direct effects of these coercive practices can be interpreted in terms of the economic concept of property rights. Analysis of the indirect effects requires consideration of the ways that groups based on gender (and other aspects of social identity) may seek to influence the formation of values, norms, and preferences.

Traditional patriarchal societies stipulate property rights that seriously constrain women's choices to specialize in anything but the provision of care services to family members. Women are denied access to the acquisition of non-home-related skills and limited to the least remunerative forms of work. Until the midtwentieth century, men in most countries had the legal right to prevent their wives from working outside the home. They retain that right in some countries today. Explicit rules can give men control over women's caring services. A late nineteenth century Prussian law gave husbands the legal right to specify how long their wives should breast feed (Bebel 1971). Even today, most legal traditions define the marriage contract in terms that are disadvantageous to wives, mothers, and children. Contrary to the concept of partnership, they are denied any specific claim to the income of a husband or father and are legally owed nothing more than subsistence support. Wives often lack any explicit protection from physical abuse or rape within marriage.

Why did such gender-biased property rights evolve? Their historical importance challenges the conservative assumption that women's specialization in the provision of care services reflects nothing more than biological instincts, God-given duty, or comparative advantage. If women had voluntarily agreed to such extreme specialization, it would have been unnecessary to establish such coercive gender-biased rules. Evidence suggests that men have engaged in rent-seeking behavior designed to lower the costs of caring services. It is not difficult to find examples of male collective action designed to exclude women from participation in the specification of property rights. Nor is it difficult to find examples of female collective action designed to combat this exclusion (Folbre 1994).

Patriarchal coercion is by no means limited to property rights. It may also take the more indirect form of gender-biased values and norms that influence preferences. Most institutional economists describe values and norms simply as solutions to coordination problems (Schotter 1981). But groups often seek to enforce social values they find beneficial, and men have much to gain by enforcing values, norms, and preferences of caring in women. Of course, the opposite is also true: Women have much to gain by enforcing values, norms, and preferences of caring in men. But our cultural constructs of appropriate behavior for men and women were largely developed at a time when strong patriarchal coercion was in effect, therefore increasing the likelihood that they serve men's interests better than women's.

Economists are just beginning to explore the possibility that women are more altruistic than men (Eckel and Grossman 1996a, 1996b; Seguino et al. 1996). Certainly, women are more likely to assume responsibility for children and other dependents, a factor that significantly lowers both their income and their leisuretime (Fuchs 1988). Some portion of this difference between men and women may be rooted in biological mechanisms. Some portion, however, may be the result of what might be termed coercive socialization. The feminist theorist Joan Tronto points out that robbing individuals of opportunities to pursue their own self-interest effectively may encourage them to live through others, using caring as a substitute for more selfish gratification (1987, pp. 647, 650). Amartya Sen hints at a similar problem: Women may not realize they are exploited when they lack a cultural conception of themselves as individuals with interests separate from those of their family members (1990). While neoclassical economists tend to avoid the gender issue, they suggest that parents may inculcate caring preferences in their children in order to ensure that they are cared for in old age (Becker 1992; Stark 1995). Men may try to inculcate caring preferences in women for similar reasons.

Coercive socialization might be interpreted, using Robert Frank's terminology (see his essay, this volume), as a "positional arms control agreement" in which relative power, as well as overall efficiency, is at stake. The imposition of limits helps prevent destructive, inefficient forms of competition. Frank describes agreements between two parties of roughly equivalent power (e.g., the United States and the Soviet Union during the Cold War). But such agreements have also been imposed by large powerful nations on less-developed countries trying to develop their own weapons systems. Similarly men may try to avert the escalation of self-interested behavior by imposing particularly strict limits on its expression by women. The costs of developing and enforcing such an agreement could be quite high; certainly such costs would likely increase as women gained more social and economic power (as we will argue in the next section).

The endogenous character of caring preferences, however, may create a circular process that greatly lowers enforcement costs. Caring may be addictive. Adults who spend time providing caring services to dependents often come to feel more affection for them than those who do not. A small initial difference in preferences may be augmented by experience. Most economic models of endogenous preferences focus on addictions with negative consequences for both the consumer and society, such as addiction to cigarettes or drugs. An addiction to caring has positive consequences for society as a whole but may have negative consequences for the individual (or group of individuals) who provide care. If addiction reflects a rational, utility maximizing choice based on full information, the addict feels no regret (Becker, Grossman, and Murphy 1991). But a combination of imperfect information and uncertain outcomes can explain why individuals sometimes conclude they made the wrong choice (Orphanides and Zeroos 1995). Sometimes, people wish they could stop caring, but find they cannot.[4]

The implications of an increase in direct coercion at the expense of other motives for the supply of caring services are fairly obvious – a probable reduction in the quality of those services, for the reasons outlined in section 1. The implications of an increase in indirect coercion, however, are ambiguous. Values, norms, and preferences that pressure women to behave in more altruistic and responsible ways than men may

---

[4] Many women consider abortion rights crucial precisely because they know that mothering preferences are endogenous. If they carry a child to term, they may then be unable to relinquish it.

successfully increase the supply of caring labor from women. On the other hand, they may decrease the supply of caring labor from men. Further, patriarchal socialization works only as long as men are able to convince women that it is "natural." As women gain economic and social power, they challenge unfair property rights. They also become more cognizant of social processes by which values, norms, and preferences are formed and begin to contest traditional norms of masculinity and femininity.

## 2.2 The contradictory effects of markets

Some economists (including the editors of this volume) suggest that the growth of markets encourages the competitive pursuit of self-interest rather than the kinds of values, norms, and preferences associated with caring labor. We agree only in part: The expansion of labor markets may have a contradictory effect, undermining patriarchal forms of coercion in ways that partially countervail the negative impact on caring motives. We would therefore expect markets to have a more positive overall effect on caring labor when and where patriarchal institutions are strong, and a more negative overall effect when and where patriarchal institutions are weak. Over time, the expansion of markets probably has a nonlinear impact on the supply of caring labor, with the shape of the curve determined by the interactions among markets, families, and the state.

The possible negative and positive effects of markets on the relative supply of caring vs. self-interested labor can be explained in terms of the list of motives developed in section 1. To the extent that markets encourage transactions motivated by contracted-for rewards (motive 5) at the expense of altruism, responsibility, enjoyment, or informal quid pro quo (motives 1–4), they decrease the relative supply of caring labor. To the extent that they enable people to avoid directly coerced care service labor (motive 6), they increase the relative supply of caring labor. By opening up avenues for exit, market institutions provide greater bargaining power and hence greater standing to those people (mainly women) who would otherwise be obliged to do care service labor for other people (mainly men) who wield more power within nonmarket institutions like the patriarchal family. The relative size of the two opposing effects of markets on caring labor depends on the extent to which both markets and coercion indirectly affect values, norms, and preferences relevant to the supply of caring labor.

The growth of wage employment destabilizes patriarchal coercion partly because it modifies the economics of family life. Changes in relative prices, including increases in the cost of raising children, make traditional patriarchal forms of control over women less advantageous to men. A traditional housewife may have less bargaining power than a well-educated professional woman, but she also contributes less income to the family. Men eventually gain from increases in their wives' labor force participation, and a more egalitarian family begins to emerge, based on ideals of quid pro quo and reciprocity rather than coercion or internalized norms of maternal responsibility. Both men and women enjoy more freedom of entry and exit into families; the percentage of individuals living together out of wedlock tends to rise, along with divorce rates.

The benefits to women, however, are uneven. Single women benefit more than mothers, whose bargaining power is limited by their tendency to take primary responsibility for children. A more egalitarian family is almost inevitably a less stable one. It is easier for women to obtain rights over their own earnings than to enforce claims on men's income. Children suffer as a result. In the United States, poor enforcement of paternal child support responsibilities, inadequate child care provision, and decreasing levels of public assistance have contributed to increased rates of poverty among all individuals under eighteen.

The impact of wage employment on women's empowerment is blunted by the fact that they tend to specialize in jobs that have a large caring component. Employers prefer to hire them for such jobs, and, as a result of the socialization processes described in the preceding section, women themselves may prefer them. To the extent that care service labor is supplied for caring motives rather than for compensation, the supply curve of labor to care service jobs such as teaching, providing day care, and nursing will be lower, as will therefore the wages paid to those who are compensated for such labor. Thus, many workers in care service jobs are exploited in the sense that they are being paid less than they would be in a world entirely lacking in altruism, responsibility, or intrinsic enjoyment of helping others. Indeed, as the sociologist Paula England has shown, the more "nurturing" a job requires, all else equal, the lower the wages paid (1992).

Over time, however, women become increasingly aware of the penalties imposed on care. Gender differences in preferences mattered less when women spent only a portion of their working life in paid employment. In most industrialized countries today, however, labor market participation rates of men and women are converging. Higher levels of education and productivity increase the opportunity cost of most activities motivated by care. As women anticipate greater dependence on their own earnings and observe the increasingly high cost of commitments to children and other dependents, they may become less altruistic. Even if they are unable to change their own preferences, they may be more likely to challenge traditional gender norms and to encourage the younger generation of women to become more oriented toward paid employment. An obvious example is the "Take Your Daughter to Work" day, organized by feminist groups in the United States.

In general, movement toward gender equality has taken the form of a shift in which women's behavior has come to resemble men's more closely. Femininity has been somewhat masculinized. There is no reason, in principle, why gender equality could not be achieved from the other direction. Masculinity could be somewhat feminized. Rather than women's increasing participation in market work, men could increase their participation in caring activities. Fathers could organize "Show Your Son How to Babysit" day. Unfortunately, it is easier for women to pursue their own self-interest than to persuade men to become more altruistic. The inertial effect of patriarchal privileges is reinforced by market processes that increase the opportunity cost of caring labor.

### 2.3    *Nice guys (and gals) finish last*

Either act like a man or be penalized for the pursuit of feminine values – this uncomfortable choice can be described in game-theoretic terms. The supply of caring labor poses a coordination problem that involves the endogeneity of norms and preferences. Without some coordination in the form of enforcement from nonmarket institutions (of which patriarchal coercion is only one example), the values, norms, and preferences that motivate caring labor may become less attractive to groups and to individuals. This problem does not conform exactly to the standard model of the prisoner's dilemma, because individuals are not making strategic decisions about how to act; they are being penalized or rewarded as a result of values, norms, and preferences over which they exercise only a small amount of control. But, insofar as they have the power to alter these in the next round of the game, their decisions are likely to be affected by their perception of what alterations other people will make.

Empirical evidence suggests that women have been much more successful at improving their access to paid employment than in persuading men to assume more responsibility for family responsibilities. Household studies show that even women who earn considerably more than their husbands seldom persuade them to depart from traditional male sex roles (Hochschild 1989). The values, norms, and preferences governing such roles have been in place for hundreds of years, and men have good reasons to resist changing them. But another difficulty lies in the crucial role of motives in the provision of caring labor. Individuals cannot be forced to care.

Consider the game called chicken. Rather than imagining two teenage men racing toward one another in their hot-rods, each hoping that the other will swerve, imagine two parents lying in bed in the middle of a night listening to their child screaming. Both care about the child but care also about their own comfort. The best outcome for the father would be if the mother would tend to the child; the best outcome for the mother would be the opposite. The worst outcome for both is if neither tends to the child. Who will go? If the mother cares more, she is likely to get up far more often (for an illustration of payoffs in a game of chicken with asymmetric preferences, see Appendix B). If caring preferences are addictive, she will begin to care even more and lose even more sleep relative to the father.

This game is a metaphor for a larger process of bargaining over the distribution of caring responsibilities. Some women may collectively decide to challenge asymmetric values, norms, and preferences, but they face the same catch-22 as any individual woman. They do not want to encourage women to start caring less unless they are sure that they can persuade men to start caring more. Given a choice between a society in which women perform most caring labor and one in which no one performs it, they may choose the former, even though they would prefer a more equal distribution of responsibilities.

A simple solution to this problem would be to adopt an egalitarian rule: Both parents take turns providing caring labor, and men and women share the larger responsibilities of providing care services to all dependents. However, women are likely to have a hard time enforcing this rule, not only for the reasons described, but also because of the impact of markets and current state policy. It may be impossible to develop gender-neutral values, norms, and preferences of caring without some form of collective intervention. Another catch-22 looms: Such intervention will, almost inevitably, be coercive.

## 2.4    *Sharing caring*

We need to develop a new social contract that generates a sense of responsibility for caring labor in all members of society. Such a social contract cannot simply be imposed from above, nor can it be fulfilled simply by transferring money or paying taxes. It cannot be defined purely in political terms, because it requires a larger cultural and economic transformation. It may be intrinsically more difficult to design, develop, and enforce than a patriarchal social contract that assigns women primary responsibility for care services. But it could equitably balance the goals of individual self-realization and social responsibility. Moreover, it appears far more likely to assure a continuing and sufficient supply of caring labor than any feasible alternative – such as an effort to strengthen patriarchal authority or to rely on a purely voluntary supply of caring labor. Indeed, it may also be the only kind of social contract that will in the long run allow market economies to prosper in a democratic environment.

In emphasizing the need for a new social contract, we are not arguing against the payment of higher wages for care service work. Higher pay could encourage and facilitate the development of caring relationships within wage employment. Higher pay alone, however, will not solve the problem that we point to: the erosion of norms and preferences by a competitive process in which those who provide care gradually realize that others are free riding on their altruism.

Consider the competitive economy – in a time-honored metaphor – as a footrace. The principles of equal opportunity suggest that all members of a society should have a fair chance to participate in a competition that rewards effort and ability, though opinions differ as to how a fair chance should be defined. Stepping back from this problem, however, consider the incentives created by a race based on speed. As the prizes increase, and more and more individuals begin to compete, it becomes apparent that offering caring labor only slows people down. Any competitor who carries a baby, or stops to assist an elderly person, or cares for someone who is sick loses valuable time. A similar disadvantage accrues to teams, or even nations, running this metaphorical race. As a result, the competition undermines norms, values, and preferences that might otherwise help supply caring labor. Yet even the most vigorous competitors will find that at some point they need to be cared for; so the decline in caring labor will ultimately impoverish everyone.

One solution to the problem of assuring sufficient caring labor is to exclude women from the race and assign them primary responsibility for caring. Another solution is to impose a new rule: Everyone can race, but everyone must also carry a fair share of the weight of caring labor. Each of these solutions involves an element of coercion, in that caring roles are assigned from above rather than voluntarily assumed. The first solution has the merit of capturing gains from specialization, but it is inequitable. The second solution has the merit of equity, but it forgoes gains from specialization. Because of its obvious inequity, the first solution is likely to require grounding in a belief system and/or a structure of authority which distinguishes sharply between those deemed to be competitors and those deemed to be carers. By contrast, the second approach suggests that everyone should have an equal opportunity to develop innate capabilities for both competing and caring; the greater equity of this solution makes it more likely to emerge from a genuinely democratic process of decision making.

In comparing the two solutions, we have thus far failed to confront a major dilemma: How can genuine caring be assured by any kind of *assignment* of responsibility? It is possible to assign responsibility for care services, but if this responsibility is fulfilled only because it has been assigned (i.e., because one would face unpleasant sanctions if one did not carry it out), then it does not qualify as caring. Indeed, it results from coercion in the sense of the sixth of the motives we distinguished at the beginning of this chapter. To assure caring means to encourage action based on the first four motives. We must ask, therefore, which solution is more likely to promote and sustain motivations of altruism, responsibility, enjoyment, and informal quid pro quo in the provision of care.

We have noted in analyzing patriarchal constraints that women who are coercively assigned the role of providing care service may come to internalize this as a responsibility willingly assumed. In other words, what originates as coercion (motive 6) is transmuted into responsibility (motive 3), thereby generating caring labor. By the same token, responsibilities for care assigned to all members of society involve a form of coercion, but one which may well transmute into a responsibility willingly accepted by individuals. Indeed, this process of transmutation appears far more likely to occur if the coercion involves an equitable assignment of responsibilities and results from a democratic decision-making process than if it involves an inequitable assignment based on a belief system linked to traditional authority. (This conclusion is only strengthened if such authority is weakening, as in the case of patriarchal authority in the modern world.)

The process of reaching a democratic agreement to define and share caring responsibilities will not be an easy one. While the social safety net policies of the type currently in effect in much of northwestern Europe may be necessary, they would certainly not be sufficient, because they define social responsibility almost exclusively in monetary terms – the payment of taxes to help provide care services that are paid for by the state. Indeed, this emphasis on money transfers may help explain waning support for redistributional policies. Taxpayers have little personal contact with those they are nominally helping to provide for.

Public policies could, following the Scandinavian example, support and reward family commitments without reinforcing traditional gender roles. But the project of encouraging caring labor should not be limited to families. Citizens could be given tax credits for contributing care services that develop long-term relationships between individuals. Many young adults benefit from public support for higher education. They could repay their fellow citizens by engaging in a period of mandatory national service that would include taking some responsibility for children and other dependents in their community. The care services they could provide would be at least as valuable as the non-care services currently emphasized by the military, and they could develop important skills, as well as reinforcing the value of care.

Policies designed to foster a greater supply of caring labor appear "unproductive" or "costly" only to those who define economic efficiency in terms of misleadingly narrow measures such as contribution to gross domestic product. The erosion of family and community solidarity imposes enormous costs that are reflected in inefficient and unsuccessful educational efforts, high crime rates, and a social atmosphere of anxiety and resentment. The care and nurturance of human capital have always been difficult and expensive. In the past, a sexual division of labor based upon the subordination of women helped minimize both the difficulties and the expense. Today, however, the costs of providing caring labor should be explicitly confronted and fairly distributed.

### Appendix A: A welfare analysis of care service labor

Our discussion of care service labor (CSL) in section 1 of this chapter suggests that there are two important respects in which CSL differs from most of the labor supplied in a market economy.

The first important difference involves the *motivation* for supplying the labor. Suppliers of labor in general expect to be compensated with a well-defined and contracted-for reward (motive 5 in our taxonomy); most often this is in the form of a wage payment. In contrast, a reward is not the major element in compensation for a substantial proportion of suppliers of care service labor. Some supply CSL voluntarily without expecting any wage (having only motives 1–4), and some supply CSL without receiving a wage because they are obliged or coerced to do so by the terms of their family arrangement (motive 6). Yet others are willing to supply CSL for less compensation than they could receive in other pursuits, because they are motivated in part by motives 1–4; in effect, they derive a form of psychic satisfaction, as well as compensation, from providing care service labor.

The second important respect in which care service labor differs from labor in general is that the *quality* of the labor supplied is functionally related to the motivation for supplying it. For most kinds of labor in a market economy there is no such relationship. In the case of care service labor, however, the motivation for supplying CSL makes a great deal of difference. To the extent that CSL is supplied for motives 1–4, it conveys to care recipients the sense that someone really cares about them; it confirms that they are loved and/or respected. In this case the care recipient receives not just the care service but also a joint product that we will call "caring," which enhances in an important respect the quality of the care service provided.[5]

The amount of caring which accompanies care service labor will vary, depending on which of the motives 1–4 is at issue; it seems likely to be considerably more substantial in the case of altruism (motive 1) than in the case of an informal quid pro quo (motive 4). For the purpose of our analysis here, however, we can safely ignore these differences and simply group together all the motives for CSL which involve some degree of caring – i.e., the motives 1–4, which we will call "caring motives." The element of caring is lacking when CSL is delivered solely for a wage (motive 5) or under coercion (motive 6).

### A.1    *The care service labor market in the context of mixed rewards*[6]

Consider now the supply of care service labor. Assuming initially that CSL is homogeneous and measurable in terms of hours of labor, we can draw a supply curve for CSL with quantity supplied ($h$ for hours) on the horizontal axis and the wage ($w$) in dollars per hour on the vertical axis. Some people will be coerced into supplying CSL, and some people will supply CSL solely out of caring motives; the combined CSL supply from these sources is represented by the horizontal line running from the origin to the point $h^*$ on the x-axis of the diagram. All other suppliers of CSL require some wage compensation in order to supply CSL. In the absence of any nonwage reward, their supply would be represented by the curve $S_x$ in Figure 1. Representing the reservation wage at which people will supply CSL, it begins at some positive wage level (directly above $h^*$) and then slopes upward to the right. The upward slope in $S_x$ reflects the fact that potential suppliers of CSL are likely to have different alternative opportunities in the labor market – either because they

---

[5] We use the term "caring" rather than "care" to distinguish the caring joint product from the care service itself. The tenderness in "tender loving care" is one form of caring, but caring may involve other forms of affection or simply respect and esteem for the care recipient.

[6] In order to simplify our exposition, we will henceforth describe a well-defined and contracted-for reward (motive 5) in terms of wage compensation alone.

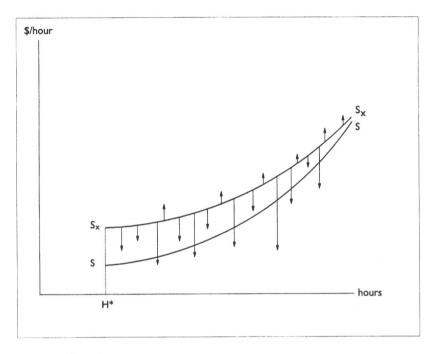

Figure 1

have different kinds and amounts of marketable skills or because they have different degrees of access to alternative job opportunities.

Those who require a wage for supplying CSL may well also, however, derive varying degrees of psychic satisfaction from supplying CSL. As we have seen, there are various kinds of noncontractual rewards which may be associated with the supply of CSL; moreover, some people may find the provision of care service distasteful and thus incur a loss of psychic satisfaction when supplying it. Taking these possibilities into account, we need to modify the curve $S_x$ by subtracting for each hour of CSL supplied the value of psychic satisfaction from the initial reservation wage reflecting only the wage reward. The arrows departing from $S_x$ in Figure 1 depict the psychic satisfaction component of the CSL supply curve. These arrows point predominantly downward (since positive psychic satisfaction will be much more common than negative psychic satisfaction), and their length varies more or less randomly along the $h$-axis (since there is no reason to posit any correlation across individuals between their alternative wage possibilities and the extent to which they derive psychic satisfaction from care service labor).

To draw a proper CSL supply curve, reflecting both psychic and wage rewards, we need to include the horizontal line from the origin to $h^*$ and then to reorder the points at the end of the arrows in Figure 1 so that they are sequential in the value of the wage $w$. The result will be a new supply curve – depicted by S in Figure 1 (we are assuming that in no case does psychic satisfaction exceed the wage). The upward-sloping segment of S begins at a lower $w$ than does $S_x$ (because some people with poor alternative opportunities will have high psychic reward), and it rises to the right to a point near to, if not above, $S_x$ (because some people with very good alternatives will have zero or negative psychic reward). Thus the rising segment of S is steeper than $S_x$.

Among CSL suppliers demanding some wage compensation, ceteris paribus, those who derive substantial positive psychic reward from care service labor will tend disproportionately to be concentrated around the lower end of the rising segment of the S curve, while those who derive little or negative psychic reward will be disproportionately clustered around the upper end. To be sure, the lower part will also include some people with poor alternatives and little or no psychic reward from supplying CSL, and the upper part will also include some people with excellent alternatives and a high degree of psychic reward. But the amount of psychic reward associated with an hour of CSL supplied will decline on average as one moves up the CSL supply curve S.[7]

Consider now the demand side of the care service labor market. For familiar reasons the demand curve for CSL will be downward-sloping; Figure 2 shows both such a demand curve D and the supply curve S from Figure 1. Typically we would expect that the D curve intersects the S curve somewhere on its upward-sloping segment (otherwise we would observe a wage of zero for care service labor). Thus we depict equilibrium in the CSL market in Figure 2 at the point $E_0$, where $h = h_0$ and $w = w_0$.[8]

---

[7] We are assuming that the distribution of positive and negative intrinsic rewards to CSL suppliers is distributed randomly, i.e., independently of their reservation wage before taking into account the effect of any positive or negative psychic rewards. It follows that when one takes those psychic rewards into account, one will find a disproportionately large number of people with positive psychic rewards among individuals with lower reservation wages. Indeed, in the whole range of the sloping segment of the S curve which lies at a lower level than the starting point of the sloping segment of the $S_x$ curve there must be only individuals with positive psychic rewards, because otherwise their reservation wage taking these into account could not possibly be lower than it was when those rewards were not taken into account.

[8] The equilibrium wage for SCL depends of course on the location of both the demand and the supply curve. The stronger is the demand for CSL, the higher will be the equilibrium wage, and the less likely it is that care service workers who derive positive psychic satisfaction from their labor will actually confront a negative compensating differential in the CSL market. We thank Julie Nelson for reminding us of this point.

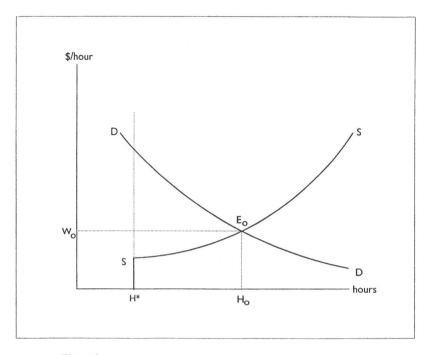

Figure 2

We can now use a comparative static analysis to study the effects of changes in the amount of caring labor supplied to the care service labor market. A decrease in the supply of caring labor can take the form of a decrease in the extent to which wage-paid CSL suppliers derive psychic satisfaction from their care service activities, or a decrease in the amount of CSL that is supplied without any compensation at all. We explore each of these changes in turn.

The effect of a *decrease in the extent to which wage-paid CSL suppliers receive psychic satisfaction* from care service labor is illustrated in Figure 3 by means of an upward shift in the sloping segment of the supply curve; the higher supply curve $S_3$ implies a new equilibrium point $E_3$ where $h = h_3 < h_0$ and $w = w_3 > w_0$. Thus, less psychic reward for CSL (by those who also demand a wage) results, ceteris paribus, in a lower supply of CSL and a higher wage paid. The overall change in consumer and producer surplus is represented by the change in area under the demand curve and above the supply curve in Figure 3; in this case it is clearly negative, since the new supply curve $S_3$ is everywhere above the old supply curve S.

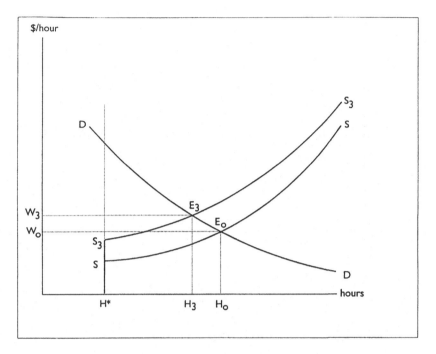

Figure 3

The effect of a *decrease in the uncompensated supply of care service labor* (relative to the compensated supply) is illustrated in Figure 4 by means of a new and lower value $h^{**}$ instead of the original $h^*$. The "newly compensated" hours of CSL (between $h^{**}$ and $h^*$) must now be accounted for in the rising portion of the supply curve. Depending on the distribution of the reservation wages now associated with these hours, the slope of the new supply curve $S_4$ will differ from that of the original curve S, but when all of those hours are accounted for (at a high enough wage to elicit their supply), the $S_4$ curve will join the S curve. The overall effect of the change is thus to shift the supply curve left, by an amount that decreases as $w$ rises, and the new supply curve $S_4$ implies a new equilibrium point $E_4$ where $h = h_3 < h_0$ and $w = w_3 > w_0$. It follows that the greater the extent to which CSL is supplied for a wage, the lower the total amount of CSL supplied and the higher the wage paid for those CSL hours that are actually compensated. The overall change in producer and consumer surplus is again clearly negative, since there is now a smaller area under the demand curve and above the supply curve.

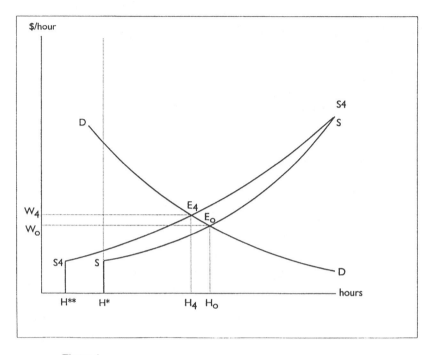

Figure 4

In both of the two cases there is clearly a decrease in consumers' surplus, for in equilibrium less CSL is supplied at higher cost. What happens to producers' surplus is not so obvious, but it can be shown that – except under highly unusual conditions – producers' surplus decreases in the first case and increases in the second case. Thus an increase in the compensated supply of care service labor pits supplier against consumer interests, benefiting suppliers while penalizing consumers.

This last conclusion, however, abstracts from any gain or loss for CSL suppliers associated with the transition between uncompensated and compensated labor. To remedy this inadequacy, we must analyze the welfare implications of such transitions. To do this we need to return to the distinction between caring motives and coercion. Suppose first that changes in the supply of compensated CSL are due to changes in the extent to which potential suppliers of CSL are coerced into supplying care service labor. Then any movement toward more compensated CSL involves an additional welfare gain for the suppliers involved; we will label this additional welfare gain the "freedom gain." The existence of freedom gains (or losses, when movement is toward more uncompensated labor) strengthens the opposition of consumer and producer interests with respect to changes in the supply of compensated CSL and shows that a transition to more compensated labor could lead to an overall welfare gain.

What if changes in the supply of uncompensated care service labor are due to changes in the number of CSL hours supplied by people for whom caring motives are the only consideration? (The people in question are not coerced into supplying CSL, nor do they believe that compensation is warranted for supplying it.) Any movement toward more (or less) compensated CSL does not involve the additional freedom gain (or loss) experienced by CSL suppliers who are being subjected to less (or more) coercion. We appear to be back in the world analyzed just before, where a leftward shift of the CSL supply curve from S to $S_3$ results in a gain of producer welfare but a loss of consumer and overall welfare.

Yet a stronger conclusion may be warranted. To this point we have treated the supply of uncoerced, uncompensated care service labor as producing substantial consumer benefits (equal to the area under the demand curve), but no supplier benefits (under the presumption that the actual wage of zero is exactly offset by the implicit reservation wage of zero where the supply curve hugs the x-axis). Our analysis of the overall welfare loss associated with a leftward (and upward) shift of the CSL supply curve from S to $S_4$ in Figure 4 is parallel to our analysis of the overall welfare loss associated with the upward shift of the CSL supply curve from S to $S_3$ in Figure 3. But we must come to grips with the fact that suppliers of uncoerced, uncompensated CSL are deriving psychic satisfaction from it; though their reward is incommensurate with wage compensation, it certainly has a positive value.

It follows that something of value is lost by CSL suppliers (and by society at large) when the suppliers choose voluntarily to offer less uncoerced and uncompensated care service labor. We will label this the "warm glow" loss. There is of course a corresponding warm glow gain associated with an increase in the amount of CSL supplied voluntarily for no compensation. Taking into account warm glow considerations, a leftward shift of the CSL supply curve of the kind analyzed in Figure 4 will not only reduce consumer welfare (as measured by the consumer surplus); it may also reduce supplier welfare, if the loss of warm glow associated with a drop in uncoerced uncompensated CSL supply is significant enough to offset the gain in producer surplus analyzed earlier.

A.2     *The supply of caring in the care service labor market*

We now address the second important respect in which care service labor differs from labor in general. In effect, a supplier of CSL motivated by caring motives produces a joint product – not only the basic care service that would be provided over the same period by a differently motivated CSL supplier, but also a certain amount of "caring" for the care service recipient. Caring as a joint product cannot be bought or sold in any market; so the total amount of caring provided in any society depends not on the demand for it but on the extent to which people with caring motives supply CSL.

Caring can contribute both directly and indirectly to overall welfare. It does so directly because it constitutes something valuable received by the care service recipient, and indirectly to the extent that it helps to resolve information and incentive problems associated with the provision of difficult-to-monitor care services. Those who wish to see good care service provided must consider not only whether the provider has the ability to supply the needed services but also whether the provider has a good incentive to do so.

A service provider motivated by caring motives will be attentive to the recipient's needs. A service provider lacking these motives will be most concerned with meeting the expectations of whoever is compensating or coercing the care service. If the latter is not the care service recipient, but instead some third party responsible for the recipient, then the information and incentive problems arise. (These problems can also arise even if the compensating or coercing party is the care service recipient, to the extent that he/she is not able to discern the quality of the care service). Because of the difficulty of measuring the quality of care services, any third party would have to invest some time and/ or resources in order to determine how good a job the care service provider was doing. Indeed, the more difficult it is to assess the quality of the care service, the more a third party responsible for the provision of care service will have an incentive to engage someone who really cares for the care recipient. It follows that caring not only adds a valuable element of affection and respect to care service; it also reduces monitoring costs.

We can gain some initial insight into the determinants of the amount of caring forthcoming with care service labor in a given situation by referring to Figure 1. We will continue to assume, for the time being, that CSL is measurable in terms of hours of labor and that it is homogeneous in terms of the basic care service provided (apart from any caring that may accompany it). Of the $h^*$ CSL hours supplied for no compensation, each of those which are not coerced is motivated by psychic reward and provides what we will identify as a full hour of caring. CSL hours supplied beyond $h^*$ are supplied for compensation but also provide varying amounts of psychic satisfaction (positive in the relatively frequent cases in which the arrows in Figure 1 point downward, but negative in some cases where the arrows point upward). It is reasonable to suggest that even those compensated CSL suppliers who derive the greatest psychic reward will not derive as much – nor convey as much caring – as do the uncoerced uncompensated CSL suppliers. Thus an hour of compensated CSL cannot provide as much as a full hour of caring.

As we noted earlier, CSL suppliers who derive substantial psychic reward from care service labor will tend to be concentrated around the lower end of the rising segment of the operative supply curve S. More generally, the average amount of psychic satisfaction associated with a marginal hour of compensated CSL will decline as one moves upward along the supply curve. Correspondingly, the amount of caring conveyed by an additional hour of CSL will tend to decline (from an initial level of less than a full hour) as the hours supplied increase from $h^*$.

Consider now the implications for the supply of caring of the changes in supply conditions in the care service labor market analyzed earlier.

*A decrease in the extent to which wage-paid CSL suppliers receive psychic satisfaction*, illustrated in Figure 3, will reduce the supply of caring; the reduction will be substantial, unless both the old and new equilibrium levels of hours $h_0$ and $h_3$ are close to $h^*$ and most of the caring is originally supplied with uncompensated labor.

*A decrease in the uncompensated supply of care service labor*, illustrated in Figure 4, will reduce the supply of caring; the reduction will be very substantial, unless the lost uncompensated hours of CSL were primarily coerced.

### A.3    *Skills and the care service labor market*

Our analysis to this point has been simplified by the unrealistic assumption that the actual care service resulting from an hour of care service labor is homogeneous (apart from any accompanying caring). A more realistic analysis would recognize that an hour of care service labor can be provided with widely differing degrees of skill, and hence with widely differing levels of productivity measured in terms of the amount of actual care service delivered per hour of CSL.

The incorporation of skilled labor into our graphical analysis of the care service labor market calls for a distinction to be made between hours of CSL supplied and units of actual care service delivered; furthermore, the productivity of skilled care labor, as well as the opportunity cost of its supply, must be carefully modeled. We have carried out such an analysis, but its additional complexity precludes our presenting it in the space available here. We will therefore limit ourselves to a discussion of the most important conclusion.

In equilibrium, ceteris paribus, the more skilled the care service labor force, the fewer will be the number of hours of care service labor supplied. This has an important implication with respect to the supply of caring. The amount of caring accompanying the provision of care service labor is clearly a function not of the number of units of actual care service delivered but of the number of hours expended in supplying care service labor. A person conveys love, affection, and respect for another person in the course of spending time with that person; whether the care service provided during any given hour is more or less skilled would seem to be quite unrelated to the amount of caring involved.

It follows that there is a diminution of caring per unit of care service delivered as the amount of skill embodied in an hour of CSL increases. The greater the extent to which care service skills substitute for care service hours, the less caring will accompany the care services which are provided. Even when an increase in care service skills allows more care service to be delivered at a lower cost per unit of such service, the gain in welfare represented by a larger total consumer plus producer surplus must be weighed against a loss in welfare associated with a decline in the amount of caring conveyed.

### A.4 The overall advantages of caring labor over compensated labor

Intuitively one can sense that a society benefits to the extent that care services are provided out of caring motives rather than in exchange for compensation. Our analysis to this point permits us to identify more precisely what are the social benefits of CSL provided out of caring motives rather than for compensation.

To identify these social benefits, let us first compare situation A in which CSL is motivated solely by compensation to situation B in which the same amount of care service is provided by people, some of whom are willing (without coercion) to provide uncompensated CSL and some of whom derive positive psychic satisfaction from the compensated CSL they provide. The demand curve for CSL in the two situations is the same. The supply curve of CSL will be lower in situation B than in situation A: To the extent that compensated CSL suppliers derive positive psychic reward from their labor, the applicable portion of the supply curve will shift down (as from $S_3$ to S in Figure 3); to the extent that there are suppliers of uncompensated CSL, the supply curve will shift to the right (as from $S_4$ to S in Figure 4, if $h^{**}$ is at the origin). Consequently, the total consumer and producer surplus will be greater in situation B than in situation A, reflecting a higher overall level of social welfare.

Indeed, this initial comparison understates the improvement in social welfare from situation A to situation B. It takes account of the gain in welfare associated with a higher level of psychic satisfaction accruing to compensated CSL suppliers; this is what shifts the supply curve down in the range of compensated CSL supply. And it takes account of the gain in consumer plus producer surplus associated with the drop in the supply curve to the x-axis in the range of uncompensated CSL supply. It does not, however, take into account the warm glow gain associated with an increase in the amount of CSL supplied voluntarily for no compensation. Nor does it take into account the overall social gain associated (directly and indirectly) with a larger supply of caring. Although these latter gains are (with the exception of savings in monitoring costs) essentially incommensurate with the gains of consumer and producer surplus, they represent additional important sources of higher social benefits in situation B as compared to situation A.

### Appendix B: Child care as a chicken game

The issue of who takes care of the kids is nicely modeled as a game of chicken with asymmetrical preferences. The standard symmetrical chicken game can be described by the following payoff matrix:

|  |  | Column player | |
|---|---|---|---|
|  |  | Cooperate | Defect |
| Row player | Cooperate | (2, 2) | (1, 3) |
|  | Defect | (3, 1) | (0, 0) |

where the cell pairs show the row player's payoff first. For each player it is best to do the opposite of what the other player does, and there is no obviously dominant outcome.

This would apply to the child care situation if a woman and a man cared equally about having the kids cared for, and if they valued equally the burden of spending time with the kids (they can actually value this positively, rather than negatively as a burden, so long as it is not so positive that taking care of the kids oneself becomes preferable to having the other party do it).

Let us assume, more realistically, that there are different payoffs for women and men. The difference may result from difference in the value placed on having the kids be cared for at all (women care more), or in the burden associated with taking care of kids (women find it less of a burden), or both. This changes the payoffs for women, but not for men. If the woman values having the kids cared for by an amount $x$ more than the man does (and is upset by the same amount more if there is no child care), then the payoff matrix will look like this:

Man

|  |  | Cooperate | Defect |
|---|---|---|---|
| Woman | Cooperate | $(2 + x, 2)$ | $(1 + x, 3)$ |
|  | Defect | $(3 + x, 1)$ | $(-x, 0)$ |

It's still a chicken game, because each party would choose the opposite of the other party, if he/she knew the other's choice, and double care is better for both than no care. But there is now a difference in the intensity of the urge to care when the other party doesn't; for the man the difference remains 1, whereas for the woman it rises from 1 to $1 + 2x$. In a probabilistic sense we can conclude that women will more often choose to care (since they have more to lose than men by not caring if the other party also turns out not to care); knowing that, and having less to lose if they guess wrong, men will more often choose not to care. So the outcome of women's caring and men's not caring will be the most likely.

If we now model the possibility that the woman views the caring as less burdensome than the man does, so that the cost to her of doing care is $y$ less than it is for the man, then we get the following payoff matrix:

Man

|  |  | Cooperate | Defect |
|---|---|---|---|
| Woman | Cooperate | $(2 + x + y, 2)$ | $(1 + x + y, 3)$ |
|  | Defect | $(3 + x, 1)$ | $(-x, 0)$ |

If $y$ is very small, this leaves us in the same situation as before – except that the woman's urge to care when the man doesn't rises even further (from $1 + 2x$ to $1 + 2x + y$), and the woman's urge not to care when the man does falls (from 1 to $1 - y$). From a probabilistic point of view, the outcome is even more likely to be women caring and men not caring. But if $y$ is large enough ($y > 1$), it would cause the woman to prefer care to no care even when the man also chooses care. In that case the payoff structure is no longer that of a chicken game; the woman always chooses to care, the man chooses not to, and the situation is completely determinate.

204     **Nancy Folbre and Thomas E. Weisskopf**

REFERENCES

Akerlof, George (1982). "Labor Contracts as Partial Gift Exchange," *Quarterly Journal of Economics* 97(4): 543–70.
Bebel, August (1971). *Women and Socialism.* Trans. Daniel De Leon. New York: Schocken Books.
Becker, Gary (1992). "Finding Fault with No-Fault Divorce," *Business Week*, December 7, p. 22.
Becker, Gary, Michael Grossman, and Kevin Murphy (1991). "Rational Addiction and the Effect of Price on Consumption," *American Economic Review* 81(2): 237–41.
Eckel, Catherine C., and Philip Grossman (1996a). "Are Women Less Selfish Than Men? Evidence from Dictator Experiments." Manuscript, Department of Economics, Virginia Polytechnic Institute and State University.
Eckel, Catherine C., and Philip Grossman (1996b). "The Relative Price of Fairness: Gender Differences in a Punishment Game." Unpublished manuscript, Department of Economics, Virginia Polytechnic Institute and State University.
England, Paula (1992). *Comparable Worth: Theories and Evidence.* New York: Aldine de Gruyter.
England, Paula, and Barbara Kilbourne (1990). "Feminist Critiques of the Separative Model of the Self: Implications for Rational Choice Theory," *Rationality and Society* 2(2): 517–25.
Ferguson, Ann (1989). *Blood at the Root: Motherhood, Sexuality, and Male Dominance.* London: Pandora Press.
Folbre, Nancy (1994). *Who Pays for the Kids? Gender and the Structures of Constraint.* New York: Routledge.
Folbre, Nancy, and Heidi Hartmann (1988). "The Rhetoric of Self-Interest: Selfishness, Altruism, and Gender in Economic Theory," in Arjo Klamer, Donald McCloskey, and Robert Solow, eds., *Consequences of Economic Rhetoric*, pp. 184–206. Cambridge: Cambridge University Press.
Fuchs, Victor (1988). *Women's Quest for Economic Equality.* Cambridge, Mass.: Harvard University Press.
Hochschild, Arlie (1989). *The Second Shift.* New York: Viking.
Orphanides, Athanasios, and David Zeroos (1995). "Rational Addiction with Learning and Regret," *Journal of Political Economy* 4(103): 740–52.
Schotter, Andrew (1981). *An Economic Theory of Social Institutions.* London: Cambridge University Press.
Seguino, Stephanie, Thomas Stevens, and Mark A. Lutz (1996). Economic Men Free Ride: How About Economic Women? *Feminist Economics* 2(1): 1–21.
Sen, Amartya (1987). *On Ethics and Economics.* New York: Basil Blackwell.
——— (1990). "Gender and Cooperative Conflicts," in Irene Tinker, ed., *Persistent Inequalities: Women and World Development*, pp. 123–49. New York: Oxford University Press.

Stark, Oded (1995). *Altruism and Beyond: An Economic Analysis of Transfers and Exchanges Within Families and Groups.* Cambridge: Cambridge University Press.

Taylor, Michael (1987). *On the Possibility of Cooperation.* Cambridge: Cambridge University Press.

Titmuss, Richard (1970). *The Gift Relationship: From Human Blood to Social Policy.* London: George Allen and Unwin.

Tronto, Joan (1987). "Beyond Gender Difference to a Theory of Care," *Signs: Journal of Women in Culture and Society* 12(4): 644–63.

CHAPTER 7

# How communities govern: the structural basis of prosocial norms

*Samuel Bowles and Herbert Gintis*

## 1    Introduction

The age of commerce and the dawn of democracy were widely thought to mark the eclipse of community. Writers of all persuasions believed that markets, the state, or simply "modernization" would extinguish the values that throughout history had sustained forms of governance based on intimate and ascriptive relationships. According to the romantic conservative Edmund Burke (1955)

> The age of chivalry is gone. That of Sophisters, economists, and calculators has succeeded. . . . Nothing is left which engages the affection on the part of the commonwealth . . . so as to create in us love, veneration, admiration or attachment.

The liberal Alexis de Tocqueville (1969) echoes Burke's fears in this comment on democratic culture in America during the 1830s:

> Each [person] . . . is a stranger to the fate of all the rest . . . his children and his private friends constitute to him the whole of mankind; as for the rest of his fellow citizens, he is close to them but he sees them not . . . he touches them but he feels them not; he exists but in himself and for himself alone.

For the socialists Marx and Engels (1972)

> The bourgeoisie . . . has put an end to all feudal, patriarchal, idyllic relations. It has pitilessly torn asunder the motley feudal ties that bound man to his "natural superiors," and has left remaining no other nexus between man and man than naked self-interest. . . . [I]n place of the numberless indefeasible chartered freedoms, it has set up that single, unconscionable freedom – free trade. (p. 475)

We are grateful to Jeff Carpenter for helpful comments and the MacArthur Foundation for financial support.

Yet communities have survived, and some have even proliferated: Residential neighborhoods, as well as voluntary and ethnic associations, are still with us.[1] Many who predicted the demise of community based their argument on the notion that communities owe their existence to a distinct set of premodern "values" that were bound to be extinguished by economic and political competition in markets and democratic states, or as Marx put it by "the icy waters of egotistical calculation." Modern writers as well have stressed that the parochialism on which communities thrive requires cultural commitments that are antithetical to modern social institutions. Talcott Parsons's sociological system, to mention one prominent example, consistently attributes "particularistic" values to more primitive levels of civilization, and "universalistic" values to the more advanced.

Fred Hirsch (1976, pp. 117–18) refers to the waning of precapitalist moral codes in similar vein:

> This legacy has diminished with time and with the corrosive contact of the active capitalist values. As individual behavior has been increasingly directed to individual advantage, habits and instincts based on communal attitudes and objectives have lost out.

We do not doubt that markets and democratic states represent cultural environments in which some values flourish and others wither. Indeed, the dismay concerning their effects, expressed so long ago by Burke, Marx, and de Tocqueville, may have been prescient. But the basis for the rise, fall, and transformation of communities, if we are correct, is to be sought not in the survival of vestigial values of an earlier age, but in the capacity of communities, like that of markets and states, to provide successful solutions to the problems that people confront in their contemporary social lives. In our view communities overcome free-rider problems, internalize external economies, and punish "antisocial" actions by supporting behaviors consistent with such prosocial norms as truth telling, reciprocity, and a predisposition to cooperate toward common ends.

These norms and values are often represented as the legacy of a particular tradition supported by intentional indoctrination and virtually universally held in a given population. But this account of community-based values is uncompelling. First, groups appear to be quite internally heterogeneous with respect to many important norms, and the theory of "deviance" from universal norms does not provide an adequate

---

[1] In addition to these obvious forms of community we would include such economic institutions as at least some firms and rotating savings and credit associations. See Putterman (1988) and Bouman (1977), for example.

understanding of the distribution of normative orientations in members of a group (Gintis 1975). Second, the implied power of intentional inculcation of values is belied by many failed experiments in the social engineering of the psyche, the attempted construction of the "new socialist man" in the former Soviet Union being the most notable. Third, value orientations appear to be subject to quite rapid shifts, as witnessed by the precipitous unravelling of indigenous cultures and the meteoric rise of modern feminism in the twentieth century, suggesting that while history may matter, particular norms are only reproduced and sustained when they meet the test of relevance and usefulness for the contemporary groups and individuals embracing them.

As an alternative to the idea that community-based values are the result of a universally inculcated legacy of the past, we here develop the view that the contemporary structure of social interactions that characterize communities, not the inertial weight of tradition or intentional indoctrination, accounts for the viability of the prosocial norms we have indicated. Communities persist under modern conditions because they solve modern problems. They do this by supporting prosocial norms and behaviors.[2]

## 2    Community governance

> Most if not all economic acts [among the Trobriand Islanders] are found to belong to some chain of reciprocal gifts and counter gifts, which in the long run balance.... The real reason why all these economic obligations are normally kept, and kept very scrupulously, is that failure to comply places a man in an intolerable position.... The honourable citizen is bound to carry out his duties, though his submission is not due to any instinct or intuitive impulse or mysterious "group sentiment," but to the detailed and elaborate working of a system, in which every act has its own place and must be performed without fail. Though no native however intelligent can formulate this state of affairs in a general abstract manner ... every one is well aware of its existence and in each concrete case he can foresee the consequences.
>
> Malinowski, *Crime and Custom in Savage Society*, p. 40

A "community" is a social institution characterized by high entry and exit costs and nonanonymous interactions among members. Communities foster frequent interaction among the same agents, partly as a result of low cost access to information about other community members, a tendency to favor interactions with members of one's own community over those with outsiders, and restricted migration to and from

---

[2] It goes without saying of course that communities as we have defined them may obstruct efficiency-enhancing economic arrangements and nonetheless persist. See, for example, Platteau (1996).

|           | Ephemeral | Enduring    |
|-----------|-----------|-------------|
| Anonymous | Markets   | States      |
| Personal  | —         | Communities |

Figure 1. The structure of interactions in different institutions

other communities. These structural characteristics contribute to the ability of communities to promote prosocial behavior.

The structure of interactions in communities contrasts with that of markets and states, at least in their idealized forms. Market interactions are characterized by ephemerality of contact and anonymity among interacting agents, while idealized state bureaucracies are characterized by long-term anonymous relationships. The relevant contrasts appear in Figure 1.

States and markets have distinctive capacities and shortcomings as governance structures, but our concern here is with communities.[3] We have identified four ways in which communities solve coordination problems.

First, a high frequency of interaction among community members lowers the cost of gathering information and raises the benefits associated with discovering the characteristics of those with whom one interacts. The more easily acquired and widely dispersed this information, the more will community members have an incentive to act in ways beneficial to their neighbors. Thus when agents engage in repeated interaction, they have an incentive to act in ways that build their "reputation" for cooperative behavior.[4] This is the "reputation effect" of community.

Second, since in a community the probability is high that members who interact today will interact in the future, there is an incentive to act favorably towards one's partners to prevent future repercussions.[5] The more multifaceted is the relationship among people involved in the interaction, the more opportunities there are for the later redress of opportunistic treatment. We refer to this as the "retaliation effect."

Third, the social segmentation typical of communities may provide a surrogate for contractual incompleteness. Prosocial and antisocial

[3] We provide an information theoretic account of the capacities and shortcomings of markets, states, and communities in Bowles and Gintis (1997). See also Farrell (1987).
[4] Reputational models are explored in Shapiro (1983), Gintis (1989), and Kreps (1990).
[5] See Axelrod and Hamilton (1981), Axelrod (1984), Taylor (1987), and Fudenberg and Maskin (1986) for models of this type.

| | Effect favoring the solution of coordination problems | Characteristic of community necessary for this effect | Variable in Model to Follow |
|---|---|---|---|
| Reputation | Enhanced value of reputations for pro-social behaviors | Low cost of information about other agents | $\delta$ |
| Retaliation | Punishment of anti-social behaviors | Frequent or long-lasting interactions | $\rho$ |
| Segmentation | Disadvantageous pairing of anti-social agents | Non-random pairing of agents | $\sigma$ |
| Parochialism | Enhanced group selection pressures favoring nice traits | Limited migration among groups; non-random new group formation | $\mu$ |

Figure 2. How communities solve coordination problems

behaviors typically involve conferring benefits and inflicting costs on others, in a situation where the costs and benefits in question are not subject to cost effective contracting. In a large population of many communities, the greater likelihood of interacting with a member of one's own community than with a randomly selected member of the population provides a mechanism for likes interacting and thus for internalizing the noncontractible benefits and costs of prosocial and antisocial activities.[6] This is the "segmentation effect."

Finally, such prosocial behaviors as altruism and reciprocal fairness may evolve if the pressure of group selection is sufficiently strong, the group benefits of the prevalence of nice traits outweighing the individual costs of the prosocial behaviors. The group selection pressures in turn vary with the degree of diversity in the distribution of traits among groups. The degree of diversity depends on the level of migration among groups and the extent to which the formation of new groups favors groups more homogeneous than the population as a whole. Impermeable boundaries and segmentation support higher levels of diversity than would be otherwise sustainable.[7] We call this the "parochialism effect."

Figure 2 summarizes these causal links between the structure of communities and the attenuation of coordination problems.

[6] Such segmentation models have been investigated by Grafen (1979), Axelrod and Hamilton (1981), and Bowles (1996), among others.

[7] Models of this type are explored in Boorman and Levitt (1980), Wilson (1980), Boyd and Richerson (1990), and Soltis, Boyd, and Richerson (1995).

Interactions among people may be structured by communities, markets, states, and families, as well as other institutions. The importance of communities in this nexus of governance will evolve in response to the balance of benefits conferred by the four community effects just identified relative to the opportunity costs of community governance and the corresponding benefits of alternative institutional structures.

Though we will not model the process here, we think it reasonable to suppose that populations whose interactions are regulated by a balance of community and other governance structures that successfully address coordination failures will tend to grow and to occupy new territories, to absorb other populations, and thus to replace less successful governance structures. The selective pressures operating in these cases may include military and economic competition as well as the possibility of rejections by the governed of unsuccessful governance structures as attempts at emulation of the successful.

## 3     Cultural evolution

> What is the nature of social selection? . . . in the process of socioeconomic change, new economic trends develop for which the traditional character is not well adapted, while a certain heretofore deviant character type can make optimal use of the new conditions. As a result the "ex-deviants" become the most successful individuals or leaders of their society or class. They acquire the power to change laws, educational systems, and institutions in a way that . . . influences the character development of succeeding generations. . . . Secondary trait personalities never fully disappear and hence . . . social changes always find the individuals and groups that can serve as the core for the new social order.
>
> Fromm and Maccoby, *Social Character in a Mexican Village*, p. 232

Suppose a community is composed of a large number of people who interact in pairs with available actions and payoffs describing a prisoner's dilemma, as indicated in Figure 3, with the familiar payoffs $a > b > c > d$ and $a + d < 2b$.[8] The actions taken by each are not subject to enforceable contracts. Universal defect is the dominant strategy equilibrium for this interaction. If the players could contract to play cooperatively, they would surely do so. But the assumption that the behaviors in question are noncontractible, namely, that the interaction is noncooperative, precludes this. How might the structure of the community nonetheless induce universal cooperation?

To answer this question we must know what behavioral norms, preferences, or other rules of thumb will be followed by people in their interactions, and how they come to acquire the traits governing these

---

[8] The second requirement simply precludes the social optimality of alternating roles of defector and cooperator.

Cooperate  Defect

|  | Cooperate | Defect |
|---|---|---|
| Cooperate | $b, b$ | $d, a$ |
| Defect | $a, d$ | $c, c$ |

Figure 3. The prisoner's dilemma

behaviors. Because many of the traits in question may be moral rules or cultural regularities that may not have been actively and purposefully chosen by the people in question, we require an approach more general than the standard view, whereby actions, or the rules governing actions, are instrumentally chosen to maximize an objective function. Instead, we adopt the evolutionary view that key to the understanding of behaviors in the kinds of social interactions we are studying is *differential replication*: Durable aspects of behavior, including norms, habits, and rules of thumb, may be accounted for by the fact that they have been copied, diffused, and hence replicated, while other traits have not.[9]

Differential replication may result from individuals' seeking to acquire traits, rules of thumb, and norms that have proved successful to others. Differential replication may also take place through less instrumental means, such as "conformism," in which individuals copy cultural forms that have high frequency in the population. The process of differential replication also may work through the exercise of power by nations, classes, or other collectivities, as when those who lose wars adopt the culture, constitutions, and the like, of winners.

By "culture" we mean a set of cultural traits. A cultural trait is a belief, value, or other acquired aspect of an individual that influences the individual's behavior in some durable fashion.[10] A predisposition to help others, or to have large families, or generally to skip breakfast is a cultural trait, as are the practices of reciprocating social invitations and always selling to the highest bidder. Cultural evolution is the process of

[9] Differential replication is of course a key to biological evolution. Many evolutionary ideas concerning culture are adapted from biological reasoning, without the underlying genetic mechanisms. Key sources on cultural evolution are Cavalli-Sforza and Feldman (1981), Boyd and Richerson (1985), and Dawkins (1982).

[10] This framework draws on the sources mentioned in footnote 9. Others defining culture often stress aspects absent here, such as the functional or legitimating role of culture, its integrated nature, and its grounding in historical tradition.

change over time in the distribution of cultural traits in a population. A cultural equilibrium is a distribution of cultural traits not subject to endogenous sources of change. A cultural environment is any social situation affecting the propensity of existing cultural traits to be adopted by others (whether willingly, consciously, or not) and new cultural traits to be introduced.

Communities, like markets and states, are environments in which cultural traits develop and change. Cultural environments may be distinguished by the way that they favor the copying and hence evolution of distinct cultural traits.[11]

Suppose cultural evolution takes place under the influence of the differential replication of traits that are perceived to be successful by members of the population.[12] Emulation of the cultural traits of individuals perceived to be socially successful is analogous to the increased reproductive success of biologically fit organisms. Emulation may be very rapid if the cultural traits correlated with success have no moral force and are embraced only because of their expected consequences. Even where there is a conflict between a deeply held moral value and the perceived success of individuals and groups who reject that value, there is a tendency for the moral value to be abandoned. This may happen through group selection, since groups that espouse the more successful value may simply displace groups that espouse the less (Soltis, Boyd, and Richerson 1995). In addition, individuals themselves may abandon inopportune values (Festinger 1957), or a new generation may simply refuse to embrace the inopportune values of the previous. Moreover, values found useful in one social setting (e.g., the workplace) may be unconsciously "transported" to another, where they threaten and possibly displace more traditional values (Kohn 1969; Bowles, and Gintis 1976). Finally, successful individuals may obtain positions, as governmental leaders, media figures, and teachers, for example, in which they have privileged access to the population as cultural models and thus may be copied disproportionately for reasons associated with their location in the social structure rather than success per se, and others deemed equally successful will be less replicated.

---

[11] Of course the structure of cultural transmission under which human societies acquire cultural traits is itself the result of both genetic and cultural evolutionary processes. For this reason, an adequate model of the differential replication of cultural traits presupposes the adaptive nature of the transmission processes in question in the relevant environments, including the present. The transmission process postulated must be capable of reproducing itself.

[12] This framework is derived from the models of cultural evolution cited, but it is also consistent with a variety of other approaches. See, for instance, Bandura (1977).

Notice a rough learning rule underlying differential replication has replaced the role usually assigned to conscious optimization. We do not specify why traits are copied. The previous paragraph leaves this issue open. Rather, we simply posit that successful traits are more likely to be copied. In the penultimate section we investigate more general approaches to the process of replication of traits, notably a model in which both the success of traits and their prevalence in the population influence the probability of their replication.

Cultural transmission based on the favored replication of successful traits may be modeled as follows: Let there be one of two mutually exclusive traits ($x$ and $y$) present in each member of a large population ($y$ may be considered to be the absence of $x$). Let $p_x$ be the fraction of members of the population that has trait $x$, and let $r_x$ be the rate of growth of $p_x$ over time.[13] The structure of the transmission process is this: In a large population with a given distribution of traits, agents implement the strategy dictated by their trait in a game which assigns benefits to each, after which the traits are replicated, generating a new population distribution. Equilibrium is defined as stationarity of the frequency of traits.

Suppose members of the population are randomly paired to interact in a two person game, the payoffs of which are denoted $\pi(i, j)$, the payoff to playing trait $i$ against a $j$-playing partner. Thus the probability of an individual's meeting an $x$ type is $p_x$, and the probability of meeting a $y$ type is $(1 - p_x)$. Thus the expected payoffs are given by

$$b_x(p_x) = p_x\pi(x,\ x) + (1 - p_x)\pi(x,\ y)$$
$$b_y(p_x) = p_x\pi(y,\ x) + (1 - p_x)\pi(y,\ y) \tag{1}$$

Read the first equation, "With probability $p$ an $x$ person is paired with another $x$ person with payoff $\pi(x, x)$, and with probability $(1 - p)$ is paired with a $y$ person with payoff $\pi(x, y)$."

Suppose at the end of each period each agent $A$, with probability $\gamma_1 > 0$, decides to reassess the value of his "type" by comparing his $b_i$ with that of a randomly chosen person $B$. If $B$ has a lower payoff than $A$, we assume $A$ does not change his cultural trait. But if $B$ has a higher payoff than $A$, and if $B$ is not of the same type as $A$, $A$ shifts to $B$'s type with a probability that is proportional to the difference in the payoffs to $A$ and $B$, with a proportionality factor $\gamma_2 > 0$. Then it is easy to show that[14]

---

[13] We assume the population is sufficiently large that we can treat $p_x$ and $r_x$ as real numbers.
[14] A proof is available to interested readers.

$$r_x = \gamma_1 \gamma_2 \left[ b_x(p_x) - \bar{b}(p_x) \right] \tag{2}$$

where $\bar{b}(p)$ is the average payoff in the society:

$$\bar{b}(p_x) = p_x b_x(p_x) + (1 - p_x) b_y(p_x) \tag{3}$$

Without going into the formal details (Bowles 1996), it is obvious that the population distribution $p$ will be unchanging if and only if $r_x = 0$, or that

$$b_y(p_x) = b_x(p_x) \tag{4}$$

Thus a condition of equilibrium (unchanging $p_x$) is that payoffs be equal. For a solution to (4), which we will call $p_x^*$, to be stable (i.e., to return to $p_x^*$ when perturbed) a small increase in $p_x$ (the fraction of those with trait $x$) must increase the replication propensity of the $y$ trait more than the $x$ trait, thereby favoring the $y$ trait in replication and lowering $p_x$. This can be written

$$\frac{dr_x}{dp_x} < 0 \tag{5}$$

requiring that

$$\pi(y, x) - \pi(y, y) - \pi(x, x) + \pi(x, y) > 0 \tag{6}$$

We turn now to a consideration of each of the four governance effects of community.

## 4    Reputation

> Honesty comes much more easily in a tiny community than it does in a great city, where misconduct always hopes that the multitude of alien tracks will cover up its own footprints.
>
> Diamond Jenness (of the 1913 Arctic expedition),
> *Arctic Odyssey*, pp. 128–29, commenting on the Eskimo lack of fear of stealing

Suppose now each agent can precommit to being one of two types of players, which we call "nice" and "nasty." An agent can determine whether a partner is "nice" by paying an inspection cost $\delta > 0$.[15] A nice agent is one who either cooperates unconditionally or inspects and responds to a nice partner by cooperating and to a nasty partner by defecting. Otherwise an agent is nasty. There are clearly six pure strategies (see Figure 4).

---

[15] This treatment of inspection and trust is adapted from Güth and Kliemt (1994). The dynamics of this model are more fully explored in Bowles and Gintis (1997).

| strategy | inspect | action | frequency |
|---|---|---|---|
| Defect | no | defect | $1 - \alpha - \beta$ |
| Trust | no | cooperate | $\beta$ |
| (a) | yes | defect | --- |
| (b) | yes | cooperate | — |
| Inspect | yes | defect if partner nasty | $\alpha$ |
|  |  | cooperate if partner nice | — |
| (c) | yes | defect if partner nice | — |
|  |  | cooperate if partner nasty | — |

Figure 4. Strategies in the inspect variant of the prisoner's dilemma

We have named only three of these strategies, since the others are strictly dominated, and hence cannot appear in a Nash equilibrium: (a) and (c) are strictly dominated by Defect and (b) is strictly dominated by Trust.

The payoff matrix to a pair of agents who agree to interact is now given by the normal form matrix shown in Figure 5.

We call a Nash equilibrium a *universal defect equilibrium* if all agents Defect, a *nontrust equilibrium* some agents Inspect but no agent Trusts, and a *trust equilibrium* if at least one agent Trusts. There are no other types of Nash equilibria.[16]

To investigate the possibility of an equilibrium with a positive level of trusting, let $\alpha \geq 0$, $\beta > 0$, and $(1 - \alpha - \beta) \geq 0$ be the probability that strategies Inspect, Trust, and Defect are used, respectively. If there were no defection, then Inspect is dominated by Trust, so all agents would Trust. But then Defect dominates Trust, which is a contradiction. Thus there is a positive level of Defect. If there were no Inspect, then again Defect would dominate Trust, which is impossible in equilibrium. Thus there must be positive levels of all three strategies if $\beta > 0$ in equilibrium.

Let $\pi^i(\alpha, \beta)$ be the expected payoff to adopting strategy $i$ in a population whose composition is described by $\alpha, \beta$. Then by (4), the payoffs to all must be equal in equilibrium. Thus we have $\pi^i(\alpha, \beta) = \pi^T(\alpha, \beta) = \pi^D(\alpha, \beta)$, or

$$\alpha(b - \delta) + \beta(b - \delta) + (1 - \alpha - \beta)(c - \delta) = (\alpha + \beta)b + (1 - \alpha - \beta)d \tag{7}$$

$$= \alpha c + \beta a + (1 - \alpha - \beta)c \tag{8}$$

---

[16] We will assume that number $x$ of players is sufficiently large that we can treat $x$ as a continuous real variable. In particular, we assume any Nash equilibrium can be supported by all players' choosing the appropriate pure strategies, and we will allow functions of $x$ to be continuous over the positive real numbers.

|        | Inspect | Trust | Defect |
|--------|---------|-------|--------|
| Inspect | $b - \delta, b - \delta$ | $b - \delta, b$ | $c - \delta, c$ |
| Trust  | $b, b - \delta$ | $b, b$ | $d, a$ |
| Defect | $c, c - \delta$ | $a, d$ | $c, c$ |

Figure 5. Payoffs for the inspect variant of the prisoner's dilemma

This implies

$$\alpha * + \beta * = 1 - \frac{\delta}{c - d} \tag{9}$$

from which it is clear that the fraction adopting prosocial strategies (Inspect or Trust) varies inversely with the cost of information $\delta$, attaining a value of unity when $\delta = 0$. Further,

$$\alpha * = \frac{1}{a - c}\left[(a - b)\left(1 - \frac{\delta}{c - d}\right) + \delta\right] \tag{10}$$

$$\beta * = \frac{1}{a - c}\left[(b - c)(b - d)\left(\frac{\delta}{c - d}\right)\right] \tag{11}$$

For such a solution to exist with $\alpha*, \beta* > 0$, equation (9) shows that we must have $\delta < c - d$. Then $\beta* > 0$ requires

$$\delta < (c - d)\frac{b - c}{b - d} \tag{12}$$

Notice that the right hand side of equation (12) is strictly positive, so such a $\delta > 0$ exists. Now $\alpha > 0$ if and only if

$$a - b > (a + d - c - b)\frac{\delta}{c}$$

which gives $(a - b)(c - \delta) + \delta(c - d) > 0$, which is true. Since equation (12) also implies $\delta < c - d$, we see that (12) is necessary and sufficient for a mixed strategy Nash equilibrium with a positive level of Trust. In this case the frequency $1 - \alpha* - \beta*$ of Defect is $(\delta/c - d)$, which is an increasing function of the cost of inspection. Also, the frequency $\beta*$ of Trust is a decreasing function of $\delta$, since

$$\frac{d\beta}{d\delta} = -\frac{b - d}{(c - d)(a - c)} < 0$$

Since the payoffs to all strategies are equal, the expected payoff to all the players is the same as to Trust, which, from (7), is $(\alpha^* + \beta^*)(b - d) + d$. Using (9), this gives

$$d + (b - d)(\alpha^* + \beta^*) = b - \frac{b - d}{c - d}\delta \qquad (13)$$

which is decreasing in the cost of inspection $\delta$.[17]

In sum, we have four distinct reputation effects based on the capacity of community to provide low cost information on the types of those with whom one interacts. First, reduced cost of information may make possible an equilibrium in which trusting behaviors occur (12). Second, in such an equilibrium the amount of trusting behavior will be greater the lower is the cost of information (11). Third, if trusting occurs in equilibrium, the average payoff to all members of the population will vary inversely with the cost of information (13). Finally, the fraction of the population defecting varied directly with the cost of information (9).

## 5    Retaliation

> Antonia did not speak to Juan for 15 years. He had offended her in public while she was mourning for her husband. . . . Through gossiping and chatting, the community of women [in Oroel, a Spanish town of 150 inhabitants] evolves a fund of information, impressions and understandings . . . which they draw on and interpret in order to make decisions about their daily interactions.
>
> Susan Harding, "Street Shouting and Shunning," p. 16.

We will show that if the prisoner's dilemma in Figure 3 is repeated with some probability, cooperation may be supported by the threat of retaliation against defectors, the threat being more effective the more likely is the repetition. If repetition is sufficiently likely, and if the time that elapses before repetition is sufficiently brief, the payoff structure is transformed to an assurance game interaction, with two equilibria, universal defect as before and universal cooperate.

Thus to the extent that the high exit and entry costs that characterize communities and entail frequent and repeated interaction with the same individuals, they may support a cooperative outcome unattainable under more ephemeral conditions.

---

[17] For completeness we should also deal with the case in which only Inspect and Defect strategies are used with positive probability. If Inspect is used with probability $\alpha^* > 0$ then Defect must be used with the strictly positive probability $1 - \alpha^*$ in equilibrium. Since the payoff to Defect is $c$, the expected payoff to Inspect must also be $c$.

|  | Tit-for-Tat | Defect |
|---|---|---|
| Tit-for-Tat | $b/\rho$ <br> $b/\rho$ | $d + (1-\rho)c/\rho$ <br> $a + (1-\rho)c/\rho$ |
| Defect | $a + (1-\rho)c/\rho$ <br> $d + (1-\rho)c/\rho$ | $c/\rho$ <br> $c/\rho$ |

Figure 6. The payoffs in the repeated prisoner's dilemma game

Repetition changes the interaction in two ways. It allows more complicated strategies, ones that take account of one's partner's prior actions, and it requires that payoffs be accounted for as expected gains over the entire interaction. Players might now want to adopt the so-called nice tit-for-tat strategy: Cooperate on the first round, and on all subsequent rounds do what your partner did on the previous round. To keep things simple let us confine the choice of strategies to just tit-for-tat ($T$) and unconditional defect ($D$). The expected payoffs may now be calculated.

Suppose that after each play the interaction is to be terminated with a given probability $\rho$, and repetitions occur over a brief enough period to justify ignoring the players' rates of time preference (an assumption of no consequence in what follows). When two tit-for-tatters meet, for example, they will both cooperate and then continue to do so until the interaction is terminated (that is, for an expected duration of $1/\rho$ iterations), giving expected benefits of $b/\rho$. When a tit-for-tatter meets a defector the former will get $d$ on the first iteration, and then both will defect until the game terminates; the expected number of iterations after the first iteration will be $(1-\rho)/\rho$, and the resulting expected payoffs thus will be $d + (1-p)c/\rho$. The resulting payoff matrix for the iterated game appears in Figure 6.

If the fraction of the population adopting tit-for-tat is $\tau$ (the remainder adopting unconditional defect) and if members of the population are paired randomly to interact so that the probability of being paired with a tit-for-tatter is $\tau$, expected returns will be

$$\pi^T(\tau) = \frac{\tau b}{\rho} + (1-\tau)\left\{d + (1-\rho)\frac{c}{\rho}\right\}$$

$$\pi^D(\tau) = \tau\left\{a + (1-\rho)\frac{c}{\rho}\right\} + (1-\tau)\frac{c}{\rho}$$

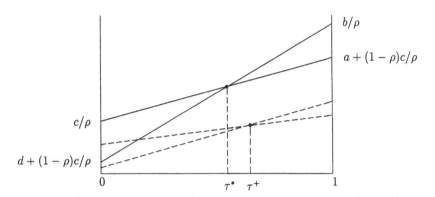

Figure 7. The retaliation effect: An increase in the probability of termination diminishes, and may eliminate, the range of attraction of the universal cooperate equilibrium.

which, when equated to determine the equilibrium population fraction $\tau^*$, yields

$$\tau^* = \frac{c-d}{2c-a-d+\left(b-c\right)/\rho} \tag{14}$$

For payoffs and termination probability such that

$$\rho < \frac{b-c}{a-c} \tag{15}$$

and for $c > d$, we have $\tau^* \in (0,1)$, giving an interior equilibrium. The second condition must be true because the single period payoffs describe a prisoner's dilemma. The first will be true when the gains to universal cooperation relative to the gains to single period defection are great relative to the termination probability. The preceding payoffs and an interior equilibrium $\tau^*$ are illustrated in Figure 7.

But unlike the equilibria in the reputation game considered, $\tau^*$ is unstable; small deviations from $\tau^*$ do not result in a convergence back to $\tau^*$. This is because

$$\frac{d\pi^D\left(\tau\right)}{d\tau} < \frac{d\pi^T\left(\tau\right)}{d\tau}$$

violating the stability condition (6). We may see this as follows: For values of $\tau$ greater than $\tau^*$ the expected return to $D$ relative to $T$ is diminished, but as the payoffs were equal at $\tau^*$ the returns to $D$ must therefore be inferior to $T$, which by the dynamic process described in section 3 will lead to further increase in $T$ rather than a return to $\tau^*$. As a result there are three equilibrium population frequencies, namely, 0, $\tau^*$, and 1. The first and third are stable. The unstable equilibrium $\tau^*$ defines the boundary between the ranges of attraction of the two stable equilibria.

Two results concerning the governance effects of community follow. First, the interaction will have an equilibrium of universal cooperation if the probability of termination is sufficiently low. This follows directly from condition (15): If an interior equilibrium exists and is unstable, $\tau = 1$ must be a stable equilibrium. Second, an increase in the probability of termination will reduce the range of attraction of the cooperative equilibrium. This is because

$$\frac{d\tau^*}{d\rho} = \frac{\left(\tau^*\right)^2\left(b-c\right)}{\rho^2\left(c-d\right)}$$

which must be positive if the initial payoffs are a prisoner's dilemma and if $\tau^* \in (0,1)$. Thus as the expected duration of interactions is reduced, the dividing line between the basin of attraction of universal defect and universal cooperation shifts toward the latter.

Condition (15) does not ensure that universal cooperation will take place. It ensures only that should universal cooperation occur, such cooperation would not unravel by the process of unilateral defection. Thus when condition (15) is fulfilled, tit-for-tat is a best response to itself and hence is a sustainable strategy.[18] This is the sense in which that continuity of interactions (low $\rho$) characteristic of communities favors cooperation.

## 6    Segmentation

> Like ethnic businesses generally, [Korean rotating credit associations] encourage the ethnic solidarity they require. . . . Bureaucratized financial institutions accelerated the atomization of the population rather than having, as previously thought, served the otherwise intractable needs of an already atomized population.
>
> Light, Kwuon, and Zhong (1990)

The high entry and exit costs that characterize communities cause populations to be segmented, as members of the communities that make up the larger population interact with outsiders less frequently than with insiders, for example when members of a population residing in villages engage in frequent exchanges with coresidents and occasionally exchange goods at a single market serving the entire population.

---

[18] Unconditional defect is also a sustainable strategy, of course.

Individuals in the larger population are either defectors or co-operators in a single period prisoner's dilemma, and as before they periodically update their type in response to the relative success of the two strategies. By contrast to the reputation and retaliation models, in which members of the population are randomly paired to interact, the segmentation model is based on nonrandom pairing. The communities into which the population is segmented are more homogeneous with respect to type than is the larger population, as likes tend to cluster with likes.

The clustering of likes attenuates coordination problems because prosocial behaviors such as cooperating in a prisoner's dilemma situation confer advantages to those with whom one interacts, while defection inflicts costs. Thus a biased pairing process that disproportionately pairs likes with likes raises the payoffs to those exhibiting the prosocial traits. The segmentation associated with community has the effect of internalizing the noncontractible benefits of prosocial behavior and thus supports a greater frequency of these traits in a population.

We define the degree of segmentation as follows: If the fraction of the population who are cooperators is $\alpha$, the probability that a cooperator will meet a fellow cooperator is no longer $\alpha$ but $\sigma + (1 - \sigma)\alpha$ where $\sigma$ is a measure of the degree of segmentation of the population. Correspondingly the probability of a defector's meeting a fellow defector is now $\sigma + (1 - \alpha)(1 - \sigma)$. The degree of segmentation $\sigma \in [0,1]$ with $\sigma = 1$ implying pairing of likes with likes whatever the population composition, and $\sigma = 0$ implying random assignment. The expected returns to each are thus

$$\pi^{C}(\alpha,\ \sigma) = \sigma b + (1 - \sigma)(\alpha b + (1 - \alpha)d)$$

$$\pi^{D}(\alpha,\ \sigma) = \sigma c + (1 - \sigma)(\alpha a + (1 - \alpha)c)$$

We take the pairing rule implied by the degree of segmentation as an exogenously given characteristic of the clustering of types supported by community and now consider its effects on the equilibrium level of cooperation. To do this we just find the value of $\alpha$ equating the two expected payoffs, or

$$\alpha^* = \frac{\sigma(d - b) + c - d}{(1 - \sigma)(b - d - a + c)}$$

Depending on the payoffs this equilibrium may be stable or unstable. In the latter case $\alpha^*$ marks the boundary between the range of attraction

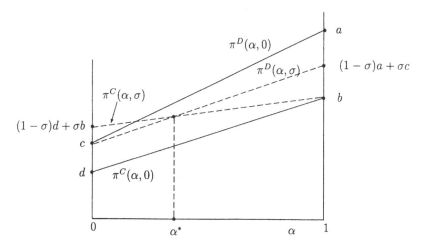

Figure 8. The segmentation effect: stable interior equilibrium case

of stable equilibria at $\alpha = 1$ and $\alpha = 0$. Figure 8 illustrates the case of a stable interior equilibrium.[19]

Four results support our interpretation of the segmentation effect of community. First, there exists some value of $\sigma < 1$ such that universal cooperation is an equilibrium, even where the interaction is a single shot prisoner's dilemma. Call this critical value of the degree of segmentation $\sigma'$, which is simply the value for which $\alpha^* = 1$. Thus

$$\sigma' = \frac{a - b}{a - c} < 1$$

where the inequality holds because the prisoner's dilemma payoffs specify $b > c$.

Second, there exists some value of $\sigma < 1$, call it $\sigma''$, such that for $\sigma > \sigma''$ some level of cooperation may be sustained as an equilibrium. This is the value of $\sigma$ for which $\alpha = 0$, or

$$\sigma'' = \frac{c - d}{b - d}$$

which is less than 1 because $c < b$.

---

[19] The condition for stability given in section 3 requires that the denominator of the preceding expression be negative, requiring for $\alpha > 0$ that the numerator also be negative; the intuition behind this result is clear from Figure 8. Stability obtains when the reward from unilateral defection $(a - b)$ is larger than the penalty of cooperation against a defector $(d - c)$.

Third, if $\alpha^*$ is stable, an increase in segmentation will increase the frequency of cooperation in the population. This is because $d\alpha^*/d\sigma$ has the sign of $(c - b)(b - d - a + c)$, which is positive for a stable equilibrium.

Fourth, if $\alpha^*$ is unstable, an increase in segmentation will enlarge the range of attraction of the universal cooperation equilibrium, for the reasons supplied.

## 7    Parochialism

> The advantages of widespread generosity [among llama herders in the Peruvian highlands] outweigh the advantages of cheating or ignoring those who are not one's kin. . . . The custom [of reciprocal generosity], once adopted, might have been strongly selected for at the group level. In our models, herd systems that practice it have larger and far more stable herds after 100 years than systems without it . . . universal adherence . . . – even if it includes giving good breeding stock to non-kin – can make it possible for one's children to pass on more animals to one's grandchildren. It does that by ensuring that there will be lots of other herds around from which the children and grandchildren can get [help] when they need it.
>
> Flannery, Marcus, and Reynolds, *The Flocks of the Wamani*, p. 202

If subgroups in a population exhibit differing levels of prosocial norms, and hence experience coordination failures of differing extents, an excessively high rate of migration into and out of a relatively prosocial group will render the cooperative equilibrium unattainable. "Parochial" cultural values that reduce the rate of migration will thus interact synergistically with the prosocial norms themselves to help maintain stable cooperative interactions in communities. We show this by adapting a model due to Boyd and Richerson (1990) to the prisoner's dilemma interaction we have used to illustrate our three previous community effects.

We return to our model of the retaliation effect, but we now embed the group studied in section 5 in a population composed of many groups. Interactions take place only within groups, but in each period some migration among groups takes place, with a fraction $\mu$ of each group relocating each period.

The migration process is the following: As before, individuals interact for an indeterminate number of periods with termination probability $\rho$, and after termination of the interaction they update their behaviors through inspection of the payoffs of others. After this updating, a fraction $\mu$ of the group leaves and is replaced by new community members drawn randomly from the larger population. The higher the entry and exit costs the lower will be $\mu$.

Suppose the frequency of those playing tit-for-tat in a particular group is $\tau$, and its change over time due to updating of behaviors is governed by

$$\tau' = \tau + \dot{\tau}\,dt$$

Migration alters the composition of the updated population, converting the postupdating, premigration frequency $\tau'$ to the postmigration frequency $\tau''$ according to

$$\tau'' = (1 - \mu\,dt)\tau' + \mu\underline{\tau}\,dt$$

where $\underline{\tau}$ is the frequency of tit-for-tat players in the larger population.

The equilibrium frequency of tit-for-tatters in the group must satisfy $\tau = \tau''$ (the frequency must be stationary) or

$$\frac{\dot{\tau}}{\tau} = \frac{\mu}{1-\mu}\left(1 - \frac{\underline{\tau}}{\tau}\right)$$

We know from (2) and (3) that the rate of growth of the population frequency $\dot{\tau}/\tau$ can be expressed

$$\frac{\dot{\tau}}{\tau} = \gamma_1\gamma_2\left[\pi^T(\tau) - \bar{\pi}(\tau)\right]$$

$$= \gamma_1\gamma_2(1 - \tau)\left[\pi^T(\tau) - \pi^D(\tau)\right]$$

Using the payoffs for the retaliation game, this may be expressed

$$\frac{1}{\tau}\dot{\tau} = \gamma_1\gamma_2(1 - \tau)\left[\tau\left\{2c - a - d + \frac{b-c}{\rho}\right\} - c + d\right]$$

Using this expression for the preceding equilibrium condition we can define an equilibrium population frequency $\tau_\mu$, as is shown in Figure 9. At the population frequency $\tau_\mu$, the effects of migration on the population composition are just offset by the effects of behavioral updating in light of the payoffs in the previous interaction.

Recall that in the retaliation model universal cooperation (by use of the tit-for-tat strategy) was a stable equilibrium for sufficiently low termination probabilities, and this being the case the higher payoffs to members of this group could have fostered the proliferation of the trait through differential growth of the favored population. The presence of intergroup migration alters this result in the following way.

First, if the frequency of tit-for-tat players at the unstable interior equilibrium $\tau^*$ is lower than that of the larger population $\underline{\tau}$, as is shown in Figure 9, then

$$\frac{d\tau_\mu}{d\mu} < 0$$

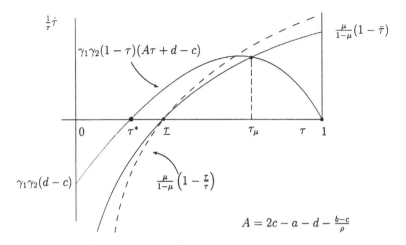

Figure 9. The retaliation effect with migration

This means that an increase in the rate of migration will reduce the frequency of tit-for-tat players and increase the frequency of defectors in equilibrium, as is indicated by the dashed line in Figure 9.

Second, if $\tau < \tau^*$ there will exist either one equilibrium with a low level of cooperation (below $\tau^*$) or three equilibria, two being stable equilibria, one with a high and one with a low level of cooperation, and an unstable equilibrium intermediate between these two.[20] In this case an increase in the rate of migration will decrease the level of cooperation at the upper stable equilibrium and increase it at the lower, while if the increase in the rate of migration is sufficiently high, it will eliminate the high cooperation equilibrium altogether.

More complicated and more realistic models of migration – those taking account of the probability that migrants will choose successful groups as their destinations, for example – would not alter these results.

## 8     Conclusion

What the entrepreneurial group of Islamic small businessmen most lacks is not capital, for . . . their resources are not inadequate, not drive, for they display the typically "Protestant" virtues of industry, frugality, independence and determination in almost excessive abundance; certainly not a sufficient market. What they lack is . . . the capacity to form efficient economic institutions. . . . Despite the advantages of such bold and rugged, not to say ruthless, individualism in

---

[20] There is a degenerate case that may occur in which two of the equilibria coincide.

stimulating creativity and destroying customary constraints on enterprise in a traditional society, it seems that . . . it also involves very important limitations on the capacity to grow . . . by limiting the effective range of collective organization.
Clifford Geertz, *Peddlers and Princes*, pp. 23, 126

Communities have properties allowing them to persist in a world of market exchanges and modern states despite their inability to exploit the efficiency-enhancing properties of markets and the advantages of universal enforcement of rules provided by states. Among these properties, and the one explored in this chapter, is the capacity of communities to foster cooperative behavior among community members and thus to avert or attenuate costly coordination problems of the prisoner's dilemma type. By inducing prosocial behaviors, communities may also support the norms and values that regularize and justify these behaviors, given that people typically seek consistency between their actions and their valuations.

We have not shown that communities have persisted for these reasons. We have shown only that they might have. Other reasons are commonly suggested, prominent among which is the view that communities and their associated values have persisted by virtue of the conformist and other inertial tendencies of the process of cultural transmission. We do not doubt that these tendencies are present and are sometimes decisive. But for reasons indicated at the outset, we do not believe that any purely inertial or backward-looking approach can provide an adequate explanation of the evolution of either the governance structures regulating social interactions or their associated social norms.

Rather our strategy has been to depict communities, like states and markets, as modern governance structures whose patterns of proliferation, diffusion, decline, and extinction are regulated by contemporary processes. Far from being vestigial anachronisms, we think communities may become more rather than less important in the nexus of governance structures in the years to come, since communities may claim some success in addressing governance problems not amenable to market or state solution.

Many have argued that as production shifts from goods to services, and within services to information-related services, and as team-based production methods increase in importance, the gains from cooperation will increase as well, on the grounds that such activities involve relatively high monitoring costs, and hence are subject to costly forms of opportunism. If, as we suspect, this is the case, we may expect the viability of communities to increase rather than to ebb. This will be especially true where communities are structured so as to minimize the tension between the universalism required for exploiting gains from trade and the parochialism which provides surrogates for missing markets.

REFERENCES

Axelrod, Robert (1984). *The Evolution of Cooperation.* New York: Basic Books.
Axelrod, Robert, and William D. Hamilton (1981). "The Evolution of Cooperation," *Science* 211 (March): 1390–96.
Bandura, Albert (1977). *Social Learning Theory.* Englewood Cliffs, N.J.: Prentice-Hall.
Boorman, Scott A., and Paul Levitt (1980). *The Genetics of Altruism.* New York: Academic Press.
Bouman, F. J. A. (1977). "Indigenous Savings and Credit Societies in the Developing World," *Savings and Development* 1(4): 181–214.
Bowles, Samuel (1996). "Markets as Cultural Institutions: Equilibrium Norms in Competitive Economies." University of Massachusetts Discussion Paper.
Bowles, Samuel, and Herbert Gintis (1976). *Schooling in Capitalist America: Educational Reform and the Contradictions of Economic Life.* New York: Basic Books.
Bowles, Samuel, and Herbert Gintis (1997). Optimal Parochialism. University of Massachusetts Working Paper, April.
Bowles, Samuel, and Herbert Gintis (1997, forthcoming). *Recasting Egalitarianism: New Rules for Markets, States, and Communities.* Ed. Erik Olin Wright. New York: Verso.
Boyd, Robert, and Peter J. Richerson (1985). *Culture and the Evolutionary Process.* Chicago: University of Chicago Press.
Boyd, Roberts, and Peter J. Richerson (1990). "Group Selection among Alternative Evolutionarily Stable Strategies," *Journal of Theoretical Biology* 145: 331–42.
Burke, Edmund (1955 [1790]). *Reflections on the Civil War in France.* New York: Bobbs-Merrill.
Cavalli-Sforza, Luigi L., and Marcus W. Feldman (1981). *Cultural Transmission and Evolution.* Princeton, N.J.: Princeton University Press.
Dawkins, Richard (1982). *The Extended Phenotype: The Gene as the Unit of Selection.* Oxford: Freeman.
de Tocqueville, Alexis (1969). *Democracy in America.* Garden City, N.Y.: Doubleday.
Farrell, Joseph (1987). "Information and the Coase Theorem," *Journal of Economic Perspectives* 1(2): 112–29.
Festinger, Leon (1957). *A Theory of Cognitive Dissonance.* Stanford, Calif.: Stanford University Press.
Flannery, Kent, Joyce Marcus, and Robert Reynolds (1989). *The Flocks of the Wamani: A Study of Llama Herders on the Puntas of Ayacucho, Peru.* San Diego: Academic Press.

Fromm, Erich, and Michael Maccoby (1970). *Social Character in a Mexican Village: A Sociopsychoanalytic Study*. Englewood Cliffs, N.J.: Prentice-Hall.

Fudenberg, Drew, and Eric Maskin (1986). "The Folk Theorem in Repeated Games with Discounting or with Incomplete Information," *Econometrica* 54(3): 533–54.

Geertz, Clifford (1963). *Peddlers and Princes: Social Change and Economic Modernization in Two Indonesian Towns*. Chicago: University of Chicago Press.

Gintis, Herbert (1975). "Welfare Economics and Individual Development: A Reply to Talcott Parsons," *Quarterly Journal of Economics* 89(2): 291–302.

——— (1989). "The Power to Switch: On the Political Economy of Consumer Sovereignty," in Samuel Bowles, Richard C. Edwards, and William G. Shepherd, eds., *Unconventional Wisdom: Essays in Honor of John Kenneth Galbraith*, pp. 65–80. New York: Houghton Mifflin.

Grafen, Alan (1979). "The Hawk-Dove Game Played between Relatives," *Animal Behavior* 27(3): 905–07.

Güth, Werner, and Harmutt Kliemt (1994). "Competition or Co-operation: On the Evolutionary Economics of Trust Exploitation and Moral Attitudes," *Metroeconomica* 45(2): 155–87.

Harding, Susan (1978). "Street Shouting and Shunning: Conflict between Women in a Spanish Village," *Frontiers* 3(3): 14–18.

Hirsch, Fred (1976). *Social Limits to Growth*. Cambridge: Harvard University Press.

Jenness, Diamond (1991). *Arctic Odyssey: The Diary of Diamond Jenness, Ethnologist with the Canadian Arctic Expedition in Northern Alaska and Canada, 1913–1916*. Hull, Canada: Canadian Museum of Civilization.

Kohn, Melvin (1969). *Class and Conformity*. Homewood, Ill.: Dorsey Press.

Kreps, David M. (1990). "Corporate Culture and Economic Theory," in James Alt and Kenneth Shepsle, eds., *Perspectives on Positive Political Economy*, pp. 90–143. Cambridge: Cambridge University Press.

Light, Ivan, Im Jung Kwuon, and Deng Zhong (1990). "Korean Rotating Credit Associations in Los Angeles," *Amerasia* 16(1): 35–54.

Malinowski, Bronislaw (1926). *Crime and Custom in Savage Society*. New York: Routledge & Kegan Paul.

Marx, Karl, and Friedrich Engels (1972 [1848]). "The Communist Manifesto," in Robert Tucker, ed., *The Marx-Engels Reader*, 2d ed. New York: W. W. Norton.

Platteau, Jean-Philippe (1996). "Traditional Sharing Norms as an Obstacle to Economic Growth in Tribal Societies," *Cahiers de la Faculté des Sciences Economiques et Sociales, Facultes Universitaires Notre-Dame de la Paix* 173: 201–23.

Putterman, Louis (1988). "The Firm as Association vs. the Firm as Commodity," *Economics and Philosophy* 4: 243–66.

Shapiro, Carl (1983). "Premiums for High Quality Products as Returns to Reputations," *Quarterly Journal of Economics* 98(4): 659–79.

Soltis, Joseph, Rob Boyd, and Peter Richerson (1995). "Can Group-Functional Behaviors Evolve by Cultural Group Selection: An Empirical Test," *Current Anthropology* 36(3): 473–83.

Taylor, Michael (1987). *The Possibility of Cooperation*. Cambridge: Cambridge University Press.

Wilson, David Sloan (1980). *The Natural Selection of Populations and Communities*. Menlo Park, Calif.: Benjamin Cummings.

CHAPTER 8

# Moral overload and its alleviation

*Timur Kuran*

## 1   Moral overload and moral dissonance

Suppose you are far away from home, traveling alone on a highway. You stop at a busy roadside restaurant for dinner. The food is decent and the service acceptable. When the bill of $13.64 arrives, an inner voice tells you that the waitress deserves the customary 15 percent tip. Reaching into your pocket, you notice that you are carrying only bills in the amounts of $5, $10, and $50. Through a quick mental calculation, you realize that a payment of $15 would leave the waitress a smaller tip than what you consider fair. Alas, being in a hurry to reach your hotel, you would rather not wait for the change on $50. Following a moment's hesitation, you drop $15 on the table and head for your car. The decision is now behind you, but not the issue. For a while, until a melody on the radio carries your thoughts elsewhere, you feel a bit guilty for having been unfair to the waitress for the sake of a little extra sleep.

You were a complete stranger in the restaurant, and you probably will not see the waitress again. What has given you trouble is not, therefore, the possibility of social sanctions. It is, rather, your conscience. Your *choice* failed to accommodate a *value* that you hold – the principle that people should receive their due. Not satisfied with the *preference* that your choice revealed, you feel that you ought to have behaved differently.

The earliest draft of this chapter was presented at the Conference on Economics, Values, and Organization, held at Yale University in April 1996. For many useful criticisms and suggestions, I am indebted to Jonathan Baron, Kaushik Basu, Roger Congleton, Tyler Cowen, Daniel Kahneman, Jane Mansbridge, Howard Margolis, John Michael Montias, Jean-Philippe Platteau, and Cass Sunstein. Murat Somer provided valuable research assistance. The chapter was completed at the George J. Stigler Center for the Study of the Economy and the State, Graduate School of Business, University of Chicago; I am grateful to the Center for financial support.

231

This interpretation of the episode rests on the view that our personal values can produce lasting psychological tensions. As such, it departs from the classical theory of individual choice, according to which one has a unitary preference ordering. In the classical theory, the decision maker judges neither his own preferences nor the choices they generate; his preferences are considered given, and his choices are presumed optimal in relation to his available options. Here, by contrast, I am proposing that we have a binary system for evaluating our available options. In addition to the preferences by which we choose among our options, I am suggesting, we have values that evaluate what we want and actually do. Values, then, are judgments about preference orderings or about the choices that preferences have generated; they are standards of rightness in either character or conduct.[1]

Values, which often form clusters called *moral systems* or *moralities*, can be interpersonal or intrapersonal. Interpersonal values consist of the judgments we make about the preferences of others. They produce moral conflict *among* us, as when you anger a friend by criticizing her stinginess toward a waitress. Intrapersonal values, our concern here, encompass the judgments we make about our own preferences. As in the tipping example, they produce moral conflict *within* us. They can make us feel bad about ourselves even when we are unlikely to be reproached.

Cognitive psychologists find that preferences are not fixed but variable. They find, in particular, that preferences depend on the framing of choices, the context in which choices are made, and the method by which choices are elicited.[2] These factors complicate the study of preferences, but the task gets simplified insofar as their expression is subject to physical and financial constraints. In the tipping example, you could have extended your sleep or paid the waitress a decent tip; you ultimately had to choose one or the other, revealing a priority. By contrast, values do not get disciplined by reality – at least not to the same extent as preferences. After opting for more sleep, you rebuked yourself for having given a small personal comfort priority over a moral obligation. Yet, had you chosen instead to delay your departure for the sake of leaving an adequate tip, you might have faulted yourself for risking your safety on the road, and thus your family's happiness, by neglecting to leave yourself enough time for rest. There is an inconsistency here, and it arises because the constraints that regulated your actual choice did not restrain

---

[1] This definition is broader than the concept of metapreference, as developed by Frankfurt (1971), Sen (1974), and George (1993), among others.

[2] See Payne, Bettman, and Johnson (1992) for an overview of the evidence. For some interpretations, see Kahneman, Knetsch, and Thaler (1991) and Tversky and Simonson (1993).

your values. Left unrestrained, your values were able to require of you an impossible set of behaviors.

The state of having values that cannot be satisfied within the prevailing physical and financial constraints may be called *moral overload*. This condition inevitably generates *moral dissonance*, psychological discomfort stemming from the feeling that one's personal values remain unfulfilled.[3] The source of moral overload may be a single moral system. For example, a religion can demand of its adherents behaviors they are unable to satisfy, and parents can instill in their children unrealistic standards of achievement. Often, however, moral overload results from poor coordination among the processes through which personal values get formed. Values rooted in biological evolution need not be mutually consistent in any given context, for they might have developed in response to separate problems. Likewise, socially shaped values might have been promoted by disconnected groups, each with its own distinct objectives. And these two categories of values need not be compatible with one another.

This chapter's main point is that moral overload generates efforts to alleviate the resulting dissonance. The efforts may involve acts chosen unilaterally. Thus, a person burdened by overly strict values might compensate for his moral failings through moral acts in some other domain of activity; or he might avoid environments that reinforce the disturbing values. Generally, however, the alleviation of moral overload also involves collective efforts, including ones featuring institutional innovation. Later sections will distinguish among three categories of such efforts. In the first category are those aimed at making it cheaper to accommodate specific values; they include *redemption, casuistry,* and *rationalization.* The second category, *compartmentalization,* consists of efforts to separate one's choices into domains to which different values apply; it has an extreme variant that involves *escape.* And the final category entails *moral reconstruction* to enhance the feasibility of individual moral systems.

The final segment of the chapter points to commonly overlooked social benefits from institutions that facilitate moral reconciliation and fusion. As we shall see, the desirability of such institutions does not conflict with cultural relativism: One can treat every culture as equally meritorious and still appreciate the mechanisms tending toward moral homogenization and simplification within each culture. The implication

---

[3] Moral dissonance differs from cognitive dissonance in that it is caused by clashes of values rather than clashes of beliefs. The seminal work on cognitive dissonance is Festinger (1957); later contributions include Akerlof and Dickens (1982), Schlicht (1984), and Rabin (1994).

does clash, however, with certain strands of the contemporary multiculturalism movement, namely, those that perceive multiculturalism as a vehicle for preserving, if not advancing, cultural heterogeneity. Insofar as the values of different cultures conflict, I will argue, this is problematic: Multiculturalism may fuel moral overload, thus provoking responses that render it unsustainable.

A positive theory about moral evolution must define value in a value-free manner; it must not equate the concept with any particular definition of virtue. Accordingly, I am not restricting what may count as a value. A person may feel that he ought to be charitable toward beggars, that helping the destitute is a basic requirement of human decency. He may feel, alternatively, that, regardless of the satisfaction one might derive from the act of giving, it is wrong to extend help to beggars, lest such help reduce their incentives to become self-supporting. Both the principle of "charity toward beggars" and that of "no help to beggars" may qualify as a value.

## 2     Moral overload defined

For a fuller definition of moral overload, imagine a person faced with a particular decision. His options lie in the *opportunity set*, $X$, determined jointly by his physical and economic constraints. He happens to have internalized values that require him to avoid a subset of his options. Of the remaining possibilities, those within $X$ form his *moral opportunity set*, $X^m$. If $X^m$ contains at least one element, the underlying morality is *feasible*. Figure 1 depicts such a case. Specifically, the individual's values instruct him to keep $a \geq \underline{a}$ and $b \geq \underline{b}$. The shaded area defined by these values overlaps with $X$, so $X^m$ is nonempty.

A person's moral system can obviously be *infeasible*. In Figure 2, the same values, when paired with a smaller opportunity set, yield an empty moral opportunity set. The situation can be caused by a shrinking of $X$ (the case shown), or a hardening of the individual's values, or some combination of these changes. Whatever the cause of the infeasibility, the result is moral overload: The individual cannot possibly live by his values.[4]

By definition, the individual would put himself morally at ease by selecting $x^m \equiv (\underline{a}, \underline{b})$, his *moral base*. Depending on the context, of course, he might derive greater satisfaction from choices for which $a > \underline{a}$, or $b >$

---

[4] A tragic example of such a situation occurs in the novel *Sophie's Choice*. Sophie, a mother of two children, is asked to turn over one of them to the Nazis. By sacrificing one child, she may save herself and the other child. No matter how she responds, she will consider her choice morally reprehensible and hate herself for making it.

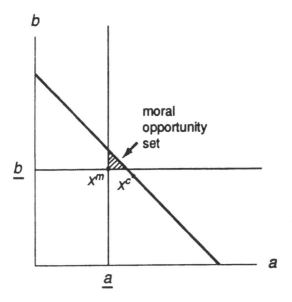

Figure 1. Choice under a feasible morality. The individual's moral base, $x^m$, lies within his opportunity set, so he is capable of making a morally satisfying choice. Nonetheless, his preferences lead him to choose $x^c$, implying that he incurs some moral dissonance.

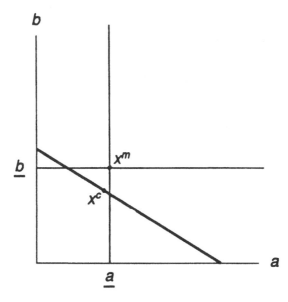

Figure 2. Choice under an infeasible morality. The individual's moral base, $x^m$, lies outside his opportunity set, so he cannot make a morally satisfying choice. His choice, $x^c$, generates moral dissonance.

$\underline{b}$, or both. What is relevant here, however, is that a choice outside $X^m$ would inevitably produce moral dissonance. The magnitude of the dissonance may depend on the distance between $x^m$ and the individual's actual choice $x^c$, determined by his preferences and constraints. In Figure 2, $x^c$ necessarily lies outside $X^m$, which means that moral dissonance is inescapable. In effect, the individual sees achieving $\underline{a}$ and reaching $\underline{b}$ as matters of principle, and, failing to live by one or more of these principles, he feels guilty.

Returning to Figure 1, we see that moral overload is a sufficient but not a necessary condition for moral dissonance: Dissonance can arise even if the moral opportunity set is nonempty. Since the individual's preferences and values need not be mutually consistent, he may avoid making a morally satisfying selection even when able to do so. The figure illustrates another important feature: Sentiments generally considered noble, like generosity and fairness, may influence both values and preferences. Suppose, in the context of Figure 1, that devoting resources to $b$ is widely recognized as moral behavior. The individual is selecting a certain amount of $b$, but his moral sense tells him that he should be opting for more. The distinction between values and preferences is not, then, that one is altruistic and the other purely selfish. As Figure 1 shows, it is that his values may judge his preferences negatively.[5]

Jonathan Baron and Mark Spranca (1996) observe that the defining characteristic of values is their resistance to trade-offs.[6] Where trade-offs are central to preference systems, it is rigidity that characterizes moralities. If one of your values is "I should get enough sleep to be able to drive safely" and another "I should compensate people fairly for their services," you will treat them both as obligatory. Moreover, insofar as you consider them absolute commitments, you may be reluctant even to rank them. By contrast, your relevant preferences necessarily embody trade-offs. Faced with an actual decision, you are forced to rank your alternatives. You have to decide whether leaving a somewhat larger tip is worth a five-minute wait when you are eager to get some sleep. Whereas your values may instruct you to do both, your preferences must make you select one over the other.

Values produce, then, judgments that are more or less independent of possibilities. Unlike preferences, which reflect an understanding of practical limitations, they can be divorced from reality. Their coexistence within the individual may help explain the commonly observed disparity

---

[5] As Rabin (1995) discusses, attempts to incorporate values into the study of individual choice have tended to treat them either as constraints or as modifiers of preference structures. The present framework rejects this crude dichotomy.

[6] They use the term "protected values" to describe what I call simply "values."

between willingness to pay (WTP) for a good and willingness to accept (WTA) its elimination. When respondents are asked what it would take to get them to accept a habitat's destruction, they typically give much higher figures than when asked what they would pay to prevent the loss.[7] None of the proposed explanations for the disparity, which generally avoid moral factors, has resolved the puzzle – although some provide insights likely to survive the test of further research.[8] One explanation that *does* invoke values has been advanced by Cass Sunstein (1997, pp. 52–53): WTA assigns responsibility for the elimination clearly to the individual whereas WTP does so ambiguously. I would add that inquiries about WTA and WTP differ in the mix of elements that they make the individual consider. A question about WTP forces the individual to think about trade-offs imposed by his budget constraint; by contrast, one about WTA makes him focus on his relevant values.[9] If he has been socialized to consider it a moral obligation to keep the environment intact, this value will come into play. Asked about what it would take for him to permit a habitat's destruction, he will be reminded of this value, and his attention to the value will draw his mind away from trade-offs.

In the tipping example, the thought process that made you leave an inadequate tip was analogous to the thinking that generates a WTP measure: You made your decision after considering the trade-offs. And your subsequent guilt-ridden thoughts were analogous to the thinking that underlies a WTA measure: Once liberated from the need to consider compromises, you restored the absoluteness of your standards, effectively reburdening yourself with the obligation to guard every minute of your sleep without being unfair to the waitress.

The proposed system of binary rankings accommodates Henry Aaron's (1994) observation that the human brain harbors no general coordinator – no mechanism that reconciles every impulse, sentiment, goal, ranking, and perception. At the same time, it recognizes that economizing is as much a part of human existence as is internal tension. The system allows, that is, for both conflict and compromise, and for both idealism and pragmatism.

---

[7] See Thaler (1980) and Hoffman and Spitzer (1993) for evidence from various experiments.

[8] For a critique of the main explanations, see Hoffman and Spitzer (1993, sect. 3).

[9] Kahneman and Knetsch (1992) identify "moral satisfaction" as a key determinant of WTP for collective goods. Their evidence does not contradict the interpretation given here, for one can obtain such satisfaction from any source and regardless of one's constraints. Moral considerations are among the determinants of preferences as well as values, so they influence both WTA and WTP. The critical difference between the two measures is that the opportunity set imposes greater restraint on the latter.

## 3    The sources of moral overload

Thus far, I have made two main points: Our preferences need not be consistent with our values, and the moralities formed by our values may be impossible to satisfy. Our next task is to explain these observations. The exercise, divided into five segments, will prepare us for the subsequent analysis of efforts we undertake to alleviate moral overload.

### 3.1    *Diversity of social pressures*

Whatever our moral capacity, the exact content of our values is determined by a vast array of social pressures. The groups responsible for the pressures work more or less independently; their efforts are not coordinated. There is no guarantee, therefore, that the results of their efforts will be mutually compatible. Just consider some of the broad values that get promoted by contemporary participants in the political process. Libertarians teach that market outcomes are fair, socialists that it is unfair to deny assistance to the victims of market competition. Internationalists promote compassion toward nations in distress; isolationists counter that our own problems should have priority. Social conservatives teach that the traditional family is the backbone of civilization, their liberal counterparts that consensual social arrangements are harmless. Moral dilemmas are among the unintended consequences of these disparate campaigns. Insofar as people absorb many such values simultaneously, they find themselves with diminished, if not extinguished, moral opportunity sets.

Just as a society may subject its members to moral overload through competing values, it may do so through overly demanding ones. The message "If you want something, you can have it" need not pose problems for those with the requisite talents. However, it can mislead modestly talented people into considering themselves failures. Think of making average gymnasts believe that with diligence they can become Olympic champions. Those lacking superb ability will be left feeling that they are falling short of their potential. A similar unintended effect arises from the tendency, which gained legitimacy through the European Enlightenment, to make people attribute their failures to themselves rather than to social, natural, or supernatural forces. If a child's obesity represents the unfolding of a humanly unfathomable divine plan, it does not become a moral burden, but if it stems from the child's upbringing, it points to parental failure.

## 3.2  *Moral inertia*

A second possible contributor to moral overload is moral inertia – the rigidity of values in the face of changing conditions. Values developed to address particular problems may continue to judge individual prefer- ences and choices long after the disappearance of these problems, and they may persist, possibly in weakened form, even after the emergence of competing values. Moreover, values can get separated from their original rationales, allowing their preservation even when the justifications have been discredited.

Bernard Lewis (1993) gives examples from the Middle East, where certain values discredited by the Westernization drives of the last two centuries continue to exert influence, creating "problems of adjustment." For example, nepotism, once the unquestioned virtue of family loyalty, is now officially treated as retrograde and uncivilized. Yet, despite this condemnation, the value lives on in individual minds, making people feel guilty when they reject opportunities to help their kin. Individuals born long after nepotism became a widespread value, and who know little about the social conditions that may once have made nepotism critical to survival, thus feel torn between an old value and its replacement.

Implicit in the two reasons just given for the commonness of moral overload is the existence of a capacity to harbor values. Why, in the first place, do we have a moral capacity?

## 3.3  *Human evolution and moral signaling*

The logic of human evolution suggests that our ancestors may have developed a capacity for self-judgment because it promoted their genetic fitness. As Robert Frank (1988) has shown, individuals known to follow principles even in the face of temptations to deviate would have found it relatively easy to make and enforce credible commitments, thus becom- ing exceptionally successful at keeping mates, friends, and partners. This argument recognizes that our ancestors enjoyed opportunities to profit by cheating and also that many succumbed to temptation. So it accom- modates the chapter's distinction between values and preferences. The more stringent a person's values, the more he would feel guilty for violating them. Of course, what our distant ancestors would ultimately have cared about was others' preferences rather than their values. If values mattered, this was probably because the physical signs of guilt made them somewhat transparent, and because the signs were correlated with the preferences that shaped actual choices. Correlation allows variation, of course. As long as people who seemed to have a strong conscience tended to act more fairly than those who seemed to have a weak one, the mechanism would have given the appropriate signals.

Even under prehistoric conditions, values could have varied across individuals, because the difficulties of making accurate character judgments would have prevented people with undesirable character traits from losing all their reproductive potential. The dispositions that became common to most people's moralities included ones of general relevance, like honesty, sympathy, fairness, self-control, and duty.[10] They also included dispositions of relevance to specific activities and relationships, such as values defining parental obligations and tribal loyalty. A major theme in evolutionary psychology, which investigates the origins of universal human values, is that they all emerged as means of helping our hunter–gatherer ancestors cope with *focused* problems of existence and reproduction. In this view, developed in essays edited by Jerome Barkow, Leda Cosmides, and John Tooby (1992) and extended by Robert Wright (1994), the mind resembles not a general-purpose computer but one hard-wired with numerous subroutines for dealing with specific problems. The subroutines equip the mind with standards of good conduct, and they also sensitize it to violations of those standards. Accordingly, we feel guilty when we engage in opportunism; devious behavior bothers us even when the victim is a stranger; and our minds are endowed with special capabilities for detecting breaches of contract.

Developed as they were to address distinct problems, our genetically shaped values did not have to be consistent with one another. In principle, an ancient human community could appeal to sympathy on one class of problems, to fairness on another, and to unrestrained selfishness on still another. Likewise, its members could be guided by one set of values in raising their children and by another during hunting expeditions. The resulting inconsistencies would remain unnoticed as long as individuals dealt with issues serially rather than simultaneously. Yet our hunter–gatherer ancestors must have had difficulty keeping their various domains of activity strictly compartmentalized; hence, they were probably no strangers to moral conflict. A father and son on the same hunting team would inevitably feel both family loyalty and tribal loyalty, facing situations rife with moral dilemmas. Today, tens of thousands of generations after the emergence of human values, the ever-finer division of labor may facilitate the mental compartmentalization necessary to prevent us from noticing conflicts among our genetically inherited values.

---

[10] Such general values are the focus of Wilson's (1993) analysis of our "moral sense."

With most of us working outside the home in organizations that often include only nonkin, our professional decisions are generally insulated from family matters. But we routinely face dilemmas in trying to allocate time between work and family.

### 3.4 *The split between values and preferences*

It is one thing to identify the evolutionary *function* of values, quite another to explain the emergence of a split between values and preferences. Why did human evolution produce a binary rather than a unitary system of rankings? My answer draws on Baron and Spranca (1996).

In seeking to control one another's behavior, early humans might have promoted rigid rules for fear that flexibility would allow others, even themselves, to break them inappropriately. Everyone must have realized that for almost any rule there are conditions that invite flexibility. Consider the rule "Try to save a drowning person, even at risk to yourself." When rescue efforts would only endanger the rescuers, with no reasonable chance of saving the victim, a relaxation of this rule might be appropriate. For example, flexible interpretation could be socially advantageous in the case of a terminally ill octogenarian who slips into Niagara Falls. Yet, replacing the rigid assistance rule with one that says, "Try to save a drowning person, but only when the risk is modest" could invite abuse. In particular, it might give individuals license to evade responsibility through self-serving interpretation.[11] Values in the form of absolute principles might have emerged, then, as a means of preventing opportunism.

The emergence of absolute standards did not mean, however, that the standards would always be followed strictly. In day to day decision making, our distant ancestors must have made trade-offs routinely. Should a mother of six risk her own life for the tiny chance of saving her great aunt, who has fallen into a thunderous waterfall? Would such behavior not violate another absolute rule, "Do everything and anything to ensure your children's survival"? A flexible interpretation of the rescue rule would have benefited her genetic fitness, and people avoiding exceptions would have hurt their own. With the flexible interpreters leaving offspring at a greater rate than the rigid ones, the system of dual rankings would have become entrenched. Their descendants would hold many absolute values, yet the preferences governing their actual choices would reflect compromises.

---

[11] The logic here is analogous to the rationale for constraining ourselves. Schelling (1984, esp. chaps. 3–4) provides insights into the uses of self-imposed constraints.

In principle, the split between values and preferences could have been avoided through highly complex rules. But our cognitive shortcomings limit the accurate communication of complexity. In practice, if rules are to be understood widely they must be simple. Absolute rules are necessarily simpler than ones with escape clauses, a characteristic which helps explain their genesis. In applying absolute rules, however, individuals would have adapted them to their own circumstances. Moreover, because of other rules, they inevitably would have made compromises. In effect, they would have subscribed to one set of rankings, identified here as values, and acted according to another, characterized as preferences.

### 3.5     *The commonness of moral overload*

To sum up, we have inherited a moral capacity, and the values that form our moral systems are rooted partly in our biological evolution and partly in social processes exhibiting inertia. If the mind contained an infinitely powerful coordinating center, it would reconcile and rank all the values that it absorbs. For example, it would distinguish clearly between contexts in which equality is to take precedence over liberty and fraternity, and those in which the reverse orderings are to hold. Yet, the powers of the mind are limited, and the possible contexts vary greatly, so nothing like a complete ranking is feasible. The mind can cope with its limitations through moral heuristics – shortcuts to simplify ranking tasks. Such heuristics are furnished by slogans, programs, and ideologies. But just as our use of judgmental heuristics to simplify estimation does not mean that information never overwhelms,[12] so our use of moral heuristics allows vast possibilities for feeling morally torn. Moreover, the more complex our moral systems, the more we will find ourselves in situations in which the demands generated by our values are incompatible.

What I am suggesting is not only that our values may point in different directions. It is also that they create psychological discomfort. The theory under construction differs, then, from theories of morality, like that of Howard Margolis (1982), that have individuals searching for a happy balance among competing claims on their resources, always successfully. In such theories, individuals divide their resources among selfish and altruistic pursuits, experiencing psychological stress only during brief adjustments. Here, by contrast, I am suggesting

---

[12] The seminal papers on judgmental heuristics are in Kahneman, Slovic, and Tversky, eds. (1982).

that we routinely encounter choices that generate persistent inner conflicts.

## 4 Personal responses to moral overload

Having investigated the causes of moral overload and explored why values come into conflict with preferences as well as other values, we can return to the decision making framework introduced earlier.

### 4.1 *Personal optimization under the threat of moral dissonance*

Remember that in Figure 2 the individual selects the option $x^c$ and then feels guilty that his moral obligations remain unmet. His *total utility* from any one of his options $x$ may be represented as $U(x) = I(x) + M(x, x^m)$, where $I(x)$ is his *intrinsic utility* and $M(x, x^m)$ the consequent *moral utility*, given his prevailing values, as represented by $x^m$. The second additive component of total utility is necessarily negative whenever the moral opportunity set is empty, and it is zero whenever $x^m$ is fully satisfied. What I have been calling moral dissonance amounts to negative moral utility.

At least in the short run, the individual's only decision variable is $x$. Accordingly, he selects $x$ to maximize $U(x)$, subject to his budget constraint and his predetermined morality. His choice $x^c$ may well produce moral dissonance. What I have been calling his preferences is his ordering of all the possible $x$, as measured by total utility, $U(x)$. This ordering takes account of any guilt that might be involved. But guilt is not decisive to the choice. Of two options that generate different amounts of guilt, the one that produces more might provide greater total utility. Hence, the possibility of conflict between preferences and values even with a morality that is feasible.

Suppose that the individual's choice happens to satisfy all his values. If the opportunity set then expands, will he spend his additional resources only on pursuits lacking a moral content? Not at all. Since a moral pursuit can also be a source of pleasure, it may absorb some, even all, of the added resources. But his return will entail only intrinsic utility, rather than both moral and intrinsic utility. Take a person who feels morally compelled to spend one thousand dollars on charity. Once this target has been met, he may make further contributions for the sheer joy of it.

We saw earlier that both preferences and values carry the influence of past social pressures. In practice, social pressures can come into play also at the time of the decision. Accordingly, our individual might be encouraged to select a feasible option different from $x^c$, that is, to engage in preference falsification.[13] Preference falsification could either dampen or aggravate his moral dissonance: It could push $x^c$ toward $x^m$ or away from it. I shall be abstracting from such complications, however. Our focus will remain on tensions among values and between values and preferences; to keep the analysis simple, those between the private and public manifestations of these variables will be suppressed. Within the present analysis, then, the immediate source of moral dissonance is always internal; ongoing social pressures do not constitute a factor.

How might a person respond to feelings of guilt generated by choices that he considers immoral? He can obviously endeavor to expand his opportunity set, but in many contexts the difficulties will be insurmountable. Alternatively, he can perform morally satisfying acts in some other context – one in which the constraints on moral behavior are not binding. Just as a person intending to see a certain play might, on learning that it is sold out, satisfy his urge for entertainment by watching a movie, someone unable to reach moral satisfaction in one domain may seek out another opportunity. In effect, he may substitute moral satisfaction in one domain for satisfaction in the other. This observation draws support from a class of experiments designed to test whether people who become conscious of having harmed others become unusually responsive to emerging opportunities for altruism. A critical review of these experiments will place in context the collective guilt-alleviation efforts that will be the focus of subsequent sections.

## 4.2   *Laboratory experiments*

In one particular experiment by Dennis Regan, Margo Williams, and Sondra Sparling (1972), the sample of subjects consisted of women walking alone in a shopping center. The experimenter would ask each to take his picture for a project. Indicating that his expensive-looking camera was rather sensitive, he would then explain its operation and strike a pose. Alas, when the subject attempted to take the picture, the shutter would not work. At this point, one of two things would happen. In one condition, the experimenter would explain that the camera "acts up a lot," assuring the subject that she did nothing wrong; thanking her for her assistance, he would walk away. In the other condition, the experimenter would imply that the jam occurred because she did something wrong; saying that the camera needed to be fixed, he would thank her perfunctorily yet politely, and then disappear. At some distance stood a confed-

---

[13] On the mechanics and consequences of preference falsification, see Kuran (1995a).

erate of the experimenter who could not tell how any given subject was being treated. She held a grocery bag whose bottom was torn. After the unsuccessful picture-taking episode, she would cross the subject's path, pretending to be unaware that groceries were spilling out of her bag. The question under investigation was whether the two classes of subjects would react differently.

As it turned out, 55 percent of the subjects accused of breaking the camera alerted the confederate to the falling groceries, compared with only 15 percent of those assured that they did nothing wrong. A plausible explanation is that the faulted subjects were more likely to feel guilty than those told that the source of the problem was the temperamental camera. Unable to expiate their guilt by helping the camera owner who had disappeared, they sought the next best opportunity. It is significant that the confederate did nothing to invite help. She did not seem to be in distress or ask for assistance. On the contrary, she appeared unaware of the falling groceries, thus allowing subjects to ignore her situation. So if the subjects charged with carelessness were statistically more likely to help her out, the reason must have been that they were trying to expiate guilt.[14]

Many of the accused subjects of the camera experiment would probably have asked the ostensibly victimized camera owner whether they could help him get the camera fixed, but he was gone before they could respond. It is as though this mishap instilled in them a new moral objective that they could not meet.[15] Their situation is analogous, then, to that of Figure 2. Our individual has somehow developed a moral base that lies out of reach, and he cannot alleviate his anxiety by correcting the troubling situation itself. The reviewed experiment is consistent, therefore, with the claim that individuals who become morally frustrated in one sphere of activity may seek to soothe their troubled consciences through deeds in some other sphere. Claude Steele (1988), who has conducted many related experiments, adds that people may differ in the instruments they use to overcome dissonance. The idealist might double his efforts in defense of a cause, the devout might turn to more vigilant

[14] That the confederate got help from 15 percent of the control group admits multiple explanations. They might not have been sure that they were blameless, in which case they, too, were seeking to compensate for their possible faults. They might have felt guilty for reasons unknown to observers. Finally, they could have been using the occasion of the falling groceries to help fulfill a general desire to help others. These alternatives are not mutually exclusive.

[15] An unattainable objective could be created even if the camera owner stayed around. If the cost of repairing the camera were sufficiently high, a subject wanting to cleanse her conscience would have no choice but to help someone other than its owner.

worship, and the aesthete might seek solace in the beauty of a new art exhibit.

In line with this insight, other experiments show that individuals made to feel bad about their actions are less likely to assist someone in distress if their induced discomfort is relieved through other means. Robert Cialdini, Betty Lee Darby, and Joyce Vincent (1973) conducted an experiment whose subjects were led to believe that its objectives were methodological. The subjects, who met the experimenter at separate times in an officelike room, were asked to be seated in a chair so rigged that, when it was pulled out, three boxes of sequenced cards sitting on the adjoining table would spill on the floor. Half the subjects caused the mishap themselves; the other half merely witnessed it as the experimenter pulled out the chair herself. In all cases, the experimenter would exclaim, "Oh no! I think it's the data from Tom's master's thesis!" and proceed to indicate that it would take "Tom" much time to reorder the cards. After these staged remarks, the experimenter would lead the subjects through the methodological task for which they had volunteered their time. In some of the cases, the subjects were then paid or warmly thanked for participating in the experiment; in the rest, they were simply told that the experiment was over. But in every case, a confederate of the experimenter then walked into the room, asking the subject to participate also in her own experiment, which would involve administering a few ten-minute phone interviews. As it turned out, the subjects who had received money or approval gave the confederate significantly less help than those who had heard only that the experiment was over.

The architects of the experiment propose that the spilling of the cards puts the subjects in a "negative affective state" that calls for relief.[16] One source of relief, they add, is benevolence. Subjects who heard that they did a favor merely by being in the experiment got their need alleviated, at least in part. By contrast, subjects who were not even thanked were left wondering whether their participation in the experiment merely created a nuisance. Accordingly, the latter group of subjects were more motivated to perform compensatory moral acts. This experiment shows, like the previous one, that the beneficiary of a compensatory act need not be the victim of the harm responsible for moral dissonance. Just

---

[16] Statistically, the subjects who observed the mishap did not behave differently from those who caused it themselves. Apparently, the mere witnessing of an injustice can create a need for psychological relief. This outcome points to the complexity of the sources of moral dissonance; evidently, the sources covered here do not exhaust the possibilities. Other ways of making an individual feel guilty include reminding him of his past moral transgressions for which he has already compensated and making his minor misdeeds seem major through appropriate framing.

as subjects in the camera experiment relieved their guilt by helping someone other than the owner of the ostensibly broken camera, those in the spilled-cards experiment helped someone other than the person ostensibly burdened with reordering a huge data set.

### 4.3 The social merits of compensatory acts

In neither of these experiments are observers likely to disapprove of the acts through which troubled subjects seek inner comfort. Who would object to helping a shopper collect her fallen groceries? Yet it is possible to identify reasons why a compensatory act would actually harm its intended beneficiaries. With regard to the last experiment, it could be that the student requesting assistance would learn more from her experiment by making all the calls herself. Room for judgment is often present also in nonexperimental contexts. In the Middle East, for example, devout traders who cannot keep afloat without violating religious precepts contribute heavily to religious causes ranging from construction of medical clinics to support for Islamist political parties.[17] How one judges the means by which guilt-ridden Muslims seek redemption will depend, of course, on one's own interpersonal values. Secularists, Muslim or not, will consider the donations to Islamists alarming. The essential implication is that compensatory acts cannot be judged without appealing, at some level, to particular values. My argument, then, is not that the inducement of psychological tension provokes responses that are incontrovertibly beneficial. It is simply that the responses will often distort activities beyond the immediate context in which the tension was generated.

Nor do compensatory moral acts necessarily succeed in eliminating the moral tensions that motivated them. The subjects of the reviewed experiments may or may not have achieved inner peace through their benevolent acts. It is likely that they continued to feel upset about the mishaps, although neither experiment tested for this possibility. Insofar as people are unable to eliminate their moral dissonance, they can be expected to develop resentment toward sources of the relevant values. To put this in terms of our simple framework, suppose that our individual is unable, despite his best efforts, to eliminate the guilt induced by the values $a \geq \underline{a}$ and $b \geq \underline{b}$. He may then resent one or both values, though without necessarily managing to liberate himself from them.

[17] I have argued elsewhere (Kuran 1995b, pp. 167–69) that the recent rise in Islam's political and socioeconomic significance is due partly to clashes between values rooted in the conditions of small communities and the exigencies of surviving in a dynamic modern economy.

Echoing a theme touched on earlier, Daryoush Shayegan (1992) attributes the anti-Westernism found among young Muslims to their troubles in reconciling their religious values with values they associate with the West. The former keep them steadily in touch with seventh-century Arabia, Islamic martyrdom, and ancient rituals; the latter, inspired partly by movies and television, urge them to seek the fast life of celebrities, high technology, and relentless change. Unable to harmonize these values and compensate adequately for the consequent frustrations, they join movements that demonize the West. The West is indeed a key source of their problems: Had the West not undergone the Renaissance, the Enlightenment, and the Industrial Revolution, it would probably not fascinate so many young Muslims today. Shayegan's logic points, however, to a potential for a massive reaction against Islamism. After all, the attractions of the West would not pose a problem were Islam interpreted more flexibly. In fact, ever since the rise of the West gained wide recognition in the Islamic world, some have dealt with the ensuing clash of ideals through open Westernization accompanied by lower religiosity.[18] If the youth in cities of the Middle East are currently seeking to escape inner turmoil by rallying against Western materialism, tomorrow they may see the solution in bashing the strict interpretation of Islam. Returning again to Figure 2, we see that dissonance caused by $x^m$ can be lessened by relaxing either the value $a \geq \underline{a}$ or the value $b \geq \underline{b}$.

Our move from laboratory experiments to the contemporary Middle East forms a bridge to the next three sections, which discuss collective responses to moral dissonance, as opposed to individual responses. In the Middle East, there are doubtless individuals who are seeking to reduce their inner tensions in their own, possibly unique, ways. But the region also exhibits broad-based social movements that offer collective solutions to the very same problem.

These movements call into question the generality of dissonance management strategies that ascribe to individuals the power to reduce, even to eliminate, discomfort by themselves. In the best known of these, Leon Festinger's (1957) argument on *cognitive* dissonance, individuals make a point of avoiding information likely to raise their dissonance and of exposing themselves to information likely to lower it. Subsequent research has generally confirmed the existence of selective exposure. But it has also raised questions about the phenomenon's commonness outside controlled laboratory experiments.[19] In noncontrolled situations people ordinarily can choose from among a wider variety of dissonance reduc-

---

[18] Islamist writers frequently endorse this observation, invariably in the form of a complaint.

[19] See Cotton's (1985) survey of research on selective exposure.

tion instruments than they do in laboratory experiments, where typically there is just a single option. Even more critical, selective exposure is not necessarily the most effective instrument. In the case of values, as opposed to beliefs of the sort tested in laboratory experiments on cognitive dissonance, a further difficulty is that selective exposure might require the individual to leave his community.

## 5 Redemption, casuistry, and rationalization

As I shall argue later, escape is among the observed responses. But it is not a common response. Especially in contexts in which moral dissonance is widespread, individuals often get relief instead through social institutions that make it cheaper to meet given values. I shall distinguish among three categories of such institutions.

### 5.1 *Redemption*

In each of the experiments discussed, the appearance of a confederate in need of help provided a convenient vehicle for expiating guilt. Outside experimental settings, the role of the confederate gets carried out by collectively furnished mechanisms for moral relief. In medieval Christendom, for example, guilt-ridden parishioners enjoyed a socially supplied menu of rehabilitation instruments. Grave sinners could do public penance; lesser ones could confess to a priest. Prayer, alms, and fasting offered additional vehicles for the remission of sins, and in certain times and places wealthy sinners could buy off their obligations through indulgences. The underlying demand for redemption was certainly not independent of church activities. The church fueled it through steady emphasis on the omnipresence of Satan, the pervasiveness of evil, the horrors of hell, and the impossibility of achieving salvation without persistent introspection and penitence.[20]

Whatever the ecclesiastical role in generating moral turmoil, church-designed compensation mechanisms lowered the price of achieving moral comfort. In effect, they allowed Christians to achieve the satisfaction of virtuous living without having to avoid behaviors that would be very costly in terms of nonreligious criteria.

The point may be illustrated through Figure 3, which shows a tradeoff between income and religious participation. Implicit in the figure is the notion that time, a scarce resource, can be converted either into

---

[20] Delumeau (1990) offers vast documentation on this dual role of the church. See also Le Goff (1984) and Ekelund, Hébert, and Tollison (1992).

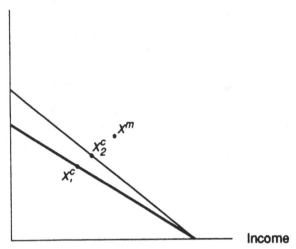

Figure 3. The effect of a fall in the price of religious participation. Initially, the individual selects $x_1^c$, which falls short of his moral target, $x^m$. A fall in the relative price of religious participation allows him to achieve $x_2^c$, lowering his moral dissonance.

business activity that yields income or into religious participation, an end in itself. The depicted trade-off could also be produced by religious restrictions on the pursuit of worldly gain, like antiusury rules and occupational limits. If the efficient operation of a business requires selling goods at interest, and interest is considered sinful, efforts to earn income will generate "negative" religious participation; and conversely, efforts to lead a pious life-style will involve sacrifices of income.[21] Whatever the source of the trade-off, the individual's moral base $x^m$ indicates that he feels morally compelled to meet two goals. He feels driven, on the one hand, to earn a particular income in order to give his family a standard of living he considers decent and, on the other, to perform a certain amount of religious activity, so as to feel that he is pursuing a Christian life-style. Under the initial opportunity constraint shown by a heavy line, the individual faces moral overload, and he selects $x_1^c$. Redemption mechanisms lower the price of moral satisfaction, expanding the opportunity set. Under the new opportunity constraint, the thin line, the individual

---

[21] By no means do all forms of religious participation exhibit such trade-offs. I am simplifying to illustrate a point.

selects $x_2^c$. He thus achieves greater religious participation along with more income, implying a fall in moral dissonance.[22]

## 5.2     Casuistry

Casuistry offers a second institutional device for making it easier to abide by guilt-producing moral injunctions. It involves the use of stratagems to circumvent a value without discarding it formally.[23] In both Christianity and Islam, the development of stratagems to overcome antiusury rules became a flourishing pursuit as economic development raised the demand for borrowing and lending at interest.[24] Another example, due to Richard and Nancy Tapper (1987), involves contemporary efforts to achieve consistency between Islam and the obligations of citizenship. In a small Turkish town that the Tappers studied, residents routinely felt torn between their civil duty to pay taxes to the state and their religious duty to pay tithes and alms. Officials helped solve these dilemmas by arguing that the state uses tax revenues to fulfill the functions once served by religious collections. The argument stretches the facts: The modern Turkish state pursues goals that are much broader and, in some respects, contrary to traditional Islamic objectives. Yet the argument serves the purpose of making it easier to satisfy religious needs, thus tempering a source of guilt.

## 5.3     Rationalization

Tapper and Tapper (1987) mention another method that the townspeople have used to consolidate their values: rationalization. It involves efforts to make incompatible values seem compatible by making rivalry in consumption seem like jointness. Ever since the Atatürk era, a common view among Westernized Turks has been that certain Islamic rituals, like praying five times a day and fasting during the month of Ramadan, are inimical to economic productivity. This view instills guilt

---

[22] Economic reasoning suggests that the rotation of the opportunity frontier will produce a substitution effect and a portfolio effect. Depending on the signs of these effects, either religious participation or income could fall as a result of a decline in the price of religious participation. Moreover, moral dissonance could actually increase. The logic of the latter possibility is that dissonance depends on each of the individual's moral shortcomings; according to the weight his moral utility function assigns them, the alleviation of one and aggravation of the other might raise his moral dissonance.

[23] There is another meaning of casuistry, developed by Sunstein (1996, chap. 5): close attention to the particulars of each situation. This meaning is closer to what I call "compartmentalization."

[24] For evidence, see Nelson (1969) and Rodinson (1973).

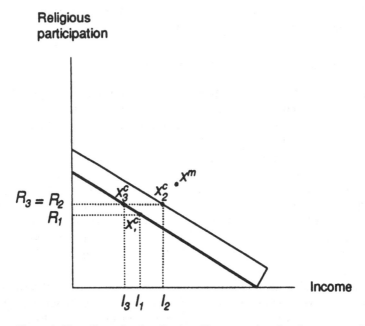

Figure 4. The effect of rationalization. The perception that frequent praying enhances economic productivity shifts the individual's choice from $x_1^c$ to $x_2^c$, lowering his moral dissonance. If the perception is spurious, he will actually have moved to $x_3^c$.

in individuals who demand of themselves both piety and hard work. Great efforts have been made, therefore, to refute it. A counterview, the Tappers found, is that Islamic rituals actually raise productivity by improving health: Frequent praying ensures regular exercise, and fasting is good for weight control. The counterview implies that the requirements of Islam are not only not inimical to modern economic needs but consistent with them. It also implies that Islam both anticipated and verifies the findings of modern medical research. As such, it helps lessen tensions by reconciling religious and secular values.[25]

In terms of our framework, this rationalization makes the individual believe that certain religious activities have a *negative* opportunity cost. His perceived opportunity set thus takes the form shown in Figure 4. Moreover, insofar as the promoted belief is grounded in reality, he is able to reduce his dissonance by moving from $x_1^c$ to $x_2^c$ – a move that

[25] Mardin (1983) offers numerous other examples involving the role of Islam in Turkish life.

increases his income and religious participation simultaneously. Interestingly, his moral dissonance could decline even if the belief in the compatibility of Islamic rituals and economic success were entirely spurious. Suppose that our individual, convinced of the economic advantages of prayer, sets his religious participation at $R_2$ in the expectation that work will then generate the income $I_2$. Suppose also that his opportunity set has not really changed, so he earns only $I_3$. Depending on how he accounts for the fall in his income, he may now feel more comfortable with his religious activities during work hours. In particular, if he attributes the decline to factors unrelated to frequent work breaks, he may find the task of allocating his work hours morally less burdensome. The illustration shows that an empirically vacuous rationalization, if accompanied by the right form of mental accounting, can make a person, in effect, restrain his preferences in favor of his values.

## 6    Escape and compartmentalization

In modifying individual opportunity sets, redemption, casuistry, and rationalization change behavior without altering the values responsible for moral discomfort. I now turn to collective responses that reshape individual values. The most extreme of these responses shields psychologically troubled individuals from the social sources of moral overload.

### 6.1    *Escape*

We saw earlier that the medieval church fostered widespread guilt through its contempt and even condemnation of earthly existence. Made to feel morally inadequate, some Christians found it impossible to attain inner harmony through means like confession and penitence. So they sought to avoid secular temptations by fleeing them. The monasteries of the Middle Ages were founded, in part, as a refuge for such individuals; they were to allow troubled Christians to abandon worldly pleasures in favor of quiet preparation for the afterlife.

One can only speculate on the degree to which this objective was reached. What is known is that, in removing themselves from church-condemned activities, monks and nuns placed themselves in social environments that condemned secular pursuits, thus heightening their exposure to the very discourse responsible for their initial anxieties. Revealingly, the Christian doctrine of *contemptus mundi,* which promoted a woeful vision of life on earth, was refined within monasteries.[26]

---

[26] See Delumeau (1990, especially chaps. 1 and 16).

Nevertheless, these establishments may well have helped many individuals alleviate guilt. Reconsider an infeasible moral base $x^m$, composed of objectives $a \geq \underline{a}$ and $b \geq \underline{b}$. By avoiding environments that reinforce one of the objectives, one may render $x^m$ feasible. It is logically possible, of course, for countervailing changes to overwhelm the potential reduction in dissonance: One's opportunity set might shrink, and exposure to a new discourse might expand a particular moral objective. Accordingly, a monk might find that in joining a monastery he has helped shrink his secular objectives yet also expanded his religious goals. But the essential point is that escape may contribute to guilt reduction.

Another example of the use of moral escape is given by Gary Becker (1996, pp. 231–33). The sight of a beggar tends to make people feel guilty, he observes, and they respond through charity. Still, they feel worse off after the encounter than if it had not occurred. They prefer, therefore, to reduce their contacts with beggars, supporting regulations that keep beggars away from them. Here, it is the source of guilt that gets transposed – not, as in the example of the monks, the victims. But from the standpoint of the victims, the result is the same: They separate themselves from a source of guilt.

### 6.2    *Compartmentalization*

Moral overload can be generated, Figure 1 showed, by the coexistence of multiple values that are each feasible by themselves. In such cases, moral dissonance may be lightened by restricting the values relevant to each of many contexts. Such a response, which amounts to *alternating* escape, may be called compartmentalization. Suppose again that, with the opportunity set fixed, the objectives $a \geq \underline{a}$ and $b \geq \underline{b}$ are both attainable on their own. If the individual can learn to consider the two values as applying to separate contexts, he may lessen, even eliminate, his guilt. For the solution to work well, of course, moral compartmentalization must be accompanied by a consistent compartmentalization of preferences: The person's intrinsic desires must tilt heavily toward $a$ in contexts in which the operative moral objective is $a \geq \underline{a}$ and toward $b$ where it is $b \geq \underline{b}$. For example, he must enjoy financially motivated work in settings where his operative moral drive is monetary gain; likewise, he must enjoy religious activity in settings where he feels morally compelled to worship.

Abortion and capital punishment are issues that, when paired, may produce moral dissonance: Allowing abortion clashes with banning capital punishment, and vice versa. In either case, then, justifying one position on the basis of the sanctity of life calls into question the moral standing of the other – as long as the two issues are considered together.

If the relevant discourses are kept separate, however, one may support either pair of policies without experiencing guilt. For instance, one can support liberal abortion in the interest of gender equality and, independently, oppose capital punishment on the grounds that nothing can justify a killing.

For moral compartmentalization to work, the society's public discourse must separate the issues that generate moral clashes. So, wherever the potential for moral overload is present, one is likely to find pressure groups trying to partition public discourse into mutually exclusive zones. The ongoing abortion debate in the United States offers an example: Activists on both sides of the divide make efforts to keep their sympathizers focused on the abortion issue, downplaying the possibility of moral conflict. For example, the prolife lobby avoids reminding its members that many of them support the death penalty, which sometimes results in the taking of innocent life. Likewise, it avoids mentioning that contraception, which many of its members practice, and restrictions on sexual activity, which many support, both take *potential* innocent lives. For its part, the prochoice lobby avoids reminding its own members that they tend to oppose the death penalty and that their ranks include many vegetarians who deplore the killing of animals. The presence of rival agendas for moral compartmentalization may cause, then, the general population to split into multiple *moral communities*. The members of each community would be reluctant to expose themselves to the other, lest they be forced to confront moral inconsistencies they are able to avoid within their own communities.[27]

A historically very significant case of moral compartmentalization has been the secularization process that began with the Christian Reformation. Whereas the medieval church strove to keep Christians constantly aware of their diverse moral failings – at work, in the marketplace, at home, in bed, at the dinner table – secularization has pushed many such domains essentially outside the realm of religion. In effect, it has partitioned human activities into spheres governed by distinct moralities.

Moral compartmentalization need not be an all-or-nothing process. It can be achieved partially through selective reductions in the social salience of particular values. If a certain moral obligation starts receiving progressively less attention in certain contexts, it becomes increasingly easy to forget within those particular contexts. At the same time, the declining emphasis on the value can reduce the intrinsic utility that

---

[27] Sunstein (1997, pp. 40–41) observes that contested norms can split a society into diverse "norm communities." Where moral communities arise from the quest for intrapersonal harmony, norm communities are rooted in efforts to foster interpersonal harmony. The two types of communities commonly overlap.

people derive from actions serving to fulfill it. This is because knowledge about an activity's advantages depends on the exposure it receives.[28] Also, insofar as past consumption enhances the intrinsic utility of present consumption through mechanisms akin to addiction,[29] a person's limited experience with an activity will compound the decline in this utility. The joint effect of all these changes will be to reduce the moral dissonance generated by the value whose salience has fallen. For an illustration, suppose that a certain transformation lowers religion's salience during weekdays. Because of the transformation, new generations are reminded of religion less frequently than their parents had been. Simultaneously, their added attention to material goods makes them increasingly aware of nonreligious sources of satisfaction, and in shifting their consumption patterns they come to desire material goods more intensely than before. The combined effect can be to lower both religious consumption and religion-based guilt.

A recent example of an attempt to lower the salience of certain values lies in the reluctance of American universities to release information on the standards they apply to the beneficiaries of affirmative action. Affirmative action puts the American ethic of individualism in conflict with the principle of group rights. As such, it can be a source of moral dissonance. In keeping the details of their affirmative action programs secret, American universities have, then, effectively permitted the programs to continue without creating moral dilemmas for their faculty.[30]

There is a revealing experiment, reported by Stanley Schachter (1951), in which groups were formed to discuss a study on a certain juvenile delinquent. The study was written to convince readers that the delinquent needed love and kindness. Each group contained several confederates who, unknown to the others, had been instructed to take predetermined positions. One of the confederates consistently disagreed strongly with the consensus, which was always that the delinquent should be treated leniently. The experiment's purpose was to discover how, at the end of the discussion, the subjects would feel about the confederates, including whether they wanted them to remain in the group. The persistent disagreer endured castigation and rejection, indicating that the subjects were bothered by the presence of someone who put them in touch

---

[28] For the underlying reasoning, see Kuran (1995a, esp. chaps. 10–11).

[29] Becker (1996, chaps. 2–6) explores various dimensions of the process.

[30] A complementary vehicle for attenuating such dilemmas has been the practice of demonizing the opponents of affirmative action. If the critics of affirmative action are miscreants, they need not be taken seriously, and their criticisms can be ignored. Attention can focus on their personal flaws, rather than on the dissonance-generating substance of their arguments.

with values other than compassion. Evidently, they found the moral compartmentalization advantageous; they understood that open moral discourse might generate moral overload.

## 7 Moral reconstruction

The dissonance-reduction measures considered thus far are all aimed at managing rather than discarding guilt-producing values. Escape entails one's physical removal from a source of guilt, and compartmentalization distances one mentally from particular values in a selective manner. As for redemption, casuistry, and rationalization, they constitute instruments for lowering the cost of abiding by a given morality. An alternative to all these measures is moral reconstruction.

The reforms that Turkey underwent in the 1920s offer an example of an attempt at moral reconstruction on a grand scale. Kemal Atatürk, the chief architect of these reforms, sought to commit Turkey to Westernization, including a form of secularism aimed at purging Islam from public life and drastically restricting its moral reach. Generations of earlier reformers had sought to reconcile Islam with Western values. As Niyazi Berkes (1964), Bernard Lewis (1968), and others have documented, they were largely unsuccessful. Rather than achieving a moral synthesis, they institutionalized a bifurcated moral system. Their education system illustrates the point. Primary schools of the late nineteenth century continued to teach traditional Islamic values, with an emphasis on community, authority, and stability, but the reorganized secondary schools promoted the values of the European Enlightenment, including individual freedom, democracy, and progress. The consequent moral overload created a constituency for moral reconstruction, and Atatürk rose to the challenge. His reforms were designed to make Turks feel free to adopt Western practices without fear of breaching religious laws, although he toyed first with the idea of reforming Islam.[31] That Islam crept back into Turkish public life after Atatürk's death does not alter the revolutionary character of his mission. Nor does it indicate that his efforts were entirely unsuccessful. While many contemporary Turks reject Atatürk's objective of disestablishing Islam, no one – not even the Islamists who demonize him – denies that his reforms permanently changed Turkish moral discourse, thus facilitating various later initiatives.

When two values or moral systems clash, the moral reconstruction through which one tries to lessen the resulting guilt may take more than one form. For example, insofar as traditional Islamic values conflict with

---

[31] Toprak (1981) offers many relevant observations and insights.

modern Western ones, the objective of moral reconstruction could be to discard the former, the latter, or even both, in favor of some new system. Accordingly, the Westernization movements within the Islamic world have always faced competition from movements dedicated to limiting, if not eliminating, Western influences. The best known anti-Westernizer of modern times has been the Ayatollah Khomeini. The revolution that Khomeini spearheaded was, above all, a cultural revolution; he never tired of stressing that his overriding objective was to expand Islam's authority in the lives of Muslims. His popularity is attributable partly to the simplicity he promised to give to Iranian life. In the Iran of his dreams, no one would be torn between East and West, old and new, tradition and progress. Nobody would suffer moral dissonance, as there would be no competing claims on behavior.

A final example of moral reconstruction is from sixteenth- and seventeenth-century Europe. The expansion of European trade in earlier centuries necessitated, in addition to the creation of new economic institutions, the replacement of medieval economic values by ones conducive to large-scale trade and investment. Individuals had to become capable of forming attachments to economic enterprises based minimally on kinship; they had to accept the spread of markets as socially beneficial; and they had to stop seeing economic success as a sign of character flaws inimical to salvation. Such new needs made the redistribution-focused, communalist economic morality of the church increasingly burdensome. The stage was set for the Protestant Reformation, which legitimized rapidly spreading economic practices so that producers and traders could carry on their activities without developing guilt.[32]

## 8     The limits of moral diversity

The instruments of dissonance reduction that have been identified in previous sections are not mutually exclusive. In the course of efforts to achieve moral compartmentalization, moral overload might get alleviated through rationalization, and compartmentalization itself might serve as a step toward moral reconstruction. Generally, however, uses of the various instruments will be uncoordinated. Just as an epidemic will bring forth diverse and possibly competing projects to arrest its advance,

---

[32] For details of this thesis, see Rosenberg and Birdzell (1986, chap. 4). The authors acknowledge that attempts to use Christianity for economic control did not end with the Reformation. All branches of Christianity have continued to harbor strains that pursue behavioral regulation for distributional ends. For related insights, see Hirschman (1977) and Delumeau (1990, chaps. 19–21).

so widespread moral dissonance will induce various possible remedies. One group of moral entrepreneurs will institute means for moral escape; going further, another will pursue moral reform. Even if trying to resolve the same problem, the groups may become rivals, disparaging each other as "extremists" or "traitors." During the Protestant Reformation, moral activists formed anything but a united front, and the same is true of the Middle East today.

In every society, the major social issues of the day – those that define individual identities, political loyalties, and the epoch – are ones that generate intense moral conflict. This is true, we have seen, because the resolution of moral strain requires social cooperation, and also because the goal can be met through various forms of cooperation. In the United States, slavery and the Vietnam War have, at different times, been preeminent social issues, and today, abortion and race relations have filled their place. These issues divided, or still divide, Americans into camps seeking to rank or restructure values differently. The divisions have been emotionally charged, precisely because each camp interferes with the other's pursuit of moral peace.

Take again the issue of abortion, which pits the sanctity of life against the rights of women. As noted earlier, both extreme camps pursue moral compartmentalization. At the same time, each seeks to frustrate the other's compartmentalization strategy, as when "prolife" activists call abortion performers "baby killers" or when "prochoice" activists characterize their rivals as "defenders of patriarchy." A common response to the induced frustrations is to seek to censor the other, while insisting on one's own right to be heard.[33] And the consequence of the competing pressures is an equilibrium whereby public discourse is carried on almost exclusively by vocal minorities committed to the supremacy of their most cherished values. Such an equilibrium can persist indefinitely, although it will create opportunities for innovative moral entrepreneurs to introduce institutions that will reduce the associated moral dissonance.

Not all intrapersonal conflicts that breed social strains have a moral dimension. Conflicting interpretations of the world may breed cognitive dissonance, which can fuel competing collective efforts to make one of them prevail. And, as a practical matter, broad social conflicts have both moral and cognitive dimensions. But insofar as a moral dimension is present, there will be evidence of efforts to cope with moral dissonance. One will find, for instance, that individuals are seeking guidance from religious authorities and help from psychiatrists, and that they are worrying about who they are. If the sole source of social conflict were cognitive

[33] From different angles, the point is developed by Hunter (1991) and Hentoff (1992).

dissonance, people would seek assistance only from experts in command of empirical knowledge; they would want to know what *is* but not what *ought to be*.

The overall argument has implications for the evaluation and design of social systems. Were it possible to develop a social system behind a veil of ignorance,[34] one might want it to harbor institutions that facilitate the reconciliation and fusion of values. Some of these institutions would give protection to individuals seeking the middle ground in polarized moral debates. Others would simplify compromises among conflicting moral agendas. And still others would frustrate efforts to conceal the potential constituency for moral reconstruction. One might also want to preserve, perhaps even to promote, socially advantageous opportunities for expiating the guilt feelings that are inevitable even in the best of all possible societies. Charities, scholarship funds, and religious endowments are possible examples of socially beneficial outlets for individuals needing to compensate for moral transgressions. Keeping certain activities dependent on voluntary donations, and at least partially uncommercialized, may thus help preserve opportunities for alleviating psychological stress.[35]

This argument for supporting tendencies toward moral uniformity and consistency does not necessarily conflict with "cultural relativism," the view that all cultural practices are equally valid and all values equally suspect.[36] In its purest form, cultural relativism implies merely the lack of a rational basis for choosing among values. It does not imply that one should obstruct tendencies toward moral uniformity, nor that one should actively promote moral diversity. Yet the latter objective is among the pillars of the contemporary multiculturalism movement,[37] whose intellectual antecedents include cultural relativism. This new movement celebrates and even promotes differences among groups, including moral ones. The multiculturalism movement is, of course, appropriately "diverse." It encompasses many who consider it a vehicle for cross-cultural understanding and cooperation, or an antidote to the cultural chauvin-

---

[34] As developed by Rawls (1971, pp. 136–42), the concept refers to ignorance about how known options will affect one's own particular situation. Such ignorance obliges one to evaluate alternatives solely on the basis of general considerations.

[35] This point complements, yet is distinct from, Frey's (1993) argument that limits on commercialization prevent the crowding out of motivations to perform tasks for their own sake. My emphasis here is on opportunity rather than motivation.

[36] The phrase was popularized by Benedict (1934), who discussed cannibalism without explicitly condemning it.

[37] The movement is sometimes called the "diversity" movement. For presentations of its goals, see Goldberg (1994, pt. 1). Ravitch (1990) and Lynch (1997) critique its American variant.

ism of the powerful, and many others who see it as a tactical device for overthrowing existing values at odds with certain agendas.

Notwithstanding such motivational differences, the movement's participants are united, at least provisionally, in opposing moral homogenization. One may distinguish here, along with Clifford Orwin (1996), between "multiculturalism as a fact" and "multiculturalism as a policy." Multiculturalism as a fact refers to the great variety of ethnically based subcultures that increasingly characterizes many modern nations. As for multiculturalism as a policy, it involves the promotion of cultural differences as a vehicle for helping culturally diverse individuals integrate into their society's mainstream. One can recognize the fact of multiculturalism and support cross-cultural tolerance without endorsing the policy. Indeed, from the prevailing cultural diversity one may infer that the world is passing through a period when moral reconciliation mechanisms have an especially great role to play.

The groups that the new multiculturalism aims to protect include individuals who suffer from moral overload. For example, the members of economically disadvantaged communities, including many formed by recent immigrants, are learning that they ought to become full participants in American public life, but also that they should never forget who they are. One can think of contexts in which these two values would be compatible, but not everyone will be equally capable of reconciling them.

Much of the debate on multiculturalism has centered on whether the cultures of poorly educated, weak, or historically dominated groups are worth preserving. Insufficient attention has been paid to the costs of subjecting individuals to moral overload. Yet, essential functions of culture are to homogenize, simplify, and rank the values by which people judge decisons, including their own. To keep alive multiple cultures may defeat, therefore, a principal reason why we have cultures. The point is not that governments should be in the business of choosing among cultures, although there do exist economic reasons for supporting particular values and opposing others – to say nothing of moral reasons. It is, rather, that cultural diversity is not an unmitigated blessing.

As a socially beneficial by-product, a clash of values can yield, it might be said, innovations that make human civilization more safe or productive. Indeed, people exposed to very different moral systems may develop diverse desires and insights which jointly foster creativity. Yet, as Freud (1961) recognized, the march of civilization entails psychological costs. I would add that such costs stimulate moral measures to alleviate them. And the search for these measures can itself be a source of innovation.

If multiculturalism generates moral tensions, can the same not be said about any group pursuing social transformation? It is certainly true that groups explicitly dedicated to moral reconstruction can create moral conflicts within anyone who internalizes contradictory values. Yet there is a major difference between monocultural and multicultural moral agendas. Whereas an attempt at monocultural moral transformation may in the long run reduce moral dissonance, a genuinely multiculturalist campaign will not. There may be good reasons, of course, for rejecting any particular monocultural agenda. But these reasons will have to be weighed against the disadvantages of multiculturalism in regard to dissonance alleviation. The argument supports a prediction: The sort of society envisioned by multiculturalists is inherently unstable. Either the societies they are trying to transform will split into separate yet morally cohesive entities or their movement will founder in the face of a new moral synthesis that erodes group-based moral differences.

In itself, the desirability of institutions that lessen cultural or moral diversity is not a new point. Going back at least to Émile Durkheim (1933), numerous sociologists have proposed that nation building requires a convergence of values. They have also argued that the homogenization of individual values contributes to social stability and economic cooperation by reducing violence. Echoing this theme in relation to the American multiculturalism movement, the historian Arthur Schlessinger (1991) worries that it promotes a "cult of ethnicity" that makes individuals focus less on their shared interests as citizens than on their group-based differences. Other social scientists, including Thomas Sowell (1994, chap. 4) and Russell Hardin (1995, chap. 4), observe that cultural differences serve as norms of exclusion. Their insight implies that moral diversity, inasmuch as it generates behavioral variation, breeds segregation and discrimination, fueling political instability. Forming yet another intellectual tradition, economists stretching from Thomas Schelling (1960) to Robert Sugden (1995) have shown how various uniformities across individuals, including moral uniformities, facilitate coordination. With respect to all such theses, this final section's contribution lies in its focus on conflicts *within* individuals as a reason why moral diversity can be socially costly.

## REFERENCES

Aaron, Henry J. (1994). "Public Policy, Values, and Consciousness," *Journal of Economic Perspectives* 8 (Spring): 3–21.

Akerlof, George A., and William T. Dickens (1982). "The Economic Consequences of Cognitive Dissonance," *American Economic Review* 72 (June): 307–19.

Barkow, Jerome H., Leda Cosmides, and John Tooby, eds. (1992). *The Adapted Mind: Evolutionary Psychology and the Generation of Culture.* New York: Oxford University Press.

Baron, Jonathan, and Mark Spranca (1996). "Protected Values." Working paper, University of Pennsylvania.

Becker, Gary S. (1996). *Accounting for Tastes.* Cambridge, Mass.: Harvard University Press.

Benedict, Ruth (1934). *Patterns of Culture.* Boston: Houghton Mifflin.

Berkes, Niyazi (1964). *The Development of Secularism in Turkey.* Montreal: McGill University Press.

Cialdini, Robert B., Betty Lee Darby, and Joyce E. Vincent (1973). "Transgression and Altruism: A Case for Hedonism." *Journal of Experimental Social Psychology* 9 (November): 502–16.

Cotton, John L. (1985). "Cognitive Dissonance in Selective Exposure," in Dolf Zillman and Jennings Bryant, eds., *Selective Exposure and Communication,* pp. 11–33. Hillsdale, N.J.: Lawrence Erlbaum.

Delumeau, Jean (1990). *Sin and Fear: The Emergence of a Western Guilt Culture, 13th–18th Centuries.* Trans. Eric Nicholson. New York: St. Martin's Press.

Durkheim, Émile (1933). *The Division of Labor in Society.* Trans. George Simpson. New York: Macmillan.

Ekelund, Robert B., Jr., Robert F. Hébert, and Robert D. Tollison (1992). "The Economics of Sin and Redemption: Purgatory as a Market-Pull Innovation?" *Journal of Economic Behavior and Organization* 19 (September): 1–15.

Festinger, Leon (1957). *A Theory of Cognitive Dissonance.* Stanford, Calif.: Stanford University Press.

Frank, Robert H. (1988). *Passions within Reason: The Strategic Role of the Emotions.* New York: W. W. Norton.

Frankfurt, Harry G. (1971). "Freedom of Will and the Concept of a Person," *Journal of Philosophy* 68 (January): 5–20.

Freud, Sigmund (1961). *Civilization and Its Discontents.* Trans. James Strachey. New York: W. W. Norton.

Frey, Bruno S. (1993). "Motivation as a Limit to Pricing," *Journal of Economic Psychology* 14 (December): 635–64.

George, David (1993). "Does the Market Create Preferred Preferences?" *Review of Social Economy* 51 (Fall): 323–46.

Goldberg, David Theo, ed. (1994). *Multiculturalism: A Critical Reader.* Oxford: Blackwell.

Hardin, Russell (1995). *One for All: The Logic of Group Conflict.* Princeton, N.J.: Princeton University Press.

Hentoff, Nat (1992). *Free Speech for Me – Not for Thee: How the American Left and Right Relentlessly Censor Each Other.* New York: HarperCollins.

Hirschman, Albert O. (1977). *The Passions and the Interests: Political Arguments for Capitalism before Its Triumph,* Princeton, N.J.: Princeton University Press.

Hoffman, Elizabeth, and Matthew L. Spitzer (1993). "Willingness to Pay and Willingness to Accept: Legal and Economic Implications," *Washington University Law Quarterly* 71 (Spring): 59–114.

Hunter, James Davison (1991). *Culture Wars: The Struggle to Define America.* New York: Basic Books.

Kahneman, Daniel, and Jack L. Knetsch (1992). "Valuing Public Goods: The Purchase of Moral Satisfaction," *Journal of Environmental Economics and Management* 22 (January): 57–70.

Kahneman, Daniel, Jack L. Knetsch, and Richard H. Thaler (1991). "The Endowment Effect, Loss Aversion, and the Status Quo Bias," *Journal of Economic Perspectives* 5 (Winter): 193–206.

Kahneman, Daniel, Paul Slovic, and Amos Tversky, eds. (1982). *Judgment under Uncertainty: Heuristics and Biases.* Cambridge: Cambridge University Press.

Kuran, Timur (1995a). *Private Truths, Public Lies: The Social Consequences of Preference Falsification.* Cambridge, Mass.: Harvard University Press.

———(1995b). "Islamic Economics and the Islamic Subeconomy," *Journal of Economic Perspectives* 9 (Fall): 155–73.

Le Goff, Jacques (1984). *The Birth of Purgatory.* Trans. Arthur Goldhammer. Chicago: University of Chicago Press.

Lewis, Bernard (1968). *The Emergence of Modern Turkey*, 2d ed. London: Oxford University Press.

———(1993). "Islam and Development: A Revaluation of Values," in *Islam in History: Ideas, People, and Events in the Middle East*, rev. ed., pp. 345–57. Chicago: Open Court.

Lynch, Frederick R. (1997). *The Diversity Machine: The Drive to Change the "White Male Workplace."* New York: Free Press.

Mardin, Şerif (1983). "Religion and Politics in Modern Turkey," in James P. Piscatori, ed., *Islam in the Political Process*, pp. 138–59. New York: Cambridge University Press.

Margolis, Howard (1982). *Selfishness, Altruism, and Rationality.* New York: Cambridge University Press.

Nelson, Benjamin (1969). *The Idea of Usury: From Tribal Brotherhood to Universal Otherhood*, 2d ed. Chicago: University of Chicago Press.

Orwin, Clifford (1996). "All Quiet on the (Post)Western Front?" *Public Interest* no. 123(Spring): 3–21.

Payne, John W., James R. Bettman, and Eric J. Johnson (1992). "Behavioral Decision Research: A Constructive Processing Perspective," *Annual Review of Psychology* 43: 87–131.

Rabin, Matthew (1994). "Cognitive Dissonance and Social Change," *Journal of Economic Behavior and Organization*, 23 (March), 177–94.

———(1995). "Moral Preferences, Moral Constraints, and Self-Serving Biases." Unpublished paper, University of California at Berkeley.

Ravitch, Diane (1990). "Multiculturalism: *E Pluribus Plures*," *American Scholar* 59 (Summer): 337–54.

Rawls, John (1971). *A Theory of Justice.* Cambridge, Mass.: Harvard University Press.

Regan, Dennis T., Margo Williams, and Sondra Sparling (1972). "Voluntary Expiation of Guilt: A Field Experiment," *Journal of Personality and Social Psychology* 24 (October): 42–45.

Rodinson, Maxime (1973). *Islam and Capitalism.* Trans. Brian Pearce. New York: Pantheon Books.

Rosenberg, Nathan, and L. E. Birdzell, Jr. (1986). *How the West Grew Rich: The Economic Transformation of the Industrial World.* New York: Basic Books.

Schachter, Stanley (1951). "Deviation, Rejection, and Communication," *Journal of Abnormal and Social Psychology,* 46 (April): 190–208.

Schelling, Thomas C. (1960). *The Strategy of Conflict.* Cambridge, Mass.: Harvard University Press.

———(1984). *Choice and Consequence: Perspectives of an Errant Economist.* Cambridge, Mass.: Harvard University Press.

Schlessinger, Arthur M., Jr. (1991). *The Disuniting of America: Reflections on a Multicultural Society.* Knoxville, Tenn.: Whittle Books.

Schlicht, Ekkehart (1984). "Cognitive Dissonance in Economics," *Gesellschaft für Wirtschafts- und Sozialwissenschaften* 141: 61–81.

Sen, Amartya K. (1974). "Choice, Orderings, and Morality," in Stephan Körner, ed., *Practical Reason: Papers and Discussions,* pp. 54–67. New Haven, Conn.: Yale University Press.

Shayegan, Daryush (1992). *Cultural Schizophrenia: Islamic Societies Confronting the West.* Trans. John Howe. London: Saqi Books.

Sowell, Thomas (1994). *Race and Culture: A World View.* New York: Basic Books.

Steele, Claude (1988). "The Psychology of Self-Affirmation: Sustaining the Integrity of the Self," *Advances in Experimental Social Psychology* 21: 261–302.

Sugden, Robert (1995). "A Theory of Focal Points," *Economic Journal* 105 (May): 533–50.

Sunstein, Cass (1996). *Legal Reasoning and Political Conflict.* New York: Oxford University Press.

———(1997). *Free Markets and Social Justice.* New York: Oxford University Press.

Tapper, Richard, and Nancy Tapper (1987). "'Thank God We're Secular!' Aspects of Fundamentalism in a Turkish Town," in Lionel Caplan, ed., *Studies in Religious Fundamentalism,* pp. 51–78. Albany: State University of New York Press.

Thaler, Richard (1980). "Toward a Positive Theory of Consumer Choice," *Journal of Economic Behavior and Organization* 1 (March): 39–60.

Toprak, Binnaz (1981). *Islam and Political Development in Turkey.* Leiden: E. J. Brill.

Tversky, Amos, and Itamar Simonson (1993). "Context-dependent Preferences," *Management Science* 39 (October): 1179–89.

Wilson, James Q. (1993). *The Moral Sense.* New York: Free Press.

Wright, Robert (1994). *The Moral Animal: Evolutionary Psychology and Everyday Life.* New York: Pantheon Books.

CHAPTER 9

# Moral diversity and specialized values: some observations

*John Michael Montias*

It is widely believed that "moral dissonance" results when individuals have preferences over material goods that conflict with the "superior values" inculcated into them by religious or other groups. Instead of delving into this conflict within individuals, one may analyze the conflicts or tensions in a society divided into groups of individuals with sharply differing preferences, as, for example, those primarily motivated by greed and those primarily motivated by superior values. The first approach is pursued by Kuran, the second by Bowles and Gintis, in their respective chapters in this volume. Bowles and Gintis look at the equilibrium properties of societies made up of individuals with and without cooperative traits ("nice" and "nasty"). In their model "agents are paired for trade through some stochastic mechanism." While there may be diversity in the societies modeled by both Kuran and Bowles and Gintis, there are no religiously, racially, or tribally defined subgroups with special sets of values that are likely to determine the patterns of interaction which will take place in those hypothetical societies. In this note,[1] I focus on groups with specialized values[2] that played a critical role in societies transiting from Gemeinschaft to Gesellschaft.

Some of the groups I am referring to are well known (the Jews in early modern Europe, the Chinese in Thailand, the Asians in East Africa, the

[1] I am grateful to Avner Ben-Ner and James Stodder for their substantive comments and for their assistance with bibliographic references.
[2] It may be useful to distinguish values derived from preferences regarding interactions with other individuals, within a group to which an individual is attached and outside it, from those regarding the process or nature of these interactions. For example, an individual may be willing to lend money without charging interest (a particular type of interaction) but only to individuals within his or her group (a preference for dealing with certain individuals). This distinction, in the spirit of the terminology developed in Avner Ben-Ner and Louis Putterman (this volume), cannot be developed further in the confines of this brief note.

267

Armenians in Turkey), others less (the Bamileke tribe in Cameroon, the Parsis in India, the Berbers in Morocco). Why are these allogens (people ethnically different from the majority) so successful in carving out an economic niche in these diverse societies? I would suggest the reason lies chiefly in that their values do not require them to behave in a charitable way toward the members of the dominant group. In some cases it may be that they have values similar to those of the dominant group when they deal with one another – say, with respect to the prohibition on usury – but that they harbor no such values when it comes to dealing with representatives of the dominant group. This makes it possible for them to be "hard-nosed" in their commercial and financial relations with members of the dominant group and to edge out members of that group in certain occupations, including moneylending and many types of commerce in which being hard-nosed yields a competitive advantage. Max Weber in his *Sociology of Religion* (Weber 1963, p. 250) had already pointed to this phenomenon in the case of the Jews: "As a pariah people, [the Jews] retained the double standard of morals which is characteristic of primordial economic practice in all communities: what is prohibited in relation to one's brothers is permitted in relation to strangers." He did not stress, however, the comparative advantage that pariahs derive from their ability to ignore the prohibitions that fetter majority entrepreneurs. To put a fine point on it, pariah entrepreneurs make better principals or quasi principals because they are not encumbered by favorable sentiments for their agents.[3]

Students of pariah entrepreneurship have shown that successful minorities share a number of common characteristics: They resist assimilation into the dominant group (and subversion to its values) by claiming "transient status"; they rarely intermarry with members of the dominant group; they tend to segregate themselves residentially (if they are not already forced to do so by the majority); they establish separate schools for their children; they maintain customs that make them distinct and reinforce their cultural isolation (Bonasich 1973, p. 589).

"Specialization of values," if I can call it that, has important consequences for the way people sort themselves out in engaging in transactions. Those with strong traditional values (against usury and

---

[3] This formulation of the pariah's comparative advantage was suggested by Avner Ben-Ner. Note that differences between in- and out-groups need not be grounded in religion or ethnic differences. The plywood cooperatives of the American West are known to hire non-member managers because such managers are believed to be more effective monitors and administrators of discipline than managers hired from the in-group of cooperants would be.

nontraditional economic activity) will reduce moral dissonance by desisting from engaging in prohibited activities (allowing the outgroup to dominate these activities) or they will engage in them only as passive partners, i.e., as borrowers rather than as lenders, as taxpayers rather than as tax collectors, as employees rather than as employers. They may try to keep transactions with pariah entrepreneurs to a minimum but still be forced into them by necessity. A Polish proverb, common in pre–World War II days, suggests that Christians dealt with Jews out of need, when they had no other choice: "Jak bieda, to do Zyda" – When there is poverty [or distress], *then* you go to the Jew (for details, see Gerber 1981, pp. 100–18).

As time goes by, and the out-group becomes increasingly proficient at performing the services it has been performing, the economic specialization that this behavior entails deepens. An interesting example of the success of a subgroup in which neither religion nor race plays a role is that of the Bamileke tribe in Cameroon, whose superior ability (and specialized values) as traders has translated into superior skills in mathematics, accounting, and economics and who have flowed with ease, in one generation, from the marketplace to the government bureaucracy and the university. So, to revert to a general situation, we have, loosely speaking, an equilibrium in which members of the out-group and those of the dominant group transact with each other in stable ways, albeit at low levels. This equilibrium, however, may be unstable in the long run because it creates moral tensions, not so much within individuals, as Kuran stresses, but across groups. The members of the dominant group who harbor traditional values get to hate the members of the out-group who seem to flout them. Envy, a common human motivation too infrequently taken into account by economists, magnifies, in the minds of the members of the in-group, the advantages the out-group are thought to derive from their behavior. Many of them believe that "these bloodsuckers [members of the outgroup] have become filthy rich by exploiting us." Eventually a pogrom or massacre breaks up the uneasy coexistence of the two groups.[4] The out-group may be eliminated altogether or thoroughly marginalized.

In any concrete historical situation, however, factors other than heterogeneous values must be taken into account to explain both the initial

---

[4] In sixteenth and seventeenth century Europe, rulers (emperors, princes, electors) who wished, for mercantilistic reasons, to give greater liberty to the Jews were frequently compelled to give in to the majority of the population who wished to maintain these curbs for the purpose of restricting competition, for religious reasons, or for both reasons (Israel 1989, p. 65 and passim).

equilibrium between the in- and the out-group and its eventual distur-
bance. Specialization in certain occupations is reinforced, if it is not
altogether brought about in the first place, by the successful pressures of
the dominant group to prevent members of the out-group from engaging
in most traditional occupations (guild restrictions in the case of crafts,
strictures against landholding in the case of agriculture). These disabili-
ties played a key role in restricting European Jews to the occupations in
which they eventually excelled, including international trade, banking,
and diamond trading.[5] In France, much the same can be said of Protestants in the seventeenth century who were not allowed to join craft guilds
and were barred from the lucrative acquisition of administrative positions (*charges vénales*).[6]

Class divisions within the dominant group add another dimension
to the historical problem, as members of the upper class used the out-
group to fend off, or more effectively exploit, the weaker members of
their own group. The classical case is that of the Romanian landowners
in the late nineteenth and early twentieth centuries who either leased
their estates to Jews or hired them as managers. An important demand
of the peasants in the Great Peasant Revolt of 1907 was the expulsion of
Jewish *arendaşi* (professional estate managers) from Moldavian estates.
Some of them were killed and most were forced to flee, at least temporarily. The landlords succeeded, at least in some areas, in deflecting the
anger of the peasants from themselves to the Jewish and Greek
*arendaşi*.[7]

---

[5] Even in the seventeenth century Dutch Republic, where Jews enjoyed a degree of
toleration that was greater than in other European countries, they were still excluded
from guild-dominated crafts. In midsixteenth century Prague, the restrictions on craft
occupations were even more severe. It is interesting that after the Emperor Rudolph II
permitted the Jews to engage in occupations from which they had formerly been excluded the Jewish population of the city witnessed an "astonishing growth." For this and
other details on guild restrictions applying to Jews, see Israel (1981, pp. 40, 68–69, 154).

[6] For an illuminating discussion of the legal and paralegal restrictions to which French
Protestants were subject under Louis XIV, even before the minimal tolerance of the Edit
de Nantes was done away with as a result of the rescission of the edict in 1685, see Lüthy
(1959, pp. 65–67).

[7] Eidelberg (1974, pp. 118, 224). The efficiency (and/or the lack of compassion) of Jewish
arendaşi was particularly resented by their native equivalents. Some of these Romanian
arendaşi claimed that they were "condemned to extinction" as a result of the "invasion
of Jews and Greeks" (p. 120). According to Eidelberg, landlords favored Jewish over
native arendaşi because the former were better at extracting short-run profits from the
estates than the latter were (p. 39). Jewish arendaşi were thought to be "particularly hard
taskmasters" (p. 202).

REFERENCES

Bonacich, E. (1973). "A Theory of Middlemen Minorities," *American Sociological Review* 38(5): 583–94.

Eidelberg, P. G. (1974). *The Great Romanian Peasant Revolt of 1907: Origins of a Modern Jacquerie.* Leiden: E. J. Brill.

Gerber, H. (1981). "Jews and Money-Lending in the Ottoman Empire," *Jewish Quarterly Review* 72: 100–18.

Israel, J. (1989). *European Jewry in the Age of Mercantilism, 1550–1670.* Oxford: Clarendon Press.

Lüthy, H. (1959). *La Banque Protestante en France de la Révocation de l'Edit de Nantes à la Révolution.* Paris: S.E.V. P.E.N.

Weber, M. (1963). *The Sociology of Religion.* Boston: Beacon Press.

# PART III
# SOCIAL NORMS AND CULTURE

CHAPTER 10

# Social norms as positional arms control agreements

*Robert H. Frank*

The term "positional arms race" refers to an escalating pattern of mutually offsetting investments undertaken by rivals whose rewards depend on relative performance. Such arms races are abundant in social and economic interaction – advertising wars, anabolic steroid consumption, cram courses for the SATs, social and professional wardrobe expenditures, even cosmetic surgery.

A variety of formal mechanisms – such as random drug testing of athletes and chronological age mandates for kindergarten students – have been used to control positional arms races. In this chapter, I explore how less formal mechanisms such as social norms have served a similar function. Examples include social ostracism of "nerds" by students, norms favoring modest standards of consumption, and implicit agreements among news organizations not to dwell on sensational or lurid news stories.

I begin with a brief description of the payoff structure that gives rise to positional arms races and then discuss why this structure often leads to inefficient outcomes. Next, I investigate the circumstances under which social norms will be sufficient to curb positional arms races. I then describe a series of examples in which social norms may be plausibly seen as achieving this purpose. Finally, I discuss economic forces that have caused many such norms to break down in recent years and suggest an alternative mechanism whereby the aims of these norms might be achieved.

## 1    Positional arms races

Economic and social life is replete with situations in which people's rewards depend not only on their absolute performance, but also on how

Portions of this essay draw on material from Frank (1985) and Frank and Cook (1995).

well they perform relative to immediate rivals. Thus, the times posted by the swimmer Mark Spitz earned him seven gold medals in the 1976 Olympic Games, but would not even have qualified him for the U.S. team in 1992.

In general, the outcome of any contest depends not only on the talent and other given characteristics of the contestants, but also on how much effort they expend and on how much they invest in performance enhancement. The former tennis great John McEnroe once complained that he had more talent in his little finger than his archrival Ivan Lendl had in his whole body. Maybe so, but Lendl's strict training regimen and long hours on the practice courts nonetheless enabled him to displace McEnroe from the top of the tennis rankings.

Few people responded sympathetically to McEnroe's graceless complaint, and even many of his most ardent fans could not help admiring Lendl's dedication. Why, then, is investment in performance enhancement something that people might wish to inhibit by social norms and other means?

In some cases – the consumption of anabolic steroids by athletes, for example – the answer appears obvious: namely, that the investment is costly and adds nothing of genuine value. On the cost side, athletes not only incur the monetary outlays needed for purchasing the drug, they also face potentially severe health consequences. In the short term, these include hair loss, skin disorders, heightened aggressiveness, and even severe psychosis. In the long term, there is at least fragmentary evidence linking steroid consumption to a variety of circulatory disorders, testicular atrophy, and higher risks of some cancers.[1]

Individual athletes are willing to endure these costs because the drugs enhance performance. According to one estimate, for example, steroid use provides a half-second advantage for a one hundred meter sprinter, more than eight times the winning margin in the 1992 Olympic Games.[2]

And yet there is no evidence whatever that steroid use enhances the value of athletic competition from a spectator's perspective. National Football League fans, for example, have little reason to prefer that opposing linemen average 300 pounds rather than 250. Of course, the advantage of larger players to any individual team can be decisive. Thus, the starting offensive linemen on the 1996 SuperBowl Champion Dallas Cowboys averaged 333 pounds, some 30 pounds more than their counterparts on the Pittsburgh Steelers. And so, in the absence of effective drug testing, widespread ingestion of steroids, with all their attendant

---

[1] Windsor and Dumitru (1988).    [2] Janofsky (1992, p. 1).

Table 1. *The relationship between the winner's reward and investment in performance enhancement*

| Winner's investment in performance enhancement ($) | Value of the winner's prize ($) |
|---|---|
| 0 | 24 |
| 1 | 28 |
| 2 | 31 |
| 3 | 32 |
| 4 | 32.02 |
| 5 | 32.03 |

health risks, is inevitable. All parties – fans and athletes alike – would benefit if effective testing methods made it possible to eliminate steroid use entirely.

In other cases, investments in performance enhancement translate into a more valuable final product. The sopranos who compete for the handful of recording contracts issued each year spend thousands of dollars on voice coaches and other forms of music instruction. These efforts translate into greater clarity, dynamic range, and other perform-ance characteristics that yield additional listener satisfaction.

In cases like these, society has an interest in performance enhance-ment, but only up to a point. The criterion for social efficiency in such cases is to invest as long as the next dollar spent raises the value of the winner's performance by at least one dollar. As the following examples will suggest, however, the incentives facing contestants tend to push investment far past the efficient level.

To illustrate the basic forces involved, I consider examples in which two identical contestants are vying for a prize whose value rises at a diminishing rate with the winner's investment in performance enhance-ment, as shown in Table 1.

What is the socially optimal investment level given the relationship in Table 1? The criterion stated earlier suggests that the first dollar spent on performance enhancement is clearly worthwhile, because it raises the winner's reward by $4, from $24 to $28. The second dollar spent is less effective, raising the winner's reward from $28 to $31, a gain of only $3. But this is still a net gain of $2 and hence worth doing. Raising the investment another dollar to $3 produces only an extra dollar of reward

– from \$31 to \$32 – and so, from a social perspective, it is worth doing, but only just. Note, finally, that the fourth dollar of investment raises the prize by only 2 cents, which would mean a net social loss of 98 cents. In this simple example, then, the socially optimal level of investment in performance enhancement is \$3.

One immediate source of waste in examples of this sort is that if there were multiple contestants each investing \$3, all but one of their investments would be superfluous. In this example with two contestants, there would thus be \$3 of waste even if each contestant limited her investment to the socially optimal level. Waste of just this kind has been attributed to patent races, and several commentators have suggested that a more efficient result could be obtained if the government were simply to assign each development project to a separate laboratory.[3]

There are obvious problems with this proposal, however, not least among which is that the government is hardly in a position to know which laboratories are the most likely sources of yet uninvented technologies. So it may be that some duplication of effort is an unavoidable cost in many cases.

But even if we accept this cost, there is still another source of inefficiency when reward depends on rank. To begin with the most extreme case, suppose that whichever contestant invests the most in performance enhancement is certain to win the prize. (In the event of a tie, let the winner be chosen by the flip of a coin.) Suppose further that each of our two identical contestants has currently invested \$3 in performance enhancement. Given the procedure for resolving ties, each thus has a 50 percent chance of winning, and thus an expected reward equal to 50 percent of \$32, or \$16.

Suppose each contestant then asks herself, "Does it pay to invest an extra dollar?" If she does so and her rival does not, she will win \$32.02 with certainty. By contrast, if she does not invest and her rival does, she will have absolutely nothing to show for her \$3 investment. So the incentives strongly favor each contestant's investing another dollar. With both contestants now investing \$4, each must decide whether to invest yet another dollar. Each knows that the extra dollar will increase the value of the winner's prize by only a penny. But again, each knows that if she invests and her rival does not, she will win the entire prize, \$32.03, with certainty; and that if her rival invests while she does not, her own \$4 investment will have gone for naught. If both invest, each will have a 50 percent chance to win \$32.03, or an expected reward of \$16.015.

---

[3] See, for example, Loury (1979).

No matter what she expects her rival to do, if she could be sure the escalation would stop with the next round, it would be better for her to invest. Of course she cannot be sure that further escalation will not ensue, for at that point the incentives to invest further will be as compellingly attractive as before.

The term "entrapment model" has been used to describe the case in which the top investor wins the prize with probability one. Laboratory experiments suggest that investments in performance enhancement reach astonishingly high levels under this incentive structure – as much as ten times the value of the prize itself when the prize is worth $20.[4]

The entrapment model is an extreme case. More generally, we would not expect the highest investor to be sure of winning. A popular alternative model in the literature on rent seeking is the "lottery" model,[5] which assumes that a contestant's probability of winning is equal to his share of total investment in performance enhancement. For present purposes, the critical difference between the lottery model and the entrapment model is that the incentives to escalate investment are weaker under the lottery model.

In the entrapment model, recall, if the two candidates had equal investments to begin with, either could tip the outcome decisively in her favor by making only a small additional investment. In the lottery model, by contrast, a slight increase in investment means only a slight increase in the odds of winning. Suppose, for example, that each candidate has $4 of investment initially, so that each initially has a 50 percent chance of winning in either model. In the entrapment model, if one candidate ups her investment to $5, her probability of winning soars to 100 percent. In the lottery model, by contrast, if one candidate invests an extra dollar, total investment will be $9; that means that her share of that total will be 5/9, or just less than 56 percent. Investing the extra dollar thus increases her odds by less than 12 percent in the lottery model.

Although the incentives for escalating investment are much weaker in the lottery model than in the entrapment model, we see excessive investment in performance enhancement even in the lottery model. Returning to the example described in Table 1, suppose each of our two contestants is currently spending $3 on performance enhancement. This means that each has a 50 percent chance of winning $32, or an expected payoff of

---

[4] Max Bazerman, personal communication.

[5] So called because of its likeness to the way in which the odds in state lotteries are determined. In a lottery, someone who buys 10 percent of all tickets sold has a 10 percent chance of winning. Likewise, in the example with two identical contestants, the lottery scheme means that someone who invests three times as much as his rival has a 75 percent chance of being the winner.

$16. If one of them invests an extra dollar while the other remains at $3, the higher investor's share of total investment will be 4/7, or just over 57 percent. She will thus have a 57 percent chance of winning $32.02, which computes to an expected payoff of $18.30. And since this is more than one dollar better than her previous expected payoff, it pays to invest the extra dollar.

What about the other contestant? If she stays at $3 while her rival moves to $4, her odds of winning will fall to 3/7. This yields an expected payoff of only $13.72. If she too moves to $4, however, her odds of winning will again be 50 percent: an expected payoff of just over $16. And since that is more than a dollar higher than she expects from standing pat, it also pays her to invest the extra dollar.

The lottery model of investment has been well studied in the literature on rent seeking and patent races.[6] When there are two identically situated contestants independently investing in pursuit of a fixed reward, each will invest one-fourth of that reward on performance enhancement. Together, they will thus squander one-half the total reward on mutually offsetting investments in performance enhancement. If there are not two contestants but $N$, each investing independently under the incentives of the lottery model, the total amount spent on performance enhancement will be $(N - 1)/N$. Thus, as the number of contestants grows, the level of total investment quickly approaches the value of the reward being sought. So even under the much weaker incentives posed by the lottery model, mutually offsetting investments in performance enhancement remain substantial.

Common sense, empirical observation, and theoretical analyses of investment incentives thus yield a common message: In contests in which investments in performance enhancement affect individual contestants' odds of winning, there will invariably be mutually offsetting, socially inefficient patterns of investment in performance enhancement.[7] Such investments bear an obvious resemblance to the purchase of armaments in the classic military arms race, and hence the term "positional arms race."

---

[6] See, for example, Congleton (1980); Frank and Cook (1993).

[7] An important potential exception to this claim involves cases in which the prize being sought substantially understates the social value of the winner's performance. In such cases, investment in performance enhancement may be insufficient despite the reward-by-rank payoff structure. In other cases, insufficient effort may be the expected result if it is too costly for employers to prevent shirking through direct monitoring of worker behavior. In these cases, employers and employees may gain through the artificial creation of a positional arms race – as in compensation schemes based in part on relative performance.

And hence, too, the attraction of collective agreements to limit these arms races. Given the obvious incentives for contestants to violate these agreements, they are destined to fail unless there is considerable power to enforce them. Appreciating this difficulty, professional sports franchises cede much of their autonomy to league officials, who impose team roster limits, revenue-sharing schemes, and other measures that constrain investment in performance enhancement. In the business world, contracting parties often sign binding agreements that commit them to arbitration in the event of disputes. By so doing, they sacrifice the option of pursuing their interests as fully as they might later wish to, but in return they insulate themselves from costly legal battles. And with a similar goal in mind, a federal judge in South Dakota recently announced – presumably to the approval of litigants – that he would read only the first fifteen pages of any brief submitted before his court.

## 2 An example: social norms that limit conspicuous consumption

Many small towns have informal norms against conspicuous consumption. The power of these norms became vividly apparent to me several years ago when they led me to pass up what would otherwise have been an irresistible consumption opportunity. A relative in California had bought a new Porsche 911 Cabriolet during a visit to France. Because the franc was then trading cheaply against dollar, he paid only twenty-six thousand dollars for essentially the same car that would have cost him seventy thousand dollars had he purchased it in the United States.

Actually, there was one important difference between the car he bought in Europe and the one he would have bought here. When he returned to California he discovered that he could not register his car there because it had been produced for the European market. California dealers had successfully lobbied for a law that made such cars illegal even if retrofitted to satisfy all California pollution regulations. As a stopgap measure, he registered it in Oregon, but in time this led to difficulty with his insurance company.

In the end, he decided to sell the car. Being a family member, I had a chance to buy it for something like fifteen thousand dollars (by that time it was three years old). And since my home state of New York does not prohibit retrofitting European car models, I could have owned and operated it in full compliance with the law.

I was sorely tempted. But as a resident of Ithaca, a small upstate town with strong norms against conspicuous consumption, I simply did not find it tenable to buy this car. I realized that unless I could put a sign on it that explained how I happened to acquire it, I would never feel comfortable driving it. I still wonder whether I made the right decision. But what is not in question is that there would have been a social price to pay if I had bought it.[8]

Why do people want to discourage conspicuous consumption? And, given that they do, what forces enable them to succeed? The first question turns out to be easier than the second, so I consider it first. The short answer is that norms against conspicuous consumption are attractive because they help to prevent the costs of mine-is-bigger consumption arms races.

All available evidence tells us that satisfaction depends at least as much on relative consumption as on absolute consumption levels.[9] The result is that consumers confront a positional arms race when they decide how to allocate their time between leisure and work. From the individual's perspective, giving up leisuretime to work longer hours gives rise to two benefits: an increase in absolute consumption and an increase in relative consumption. From a collective perspective, however, the second of these benefits is spurious, for when everyone works longer hours, relative consumption levels remain unchanged. And hence the utility of collective agreements to weaken incentives to work longer hours.

In the legal arena, one strategy is to penalize firms whose employees work more than a specified number of hours, as the Fair Labor Standards Act does through its overtime provisions. Less formally, the community can attempt to discourage consumption by the adoption of social norms against excessive consumption. Such norms, if enforceable, would enable people to spend more time with their families, to save more, and in other ways to achieve more balance in their lives.

### 3    The enforcement problem

How are social norms enforced? In particular, what sanctions can be brought to bear against those who violate them? And if these sanctions are costly to impose, what prevents potential enforcers from free riding? As James Coleman has observed, the mere fact that a norm might be nice to have is by no means sufficient to bring about its existence.[10] The

---

[8] Of course, the particular consumption norms that a community adopts will depend not only on its size, but also on other factors like its income level and the degree of interpersonal contact between its members. An Ithaca-size community in Marin County, California, for example, would thus be unlikely to impose comparable social sanctions on its members who drive expensive automobiles.

[9] For an extensive summary of this evidence, see Frank (1985, chap. 2).

[10] Coleman (1990, chap. 10).

demand for norms arises from externalities and other collective action problems, yet there are many externalities for which there are no corresponding norms.

In Coleman's view, the free-rider problem can be overcome through "connectedness," his term for closely linked networks of personal relationships. Thus, if A benefits from B's efforts to enforce a social norm, it may be possible for A to reward B with a favor in some other context. But even in small, close-knit communities, the reciprocal exchange of favors appears hardly sufficient to assure the enforcement of a social norm against conspicuous consumption.

In the exchange theory view, people associate with one another because – and only because – of the exchange benefits they expect to reap in the process. Someone who abstains from associating with the violator of a social norm thus punishes not only the violator but also himself. Suppose this cost deters a potential enforcer from taking action. Failure to enforce is itself an offense, but one that is both less serious and more difficult to observe than the original violation. Yet the costs required to punish this secondary offense will be on a par with those required to sanction the original violator. If that cost deterred potential enforcers in the first instance, it will perforce deter them from taking action against delinquent enforcers. And once it becomes known that delinquent enforcers face no discipline, the prospects for action against the original norm violators become even more tenuous.

On the adherence side of the norm market, there are similar contradictions, for we know that people often follow norms even when external sanctions are not a credible threat. For example, the norm to tip in restaurants is almost impossible to enforce by external sanctions in the case of people who eat at restaurants along interstate highways, yet the observed tipping rates in such restaurants are little different from those in restaurants patronized mostly by local diners.

An alternative approach is to suppose that both adherence to and enforcement of social norms are motivated not only by the material rewards and penalties inherent in exchange relationships but also by internal, nonmaterial rewards. Thus, people may incur costs to enforce social norms simply because it gives them satisfaction to take action against violators; similarly, people may follow social norms simply because they feel uncomfortable, even in the absence of material sanctions, when they violate them.

At first blush, this approach seems to abandon the discipline of the purposive rational actor model, a step that many rational choice theorists are understandably reluctant to take. Thus, as James Coleman wrote: "To examine the process whereby norms are internalized is to enter waters that are treacherous for a theory grounded on rational choice. Asking the question of how individuals come to have the interests they exhibit is ordinarily not possible in constructing such a theory."[11]

Yet this is a step that behavioral scientists ultimately cannot avoid.[12] Elsewhere I have argued that it is fruitful to view preferences, or internal motivational states, not just as ends in themselves, but as means for achieving important material objectives.[13] Concern about relative wealth, for example, proves helpful in interpersonal bargaining contexts.

The logic behind this claim is illustrated by the elegant experiment known as the "ultimatum bargaining game."[14] The game is played by two players, Proposer and Responder. It begins with Proposer's being given a sum of money (say, $100) that he must then propose how to divide between himself and Responder. Responder then has two options: (1) he can accept, in which case each party gets the amount proposed; or (2) he can refuse, in which each party gets zero and the $100 goes back to the experimenter.

If Proposer believes that Responder cares only about absolute wealth, his own wealth-maximizing strategy is clear: He should propose $99 for himself and $1 for Responder (only integer dollar amounts are allowed). If Proposer's assumption about Responder is correct, Responder will accept this one-sided offer because he will reason that getting $1 is better than getting nothing.

But suppose Proposer believes that Responder cares not only about absolute but also relative wealth levels. Responder might then refuse the one-sided offer, even though he stands to gain from it in absolute terms, because he finds the relative terms so distasteful. The irony is that the effect of Proposer's believing that Responder cares about relative wealth is substantially to boost the amount that Proposer offers Responder. By virtue of his concern about relative wealth, Responder becomes a much more effective bargainer.

But this benefit has a cost. In the context of the ultimatum game, for example, if Proposer miscalculates and does make a one-sided proposal, Responder will incur the cost of refusing it. Likewise, someone who cares about relative position may willingly incur the cost of sanctioning the violator of a consumption norm, whereas someone who cares only about absolute wealth will not incur this cost. But the latter person will also be a much less effective bargainer in other contexts.

As a descriptive matter, it is clear that most people have at least a limited willingness to incur costs both to enforce and to adhere to social

[11] Coleman (1990, chap. 11).    [12] See Frank (1992).
[13] Frank (1988).    [14] See Guth, Schmittberger, and Schwarze (1982).

norms. And so there are neither compelling theoretical nor empirical grounds for insisting that implementation of social norms be rooted only in mutually beneficial exchange relationships.

Of course, considerations of exchange need not be excluded from the implementation of social norms. Indeed, the same internal motivations that lead a person to incur the costs of sanctioning the violator of a social norm are likely also to help cement alliances with others who incur these costs. In practice, then, internal motivations and exchange relationships will often act in mutually reinforcing ways. This observation may help explain why a norm against conspicuous consumption has considerably more force in small communities than in large urban areas.

The importance of internal motivations is attested to by the resources devoted to efforts aimed at molding these motivations. Thus, a portion of the curriculum in public schools is devoted to inculcating the duties of citizenship. A major purpose of organized religion is to help foster the development of feelings that promote prosocial behavior and inhibit antisocial behavior. Similar themes receive consistent emphasis in political campaign rhetoric. And as Edward Banfield has observed, the societies that succeed in these efforts appear far more likely than others to succeed in the economic domain as well.[15]

## 4    Further examples

The Academy Award–winning film *Chariots of Fire* portrays British collegiate track and field competitors who have developed an implicit norm that limits their training and practice time. Their apparent understanding is that since the most talented runner will win whether all train arduously or none does, the sensible thing is for no one to train very hard. This arrangement is challenged by an outsider with a rigorous training regimen. In response, the incumbents bring considerable social pressure to bear upon the maverick. In the face of such pressure, most normal challengers might have succumbed. But this particular runner is tough, and he goes on to win in the end.

This is not to say that the social norm he helped to destroy in the process was a desirable one. Deciding races on the basis of talent alone may be efficient, but it is not necessarily fair. The underlying distribution of running talent, after all, is essentially a matter of luck. Even so, many of us who believe that effort should also matter are troubled by the types of efforts that emerge when competition is completely unregulated.

---

[15]  Banfield (1958).

### 4.1    *Norms against exceeding piece-rate quotas*

Social norms for curtailing effort are also common on the shop floor. In many manufacturing and sales jobs, it is possible to measure with reasonable precision what each worker produces. According to traditional economic theory, such conditions strongly favor the use of piece-rate pay schemes, which reward workers in direct proportion to the amounts they produce. One of the enduring puzzles in labor economics is the relative scarcity of these pay schemes. Even in sales, perhaps the easiest activity in which to monitor productivity, a National Industrial Conference Board study found that more than half of all compensation plans imposed caps on total sales commissions.[16] Similar pay ceilings are described in a large literature that examines the widespread practice whereby workers on piece rates establish their own informal production quotas and impose strong sanctions against those who violate them.[17] Cases have even been reported in which firms themselves impose limits on production.

Worker-imposed production quotas have been described as devices whereby employees fool managers about the difficulty of their production tasks, in the fear that if they earn too much under existing piece rates, management will simply lower the rates.[18] In support of this interpretation, the sociologist Donald Roy describes the following conversation in which Starkey, an experienced worker, counsels Tennessee, a new man on the job, about the need to work slowly in the presence of the time-study man:

> "Another thing," said Starkey, "you were running that job too damn fast before they timed you on it! I was watching you yesterday. . . ."
>
> "I don't see how I could have run it any slower," said Tennessee. "I stood there like I was practically paralyzed!"
>
> "Remember those bastards are paid to screw you," said Starkey. "And that's all they think about. They'll stay up half the night figuring out how to beat you out of a dime. They figure you're going to try to fool them, so they make allowances for that. They set the prices low enough to allow for what you do."
>
> "Well, then, what the hell chance have I got?" asked Tennessee.
>
> "It's up to you to figure out how to fool them more than they allow for," said Starkey.
>
> "The trouble with me is I get nervous with that guy standing in back of me, and I can't think," said Tennessee.
>
> "You just haven't had enough experience yet," said Starkey. "Wait

---

[16] NICB (1970, p. 79).    [17] For a survey of this literature, see Frank (1985, chap. 5).
[18] See, for example, W. F. Whyte (1955, p. 201).

until you have been here a couple of years and you'll do your best thinking when those guys are standing behind you."[19]

It would be foolish not to suppose that workers slow down when the time-study man visits the factory to establish quotas for piece rates. Yet to suppose that managers have no way to discover that a quota has been set too low is to credit them with none of the ingenuity demonstrated by workers in their skirmishes with the time-study man. In fact, management has ample means for discovering how much time production tasks require. Thus, one author describes an electrical assembly plant strike during which supervisors were easily able to double existing production quotas.[20]

There are other cases in which management clearly knows that workers could easily exceed their production quotas. In one factory, for example, workers routinely met their quotas by midafternoon and spent the remainder of their workday playing cards in the restrooms, prompting several wives to complain to management about their husbands' gambling losses.[21]

So if these quotas substantially understate what workers are capable of producing, and management knows it, why doesn't management elicit higher production by simply reducing current piece rates? Management's implicit tolerance of production quotas makes much more sense if we interpret such agreements as social norms whereby workers attempt to curb positional arms races with one another. The difficulty is that if each worker's chances of promotion depend in part on relative productivity, the conditions are ripe for a mutually offsetting effort pattern. Each worker attempts to produce more in the hope of gaining ground relative to the others, yet when all workers double their efforts, relative promotion prospects remain largely the same. From a collective vantage point, the extra output summoned by unregulated piece rates is not sufficient to compensate for the extra effort required to produce it. When promotion prospects depend on relative effort, social enforcement of informal production quotas may bring private incentives more in line with collective interests.

## 4.2    Nerd norms

We also see social norms against excess effort in the world of education. Consider, for example, the positional arms race that arises when students are graded on the curve. From students' perspective, grading on the curve makes extra effort more attractive to each individual student than

---

[19] Roy, quoted in Whyte (1955, p. 15).    [20] Mangum (1964, p. 48).    [21] Ibid.

it is to students as a whole, for if all students increase their efforts in an attempt to improve their grades, the aggregate grade distribution will remain much the same as before.

Whether a positional arms race is inefficient depends, of course, on the perspective from which it is viewed. Students think grading on the curve leads to excessive effort. Parents and teachers, by contrast, are more likely to view the competitive struggle for higher grades as benign. Recalling their own youth, many are inclined to believe that students would tend to spend far too little time on their studies in the absence of competitive pressures. In their view, a positional arms race is just what the doctor ordered.

It is not surprising, then, that different social norms about academic effort have evolved among students, on the one hand, and concerned adults, on the other. Students are quick to brand as "nerds" or social misfits those among them who "study too hard," or in other ways attempt to curry favor with teachers. Parents and teachers, for their part, try to counter this norm with norms of their own that extol the virtues of academic achievement.

### 4.3    *Sabbath norms*

Judaism, Christianity, and other religions of the world embrace Sabbath norms, which enjoin practitioners to set aside a day each week for rest and worship. Such norms may be viewed as early precursors of blue laws, which mobilized the state's enforcement powers toward similar ends. Each may plausibly be seen as a device for limiting the extent to which people can trade leisuretime for additional income. To the extent that utility depends strongly on relative income, Sabbath norms and blue laws thus help bring individual and collective incentives into closer alignment.

### 4.4    *Norms governing dueling*

In centuries past, a European gentleman's response to a profound insult was to challenge the offending party to a duel. Accompanied by their seconds, the antagonists would typically assemble at dawn for their contest, which was governed by several formal rules. On examination, each of these rules is most plausibly interpreted as a positional arms control agreement.

One rule, for example, specified the physical distance between the antagonists at the actual moment of the duel itself. It called for them to stand back to back, then march off a given number of paces before each turned to fire. The transparent purpose of this rule was to reduce the odds of being killed. Establishing physical separation between the duelists made it more likely that their shots would miss than if they simply turned and fired at point-blank range.

A second rule governed the characteristics of the guns employed. Among other things, it specified that the barrels of the guns must be smooth, as opposed to having spiral grooves, and it called for weapons that fired only a single shot. The purpose of requiring smooth gun barrels was to make the trajectories of the bullets less true. Rifling – the engraving of spiral grooves on the inner surface of a gun barrel – imparts a spin to the bullet as it leaves the weapon. This causes the bullet to follow a much straighter trajectory than it would if the barrel had been smooth, much as a football thrown with a tight spiral tends to be more accurate than one without. Projectiles that lack spin tend to wobble and flutter erratically, like the knuckleball in baseball. To appreciate the utility of the single-shot restriction, we need only contemplate the fate of duelists who faced off with hundred-shot assault rifles.

These restrictions served their intended purpose. Thus, one study of some two hundred British duels concluded that only one in six duelists was even hit by his opponent's bullet, and only one in fourteen was killed.[22] These figures probably overstate the true casualty rates, since "very many duels which left no business for the coroner must have gone unregistered."[23] Yet even these odds were a high price to pay for defending one's honor. And indeed, virtually all industrial societies have now made dueling illegal.

## 4.5    *Fashion norms*

Many social norms regarding dress and fashion may also be interpreted plausibly as positional arms control agreements. This claim springs from the well-documented finding in experimental psychology that perception and evaluation are strongly dependent on the observer's frame of reference.[24] Consider, for instance, the person who wishes to make a fashion statement that he or she is among the avant garde, someone on the cutting edge. In some American social circles during the 1950s, that could be accomplished by wearing earrings for pierced ears. But as more and more people adopted this practice, it ceased to communicate avant-garde status. At the same time, those who wanted to make a conservative fashion statement gradually became more free to wear pierced earrings.

---

[22] Wilkinson (1979, pp. 45, 46).    [23] Kiernan (1988, p. 144).

[24] See, for instance, Helson (1964).

For a period during the 1960s and 1970s, one could be on fashion's cutting edge by wearing two pierced earrings in one earlobe. But by the 1990s multiple ear piercings had lost much of their social significance, as the threshold of cutting-edge status had drifted to upwards of a dozen pierced earrings, or a smaller number of piercings of the nose, eyebrows, or other parts of the body. A similar escalation has taken place in the number, size, and placement of tattoos that define avant-garde status.

It is unlikely, however, that there has been any corresponding increase in the value of avant-garde fashion status to those who desire it. Being in the right-hand tail of the fashion distribution means pretty much the same now as it once did. So to the extent that there are costs associated with body piercings, tattoos, and other steps required to achieve avant-garde status, the current situation is wasteful compared to the earlier one, which required fewer steps. In this sense, the erosion of social norms against tattoos and body piercings has given rise to a social loss. Of course, the costs associated with this loss are small in most cases. Yet since each body piercing carries with it a small risk of infection, the costs will continue to rise as the number of piercings rises. And once these costs reach a certain threshold, support may again mobilize on behalf of social norms that discourage body mutilation.

Similar cycles occur with respect to behaviors considered to be in bad taste. In the 1950s, for example, prevailing norms prevented major national magazines from accepting ads that used nude photographs to draw readers' attention. Advertisers naturally have powerful incentives to chip away at these norms, for they must compete vigorously for the buyer's limited attention. And indeed, norms regarding good taste have evolved in a way similar to those regarding body mutilation.

Consider, for instance, the evolution of perfume ads. First came the nude silhouette, then increasingly well-lighted and detailed nude photographs, and more recently, photographs of what appear to be group sex acts. Each innovation achieved exactly the desired effect – drawing the reader's instant and rapt attention. Inevitably, however, competing advertisers have followed suit and the effect has been merely to shift our sense of what is considered attention-grabbing. Photographs that once would have shocked readers now often draw little more than a bored glance.

Whether this is a good thing or a bad thing naturally depends on one's view about public nudity. Many believe that the earlier, stricter norms were ill advised in the first place, the legacy of a more prudish and repressive era. And yet even those who take this view also are likely to believe that there are some kinds of photographic material that ought not to be used in advertisements in national magazines. Where this limit lies will obviously differ a great deal from person to person. And each person's threshold of discomfort will depend in part on the standards currently observed. But we should not be surprised that as advertisers continue to break new ground in their struggle to capture our attention, the point may come when social forces again mobilize in favor of stricter standards of "public decency." Such forces are yet another example of a positional arms control agreement.

## 4.6    *Norms against vanity*

A similar claim can be made on behalf of social norms that discourage cosmetic surgery. Cosmetic and reconstructive surgery has produced dramatic benefits for many people. It has enabled badly disfigured accident victims to recover a more normal appearance and so to continue with their lives. It has also eliminated the extreme self-consciousness felt by people born with strikingly unusual or unattractive features. Such surgery, however, is by no means confined to the conspicuously disfigured. "Normal" people are increasingly seeking surgical improvements in their appearance. There were some two million cosmetic "procedures" done in 1991, six times the number just a decade earlier.[25] Once carefully guarded secrets, these procedures are now offered as prizes in charity raffles in Southern California. And Southern California morticians now complain that the noncombustible silicon implants used in breast and buttocks augmentation have begun to clog their crematoria.

In individual cases, cosmetic surgery may be just as beneficial as reconstructive surgery is for accident victims. Buoyed by the confidence of having a straight nose or a wrinkle-free complexion, patients sometimes go on to achieve much more than they ever thought possible.

But the growing use of cosmetic surgery also has an unintended side effect – it has altered our standards for normal appearance. A nose that would once have seemed only slightly larger than average may now seem jarringly big; the same person who once would have looked like an average fifty-five-year-old may now look nearly seventy; and someone who once would have been described as having slightly thinning hair or an average amount of cellulite may now feel compelled to undergo hair transplantation or liposuction. Because such procedures shift our frame of reference, their payoffs to individuals are misleadingly large, and from a social perspective, reliance on them is therefore likely to be excessive.

[25] *The Economist*, January 11, 1992, p. 25.

It is difficult to imagine legal sanctions against cosmetic surgery as a remedy for this problem. But at least some communities embrace powerful social norms against cosmetic surgery, heaping scorn and ridicule on the consumers of face lifts and tummy tucks. In individual cases, these norms may seem cruel. And yet, without them, many more people might feel compelled to bear the risk and expense of cosmetic surgery.

## 5     The breakdown of social norms

For most of the history of print journalism, and for the first several decades of electronic journalism, there were strong social norms opposing the exploitation of lurid or sensational news stories. Thus, as recently as the early 1960s, journalists abided by a tacit agreement not to publicize a sitting American president's flagrant acts of marital infidelity. In the 1990s, needless to say, such topics are fair game, not only in the tabloid press but also in mainstream news outlets. Why this dramatic transformation?

One important change has been an increase in the economic incentives to violate implicit norms. Television executives, for example, now realize that a top-rated news program is an important ingredient for a successful schedule of prime time programming, whose advertising revenues now measure in the hundreds of millions of dollars. And newspaper editors, for their part, recognize the growing trend for the most popular local paper to capture the entire market.

Another important change in recent years has been the movement toward more open competition for audiences. In television, this has resulted from the proliferation of cable and the addition of a fourth major broadcast network. The print media, for their part, have faced growing competition from television, from magazines targeted at specialty audiences, and from the addition of one new national newspaper (*USA Today*) and the increased availability of two others (*The New York Times* and *The Wall Street Journal*).

Both the larger prizes and the more competitive environment have worked in tandem to fuel the growing trend toward sensationalism. In the past, a relatively small number of competitors interacted repeatedly with one another. With only three TV networks, a small number of movie studios, and a handful of major publishers, it was possible for the news and entertainment industries to implement implicit social norms about the kind of material that could be shown or written about. The fact that the prizes were relatively small, moreover, kept the temptation to violate these norms within reasonable limits.

Thus, each publisher knew it could make extra profits in the short run by publishing lurid books or reporting candidates' sexual indiscretions. But each also knew that the advantage would be short-lived because its defection would spell the breakdown of their implicit agreements. And in the smaller markets of yesteryear, the potential gains from breaking ranks were not all that large anyway. In today's competitive climate, such restraint has proved virtually impossible to sustain. There is simply too much at stake and too many peripheral actors with little to lose.

Many of the same forces that have undermined social norms in the news media have undermined norms in other arenas as well. For example, just as the top prizes have escalated in the news media, so too have the top prizes in the labor market overall. During the last two decades, for example, the top 1 percent of U.S. earners have captured more than 40 percent of all earnings growth.

Personal injury lawyers who used to file lawsuits seeking ten thousand dollar damage payments for clients with stiff necks now head up teams that compete for a share of multibillion dollar class action judgments. Can anyone doubt that the decorum of lawyers competing for such prizes is little constrained by social norms?

CEOs who earned thirty times as much as the average worker twenty years ago now earn almost two hundurd times as much. The top performers' salaries have also escalated sharply in sales, journalism, medicine, dentistry, design, and even academia. With such large rewards at stake, social norms are increasingly less able to restrain individual interest.

Changes in the reward structure in private markets have indirect as well as direct effects on the enforceability of social norms. By "direct effect," I mean that when the monetary payoff for violating a norm increases, a rational actor becomes more likely to violate it. But holding payoffs and other relevant factors constant, the willingness to obey a norm is also indirectly influenced by the overall frequency with which people comply with it. Because they entail potentially explosive positive feedback processes, the indirect effects often turn out to be far more important than the direct effects. Thus, when a change in payoffs leads marginal actors to violate a social norm, their defections lead others also to violate that norm, and these defections have ramifications of their own. In this manner, seemingly trivial changes in direct financial incentives may result in the complete breakdown of specific social norms.

## 6    Consumption taxes: an alternative or supplement to social norms

The positional arms races described occur because certain forms of consumption or behavior are more attractive individually than collectively. When social norms break down, or are simply insufficient in producing the desired realignment of incentives, we often undertake more formal interventions, such as taxation or prescriptive regulation. Experience with environmental pollution has taught us that taxation has two advantages over prescriptive regulation: First, unlike regulation, which often requires that bureaucrats have detailed knowledge of people's production and consumption alternatives, taxation requires no such knowledge; second, whereas regulation imposes the cost of curtailing harmful activities on all parties indiscriminately, taxation concentrates this cost in the hands of those parties who can curtail the activities in the least costly way. Taxing misleadingly attractive activities alters overall incentives in the desired direction, while preserving for individuals the latitude to take their own circumstances into account.

The standards that define acceptable schools, houses, wardrobes, complexions, cars, vacations, and a host of other important budget items are inextricably linked to the amounts other people spend on them. Because individual consumers do not take positional externalities into account in their choices, the result is that such commodities appear much more attractive to individuals than to society as a whole. For the same reasons it is often efficient to tax pollution, it will be efficient to tax many of these forms of consumption. On efficiency grounds, such taxes would be an attractive substitute for existing regulations and taxes that interfere with efficient resource allocation. And they would also help bolster the effects of increasingly tenuous social norms.

Proposals to tax positional consumption raise the specter of forbidding complexity – of citizens having to save receipts for each purchase, of politicians and producers bickering over which products are to be classified as positional consumption items, and so on. Yet a system of positional consumption taxation would entail no greater complexity than do the usual systems of income taxation. The need to keep expenditure receipts can be easily prevented by calculating overall consumption as the difference between current income and current savings. There is simply no need to sum the value of each item purchased. The need to debate which items are positional can be avoided by having a standard deduction – by making the first, say, twenty thousand dollars of annual consumption expenditures exempt from taxation. This feature would serve two purposes: (1) It would shield nonpositional consumption items – including necessities like food, basic clothing, shelter, and transportation – from taxation; and (2) it would make the tax system progressive. The positional consumption tax, like any other tax, invites debate in the political arena about special exemptions. But this tax is no more complex than the existing taxes employed in the United States and Europe.

REFERENCES

Banfield, Edward (1958). *The Moral Basis of a Backward Society.* Glencoe, IL: Free Press.

Coleman, James S. (1990). *Foundations of Social Theory.* Cambridge, Mass.: Harvard University Press.

Congleton, Roger (1980). "Competitive Process, Competitive Waste, and Institutions," in J. Buchanan, R. Tollison, and G. Tullock, eds., *Toward a Theory of the Rent-Seeking Society,* College Station, TX: Texas A&M Press.

*The Economist* (1992), January 11, p. 25.

Frank, Robert H. (1985). *Choosing the Right Pond.* New York: Oxford University Press.

———(1988). *Passions within Reason.* New York: W. W. Norton.

———(1992). "Melding Sociology and Economics: James Coleman's *Foundations of Social Theory,*" *Journal of Economic Literature* 30: 147–70.

Frank, Robert H., and Philip J. Cook (1993). "Winner-Take-All Markets," Unpublished manuscript. Cornell University.

Frank, Robert H., and Philip J. Cook (1995). *The Winner-Take-All Society.* New York: Martin Kessler Books at The Free Press.

Guth, Werner, Rolf Schmittberger, and Bernd Schwarze (1982). "An Experimental Analysis of Ultimatum Bargaining," *Journal of Economic Behavior and Organization* 3: 367–88.

Helson, Harry (1964). *Adaptation Level Theory.* New York: Harper & Row.

Janofsky, Michael (1992). "Devers and Christie Get to Dazzle in the Dash," *New York Times,* August 2, sect. 8, p. 1.

Kiernan, V. G. (1988). *The Duel in European History: Honour and the Reign of Aristocracy.* New York: Oxford University Press, 1988.

Loury, Glenn C. (1979). "Market Structure and Innovation," *Quarterly Journal of Economics* 93: 395–410.

———(1995). *One by One from the Inside Out: Essays and Reviews on Race and Responsibility in America.* New York: Free Press.

Mangum, Garth L. (1964). *Wage Incentive Systems.* Berkeley: Institute of Industrial Relations, University of California.

National Industrial Conference Board (1970). "Incentive Plans for Salesmen," *Studies in Personnel Policy* 217: 75–86.

Schelling, Thomas (1978). *Micromotives and Macrobehavior.* New York: W. W. Norton.

Whyte, William F. (1955). *Money and Motivation.* New York: Harper & Brothers.

Wilkinson, F. (1979). The *Illustrated Book of Pistols.* London: Hamlyn.

Windsor, Robert, and Daniel Dumitru (1988). "Anabolic Steroid Use by Athletes: How Serious Are the Health Hazards?" *Postgraduate Medicine* 84: 37–49.

CHAPTER 11

# Bribes and gifts

*Susan Rose-Ackerman*

One person's bribe is another's gift. When disparaging a monetary quid pro quo, critics call it a bribe, whatever its legal status. Bribes are bad, and gifts are good. Being too mercenary is suspect, but living off the generosity of others is also disreputable. Into this set of rough and ready judgments comes the cheerfully philistine economist to argue that bribes are good and gifts are payments for expected benefits. Corrupt officials are efficient, and pure altruism does not exist.

But such reductionism ignores the moral force of labels. If a payment is viewed as an immoral bribe, many people will refuse to pay or accept one even if someone explains to them that the transaction is efficient and fair. Conversely, if a payment is described as a gift, people who try to be good and generous may be eager to contribute even if the consequences are pernicious.

Values are not, however, immutable. Society delimits the boundaries between unacceptable bribes and acceptable gifts and prices. It does this with legal strictures and social norms. The state can signal the seriousness of an infraction by the level of law enforcement and the size of the penalties. People are deterred from bribery, not just by the fear of being caught, but also by the state's clear signal that such behavior is unacceptable. Similarly, gifts can be encouraged through subsidy programs and tax breaks. People are encouraged to give not only because of the subsidy itself, but also because the subsidy signals that giving is a good thing to do.

Because of the state's ability to shape norms and influence behavior through law, it is important to determine the economic consequences of alternative types of payments. If, for example, many payments com-

I am grateful to the editors; to Avner Greif and Viviana Zelizer, the conference discussants; and to Peter Cramton and Burton Weisbrod for helpful comments.

monly labeled as bribes actually serve a useful economic purpose, then their legal and moral status should be reconsidered. If transfers viewed as praiseworthy gifts impose costs, the state should not encourage them.

This chapter explores the question of where the line between legal and illegal payments should be drawn. It sorts out the characteristics of payments and attempts a more sophisticated analysis of their normative properties. Section 1 begins with a simple taxonomy of gifts, bribes, tips, and prices that distinguishes between principals and agents and asks whether or not an explicit quid pro quo exists. Although gifts and bribes are at the opposite ends of my taxonomy and have very different normative properties, section 2 demonstrates their fundamental similarity. In general, neither payment creates a legally enforceable quid pro quo. Thus the literature on implicit contracts helps model both bribes and gifts. Trust and reputation play an important role. Other strategies, analogous to those in the implicit contracting literature – such as hostage taking and reciprocal obligations – have their uses in corrupt and donative deals. With this background section 3 considers how to put the market in its proper place and reward agents for high quality performance. If a society wants to use law and moral suasion to influence the public's view of acceptable and unacceptable payments, this section of the chapter provides some guidance.

As the discussion of implicit contracting makes clear, personal relationships between those who make payments and those who accept them can facilitate both legal and illegal transactions. If one is primarily concerned with the efficiency and fairness of the economic system, close, trusting bonds between people are not inevitably valuable. Tensions persist between ties based on family and friendship, on the one hand, and the operation of competitive markets and professional bureaucracies, on the other. These tensions are likely to be especially acute in developing countries.

Section 4 explores the difficulty of finding a balance between traditional norms favoring close personal ties and modern efforts to create impersonal markets and government institutions. A gift in one context becomes a bribe in another. If traditional values stress close interpersonal ties, market institutions and public bureaucracies may function very differently than they do in societies that distinguish among impersonal markets, technocratic bureaucracies, and links based on family and friendship. Economic development may require that a country's traditional values change to create distinctions among bribes, gifts, prices, and tips. But how can values be changed? Will the development of modern organizational forms change values, or, conversely, does a change in values produce the preconditions for organizational change? We do not know the answer to this question, but both virtuous and vicious cycles seem possible. The wrong starting point can produce a downward spiral in which poorly operating institutions undermine traditional values without putting functional substitutes in their place.

## 1    The simple economics of gifts, bribes, tips, and prices

Payments, whether in money or in kind, can be characterized along two dimensions. First, does an explicit quid pro quo exist? If so, the transaction can be labeled a sale even if there is a long time lag between payment and receipt of the benefit. Both market sales and bribes involve clear reciprocal obligations. Gifts to charities or loved ones often do not explicitly involve reciprocity – although many do generate implicit obligations.

My second focus is on the institutional positions of payers and payees. Are they agents or principals? A restaurant bill is paid to the owner; a tip, to the waiter. A speeding ticket is paid to the state; a bribe, to the policeman. Employers, sales agents, and customers can pay agents. Bosses give Christmas gifts to their employees, salesmen give gifts to purchasing agents, and customers tip sales people for good service.

Some people, however, have duties to the public, or to some other amorphous group that lacks well-specified, sharp-eyed principals. Politicians, for example, can be described as the representatives of the public interest or of the citizens who elected them. Under either view, they have considerable discretion. The desire for reelection is a constraint, but one that does not always prevent lucrative side deals. Since the quid pro quo is often vague, those who transfer money to politicians commonly say they are giving gifts. Others disagree.

Concentrating only on these two dimensions – the existence of a quid pro quo and the presence or absence of agents – produces four categories, labeled bribes, tips, gifts, and market prices in Table 1. The table recognizes that even when no explicit quid pro quo is involved, there may be an implicit expectation of reciprocal behavior. Although the categories include the morally loaded terms "bribes" and "gifts," the table identifies payments only in terms of the agency relation and the existence of a quid pro quo.

### 1.1    *Gifts and prices*

In Table 1, gifts are distinguished from prices by the lack of an explicit quid pro quo. But there may be more subtle links between gifts and

Table 1. *Payments by clients or customers*

|  | Quid pro quo | No explicit quid pro quo |
|---|---|---|
| Payment to principal | Price | Gift |
| Payment to agent | Bribe | Tip |

beneficiaries' behavior. A university may start a new professional school in the hope of attracting donations, and a child may work hard in the hope of attracting parental gifts. Nevertheless, many gifts are purely altruistic transfers with no expectation of a material reward. They may provide psychological benefits such as the "warm glow" of sympathy, or the satisfaction of living up to a moral commitment (Andreoni 1988; Rose-Ackerman 1996; Sen 1977) but no tangible gains. Some self-sacrificing gifts harm the giver, as when a person imposes sacrifices on family members or gives up his or her life for another person or for a cause.[1]

When individual gifts are large enough to have a marginal impact on the recipient's behavior, a quid pro quo is implicit. This will be true of many gifts to family members and some large donations to charities. In that case there is little functional difference between gifts given to further announced goals and those given under the condition that such goals be established. When conditional gifts create enforceable obligations, they are like sales except that the benefit given in return must be something that accords with the charity's purpose.[2] Such gifts belong in the "price" box.

In terms of standard economic analysis, as gifts move down the scale from gifts to charitable organizations and causes, to gifts to needy, but unknown individuals, to gifts to friends and relatives, to gifts to people and institutions in a position to benefit you, they come closer and closer to being prices or, depending upon the nature of the trade, bribes. But simple economics is only part of the story. Personal relations between giver and receiver or buyer and seller are an important dimension of

---

[1] See Monroe (1996), who interviewed people concerning their altruistic behavior and distinguishes among entrepreneurs, philanthropists, heroes, and rescuers. Those in the last category included rescuers of Jews in Nazi Europe whose personal and familial sacrifices were extreme.

[2] For gifts, some quid pro quos are legally enforceable, but others are not (Eisenberg 1979; Gordley 1995).

many transactions that have a value independent of their instrumental functions in regulating transactions.[3]

## 1.2     *Bribes and tips*

Now consider agency relationships. Agents are generally paid by their principals, not outsiders, such as customers or sales agents. The principal needs to develop a system of remuneration and monitoring that gives agents an incentive to perform well. A large literature in labor economics and game theory deals with the relative merits of remuneration schemes. The models assume that the principal cannot perfectly measure the agent's effort, but must use such imperfect measures as output produced or hours worked. The relative merits of a wide range of incentive contracts and pay schemes have been discussed – from hourly wages, to piece rates, to contingent fees, to bonuses and pensions contingent on a lifetime of good performance. When many agents report to a single principal, "tournaments" in which rewards are based on relative performance are frequently recommended. This is not the place to review this material, except to observe that most scholars assume that laziness and shirking are the problem to be remedied, rather than active inducements offered by a third party. Most work assumes a two-sided relationship between principal and agent where the agent's environment has certain externally generated random elements.[4]

Jean-Jacques Laffont and Jean Tirole bring in a third party. Their research focuses on the case of an owner, a foreman, and a worker (an "agent" in their terminology) in which the worker and the foreman can collude to fool the manager (Laffont 1990; Tirole 1986, 1992). As Laffont and Tirole realize, their work can be recast as a model of corruption with a little redefining of terms. The foreman is renamed the "agent" and the worker is renamed the customer or client who is the potential briber (Tirole 1986, 1992; see also Becker and Stigler 1974; Rose-Ackerman 1978). Bribes are then payments made to *agents* by people who are not their principals in return for a well-understood quid pro quo. For corruption to occur, the agent must have both discretion and monopoly power.[5]

Pervasive bribery may indicate that society has structured the agency

---

[3] In sociological analyses, personal connections are the key to gift giving. Donations to charitable organizations are not labeled gifts *because* they do not involve a personal connection (Zelizer 1994, 77–85).

[4] For citations to this work see Laffont (1990); Rasmusen (1990, chaps. 6–9, pp. 133–222); Rose-Ackerman (1986); Tirole (1986).

[5] See Rose-Ackerman (1978) and Klitgaard (1988).

relationship inefficiently. If customers commonly bribe agents, perhaps it would be more efficient to have the customers hire the agents to deal with their old principals. For example, suppose an automobile company provides free repair service to those who purchase its cars. In practice, customers eager for good service bribe repairmen to provide speedy high quality work. The fact that the customer is better at monitoring the repairman than the automobile company suggests that the service can be more efficiently provided by a contract between the customer and the repairman than by a contract between the repairman and the automobile company. In spite of this incentive for commercial bribery, the automobile company might continue to provide free repairs as part of the warranty provided ex ante to buyers. Warranties improve a firm's competitive position by reducing the risk faced by customers, but like all insurance policies, they create monitoring costs ex post (Cramton and Dees 1993, pp. 366–67).

Similar issues arise in many professional service industries in which customers buy the expertise of others. They can judge output – good health, a large damage award in a lawsuit – but cannot directly observe the quality of inputs. Is it more efficient to hire the professional directly or to pay a lump sum to a large organization (an insurance company, say) that then monitors and reimburses the professionals? Should the outright sale of lawsuits to attorneys be permitted, thus avoiding the agency–principal problem altogether?[6] Should the state subsidize legal services across the board?

To see the difficulties of the last possibility, suppose that the state provides free lawyers at fixed fees to anyone who brings a lawsuit. Suppose further that many clients make secret payments to their lawyers to induce greater work. If this type of commercial bribery is common, the implication is that the sale of legal services should be privatized with a residual subsidized program for the indigent. In contrast, evidence that the parties to a lawsuit are paying judges to get favorable rulings does not imply that one should legalize such payments. They undermine the very idea of an impartial judiciary issuing rulings not influenced by financial incentives.[7] Even private commercial arbitration services structure their payment systems to prevent links between substantive decisions and the arbitrators' financial rewards.

[6] For an argument in favor of the sale of tort suits see Choharis (1996).

[7] For example, consider Egypt under Muhammed Ali in the 1820s. According to Edward William Lane, an Englishman living in Egypt at that time, judges' decisions were influenced by the rank of the plaintiff and the defendant or a bribe from either. "On some occasions, particularly in long litigation, bribes are given by each party, and a decision is awarded in favour of him who pays the highest." Quoted by Johnson (1991, p. 686).

A franchise arrangement is an intermediate solution. The ultimate sellers are independent businesses whose behavior is constrained by a franchise contract. If the principal – in this case the franchiser – benefits when "sales people" – in this case the franchisees – take a personal interest in selling the product, such arrangements may make sense. Franchisees earn profits for providing good service, rather than taking bribes for the same thing. This option may not always be available to the government. The National Park Service can sign franchise arrangements with companies that provide food and lodging. A public authority that supplies housing units cannot do the same unless it writes a complex contract to assure that the goal of providing shelter to the needy is met.

The state's lack of organizational flexibility limits its ability to reorganize the agency relationship. A government uses agents where private businesses would simply sell their services directly. Conversely, the public sector uses contracts where private firms would vertically integrate because of monitoring difficulties. Sometimes deregulation and privatization can correct these difficulties, but some constraints are inherent in the special nature of government services. A state can privatize its cement plant, steel mill, or telephone system with net gains all around, but it needs bureaucrats to maintain an army, a police force, and a school system or to regulate environmental pollution, automobile drivers, and land use. Legitimate public functions cannot by their nature be organized like private markets. This fact implies that all incentives for corruption in public programs cannot be eliminated.

With tips, the quid pro quo is vague and service is usually delivered before the tip is paid. Tips are "legally optional, informally bestowed, the amount unspecified, variable, and arbitrary" (Zelizer 1994, p. 91). Tips permit customers to pass judgment on the quality of service in situations in which business owners may have difficulty evaluating quality. If customers are better monitors than managers, tips make sense. In contrast, if management can infer good service from high levels of individual sales, it can give out the rewards itself. A restaurant might, for example, reward its waiters on the basis of the number of meals served, much as tips do. But such a scheme would be less effective than tips. Basing rewards only on volume induces waiters to create bad feelings by rushing people out the door. Tying rewards to a mixture of volume and quality is better for profit-maximizing restaurants. Allowing customers to pay agents directly for good service is one way to do this. Such payments would not, however, be desirable for owners if they caused agents to discriminate between customers in a way that undercuts the revenues flowing to the principal. Imagine, for example, that waiters, like corrupt customs agents, gave diners discounts on their meals or served extra dishes in return for payoffs.

## 2 Gifts and bribes: extralegal enforcement

Although they appear as distinct categories in Table 1, gifts and bribes have one important similarity. In neither case can a disappointed individual go to court to demand payment or to insist on performance of the implicit contract. Alternative methods of assuring compliance must be designed if one wishes to induce others to act. In some cases, these extralegal mechanisms may be more effective and perhaps cheaper than those available to market traders. When these conditions hold, even people without altruistic feelings or a criminal mentality will have an incentive to use alternatives to legally enforceable contracts.[8]

Several familiar informal enforcement mechanisms seem most relevant: trust, reputation, hostage taking, and reciprocal obligations (Cramton and Dees 1993; Williamson 1975, 1979). In many ordinary contracting contexts, these mechanisms are highly desirable. But they can facilitate corrupt deals as well as altruistic transfers. There may be a conflict between traits that seem virtuous in and of themselves, like trustworthiness, and the undesirable consequences they produce. An examination of bribery and gift giving helps one to see that otherwise admirable norms of behavior can, under some conditions, prove costly for economic efficiency and development.

---

[8] Even gifts and bribes can sometimes give rise to legally enforceable obligations. In the case of gifts, both Anglo-American and Continental law make it quite easy to convert a gift into a legally binding transfer that also imposes obligations on the recipient (Eisenberg 1979; Gordley 1995; Posner 1977). If the donor wishes to assure that the payment will be viewed as a gift and not as a price, he or she will be limited in what can be demanded in return. The donor can require that a university build a sports complex and name it after him. He cannot receive a charitable tax deduction for a private residence that the university constructs for him to live in during his visits to campus.

Although no one can go to court to require payment from delinquent bribers, the quid pro quo demanded may be legally enforceable even if the corruption is discovered. For example, a corrupt land sale approved by the state of Georgia in the early 1800s was upheld by the United States Supreme Court. The court was unmoved by the fact that all but one of the legislators had been bribed (*Fletcher v. Peck*, 1810). When the scandal was revealed, the entire legislature lost office in the next election, but the court held that the contract was a legal obligation of the state of Georgia (Coulter 1933). Of course, if the bribery itself remains secret, courts treat contracts and concessions obtained through payoffs as ordinary commerical deals. In fact, the most favorable conditions for large-scale corruption are those in which a well-functioning, honest judiciary enforces public contracts, but the prosecution of white-collar crime is very lax.

## 2.1     *Trust*

In discussing the Sicilian Mafia, Diego Gambetta (1993) emphasizes the pervasive lack of trust in the Italian state. An increase in private property transactions occurred at a time when the state lacked the capacity to handle such transactions. The state failed to provide a reliable method of resolving disputes and managing private property transfers. The Mafia arose as a substitute. Other observers view the rise of "mafias" in Russia as due to a similar weakness of the state (Varese 1994).

Gambetta uses the word "trust" in two senses best kept separate. First, he points to the state's lack of competence and legitimacy. People do not trust the state to resolve disputes fairly and efficiently, so they look to alternatives. This meaning of trust has nothing to do with close personal ties. The relationship may be entirely at arm's length. In fact, one's trust in the state may be higher if officials are dispassionate and objective.[9] Second, people may trust each other because of close personal ties that depend on kinship, business links, or friendship. A person may trust his powerful friend to help him, not because the friend will apply the law fairly, but because he is known to favor his friends.[10] Gambetta emphasizes how the failure of trust in either sense produces a demand for private protective services such as the Mafia. I want to stress how the second type of trust, based on personal ties, facilitates both corrupt and donative transfers.[11] My analysis complements Gambetta's discussion of the internal organization of Mafia "families" who demand unswerving loyalty from members. My concern is not with organized crime per se, but with the way trusting, personalized relations facilitate deals in the absence of legal enforcement.

Gift giving and bribery will be more common when legal dispute resolution mechanisms are costly and time consuming. When legal guarantees are not possible, trust is correspondingly more important. But the lack of a legal backup means that some transactions are unlikely to be carried out. Deals in which the bribe must be paid before the bribee

---

[9] Empirical work has found that in the workplace trust can only be created by "procedural justice." Decisions must be fair and must be seen to be fair with opportunities for appeal (Kim and Mauborgne 1995).

[10] Consider the following Latin American quip: "A los amigos todo, a los enimigos nada, al extrano la ley" ("For my friends everything, for my enemies nothing, for strangers the law").

[11] Barney and Hansen (1994) call this "strong form trustworthiness" and discuss how it can give firms a competitive advantage (pp. 184–86). Hood (1996, pp. 211–14) discusses how "contrived randomness" in the form of staff rotation and division of authority can help break up systematic cooperation that produces corruption and other "anti-system 'networking' activity."

performs may be too risky. The corrupted official who fails to deliver can claim that the payment he received was just a gift from a friend or admirer. Similarly, the recipient of a gift with implicit strings can characterize it as a bribe if the relationship sours. Both sides to the deal have an interest in blurring the meaning of the payment in the eyes of the outside world while being quite explicit between themselves. Bribes will frequently be disguised as gifts to limit criminal liability.[12] But duplicity may make it difficult to insist that the official follow through.

Gifts that involve an unenforceable quid pro quo will be more likely if a trusting relationship between the parties already exists by reason of family ties or friendship. Thus gifts are often given to family members, not only because the giver feels special affection, but also because the *recipient* has emotional bonds with the donor and may be more willing to carry out his or her side of the obligation.

By the same token, trust is important in corrupt deals. Gambetta stresses how the lack of trust in government leads to the demand for private protective services. I emphasize how the ability to establish trust based on close personal relationships helps reduce the risks of disclosure. It provides a guarantee of performance when payment and quid pro quo are separated in time. A public official may favor his own relatives in allocating concessions and other public benefits in return for a share of the benefits. He may do this not only because he cares about *them*, but also because they care about *him* and will be less likely than strangers to reveal the corrupt deal or to try to renege on the agreement. The interdependency of utilities reduces the risks to both participants (Schmid and Robison 1995).

The risk, of course, is that disgruntled family members may be especially dangerous. The interdependency of utility can mean that a bitter relative gets special pleasure in exposing a corrupt kinsman.[13] The corrupt ruler may end up wishing he had dealt with cool headed, opportunistic business people unlikely to upset a lucrative arrangement.

---

[12] In Japan great care is taken to differentiate "gifted" monies by using only new bills and using special envelopes. As a result, "bribes are often disguised as gifts by placing clean bills in a money envelope or by using properly wrapped gift certificates sold by department stores" (Zelizer 1994, p. 117). In Japan, the merging of bribes and gifts apparently has a long history. Writing about the shogunate in the early part of the nineteenth century, Paul Johnson (1991, p. 805) indicates that every official had his hangers-on and that "all had to be bribed to get any action. Officials and courtiers constantly gave each other costly presents."

[13] In Brazil the corruption of President Fernando Collor de Mello was revealed by a disgruntled brother angry at Collor's attempt to create a newspaper to rival the one that he owned (Manzetti and Blake 1996).

## 2.2    *Reputation*

Just as in legal markets, reputations developed from repeat play can substitute both for the law and for trusting personal relationships.[14] A reputation for generously rewarding those who help you will induce others to do you favors (Barney and Hansen 1994, pp. 178–79). A reputation for maiming defaulters will help assure performance of corrupt deals. It will, however, also discourage people from contracting with you.

Reputation acts on both sides of the transaction for both gifts and bribes. The reputation of the person who responds second is important to the one who makes the first move. A campaign contributor is more likely to give to someone with a reputation for rewarding donors after his election. A child is more likely to behave obediently if his parents have a reputation for making generous gifts to their well-behaved children. Bribery can be more easily institutionalized if bribers can observe the past performance of corrupted officials and these officials have stable long-term employment prospects. Sometimes the reputation of the *first* mover is important. Extortionary demands for payment may be more readily accepted if the extortioner has a reputation for carrying out vengeful acts. For example, police can maximize bribes by credibly threatening to beat up nonpayers or to arrest honest people for crimes such as making illegal payoffs.

The illegality of bribes and the legality of gifts make reputations more difficult to establish in the former case than in the latter. Gift giving can be public knowledge unless the implicit favor looks too much like an illegal quid pro quo. Donors can announce their gifts in the hope of gaining a reputation for generosity. However, a reputation as an altruist has costs and benefits. One obtains praise and respect but also encourages a broader range of organizations to ask for aid. Charitable organizations may publish lists of donors as a way of persuading others to give as well. The ability to attract gifts from prominent people helps establish the respectability of the organization. In short, both donors and charities have a reputational interest in announcing gifts, and the two can feed off each other. A well-respected charity attracts gifts because it gives donors an aura of virtue, and past donors' reputation for virtue is then a fundraising tool to attract more gifts.

[14] Experimental work on the development of reputations among traders shows that they are more likely to arise when product quality is difficult for buyers to judge before purchase (Kollock 1994). In the experiments subjects did not meet face to face, and there was no outside source of appeal. Thus the conditions were in some ways similar to corrupt or donative exchanges that lack the element of personal trust.

Gifts or tips to service providers may have a different reputational dynamic. Suppose that the official price is uniform, but that agents can provide special favors or benefits to some customers. If they do this, others may experience declines in service. Then gifts from some customers may induce others to give as well. This seems to be the aim of parking garage attendants who publicly list gifts from monthly parkers (Tierney 1995). The spiral in gift giving will be especially powerful if there is a scarcity of desirable parking spots. Parkers are engaged in what game theorists call a "war of attrition."[15] They are induced to give not only to avoid appearing stingy, but also to assure good service. Parking lot owners may try to capture some of these gains by charging different prices for different quality spaces. The inevitable discretion exercised by the attendants, however, means that even if owners follow this strategy, they will not be able to extract all of the gains.

Some corrupt "markets" operate the same way but are less effective since bribes cannot usually be posted. This is an advantage of gifts over bribes. Campaign contributions frequently skirt the narrow line between gifts and bribes and fall on one side or the other, depending upon the vagaries of campaign finance laws.[16] Potential contributors may be more likely to donate if they are informed about the donations of others. The possibility of an escalating spiral of donations suggests that a politician may publish a list of her contributors even if the law does not require it.

The stricter the laws governing private contributions and defining bribery, the more difficult it will be to establish a reputation. Bribers and bribees can develop a word of mouth reputation for strong arm tactics, but they also want to be viewed as people who will make deals and not report corrupt offers. Since legal advertising and official certification are out, corrupt officials need to communicate by other means. The difficulty of establishing a reputation may lead crooks to deal only with known partners. Limiting the range of people who can pay bribes also reduces the risk of being exposed by newcomers. Establishing a corrupt relationship between strangers is risky since the first one who is explicit about wanting to make or accept a payoff is at the mercy of the others if they threaten to report the illegal act. Introductions by third parties are important, and in some cases the language of bargaining is veiled and ambiguous except to the initiates (Gambetta 1993).

---

[15] War of attrition games are analyzed in Bishop, Cannings, and Smith (1978); Krishna and Morgan (1994); and Rasmusen (1990, pp. 74–76). I am grateful to Peter Cramton for pointing out this connection.

[16] See Jane Fritsch, "A Bribe's Not a Bribe When It's a Donation," *New York Times*, News of the Week in Review, January 28, 1996, p. 1.

The bribery market may work very imperfectly compared to a legal market since the number and identity of buyers and sellers will be limited by the need for secrecy. It is difficult for a newcomer to establish a reputation. Furthermore, bribe prices may be sticky rules of thumb that do not respond well to changes in underlying economic conditions.[17]

Stable corrupt systems will be easier to maintain in small local markets than in large national or international ones. The need for secrecy favors systems in which a limited number of actors communicate easily. Thus corruption is more likely to be endemic in industries whose producers are locally based, must deal with government on an ongoing basis, and have no choice about where to operate. In many cities construction firms, trash haulers, and vendors in city-owned markets are required to pay off city officials to obtain contracts and licenses to operate. In some areas of the world, local politicians are in league with criminal gangs who enforce payoff schemes with threats of violence (Gambetta 1993). These businesses cannot easily exit the market and move to a less corrupt community elsewhere. Reform city governments have occasionally tried to limit corruption by bringing in large national or multinational firms to challenge the corrupt local operators. In New York City, for example, national waste management firms have been given trash hauling contracts as a way of reducing corruption and organized crime influence in the city.[18]

---

[17] Cartier-Bresson (1995). In many countries fairly standardized illegal payoffs are required both to induce policemen to overlook routine legal violations and to obtain basic government services from officials. Some of these payoffs are fixed fees; others are calibrated as a percentage of the value of the deal. An Indian newspaper recently published a list of the standard payoffs required for various government services. For example, a new driver's license costs one thousand to two thousand rupees while installation of an electric meter costs twenty-five thousand to thirty thousand rupees ("Bribe Index," *Sunday Times of India*, December 17, 1995). Kaufman and Kaliberda (1996) report the standard payoffs required of firms in the Ukraine to license a new business, engage in foreign trade, obtain credit, etc. Contractors in the Pakistani state of Peshawar admit to paying a standard 7 percent "commission." When such payments become routine, both demands for "excessive" payments and attempts to eliminate them meet resistance. In Peshawar, the Government Contractors Association rejected a government demand that its members refuse to pay commissions. The association president applauded the recent fall in the rate from 18 percent to 7 percent, supported the eventual elimination of payoffs, but stated that a sudden cutoff would be costly for contractors. However, any member paying more than 7 percent would be blacklisted by the association (*International News*, December 16, 1993. Summarized in *TI Newsletter*, December 1994, p. 2).

[18] "Judge Backs Competition in Trash-Hauling Industry," *New York Times*, February 28, 1994, p. 3; "The Garbage Wars: Cracking the Cartel," *New York Times*, Money and Business, July 30, 1995, p. 1; "Monitors Appointed for Trash Haulers," *New York Times*, December 23, 1995, p. 3.

Furthermore, corrupt relationships may be easier if the same small group deals with each other in numerous different contexts. Reputations for honesty, reliability, or violence will be inexpensive to establish, making gift giving and bribery relatively advantageous. Trust is not necessary since everyone is always checking up on everyone else. Although such networks are common in local governments everywhere, even quite large polities may be governed by small elites. Considerable wealth in countries like Italy, Brazil, Mexico, or Argentina may be controlled by a small number of insiders.[19] Reputations can be firmly established within such a group for better or for worse.

The costs of establishing a reputation are less severe when bribery is widely accepted and credible law enforcement does not exist. Bribes may be a relatively efficient way to transfer rents from private individuals and organizations to public officials. Corruption is then a symptom of the underlying rent generating character of the state. In an honest world, private actors seek publicly provided rents through wasteful spending programs and regulations that create monopoly rents. In a fully corrupt world, they would not bother seeking legal benefits because the monopoly gains would be extracted by public officials at the implementation stage. There is an intimate connection between the incentive to create rents and the distribution of those rents. In less corrupt countries, private actors seek to use the state to get benefits for themselves. In more corrupt ones, public officials use the state to extract rents from private individuals and firms. They may do this by creating monopolies or by imposing restrictions. Alternatively, they may collude with private interests to extract benefits from foreign and domestic sources that are then shared between the corrupt public officials and their private sector allies.[20]

---

[19] Anecdotal evidence on Italy and Argentina is provided in Colazingari and Rose-Ackerman (1995). Latin American countries have some of the most unequal distributions of income and wealth (Berry, Bourguignon, and Morrison 1991; Fields 1988).

[20] Tirole (1996) has a model of corruption that focuses on a group's reputation for honest or corrupt service to the principal. The difficulties of managing the corrupt transaction are not modeled. Rather, the only choices are the lower level officials' decisions about whether to be corrupt and the principal's decision about whether to assign agents tasks that can be exploited for corrupt gain. The group's past reputation influences the principal's choice, which in turn influences the agents' choices. Multiple equilibria are possible with high and low corruption levels. This model could be adapted to the situation discussed here. If agents as a group have a reputation for being venal, only agents with strong moral scruples will remain honest. Opportunistic agents who balance the costs and benefits will take bribes if the pervasiveness of corruption lowers the costs of being corrupt and increases the chances that private individuals will offer bribes.

## 2.3     *Reputational hostage taking*

Hostage taking is a familiar device for guaranteeing performance. The reality is likely to be less dramatic than the princess kept in the tower, but the principle is the same. Given a time inconsistency in the deal, the first mover demands that the second mover give him something of value to hold in trust. Hostage taking works best as a commitment device when the parties can appeal to a fair and honest tribunal to decide uncertain cases (Cramton and Dees 1993).

Such tribunals are hard to create for corrupt deals. However, bribe payments create the possibility of a special kind of hostage taking. The "hostage" is the reputation of the other person. The first mover may keep secret records of the other person's actions.[21] If, for example, officials are punished more severely than business people, entrepreneurs can pay bribes for future favors and threaten to expose the payoff unless the official delivers. If bribes are paid for routine legal benefits, holding the official's reputation hostage is more difficult than when he provides an illegal or illicit benefit. In general, the greater the symmetry between the losses suffered by briber and bribee from exposure, the less credible is the threat to destroy the other's reputation.

If, however, the briber's reputation has already been destroyed, then he may reveal his corrupt payoffs as well. For example, a member of a Colombian drug cartel turned himself in to the police to save his own life and helped U.S. authorities decipher records of payoffs to Colombian officials.[22] This case illustrates the importance of overlapping law enforcement authorities. If only some are corrupt, those who are honest will limit the malfeasance of the others both by raising the risk of detection and by lowering the illegal benefits any one police force can provide (Rose-Ackerman 1978, pp. 159–63).

Reputational hostage taking can also occur in charitable giving. A donor may seek to hold a university to its promised use of his money by threatening a campaign of negative publicity if the terms of the gift are violated. But a university might be reluctant to threaten negative publicity about a deadbeat donor for fear of discouraging others' gifts. However, it can take steps to reduce the time inconsistency of the deal, for example, by not naming a building after a donor until all of her gift has been legally committed.

[21] For example, in India a businessman accused of corruption had kept careful records of those he paid off. "Indian Premier Shrugs Off Scandal," *New York Times*, February 25, 1996, p. 14.

[22] "Informant's Revelations on Cali Cartel Implicate Colombian Officials," *Washington Post*, January 28, 1996, p. A24.

## 2.4 *Reciprocal obligations*

Many business people develop long-term reciprocal obligations. Each person has an incentive to act responsibly when he is an agent so that he can employ his current principal as an agent in the future. For example, Karen Clay (1997) studied the merchants in California between 1830 and 1848, when it was nominally under Mexican control but lacked a functioning system of contract enforcement. There were few traders, and an individual located in one city was likely to need the help of people in other cities. Instead of sending out his own agents, each used merchants in other cities to perform tasks. Direct bilateral deals were not necessary. Merchant A might act as an agent for merchant B, and B might be an agent for C, who acted as an agent for A. These arrangements were sustained by an active correspondence that communicated information about the reputation of traders along with news about arrivals and departures of ships and the prices and qualities of goods.[23]

How might such systems operate in a corrupt world? To function, the favors must not all go in one direction. Politician A votes for a project that will line the pocket of politician B and relies on B to support him in a similar project later on. The minister of planning favors a company partially owned by the minister of highways, and later, the minister of highways grants a contract to construct a new road to a firm in which the minister of planning has an interest. As in the cases described by Clay, the obligations need not be either bilateral or legally enforceable so long as the relevant group can easily identify defaulters and exclude them from future favors.

In these cases, the distinction between gifts and bribes is particularly difficult to draw. The quid pro quo is paid in the same "currency" as the initial benefit – votes on bills, favoritism on contracts. Taken in isolation the behavior looks like favoritism, not corruption. A gift has been given or a favor done that some may view as inappropriate. The gain to the person who does the favor is not easy to identify. Only the reputation for doing well by those who have helped you in the past sustains the system.

The California system broke down during the gold rush, when the number of merchants increased dramatically. This can also be a cure for corrupt mutual back scratching. As the number of players increases, the accurate communication of reputation becomes more difficult. Some, for example, suggest that the elaborate set of connections characteristic of

---

[23] Clay's work builds on an earlier study by Greif (1989, 1993) of the Maghribi traders in the Mediterranean in the eleventh century.

the overseas Chinese business community in Asia may break down as the Asian market expands.[24] Another solution is a more centralized system of bureaucratic decision making that reduces the opportunities for reciprocal deals spread out over time. This will not, however, succeed if it just consolidates all deals in a single omnibus package. The hope, however, is that bundling will reveal more clearly any quid pro quos that remain. Both market enlargement and improved oversight are moves in the direction of a more impersonal economic and political system. These changes can undermine corrupt networks, but, of course, they can also undermine whatever desirable functions such networks served as well.

## 3     Regulating payments and payoffs

Suppose a society is writing on a clean slate and wishes to establish a legal regime determining which payments should be legal prices, gifts, and tips and which, illegal bribes. The purpose of the legal regime is both to signal to the population what kinds of behavior are acceptable and to deter those for whom legal rules are meaningless unless backed up by credible enforcement measures. My discussion assumes that legal rules have moral meaning for the citizenry. Since, however, some people will only be deterred by costly enforcement measures, a fuller discussion would need to analyze the relative costs and benefits of alternative law enforcement strategies (Pope 1996; Rose-Ackerman 1978). Similarly, if a government wishes to encourage gift giving, subsidies may be needed (Rose-Ackerman 1996).

### 3.1     *Gifts versus sales*

Consider first the distinction between gifts and sales, ignoring the problems of agency. Does economic analysis favor the use of market trades over gifts? When viewed in utility maximizing terms, the answer is simple. There is no reason to restrict gift giving. Many people get positive utility from giving and receiving gifts, unwanted gifts can be refused or at least discarded, and in many cases there are no external costs imposed on others from permitting altruistic transfers. Subsidizing such actions, however, presents a different and more complex issue whose value turns on the existence of beneficial external effects.

Conversely, would an economist ever want to outlaw sales and permit gifts? Only when the expectation of payment would lower product qual-

---

[24] "Inheriting the Bamboo Network," *The Economist*, December 23, 1995–January 5, 1995, pp. 79–80.

ity or quantity. When sellers know product quality and cannot credibly communicate it to buyers, the market may work poorly (Akerlof 1970). In extreme cases, it may be most efficient to outlaw sales and encourage uncompensated gifts (Arrow 1972; Rose-Ackerman 1985). The number of cases in which such conditions hold is likely to be small. On the one hand, appeals to altruism must be feasible, and on the other hand, alternative strategies – such as the provision of information or the imposition of tort liability – must be costly and ineffective. Some have argued, for example, that human blood should only be acquired through donations in the absence of fully effective tests for contaminants such as hepatitis or acquired immunodeficiency syndrome (AIDS) and that human organ donations would fall if sales were also permitted. Richard Titmuss (1970), for example, stresses the problem of the transmission of hepatitis through contaminated blood. This raises the possibility that an entirely donative system of supply might be more efficient than a world which permits both gifts and sales. We do not have good data, but such results are, at least, possible (Thorne 1994).

Titmuss (1970) argues that altruistic behavior is undermined by the introduction of the market. In general, however, this result does not follow (Zelizer 1994). Markets in some goods and services can easily coexist with altruistic transfers. People give food, clothing, and shelter to the poor undeterred by the existence of a market in these commodities. Others support cultural institutions in music and art despite an active for-profit entertainment sector. College graduates give to their alma mater even though most students also pay tuition.

But it does seem likely that market substitutes reduce giving in areas in which people are urged to sacrifice for the public good. Why should you sacrifice if others are being paid to do the same thing? Thus if blood and body parts are purchased from some, donations can be expected to fall (Thorne 1994).[25] The same may be true when mandatory retirement ages are outlawed, as has recently happened in the United States. If some employees demand large severance payments in return for retiring, even employees who believe that older workers have a duty to their employers to retire at a specified time may demand a similar payoff. One's feelings of moral obligation may be undermined by the payment of compensation. Instead of feeling an obligation to take an action or accept a burden without payment, one may feel entitled to compensation. The debate over regulatory takings in the United States can be analyzed in similar

---

[25] One exception may be the widespread coexistence of volunteer and paid labor in the nonprofit organizations. Many organizations with paid staff are nevertheless able to attract volunteers, although they frequently perform different tasks.

terms. In the past, people felt obligated to accept regulatory costs imposed by statutes. Those who favor a doctrinal shift argue that the state has an obligation to pay compensation whenever public actions lower the value of private property (for discussions of the pros and cons see Cordes and Weisbrod 1979, 1985; Rose-Ackerman 1992, pp. 132–43).

### 3.2    *Bribes*

Now consider payments to agents by clients or customers. If the agent provides a quid pro quo, should such payments be illegal? For some economists the fact that bribes are payments for services argues in their favor (Bayley 1966; Leff 1964). They look like prices. But this is carrying the market analogy too far. The problem is the agency relationship in which bribery occurs. Even when agents carry out their duties only in return for bribes, they are being paid twice for the same service – once by their employer and once by clients. The service is inefficiently costly to society and too little of it is demanded.

In many situations commonly labeled corrupt, quid pro quo payments by clients to agents have serious costs (Alam 1991; Rose-Ackerman 1978, 1994, 1997, 1998). Consider, first, transactions that are costly for society at large, but beneficial to both the payer and the receiver of bribes – that is, transactions that impose external costs. Payments to reduce customs duties or taxes, to get inside information before a privatization auction, or to induce officials to overlook regulatory violations are examples. A corrupted tax system may produce an inefficient pattern of tax collections or lead to an inefficiently small state. Inside information can lead a state firm to be sold to an inefficient investor if some potential bidders stay away. Regulations designed to correct market failures may be undermined by payoffs. One pair of commentators describes this type of corruption as "bribery with theft" (Shleifer and Vishny 1993). In such cases, agents face two conflicting sets of incentives – those imposed by the principal seeking to control the agents' behavior and those offered by clients.

Officials may also demand payments simply for doing their job. They may impose delays and fines on those who refuse to pay. If everyone pays and if the official can price discriminate, the result will approximate an honest system based on willingness to pay, but with most of the rent going to the official instead of the private individuals and firms. If bribes replace other transaction costs in such cases, they improve efficiency even if the distribution of gains is unlikely to please anyone except the corrupt officials. Bribers are at least as well off as they would be if no program existed, but they are obviously worse off than in a world with an honest, well-functioning government. The evaluation of such cases involves both a decision about the allocation criterion and a judgment about who should receive the payments. Do the payoffs give agents a better motivation to perform efficiently, or does the search for payoffs lead them to create costly obstacles?

Given a fixed quantity of services, payments to agents may be an efficient method of allocation. If so, they should be treated as legal tips, not illegal bribes. Bribery implies secrecy, and secrecy implies that "price" information will not be widely available. Furthermore, those with moral scruples about disobeying the law will not participate in bribery but would pay legal tips. However, the conditions under which direct payments to public officials are efficient are limited. Officials can frequently create situations that permit them to extract economic rents from private individuals and businesses. In the short run, this is "just" a transfer; in the long run it will discourage people from investing in areas that require contact with the state. Those with the authority to impose costs, such as policemen, are especially likely to use these tactics.[26]

The difference between ordinary officials and law enforcement agents, however, is one of degree rather than of kind. When ordinary officials are involved, no one will pay more than the individual license or other benefit is worth. If the required bribe is too high, the bribee selects another line of business. Police, however, can threaten violence and imprisonment. Since people will pay to avoid such costs, the rent extraction possibilities available to the police are not as limited as those of clerks issuing drivers' licenses. Extortionary possibilities increase if the potential briber is himself breaking the law in other ways, i.e., selling illegal drugs or running a gambling operation. He cannot complain to a higher authority about bribery demands. The police official, however, faces a corresponding risk. The criminal may resist bribery demands with his own threats of violence backed up by his criminal organization. Those most vulnerable to extortion are nominally respectable people with illegal businesses on the side or legitimate business people in a weak state who have no recourse against the corrupt demands of officials operating in connection with violent criminals (Rose-Ackerman 1994; Varese 1994).

Since a number of people have canvassed possible policy responses to systemic corruption, I will not repeat these recommendations here (Klitgaard 1988; Pope 1996; Rose-Ackerman 1978, 1997, 1998). What should be clear is that strategies that reduce the opportunities for payoffs should be part of any realistic reform plan. Campaigns that seek to raise

---

[26] For a fuller discussion of these issues see Rose-Ackerman (1997, 1998).

moral consciousness and to punish wrongdoers without a change in the underlying structure of incentives are, at best, a stopgap. Rather than agonize over the proper definition of bribes and gifts, reformers should try to reduce opportunities for engaging in outright corruption and for providing favors to friends and relations. This implies both a reduction in the role of the state and a reform in the way it does business. A strong libertarian stance under which the state simply withers away is unrealistic and unwise in a world of pervasive market failures and inequities. The alternative is to reduce discretion within the public sector without introducing stultifying controls. One way to do this is to introduce legal incentives and market-based systems within the government. This means transparent procedures for allocating contracts and privatized firms. It means giving serious consideration to such reforms as effluent charges or tradable rights in the environmental area or the auction of scarce benefits such as the microwave spectrum, stalls in urban markets, and import licenses.

When, however, the government cares about the quality of the output produced, it cannot simply auction off the scarce benefit. For example, research grants can be awarded corruptly, but the solution is not to provide them to the researchers willing to supply the highest level of matching funds. Agencies that approve grants must exercise discretion over the quality of the promised research. Devices such as peer review by outside panels, however, are frequently used as a way of distancing career bureaucrats from these decisions and reducing their corruption opportunities.

Each of these reforms is a step toward a more impersonal, objective method of governing. All have little chance of success, however, if everyone operates on the presumption that personal ties deserve the highest value. Those operating the new system will simply try to convert it into a variant of the old one. Reform programs cannot presume that citizens have attitudes that facilitate the development of legal markets and discourage illegal corruption. If, however, a successful market economy and an honest well-functioning bureaucracy convince people to change their views, then once that transformation has been accomplished, other more subtle applications of economic incentives to public service provision can be attempted.

### 3.3    *Tips*

Finally, consider tips, that is, gifts to agents. In the early 1900s a few state legislatures in the United States made tipping a misdemeanor and some reformers urged the formation of antitipping leagues. The objections were based on the socially demeaning nature of the gift (Zelizer 1994, pp. 94–99). The demand for legal controls was based on fears of moral decay, not a claim of inefficiency. Presumably, managers will try to construct remuneration schemes for their employees that mix wages and tips in a profit maximizing way. Those who feel demeaned by accepting tips can select jobs with fixed wages. However, managers, employees, and customers are embedded in society. Employers may face the problem of encouraging a social norm of tipping when the practice is by its nature voluntary. Workers may not have the option of refusing jobs that include tips. Legal regulation, for or against the practice, does not, however, appear worthwhile except to assure proper tax collection when tips are easy to conceal.

Problems arise when the principal is incapable of effective monitoring. Thus, one might view campaign contributions as "tips" given to politicians who have provided good service to donors in the past. The quid pro quo is only implicit. The politician's principal is a diffuse group of voters in his or her district. Unlike the restaurant owner who stays in business by satisfying his customers, a representative who only satisfies the narrow interests of campaign contributors will not generally be reelected. But voters cannot effectively monitor such implicit quid pro quos on their own. The lack of correspondence between the interests of voters and the interests of contributors will lead to secret donations unless publicity is required. Opponents have an incentive to monitor the political contributions others receive, but their joint interest in maintaining a system of private donations may make public regulation or public funding of campaigns desirable.

Similarly, gifts from clients to bureaucrats may, as a practical matter, be difficult to distinguish from bribes. In such cases simple rules of thumb outlawing gifts of substantial value may be the most realistic option. Since gifts are per se forbidden, there is no need to demonstrate that the official actually favored the gift giver over other applicants or that any illegal benefits were dispensed.

## 4 Gifts, bribes, and prices in the developing world[27]

In the developed world, where impersonal markets and technocratic bureaucracies are pervasive, we have seen that the distinctions among prices, bribes, gifts, and tips are difficult both to draw and to evaluate normatively. In the developing world the problem is much more vexing.

---

[27] Sarah Dix, a graduate student in the Department of Political Science, Yale University, provided very helpful research assistance on this portion of the chapter.

The line between market and family and between the public and the private sectors is often blurred and uncertain. The transition from a situation in which personal ties are the norm to a more impersonal society with strong market and public sector institutions may be a painful one. How is a country to make such a transition without giving up what is valuable in its older traditions and practices?

Standard neoclassical economics assumes away personal ties between buyers and sellers and argues that the impersonality of the market is one of its advantages. Trade is efficiently carried out by individuals who base their trading decisions on the characteristics of products and the prices charged. Markets conserve on information, and their impersonality assures that sales are made to those who value the goods most. One does not need to like or respect a person in order to trade with him. The process of trading is not itself a source of utility.

Even in highly developed societies, however, the identity of buyers and sellers is often an important piece of information that establishes reputation and trust. The implicit contracting literature highlights the importance of personal relationships between buyers and sellers in complex contracting situations. The connection may be one of love, affection, and respect or may be based on fear and intimidation. If personal relations are relatively easy to establish, problems of fraud and shoddy merchandise may be reduced by efforts to create a reputation for quality and fair dealing. Free-rider problems can be overcome by cooperation among interrelated groups (Bardhan 1993; Ostrom and Gardiner 1993).

Nevertheless, as we have seen, personalized ties are not always compatible with efficiency. Trust, reputation, and reciprocal obligations can facilitate corruption and undermine attempts to improve the operation of the state. If people will only deal with those they know personally, this will limit entry into the market to those with inside connections and lead sales and purchasing agents to favor their relatives and friends. The monitoring and quality control provided by personalized links also entail increased entry costs for those not "in the loop." Furthermore, if private economic interests have personal links to public officials, patrimonial or clientelistic systems built on favors and payoffs can undermine the transparency and effectiveness of public and private institutions.[28]

---

[28] Mushtaq Kahn (1996) makes a distinction between corruption in patrimonial and in clientelist states. In the former, public officials are the patrons and private interests are the clients. In the latter, "the property rights defined by the state are weakly-defined and are contested by well-organized social groups who are able to challenge the rights being enforced by the state" (p. 18). Bangladesh appears to be an example of a patrimonial state. After its separation from Pakistan almost no locally powerful business leaders

In such societies those embedded in dense interpersonal networks may care little about market and public sector efficiency. They may view impersonal markets as illegitimate and morally bankrupt. In the extreme, the idea of an explicit quid pro quo may be questionable. People may believe they should give freely to others in their family or group and will expect that return "gifts" will also be made. Although an outsider may observe what appears to be an active trading culture, those within the system may not see it that way. Trade, for them, is legitimate only if one has an individual connection with the person on the other side of the transaction. A society based on such highly personalized relations will have difficulty developing large-scale capitalist enterprise or supporting active cross-border trade but may produce a viable, if quite poor, autarky. Attempts by development experts to introduce more formal and impersonal mechanisms may not succeed without a change in attitudes. If such a change does occur, however, the end result can have costs as well as benefits. As Richard Titmuss (1970) has argued with respect to the supply of blood for transfusions, a greater role for the market may be accompanied by a lower sense of obligation to help one's relatives and friends. Cooperation to solve common problems may fall, and those in need may suffer (Dia 1996).

Societies based on strong interpersonal relations may have little notion of formal agency–principal relations and the obligations they impose on agents. The idea that one has distinct responsibilities to a superior separate from ties of loyalty, friendship, and kinship may seem strange and unnatural. Such societies will have difficulty establishing modern bureaucracies whose civil servants are hired on the basis of skills and are expected to separate their role as official from their role as friend or relative. Citizens expect that personal ties with officials are needed to get anything done and think it quite appropriate to reward those who help them with gifts and tips. Similarly, higher-ups in government seek to assure the support of lower level officials by appointing loyal subordinates who will resist offers of payment unless the superior approves. They will set up systems for sharing payoffs up and down the hierarchy.

existed, and those who eventually became established were very dependent on government patronage. According to Stephen Kochanek (1993), the level of patronage and corruption in Bangladesh has held down growth.

Other examples of states where strong patron–client connections exist are easy to find. Merilee Grindle's (1996) comparison of Mexico and Kenya in the 1980s and 1990s emphasizes the importance of patron–client links in both countries and the negative impact of corrupt networks on growth. See also Robison (1996) on Indonesia and Pinches (1996) on "crony capitalism" in the Philippines. Pinches points out that although many of the "cronies" were pure rent seekers, others were genuinely interested in developing productive business enterprises.

Payments made at the top will be shared down the line and those collected at the bottom will be divided up with superiors. Loyalty to family, friends, and coworkers, not the state, is the primary value.[29]

Strong networks based on trust and reputation can be invaluable during periods when formal state institutions are weak and ineffective. In the early postrevolutionary period in the Soviet Union, for example, informal social networks substituted for formal organizational structure (Easter 1996). Cadres who had been members of tight-knit underground organizations carried their loyalties and connections over into the new Soviet state. Over time, however, as the state structure developed, networks became sources of corruption and favoritism. Stalin complained that informal social structures undermined formal ones, and Gorbachev's efforts at reform in the 1980s were hampered by informal networks that reduced the center's capacity to implement policies (pp. 574, 576–77). Similarly, in the recent period of flux and change in Eastern Europe, corruption facilitated by personal ties helped ease the transition. The long-run consequence of these habits of behavior is to make the creation of effective state structures difficult (Verheijen and Dimitrova 1996). These cases suggest that, whatever one thinks of the merits of a government's announced policies, personal links that survive from a previous era can make state action difficult.

Will the introduction of free market institutions and governance structures imported from developed modern states change underlying attitudes?[30] Both vicious and virtuous cycles seem possible. The intro-

---

[29] For a description of a country that fulfills many of these conditions see Kochanek's (1993) discussion of Bangladesh. Verheijen and Dimitrova (1996, pp. 205–6) argue that the lack of understanding of public administration principles has hindered bureaucratic development in post-Soviet societies in Eastern Europe. Loyalty to other members of the organization is as important as or more important than good administration. According to them, "civil servants from the core ministry of finance in Bulgaria still feel that they have to protect their colleagues at the customs offices, rather than launch a serious inquiry into what seem to be corrupt practices by customs officials." Robert Scalapino (1989, p. 4) argues that Western colonizers in Asia faced a daunting task in creating a new civilian elite "in the image of the Western Civil servant" since such concepts "as considering office holding to be a public trust, applying rules without fear or favor, and abiding by the verdict of the people as expressed through their elected representatives" were foreign to traditional Asian officials. This task was made more difficult by the inconsistency of Western efforts as colonizers whose legitimacy was dependent on military power.

[30] According to Scalapino (1989, p. 107): "One must reject the argument that the cultural as well as economic changes required for . . . (a more open and democratic Japanese society) are too great to be expected. Rapid cultural change is an inextricable aspect of the era in which we live, especially within the avant-garde societies." Studies of political culture suggest that attitudes are subject to change as circumstances change. The

duction of new institutions that fit poorly with underlying norms can make gradual changes in attitudes unlikely as people observe the costs of markets and bureaucracies. Developed market economies draw many formal and informal lines between impersonal market trades and official functions, on the one hand, and personal ties, on the other.[31] Conflict of interest and campaign finance laws regulate the links between money and politics. Norms of behavior limit the intrusion of the market into family relationships and friendship. Journalism standards prevent reporters from accepting money to write particular stories.

In contrast, complex boundaries between market and nonmarket activities do not exist in countries that have relied little on the impersonal free market in the past. If such countries dramatically increase the role of the market and at the same time try to establish a modern bureaucracy and a democratic polity, the resulting system may work poorly. Payoffs to state officials may be common; many market trades may be based on personal connections; and state purchases and personnel appointments may continue to be part of a web of patronage.[32] On the one hand, the market may lose its fragile legitimacy by intruding into areas in which it is viewed as illegitimate even in developed market economies. On the other hand, the market may have difficulty becoming established even in those areas where it produces clear efficiency gains elsewhere.

Virtuous cycles are also possible. If those operating in the modern sector benefit, others may be induced to try it out, however reluctantly. In China, for example, the success of regions that liberalized their economies encouraged other more conservative regions to copy them (Shirk 1994). A successful small and medium sized business sector operating free of excessive controls can encourage others to try their luck as entrepreneurs. Robert Scalapino (1989, p. 77) worries that entrepreneurs

causality works both ways. As Larry Diamond writes, in summarizing recent work by Gabriel Almond, "the cognitive, attitudinal, and evaluational dimensions of political culture are fairly 'plastic' and change quite dramatically in response to regime performance, historical experience, and political socialization. Deeper value and normative commitments have been shown to be more enduring and change only slowly" (Diamond 1993, p. 9). See, for example, Seligson and Booth's (1993) study of Costa Rica and Nicaragua. They conclude that "political culture is far more contingent, utilitarian, and malleable than has previously been assumed" (p. 790).

[31] For a discussion of this issue focusing on the role of money see Zelizer (1994).

[32] In China the reallocation of resources from the state to private hands has increased efficiency and improved productivity. However, "the line between corruption and the more acceptable transfer of resources has not been clearly defined" (Goodman 1996, p. 241). An important task for government is to redraw "the distinctions between legitimacy and corruption in the private sphere . . . in a new atmosphere, and as a new entrepreneurial class emerges" (Scalapino 1989, pp. 114–15).

drawn from the ranks of Chinese officialdom will maintain long-established habits and depend "extensively upon political contacts and an exchange of favors." However, he sees hope in an underlying spirit of pragmatism and of "creativity and independent entrepreneurship." In other words, deep-seated cultural norms favor the development of a competitive market economy but have been suppressed by the all-persuasive socialist state.

A common source of corruption and patronage in the developing world is in credit and banking services.[33] Given the fundamental character of credit in the development process, this is worrisome if some potential entrepreneurs are unable to borrow at market rates. Thus one way to encourage a virtuous cycle may be the provision of credit outside existing patronage networks. Recent experiments do not, however, seek to re-create the institutional forms common in the developed world. Instead, close ties between neighbors are used to complement efforts to establish a banking system. Social pressure encourages people to repay, but the initial loans are made to those outside the existing circle of borrowers.[34]

Do efforts to limit personalized dealings by public officials and market actors undermine the desirable features of interpersonal links based on trust and respect? If a trade-off exists, it does not appear to be a stark one.[35] In spite of the jeremiads of some writers, the United States has a remarkably dense network of nonprofit organizations and a strong tradition of private gift giving both to charities and to relatives.[36] Many

---

[33] In Bangladesh Kochanek (1993, p. 264) claims that under General Zia industrial loan funds provided by the World Bank and the Asian Development Bank were handed out as a form of patronage. "Of 3718 units financed under Zia from 1976 to 1981–82, fewer than half became operational. There exists no trace of some 898 or 24 percent of the units financed, and another 495 or 13 percent failed." In Africa development finance institutions founded on external loans have experienced problems of illiquidity and insolvency with nonperforming portfolios and high default rates (Nissanke 1991, p. 143). In both China and the countries of Eastern Europe corruption in the granting of loans is common (De Melo, Ofer, and Sandler 1995; Johnston and Hao 1995; Webster 1993; Webster and Charap 1993). Corruption frequently arises because the state has fixed interest rates too low. This explains the incentives to pay bribes, but it also leaves the way open for loan officers to use criteria other than efficiency to allocate scarce supplies.

[34] A number of experiments along these lines are in progress in Africa and Asia (Dia 1996, pp. 194–219). The most well known is the Grameen Bank developed in Bangladesh for lending to people lacking ordinary sorts of collateral. The benefit of mutual surveillance by peers in bureaucratic settings is discussed by Hood (1996, pp. 214–16).

[35] Zelizer (1994, pp. 71–118) stresses the coexistence of different forms of exchange in modern societies.

[36] For a summary of the facts see Rose-Ackerman (1996) and Hodgkinson and Weitzman (1994).

private business relations rely on trust and reputation to assure high quality performance. Regulation of political campaigns and bureaucratic behavior limits self-dealing, although private wealth, of course, remains an important influence on political life. In Africa some observers, frustrated with past development failures, are urging a more careful study of indigenous institutions. The aim is not to accept them uncritically, but to ask how new and old institutional forms and practices might be blended.[37]

The definition of bribes and gifts is a cultural matter, but "culture" is not a fixed, immutable entity. One role economists can play is to demonstrate the costs and benefits of alternative ways of organizing economic transactions and of paying agents. This work can clarify the costs in economic well-being of certain ingrained practices and attitudes. If some behavior labeled "corrupt" by outsiders is, nevertheless, viewed as acceptable gift giving or tipping within a country, it should simply be legalized and reported. If, however, these practices are imposing hidden or indirect costs on the populace, outsiders can, at least, clarify and document these costs. Definitions of acceptable behavior may change once people are informed of the costs of tolerating payoffs to politicians and civil servants. Conversely, experts from the developed world may learn something new about the organization of economic and social activity by studying systems in which "implicit contracting" is the only form of contracting that exists and interpersonal relationships are central to economic life.

## Conclusions

This chapter begins with the premise that values affect the behavior of organizations and the meaning of legal forms, and that, in turn, organizations and laws shape human values. One important value that reverber-

---

[37] This is the theme of Dia (1996), who writes that Africa faces a crisis of institutions. The crisis is "mainly due to a structural and functional disconnect, or lack of convergence, between formal institutions that are mostly transplanted from outside and informal institutions that are rooted in African history, tradition, and culture and that generally characterize the governance of civil society" (p. 29). Recent World Bank research on Africa suggests "that when informal institutions are open to modern technology and challenges (renovation) and formal institutions integrate local cultural values and practices (adaptation), then transformation and transaction costs can be minimized and the performance of the public and private sectors can be improved" (p. 29). Dia's book provides a number of case studies of successful efforts along these lines. See especially his discussion of the public electric company in Côte d'Ivoire, where a systematic effort was made to reconcile corporate and societal culture without an unquestioning devotion to either (pp. 222–27).

ates through modern society is the moral status of monetary payments and transfers. The way the line is drawn between acceptable and unacceptable monetary transfers will affect the performance of both the economy and the polity.

Bribery and corruption are associated with immorality and evil. Gift giving and altruism are associated with goodness. Those who can successfully attach the label "corruption" to some type of behavior have gone a long way toward discouraging it. Those who can label something a gift give it moral approval. Because of the power of these labels, it is important to understand the consequences of payments to principals and to agents both with and without a quid pro quo. One can then ask whether society has drawn the lines between acceptable and unacceptable payments in a way that makes sense in terms of the consequences.

This chapter has provided an economic analysis of such payments. It has aimed both to describe the economic consequences of prices, bribes, gifts, and tips and to guide those seeking to draw the legal boundaries in a functional way. Although I reject the view that corruption is a benign manifestation of the price system, the analysis points to some subtle distinctions between different types of payments to agents. It demonstrates that trust and a reputation for keeping one's word are not always beneficial traits. They can undermine the legitimacy and efficiency of state action if they facilitate corrupt collusive relationships between public and private actors. The chapter highlights the tension between close personal ties and the impersonal agency relations that are an integral part of modern states and modern economic systems.

## REFERENCES

Akerlof, George A. (1970). "The Market for Lemons," *Quarterly Journal of Economics* 84: 488–500.

Alam, M. Shahid (1991). "Some Economic Costs of Corruption in LDCs," *Journal of Development Studies* 27: 89–97.

Andreoni, James (1988). "Privately Provided Public Goods in a Large Economy: The Limits of Altruism," *Journal of Public Economics* 35: 57–73.

Arrow, Kenneth (1972). "Gifts and Exchanges," *Philosophy and Public Affairs* 1: 343–62.

Bardhan, Pranab (1993). "Symposium on Management of Local Commons," *Journal of Economic Perspectives* 7: 87–92.

Barney, J. B., and Hansen, M. H. (1994). "Trustworthiness as a Source of Competitive Advantage," *Strategic Management Journal* 15: 175–90.

Bayley, David H. (1966). "The Effect of Corruption in a Developing Nation," *Western Political Quarterly* 19: 719–32.

Becker, Gary, and George Stigler (1974). "Law Enforcement, Malfeasance, and Compensation of Enforcers," *Journal of Legal Studies* 3: 1–19.

Berry, Albert, François Bourguignon, and Christian Morrison (1991). "Global Inequality and Its Trends Since 1950," in Lars Osberg, ed., *Economic Inequality and Poverty*, pp. 60–90. Armonk, N.Y.: M. E. Sharpe.

Bishop, D. T., C. Cannings, and J. Maynard Smith (1978). "The War of Attrition with Random Rewards," *Journal of Theoretical Biology* 74: 377–88.

Cartier-Bresson, J. (1995). "L'Economie de la Corruption," in D. Della Porta and Y. Mény, eds., *Démocratie et Corruption en Europe*, pp. 149–64. Paris: La Découverte.

Choharis, Peter Charles (1995). "Creating a Market for Tort Claims," *Regulation* no. 4: 38–45.

Clay, Karen (1997). "Trade without Law: Private-Order Institutions in Mexican California," *Journal of Law, Economics, and Organization* 13: 202–31.

Colazingari, Silvia, and Susan Rose-Ackerman (1995). "Corruption in a Paternalistic Democracy: Lessons from Italy for Latin America." Draft prepared for a lecture in the Trinity College Italian Programs, Hartford, Conn.

Cordes, Joseph, and Burton Weisbrod (1979). "Government Behavior in Response to Compensation Requirements," *Journal of Public Economics* 11: 47–58.

——— Cordes, Joseph, and Burton Weisbrod (1985). "When Government Programs Create Inequities: A Guide to Compensation Policies," *Journal of Policy Analysis and Management* 4: 178–95.

Coulter, E. M. (1933). *Short History of Georgia.* Chapel Hill: University of North Carolina Press.

Cramton, Peter C., and J. Gregory Dees (1993). "Promoting Honesty in Negotiation: An Exercise in Practical Ethics," *Business Ethics Quarterly* 3: 360–94.

De Melo, Martha, Gur Ofer, and Olga Sandler (1995). "Pioneers for Profit: St. Petersburg Entrepreneurs in Services," *World Bank Economic Review* 9: 425–50.

Dia, Mamadou (1996). *Africa's Management in the 1990s and Beyond: Reconciling Indigenous and Transplanted Institutions.* Washington, D.C.: World Bank.

Diamond, Larry (1993). "Introduction: Political Culture and Democracy," in Larry Diamond, ed., *Political Culture and Democracy in Developing Countries*, pp. 1–33. Boulder, Colo.: Lynne Rienner.

Easter, Gerald (1996). "Personal Networks and Postrevolutionary State Building: Soviet Russia Reexamined," *World Politics* 48: 551–78.

Eisenberg, Melvin Aron (1979). "Donative Promises," *University of Chicago Law Review* 47: 1–33.

Fields, Gary (1988). "Income Distribution and Economic Growth," in G. Ranis and T. P. Schultz, eds., *The State of Development Economics: Progress and Perspectives*, pp. 459–85. Oxford: Basil Blackwell.

*Fletcher v. Peck*, U.S. Supreme Court, 87–148, February 1810; 3 L. Ed. 162–81.

Gambetta, Diego (1993). *The Sicilian Mafia.* Cambridge, Mass.: Harvard University Press.

Goodman, David S. (1996). "The People's Republic of China: The Party-State, Capitalist Revolution and the New Entrepreneurs," in Richard Robison and

David S. G. Goodman, eds., *The New Rich in Asia*, pp. 225–43. London: Routledge.

Gordley, James (1995). "Enforcing Promises," *California Law Review* 83: 547–613.

Greif, Avner (1989). "Reputation and Coalitions in Medieval Trade: Evidence on the Maghribi Traders," *Journal of Economic History* 59: 857–82.

———(1993). "Contract Enforceability and Economic Institutions in Early Trade: The Maghribi Traders Coalition," *American Economic Review* 83: 525–48.

Grindle, Merilee S. (1996). *Challenging the State: Crisis and Innovation in Latin America and Africa*. Cambridge: Cambridge University Press.

Hodgkinson, Virginia Ann, and Murray S. Weitzman (1994). *Giving and Volunteering in the United States*. Washington, D.C.: Independent Sector.

Hood, Christopher (1996). "Control over Bureaucracy: Cultural Theory and Institutional Variety," *Journal of Public Policy* 15: 207–30.

Johnson, Paul (1991). *The Birth of the Modern: World Society, 1815–1830*. New York: HarperCollins.

Johnston, Michael, and Yufan Hao (1995). "China's Surge of Corruption," *Journal of Democracy* 6: 80–94.

Kahn, Mushtaq H. (April 1996). "A Typology of Corrupt Transactions in Developing Countries," *IDS Bulletin* 27(2): 12–21.

Kaufman, Daniel, and Aleksander Kaliberda (1996). "Integrating the Unofficial Economy into the Dynamics of Post-Socialist Economies: A Framework of Analysis and Evidence," in Bartlomej Kaminski, ed., *Economic Transitions in the Newly Independent States*, pp. 81–120. Armonk, N.Y.: M. E. Sharpe.

Kim, Chan, and Renée Mauborgne (1995). "A Procedural Justice Model of Strategic Decision Making," *Organization Science* 6: 44–61.

Klitgaard, Robert (1988). *Controlling Corruption*. Berkeley, Calif.: University of California Press.

Kochanek, Stephen A. (1993). *Patron-Client Politics and Business in Bangladesh*. New Delhi: Sage Publications.

Kollock, Peter (1994). "The Emergence of Exchange Structures: An Experimental Study of Uncertainty, Commitment, and Trust," *American Journal of Sociology* 100: 313–45.

Krishna, Vijay, and John Morgan (1994). "An Analysis of the War of Attrition and the All-Pay Auction," Working paper, Pennsylvania State University.

Laffont, Jean-Jacques (1990). "Analysis of Hidden Games in a Three-Level Hierarchy," *Journal of Law, Economics, and Organization* 6: 301–24.

Leff, Nathaniel (1964). "Economic Development through Bureaucratic Corruption," *American Behavioral Scientist* 8: 8–14.

Manzetti, Luigi, and Charles Blake (1996). "Market Reforms and Corruption in Latin America: New Means for Old Ways," *Review of International Political Economy* 3: 662–97.

Monroe, Kristen Renwick (1996). *The Heart of Altruism*. Princeton, N.J.: Princeton University Press.

Nissanke, Machiko (1991). "Mobilizing Domestic Resources for African Development and Diversification," in Ajay Chhibber and Stanley Fischer, eds., *Economic Reform in Sub-Saharan Africa*, pp. 137–47. Washington, D.C.: World Bank.

Ostrom, Elinor, and Roy Gardiner (1993). "Coping with Asymmetries in the Commons: Self-Governing Irrigation Systems Can Work," *Journal of Economic Perspectives* 7: 93–112.

Pinches, Michael (1996). "The Philippines New Rich: Capitalist Transformations amidst Economic Gloom," in Richard Robison and David S. G. Goodman, eds., *The New Rich in Asia*, pp. 105–33. London: Routledge.

Pope, Jeremy, ed. (1996). *National Integrity Systems: The TI Sourcebook*, Berlin: Transparency International.

Posner, Richard (1977). "Gratuitous Promises in Economics and Law," *Journal of Legal Studies* 6: 411–26.

Rasmusen, Eric (1990). *Games and Information: An Introduction to Game Theory*. Oxford: Basil Blackwell.

Robison, Richard (1996). "The Middle Class and the Bourgeoise in Indonesia," in Richard Robison and David S. G. Goodman, eds., *The New Rich in Asia*, pp. 79–101. London: Routledge.

Rose-Ackerman, Susan (1978). *Corruption: A Study in Political Economy*. New York: Academic Press.

——— (1985). "Inalienability and the Theory of Property Rights," *Columbia Law Review* 85: 931–69.

——— (1986). "Reforming Public Bureaucracy through Economic Incentives?" *Journal of Law, Economics, and Organization* 2: 131–61.

——— (1992). *Rethinking the Progressive Agenda: The Reform of the American Regulatory State*. New York: Free Press.

——— (1994). "Bribery in the Public Sector," in Duc V. Trang, ed., *Corruption and Democracy: Political Institutions, Processes, and Corruption in Transition States in East-Central Europe and in the Former Soviet Union*. Budapest: Institute for Constitutional and Legislative Policy.

——— (1996). "Altruism, Nonprofits and Economic Theory," *Journal of Economic Literature* 34: 701–28.

——— (1997). "The Political Economy of Corruption," in Kimberley Elliott, ed., *Corruption in the World Economy*. Washington, D.C.: Institute for International Economics.

——— (1998, forthcoming). "Corruption and Development," in Joseph Stiglitz and Boris Pleskovic, eds., *Annual World Bank Conference on Development Economics*. Washington, D.C.: World Bank.

Scalapino, Robert (1989). *The Politics of Development: Perspectives on Twentieth-Century Asia*. Cambridge, Mass.: Harvard University Press.

Schmid, A. Allan, and Lindon J. Robison (1995). "Applications of Social Capital Theory," *Journal of Agriculture and Applied Economics* 27: 59–66.

Seligson, Mitchell A., and John A. Booth (1993). "Political Culture and Regime

Type: Evidence from Nicaragua and Costa Rica," *Journal of Politics* 55: 777–92.

Sen, A. K. (1977). "Rational Fools: A Critique of the Behavioral Foundations of Economic Theory," *Philosophy and Public Affairs* 6: 317–44.

Shirk, Susan L. (1994). *How China Opened Its Door: The Political Success of the PRC's Foreign Trade and Investment Reforms.* Washington, D.C.: Brookings Institution.

Shleifer, Andrei, and Robert Vishny (1993). "Corruption," *Quarterly Journal of Economics* 108: 599–617.

Thorne, Emmanuel David (1994). "The Economics of Market-Inalienable Human Organs." Ph.D. dissertation, Yale University, New Haven, Conn.

Tierney, John (1995). "Holiday Bribery" *New York Times Magazine*, December 17, pp. 42–44.

Tirole, Jean (1986). "Hierarchies and Bureaucracies: On the Role of Collusion in Organizations," *Journal of Law, Economics, and Organization* 2: 181–214.

——— (1992). *Collusion and the Theory of Organizations, in Advances in Economic Theory: Sixth World Congress*, Vol. II, pp. 151–206. Cambridge: Cambridge University Press.

——— (1996). "A Theory of Collective Reputations (with Applications to the Persistence of Corruption and to Firm Quality)," *Review of Economic Studies* 63: 1–22.

Titmuss, Richard (1970). *The Gift Relationship.* London: Allen and Unwin.

Varese, Federico (1994). "Is Sicily the Future of Russia? Private Protection and the Rise of the Russian Mafia," *Archives of European Sociology* 35: 224–58.

Verheijen, Tony, and Antoaneta Dimitrova (1996). "Private Interests and Public Administration: The Central and East European Experience," *International Review of Administrative Sciences* 62: 197–218.

Webster, Leila M. (1993). *The Emergence of Private Sector Manufacturing in Hungary.* World Bank Technical Paper 229, Washington, D.C.: World Bank.

Webster, Leila M., and Joshua Charap (1993). *The Emergence of Private Sector Manufacturing in St. Petersburg.* World Bank Technical Paper 228, Washington, D.C.: World Bank.

Williamson, Oliver (1975). *Markets and Hierarchies: Analysis and Antitrust Implications.* New York: Free Press.

———(1979). "Transaction-Cost Economics: The Governance of Contractual Relations," *Journal of Law and Economics* 22: 233–61.

Zelizer, Viviana A. (1994). *The Social Meaning of Money.* New York: Basic Books.

# CHAPTER 12

# How do we know whether a monetary transaction is a gift, an entitlement, or compensation?

*Viviana Zelizer*

After millennia during which officially sanctioned monies multiplied but large areas of social life remained outside the zone of monetary exchange, over the last two centuries governments have standardized legal tenders, and the range of monetized social transactions has enormously expanded. These days the highly commercialized economies of Europe are seriously contemplating the imposition of a single money in place of the national currencies that now hold sway in the countries of the European Union. That combination of multiple uses and standardized currency presents living, working social beings with an unrecognized but acute dilemma: how to distinguish unambiguously among forms of payment that have deeply different meanings for their participants. Given the apparent anonymity of bank notes, for example, how do we distinguish among bribes, gifts, tips, allowances, and payments for goods and services?

What is at issue? In my investigation of payment systems, I have found it useful to distinguish among three possible ways of organizing monetary payments of any kind: as *compensation* (direct exchange), as *entitlement* (the right to a share), and as *gift* (one person's voluntary bestowal on another). Money as compensation implies an equal exchange of values, and a certain distance, contingency, bargaining, and accountability among the parties. Money as an entitlement implies strong claims to power and autonomy by the recipient. Money as a gift implies intimacy and/or inequality plus a certain arbitrariness.

What distinguishes such categories of payments? Two elements seem essential: first, the relational content and meaning of the transaction, and second, the time duration of the relation. Payment systems are relational; they affirm or define the quality of social relations between the parties. Thus, gift, entitlement, and compensation each correspond to a significantly different set of social relations and systems of meanings. On the

329

whole, entitlements and gifts imply a more durable social relation between them than does compensation.

But how does the relational content of the transaction help us identify the category of payment? Suppose a man gives a woman one hundred dollars cash: How do we know whether the payment is a birthday present (a gift), alimony (an entitlement), or payment for sexual services (compensation)? Or could it be a bribe or a tip? To define the transaction, we need information about the social relation of the parties involved: Are the pair husband–wife, divorced spouses, friends, lovers, patron–prostitute, diner–waitress, driver–traffic cop? In each case, how long have they known each other?

In fact, such questions often become the subjects of legal dispute. Consider the case of *United States v. Harris* (942 F.2d 1125, 7th Cir. 1991). David Kritzik, a wealthy widower, "partial to the company of young women," had over the course of several years given Leigh Ann Conley and Lynnette Harris, twin sisters, more than half a million dollars, in kind and cash: In fact, he regularly left a check at his office, which Conley picked up every week to ten days, either from Kritzik himself or from his secretary.

The case raises the issue of the taxability of transfers of money to a mistress in long-term relationships. Were those transfers gifts or compensation? If gifts, Kritzik had to pay gift tax on the money; if compensation, the sisters had to pay income tax. The United States claimed that the money was compensation: As part of its evidence, the government argued that the form of transfer, the regular check, was that of an employee paid regular wages. Harris and Conley were convicted of evading income tax obligations and sent to jail. After Kritzik's death, however, Harris and Conley appealed the case. Although the government insisted that the form of monetary transfer established that it was compensation, the appellant pointed out that it could just as easily have been an entitlement: "This form of payment . . . could be that of a dependent picking up regular support checks." The court finally agreed that it was a gift. Invoking legal precedent, the appeal successfully argued that "a person is entitled to treat cash and property received from a lover as gifts, as long as the relationship consists of something more than specific payments for specific sessions of sex." A number of Kritzik's letters to Harris were shown as evidence of his continuing affection and trust, such as "I love giving things to you and to see you happy and enjoying them."

What was the appeal's author doing? The attorney was demonstrating that distinctions between categories of payment, in this case between a gift and compensation, hinge on the type of relationship between the parties involved: lover–mistress vs. patron–prostitute. Of course, if Kritzik and Harris had been husband and wife, rather than lover and mistress, the transfers of money would have been tax-free domestic transactions.

Domestic transfers, however, are subject to their own forms of contention and definitional struggles. As Susan Rose-Ackerman (this volume) notes, the same parents who spend thousands of dollars for their children's education often balk at paying their children for shoveling snow or getting good grades. Such payments, she tells us, are considered inappropriate bribes. We might clarify her point as follows: Bribes are improper payments, either because they compensate the recipient for a performance not authorized by the relationship between payer and recipient or because they compensate the recipient for a performance the relationship requires without payment. Bribes fall into the portion of compensation territory that lies near the boundaries of entitlements and gifts. Indeed, payers of bribes often disguise them as entitlements and gifts. Similarly, tips cluster at the intersection of compensation, gift, and entitlement, with the services charge built into many European restaurant checks sweeping it across the frontier into compensation, the quarter given to the urchin who opens a taxi door for you qualifying as almost pure gift, and the holiday check to an apartment doorman bearing the strong odor of entitlement.

Let me take an example from my research on household economies (Zelizer 1994). At the turn of the century, as the consumer economy multiplied goods, at the same time the discretionary income of households rose, the proper definition, allocation, and disposition of family income became urgent and contested matters. A housewife's money became the most problematic currency, precisely because relations between wives and husbands were in transition and at issue. In middle-class households, where men earned the wages while their wives took over the shopping, the monetary transfer from husband's wage to wife's spending was undergoing a change of definition. Was it a gift, compensation, or entitlement? The nineteenth century gift method, in which husbands doled out money to their wives, became not only inefficient but also inappropriate in increasingly egalitarian marriages. But neither could the husband–wife monetary transfer be a compensation for the woman's household services. The law made sure to prevent that confusion. In her historical analysis of nineteenth century earnings statutes, Reva Siegel (1994) offers a powerful account of legal resistance to monetizing housework. While earnings statutes gave wives a right to income from their "personal labor" for third parties, they excluded the household labor performed for her husband or family. Courts, Siegel (1994, pp. 2139–40) tells us, "refused to enforce interspousal contracts for household labor, reasoning that such contracts would transform the marriage relationship into a market relationship."

In the first few decades of the twentieth century, the weekly or monthly allowance – an entitlement to a portion of the domestic income – was declared a more equitable and proper form of money income for wives than the gift method. Of course, allowances were in turn later condemned by the home-efficiency experts of the 1920s and 1930s as an unsatisfactory form of payment for modern wives. As the preferred relationship between husbands and wives changed, so did the preferred forms of payment.

What is at issue in these cases? What makes the payments contestable? Certainly not the amount of the payment, or the quid pro quo, or the principal or agent status of the recipient. It is the social relations between the parties involved that makes the crucial difference. The definitions of such social relations do not flow from the economic logic alone, but also from the histories and cultures in which they are embedded. This means of course that both the boundary lines and the relations among gift, compensation, and entitlement vary from one country and era to another. As Richard Biernacki's (1995) detailed analysis of differences between British and German systems of payment for work illustrates, compensation is just as subject to cultural variation as are gifts and entitlements (for a more general treatment of this question, see Zelizer 1996).

To take one extreme contrast from the realm of gifts, consider the anthropologist Maurice Bloch's account of the Merina in Madagascar, where a man is expected to give his lover, and often his own wife, a gift of money or goods after sexual intercourse. Prostitution does exist among the Merina, but what distinguishes it from other relations is not the object exchanged or the payment but the casualness of the relationship. For the Merina, Bloch (1989, p. 166) tells us, "the transfer of money in cash is not a sign defining the relationship involved."

In summary, the propriety and labeling of a payment depend very heavily on the social relation involved between payer and recipient and often third parties. Payments differ significantly in meaning according to such factors as duration, intimacy, and equality. Economists have commonly approached such interactions among values, institutions, and monetary transactions by searching for the hidden but precise exchanges of valued objects presumed to underlie them. A close examination of actual monetary payments, in their many subtle forms, suggests another strategy: a deliberate analysis of the culture and social relations that frame every human interchange.

REFERENCES

Biernacki, Richard (1995). *The Fabrication of Labor*. Berkeley: University of California Press.

Bloch, Maurice (1989). "The Symbolism of Money in Imerina," in Maurice Bloch and Jonathan Parry, eds., *Money and the Morality of Exchange*. New York: Cambridge University Press.

Siegel, Reva B. (1994). "The Modernization of Marital Status Law: Adjudicating Wives' Rights to Earnings, 1860–1930," *Georgetown Law Journal* 82: 2127–211.

Zelizer, Viviana A. (1994). *The Social Meaning of Money*. New York: Basic Books.

—— (1996). "Payments and Social Ties," *Sociological Forum* 11: 481–95.

# PART IV

# THE ORGANIZATION OF WORK, TRUST, AND INCENTIVES

CHAPTER 13

# How effective are trust- and reciprocity-based incentives?

*Ernst Fehr and Simon Gächter*

## 1    Introduction

In modern economics people are conceptualized as being rational and selfish. On the basis of assumptions of rationality and selfishness economists have constructed a remarkable body of theoretical knowledge that allows precise predictions in a wide variety of circumstances. However, there remains the question whether the exclusive reliance on rationality and selfishness is capable of explaining people's actual behavior. We are convinced that there are conditions in which standard economic theory predicts and explains behavior quite well. On the basis of our research, we also believe that there are important and identifiable conditions in which these assumptions lead to empirically false predictions and may, therefore, generate wrong normative advice.

In this chapter we argue that there is an important class of conditions in which predictions that are based on purely selfish behavior are systematically violated. Such conditions regularly arise when it is impossible to enforce agreements completely. Standard economic theory predicts that agreements that are not fully enforceable will never be concluded because at least one of the involved parties will not meet its obligations. But, in turn, this will in general induce the other parties not to meet their obligations. Since everybody will anticipate that the parties will not meet their contractually specified duties it makes no sense to conclude the contract in the first instance. The fact that under conditions of incom-

We gratefully acknowledge financial support from the Swiss National Science Foundation (NO. 12-43590.95) and very helpful research assistance by Martin Brown, Armin Falk, Urs Fischbacher, Jean-Robert Tyran, and Paolo Vanini. We thank J. Baron, D. Messick, A. E. Roth, A. Ben-Ner, L. Putterman, and an anonymous referee for valuable comments.

337

pletely enforceable contracts many agreements cannot or will not be concluded gives rise to severe efficiency losses.[1]

This conclusion is radically changed if one assumes that people do not always fully exploit their opportunities to violate agreements at the expense of others. It may then become rational to enter agreements that are *not* fully enforceable. The major aim of this chapter is to show that under well controlled laboratory conditions this is the rule rather than the exception. Moreover, our results indicate that these deviations from the standard predictions are closely related to the notion of trust and reciprocity.

## 2     Trust and reciprocity under incompletely enforceable contracts

In the following we outline our main arguments in the context of a simple labor contracting example. We would like to stress, however, that our argument is more general and also applies to contractual relations beyond the employment relationship.

Suppose that a firm stipulates a contract which specifies a wage $w$ and a required effort level $\hat{e}$. The firm has an enforcement technology that allows it to elicit *at most* an effort level of $e_0$ from selfish and rational workers. This means that, in case of $\hat{e} > e_0$, a worker who reduces effort below $\hat{e}$ will increase his net utility. Therefore, a rational profit maximizing firm who faces a selfish and rational worker cannot enforce $e > e_0$. How can the existence of reciprocity help the firm to elicit effort levels above $e_0$? To answer this question we have to define this term. Roughly speaking, reciprocity means that people respond to kind acts with kind behavior and if they are treated badly try to strike back. Moreover, they are willing to engage in such reciprocal behavior even if it is costly for them. To judge whether a certain behavior is kind or mean it is necessary to fix a reference standard. This standard may itself be affected by, e.g., the history of a relationship, the behavior in other similar relations, or the institutional environment.

For our present purposes it suffices to assume that the kindness of a certain contract offer $(w, \hat{e})$ is determined by the rent the worker receives from the firm. This rent is given by the utility from $(w, \hat{e})$ minus the opportunity costs of accepting $(w, \hat{e})$. If a worker is motivated by reciprocity considerations she will choose higher levels of $e$ in response to

---

[1] By efficiency we mean the total gains that arise from trading between two parties. Throughout the chapter the notion of efficiency is only applied to the bilateral case. Thus, we do not consider cases in which two parties (e.g., two duopolists) strike an agreement at the expense of third parties (e.g., consumers).

higher rents offered. Thus, by paying sufficiently high rents firms may be capable of eliciting effort levels above $e_0$. From a psychological perspective there may be several reasons for workers' willingness to respond reciprocally. According to equity theory (Adams 1963, 1965) people try to equalize the ratio of perceived inputs (e.g., effort) and outputs (e.g., the rent) from a trade with the ratio that prevails in a relevant reference trade. Therefore, if the perceived output (rent) from a trade increases, people tend to raise their input (effort). A different explanation for reciprocal behavior is put forward by Rabin (1993), who argues that people's behavior vis-à-vis others is partly determined by their interpretation of the intentions that drive the behavior of others. They reward good intentions and punish bad intentions. Since the payment of a high rent is naturally interpreted as an action that is driven by a friendly intention workers may well reward this intention by a high effort level.

In the preceding example the firm offers a contract $(w, \hat{e})$. Once the worker has accepted the contract she chooses the actual effort level. Now suppose that after a worker's effort choice a firm has the option to reward or punish a worker. Both rewarding and punishing are costly for the firm. A rational and selfish firm will, therefore, never punish or reward. However, if the firm, i.e., the person acting on behalf of the firm, is motivated by reciprocity considerations, it may well reward $e \geq \hat{e} > e_0$ and punish $e < \hat{e}$. As before there may be several reasons for a firm's willingness to respond reciprocally. Firms may reward or punish for the reasons put forward by equity theory or by Rabin. There may, however, also be a third reason that has to do with the fact that contractual agreements usually have some normative force. If a worker accepts a contract $(w, \hat{e})$ with $\hat{e} > e_0$ she agrees to provide $e = \hat{e}$ even though only $e = e_0 < \hat{e}$ is in her selfish interest. The mere fact that she accepts the offer $(w, \hat{e})$ may be perceived by both parties as a kind of obligation to provide $\hat{e}$. It seems, moreover, likely that the perception of an obligation is the stronger the higher the rent implied by $(w, \hat{e})$. Since the violation of an obligation is likely to provoke moralistic aggression the firm may well be willing to punish the underprovision of effort. Analogously, the overfulfillment of an obligation may well trigger sympathy and, hence, a reward.

There are thus several potential reasons for reciprocal behavior. Our question in this chapter, however, is whether reciprocal behavior is indeed sufficiently strong to improve the enforcement of agreements significantly. During the last ten to fifteen years many experiments and several questionnaire studies which suggest that reciprocal behavior is quite common have been conducted. As indicated by Fehr, Kirchsteiger, and Riedl (1993, 1998), Fehr et al. (1998), and Berg, Dickhaut, and McCabe (1995), people often respond reciprocally if they receive a gift (rent). People's propensity to strike back if they are badly treated is suggested by the results of ultimatum games (see Roth et al. 1991; Güth and Tietz 1990; Roth 1995; Camerer and Thaler 1995). Questionnaire studies conducted by Agell and Lundberg (1995), Bewley (1995), Blinder and Choi (1990), and Kahneman, Knetsch, and Thaler (1986) also show that ordinary people as well as personnel managers believe that fairness, work morale, and reciprocity considerations are very important determinants of people's conduct and, in particular, of workers' effort behavior.

The evidence cited suggests that reciprocal behavior might also be relevant in the context of contract enforcement. The results of our experiments indicate that this is indeed the case. The observed regularities provide rather strong support for the relevance of reciprocal behavior to the enforcement of agreements. Even among anonymous strangers reciprocal interactions constitute a powerful means for the elicitation of effort levels above $e_0$. Subjects in the role of firms persistently demanded $\hat{e} > e_0$. Moreover these demands were associated with an appeal to reciprocity. Firms offered higher rents if they demanded more effort. This trust in reciprocal responses was justified in the sense that workers' *actual* effort is, on average, also positively related to the rent offered. If firms have *no* opportunity to punish or reward workers' effort choice, the underprovision of effort is quite common although much smaller than predicted by the standard approach. However, if firms can punish or reward ex post they are capable of substantially reducing the frequency of shirking. In fact, under these circumstances excess effort $(e > \hat{e})$ was more often observed than shirking $(e < \hat{e})$.

In the remainder of this chapter we describe the experimental design (section 3) and our results (section 4) in more detail. Section 5 concludes with a summary and raises some questions that have to be addressed by future work.

## 3     Experimental design

In this section we describe our experimental design.[2] To test for the impact of trust and reciprocity on workers' performance we developed two treatments: a two-stage treatment, in which only workers had a possibility to reciprocate, and a three-stage treatment, in which both workers and firms[3] had the opportunity to behave reciprocally.

---

[2] Instructions are available on request.

[3] In the experiment we did not use the possibly value-laden terms "workers" and "firms," but called them "buyers" and "sellers," respectively. The whole experiment was framed in goods-market terms. When we speak of "firms" and "workers" we mean of course subjects acting in the roles of firms and workers. For expositional simplicity we stick to the terms "firm" and "worker".

## 3.1    *Common features in both treatments*

In total we conducted four experimental sessions (two sessions in both treatment conditions), which all took place at the University of Zurich in February 1996. Our subjects were students from the University of Zurich and the Federal Institute of Technology in Zurich. They were from different fields, yet no economists were among them. They were recruited via telephone calls to minimize the probability that subjects knew each other.[4] All of them received a show-up fee of 15 Swiss francs (about U.S.$12.5) plus their earnings in the experiment. During the experiment earnings where denoted in "points" and at the end of the experiment exchanged into Swiss francs with an exchange rate of 8 rappen (approximately 6 cents) per point.

The experiments were manually conducted and in all sessions we had eight workers and six firms, which were located in different rooms. In both treatments, at the very beginning of the experiment subjects were randomly allocated to rooms. After reading the instructions subjects had to answer a control questionnaire which tested their understanding of payoff calculations. We did not start an experiment before all subjects had correctly answered all questions. Both treatments involved a trial period which allowed subjects to become acquainted with the experimental procedures. To allow for learning and convergence we replicated the constituent stage games for an additional twelve periods. In all periods except the trial period subjects were paid according to the schedules detailed later.

## 3.2    *The two-stage treatment*

In both treatments the *first stage* was a posted-bid market. Firms posted an employment contract which consisted of a *wage* and a *desired effort level* $\hat{e}$.[5] Wages had to be integers between 0 and 100 and the available effort levels were between 0.1 and 1 with increments of 0.1 (see Table 1). In a given period each firm could offer only one employment contract; that is, each could employ only one worker. Firms made their decisions

---

[4]  At the end of the experiments we asked subjects about their knowledge of other participants. It turned out that almost all of them had never met another participant before.

[5]  In the experiments effort was framed as the "quality" of the experimental good and the term used for the desired effort level was "desired quality." We deliberately used goods-market terms instead of labor-market terms in the experimental instructions because we thought that labor-market terms might evoke more emotions and value-oriented behavior. Therefore, if trust and reciprocity show up in a goods-market framework we have a stronger result.

Table 1. *Effort levels and costs of effort*

| effort $e$ | 0.1 | 0.2 | 0.3 | 0.4 | 0.5 | 0.6 | 0.7 | 0.8 | 0.9 | 1 |
|---|---|---|---|---|---|---|---|---|---|---|
| costs of effort $c(e)$ | 0 | 1 | 2 | 4 | 6 | 8 | 10 | 12 | 15 | 18 |

privately but announced them publicly afterward. One experimenter in the firms' room wrote the offers on the blackboard whereas another experimenter listed the offers on a documentation sheet. After completion of all offers this documentation sheet was passed to the workers' room, where an experimenter wrote the offers on the blackboard in a randomly assigned order. This procedure was implemented to inhibit identification of firms. After all offers had been written on the blackboard, workers could choose among them in a randomly determined order. A worker could only accept one offer. As there were eight workers and six firms, we always had an excess supply of two workers. Therefore, in any period at least two workers could not or did not accept a contract.[6]

After the acceptance of offers the first stage was completed and the *second stage* started. Workers who had accepted an offer had to determine their *actual effort level*. A worker's choice of an effort level was associated with costs for the worker as indicated in Table 1. Of course, firms had the same effort levels available when choosing their desired effort, and they were informed about the associated costs for the worker. Table 1 was common knowledge. Workers privately determined their effort levels by inserting them into a decision sheet which was distributed to them at the beginning of the experiment. An experimenter collected the effort decisions and passed them to the firms' room. No worker was informed of the effort decision of fellow workers. Except the experimenter, only the firm with whom a worker concluded an employment contract was informed of the effort decision of the worker. However, firms were not informed of the identity of "their" worker.

Our second stage reflects a basic feature of most employment relationships, namely, the incompleteness of the labor contract. Workers in

---

[6] If, for example, the first six workers accepted an offer there were no available offers for the last two workers and, hence, they could not accept an offer. A worker was of course free to reject any available offer.

the real world almost always have considerable discretion in determining their actual effort.[7] Therefore, in our design firms could only stipulate a *desired* effort level without being able to enforce it (e.g., with the help of courts). The only effort level which was enforceable was the minimum effort level of 0.1.

After firms had been informed about the effort decision of their worker the second stage was completed and payoffs could be calculated. A worker's payoff at the end of the second stage was given by

$$u = w - c(e)$$

where $w$ denotes the accepted wage and $c(e)$ the costs of the worker's actual effort. If a worker did not trade, she earned nothing. A firm's payoff was given by

$$\pi = ve - w$$

where $v$ denotes a firm's redemption value. In all sessions $v$ was equal to 100.

It is immediately apparent from this payoff function and Table 1 that firms may suffer a (severe) loss if they offer a wage which is higher than 10 and if they get an actual effort level of 0.1.[8] We therefore gave subjects – in addition to their show-up fee – an endowment of 112.5 points. Hence, given our exchange rate, subjects had – together with their show-up fee – a total start-up endowment of 300 points. Subjects were told that if their total earnings (including the 300 points) became negative they would have to leave the experiment.[9] To prevent a loss of control over subjects' preferences (possibly because of feelings of envy) both workers and firms received 112.5 points as a start-up endowment. Because this is a lump-sum payment, marginal incentives are not affected.

Our research concerns the potential of trust and reciprocity in enhancing enforceable effort levels. As reciprocity means kindness to those who are kind to you and meanness to those who are mean to you, it requires the possibility of judging the generosity of an employment offer. Therefore, payoff functions were common knowledge.

[7] See for example the interview studies by Levine (1993) and Bewley (1995). In both studies the interviewed personnel managers pointed out the importance of "worker morale," which is only partly under a firm's control.

[8] Of course firms could avoid losses with certainty by offering a wage below 10.

[9] In fact, in our experiments not a single subject had a loss which would have forced him or her to leave the experiment.

## 3.3    *The three-stage treatment*

Notice that in our two-stage design it is basically the workers who have the opportunity to respond reciprocally to a firm's offer. However, most actual labor relations are long-term relationships and firms also have opportunities to react to a worker's effort decision. For example, firms usually have many possibilities to influence a worker's utility of a given job, e.g., promotion policies, access to fringe benefits, and social sanctioning. To prevent the problems of modeling a repeated game, we introduced a *third stage* into our design, in which firms had the opportunity to punish or to reward their worker at some cost. In particular, after having learned a worker's effort decision, a firm could choose a punishment/reward variable $p \in [-1, 1]$. Punishing ($p < 0$) or rewarding ($p > 0$) was costly for a firm. Only in the case of $p = 0$, i.e., when the firm neither rewards nor punishes, would no costs arise. A firm could only punish its worker if she had shirked. Likewise, rewarding was only possible if the worker chose at least the desired effort level. A punishment effected a reduction of a worker's gain at the end of the second stage by $25p$, whereas a reward gave the worker an additional payment of $25p$. The feasible punishment/reward levels as well as firm's costs are depicted in Table 2, which was common knowledge. Workers were privately informed about the punishment/reward choice of "their" firms. The payoffs at the end of the third stage were given by

$$u = w - c\left(e\right) + 25p$$

for a worker and by

$$\pi = 100e - w - k\left(p\right)$$

for a firm, where $k(p)$ denotes the firm's cost of punishing or rewarding.[10] To get some insight into workers' expectation formation when determining their actual effort at the second stage we asked workers in our three-stage treatment to insert into their decision sheet the *punishment/reward level they expect from their firm, given their effort decision*. Firms were not informed of the expected punishment/reward level.

In all other respects the first and the second stages were identical to our two-stage design. The Appendix summarizes our experimental procedure.

---

[10] In the experiment we called punishment and reward variables "negative" and "positive factors," respectively. Costs were framed as "costs of the factor." The payment to the worker was called "additional payment."

Table 2(a). *Punishment variable and costs of punishment for the firm*

| punishment variable | 0 | -0.1 | -0.2 | -0.3 | -0.4 | -0.5 | -0.6 | -0.7 | -0.8 | -0.9 | -1 |
|---|---|---|---|---|---|---|---|---|---|---|---|
| costs for firm $k(p)$ | 0 | 1 | 2 | 3 | 4 | 5 | 6 | 7 | 8 | 9 | 10 |

Note: The punishment levels -0.1 to -1 were only available to a firm if a worker had shirked, i.e., if the actual effort level fell short of the desired effort level $\hat{e}$.

Table 2(b). *Reward variable and costs of rewarding for the firm*

| reward variable | 0 | +0.1 | +0.2 | +0.3 | +0.4 | +0.5 | +0.6 | +0.7 | +0.8 | +0.9 | +1,0 |
|---|---|---|---|---|---|---|---|---|---|---|---|
| costs for firm $k(p)$ | 0 | 1 | 2 | 3 | 4 | 5 | 6 | 7 | 8 | 9 | 10 |

Note: The reward levels 0.1 to 1 were only available to a firm if a worker had chosen an actual effort level at least as high as the desired effort level $\hat{e}$.

## 4    Experimental results

In each of our two treatments there were in total 144 possible trades, of which 141 trades were realized in both treatments. The two-stage experiments lasted about 2.5 hours and the three-stage experiments about 3 hours. On average, a subject earned $48 in a two-stage and $58 in a three-stage session. In section 4.1 we describe our main results, which are followed by our results on effort elicitation in the two-stage treatment (section 4.2) and the three-stage treatment (section 4.3). Section 4.4 presents results on the distribution of incomes in our two treatments.

### 4.1    *Main results*

In our treatments the game-theoretic predictions are straightforward: In the two-stage treatment a worker will in each period choose the lowest possible effort level ($e = 0.1$), because higher effort levels are increasingly costly (see Table 1). Firms anticipate this effort choice and make a job offer with a desired effort of 0.1 and a zero wage. This prediction is not changed in the three-stage design, because the third stage only adds dominated strategies. To punish or to reward is a "noncredible threat," which, therefore, does not alter decisions at the first and the second stage of the game.

 In the following we confront these predictions with the results of our experiments. The first result concerns firms' *desired* effort levels, whereas the second result documents workers' *actual* effort decision.

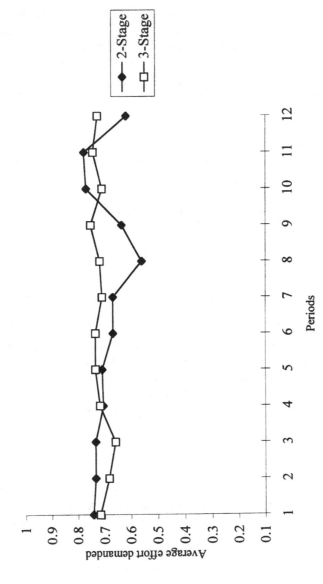

Figure 1. Firms' average desired effort in the two- and three-stage treatment

*Result 1: In the two- as well as in the three-stage treatment firms demand effort levels that are not incentive compatible.*

Figure 1 shows that desired effort levels are clearly above the theoretically predicted level of 0.1: On average firms demand an effort level of 0.70 in the two-stage treatment and of 0.72 in the three-stage treatment, with standard deviations of 0.25 and 0.13, respectively.[11] Moreover, in both treatments, firms' desired effort levels do not change very much over time. If anything, their desired effort level in the two-stage treatment is a bit more volatile than in the three-stage treatment. In addition, Figure 1 reveals that in both treatments there is clearly no convergence to the theoretically predicted level of 0.1. How successful were firms in the elicitation of actual effort levels? Our second main result shows that firms indeed succeeded in eliciting higher than incentive-compatible effort levels.

*Result 2: In the two- and in the three-stage treatment firms are capable of eliciting non-incentive-compatible effort levels.*

In the two-stage treatment firms were able to elicit an average actual effort level of 0.44 (with a standard deviation of 0.27), whereas in the three-stage treatment they could enforce an even higher mean actual effort level of 0.63 (standard deviation of 0.29). Figure 2 shows that actual effort levels as well do not converge to 0.1 even though in both treatments actual efforts are more volatile than desired effort levels.

Our third main result concerns the effectiveness of the third stage, which, from a game-theoretic point of view, should have no behavioral influence.

*Result 3: Actual effort is on average higher in the three-stage treatment compared to the two-stage treatment.*

This result confirms that the third stage is indeed behaviorally relevant. In the three-stage design firms can enforce effort levels which are on average 0.21 unit higher than in the two-stage treatment. This difference is significant at any conventional level (Mann-Whitney U test; trades as observations). Moreover, in the third stage shirking is considerably reduced compared to that in the second stage, as the following result shows.

---

[11] A Mann-Whitney U-test shows that the null hypothesis of equal means cannot be rejected at the 5 percent significance level. For a discussion of all nonparametric tests used in this chapter see Siegel and Castellan (1988).

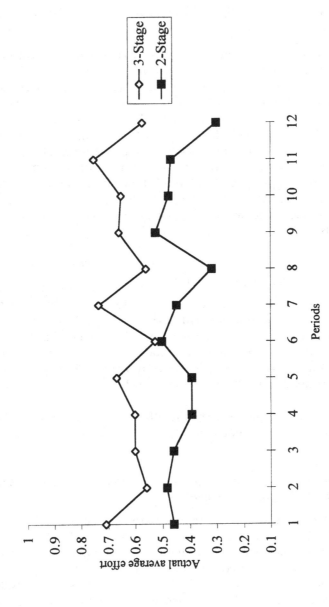

Figure 2. Workers' average actual effort in the two- and three-stage treatment

Table 3. *Effort behavior in the two- and three-stage treatment*

| treatment | No. trades | shirking $e < \hat{e}$ | | no shirking $e = \hat{e}$ | excess effort $e > \hat{e}$ | |
|---|---|---|---|---|---|---|
| | | % of trades with $e < \hat{e}$ | average amount of $(\hat{e}\text{-}e)$ | % of trades with $e = \hat{e}$ | % of trades with $e > \hat{e}$ | average amount of $(e\text{-}\hat{e})$ |
| 2-stage | 141 | 82.98 | 0.31 | 14.18 | 2.84 | 0.18 |
| 3-stage | 141 | 26.24 | 0.54 | 36.17 | 36.88 | 0.16 |

*Result 4: The existence of a third stage reduces shirking significantly and generates excess effort in many trades.*

This result follows from Result 3 and the fact that desired effort levels do not differ on average across treatments. To gain more insights into the effects of stage three we analyzed workers' effort behavior in more detail. Logically effort decisions fall into three categories: A worker has shirked (i.e., the actual effort $e$ fell short of the desired effort $\hat{e}$ [$e < \hat{e}$]), she has just delivered the desired effort ($e = \hat{e}$), or she has delivered a higher effort than asked for ($e > \hat{e}$). In Table 3 we discuss shirking behavior separately for each of these categories.

Table 3 reinforces Result 3. Shirking rates are considerably reduced in the three-stage treatment compared to the two-stage treatment. In the two-stage treatment we observed some shirking in 82.96 percent of all trades (with an average shirking of 0.31).[12] Excess effort was very rarely observed: Workers delivered an average excess effort of 0.18 (2.84 percent) in only 4 trades. No shirking was a bit more common: It occurred in 14.18 percent of all trades.

This picture is completely different in the three-stage treatment. Shirking occurred in considerably fewer trades than in the two-stage treatment. Workers only shirked in 26.24 percent of trades. Yet, if they shirked, the amount of shirking was larger than in the two-stage treatment. No shirking happened in 36.17 percent of the trades, and, what is particularly interesting, in 36.88 percent of trades we observed excess effort. In view of the already rather high levels of the desired effort this large number of excess effort choices is remarkable.

[12] Shirking behavior in the two-stage treatment may have been influenced by a subject's normative considerations of contract fulfillment. The fact that somebody accepted a contract renders it more difficult to behave opportunistically ex post. For psychological explanations of self-commitment see Cialdini (1993, chap. 3).

4.2    *Effort elicitation in the two-stage treatment*

Given our main results the question of how firms were able to enforce non-incentive-compatible effort levels arises. On the basis of evidence from previous research (Fehr, Kirchsteiger, and Riedl 1993; Fehr et al. 1998; Fehr, Gächter, and Kirchsteiger 1997) we believe that the impulse to behave reciprocally constitutes an important part of the answer to this question. For most human beings reciprocal responses are a "natural" part of their behavioral dispositions. To be kind (mean) to those who have been kind (mean) to us seems to be a natural behavioral response. Moreover, the higher the level of kindness that somebody experiences, the stronger will, in general, be the impulse to reciprocate.

To operationalize the concept of reciprocity it is of course necessary to define how kind or mean an action is. In our context the rent $\hat{u} = w - c(\hat{e})$ that is offered to the workers can be taken as an indicator of "generosity." The higher the rent $\hat{u}$, the kinder is the firm to the worker. The kindness of the worker is in turn indicated by the actual effort level. In our two-stage treatment reciprocity, therefore, means that workers choose higher effort levels if firms offer them higher rents. In addition, an appeal to workers' reciprocity requires that firms offer higher rents if they want to induce higher effort levels, i.e., if they desire a higher $\hat{e}$. This subsection investigates whether these predictions are met by the data. Our first result in this respect is related to firms' behavior.

*Result 5: Firms appeal to workers' reciprocity; i.e., the rent offered is positively related to the desired effort level in the two-stage treatment.*

Figure 3 shows the average offered rent for a given level of effort demanded in the two-stage treatment. The higher the desired effort level, the higher was on average the offered rent. This is also confirmed by the nonparametric Spearman rank-order test (correlation coefficient $\rho = 0.73$, $p < 0.001$).

Notice that this result means that firms overcompensate their workers. When they demand higher levels of $\hat{e}$ they increase the wage by more than the cost increase for the worker. This result directly contradicts the prediction of the theory of compensating wage differentials. Our next result confirms that the appeal to reciprocity was indeed a successful strategy.

*Result 6: Workers respond reciprocally; i.e., actual effort is positively related to the offered rent in the two-stage treatment.*

Figure 4 documents workers' average actual effort as a function of firms' offered rents (depicted in intervals of 5). It clearly shows a positive

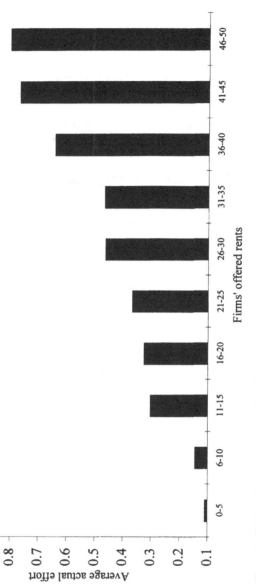

Figure 3. Workers' average actual effort given firms' offered rents

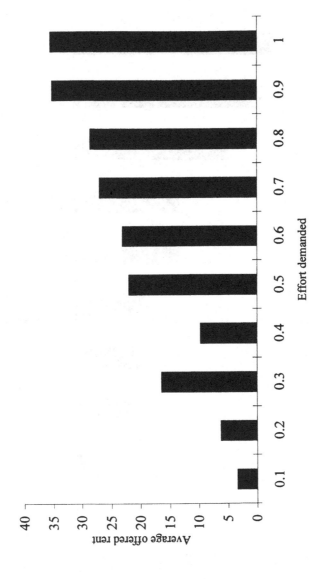

Figure 4. Firms' average offered rents per effort demanded

Table 4(a). *Firms' punishment/reward decision at stage three, given workers' effort decision*

| actual punishment/reward | shirking $e < \hat{e}$ 37 trades | no shirking $e = \hat{e}$ 51 trades | excess effort $e > \hat{e}$ 53 trades |
|---|---|---|---|
| $p < 0$ | 67.6 % (-0.71) | not possible | not possible |
| $p = 0$ | 32.4 % | 58.8 % | 29.7 % |
| $p > 0$ | not possible | 41.2 % (0.45) | 70.3 % (0.7) |

Note: Number in parentheses indicates average level of $p$.

relationship between offered rents and workers' actual effort. This is also confirmed by a Spearman rank correlation using trades as observations ($\rho = 0.67$, $p$-value < 0.001).

We now turn to the three-stage treatment, in which firms also have an opportunity to behave reciprocally, because they can punish or reward their worker for his or her effort decision.

### 4.3 Effort elicitation in the three-stage treatment

We have already seen in Results 3 and 4 that the third stage was quite effective with respect to the elicitation of effort levels. We now analyze the behavior of firms at stage three. Remember that from a game-theoretic point of view rational firms will never punish or reward, because this is costly for them; see Tables 2(a) and 2(b), respectively. The actual behavior of firms in our experiment, however, is succinctly summarized by our Result 7.

*Result 7: Firms behave reciprocally at stage three; i.e., they reward excess effort and punish shirking.*

We substantiate this result in two steps. In Table 4(a) we summarize firms' actual punishment/reward behavior given workers' effort decision at the second stage. We then discuss some regularities of firm behavior using nonparametric correlation analysis. Table 4(a) shows firms' punishment/reward behavior given workers' effort choices at stage two. In 37 trades workers have shirked, whereas in 51 trades workers have just delivered the desired effort. In 53 trades workers have delivered a higher effort than asked for.

Only in a case in which a worker has actually shirked did a firm have the possibility of punishing the worker by choosing $p < 0$; see Table 2(a). Firms punished shirking workers in 25 trades (67.6 percent) and chose an average punishment level of $-0.71$. In case workers did not shirk or even exerted an excess effort, firms had the possibility of rewarding the workers by choosing $p > 0$. In 70.3 percent of the trades in which workers delivered excess effort, firms actually rewarded their workers, by choosing on average $p = 0.7$. In both the shirking and excess effort cases the selfishly rational choice of $p = 0$ was taken in less than a third of these cases. Firms also rewarded workers (with an average of $p = 0.45$) in 42.5 percent of the no-shirking trades.[13]

Table 4(a) clearly substantiates the importance of firms' reciprocal behavior. Firms exhibited *positive reciprocity* when workers chose excess effort and *negative reciprocity* when workers shirked. Chi-square tests [which test the null hypotheses that $p < (>) 0$ is equally as likely as that $p = 0$ in the cases of shirking and excess effort, respectively] confirm that reciprocal behavior is more likely than the money maximizing choice of $p = 0$. In both cases the null hypothesis has to be rejected at conventional significance levels in favor of the alternative hypotheses, $p < 0$ and $p > 0$, respectively.[14]

As Result 6 shows, *workers'* behavior in the two-stage treatment shows clear regularity. Not only do they choose nonminimal effort levels in response to positive rents, but there is also a strong positive correlation between the actual effort and the rent level. Although Table 4(a) demonstrates the importance of firms' reciprocity, one may ask whether a similar regularity to that in workers' effort decisions shows up in firms' punishment/reward choice. In particular, we investigated whether

(i)   in case of shirking there is a negative relationship between the degree of shirking $(\hat{e} - e)$ and the level of punishment $(p \leqslant 0)$, and whether

(ii)  in case of excess effort there is a positive relation between the degree of excess effort $(e - \hat{e})$ and the level of reward $(p \geqslant 0)$.

According to Spearman rank-order tests using trades as observations the answer is clearly positive in the case of shirking. Firms punish more

---

[13] An interpretation of this behavior is that firms have rewarded workers for not exploiting their second mover advantage.

[14] In the case of no shirking the null hypothesis of an equal number of observations of $p = 0$ and $p > 0$, has to be rejected in favor of the alternative $p = 0$, which means that in the case of no shirking (but no excess effort) it is more likely to receive no reward.

Table 4(b). *Workers' expectation formation: Do they anticipate firms'*
*reciprocity?*

| expected punishment/reward | shirking $e < \hat{e}$ 37 trades | no shirking $e = \hat{e}$ 51 trades | excess effort $e > \hat{e}$ 53 trades |
|---|---|---|---|
| $p^e < 0$ | 54.1 % (-0.42) | not possible | not possible |
| $p^e = 0$ | 45.9 % | 37.3 % | 1.9 % |
| $p^e > 0$ | not possible | 62.7 % (0.36) | 98.1 % (0.64) |

Note: Number in parentheses indicates average level of $p^e$.

the higher the degree of shirking ($\rho = -0.49$, $p$-value < 0.001). In the case
of excess effort there is no such monotonic relation ($\rho = -0.07$, $p$-value =
0.339). However, if we restrict the analysis to cases in which firms
actually punish ($p < 0$) or reward ($p > 0$) firms clearly punish more the
higher the degree of shirking and reward more the higher the excess
effort ($\rho = -0.59$, $p$-value < 0.001, and $\rho = 0.41$, $p$-value < 0.001, respectively). We take this as further evidence for firms' reciprocal behavior at
stage three.

Next we ask whether workers' expectations concerning firms' punish-
ment/reward behavior are "rational" given firms' actual behavior at
stage three. Remember that we asked workers to report their expected
punishment/reward after making their effort decisions (see section 3.3).
Table 4(b) summarizes workers' expectations concerning firms' reciprocity. In those cases in which workers delivered an excess effort,
they expected in 98.1 percent of the trades that they would be
rewarded. In those trades they expected an average reward of 0.64.
Shirking workers expected only in 54.1 percent of the trades to be
punished (with an expected level of –0.42), whereas in 45.9 percent
of the trades they believed that their firm would choose $p = 0$.
According to a chi-square test one cannot reject the null hypothesis
that shirking workers regarded punishment and no punishment as
equally likely. Interestingly, however, workers who delivered exactly
the desired effort expected in almost two-thirds (62.7 percent) of
these trades that they would be rewarded (on average with 0.36).
A chi-square test reveals that reward is indeed regarded as more
likely than no reward in those trades in which workers delivered
$e = \hat{e}$.

To summarize, workers *correctly expected* that they would be rewarded in the case of excess effort. They were, however, too optimistic in the other cases. When they exactly met the effort requirement they too often expected a reward, and when they shirked they underestimated the actual number of trades in which they would be punished. One can also ask how "rational" workers' expectations were concerning the *level* of punishment or reward, respectively. A comparison of the excess effort columns of Table 4(a) and Table 4(b) reveals that on average workers expected a reward of 0.64. Actually they received an average reward of 0.55.[15] To test whether expected and actual reward levels are equal, we conducted a Mann-Whitney test. In this test we compared levels of *expected* reward with levels of *actual* reward over all periods. The results of these tests do not allow us to reject the null hypothesis that expected and actual reward levels are equal ($p$-value = 0.5644). In other words, workers not only correctly expected rewards but also anticipated actual *levels* of firms' reward choices.[16]

In the case of shirking, however, the Mann-Whitney test reveals that shirking workers underestimated not only firms' propensity to punish shirking behavior at all, but also the level of actual punishment. In particular, the null hypothesis that expected and actual levels of punishment are equal has to be rejected in favor of the alternative hypothesis that actual punishment is more severe than expected punishment ($p$-value = 0.0109).

We summarize our findings about workers' expectations in the following.

*Result 8: Workers correctly anticipate firms' rewards but underestimate firms' willingness to punish shirking.*

### 4.4    *Do "noncredible" threats affect the distribution of income?*

The opportunity for firms to punish or reward their workers at stage three is, in the absence of reciprocity considerations, an irrelevant option. It constitutes, so to speak, a noncredible threat that should not affect behavior in a systematic way. As a consequence it should leave the distribution of earnings unaffected. Yet, our results show that this prediction of the standard model is clearly violated.

---

[15] Firms who rewarded workers for their excess effort chose on average $p = 0.7$. In 29.7 percent of trades with excess effort firms did not reward; i.e., they chose $p = 0$; see Table 4(a). The average reward level was 0.55.

[16] Of course, there remains the possibility of a type II error.

Table 5. *Realized gains from trade*

| treatment | firms | workers | sum |
|-----------|-------|---------|------|
| 2-stage   | 994   | 4398    | 5392 |
| 3-stage   | 4509  | 3067    | 7576 |

*Result 9: In the two-stage treatment workers earn on average more than firms while the opposite holds in the three-stage treatment.*

This result is best illustrated in Table 5, which shows total effective earnings in experimental money units over all twelve periods of workers and firms, respectively. In the three-stage treatment firms are considerably better off than in the two-stage treatment and better off than workers. For workers the opposite is true: They are in a better position in the two-stage treatment than in three-stage treatment and earn less than firms in the three-stage treatment. The total of realized gains from trade, however, is considerably higher in the three-stage treatment than in the two-stage treatment.

Figures 5(a) and 5(b) illustrate these facts by showing periodwise profits in the two treatments. From this we conclude that threats that are not credible in the absence of reciprocity are indeed capable of affecting the distribution of income when people are motivated by reciprocity considerations. Contrary to what the standard model predicts, having the "last word" is a valuable option in our experiments.

## 5        Interpretation and concluding remarks

The data of our experiments exhibit a pattern that clearly violates the predictions of the standard approach and that is in accordance with a reciprocity-based approach. Firms persistently offer contracts with large rents and non-incentive-compatible effort requirements. In the two-stage design they try to elicit workers' reciprocal responses by offering higher rents when they desire higher effort levels. Workers, in turn, behave reciprocally by choosing higher effort levels in cases in which they are offered higher rents. Workers underprovide effort relative to $\hat{e}$, but this underprovision is much smaller than predicted by the standard approach. In the three-stage design we observe that firms respond reciprocally and that workers (partly) anticipate firms' responses correctly. Moreover, firms' opportunity to punish and reward has a large effect on workers' shirking behavior. In many instances workers even overprovide effort to elicit rewards.

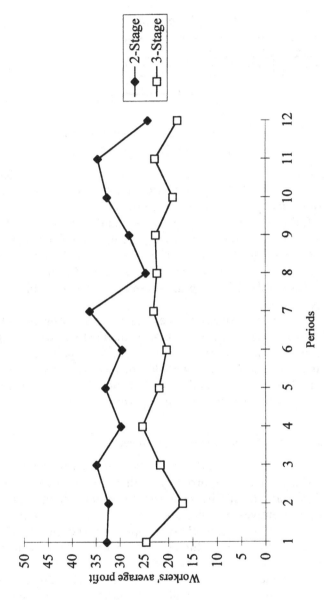

Figure 5(a). Worker's profit in the two- and three-stage treatment

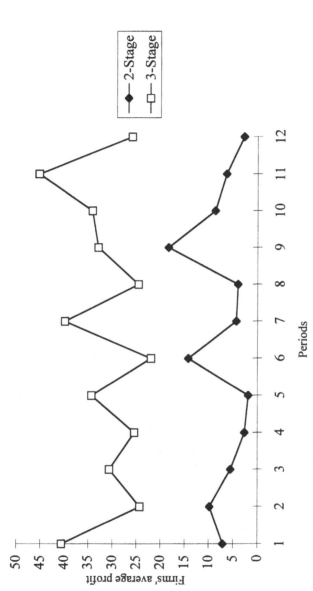

Figure 5(b). Firms' profit in the two- and three-stage treatment

These results indicate that, on average, both firms and workers try to elicit reciprocal responses. They anticipate such responses and, given the opportunity, themselves respond reciprocally. Overall these behavioral and experimental patterns result in a large increase in the total gains from trade relative to the standard prediction.

According to our interpretation the data indicate a true willingness to pay for reciprocity; that is, subjects exhibit a preference for acting reciprocally. An important objection to our interpretation concerns the fact that we had twelve market periods in each treatment. In principle, this could create opportunities for strategic and reputational spillovers across periods. However, we have taken great care in preventing such spillovers by enforcing strict anonymity between trading partners. Because of our anonymity requirements it was definitely impossible in our design that *individual* firms or workers developed a reputation. Nor was it possible that the actions of any *specific* firm or worker in previous periods could be rewarded in the present period.

A firm could, for example, not reward a high effort in period $t$ by a high job rent offer in period $t + 1$ because it did not know the worker's identity in period $t$; nor could the firm address the offer in $t + 1$ to any specific worker. Nonetheless, in case that firms – for whatever reason – respond to high effort in $t$ with high rent offers in $t + 1$ workers' effort choices could be interpreted as an investment in *group* reputation. A worker who chooses high effort levels would then provide a public good because he induces firms to make generous offers to the group of workers. This behavior is, of course, also incompatible with conventional theory because it requires nonselfish cooperation among workers. Moreover, as we will argue, the desire to establish a group reputation through nonselfish cooperation among workers cannot account for one of the major regularities of our data, that is, for reciprocal effort choices.

In our view, the fact that workers respond reciprocally to the *current* job rent is evidence against the group reputation hypothesis. Suppose, for a moment, that firms respond positively to last period's effort. Under these conditions workers should *not* respond reciprocally to the current job rent if they want to induce high future rents. If they choose low effort levels in response to low current job rents they cause low rent offers in the next period which (in the case of reciprocal effort choices) give rise to low future offers, etc. Thus, the desire to induce high future job rents by high present effort levels requires *unconditionally* high effort levels, which are, however, not observed.

An additional argument against the group reputation hypothesis arises from the evolution of effort over time. Since toward the end of the experiment the value of a group reputation decreases continuously we should observe that effort levels converge toward the minimum level of $e = 0.1$. As Figure 2, however, shows, there is no such downward trend. Even in the final period the average effort is significantly above the minimum effort level. Therefore, the data do not support the group reputation hypothesis.

Further evidence against the group reputation hypothesis comes from a series of experiments conducted by Fehr, Kirchler, Weichbold, and Gächter (FKWG) (1998). In their paper the results of a one-shot reciprocity treatment are reported. The FKWG design has the following features: Ten firms interact with ten workers over ten periods, but each firm is matched bilaterally with each worker only once. This matching procedure is common knowledge. A firm makes a wage proposal to a worker. If the worker accepts he has to choose effort and bears costs $c(e)$ according to Table 1. If he rejects the offer, both players earn zero. Because of the one-shot nature of these experiments it never pays for a subject to invest anything in group reputation. FKWG also conducted competitive market experiments with reciprocation opportunities (like our two-stage treatment) to allow for a comparison of the bilateral one-shot experiments with the competitive market experiments. Their results indicate that workers also respond reciprocally in a one-shot situation. Workers' response pattern in the one-shot situation is rather similar to their behavior in a competitive market with reciprocation opportunities. This indicates that group reputation is – if at all – not very important in the competitive market with reciprocation opportunities.

In our view the regularities of our data indicate that the neglect of reciprocal behavior may induce economists to make wrong predictions. Moreover, they may give wrong advice regarding the design of contracts and institutions. It may well be that, instead of aiming at stronger pecuniary incentives, or improving the enforcement technology, increasing the scope for reciprocal interactions is a better or an equally good means to improve the performance of agents. Likewise, it may turn out that traditional pecuniary incentives are in conflict with reciprocal incentives. Strengthening of pecuniary incentives may weaken reciprocal incentives and vice versa. An example for this is provided by Fehr, Gächter, and Kirchsteiger (1997). They report the results of experiments that are similar to the ones discussed in this chapter. The experiments differ, however, in one important respect. In Fehr, Gächter, and Kirchsteiger (1997) firms could credibly threaten ex ante to fine shirking workers. That is, their contract offers could condition wage reductions on the verifiable underprovision of effort. It turns out that in the two-stage design the opportunity of explicitly threatening a fine leads to *lower* effort levels. Thus, it seems that the introduction of traditional pecuniary incentives into a reciprocal relationship may weaken *total* incentives for effort provision. Of course, more evidence is needed. But the strong patterns of reciprocal behavior in our data suggest that the interaction between pecuniary incentives and incentives for reciprocal behavior deserves further empirical and theoretical study. A very good example for theoretical progress in this area is Rabin's (1993) model of fairness.

## Appendix: A summary of our experimental procedure

Worker and firms in two different rooms; 12 periods plus a trial period

*1st stage:*

1. Firms choose wage $w \in [0, 100]$ and desired effort $\hat{e} \in [0.1, 1]$.
2. Workers accept in randomly determined order.

*2nd stage:*

3. Workers privately determine actual effort $e \in [0.1, 1]$.
3'. *(In three-stage design only)* Worker privately states expected punishment/reward level.
4. Firm is privately informed about the worker's actual effort level.

Payoffs are calculated in the two-stage treatment.

*3rd stage:*

5. Firm privately chooses punishment/reward level $p \in [-1, 1]$.
6. Worker is privately informed about the punishment/reward level.

Payoffs are calculated in the three-stage treatment.

REFERENCES

Adams, J. St. (1963). "Wage Inequities, Productivity and Work Quality," *Industrial Relations* 3: 9–16.
———(1965). "Inequity in Social Exchange," in Leonhard Berkowitz, ed., *Advances in Experimental Psychology* 2, pp. 267–99. New York: Academic Press.
Agell, J., and P. Lundberg (1995). "Theories of Pay and Unemployment: Survey Evidence from Swedish Manufacturing Firms," *Scandinavian Journal of Economics* 97: 295–308.

Berg, J., J. Dickhaut, and K. McCabe (1995). "Trust, Reciprocity and Social History", Games and Economic Behavior 10, 122–42.

Bewley, T. (1995). "A Depressed Labor Market as Explained by Participants," *American Economic Review* (Papers and Proceedings) 85: 250–54.

Blinder, A., and D. Choi (1990). "A Shred of Evidence on Theories of Wage Stickiness," *Quarterly Journal of Economics* 105: 1003–16.

Camerer, C., and R. Thaler (1995). "Ultimatums, Dictators, and Manners," *Journal of Economic Perspectives* 9: 209–19.

Cialdini, R. (1993). *Influence: The Psychology of Persuasion.* New York: William Morrow.

Fehr, E., S. Gächter, and G. Kirchsteiger (1997). "Reciprocity as a Contract Enforcement Device: Experimental Evidence," *Econometrica* 65(4): 833–60.

Fehr, E., G. Kirchsteiger, and A. Riedl (1993). "Does Fairness Prevent Market Clearing? An Experimental Investigation," *Quarterly Journal of Economics* 108(2): 437–60.

Fehr, E., G. Kirchsteiger, and A. Riedl (1998). "Gift Exchange and Reciprocity in Competitive Experimental Markets," *European Economic Review*, 42, 1–34.

Fehr, E., E. Kirchler, A. Weichbold, and S. Gächter (1998). "When Social Norms Overpower Competition – Gift Exchange in Experimental Labour Markets," *Journal of Labor Economics*, 16, 324–51.

Güth, Werner, and Reinhard Tietz (1990). "Ultimatum Bargaining Behavior – a Survey and Comparison of Experimental Results," *Journal of Economic Psychology* 11: 417–49.

Kahneman, D., J. Knetsch, and R. Thaler (1986). "Fairness as a Constraint on Profit Seeking: Entitlements in the Market," *American Economic Review* 76(4): 728–41.

Levine, D. (1993). "Fairness, Markets, and Ability to Pay: Evidence from Compensation Executives," *American Economic Review* 83: 1241–59.

Rabin, M. (1993). "Incorporating Fairness into Game Theory and Economics," *American Economic Review* 83: 1281–1302.

Roth, A. E. (1995). "Bargaining Experiments," in A. E. Roth and J. H. Kagel, eds., *Handbook of Experimental Economics.* Princeton, N.J.: Princeton University Press.

Roth, A. E., V. Prasnikar, M. Okuno-Fujiwara, and S. Zamir (1991). "Bargaining and Market Behavior in Jerusalem, Ljubljana, Pittsburgh, and Tokyo: An Experimental Study," *American Economic Review* 81: 1068–95.

Siegel, S., and N. J. Castellan, Jr. (1988). *Nonparametric Statistics for the Behavioral Sciences.* New York: McGraw-Hill.

CHAPTER 14

# Worker trust, system vulnerability, and the performance of work groups

*Andrew Schotter*

## 1    Introduction

Economists and social psychologists have struggled long and hard in an effort to understand the characteristics of situations in which workers will act cooperatively in the workplace instead of shirk. Like all public goods problems, the temptation to free ride on the effort of others is many times too tempting for workers, and once shirking begins, it snowballs through the organization. But such low effort outcomes need not and do not always occur. The puzzle for us to unravel is why, in some organizations, are groups successful in selecting the high effort equilibrium while in others shirking is the commonly established norm?

It is our claim that economic systems are characterized by two properties which determine their success. One is a characteristic of the workers functioning in the system and the norms of work they have established among themselves. The other is a property of the incentive structure defined, either implicitly or explicitly, by the economic system itself. It is the match between these norms and the characteristics of the incentive program imposed on the group that is the key ingredient in determining whether an incentive system works well.

More precisely, most incentive systems define games for workers to play in which there is both strategic and stochastic uncertainty. For example, in target based group incentive systems, like profit sharing, where the group's output must equal or exceed a target before the group is able to realize the full benefits of their work, workers face the prospect of working hard only to find out that, because either others have shirked

The author would like to thank the Davidson Institute for their financial support in writing this chapter. In addition, he would like to thank the C. V. Starr Center for Applied Economics at New York University for their technical assistance. The research support of Jeff Davis and Alan Corns is greatly appreciated, as are the comments of Louis Putterman, Avner Ben-Ner, Barry Nalebuff, who pointed out an oversight in an earlier version, and Jonathan Baron.

or a negative stochastic shock to output has occurred, the target has not been met. Those who worked hard find themselves vulnerable to the laziness of others. This vulnerability, however, could be overcome by a group of workers if, depending on their history together and the work norm they have developed, they trust each other and have some faith that each will try hard to achieve the target. Hence, trust and vulnerability must be matched with each other in order to have a group or economic system perform well.

It is this match between the trust that a group of workers have developed among themselves and the vulnerability of the economic system they are functioning under that we investigate in the experiments to be reported on here. What we find is that the match between vulnerability and trust is a key ingredient in what makes a group of workers work well together along with the type of coordination problem that is created by the equilibrium of the incentive scheme.

In this chapter we will proceed as follows: In section 2 we will present our definition of the "vulnerability" of an incentive system in terms of the vulnerability of the Nash equilibrium of the game it defines. In section 3 we present our experimental design aimed at inducing different levels of trust and controlling for different levels of vulnerability among the subjects and games we have them play. In section 4 we present the results of our experiment. This is first done descriptively and then more formally by presenting a set of formal hypotheses to be tested. Section 5 presents some conclusions.

## 2      Vulnerability and trust

### 2.1     *Vulnerability*

Vulnerability is a concept which attempts to capture what we consider to be the riskiness of a mechanism's equilibrium. It is our feeling that incentive mechanisms which hold out the prospect of workers' being severely hurt financially when they put out high effort levels while others shirk are unlikely to elicit such equilibrium effort levels from their workers.[1]

---

[1] There has been a great deal of experimental evidence presented recently by Van Huyck et al. (1991, 1990) and Cooper et al. (1989) that the riskiness of an equilibrium and the out-of-equilibrium payoffs it determines when one's opponents tremble or make mistakes can have a dramatic effect on the likelihood that that equilibrium will be realized in any play of the game. Van Huyck et al. (1992) and Brandts and MacLeod (1991) even present evidence that an outside arbiter, with the power to suggest equilibria, may have a difficult time getting experimental subjects to coordinate on Pareto-dominant equilibria if those equilibria are too risky.

To define our concept of the vulnerability of an equilibrium more precisely consider two group incentive plans, denoted plan A and plan B. It should be noted that each such plan defines a game for economic agents to play in which their strategies are their effort levels and their payoffs are defined by the group incentive formula and depend on their own effort levels and those of their colleagues. (In the plan we investigate, the payoff to one agent depends on his effort level and the *sum* of the effort levels of his colleagues at work.) For the sake of argument say that both group incentive schemes have two equilibria in the games they define, a unique and symmetric *low effort* equilibrium (which we will assume involves complete shirking and zero effort levels) and a unique and symmetric *high effort* interior equilibrium. (By interior equilibrium we mean an equilibrium in which workers are choosing efforts in the interior of their feasible effort level sets and in which the probability of reaching the target is strictly less than 1. We will also define vulnerability for games in which the equilibrium is asymmetric and dictates that targets are met with surety, but the intuition of our vulnerability concept is most easily described for the interior unique-symmetric equilibrium case, and it is relatively easy to extend the intuition to the multiple equilibrium asymmetric case.)

Since their payoffs are greatest at the high effort equilibrium workers would like to see this equilibrium chosen. It is our contention, however, that the likelihood such an equilibrium will actually materialize depends on its vulnerability. To define vulnerability we ask the following question: If agent $i$, an individual agent in the organization, were to play according to the high effort equilibrium and put out a high level of effort (with an associated high level of disutility or cost) how fast would his payoff fall if others decreased their effort levels below that associated with the high effort equilibrium? If agent $i$'s payoff would everywhere fall more steeply under plan A than under plan B, for identical reductions in others' efforts, we say that player $i$ is more vulnerable at the equilibrium of plan A than plan B. More simply, people may be reluctant to choose the high effort equilibrium under plan A if they fear that even a small amount of shirking by their peers will have disastrous consequences for their payoff – they are vulnerable at the equilibrium. The problems associated with such strategic vulnerability are generally compounded when there is a stochastic element affecting the group revenue function itself.

More formally, let us denote the payoff function to agent $i$ in a group incentive program as $\pi_i(e_i, \Sigma e_{-i})$ where $e_i$ is the effort level of agent $i$ and $\Sigma e_{-i}$ is the sum of effort levels for all agents in the group other than $i$. Note that all group incentive plans discussed in this chapter have symmetric and anonymous payoff functions of this type in the sense that a player's payoff is a function only of his effort level and the *sum* of the efforts of others in the group. The identity of who puts out what effort is not important. Consider now incentive plans A and B and consider the payoffs $\pi_i^A(e_i^*, \Sigma e_{-i}^*)$ and $\pi_i^B(e_i^*, \Sigma e_{-i}^*)$ that each agent gets at the high effort interior equilibrium of each plan, which we will assume exists and is unique and symmetric across agents. Looking at $\pi_i^A(e_i^*, \Sigma e_{-i})$ and $\pi_i^B(e_i^*, \Sigma e_{-i})$ as a function of $\Sigma e_{-i}$ (holding $e_i$ at its high effort Nash equilibrium level $e_i^*$), we say that player $i$ is more vulnerable at the high effort Nash equilibrium of plan A than plan B if $\pi_i^A(e_i^*, \Sigma e_{-i})$ is everywhere below $\pi_i^B(e_i^*, \Sigma e_{-i})$ over the domain of the function from $\Sigma e_{-i}^*$ to 0.

The preceding definition of vulnerability is absolute in the sense that it does not judge the vulnerability of the equilibrium choice of a mechanism in comparison to other choices the agent could make. We might want to take these other choices into account, however, since the decision to adhere to a high effort equilibrium might depend on an agent's other options in the organization. For example, say that a mechanism has two equilibria, one a "good" high effort interior equilibrium and one a "bad" shirking equilibrium or even, perhaps, a secure minimax payoff (in the schemes we investigate here, secure payoffs are achieved by behavior consistent with the "bad" equilibrium – by shirking completely). Let the low Nash or secure payoff be $\pi_i$ (low) and the payoff at the good equilibrium be $\pi_i$ (high). Returning to our functions $\pi_i^A(e_i^*, \Sigma e_{-i})$ and $\pi_i^B(e_i^*, \Sigma e_{-i})$ find, for each function, that $\Sigma e_{-i}$ which equates $\pi_i(e_i^*, \Sigma e_{-i})$ with $\pi_i$ (low). $\Sigma e_{-i}^* - \Sigma e_{-i}$ would then measure the amount that others in a group could fall below their Pareto optimal equilibrium effort before player $i$ would be better off at his or her secure or low Nash payoff level. Defining $D^{*A}$ and $D^{*B}$ to be these deviations, we say that player $i$ is more vulnerable at the high effort Nash equilibrium of plan or mechanism $A$ than mechanism $B$ if $D^{*A} < D^{*B}$. In other words, under plan $A$ player $i$ is more vulnerable than under plan $B$ if smaller deviations away from the Pareto optimal level by other agents would yield a payoff equal to the secure or low Nash payoff of the mechanism. In short, we would expect that agents using plan $B$ would be more likely to choose the good equilibrium since they are better off at it than they are at the low equilibrium for a larger set of deviations by their group members. Note, however, that this definition does not take the levels of these payoffs into account, so one might want to normalize these payoffs in some manner.

To illustrate these two vulnerability concepts, consider two hypothetical incentive schemes ($A$ and $B$) which define two games each with a symmetric high effort interior equilibrium each with identical payoffs.

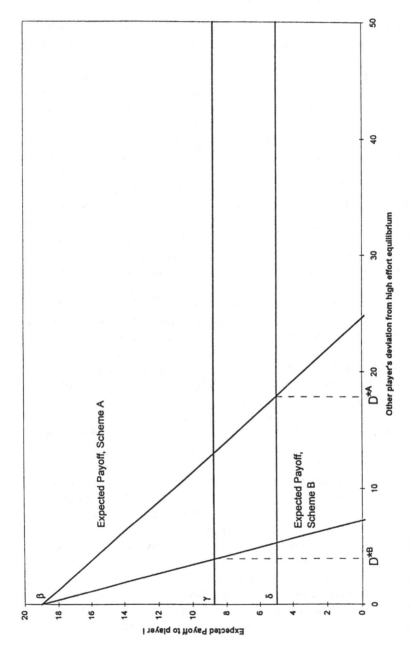

Figure 1. Vulnerability

Such a situation might be depicted by Figure 1, which places the payoff to any agent $i$ who adheres to the high effort equilibrium (i.e., set his/her effort level at the effort level dictated by the symmetric high effort equilibrium) on the vertical axis and places the sum of the deviations of the other agents from the high effort equilibrium on the horizontal axis.

Point $\beta$ obviously represents the payoff to agent $i$ at the high effort Nash equilibrium of both schemes since at $\beta$ all other agents are adhering to these equilibria as well (deviations are zero). The two straight lines emanating from $\beta$ define the payoff to agent $i$ under the two incentive schemes as the other agents deviate and choose effort levels below the equilibrium levels.

As we can see, according to our first vulnerability definition, the high effort equilibrium for scheme $B$ is more vulnerable than that of scheme $A$ since the expected payoff function for scheme $B$ is everywhere below that of scheme $A$. If we let $\gamma$ and $\delta$ be the secure payoffs that agents can guarantee themselves in schemes $B$ and $A$, respectively, then we see that again the high effort equilibrium of scheme $B$ is more vulnerable than that of scheme $B$ since $D^{*A} > D^{*B}$, meaning that it would take a larger deviation of effort away from the high effort equilibrium for agents in scheme $A$ than scheme $B$ in order to make agents regret they had selected the high effort equilibrium.

While for purposes of exposition these concepts have been defined for symmetric interior equilibria, in our experiments we have employed incentive schemes in which the equilibria are potentially asymmetric corner equilibria. After specifying the exact schemes used, we will redefine our vulnerability concepts appropriately.

To make this discussion more concrete, consider the following profit sharing incentive scheme for a group with six workers which we used in our experiment. Under this scheme each worker chooses an effort level which we will represent as a choice of a number in the closed interval $e_i \in [0, 100]$. The output of the group, $Y$, is the sum of the efforts chosen by the members of the group plus a random shock drawn from a uniform distribution with support $[-a, +a]$. When the group output is produced we can assume it is sold for a price of \$1.5 so that group revenue is $R = \$1.5Y$. Given this setup, a profit sharing group incentive scheme defines a target $R^*$ and a penalty wage for each worker $B$ such that if the revenue of the group is greater than $R^*$ the workers divide all of this revenue among them equally while if it is less than $R^*$ each worker gets $B$.

More formally, the payoff to workers under this kind of forcing contract scheme is defined as follows:

$$\pi_i = \begin{cases} \left[ 1.5\left( \sum_1^6 e_i + \epsilon \right) \middle/ 6 - e_i^2/100 \right] & \text{if} \quad 1.5\left( \sum e_i + \epsilon \right) \geq R^* \\ B & \text{otherwise} \end{cases} \tag{1}$$

Such forcing contracts have many Nash equilibria, each characterized by a different $Y^* - B$ pair. To find these Nash equilibria, let $P(e_i, \Sigma_{j\neq i} e_{-i})$ denote the probability that a group meets its target of $Y^*$ given an effort level of $e_i$ by agent $i$ and $\Sigma_{j\neq i} e_{-i}$ by the other agents excluding $i$. Note that for a fixed $e_i$ and $\Sigma_{j\neq i} e_{-i}$, the expected value of the firm's output, conditional on meeting the target, is

$$E\left(Y|Y > Y^*\right) = \frac{\left( e_i + \sum_{j\neq i} e_j + Y^* + a \right)}{2} \tag{2}$$

where the constant $a$ represents half of the support of the random variable $\epsilon$.[2]

Consequently each worker faces a payoff function of

$$\pi_i\left( e_i, \sum_{j\neq i} e_j \right) = B + P\left( e_i, \sum_{j\neq i} e_j \right) \times$$
$$\left[ \frac{(1.5/6)\left( e_i + \sum_{j\neq i} e_j + Y^* + a \right)}{2} - B \right] - \frac{e_i^2}{100} \tag{3}$$

For a Nash equilibrium the following first-order condition must hold for each $i$:

---

[2] This expression is derived as follows: Assume that the sum of the effort levels for the agents is $\Sigma_i e_i$. (Assume that $\Sigma_i e_i$ is large enough that for some subset of positive random realizations of $\epsilon$ the target can be met or surpassed.) The expression tells us what the expected output of the group will be conditional on meeting the target. Since $\Sigma_i e_i$ is the sum of the efforts of agents we know that the maximum effort possible is $\Sigma_i e_i + a$, where $a$ is the largest positive random shock. The lowest possible observable output that meets the target is $Y^*$. Since the shocks are uniformly distributed, asking what the expected output of the group will be conditional on the target being surpassed is equivalent to asking what is the expected value of a uniform random variable defined over $[Y^*, \Sigma_i e_i + a]$, which is what the expression defines.

$$\frac{\partial \pi_i}{\partial e_i} = -P'(\cdot)B + P'(\cdot)\left[\frac{1.5}{6}\left(\frac{e_i + \sum_{j \neq i} e_j + a + Y^*}{2}\right)\right]$$

$$+ P(\cdot)(0.125) - \frac{2e_i}{100} = 0, \quad i = 1, 2, \ldots, 6 \tag{4}$$

However, given our parameters no Nash equilibrium can entail effort levels such that $(\Sigma_i e_i - Y^* + a)/(2a) \geq 1$ since beyond this point the probability of reaching the target is 1 and any agent could increase his payoff by reducing his effort, thereby saving on effort cost with no reduction in the probability of reaching the target. Hence we must supplement the first-order condition with the preceding constraint.

In one of the experiments we ran we set $a = \pm 40$, $B = 5$, while in the other we set $a = \pm 10$ and $B = 8.75$. As Appendix A demonstrates, these profit sharing schemes have multiple asymmetric equilibria, all of which entail meeting the target with probability 1. In the first, ±40, any effort levels summing to 280 in which all agents select effort levels from the interval [45.625, 46.875] define a high effort equilibrium (with a symmetric equilibrium of 46.66), while in the second scheme any set of effort levels adding up to 250 in which all agents choose in the interval [12.5, 73.314] is an equilibrium with a symmetric equilibrium of 41.66. In both experiments there exists a zero effort equilibrium as well.

Note that these two schemes pose very different coordination problems for their agents to solve. In the ±10 high vulnerability experiment there is a wide variety of behavior that is consistent with the high effort equilibrium with effort levels varying from 12.5 to 73.314. The only problem remaining is one of coordinating who is going to choose a high and who a low effort level if the symmetric equilibrium is not selected. In the ±40 low vulnerability experiment the range of high effort equilibrium behaviors is severely limited to [45.625, 46.875]. Such differences should make it easier to achieve a high effort equilibrium in the ±40 case, and that is what we in fact see in our data.

To investigate the vulnerability of the equilibria of these profit sharing schemes consider Figure 2, which is the analogue of Figure 1, except that in these games we have multiple asymmetric equilibria. For each specification of our profit sharing scheme we have two payoff functions depicting the payoff to a player in either scheme as the others in the group deviate from the high effort equilibrium. Since there are multiple

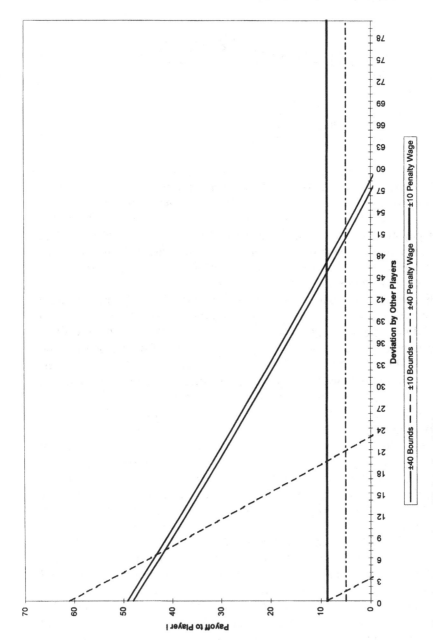

Figure 2. Asymmetric equilibria vulnerabilities

equilibria here involving asymmetric behavior of agents, we no longer have a single function depicting the payoff for any agent given the choice of the high effort equilibrium. Rather we have a continuum of such functions, each conditional on a specific effort level chosen by the agent. For either scheme, the line farthest to the right is the payoff function for an agent in such a scheme when he/she is adhering to the equilibrium but at the lowest effort consistent with it (i.e., for an agent choosing $e_i = 12.5$ or 45.625 in the $a = \pm10$ and $a = \pm40$ cases, respectively). The line closest to the origin for either scheme represents the same functions for an agent using the highest effort level consistent with that equilibrium (i.e., for an agent choosing $e_i = 73.314$ and 46.875 in the $a = \pm10$ and $a = \pm40$ cases, respectively).

Note that in this particular case our first vulnerability definition is not applicable since the payoff functions of the two schemes cross so that neither is everywhere below the other. However, our second definition is applicable because as we can see, given a secure payoff of 5 for the $\pm40$ case and 8.75 for the $\pm10$ case, a much larger deviation is required by the $\pm40$ case to make any agent adhering to the high effort equilibrium regret his/her decision and wish she or he had shirked and set $e_i = 0$. In fact for the $\pm40$ case if an agent was choosing the highest effort level (46.875) consistent with a high level equilibrium he could tolerate a deviation away from that equilibrium by his cohorts of 50.08 before he wished he had chosen differently, while for the $\pm10$ case no deviation (i.e., the deviation is zero) would cause similar regret for such a high effort agent (i.e., one who at the high effort equilibrium was choosing 73.314). For agents choosing the lowest possible efforts consistent with high effort equilibria in these two schemes the comparable deviations are 51.56 and 19.39 in the $\pm40$ and $\pm10$ cases, respectively.

## 2.2    Trust

While vulnerability can be defined deductively in terms of the properties of the payoff functions existing in a game, by trust we mean an inductively derived (empirical) belief that people have about each other's behavior.[3] In our profit sharing game high levels of trust correspond to

---

[3] The concept of trust has alternatively been called social capital by Coleman (1988) and more recently discussed by Putnam (1993, 1995) and Fukyama (1995). For all intents and purposes we can interchange these notions although it might make more sense to think of our experiments as inducing differential levels of social capital rather than trust since the idea of social capital is more inclusive or broad than that of trust and hence may capture feelings shared among people that are not strictly feelings of trust.

assignment of significant amounts of probability mass on the event that your cohorts choose effort levels consistent with those dictated by the high effort symmetric Nash equilibrium of the profit sharing game or more. So when workers "trust each other" they trust that if they play their part in the high effort Nash equilibrium, others will as well. (Note that this obviously leaves a huge coordination problem for the agents since despite their desire to cooperate, especially in the high vulnerability case, there are a broad range of effort levels consistent with this goal, depending on one's beliefs about one's cohorts.) Trust is a common shared belief. The experimental design described in the next section attempts to operationalize these two concepts and demonstrate their impact of the effort choices of subjects.

## 3     The experimental design

In the experiments performed, undergraduate subjects were recruited from economics courses in groups of twelve and asked to report to a computer lab, where the experiment was to take place. When they arrived, subjects were divided randomly into groups of six and these were the groups they were to remain with for the entire experiment. Each experiment performed had two parts. Part I was a trust-inducing experiment aimed solely at influencing the beliefs that subjects would have about each other as they entered Part II of the experiment. It presented the subjects with a coordination game, to be described later, which they played ten times in succession.[4] After Part I was over, the instructions for Part II were handed out and read aloud, and questions about them were answered. In Part II, subjects engaged in a profit sharing (forcing contracts) experiment of the type described in which the support of the random shock term was either [−10, +10] or [−40, +40]. The final payoff of subjects was the sum of their payoffs in both Parts I and II of the experiment along with a $5.00 payment they received just for showing up. Average payoffs were $13.75 for about one hour and fifteen minutes and motivation was extremely high as measured by postexperiment interviews.

To give a better description of the decision tasks performed in Part I and Part II of our experiment, let us break up our discussion into two parts.

### 3.1     *Part I – the minimum and median games*

As stated, Part I of our experiment was run simply to influence the experience of subjects at their entrance into Part II. For that reason we

---

[4] The instructions for the minimum game in Part I are provided in Appendix B.

Table 1. *The minimum game*

| Your Choice | | | | Mini- mum Chosen | | | |
|---|---|---|---|---|---|---|---|
| | 7 | 6 | 5 | 4 | 3 | 2 | 1 |
| 7 | 1.30 | 1.10 | 0.90 | 0.70 | 0.50 | 0.30 | 0.10 |
| 6 | | 1.20 | 1.00 | 0.80 | 0.60 | 0.40 | 0.20 |
| 5 | | | 1.10 | 0.90 | 0.70 | 0.50 | 0.30 |
| 4 | | | | 1.00 | 0.80 | 0.60 | 0.40 |
| 3 | | | | | 0.90 | 0.70 | 0.50 |
| 2 | | | | | | 0.80 | 0.60 |
| 1 | | | | | | | 0.70 |

chose to have them play either the minimum game (see VanHuyck et al. 1990) or a particular version of the median game (VanHuyck et al. 1991) before engaging in Part II. We chose these games because they were coordination games with Pareto-ranked equilibria which had proved to be reliable producers of Pareto-worst (in the case of the minimum game) and Pareto-best (in the case of our particular median game) outcomes. Hence, we rely on experience in the minimum game to produce "low trust" norms in which people share a common history in which it is common knowledge that they all failed to cooperate with each other and provided themselves with the worst outcome available to themselves. The median game (at least the version we employed) was used in order to induce a "high trust" norm since it has proved to be a reliable producer of Pareto-best outcomes (VanHuyck 1991).

In the minimum game, six subjects are asked to choose an integer, $e_i$, between 1 and 7 and write this number on a piece of paper. The papers are then collected and the minimum of these numbers $\{e_1, e_2, e_3, e_4, e_5, e_6\}$ revealed. The payoff for any subject in this minimum game is $\pi_i = a \cdot \min\{e_1, e_2, e_3, e_4, e_5, e_6\} - be_i + c$. With $a = 0.2$, $b = 0.10$, and $c = 60$ our subjects in Part I faced the game matrix depicted in Table 1.

As can be seen here, any set of choices in which subjects choose the same number is a Nash equilibrium, yet the equilibria are Pareto-ranked with the choice of all 7's being best and that with all 1's being worst. VanHuyck et al. found that when this game was played among a set of fourteen to sixteen subjects repeatedly for ten rounds, the equilibrium consistently converged to the worst (all 1's) equilibrium.[5] Hence, it was our hope that with six subjects we could replicate this result and therefore use this Part I experiment as a control for a low trust norm among our subjects.[6]

The median game has exactly the same structure as the minimum game except for the payoff function, which is

$$\pi_i = a \cdot (\text{median}) - be_i + c \quad \text{if } e_i = \text{median}$$

$$\pi_i = 0 \qquad\qquad\qquad\qquad \text{if } e_i \neq \text{median}$$

Here again any configuration of choices in which all subjects choose the same number is an equilibrium, yet the Pareto-best equilibrium is the one in which every subject chooses 7. The payoff matrix facing subjects in this game is presented in Table 2.

Note that a compelling incentive exists to choose the all-7 equilibrium here since the out-of-equilibrium payoffs for all equilibria are zero so choosing the best equilibrium presents no additional risk yet provides the best payoff. Since this game had proved to be a reliable producer of Pareto-best outcomes (see VanHuyck, Battalio, and Beil 1991) we used it in Part I to provide what we felt would be a high trust control for Part II. Note also that the equilibrium payoffs for the median game are the same as those for the minimum game although the out-of-equilibrium payoffs differ. This was done to ensure that the act of coordinating choices on any number would be equally profitable across these two games.

Part I of the experiment was not done using a computer network but by hand. Subjects recorded their own choices on a worksheet and calculated their own payoffs, which were checked by the experimental administrator after the experiment was over.

### 3.2     *Part II – profit sharing*

After Part I of the experiment was over, a new set of instructions was handed out and read to the same set of subjects. While subjects knew that there would be another part to the experiment they did not know what it would involve until these instructions were given to them. The experiments engaged in Part II were direct implementations of the profit sharing schemes (with random shocks [−10, +10] or [−40, +40]) described

---

[5] See Vince Crawford (1991) for an evolutionary explanation for why the worst equilibrium emerges. Basically, among the set of equilibria only the all 1's equilibrium is evolutionarily stable.

[6] It can be debated whether this was a treatment for trust or simply a treatment in which the subjects did badly and that their mutual trust was not affected at all.

Table 2. *The median game*

**Median**

| Your Choice | 7 | 6 | 5 | 4 | 3 | 2 | 1 |
|---|---|---|---|---|---|---|---|
| 7 | 1.30 | 0 | 0 | 0 | 0 | 0 | 0 |
| 6 | 0 | 1.20 | 0 | 0 | 0 | 0 | 0 |
| 5 | 0 | 0 | 1.10 | 0 | 0 | 0 | 0 |
| 4 | 0 | 0 | 0 | 1.00 | 0 | 0 | 0 |
| 3 | 0 | 0 | 0 | 0 | 0.90 | 0 | 0 |
| 2 | 0 | 0 | 0 | 0 | 0 | 0.80 | 0 |
| 1 | 0 | 0 | 0 | 0 | 0 | 0 | 0.70 |

in section 2.[7] Subjects were seated at computer terminals, and when the experiment began they were asked to type a number between 0 and 100 into their computer terminals. Such a number can be interpreted as their unobservable effort levels, although in the instructions only neutral language was used. After these numbers were entered by each subject, the program guiding the experiment added up all of these numbers and drew a random number uniformly distributed between ±10 and ±40, depending on the experiment. The random numbers for the group were added to the sum of their effort levels. In the instructions subjects were told that the higher the decision number they chose the higher their costs would be and they were given a cost table illustrating the cost of each integer between 0 and 100. (This table was an integer representation of the cost function $e_i^2/100$.)

The payoffs for each experiment were then determined according to the rules of the profit sharing scheme, which specified that if the target was met the group revenue would be split among them and their cost of effort subtracted to determine their payoff. On the other hand, if the target was not met, each subject would receive the penalty wage of either 8.75 (in the [−10, +10] experiment) or 5 (in the [−40, +40] experiment). After each round subjects could see only their own effort levels and the output levels of their own group for the past fifteen periods. No information about the individual effort levels of other subjects was ever revealed.

[7] See Nalbantian and Schotter (1997) for tests of other group incentive mechanisms.

Table 3. *Experimental design*

| Experiment | Part I | Part II | Number of Groups of Six | Number of Subjects |
|---|---|---|---|---|
| 1 | Minimum Game: (Low Trust) | Profit Sharing: [-10,+10]- High Vulnerability | 9 | 54 |
| 2 | Median Game: (High Trust) | Profit Sharing: [-10, +10] | 10 | 60 |
| 3 | Minimum Game: (Low Trust) | Profit Sharing: [-40,+40]- Low Vulnerability | 5 | 30 |
| **Total** | | | **24** | **144** |

When round 1 of the experiment was over, round 2, which was identical to round 1, started. Each experiment lasted for 25 rounds, which we felt was a sufficient length of time to foster learning if any was to occur. The payoffs at the end of the experiment were simply the sum of the payoffs of the subjects over the two parts plus a $5.00 participation fee. Payoffs in each round were made in terms of points, which were converted into dollars at a rate which was known in advance by all subjects.

A total of twenty-four groups of six subjects each were recruited to do this experiment under three different sets of parameters. The experimental design is spelled out in Table 3.

As the experimental design indicates, we are looking at the interaction between trust and vulnerability. Subjects play a trust-inducing game in Part I, followed up by group incentive games whose equilibria exhibit varying levels of vulnerability. While we have provided a definition of vulnerability for the game played in Part II we have not attempted a definition of trust for our Part I game. However, if our a priori expectations about behavior in the median and minimum games are borne out, we would expect that subjects in the median game would converge on medians in the range 5–7 while those in the minimum game would converge on choices of 2 or below. Hence, we can expect that groups coming out of the median and minimum games will have very different experiences with each other. While one would have been successful in capturing practically all of the cooperative gains available to them, the other would have left quite a bit of money on the table. Our point is that after this conditioning the level of group solidarity across these two groups would be very different. While it would be common knowledge in one group that they had successfully coordinated their choices, in the other it would be common knowledge that they had failed to do so. Whether one calls the resulting state of mind "trust" will be left to interpretation. However, from extensive oral exit interviews we got a clear sense that these different experiences did have the impact on their expectations that we predicted.

## 4 Results

### 4.1 *Descriptive results*

In this section we will proceed by first describing the results of the three experiments performed and then testing a set of six hypotheses which follow naturally from our experimental design.

*Part I result:* The results of the experiments are presented in Tables 4(a)–(g) and Figures 3(a)–6. We will first look at the results of the Part I minimum and median games. As we can see from Table 4 and Figures 3(a) and 3(b), subject behavior was dramatically different in the median and minimum games which preceded our high vulnerability Part II experiment. While in six of the ten minimum games performed the group converged to a minimum of 1 by the tenth round,[8] in the remaining four games the last round minimums were 3, 3, 4, and 3. Since in these four games the minimum game failed to achieve the purpose of inducing a low cooperation outcome, in the analysis of the data for Part II we will exclude these groups and analyze only those Part II experiments which followed minimum 1 games.

In the nine median games the last round median was 7 in two experiments, 6 in three experiments, and 5 in four experiments. Despite the failure to reach 7 in all experiments, we will use all of these observations in the Part II experiments which followed these games since median choices of 5 or above are sufficiently far from the behavior of subjects in the minimum game to offer a good comparison.

Figures 3(a) and 3(b) show a three-dimensional picture of the choices of subjects over the nine Part I median and six Part I minimum games that preceded the high-vulnerability Part II experiments. As we can see there is quite a difference in the distribution of choices over time between these two experiments. While the majority of the mass of the frequency distribution is skewed above decision number 4 for the median game, at least from round 5 on, for the minimum game the mass is skewed below 4 over those same rounds. While this bifurcation in the

---

[8] In three of the six games there was a unanimous choice. In the remaining three it was unanimous except for one choice in two of the games and two choices in one game.

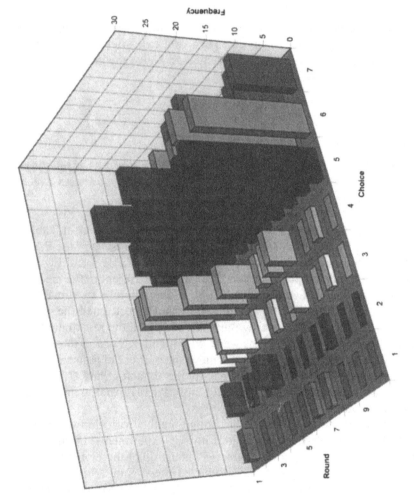

Figure 3(a). Choices by round, median game

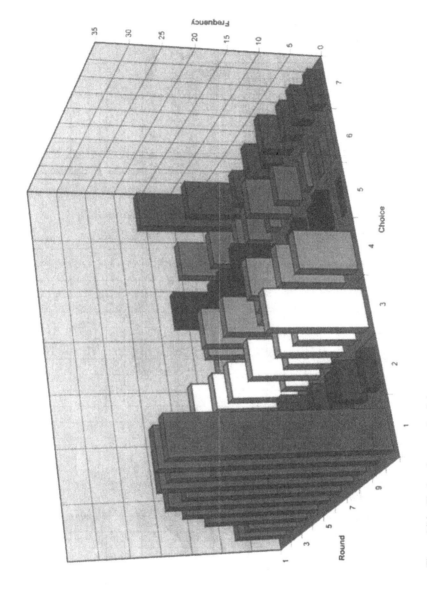

Figure 3(b). Choices by round, minimum game

Table 4(a). *Minimum of group (minimum game preceding low vulnerability Part II game)*

| Group | Round | | | | | | | | | |
|---|---|---|---|---|---|---|---|---|---|---|
| | 1 | 2 | 3 | 4 | 5 | 6 | 7 | 8 | 9 | 10 |
| 1 | 1 | 1 | 1 | 1 | 1 | 1 | 1 | 1 | 1 | 1 |
| 2 | 1 | 1 | 1 | 1 | 1 | 1 | 1 | 1 | 1 | 1 |
| 3 | 1 | 1 | 1 | 1 | 1 | 1 | 1 | 1 | 1 | 1 |
| 4 | 1 | 1 | 1 | 1 | 1 | 1 | 1 | 1 | 1 | 1 |
| 5 | 1 | 1 | 1 | 1 | 1 | 1 | 1 | 1 | 1 | 1 |

Table 4(b). *Minimum of group (minimum game preceding high vulnerability Part II game)*

| Group | Round | | | | | | | | | |
|---|---|---|---|---|---|---|---|---|---|---|
| | 1 | 2 | 3 | 4 | 5 | 6 | 7 | 8 | 9 | 10 |
| 1 | 1 | 1 | 1 | 1 | 1 | 1 | 1 | 1 | 1 | 1 |
| 2 | 2 | 3 | 3 | 3 | 3 | 3 | 3 | 3 | 3 | 3* |
| 3 | 2 | 1 | 1 | 1 | 1 | 1 | 1 | 1 | 1 | 1 |
| 4 | 1 | 2 | 3 | 1 | 1 | 3 | 3 | 3 | 2 | 3* |
| 5 | 1 | 1 | 1 | 1 | 1 | 1 | 1 | 1 | 1 | 1 |
| 6 | 5 | 3 | 2 | 1 | 1 | 1 | 1 | 1 | 1 | 1 |
| 7 | 1 | 1 | 1 | 1 | 1 | 1 | 1 | 1 | 1 | 1 |
| 8 | 1 | 1 | 1 | 1 | 1 | 1 | 1 | 1 | 1 | 1 |
| 9 | 4 | 4 | 4 | 4 | 4 | 4 | 4 | 4 | 4 | 4* |
| 10 | 5 | 3 | 2 | 3 | 4 | 3 | 3 | 3 | 3 | 3* |

*These groups were eliminated from later analysis

Table 4(c). *Median of group (median game preceding high vulnerability Part II game)*

| Group | Round | | | | | | | | | |
|---|---|---|---|---|---|---|---|---|---|---|
| | 1 | 2 | 3 | 4 | 5 | 6 | 7 | 8 | 9 | 10 |
| 1 | 4 | 5 | 6 | 7 | 6 | 5 | 6 | 6 | 5 | 6 |
| 2 | 5 | 6 | 6 | 6 | 6 | 6 | 6 | 6 | 6 | 6 |
| 3 | 5 | 5 | 5 | 5 | 5 | 5 | 5 | 5 | 5 | 5 |
| 4 | 5 | 6 | 7 | 6 | 7 | 6 | 7 | 6 | 7 | 6 |
| 5 | 5 | 4 | 5 | 5 | 5 | 5 | 5 | 5 | 5 | 5 |
| 6 | 6 | 7 | 6 | 7 | 6 | 7 | 6 | 7 | 6 | 7 |
| 7 | 6 | 5 | 5 | 6 | 5 | 5 | 5 | 5 | 5 | 5 |
| 8 | 4 | 5 | 5 | 6 | 7 | 6 | 6 | 6 | 6 | 7 |
| 9 | 5 | 6 | 5 | 5 | 6 | 5 | 6 | 5 | 6 | 5 |

Table 4(d). *Fraction of potential gains captured (minimum game preceding low vulnerability Part II game)*

| Group | Round | | | | | | | | | |
|---|---|---|---|---|---|---|---|---|---|---|
| | 1 | 2 | 3 | 4 | 5 | 6 | 7 | 8 | 9 | 10 |
| 1 | 0.33 | 0.44 | 0.49 | 0.49 | 0.51 | 0.51 | 0.46 | 0.49 | 0.51 | 0.46 |
| 2 | 0.31 | 0.37 | 0.35 | 0.45 | 0.42 | 0.50 | 0.44 | 0.53 | 0.54 | 0.53 |
| 3 | 0.26 | 0.41 | 0.45 | 0.49 | 0.47 | 0.45 | 0.47 | 0.51 | 0.51 | 0.45 |
| 4 | 0.36 | 0.41 | 0.49 | 0.47 | 0.54 | 0.53 | 0.54 | 0.54 | 0.53 | 0.54 |
| 5 | 0.31 | 0.35 | 0.38 | 0.45 | 0.49 | 0.53 | 0.54 | 0.44 | 0.54 | 0.51 |
| Mean | 0.31 | 0.40 | 0.43 | 0.47 | 0.49 | 0.50 | 0.49 | 0.50 | 0.53 | 0.50 |

Table 4(e). *Fraction of potential gains captured (minimum game preceding high vulnerability Part II game)*

| Group | Round | | | | | | | | | |
|---|---|---|---|---|---|---|---|---|---|---|
| | 1 | 2 | 3 | 4 | 5 | 6 | 7 | 8 | 9 | 10 |
| 1 | 0.27 | 0.42 | 0.46 | 0.50 | 0.54 | 0.53 | 0.54 | 0.54 | 0.54 | 0.54 |
| 3 | 0.44 | 0.38 | 0.44 | 0.46 | 0.46 | 0.53 | 0.54 | 0.50 | 0.53 | 0.53 |
| 5 | 0.15 | 0.33 | 0.46 | 0.47 | 0.53 | 0.51 | 0.53 | 0.49 | 0.51 | 0.49 |
| 6 | 0.74 | 0.44 | 0.36 | 0.31 | 0.29 | 0.37 | 0.44 | 0.49 | 0.51 | 0.49 |
| 7 | 0.32 | 0.38 | 0.53 | 0.54 | 0.54 | 0.54 | 0.54 | 0.54 | 0.54 | 0.54 |
| 8 | 0.22 | 0.42 | 0.46 | 0.44 | 0.42 | 0.40 | 0.37 | 0.46 | 0.46 | 0.46 |
| Mean | 0.36 | 0.40 | 0.45 | 0.45 | 0.46 | 0.48 | 0.49 | 0.50 | 0.52 | 0.51 |

Table 4(f). *Fraction of potential gains captured (median game preceding high vulnerability Part II game)*

| Group | Round | | | | | | | | | |
|---|---|---|---|---|---|---|---|---|---|---|
| | 1 | 2 | 3 | 4 | 5 | 6 | 7 | 8 | 9 | 10 |
| 1 | 0.51 | 0.42 | 0.46 | 0.50 | 0.36 | 0.42 | 0.15 | 0.15 | 0.56 | 0.77 |
| 2 | 0.28 | 0.46 | 0.46 | 0.62 | 0.31 | 0.92 | 0.92 | 0.92 | 0.92 | 0.62 |
| 3 | 0.28 | 0.14 | 0.42 | 0.56 | 0.85 | 0.85 | 0.56 | 0.85 | 0.71 | 0.85 |
| 4 | 0.28 | 0.77 | 0.50 | 0.31 | 0.50 | 0.46 | 1.00 | 0.77 | 1.00 | 0.92 |
| 5 | 0.28 | 0.38 | 0.42 | 0.85 | 0.85 | 0.85 | 0.85 | 0.85 | 0.85 | 0.85 |
| 6 | 0.15 | 0.50 | 0.15 | 0.50 | 0.46 | 0.67 | 0.62 | 0.83 | 0.77 | 1.00 |
| 7 | 0.15 | 0.42 | 0.26 | 0.46 | 0.56 | 0.42 | 0.42 | 0.85 | 0.71 | 0.71 |
| 8 | 0.13 | 0.56 | 0.28 | 0.46 | 0.50 | 0.31 | 0.31 | 0.46 | 0.62 | 0.50 |
| 9 | 0.14 | 0.31 | 0.28 | 0.28 | 0.46 | 0.56 | 0.62 | 0.71 | 0.46 | 0.71 |
| Mean | 0.24 | 0.44 | 0.36 | 0.50 | 0.54 | 0.61 | 0.61 | 0.71 | 0.73 | 0.77 |

Table 4(g). *Summary statistics, Part II game*

| Round | 1 | 2 | 3 | 4 | 5 | 6 | 7 | 8 | 9 | 10 | 11 | 12 | 13 | 14 | 15 | 16 | 17 | 18 | 19 | 20 | 21 | 22 | 23 | 24 | 25 |
|---|---|---|---|---|---|---|---|---|---|---|---|---|---|---|---|---|---|---|---|---|---|---|---|---|---|
| **Median, High Vulnerability (9 groups)** | | | | | | | | | | | | | | | | | | | | | | | | | |
| Average Group Revenue | 320 | 320 | 322 | 309 | 303 | 295 | 278 | 282 | 266 | 231 | 249 | 223 | 231 | 232 | 235 | 221 | 245 | 252 | 246 | 212 | 182 | 182 | 167 | 177 | 198 |
| Number of Groups made target | 4 | 4 | 4 | 4 | 5 | 4 | 3 | 4 | 3 | 3 | 3 | 3 | 3 | 3 | 3 | 4 | 3 | 3 | 3 | 3 | 3 | 2 | 3 | 3 | 3 |
| Average Individual Choice | 35 | 36 | 36 | 34 | 34 | 33 | 31 | 31 | 30 | 26 | 28 | 25 | 26 | 26 | 26 | 25 | 27 | 28 | 27 | 23 | 20 | 21 | 18 | 20 | 22 |
| % choosing 40 and above | 56 | 56 | 50 | 48 | 46 | 48 | 41 | 43 | 39 | 33 | 37 | 35 | 37 | 37 | 37 | 33 | 31 | 41 | 39 | 35 | 28 | 30 | 26 | 30 | 39 |
| **Minimum, High Vulnerability (6 groups)** | | | | | | | | | | | | | | | | | | | | | | | | | |
| Average Group Revenue | 359 | 323 | 328 | 267 | 225 | 243 | 194 | 150 | 116 | 92 | 81 | 94 | 89 | 65 | 44 | 52 | 48 | 49 | 56 | 55 | 56 | 62 | 82 | 44 | 47 |
| Number of Groups made target | 3 | 2 | 2 | 1 | 0 | 0 | 0 | 0 | 0 | 0 | 0 | 0 | 0 | 0 | 5 | 0 | 0 | 0 | 0 | 0 | 0 | 0 | 0 | 0 | 0 |
| Average Individual Choice | 40 | 36 | 37 | 30 | 24 | 28 | 22 | 16 | 13 | 10 | 9.2 | 10 | 9.6 | 7.5 | 5 | 5.4 | 5.9 | 5.4 | 7 | 6.3 | 6.8 | 6.7 | 9 | 4.4 | 5.1 |
| % choosing 40 and above | 67 | 56 | 56 | 42 | 33 | 42 | 31 | 22 | 14 | 8.3 | 14 | 14 | 8.3 | 5.6 | 0 | 0 | 2.8 | 5.6 | 5.6 | 2.8 | 2.8 | 2.8 | 5.6 | 2.8 | 2.8 |
| **Minimum, Low Vulnerability (5 groups)** | | | | | | | | | | | | | | | | | | | | | | | | | |
| Average Group Revenue | 418 | 399 | 334 | 294 | 356 | 346 | 318 | 287 | 284 | 384 | 316 | 339 | 306 | 297 | 328 | 337 | 314 | 317 | 353 | 269 | 307 | 309 | 346 | 348 | 323 |
| Number of Groups made target | 4 | 3 | 3 | 1 | 4 | 4 | 3 | 1 | 2 | 3 | 3 | 4 | 2 | 1 | 2 | 3 | 3 | 3 | 4 | 2 | 3 | 4 | 4 | 3 | 3 |
| Average Individual Choice | 46 | 43 | 39 | 33 | 36 | 37 | 35 | 33 | 34 | 38 | 36 | 35 | 33 | 35 | 39 | 40 | 40 | 36 | 39 | 34 | 34 | 38 | 40 | 39 | 34 |
| % choosing 40 and above | 77 | 67 | 63 | 50 | 57 | 53 | 57 | 47 | 47 | 53 | 63 | 57 | 53 | 57 | 63 | 63 | 60 | 50 | 53 | 50 | 53 | 50 | 57 | 57 | |

results of these experiments is certainly as we predicted, the fact that subjects fail to coordinate their actions unanimously in a mutually best-response manner (even in round 10) indicates that we were not observing consistent Nash behavior.

To illustrate the difference between these games in a different manner, let us look at the fraction of the potentially available gains from trade that groups in these Part I games have captured. This is calculated by taking the maximum monetary payment available for the group $78.00 = (6 \times \$1.30) \times 10$ and dividing it into the actual amount of money the group has achieved for itself. Hence define

$$\Lambda = \text{(Actual Monetary Payment Received)}/$$
$$\text{(Potentially Available Monetary Payment)}$$

This is demonstrated in Figure 4, where the top line represents the mean fraction of the gains from cooperation attained by the group of subjects playing the median game over the ten rounds of their experience while the bottom two lines represent the same statistic for the groups playing the minimum game. As we can see, over the course of their interaction and especially in the last ten rounds, a considerable difference exists between the payoff experiences of these two groups. For instance, in round 10 the fraction of the gains from cooperation captured in the median game was 0.77 while in the minimum game it was 0.508. This difference exists despite the fact that when a subject's decision number does not match the median in the median game his/her payoff is 0 while such out-of-equilibrium payoffs always provide positive payoffs for subjects in the minimum game. Hence, life outside equilibrium is more profitable in the minimum game than in the median game and that fact allows subjects in that game to capture some of the potentially available gains from cooperation more easily.

*Part II results*[9]*:* The results of Part II are presented in Tables 4(a)–(g) and Figures 5 and 6. In Figure 5 we see the mean revenue of groups participating in the Part II high vulnerability profit sharing game conditional on playing a previous minimum or median game. These figures

---

[9] The results reported here are carried out mostly at the individual level. Perhaps a better analysis could be done at the group level since the variance across groups is significant. However, for proper statistical significance, since it takes six subjects to furnish one data point, an extremely large number of subjects would be needed to provide the proper power to statistical tests. While we have recruited 144 subjects and test pooled individual behavior across treatments, a number of our results could still be artifacts of a few groups within the data set. In the future we might try to extend this study by recruiting sufficiently large samples of subjects.

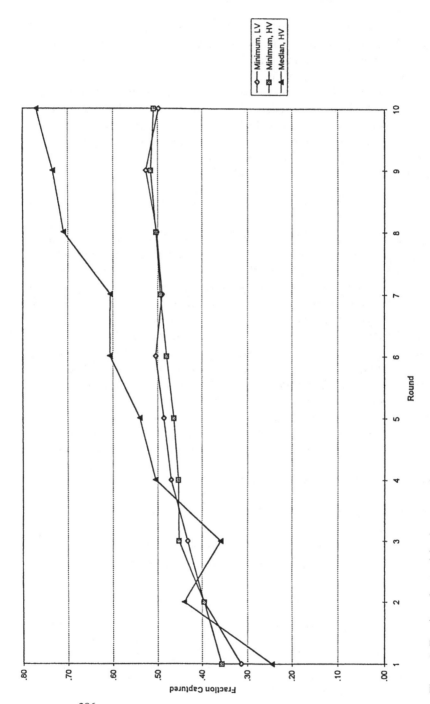

386

Figure 4. Fraction of potential gains captured

387

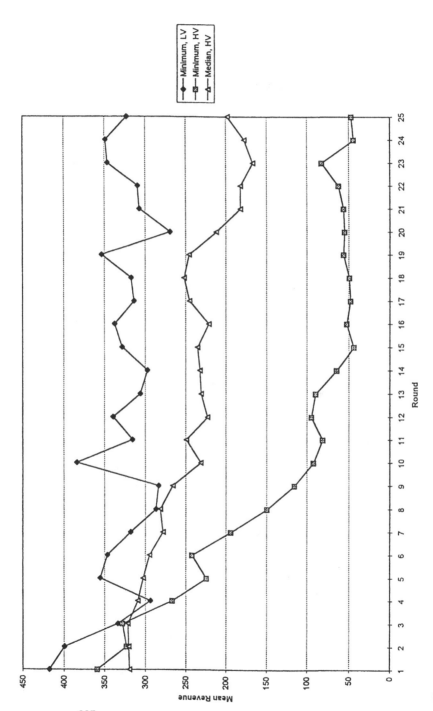

Figure 5. Mean group revenue

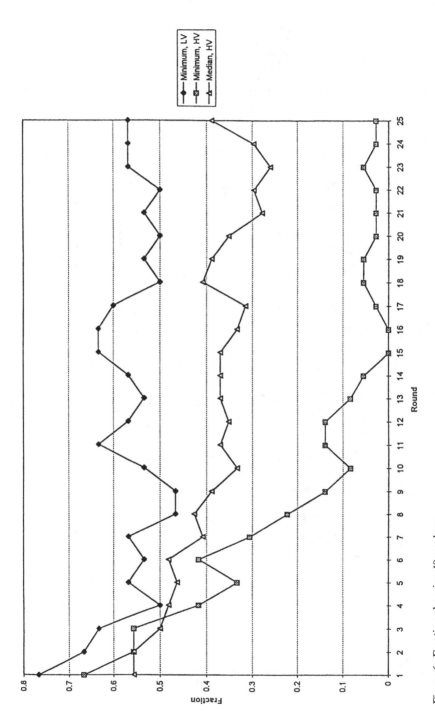

388

Figure 6. Fraction choosing 40 or above

graph the round-by-round mean revenue data pooled over all nine median group experiments and those six Part I minimum experiments whose last period minimum had converged to 1 as well as those groups who played the minimum game in Part I and then the low vulnerability profit sharing game in Part II. Figure 6 presents the fraction of subjects choosing 40 or more in any round of these low and high vulnerability experiments; it is offered to demonstrate how the Phase I game affects the attempt of subjects in the Phase II high vulnerability experiment to coordinate on a high vulnerability equilibrium.

The impact of trust on this attempted coordination is unclear. Subjects who trust others but are still self-regarding may expect others to choose high effort levels in the equilibrium range [12.5, 73.314] and hence best respond by choosing low (yet still equilibrium) effort levels. However, trust may be regarded not only as a probability belief about the actions of others but as actually part of an other-regarding norm.[10] In this case, such an other-regarding norm could carry over to behavior in the Phase II experiments. In this case we might expect high effort levels from everyone. Hence, we split the equilibrium effort level range in this experiment into high effort choices $e_i \geqslant 40$ and low effort choices $e_i \leqslant 40$ (roughly the midpoint of the range) and checked whether our high trust treatment led to relatively high choices in the high vulnerability experiments.

In comparing the behavior of subjects in the high vulnerability game, there seems to be little difference in their behavior in the first round of the profit sharing experiments conditional on their experience in Part I. In fact, the number of subjects choosing 40 or more in round 1 was greater among the subjects who played the minimum game than it was among those who played the median game. More precisely, as we see in Tables 4(a)–(g), 67 percent of the subjects who played the minimum game and then the high vulnerability profit sharing game chose 40 or more in the first round of the profit sharing game, while only 56 percent of those who previously played the median game did. Hence, it does not appear that the Part I game had any effect on the exhibited trust existing among the subjects at least in the first round of their Part II experiment. However, by round 8 a dramatic difference appears with 43 percent of the median game subjects choosing 40 or more but only 22 percent of the minimum game subjects doing so. From round 8 on the difference increases until in round 25 only 2.8 percent of the subjects in the Part I minimum game experiment attempted to choose 40 or more while 39

---

[10] For an elaboration of this point see the thoughtful comments of Jonathan Baron in this volume.

percent of the median game subjects were still attempting to do so. The same stylistic facts appear for mean revenue, where mean revenue for the minimum game groups in period 1 was 359 while for the median groups it was 320. By round 25 these revenues had decreased to 47 and 198 for the minimum and median groups, respectively.

Counter to our expectations, the impact of the Part I experience was not detectable in the round 1 play of the profit sharing game but rather in the robustness of cooperative play after the first round. This is a very significant finding since trust can mean a willingness to absorb disappointment in the group's failure to reach a goal and keep on playing cooperatively. While the minimum game subjects exhibited high levels of trust in their round 1 (and first five round) behavior, this trust was superficial and quickly evaporated once the target was not met. Subjects in the median game attempted high effort Nash play for far longer durations than did their cohorts in the minimum game experiment.

The results of the low vulnerability experiment were confounded by the type of coordination problem this scheme implied for the high effort equilibrium. Remember that this experiment was run on subjects completing the minimum game but then playing the profit sharing game with a random term of ±40. Hence, while the Phase I treatment could be expected to lead to a lack of trust and therefore low efforts in the Phase II game, the fact that it is relatively easy to coordinate actions at the high effort equilibrium might counteract this lack of trust and lead them to attempt to achieve a high effort equilibrium. The second factor seemed to have dominated the first. For example, not only did first round group revenue of subjects in this experiment exceed that of any high vulnerability experiment (the mean revenues for the minimum game and median game groups were 359 and 320, respectively, while for the low vulnerability group it was 418), but it remained higher throughout the 25 rounds, ending at an average rate of 323 as opposed to 47 for the minimum game high vulnerability subjects and 198 for the median game high vulnerability experiments. Furthermore, four of the five low vulnerability groups made the target of 360 on an average of 17.5 of the 25 rounds (the remaining group never surpassed the target at all).

To get a different view of how the Phase I minimum and median games affected choice in the Phase II high vulnerability experiment consider Figures 7 and 8. In Figure 7 we present the fraction of subjects who in any round of the high vulnerability experiment chose an effort level consistent with the high effort equilibrium conditional on the game they played in Phase I. Figure 8 presents the fraction of subjects choosing the low effort equilibrium (i.e., choosing 1 or 0). As we can see, at the pooled individual level after round 5 it is clear that subjects who partici-

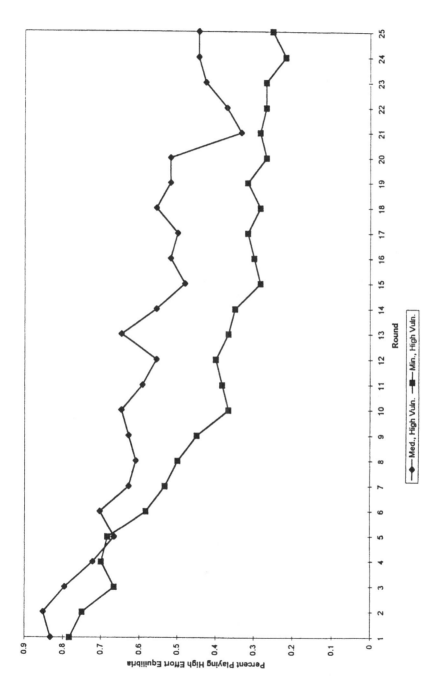

Figure 7. High effort equilibria plays in high vulnerability treatments

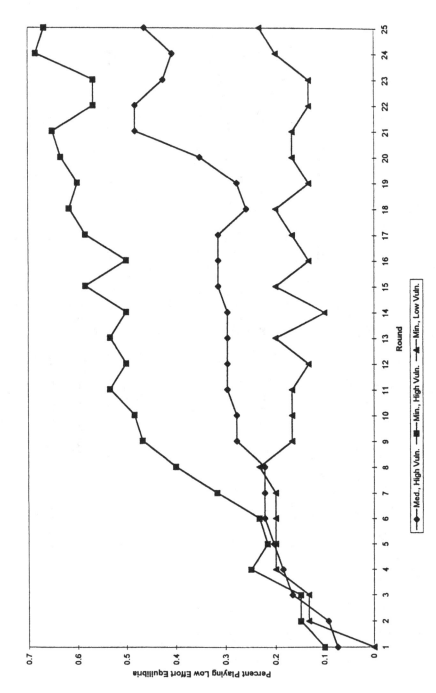

Figure 8. Low effort equilibria plays

pated in the median game in Phase I chose effort levels consistent with the high effort equilibrium with far greater frequency than did those subjects who had previously played the minimum game. Likewise, looking at Figure 8 it is evident that subjects who played the minimum game in Phase I and then the high vulnerability experiment in Phase II were much more likely to shirk and play the low effort equilibrium in Phase II as time progressed. Subjects playing the low vulnerability experiment in Phase II were the least likely to choose 0 or 1 in the Phase II game, doing so less than 20 percent of the time at the end of the experiment, while practically 70 percent of the high vulnerability minimum game subjects chose to do so.

The results of this experiment actually introduce a new variable into the picture since now it appears that even in a low trust environment, if the high effort equilibrium provides clear guidance as to how to coordinate equilibrium behavior (as in the ±40 experiment, where the high effort equilibrium specifies a small band of actions consistent with it), such equilibria may still be achievable. Hence, coordination difficulties must be added to vulnerability and trust as a determining characteristic of when cooperation will be observed.

### 4.2    *Formal hypothesis tests*

In this section of the chapter we will formally test some implications derived from the descriptive statistics presented previously. These hypotheses can be considered as substantiation of the more impressionistic evidence presented.

*Part I hypotheses:* Since Part I of the experiment was run only to induce a sense of trust among the subjects, in our hypothesis testing we will only concern ourselves with whether subjects in the median and minimum games experienced different histories by asking whether they converged to different choices in their last rounds. In addition, we will ask whether we can characterize these different Part I games as being more or less cooperative by comparing the fraction of the gains from cooperation they capture. These concerns are summarized by the following two null hypotheses.

*Hypothesis 1: The distribution of last round choices in the Part I minimum game is identical to the distribution of last round choices in the Part I median game.*

To investigate Hypothesis 1 we use a Kolmogorov–Smirnov test to compare the distribution of last round choices of subjects in their respective games (see Figures 3[a] and 3[b]). Comparing the last round sample of nine median game and six minimum game experiments (samples of 54 and 36, respectively) we see that there is a significant difference between the last round choices of the minimum and median game subjects ($p \leq 0.0001$).

*Hypothesis 2: The fraction of the potentially available gains from cooperation captured by subjects in the median game experiment is equal to that captured in the minimum game experiment.*

To test this hypothesis we employ a Wilcoxon test using the pooled data generated by all six minimum game experiments and all nine median game experiments over the 10 rounds of their existence. On the basis of this test we can reject the null hypothesis that the fractions of gains achieved in these two experiments were identical in favor of the alternative hypothesis that the gains captured were greater in the median experiment at the 5 percent level of significance ($z$ statistic 1.94, $p = 0.0529$).

*Part II hypotheses:* In Part II of Experiments 1 and 2 we investigate whether the experience subjects had in Part I of the experiment created differential degrees of trust among the subjects to the point that it affected their behavior in Part II. Our first hypothesis investigates probably the purest trust effect induced by our Part I games by looking at the round 1 choices of subjects in the Part II profit sharing game. We expect this first round (first five round) behavior to be insightful since it should reflect only the expectations of subjects about the choices of their cohort since, at least in this Part II game, they have no history together. We are interested in two questions: Are the choices in Part II higher for subjects with experience in the median game, and how many subjects in the first rounds of these experiments attempted to choose an effort level greater than or equal to 40 (i.e., that effort level dictated by the Nash equilibrium)?

*Hypothesis 3: The sample of first round choices in the Part II ±10 profit sharing experiment is not affected by which Part I experiment subjects took part in.*

Here we use a $\chi^2$ test to test for differences between the samples of first round choices in the Part II ±10 forcing contract experiment. What we find is that no significant differences (at the 5 percent level of significance) exist ($p = 0.087$) in the way in which subjects make their choices in the first round of the Part II high vulnerability games. Hence, if there was a difference in levels of trust, it did not manifest itself in the first round behavior of subjects in their Part II experiment. Looking at the first five rounds and all subsequent five round periods, however, we do see a significant difference between the choices of subjects who had previously played the median and minimum games, with the median game subjects choosing significantly higher in all five round periods. Hence, trust seems to manifest itself more dramatically in the ability of Part I median groups to choose higher effort levels later in the experiment than did those subjects who played the minimum game in Part I.

The fact that we could not detect any difference in the way our subjects started off their play in the Part II ±10 profit sharing game between the minimum and median game treatments is not surprising since such a broad range of behavior is consistent with high effort equilibrium behavior. As we have said, even if a subject chooses an effort level as low as 12.5, such behavior would be consistent with a high effort equilibrium if the subject thought that others would exert sufficiently high efforts. In fact, with such a big coordination problem it is not even clear what the impact of trust is on behavior. For example, as we have said, high trust levels combined with self-regarding behavior might lead to low effort levels since high trust indicates a high probability that others will exert high effort levels and exerting a low effort level can be rationalized given those beliefs. On the other hand, low trust might lead a subject to think that if the target is going to be reached he or she will have to contribute relatively more since others cannot be relied on. This would predict higher effort levels in low trust groups. To help sort this out we divided the range of equilibrium effort levels in the high vulnerability experiments [12.5, 73.314] into a high effort subset $e_i \geq 40$ and a low effort subset $e_i \leq 40$. The impact of trust on behavior could possibly be seen in the willingness of subjects to offer "high" effort levels above 40 in the first (or first five) rounds since in these rounds the influence of their trust game experience might be paramount in their minds and their effort choices there might simply be responses to it.

But first round (or first five round) behavior is not the entire story. From previous experiments using the profit sharing scheme[11] we know that this scheme is particularly sensitive to the failure of the group to make the target early on in their experience with each other. When the group falls short of the target, effort levels tend to tumble and group output many times quickly approaches the bad 0 effort equilibrium. However, if subjects trust each other they should be willing to persist in

---

[11] See Nalbantian and Schotter (1997).

their high effort choices for a longer time and their cooperativeness should be more robust to failures of the group to reach the target and we should observe higher output persisting longer in the groups. These considerations lead to Hypothesis 4.

*Hypothesis 4: The fraction of subjects who choose an effort level of 40 or more in the first round or in each of the five five-round periods of the Part II ±10 high vulnerability experiments should be independent of the Part I game these subjects played.*

This hypothesis presents a rather static test of the idea that even if there is no observable difference between the behavior of subjects in the first round or perhaps the first five rounds of the Part II experiment conditional on which game they played in Part I, differences may be detectable later on in the Part II game, and therefore the trust built up in Part I may manifest itself in better staying power or persistence for the Part I median game subjects in Part II. Using a $\chi^2$ test once again we see that the fraction of subjects choosing 40 or more in the first five rounds of the Part II experiment is independent of which game was played in Part I ($p = 0.936$). However, for the first round there was a significant difference, with Part I minimum subjects attempting choices of 40 or more with greater frequency ($p = 0.027$). Starting with the third five round period we do detect significant differences in the behavior of subjects, depending on their Part I experience. For example, a $\chi^2$ test indicates that significant differences do exist between the two groups of subjects in each of the five round periods starting in period 10 ($p \leqslant 0.001$ in all three remaining five round periods). What this indicates, perhaps, is that given the coordination problem presented to subjects by the high vulnerability experiment, subjects in the high trust median game condition were more willing to attempt coordination later into the experiment while low trust subjects gave up earlier.

As stated, Hypothesis 4 presents a static view of the persistence phenomenon by looking at five round snapshots of behavior on a group level. In Hypothesis 5 we present a more dynamic examination of the persistence question by estimating discrete-time hazard functions on individual pooled data. These discrete-time hazard functions are in essence conditional probability functions indicating the probability of cooperating in period $t$ (choosing 40 or more) conditional on the fact that you had been cooperating in period $t - 1$. This hazard function was estimated as a probit regression using the pooled set of individual observations of subjects in each of our two Part II experiments. What we are looking for is a difference in the time variable coefficient across these two regressions since that would indicate whether the probability of

Table 5(a). *Hazard function estimates: Part II high vulnerability following minimum game (probit estimates)*

| y | Coefficient | Std. error | t | $P > |t|$ | 95% confidence interval | |
|---|---|---|---|---|---|---|
| Time | −0.04083 | 0.0196 | −2.081 | 0.039 | −0.0795 | −0.0208 |
| Constant | 0.6419 | 0.1746 | 3.675 | 0.000 | 0.2969 | 0.9870 |

Log likelihood = −100.683; pseudo $R^2$ = 0.0212; number of observation = 157.

Table 5(b). *Hazard function estimates: Part II high vulnerability following median game (probit estimates)*

| y | Coefficient | Std. error | t | $P > |t|$ | 95% confidence interval | |
|---|---|---|---|---|---|---|
| Time | −0.00809 | 0.0103 | 0.784 | 0.433 | −0.0121 | 0.0283 |
| Constant | 1.0363 | 0.1418 | 7.305 | 0.000 | 0.7576 | 1.315 |

Log likelihood = −193.714; pseudo $R^2$ = 0.0016; number of observation = 506.

persisting in cooperation in period $t$, conditional on cooperation in period $t - 1$, was different for these two groups as time progressed.

*Hypothesis 5: Equilibrium effort persistence (hazard functions): The probability that an individual persists in choosing an effort level of 40 or greater (i.e., an effort level consistent with the symmetric high effort equilibrium) conditional on his or her previous round high equilibrium effort choice will be independent of the Part I game the subject engaged in when playing the Part II high vulnerability profit sharing game.*

The regression results used to test Hypothesis 5 are presented in Table 5.

As we see, while the time coefficient is significant and negative in the regression run on the Part I minimum game subjects, it is not significant for subjects who played the median game in Part I. This is not surprising since cooperative persistence did not seem to diminish at all for subjects who first experienced the median game while it dropped dramatically for those whose first interaction was with the minimum game. Such a finding is consistent with our a priori expectations since the lack of trust among minimum game subjects could be expected to yield a decay of cooperative persistence over time while such a decay may not be observed if our subjects actually built up significant levels of trust in their Part I experience together.[12]

### 4.3    *The effect of vulnerability*

As you recall, one of the motivations for this chapter is that we expect the match between the level of trust existing between workers and the vulnerability of the incentive plan they are placed in to be an important predictor of the performance of that group incentive plan. Hence, we expect that low trust groups would perform better when placed in low vulnerability incentive plans than in high ones since such low vulnerability plans rely less on trust for proper performance. This proposition can be tested by a comparison of the results in Experiments 1 and 3 since in each of these experiments subjects play the identical minimum game in Part I of the experiment but then face forcing contract schemes with differing levels of vulnerability. These considerations yield a set of hypotheses which compare the results of Experiments 1 and 3 as opposed to Experiments 1 and 2.

While Hypotheses 3–5 test the impact of trust on the performance of subjects in high vulnerability games, Hypothesis 6 investigates the impact of vulnerability on the behavior of subjects conditioned with the same low trust minimum game in Part I. Hence in the hypotheses that follow we are comparing the behavior of subjects in two different Part II experiments (one with low and one with high vulnerability) who participated in identical Part I minimum games. For these games we ask the same questions we asked in Hypotheses 3 and 4 as summarized in Hypothesis 6.

*Hypothesis 6: The sample of effort choices in either the first round, the first five rounds, or each of the five five-round periods in the low vulnerability game is not significantly different from the sample of choices in the high vulnerability game. In addition, the fraction of subjects who choose an effort level of 40 or more in the first round or in each of the five five-*

---

[12] It should be noted that persistence is not the same as cooperation. For example, we ran an unconditional probit regression on the probability of cooperating in any given round unconditional on cooperation in the previous period and found that in both of those regressions the time variable was significant and negative in both the minimum and median game group subjects. Hence, time does lead to a decay of cooperativeness. It only affects the persistence of such cooperation in the minimum game subject group.

*round periods does not differ according to the vulnerability of the Part II experiment.*

As we saw in the descriptive statistics offered earlier, there were dramatic differences in the behavior of subjects performing the low and high vulnerability experiments after experiencing the minimum game in Part I. For example, using a $\chi^2$ test we can reject the hypothesis that the distribution of choices in the first round or first, second, third, fourth, or fifth five-round periods of the Part II profit sharing game was identical whether or not the game played was a high or low vulnerability game ($p = 0.001$, $p = 0.012$, $p \leq 0.001$, $p \leq 0.001$, $p \leq 0.001$, $p \leq 0.001$, respectively). We can also reject the hypothesis that the fraction of subjects attempting cooperation (effort choices above 40) was the same for these two groups over the same periods ($p = 0.033$, $p = 0.021$, $p \leq 0.001$, $p \leq 0.001$, $p \leq 0.001$, $p \leq 0.001$, respectively).

As mentioned, we expect that these results differ so dramatically from those of the high vulnerability experiments because the low vulnerability experiment presented subjects with a very different coordination task in adhering to a high effort equilibrium. In this experiment the range of equilibrium behavior was severely restricted when compared to that in the high vulnerability experiment. With subjects making choices over a smaller set of equilibrium effort levels we might expect that the probability of reaching the target would be significantly increased while the temptation to free ride on the high effort equilibrium effort levels of others would be significantly decreased.

## 5    Conclusions

This chapter has investigated the complementary nature of worker trust and system vulnerability in the behavior of laboratory subjects. As indicated in the introduction, the performance of workers on the job is influenced not only by the incentive properties of the incentive mechanism they are functioning under, but also by the norms of trust they have developed with their fellow workers. Worker groups with low levels of trust or with common histories of shirking on the job should be matched with incentive systems which do not make the workers excessively vulnerable to the free riding of their colleagues.

In addition, when multiple high effort equilibria exist, the task of coordination on one equilibrium confounds the effects of trust and vulnerability. A fuller analysis of the relationships among these three influences has yet to be carried out but should provide an interesting research agenda.

### Appendix A: Derivation for range of asymmetric equilibria

The problem facing each individual is to choose $e_i$ to maximize

$$\left(\frac{Y^* - \sum_{j \neq i} e_j - e_i + a}{2a}\right) B + \left(\frac{\sum_{j \neq i} e_j + e_i - Y^* + a}{2a}\right)$$

$$\left(\frac{\sum_{j \neq i} e_j + e_i + Y^* + a}{8}\right) - \frac{e_i^2}{100}$$

s.t.

$$\frac{\sum_{j \neq i} e_j + e_i - Y^* + a}{2a} \leq 1$$

$$e_i, \lambda \geq 0$$

Let the Lagrangian be denoted as $Z$ with shadow value $\lambda$.
First-order conditions (FOCs) give

$$\frac{\partial Z}{\partial e_i} = \frac{-B}{2a} + \frac{1}{8}\left(\frac{\sum_{j \neq i} e_j + e_i - Y^* + a}{2a}\right) + \frac{1}{2a}\left(\frac{\sum_{j \neq i} e_j + e_i + Y^* + a}{2a}\right)$$

$$- \frac{e_i}{50} - \lambda \geq 0$$

$$\frac{\partial Z}{\partial \lambda} = \sum_{j \neq i} e_j + e_i - Y^* - a \leq 0$$

We know that all equilibria that are corner solutions will have the feature that $\Sigma e_i = Y^* + a$ (surety payoff) or $\Sigma e_i = 0$. We are looking at situations involving the former.

Consider the case when we have $a = 40$, $B = 5$, $Y^* = 240$. First-order conditions become

$$\frac{\partial Z}{\partial e_i} = \frac{-1}{16} + \frac{1}{8}\left(\frac{\sum_{j \neq i} e_j + e_i - 200}{80}\right) + \frac{1}{80}\left(\frac{\sum_{j \neq i} e_j + e_i + 280}{8}\right) - \frac{e_i}{50} - \lambda \geq 0$$

$$\frac{\partial Z}{\partial \lambda} = \sum_{j \neq i} e_j + e_i - 280 \leq 0$$

We can see that the only consistent case here is $e_i > 0$, $\lambda > 0$, which is a corner solution. The maximum value $e_i$ can take on then is (in the limit) that in which we set $\lambda$ equal to 0 in the first FOC with the condition that the second is met with equality

$$\frac{-1}{16}+\frac{1}{8}\left(\frac{\sum_{j\neq i}e_j+e_i-200}{80}\right)+\frac{1}{80}\left(\frac{\sum_{j\neq i}e_j+e_i+280}{8}\right)-\frac{e_i}{50}=0$$

$$\frac{-1}{16}+\frac{1}{8}+\frac{7}{8}-\frac{e_i}{50}=0$$

which gives the solution $e_i = 46.875$ as the maximum possible value. If this is then the maximum value possible, we can calculate the minimum by showing that if five players chose this maximum value, then the sixth would choose the minimum and that this vector of choices is a Nash equilibrium. Since we know from the second FOC that the sum of efforts is 280, the minimum possible value must be $e_i = 45.625$. Therefore, the range of possible asymmetric equilibrium choices for these parameters fall in the interval [45.625, 46.875] with the symmetric equilibria being $e_i = 46^2/_3$, $\forall i$.

Now consider the case when $a = 10$, $B = 8.75$, $Y^* = 240$. This gives first-order conditions

$$\frac{\partial Z}{\partial e_i}=\frac{-7}{16}+\frac{1}{8}\left(\frac{\sum_{j\neq i}e_j+e_i-230}{20}\right)+\frac{1}{20}\left(\frac{\sum_{j\neq i}e_j+e_i+250}{8}\right)-\frac{e_i}{50}-\lambda\geqslant 0$$

$$\frac{\partial Z}{\partial\lambda}=\sum_{j\neq i}e_j+e_i-250\leqslant 0$$

Again $e_i > 0$, $\lambda > 0$, will be the only consistent case. With these parameters the same technique used earlier will not give desirable results:

$$\frac{-7}{16}+\frac{1}{8}\left(\frac{\sum_{j\neq i}e_j+e_i-230}{20}\right)+\frac{1}{20}\left(\frac{\sum_{j\neq i}e_j+e_i+250}{8}\right)-\frac{e_i}{50}=0$$

$$\frac{-7}{16}+\frac{1}{8}+\frac{25}{8}+\frac{e_i}{50}=0$$

which would give a solution of $e_i = 140.63$. This is clearly inconsistent with incentive compatibility. Such an answer does make sense, however, as we know with $a = 10$ there won't be interior solutions. Thus we need to look to incentive compatibility constraints to find the maximum and the minimum anyone is willing to exert.

Again we need to use the second FOC, equal to 0 (i.e., $\lambda > 0$), to establish that in any equilibrium it must be that the sum of the efforts is equal to 250. This then being the case, we can find the maximum effort level by setting the expected wage equal to the penalty wage and solving for $e_i$.

$$\left(\frac{250 - \sum_{j \neq i} e_j - e_i}{20}\right) 8.75$$

$$+ \left(\frac{\sum_{j \neq i} e_j + e_i - 230}{20}\right)\left(\frac{\sum_{j \neq i} e_j + e_i + 250}{8}\right) - \frac{e_i^2}{100} = 8.75$$

$$\frac{500}{8} - \frac{e_i^2}{100} = 8.75$$

Solving for $e_i$ we get $e_i = 73.314$. Now clearly we again cannot find the minimum by assuming that five players exert the maximum, and taking the difference from the equilibrium total as we did above, as this would result in a negative effort level. What we need to do in this case is to remember that the efforts must sum to 250, which gives the high payoff with surety, and find the level of effort that sets the maginal revenue from the surety payoff equal to the marginal cost of the individual. The payoff of individuals, *given that the high payoff is reached with surety*, is

$$\left(\frac{1.5\left(\sum_{j \neq i} e_j + e_i + \varepsilon\right)}{6}\right) - \frac{e_i^2}{100}$$

taking first-order conditions with respect to $e_i$ we get

$$\frac{1}{4} - \frac{e_i}{50} = 0$$

Solving, we get $e_i = 12.5$ as the minimum any worker is willing to exert. Thus in this case the asymmetric equilibria can fall in the range [12.5, 73.314] with the symmetric equilibrium being $e_i = 41^2/_3$, $\forall i$.

To establish vulnerabilities simply use these values of $e_i$ in the payoff function and vary the contributions of others away from equilibrium.

### Appendix B: Instructions

*Minimum game instructions*

This is an experiment in decision making. The instructions are simple. If you follow them closely and make appropriate decisions you may

Table 6. *Payoff table; smallest value of X chosen*

| Your choice of X | 7 | 6 | 5 | 4 | 3 | 2 | 1 |
|---|---|---|---|---|---|---|---|
| 7 | 1.30 | 1.10 | 0.90 | 0.70 | 0.50 | 0.30 | 0.10 |
| 6 | — | 1.20 | 1.00 | 0.80 | 0.60 | 0.40 | 0.20 |
| 5 | — | — | 1.10 | 0.90 | 0.70 | 0.50 | 0.30 |
| 4 | — | — | — | 1.00 | 0.80 | 0.60 | 0.40 |
| 3 | — | — | — | — | 0.90 | 0.70 | 0.50 |
| 2 | — | — | — | — | — | 0.80 | 0.60 |
| 1 | — | — | — | — | — | — | 0.70 |

make an appreciable amount of money, which will be paid to you at the end.

In this experiment you will participate in a decision problem with 6 people. There will be 10 rounds which will occur one after the other. In each round, every participant will choose a decision number between 1 and 7. The value of your payoff will be determined by both the value of the decision number you choose and the minimum of the decision numbers chosen by the other members of the group.

The minimum choice is simply the lowest number chosen by any member of the group. For example, the minimum of the six numbers 33, 30, 34, 32, 34, 32 is obviously 30.

To determine your payoff in any round, look at Table 6, which is attached to these instructions. In this table, your decision choice is listed down the left hand side, and across the top is listed the minimum choice of the group. To find your payoff in any round, locate the row associated with the decision number you have chosen. Looking across this you will see what your payoff will be, depending upon what the minimum choice of the group is. For example, if you choose 4 and the minimum value of the group is 2, you will earn 60 cents that round.

At the beginning of every period, you will write on a reporting sheet (Table 7) your participant number (which appears in the upper right hand corner of your instructions) and the value of the decision number you have chosen. These sheets will be collected by the experimental administrator and brought up to the front of the room, where they will be inspected. In addition, you must be sure to write your decision number on the worksheet provided you under the column labeled Your decision number. The experimental administrator will then calculate the mini-

Table 7. *Worksheet*

| Round | Your decision number (1, 2, 3, 4, 5, 6, 7) | Minimum of group | Payoff |
|-------|---------------------------------------------|------------------|--------|
| 1 | | | |
| 2 | | | |
| 3 | | | |
| 4 | | | |
| 5 | | | |
| 6 | | | |
| 7 | | | |
| 8 | | | |
| 9 | | | |
| 10 | | | |
| | Total payoff | | |

mum of these choices and announce it to the group. From this announcement you should be able to look at your payoff table (Table 6) and determine your payoff. At this point you should write down the announced minimum and your payoff for that round in columns labeled Minimum value of $X$ and and Your earnings, respectively.

When this round is over we will proceed to the next round, which will occur in an identical manner.

*Final payoffs:* Your final payoff in this part of the experiment will be equal to the $5.00 payment we will give you for showing up plus the sum of what you have earned over the 10 rounds of the experiment.

When this experiment is over, we will proceed to another experiment, which will be described to you at that time. Your final payoff from engaging in both experiments will equal the sum of your payoffs in each experiment plus your initial $5.00 show-up fee. Hence, if you earn $X$ in the first experiment and $Y$ in the second, your final payoff on leaving will be $Z = \$5 + \$X + \$Y$.

### High vulnerability (±10) instructions

*Introduction:* You are about to participate in an experiment on group decision making. A number of research foundations have provided funds to run these experiments. Depending on the decisions you and other participants in the experiments make, you may be able to earn a considerable payoff, which will be given to you as you leave.

*Your task in this experiment:* As you walked into the room you were randomly assigned to a group of six subjects. You will be in this group for the entire experiment, which will last for 25 rounds.

When you sit down at your computer terminal, your screen will appear as follows:

| Round | Decision No. | Group Rev. | Target Rev. (360 fr.) | Payment | Cost | Earnings paym − cost |
|---|---|---|---|---|---|---|
| 1 | | | | | | |
| 2 | | | | | | |
| 3 | | | | | | |
| 4 | | | | | | |
| 5 | | | | | | |
| 6 | | | | | | |
| 7 | | | | | | |
| 8 | | | | | | |
| 9 | | | | | | |
| 10 | | | | | | |
| • | | | | | | |
| • | | | | | | |
| • | | | | | | |
| • | | | | | | |
| 25 | | | | | | |

*DO NOT TOUCH any computer key until we instruct you to.*

In round 1 of the experiment, you and the other five subjects in your group will be asked to type in a number between 0 and 100. The computer will prompt you to do so by stating,

*Please enter a number between 0 and 100.*

We call the number you enter your decision number. You enter your decision number by typing it on the number keys and hitting the return key when you are finished. The computer will then confirm your choice by stating:

*You have chosen . Is that what you wanted?*

If this is, in fact, the decision number you want to enter, push the Y (Yes) key. Your participation in this round of the experiment will then be over. If you wish to change your mind, or you made a mistake in your typing, type N (No), and you will be prompted to choose another number. When you have successfully decided on a decision number and entered it, your participation in this round of the experiment will be over.

*Round-by-round payoffs:* In each round of the experiment you will receive a payment in a fictitious currency called "francs." (The francs you earn will be converted into dollars at the end of the experiment at a rate to be described shortly.) The payment you receive will depend on your decision number and those of the other members of your group as well as the realization of a random number. Precisely how the random number influences your payment is described in the next section. Your actual payoff (or earnings) in any round is the difference between the payment you receive and the direct cost to you of the decision number you selected as given by the cost schedule of Table 1 [not included here]. In other words:

Earnings = payment − decision cost

Let us see specifically how both these components determine your earnings.

*How your payment is determined:* When you and the other members of your group have entered your decision numbers (in column 2), the computer will add them up. We will call the resulting number the *Group Total*. The computer will then randomly choose a number between −10 and +10 and add it to the group total. When we say "randomly," we mean that each number in the interval −10 to +10 has an equal chance of being chosen. Hence the chance of −10 being chosen is equal to the chance of +5 being chosen, which in turn is equal to the chance of 0 being chosen, and so on. Finally, the sum of this random number and the *Group Total* will be multiplied by the number 1.5 (francs) to get what we call *Group Revenue*, which will appear in column 3 on your screen as "Group Rev." For example, say that the decision numbers of the six members of your group are $z_1, z_2, z_3, z_4, z_5$, and $z_6$, where $z_1$ is the decision number of subject #1, $z_2$ is the decision number of subject #2, and so on. Further suppose that the random number generated by the computer is +5. Then the *Group Total* would be $(z_1 + z_2 + z_3 + z_4 + z_5 + z_6 + 5)$ and the *Group Revenue* would be $1.5 (z_1 + z_2 + z_3 + z_4 + z_5 + z_6 + 5)$. As you can see, Group Revenue will thus reflect both the choices of each group member regarding his/her decision number and the realization of the random number, namely, pure chance.

Group Revenue (Group Total) is the basis of your individual payment. Specifically, in each round of the experiment, your group will be assigned a target Group Revenue of 360 francs. (NOTE THAT IN

ORDER FOR YOUR GROUP TO REACH THE GROUP REV-
ENUE TARGET OF 360 IT IS NECESSARY THAT ON AVERAGE
EACH OF YOU CHOOSE A DECISION NUMBER OF 40 SINCE 6
× 40 = 240 (GROUP TOTAL) AND 240 × 1.5 = 360 (GROUP REV-
ENUE). [On average the random number will be zero].) If your Group
Revenue equals or exceeds 360 francs, each of you will receive a payment of one-sixth of that Group-Revenue. In other words, each member
of your group will receive an equal share of the Group Revenue that is
realized. If Group Revenue is less than 360 francs, each member will
receive the fixed amount of 8.75 francs.

REFERENCES

Brandts, J. and W. B. MacLeod (1991)."Equilibrium Selection in Experimental
Games with Recommended Play." Mimeo, Department d'Economia i
Historia Economica, Universitat Autonoma de Barcelona.
Coleman, J. (1988). "Social Capital in the Creation of Human Capital,"
*American Journal of Sociology* 94(Suppl.): S95–S120.
Cooper, R., D. DeJong, R. Forsythe, and T. Ross (1989). "Communication in the
Battle of the Sexes Game," *Rand Journal of Economics* 20: 568–87.
Crawford, V. (1991). "An Evolutionary Interpretation of VanHuyck, Battalio,
and Beil's Experimental Results on Coordination," *Games and Economic
Behavior* 3: 25–59.
Fukayama, Francis (1995). *Trust*. New York: Free Press.
Nalbantian, H. and A. Schotter (1997). "Productivity under Group Incentives:
An Experimental Study," *American Economic Review* 87(3).
Putnam, Robert (1993). "The Prosperous Community: Social Capital and Public
Life," *The American Prospect* 13: 35–42.
———(1995). "Bowling Alone: America's Declining Social Capital," *Journal of
Democracy* 6(1): 65–78.
VanHuyck, J., R. Battalio, and R. Beil (1990). "Tacit Coordination Games,
Strategic Uncertainty, and Coordination Failure," *American Economic Re-
view* 80: 234–48.
VanHuyck, J., R. Battalio, and R. Beil (1991). "Strategic Uncertainty, Equilib-
rium Selection Principles, and Coordination Failure in Average Opinion
Games," *Quarterly Journal of Economics* 106: 886–910.
VanHuyck, J. B., A. B. Gillette, and R. C. Battalio (1992). "Credible Assign-
ments in Coordination Games," *Games and Economic Behavior* 4(4): 606–
26.

# CHAPTER 15

# Trust: beliefs and morality

*Jonathan Baron*

Trust is necessary for organizations to function well, both internally and in their relations with each other. Trust has been considered a form of human capital, a public good. Few if any social scientists or political leaders complain about there being too much trust. Many contributors to this volume are concerned with trust as a good.

Trust is important in the functioning of firms and institutions. One of the qualities of good academic departments, for example, is that people do their work for real, without pretending or excessive complaining.

Trust is also important in relations between citizens and government. Giving power to the government requires believing, or acting as if one believed, that the government officials involved will use the power correctly. Ultimately, this involves trust in one's fellow citizens. They must be trusted not only to do their jobs when they are government employees, but also to recognize and correct future errors of policy. Without such trust, change becomes difficult. People are afraid to risk giving power to the government for fear of some error that will not be corrected, so they become attached to the status quo.

Breyer (1993) has described a vicious circle resulting from mistrust of government: simplistic laws that tie the hands of government, government abuses that result from trying to apply those laws, more mistrust, more laws, etc. So trust in government may also require trust in the ability of government officials to make wise judgments. Of course, the officials must deserve such trust, and Breyer discusses ways to bring about a situation in which they do deserve it.

Trust is also important at an international level. We must trust people from other countries to negotiate honestly, to try to keep their commitments to treaties and other agreements, and not to use military force except in self-defense. International commerce clearly depends on trust in foreign business associates to be as honorable toward foreigners as toward compatriots. International trust will become more important as the world moves to solve environmental, population, and resource problems that affect many nations.

If trust is a good, and if we want to promote it, what exactly do we want to promote? In one sense, trust is a belief about the goodness or rationality of others. If we want person X to believe that others are good (or rational), and if X's beliefs about others are generally accurate, then either we must make sure that the other people *are* good or we must deceive X into having inaccurate beliefs. Of course, if X is cynical to the point of inaccuracy, then we can increase her trust by bringing her beliefs into line with the facts.

However, trust is not just a belief. It is also a behavioral disposition that is somewhat independent of belief. In this sense, we can make X more trusting by changing her behavior alone. We can promulgate a norm of trust as a behavioral disposition. Of course, such dispositions are affected by beliefs, and beliefs are affected by reality, but there is slippage at each of these links. Although the effort to influence beliefs independently of reality may require deception, the effort to influence behavior independently of beliefs requires nothing necessarily immoral or irrational.

We may thus speak of two kinds of trust. The first is believing something about others. The second is behaving as if you believed this. Although the second sense may be derivative, it is no less real or important.

In this note, I discuss the nature of trust. Then I review some laboratory measures that could be interpreted as telling us about trust. Use of these measures may help to inform us about the psychology of trust, so that we can promote it better. I conclude with some comments about what sort of trust we ought to promote.

### What we trust people to do

If we want to promote trust in society or in organizations, either as a belief or as a disposition, then we need to know more precisely what kind of trust we want to promote. Different kinds of trust correspond to different beliefs about the behavior of others.

There are several things we can believe about others. First, we can believe that others will not "tremble," that is, that they will pursue their goals without error. This is a kind of belief in the competence of others. Second, we can believe that others are not myopic, that they are sufficiently concerned about their long-run self-interest. Third, we can believe that others will be sufficiently altruistic, that is, willing to sacrifice their own self-interest for some greater good. This category includes a belief that people are not sadistic or competitive in a way that leads them to rejoice in the losses of others.

Each of these dispositions might be limited in some way. In particular, it might be limited to some group of others, such as members of one's firm, institution, or nation. Other classifications of the limits of trust are possible.

Of particular interest is the classification of trust in the altruism of others. We can have different beliefs about the conditions under which this altruism will be displayed. The altruism of others might be limited to members of a certain group, or to those who also have an opportunity to display the same kind of altruism in a way that might be seen as reciprocal (even when each person must decide without knowing the other's decision). I shall call the last kind of situation "cooperative." Cooperation is a response open to each of several people, such that each cooperative response is better for this group on the whole but worse for the person who makes it. Trust in people's willingness to cooperate is especially important, for reasons I shall discuss.

Altruistic behavior – and hence trust in others' altruism – can also be classified in terms of the object of the self-sacrifice. Self-sacrifice can serve the interest of others, when some behavior involves a small sacrifice for self and a great benefit to others. Or it can serve some principle, such as obligation to keep a promise, even when nobody benefits immediately. The principle in question might also be some form of fairness. Fairness might require one subject in an ultimatum game to give up half of her money, even though the other subject is much richer and thus benefits less from the money. Another principle that people might be trusted to follow is that of contingent cooperation, which specifies that you should cooperate when you believe that most others in your position will also cooperate (Baron 1994). This might be called pitching in and doing your share.

Sometimes the various forms of trust are difficult to distinguish because the behaviors in question are motivated in more than one way. In organizations, for example, altruism and concern for long-run self-interest often work together to produce the same other-regarding behavior. So trust in long-term prudence and trust in cooperative altruism are indistinguishable. Workers might expect to be rewarded with promotions and raises for contributions they make to the organization. Often, though, the most effective workers seem to be motivated by a sense of duty or concern for others rather than their long-run self-interest, although they may occasionally think to themselves that their efforts will in the end be rewarded. Sometimes people are motivated by simple altruistic concern for their fellow workers. When people can be trusted to behave altruistically or cooperatively, many types of enforcement become superfluous.

## Trust as morality

Trust is a virtue, not just a belief. The virtue of trust is the tendency to behave *as if* one believes that others will behave in the right way, and the tendency to value such behavior in oneself and others. A virtue is a kind of social norm that we endorse for others, and, by implication, for ourselves (Baron 1996b).

Such a norm could take the form of endorsing self-deception. It could tell us to change our belief so as to think well of others. Although some people could interpret it this way, I do not. I think that the norm tells us to give others the benefit of the doubt *in our behavior*, whatever we might think privately. It tells us to have courage, to lie down and bare our necks, even when we are trembling inside.

A competing norm might be called the norm of suspiciousness. It tells us to watch out, to avoid entanglements, to have everything in writing, to hire a lawyer. People who violate this norm are seen as saps or suckers, as weak. If the norm of suspiciousness is a virtue, then it is a personal virtue, not a moral one. It does us little good to have a society filled with people like this. It benefits only the individuals, and, even then, only if others tolerate those who follow this norm. It is the kind of norm that parents might teach their children out of a concern for their children's welfare, but we don't hear preachers or university presidents tell us to watch our wallets.

The distinction between trust as belief and trust as a norm of behavior may seem somewhat artificial. People, after all, adjust their behavior to follow their beliefs, and they adjust their beliefs to be congruent with their behavior (e.g., Ellsworth and Ross 1983). But not entirely. Moreover, thinking of trust as a norm leads us to think of different ways to increase it aside from deceiving people about what other people are likely to do, or aside from fomenting revolutions.

Following the norm of trust has an effect on both the beliefs and the norms of others. It creates a virtuous circle opposite to the vicious one I have described. My evidence that this norm exists in society comes from my own experience. It was explicitly taught to me, over and over, by Leslie Cheek, the head of a school I attended in the eighth grade. He said that, if we act as if we expect the best from others, they will often behave better as a result. I have tried to follow this principle, when I remember it.

## Use of games to measure trust

Various experimental games are sensitive to various forms of trust. In the general form of these games a subject chooses between two options, call them trusting and cautious. The trusting option leads to a better outcome than the cautious option if the other subjects behave in a "good" way, and to a worse outcome if they do not. The choice of the trusting option thus suggests either a belief in the goodness of others or a willingness to behave as if one had this belief. The goodness may take the various forms I have sketched, from rational pursuit of self-interest to altruism. Only a few of the various kinds of trust have been explored in laboratory games, mostly those dealing with trust in the cooperativeness of others.

Berg, Dickhaut, and McCabe (1995) studied a simple trust game that took the form of an investment. In each round, one subject was given ten dollars. This subject could send some or all of that to a second subject, and the money would triple in value. The second subject could give back some money to the first. On average, the first subject invested about half of the money, and the second subject gave back about the same. The kind of trust at issue is cooperation, but a specific sort of cooperation in which the second player knew that the first had first behaved cooperatively to some extent.

Orbell and Dawes (1993; see also Orbell, Dawes, and Schwartz-Shea 1994) studied trust with a prisoner's dilemma game in which each subject could choose to play or not. The payoffs for mutual cooperation or free riding were positive, but those for mutual defection or being a "sucker" were negative. The decision to play was thus a sign of trust in the other player to cooperate. Cooperation was greater when the option not to play was available, mostly because defectors, expecting others to be like them, tended not to play.

In these kinds of games, it is important to ask subjects about their beliefs, which cannot easily be inferred from behavior alone. Subjects may, for example, cooperate because of a moral belief that this is the right thing to do, even if their belief that cooperation is in their self-interest would be insufficient to motivate cooperation on its own.

## Evidence for attitudinal effects

Some evidence suggests that trust – in the form of trusting behavior – can be affected by experience with the behavior of other players in experimental games, as argued by Schotter (this volume). This suggests that trust as a belief about others plays some role in trusting behavior.

Fleishman (1988) gave subjects false feedback about the behavior of others in order to manipulate their expectations. The effects of this feedback depended on whether the situation was described to the subjects as a "give some" game or a "take some" game. In the give-some game, each subject in a five-person group was given 100 points (each worth 1/3 cent) on each trial. The subject could give any number of those points to a central pool or stock. At the end of each trial, the number of points in the pool was doubled and divided among all the subjects. (Each subject would thus get 200 points per trial, if all contributed all their points.) In the take-some game, 500 units were given to the pool at the beginning of the trial, and each subject could take up to 100 units. Formally, the games are identical, except for the description in terms of giving or taking. Not giving a unit is the equivalent of taking it, and vice versa. To manipulate expectations about others, the experimenter told subjects after the first trial that the pool contained either 380 or 120 units. In the give-some game, subjects *gave less* on subsequent trials when they thought that the pool contained 380 after the first trial than when they thought it had 120. That is, behavior was opposite that of what others were perceived as doing. In the take-some game, they *took less* when they thought that the pool had 380. Behavior was the same as what others were perceived as doing. (These effects were small and should be replicated, but they are consistent with previous conflicting results cited by Fleishman. [1988].)

These results can be understood in terms of conflicting rules for behavior, which have been called fear and greed. Fear is fear of being a sucker. It induces behavior that is similar to the behavior of others, cooperating when others are perceived as cooperating and defecting when others are perceived as defecting. Greed is the tendency to take advantage of others' goodwill. Evidently, give-some subjects reasoned, "If nobody else is giving anything, then I'd better do it, but if others are giving a lot, I can take advantage of them." This is greed. Take-some subjects seemed to reason, "If nobody else is taking, then I'd better not take either, but if others are taking, then I can take too." This is fear. It seems to prevent harmful actions but not harmful omissions.

Other research has examined the continuity between laboratory measures and measures of attitudes about real-world analogues. Yamagishi and Sato (1986) found evidence for individual differences in fear and greed. On every trial, each of five subjects was given a number of points (worth money), some of which the subject could contribute to a common pool. All subjects received bonus points that depended on these contributions.

Two conditions were of special interest. In the *minimum* condition, the number of bonus points was determined by the size of the contribution of the subject who had contributed the *least*. Here, fear would be the major cause of defections: If you think that someone else is going to be a fink and give very little, there is no advantage to anyone from your not "finking out" yourself by giving nothing or very little. Greed would play only a small role here, because too much of it would penalize you as well as everyone else. In the *maximum* condition, the bonus depended on the amount given by the highest contributor. This is like volunteering for a dangerous mission on behalf of a group, when only a few volunteers are required. Here, one is little affected by a few defectors, so fear of someone else's defecting plays little role. One need not fear that one's own cooperative action will be useless to the group, either. Greed, however, may play a larger role, for one's own contribution also matters little, except in the unlikely event that one is the highest contributor.

Yamagishi and Sato found that friends cooperated more than strangers in the minimum condition but not in the maximum condition. Presumably friends were less afraid that they would cheat each other by giving less money, but friendship had no effect on personal greed. Subjects (Japanese students) were also given a questionnaire about their attitudes toward public questions, with items designed to assess both fear and greed as general motives in the subjects. Here are some "fear" items (pp. 69–70):

Help to developing nations should be limited to the minimum, because it is only exploited by a small group of people.
During the oil shock, people rushed to stores to buy a stock of toilet paper because people are concerned only with their own interest and not with the benefit of society.
There will be more people who will not work, if the social security system is developed further.

Here are some greed items (p. 70):

In order to be a successful person in this society, it is important to make use of every opportunity.
It is not morally bad to think first of one's own benefit and not of other people's.

The score on the fear scale correlated with defection in the minimum condition, but not in the maximum condition. In the minimum condition, where only one "fink" could prevent everyone from getting a bonus, subjects who expressed fear and distrust in the questionnaire were more likely than other subjects to defect. The score on the greed scale correlated with defection in the maximum condition, but not in the minimum condition. In the maximum condition, subjects who were greedy according to the questionnaire were the ones more likely to defect. These results not only indicate the existence of individual differences in the motives in question but also suggest that the motives are quite general, affecting attitudes toward public issues as well as behavior in laboratory experiments.

In the minimum condition, subjects' *expectations* about what others would do correlated highly with their own behavior; this was less true in the maximum condition. The minimum condition thus seems more sensitive to trust as a belief that others are cooperative.

In another study, Yamagishi (1986) used a short questionnaire to measure individual differences in trust. Subjects indicated their agreement with the following items, which are concerned with a variety of altruistic (vs. selfish) behaviors:

Most people tell a lie when they can benefit from doing so.
Those devoted to unselfish causes are often exploited by others.
Some people do not cooperate because they pursue only their own short-
    term self-interest. Thus, things that can be done well if people
    cooperate often fail because of these people.
Most people are basically honest (reversed item).
There will be more people who will not work if the social security system
    is developed further.

Each subject could contribute points to a public pool, where the points doubled in value and were then distributed among the four subjects. In some conditions, subjects could also contribute points toward a punishment fund to penalize the lowest contributor to the original pool, in proportion to the amount contributed to this fund. Subjects who were trusting, according to the trust scale, made higher contributions to the public pool when the punishment fund was not available. When the punishment fund was available, low trust subjects contributed more to it than high trust subjects, and the differences in contributions to the public pool disappeared. The low trust subjects' contributions to the public pool were more affected by the availability of the punishment fund.

Parks and Hulbert (1995) used Yamagishi's trust scale to study individual differences in cooperation in public good and resource dilemma games. In the public good game, three of five subjects had to "contribute" in order for all the subjects to get a bonus. On each trial of the resource dilemma, subjects could withdraw from a common pool, which increased by 10 percent after the withdrawals. Each game had a "no fear" condition, in which a payoff of zero was impossible. (In the public good game, for example, contributors got their contribution returned if the bonus was not provided.) The trust scale correlated with contributions only when fear was present, in both games. The trust scale thus behaved like the fear scale of Yamagishi and Sato (1986), with which it shared a couple of items.

Note that the trust scale is ostensibly about beliefs. This does not mean that beliefs, rather than moral values, account for the correlations with behavior. People bring their beliefs into line with their values, as I noted earlier. So the correlation with behavior could be mediated partly by values.

These results say little about where the individual differences arise. Solodkin, Chaitas, and Baron (1995) examined individual differences as a function of national culture. We gave hypothetical social dilemmas to college students in Argentina, Mexico, and the United States. For example, one dilemma read, "Imagine yourself living in a very polluted city, a city with so much pollution that many new laws have been made to fight it. One of these laws requires everyone to have his or her car inspected every six months, and if the emission levels are high, the car has to be fixed. Suppose your car fails the inspection, and imagine you have two alternatives: One is to pay one hundred dollars to have your car fixed. This will not make it less likely that you will need it fixed after the next inspection, six months later. The other is to pay forty-five dollars to the mechanic so that he gives you a permit to drive for six months." After each dilemma, we asked subjects (along with other questions) what they would do, what proportion of people in the same situation would pay the one hundred dollars, whether they would be more likely to pay the one hundred dollars if they thought that almost everyone else would do it, and whether paying the one hundred dollars would be in their long-run self-interest.

Latins (Argentinians and Mexicans) did not differ from North Americans (U.S. subjects) (or from each other) in stated willingness to pay the one hundred dollars. But Latins were less inclined to believe that *others* would pay it. This was so despite the fact that beliefs about others generally correlated with the subject's own willingness to cooperate. There is evidently some other determinant of willingness to cooperate aside from beliefs about what others will do.

A hint about what it might be was in the answers to the question about whether cooperation was in one's long-term self-interest. Subjects generally answered this affirmatively, but Latins were especially likely to do so. And the affirmative answer also correlated with stated willingness to cooperate. Thus, the willingness of Latins to cooperate may be decreased by their belief about others but increased by their belief in long-run benefits. Unfortunately, we did not ask about the nature of these long-run benefits, but another study suggests that subjects confuse the benefit of their own cooperation with the benefit of everyone's cooperating (Baron 1996c). For example, in response to a scenario about overfishing, one subject said, "By not cutting back on my current level of fishing I would more than likely be hurting myself in the future, for sooner or later the fish population would dwindle down to zero, leaving me with absolutely no income. I am willing to give up short-term financial growth for long-term financial stability." Such a confusion supports a moral norm of cooperation.

### Other effects of trust

If trust in others is a norm, what form should this norm take? Should we act as if we believe that people are perfect utilitarians? rational pursuers of their self-interest? contingent cooperators?

I suggest the following norm as something worth encouraging. We should think of each other as willing to sacrifice somewhat, but not excessively, for the common good. Thus, when setting up cooperative agreements, some enforcement mechanism may be needed, but it need not be draconian. Spot audits of taxpayers together with small penalties for violations may be sufficient, for example. We should also think of each other as willing to cooperate to set up such reasonable enforcement mechanisms, that is, to solve second-order social dilemmas. We should endorse such willingness as a social norm, and we should behave as if we expect it from each other.

Norms of good citizenship should also include trust in government and in the ability of democratic government to correct errors. We should discourage arguments based on mistrust in government, especially when these arguments are used to oppose an otherwise good solution to some social problem.

Norms of this sort could be taught as part of civics in school. They could be supported by politicians, journalists, and professors. Such support could work against the kind of vicious circle that leads to waste and disorder.

REFERENCES

Baron, J. (1994). *Thinking and Deciding*, 2d ed. New York: Cambridge University Press.

———(1995). "Blind Justice: Fairness to Groups and the Do-No-Harm Principle," *Journal of Behavioral Decision Making* 8: 71–83.

—— (1996a). "Political Action vs. Voluntarism in Social Dilemmas and Aid for the Needy." Unpublished manuscript, Department of Psychology, University of Pennsylvania.

—— (1996b). "Norm-Endorsement Utilitarianism and the Nature of Utility," *Economics and Philosophy* 12: 165–82.

—— (1996c). "The Long-Run Fallacy as a Reason to Cooperate in Social Dilemmas." Unpublished manuscript, Department of Psychology, University of Pennsylvania.

Berg, J., J. Dickhaut, and K. McCabe (1995). "Trust, Reciprocity, and Social-History," *Games and Economic Behavior* 10: 122–42.

Breyer, S. (1993). *Breaking the Vicious Circle: Toward Effective Risk Regulation.* Cambridge, Mass.: Harvard University Press.

Ellsworth, P. C., and L. Ross (1983). "Public Opinion and Capital Punishment: A Close Examination of the Views of Abolitionists and Retentionists," *Crime and Delinquency* 29: 116–69.

Fleishman, J. A. (1988). "The Effects of Decision Framing and Others' Behavior on Cooperation in a Social Dilemma," *Journal of Conflict Resolution* 32: 162–80.

Orbell, J. M., and R. Dawes (1993). "Social Welfare, Cooperators Advantage, and the Option of Not Playing the Game," *American Sociological Review* 58: 787–800.

Orbell, J., R. Dawes, and P. Schwartz-Shea (1994). "Trust, Social Categories, and Individuals: The Case of Gender," *Motivation and Emotion* 18: 109–28.

Parks, C. D., and L. G. Hulbert (1995). "High and Low Trusters' Responses to Fear in a Payoff Matrix," *Journal of Conflict Resolution* 39: 718–30.

Solodkin, A., S. Chaitas, J. Baron (1995). "Students' Attitudes Toward Social Dilemmas in Argentina, Mexico, and the United States." Unpublished manuscript, Department of Psychology, University of Pennsylvania.

Yamagishi, T. (1986). "The Provision of a Sanctioning System as a Public Good," *Journal of Personality and Social Psychology* 51: 110–16.

Yamagishi, T., and K. Sato (1986). "Motivational Basis of the Public Goods Problem," *Journal of Personality and Social Psychology* 50: 67–73.

CHAPTER 16

# Institutional commitment: values or incentives?

*Russell Hardin*

A key question in trying to understand organizations is how they induce their members to do what produces organizational successes. In many organizations, it is assumed that the main device is simply the incentive of pay for work, although it often seems that monitoring is inadequate to establish workers' reliability and, hence, inadequate to relate personal reward to organizational contribution. In other organizations, it is commonly supposed that members have their own personal commitments to values that induce them to perform. This latter view is especially common in accounts of governmental organizations. It is a lesser version of Emile Durkheim's view that social order depends on pervasive normative commitments by citizens.

A standard economist's response to such claims is that motivational systems are unlikely to shift from one realm to another and that people perform well or badly in both economic and governmental organizations largely for the same reasons: personal benefits. The economist's view is that organizations merely impose a system of incentives to get individual members to commit themselves in ways that benefit the organizations or fulfill the purposes of the organizations. In contemporary public choice analysis, the economist's view is pushed to the limit and it is commonly assumed that all role holders in government (or other) institutions will seek rents from their positions. That is, they will attempt to profit personally as much as possible from the powers they have in their positions.

The writing of this chapter has been supported by the Center for Advanced Study in the Behavioral Sciences, the Guggenheim Foundation, the National Science Foundation (grant number SBR-9022192), and New York University. Some of its argument is borrowed from Hardin (1988a), a review essay of Brennan and Buchanan (1985). I am grateful to an anonymous reader and to colleagues in the rational choice seminar of the Center for Advanced Study for unusually useful comments on an earlier draft.

419

Those who think government officials must act normatively or public-spiritedly can defend their supposition by pointing to the apparent success of many government agencies in carrying out some policies for public benefit. If self-interest entails the massive rent-seeking of the public choice thesis, then self-interest cannot be the central motivation of government officials.

Moreover, within the economic account, a critic may wonder how an organization finds people to fill the roles of monitors if these people, too, must be motivated merely by the monitored matching of their rewards with their contributions. Joseph Schumpeter's claim that economic analysis applies as well to government can be matched by a claim that the problems of government are also the problems of economics. The traditional political question – Who is custodian of the custodians? – seems as apt for many economic organizations as for governmental organizations. After all, both kinds of organizations often are intended to serve the interests of people other than their members. The too easy answer for a simplistically conceived economic organization that is wholly owned by an entrepreneur is that the entrepreneur's self-interest perfectly matches the interest of an ideal custodian for the organization. For more complex economic organizations or for typical public agencies, this simplistic resolution of the custodial task is not plausible.

It is a perhaps gross but still instructive simplification to suppose that an organization is simply a collection of individuals coordinated by a strategic structure. Ideally, that structure could be designed in ways that avoid the need for custodians who are motivated by considerations different from the ordinary interests of other members of the organization. The structure that is implicit in many incentive models of organizational behavior is essentially exchange, which is aptly modeled by the prisoner's dilemma. Unfortunately, prisoner's dilemma interactions often require external enforcement to make them go cooperatively. I wish to propose, however, that the more compelling structure in many organizations is simple coordination, which works in large part by de facto imposing costs on individuals for not going along with the relevant coordination. In addition, an initial coordination blocks group violations of relevant coordination behavior because it makes the costs of recoordination high. Recoordination would have to take the initial form of collective action to resolve a large-number prisoner's dilemma, which would be subject to the commonly prohibitive logic of collective action.

To see the structure of this argument, first let us consider the motivational structure of a public agency, that is, an agency in which the overall purpose of the organization is not plausibly the purpose of its self-interested members or of any potential custodian. In such a structure, incentives for relevant behavior must be internalized in the organization itself. That is to say, various members must somehow impose incentives on each other in lieu of a simple hierarchy of control. In general, there are two distinct problems at issue: internal and external matching. Most of the focus here will be on the institution, on its internal incentive structure. The most important problem for social order is the external problem of getting institutions to serve some general interest or purpose for the larger society.

At first thought, it might seem that, for an organization that serves the interests of its members or role holders, compliance with organizational objectives would be easy. But this is generally false, as is most obvious perhaps when there is a problem of the logic of collective action. To a substantial extent, therefore, the internal and external matching problems are basically similar. This leaves open a difficult issue, which is how institutions with public purposes could get established at all. At the stage of origination, one might suppose the expansion of an individual or family entrepreneurial enterprise into a larger and eventually quite large organization poses a problem of matching incentives that is quite different from the matching problem in the creation of a public agency. I will address this issue only briefly (in the section, Unequal Coordination) and will not consider its resolution here, although David Hume, Adam Smith, Elizabeth Colson, and others, have discussed it in ways that suggest that the problems of creating economic and state agencies are not radically different. Indeed, Margaret Levi (1988) and Mancur Olson (forthcoming) have presented articulate theories of the state that make its creation an analogue of the creation of an entrepreneurial profit-making organization. My chief focus will be on the maintenance of incentives within organizations to do what serves the ostensible purposes of the organizations.

If coordination devices are the solution to the internal institutional problem of getting incentives and commitments in line, then *among the chief obstacles to the success of those devices will be problems specific to coordination*. These include varied possible coordinations or subcoordinations on contrary patterns of action, as discussed later. The solution to these is to block such subcoordination.

## Institutional commitment

For organizations, groups, and institutions as much as for individuals, the ability to commit themselves enables them to achieve their purposes. For example, mobs are collectively incapable of committing themselves to future actions and can therefore extract gains only instantly. Hence, they cannot extract real commitments from, say, the officials against whom they might organize or from the individuals or institutions whom they might support. The mobs in Teheran at the end of the regime of the shah could topple that regime; they could not put another in its place. And many of the people in those mobs paid dearly for the peculiar combination of their capacity and their incapacity. Organizations riven with dissent often fail to achieve any significant part of what any faction wants, as the National Association for the Advancement of Colored People (NAACP) in recent years has failed almost across the board in every program. And a government on the verge of revolution, such as that of the shah or those of many nations, cannot make credible commitments because it cannot convince people that it will be around long enough to fulfill them. Yet many collectivities, organizations, and institutions seem to be able to make credible commitments and to convince relevant people that they will fulfill them. They convince us that our efforts to do things under their auspices can be expected to bear fruit. How do they do this?

Let us go back to individuals for a moment. When individuals keep their commitments, they may do so for one of at least two reasons: They may find it costly to renege because they will suffer specific sanctions, or they may simply find it in their direct interest to do what they have committed themselves to do. When an institution keeps its commitments, the reasons are parallel but more complex in structure. An institution keeps commitments because relevant individuals in the institution can be motivated to do what is necessary for the institution to follow through. There are at least two ways the relevant individuals may be motivated: They may face sanctions, and they may find it of no interest to try to push the institution in other directions. The first of these may generally be necessary when the individual can be a free rider and when free riding can undercut institutional commitment. The second has more the character of a convention, a coordination on a mutually beneficial policy. The particular form the coordination takes, however, may be a failure to coordinate on an alternative policy, a failure that stems from the high individual costs of organizing such a coordination.

Consider a case in which firing recalcitrants is not an option, so that the costs of recoordination on a new convention may be the chief incentive to comply with the going convention. Kenneth Shepsle argues that congressional committees are a very important source of the seeming stability of congressional actions from year to year in the face of constant turnover of membership (Shepsle 1991). Superficially, committees are important because they can commonly block legislation in their areas. If

I wish to overturn last year's legislation, I may face an enormous burden of organizing enough support to override the relevant committee. If the relevant committee likes what I want to do, I can get my bill through with far less organizational effort – the organization has been done in advance for my bill.

But why does all this work when some congressional majority might support a change in legislation? Because of the costs of changing the whole system from one in which committees play a central role to one in which committees can be turned over willy-nilly as majorities choose. These costs are far larger than merely the benefits that a majority might receive this moment from getting a particular bit of past legislation changed. For example, many individual members of Congress would be losers from a reform of the committee structure, as many Republicans with long tenure were losers when Newt Gingrich ignored seniority principles in appointing some committee chairs after the first Republican majority in forty years was elected in the House of Representatives in 1994. Hence, it will only be in the face of radically important changes that we can expect majorities to rise to strike against the committee structure. Typical legislative enactments will be allowed to continue as the relevant committees wish for want of a recoordination on an alternative.

This argument is roughly the same as the argument for why a particular constitutional regime works at all. Once it is in place and is working, no majority may object strongly enough to the way it works to bear the costs of recoordination on an alternative (Hardin 1989b). The argument also fits the more general argument of Thomas Hobbes for how citizens rationally ought to behave under a going regime (Hardin 1991).

The other device, the invocation of sanctions to punish free riding, may itself depend on coordination as well in the following way: It is through coordination that we elevate some people to the power to sanction others. I might strongly object to the use of sanctions against me, but I cannot motivate opposition to the sanctioning power to get us recoordinated on a system in which I would escape sanction. Indeed, because the costs of recoordination may be very great, I may personally simply bow to the sanction without any effort to change the structure that supports it. The device of sanctioning is often enough used in Congress (Lyndon Johnson and Sam Rayburn were noted for their punishment of defectors), although it may be far less important in the daily decisions on legislation than is the more direct failure of recoordination on alternative regimes to change legislative outcomes. Sanctioning may most widely be used against subjects of an institution than against role holders within the institution. For example, a legal system that regularly uses sanctions against errant citizens may seldom use sanctions against role holders in the legal system itself.

### Values or incentives?

The Durkheimian challenge is commonly put to rational choice theorists who study politics. If people are rational, such theorists are asked, how then do we explain the success of public agencies in motivating officials to carry out public programs? Indeed, this is more nearly framed as a taunt than as a question, because it is commonly assumed there can be no rational choice answer to it. Rather, we must give a normative answer, a claim that people just are moral to a sufficient extent to allow them to carry out their public duties properly. Steven Kelman thinks public-spiritedness is necessary for good bureaucratic actions (Kelman 1990); Paul Quirk thinks our salvation turns on officials' concern with what constitutes good public policy (Quirk 1990).

Although these are glib and ill-defined notions not backed by much argument, they may capture some of what motivates public officials. And no doubt there is a great deal of morally motivated behavior of other kinds by public officials, at least as much on average as by ordinary people. Perhaps public officials have even a bit more than average levels of moral commitment if there are self-selection biases – at the extreme, public agencies presumably do not typically hire criminals in numbers proportional to their numbers in the society (although they often do enable people to become criminals). But one wonders whether there is radically more than among ordinary people, as though we were somehow very good at selecting moral people for public roles or only moral people sought to fill such roles.

Conventional coordination may be the chief answer to the anti-rational-choice taunt. People do not have to be fundamentally public-spirited to be good public servants. They can be primarily interested in self, especially in income and career. As Madison advised, ambition is made to counter ambition (Madison 1987). Both bureaucratic and judicial systems generally include many checks on behavior, checks that make it easy for some to advance their careers or to block the careers of others by calling the others' actions properly to account. I block your wrong action in part because doing so benefits me personally. One of the most important incentives for sustaining the norm is that others cannot generally see benefits in ignoring or cooperating with dereliction by their colleagues and superiors.

Getting such a system established and working well may take several generations of officeholders. Once we have this system in place well enough, all have strong motivation to do roughly what is right from an institutional perspective. Such a conventional norm system may not work equally well at all levels or in all circumstances. But its force can be seen in recent decades in the forced removal from office of legislators, high ranking bureaucrats, presidential advisers, a president, and a vice president in the United States, and of ministers and other high ranking officials in England. Of course, we may occasionally judge, rightly or wrongly, that our interests can be furthered by acting against the institutional mandate. Then it may seem that we depend on direct sanction rather than this conventional underpinning for our behavior. However, even then, the sanctioning power is grounded in conventional coordination.

Although its rationale in part is similar, this is not the system of checks and balances envisioned by Montesquieu. It is, again, a finer grained application of Madison's injunction to counter ambition with ambition. In some ways it has more in common with competition among producers in a market than among departments of a government. To be sure, I block your action because I think it is wrong. But I do so with substantial support that makes my action costless or even beneficial to me. Similarly, I do my job well because others will generally support and reward me for working well. Moreover, it would be difficult to disrupt this system to anyone's benefit, including that of a national president or prime minister.

This is not to say that such a system can never be abused for essentially self-interested purposes. In addition it can be abused in a way that is peculiar evidence of how well the relevant norms can be conventionally created and enforced. It can be subject to what the French call *déformation professionnelle* – the tendency to support one's organization's supposed interests to the detriment of larger public purposes. The organized military is notoriously prone to such deformation, as in the Dreyfus Affair. But other bureaucracies, such as regulatory and welfare delivery agencies, are also often accused of such deformation. The oddity of this behavior is that the enlargement of an agency's mission is essentially a collective benefit to its staff and therefore must suffer from the logic of collective action. We individually have better career and income prospects from the expansion of our agency's mission. But, by the logic of collective action, I cannot be motivated by self-interest to take any risk to contribute to this general expansion in return for my paltry share of the expansion that results from my contribution. My incentive to contribute comes rather from the specific support I personally receive from colleagues in the agency, perhaps especially from superiors, who are all driven by our agency-specific conventional norm. It would be odd to suppose that such behavior was merely norm-directed.

Much of the criticism of government by economists of the Scottish Enlightenment and the so-called Chicago School has been directed at the problems of having self-interested officials administer government programs. Adam Smith extensively discussed the problem of self-interested officials. Geoffrey Brennan and James M. Buchanan allude to the issue in their discussion of a despotic government of one person who, given the power to decide on distributional issues, is essentially given ownership over all that is to be distributed (Brennan and Buchanan 1985, p. 115; also see p. 48). (Brennan and Buchanan briefly address this issue in a discussion of who will seek public office (p. 64), although here their central concern seems to be with those who seek elective office.)

The actual problem we face is how to make many, indeed, millions, of officials act in our interest. We seemingly resolve the problem through the force of norms for substantially disinterested behavior. However, to a large extent, the relevant norms can be established and enforced by convention, so that we can see them as essentially self-interested or at least as congruent with self-interest. And we can see them as largely internally generated within, not externally imposed on, public agencies (see further, Calvert forthcoming). The chief difficulty with this general conclusion is that the actual incentives faced by some agents might not fit the modal incentive of most agents to coordinate. Let us turn to several complicating considerations.

### Modal and nonmodal incentives

One cannot give a neat specification of the forms of coordination involved in the interactions that underlie major social institutions. One might suppose this is a failure of theory. But it is not. It is a deep problem of social life. The usual move in social theory is to focus on a very little piece of social order and to deal with it as a problem of multiple equilibria, as for example in David Hume's discussions of the rules of inheritance and of monarchical succession, both of which are extremely varied across even ostensibly similar societies (Hume 1978, 3.2.3, 504–13nn, 3.2.10, 553–67; cf. Hardin 1988b, pp. 34, 36, 48–50).

In a general game-theoretic account of social interactions, there are often disastrous equilibria, as in many prisoner's dilemma and collective action interactions. A natural supposition is that in such games, reaching equilibrium is bad, while in coordination games it is good. But the latter supposition is false. In the institutional coordination on a way of accomplishing some purpose there can also be disastrous or at least very inefficient equilibria even when the problem has the more benign structure of a coordination game. For a very simple but therefore very clear example consider Sweden's historical coordination on driving on the left, as in England. Most of Europe historically coordinated on driving on the right, and this made for severe problems in Sweden. Yet the coordination on driving left was a very strong equilibrium that could not be changed spontaneously even though it evidently had been established spontaneously. It required state intervention in 1967 at substantial cost to change from one coordination equilibrium to the other (Hardin 1988b, pp. 51–53). Suboptimal coordination is the bugbear of coordination problems.

The beauty of the example of the driving convention is that it is pristine and clear. It is the rare case of an objective instantiation of an ideal type. There are de facto two possible coordinations: All drive left or all drive right. They are in principle equally good, so that the only issue is to get the society onto one rather than neither. And no one would think it generally sensible to violate the convention that has been established in any given jurisdiction. North Americans might hate it that they have to take extra pains to drive left in Australia, but they recognize that they do have to if they wish to survive.

If there were only one jurisdiction, the left and the right convention would be equally beneficial, and the game of driving would be a matter of harmony, or pure coordination. Because most other nearby jurisdictions had the opposite convention, Sweden's drive-left convention was inferior to the drive-right convention. Most $n$-player game structures and most $n$-person social interactions are likely to be more nearly like the multiple-jurisdiction driving convention than like the ideal type of a single jurisdiction. Hence, it will be possible and even common that we will settle on suboptimal coordinations. These will commonly be better than other plausible outcomes, but they will not be the best possible.

A general characterization of the plausible game structures for the problem of institutional incentives for coordination would be extremely messy even though, modally, it might resemble the ideal type of the driving convention. Any particular game structure would be far too constrained to give a credible representation of general social order. Therefore one can compellingly object that we might as soon see poor as good outcomes. Consider several ways the game structure for a given institution can diverge from simple coordination – even from coordination that can be quite suboptimal – and responses to these.

The problem of social order (game theoretically) is how to get us onto coordination institutions and patterns of behavior, including institutions that can regulate noncoordination interactions such as prisoner's dilemma. Prisoner's dilemma interactions are pervasive in Hobbes's state of nature, which is itself an equilibrium in which life is nasty, brutish, and short. But *it is coordination on an institution of government* – not cooperation in a prisoner's dilemma – that overcomes the state of nature and produces good outcomes from many of the potential prisoner's dilemma interactions by legally, coercively blocking the extreme outcomes in which, essentially, one player steals from another rather than making an exchange (Hardin 1991).

Consider three ways the actual incentive structure of an institution or of a generalized behavior might differ systematically from the ideal type. First, the interaction might be coordination for most persons but prisoner's dilemma or otherwise noncoordination for some persons. For example, ethnic and other groups are often maintained by the imposition of norms of exclusion on the fringe members who do not have an interest in committing fully to the group (Hardin 1995, chap. 4). Second, the completely represented game structure of the interaction might be quasi prisoner's dilemma for everyone or for many, and cooperation in the piecemeal prisoner's dilemmas would undercut the institutional purpose. For example, police forces, particularly those that deal extensively with so-called vice, are subject to corruption. Such corruption might become endemic to whole units that are organized informally to maintain the cooperation on violating institutional purposes. Third, the full interaction might be coordination for all, but there might be a substantial group or groups whose best outcome is not the best outcome of some other group, so that the interaction is an unequal coordination. This problem is often acute for social coordination but may not be a major issue within institutions except insofar as an institution mirrors larger unequal social coordination.

### Modal coordination with some contrary incentives

Thrill seekers and risk takers might occasionally violate the driving convention **and** drive left in North America in order to pass others or merely for the hell of it. But they will be relatively extreme cases. Most drivers who discover they are on the wrong side of the road will hasten to correct their error. Many interactions will have this slightly mixed form: modally coordination but partially conflictive. Indeed, for any problem of general social order it would be odd to expect completely similar strategy preferences for all. Off the road, life is not an ideal type.

Moreover, even when certain outcomes represent coordination equilibria for most players, they may have a somewhat different structure for other players, as for the thrill-seeking driver who likes to tempt danger by driving on the wrong side of the road. Social institutions that are to work well will typically have to be *designed for the citizen with modal incentives to coordinate* and, often, with backup systems of enforcement to change the incentives of those whose incentives would otherwise be to violate the general coordination. H. L. A. Hart argued that social order depends on the generally normative commitments of the many in order to allow the coercion of the few. He sensibly supposed that coercion of the many would be impossible (Hart 1961, p. 88).

## Coordination with pervasive prisoner's dilemma incentives

In many organizations there is some prospect for individual role holders to engage in exchanges contrary to the organization's mission. If incentives for such behavior are pervasive, the organization's mission is at risk from individual violations and even more so from the possibility of subgroup coordination on protecting individuals against standard organizational sanctions for miscreant behavior. In an extreme case of such subgroup coordination, the subgroup might even coordinate on a system for forcing organizational members to cooperate in violating the organization's mission.

A well-known example of a substantial subgroup recoordination against the larger institution is the police force that is partially governed by an informally organized power structure to enforce cooperation in vice. By threatening sanctions against recalcitrants, that power structure can induce officers who do not otherwise think it in their interest to do so to engage in payoffs or other corrupt practices. The informal power structure itself might most commonly be a successful coordination by enough officers to give them effective sanctioning ability. Once they establish a core of cooperators in this enterprise, however, the structure of their further interaction with each other is coordination. Because it is informal and might be opposed by contrary interests, their coordination might be unstable. The strategic structure of the renegade group is therefore analogous to the general structure of the police force itself. This is the reason for its radically destructive quality: that it openly competes on similar terms with its parent institution.

Of course, we might think that an insurgency within some institution was good if viewed from an outside perspective of support for some purpose or value. But if we want an organization to accomplish the goals for which it is established, as typically most citizens must want their police forces to maintain order and to work against, not for, crime, then we would want the organization to have devices to block insurgent countercoordination.

## Unequal coordination

In larger social contexts, it is commonly possible that one group would benefit most from coordination on one outcome while another benefited most from coordination on another outcome even though both groups would strongly prefer coordination on either of these outcomes to any other (Hardin 1989a). There are numerous politically important examples of such unequal coordination, including coordination on sex roles, on differential ethnic positions within a going political order, and on a dominant language in the context of multilingual society with at least one secondary language in use, as in the case of francophones in the larger anglophone Canada.

(In the vocabulary of early game theory, the game of unequal coordination is called "battle of the sexes." As in much of verbal game theory, this is an objectionable name not merely because it is stupid but also because it fails to communicate the nature of the game. It may be impossible at this date spontaneously to recoordinate on a more appealing and more informative label for the very widely recognized prisoner's dilemma, which is a catchy but narrowly distorting name for the very general, fundamentally important strategic interaction of exchange. But perhaps the name "battle of the sexes" can be discreetly dropped from usage. There is some hope that it will be in the way linguistic coordinations typically do change, that is, intergenerationally.)

Within an organization, one might also often find a group whose position is less beneficial to its members than would be their position under some alternative structure for the organization. Indeed, organizational hierarchy generally is far more beneficial to some than to others, often arguably for reasons unrelated to the effectiveness of the organization in achieving its outcomes. But we may commonly find that the unequal coordinations of the larger society are directly mirrored within organizations, so that, for example, one social group fills managerial roles and another fills menial roles. Insofar as merit matters for the success of the organization's mission, this kind of unequal coordination might be suboptimal for the organization even while it is optimal for some subgroup within it.

The structure of unequal coordination is often the strategic structure of the more general game of social order, with the people in some organization in either the preferred or the less preferred position. Ideally, this is the level of theory we would need to handle the endogenous creation and maintenance of institutions within a society. There is coordination within an institution on coordinating the larger society. The trick in organizational design is to make the internal coordination optimal for the larger society by structuring intraorganizational incentives properly. Even when the structural match is not ideal, however, it may still be better than what would follow from not having the organization in place.

Consider a complex and richly debated example, on which serious students strongly disagree: the American Bar Association (ABA). The ABA has historically controlled lawyers and the whole of legal practice in the United States through its control of licensure, advertising, and sanctioning. In practice, this has meant that it coordinates the legal profession through devices that benefit lawyers by raising costs to the larger society. Defenders of the ABA claim that its devices are good because they protect clients. Critics claim these devices are tricked up protections of lawyers themselves. We might hold the intermediate view that ABA regulation of legal practice is generally beneficial to users of legal services despite its implications for higher costs, and we might therefore merely wish there were a less expensive way to coordinate lawyers on good practice.

### Concluding remarks

The grand problem of making an institution work well is coordinating the activities of its members. A successful organization need not and likely cannot be expected to coordinate everyone optimally, but it must coordinate modally so that piecemeal violations of the coordination are not very disruptive. Organizations of any scale cannot plausibly be expected to be fully modeled as games of harmony. But if enough of its members are well enough coordinated on the tasks that achieve an organization's purpose, the organization can use its limited sanctioning power to reduce the threat of disruptive behavior from others for whom the incentives are not to coordinate. This is a self-interest variant of Hart's claim, cited earlier, that social order is enabled by the normative commitments of the many, thereby allowing the society's limited sanctioning power to be used to keep miscreants in line. Again, the fundamental trick is that of Hobbes, not that of Durkheim: to coordinate the interests, not the morality, of participants.

There are at least three game-theoretically distinct ways to stabilize commitments of collectives and institutions if their success depends on the use of the incentives of a coordination game:

1.  We may create structures, such as legislative committees, that can be changed only by coordinating a large group to vote or work against them in order to put alternative structures in place.

The costs of such recoordination then weigh heavily against change and in favor of the current structure and, hence, in favor of the general outputs of that structure.

2. We may create structures, such as very open information systems and multiple involvements in varied areas of organizational action, that make destructive cooperation in piecemeal prisoner's dilemmas difficult. Such structures turn the prisoner's dilemmas into larger-number collective action problems that are harder to resolve than are smaller-number collective actions.

3. We may create sanctions to punish or deter free riding. The force of such sanctions is itself backed by structures similarly grounded in coordination.

In all cases, the fundamental move is the prior coordination on a structure or a power, either for decision making or for sanctioning, that then stabilizes the policies or actions of the institution or collective. And in all cases, the ultimate source of incentives for relevant, modal behavior is internal to the organization whose members have been coordinated. And in all cases, but especially the second, the admixture of even a modest complement of public-spirited or moral commitment would make the task easier even though pervasive public-spirited or moral commitment is not necessary to make any of these devices work in many contexts.

Contrary to the widespread view that our principal public difficulty may be the positive resolution of prisoner's dilemma or collective-action problems, the main grounding for social order and stability may be virtually the contrary. Instead of needing to ease the way to cooperation in collective actions, what we need are coordinating devices that make collective action *too hard* for it to be disruptive to good institutions. And that is largely what we have in our successful public agencies. Otherwise, we are condemned, like the narcissist, to be victims of our momentary urges and passions rather than masters of our larger lives.

An ironic twist here, of course, is that this dependency on commitment turns the supposedly conservative value of sticking with the status quo into a much more generally compelling value. Even one who wants constructive policies for change must want persistent and stable commitments to those policies. Such commitment requires stable institutional structures. For example, the radical restructuring of American government by President Franklin Roosevelt in the 1930s had a point only if the newly created institutions could be reliably expected to carry out their missions. The best hope for creating such structures is to make them dependent not on small numbers of properly motivated custodians but on large-number coordination interactions, that is, to endogenize them broadly through the institutions.

## REFERENCES

Brennan, Geoffrey, and James M. Buchanan (1985). *The Reason of Rules: Constitutional Political Economy.* Cambridge: Cambridge University Press.

Calvert, Randall (forthcoming). "Explaining Social Order: Internalization, External Enforcement, or Equilibrium?" in Virginia Haufler, Karol Soltan, and Eric Uslaner, eds., *Institutions and Social Order.* Ann Arbor: University of Michigan Press.

Hardin, Russell (1988a). "Constitutional Political Economy: Agreement on Rules," *British Journal of Political Science* 18: 513–30.

——(1988b). *Morality within the Limits of Reason.* Chicago: University of Chicago Press.

——(1989a). "Political Obligation," in Alan Hamlin and Philip Pettit, eds., *The Good Polity*, pp. 103–19. Oxford: Basil Blackwell.

——(1989b). "Why a Constitution?" in Bernard Grofman and Donald Wittman, eds., *The Federalist Papers and the New Institutionalism*, pp. 100–20. New York: Agathon Press.

——(1991). "Hobbesian Political Order," *Political Theory* 19 (May): 156–80.

——(1995). *One for All: The Logic of Group Conflict.* Princeton, N.J.: Princeton University Press.

Hart, H. L. A. (1961). *The Concept of Law.* Oxford: Oxford University Press.

Hume, David (1978). *A Treatise of Human Nature*, ed., L. A. Selby-Bigge and P. H. Nidditch. Oxford: Oxford University Press.

Kelman, Steven (1990). "Congress and Public Spirit," in Jane J. Mansbridge, ed., *Beyond Self-Interest*, pp. 200–06. Chicago: University of Chicago Press.

Levi, Margaret (1988). *Of Rule and Revenue.* Berkeley: University of California Press.

Madison, James G. (1987 [1788]). Federalist, no. 51, in Philip B. Kurland and Ralph Lerner, eds., *The Founders' Constitution*, vol. I, pp. 330–31. Chicago: University of Chicago Press.

Mansbridge, Jane J., ed. (1990). *Beyond Self-Interest.* Chicago: University of Chicago Press.

Olson, Mancur, Jr. (forthcoming). "Capitalism, Socialism, and Dictatorship: Outgrowing Communist and Capitalist Dictatorships." Manuscript, University of Maryland.

Quirk, Paul (1990). "Deregulation and the Politics of Ideas in Congress," in Jane J. Mansbridge, ed., *Beyond Self-Interest*, pp. 183–99. Chicago: University of Chicago Press.

Shepsle, Kenneth (1991). "Discretion, Institutions, and the Problem of Government Commitment," in Pierre Bourdieu and James S. Coleman, eds., *Social Theory for a Changing Society*, pp. 245–63. Boulder, Colo.: Westview Press.

PART V

MARKETS, VALUES, AND WELFARE

CHAPTER 17

# Institutions and morale: the crowding-out effect

*Bruno S. Frey*

## 1    Do economists have the right answers?

Consider the following two important policy areas:

*Siting of NIMBY projects:* The "Not in My Back-Yard" syndrome relates to projects which are socially desirable (they increase aggregate
welfare) but which impose considerable net costs on the persons living in
the vicinity where they are located. Examples include incinerators, air-
ports, railway tracks and roads, prisons, clinics for the physically and
mentally handicapped, and nuclear waste repositories. The citizens at the
same time demand the completion of such projects but refuse to have
them located in their vicinity. But building such a facility is not possible
without local consent (see, e.g., Easterling and Kunreuther 1995; Portney
1991). In most countries, it is either extremely difficult or even impossible to find sites for NIMBY projects. In the United States, for example,
hundreds of sites for hazardous waste repositories are urgently sought,
but extremely few have been found (Gerrard 1994). The situation is
similar in many European countries.[1]

   Economists have a handy tool to deal with such a situation. As the
aggregate net benefits of undertaking the project are positive, one must

I was able to discuss the ideas contained in this chapter with a large number of scholars, in
particular Iris Bohnet, Isabelle Busenhart, Bob Cooter, Reiner Eichenberger, Hartmut
Kliemt, Allan Lind, Richard Musgrave, Felix Oberholzer-Gee, Margit Osterloh, Daniel
Rubinfeld, Fritz Scharpf, Amartya Sen, Tom Tyler, Oliver Williamson, and Gordon
Tullock. Financial support is acknowledged to the Swiss National Fund, Project No. 12-
42480.94. Parts of this chapter draw on my *Not Just for the Money: An Economic Theory of
Personal Motivation* (1997).
[1] The search in the United States for locations for noxious facilities is discussed, e.g., in
  Hamilton (1993) and Mitchell and Carson (1986); the European situation is dealt with in
  Linnerooth-Bayer et al. (1994) and Oberholzer-Gee et al. (1995).

simply redistribute them in an appropriate way. The communities can be induced to accept the undesired project within their borders by offering a *compensation* large enough to make their net benefits positive, while the other communities must be taxed to raise the sum of compensation.[2]

The question is, Are compensations effective in overcoming the resistance to accept NIMBY projects?

*Tax Evasion:* In many countries, tax noncompliance is a rampant problem. Billions of dollars or Euros are lost each year to the government because the citizens cheat on taxes (see, e.g., Roth, Scholz, and Witte 1989; Pyle 1990; Slemrod 1992).

Again, economists have a straightforward suggestion to make: As the incentive to cheat negatively depends on expected punishment, the government should raise the probability of detection and/or the penalty for tax fraud.[3]

The question is, Does increased deterrence raise (gross) tax revenue?

This chapter argues, and will present empirical evidence, that these questions in general cannot be answered positively though they are based on the most fundamental proposition (Alchian 1977, chap. 7; Becker 1976, p. 5) in economics, the relative price effect. Thus, according to Coase (1978, p. 35), "An economist will not debate whether increased punishment will reduce crime; he will try to answer the question, by how much." Indeed, in many circumstances, compensations do not help to overcome the NIMBY problem, nor does increased deterrence raise (gross) tax revenue.

The relative price effect states that, ceteris paribus, a price increase (compared to other relevant prices) systematically reduces the demand, and raises the supply, of a good or an activity.[4] Institutions determine the size of the relative prices (see, e.g., North 1981, 1991; Eggertsson 1990). A change in institution systematically affects human behavior through an induced change in relative prices. An institutional change may take place over time, or across society at a given moment of time.

---

[2] The use of monetary compensation to overcome the siting problem was first suggested by O'Hare (1977). Since then this proposition has become standard; see, e.g., Kunreuther and Kleindorfer (1986); Kunreuther and Portney (1991).

[3] The model on which this advice is based is due to Becker's (1968) economic theory of crime and has been applied to taxation by Allingham and Sandmo (1972).

[4] Ingenious theoreticians have been able to construct cases in which this does not apply (e.g., when price is an indicator of quality), but these cases are rather irrelevant exceptions. The rational choice approach is used in economics, and parts of sociology, political science, and law (Becker 1976; Coleman 1990; Kirchgässner 1991; Frey 1992).

Institutions may be understood in various ways; they are manifestations of social regularities. They include (1) decision-making systems, e.g., market vs. democracy, or more narrowly, consensus vs. simple majority voting; (2) rules, which may be formal (legal) such as those included in constitutions, laws, or regulations, or they may be informal, such as social norms or traditions; and (3) organizations, such as firms, the government, or bureaucracies.

Four basic propositions concerning the relationship of institutions to human behavior shall be advanced.

*Proposition 1:* While the relative price effect is of great importance, it does not exhaust the determinants of human behavior. As a consequence, economists (or rational choice social scientists) risk making false predictions and offering erroneous policy advice.

*Proposition 2:* Noncalculative human motives and values such as (work and tax) morale, civic virtue, social capital, trust, and intrinsic motivation need to be taken into account to account more satisfactorily for human behavior.

*Proposition 3:* (Generalized) relative prices affect noncalculative human motives; noncalculative motives therefore cannot be assumed to remain constant but are endogenously determined.

*Proposition 4:* A specific, and crucial, interaction between relative prices and noncalculative motives is called the crowding-out effect: External interventions undermine intrinsic motivation under identifiable conditions. This effect is theoretically and empirically well grounded.

Provided these propositions are tenable, a so far disregarded relationship between institutions and (ethical and other) values is established without giving up the rational choice framework. Section 2 discusses noncalculative human motives and their relevance. The crowding-out effect is introduced in section 3. Section 4 presents empirical evidence and applies the crowding-out effect to the NIMBY and taxation issues introduced in the beginning. Section 5 draws conclusions.

## 2    Noncalculative motives

### 2.1    *Various concepts*

Human beings act in a noncalculative way when they are motivated by considerations beyond (short-run) benefits and cost. They act because they consider it to be ethically required, or even more simply because they just desire so to behave. This does *not* imply at all that (1) they are unresponsive to relative price changes. Noncalculative behavior is an *additional* motive perfectly compatible with what has so far been assumed in economic theory. (2) Noncalculative behavior is not inconsistent with rationality or with optimization behavior by individuals; and (3) there is no strict separation between calculative and noncalculative behavior. It is vain to seek a strict difference. It is always possible to interpret a particular motive as either calculative or noncalculative. What matters is that even a scholar who is devoted to attributing as much behavior as possible to (explicit or implicit) calculation will not be able to account for all that is observed satisfactorily. The same applies to a scholar who is committed to a program favoring the opposite. Most importantly, noncalculative motives exclude market and pseudo market exchanges (e.g., political vote trading). Reciprocity (e.g., Homans 1958; Blau 1964; Fehr, Gächter, and Kirchsteiger 1995) is also calculative because it is based on social exchange. On the other hand, noncalculative behavior is (for the time being) offered one-sidedly and does not depend on a quid pro quo response from other persons. Thus, true love is incompatible with calculative motives as has forcefully been argued by Nozick (1989, p. 78): "The intention of love is to form a *we* and to identify with it as an extended self. . . . A willingness to 'trade up,' to destroy the *we* you largely identify with, would then be a willingness to destroy yourself in the form of your extended self." As with many other terms used in the social sciences (e.g., the distinction between consumption and investment) the productivity of its use does not depend on whether it is *always* possible neatly to separate the two; indeed in *most cases* it is rather obvious to an undogmatic observer whether a motive is more or less calculative along a continuum of possibilities.[5]

Important instances of noncalculative human motives are the following:

(1)  Morale as it is used, e.g., when one speaks of work morale or tax morale[6]
(2)  Civic virtue or public spirit[7]

---

[5] The term is borrowed from Williamson (1993), who applies it to trust.

[6] For work morale, see e.g., Frey (1993). Tax morale will be extensively discussed later.

[7] Civic virtue has a long history in political philosophy, dating back to the time of Aristotle. It has been conceptualized in quite different ways, ranging from "a renunciation of purely private concerns for the greater good of the community" to a "critical distance from prevailing desires and practices" (Sunstein 1989, p. 1549; Michelman 1967). A survey is provided in Burtt (1993). For communitarians civic virtue simply stands for "the moral and political qualities that make a good citizen" (Walzer 1980, p. 55). Public spirit is a corresponding term used, e.g., by Kelman (1987) and Mansbridge (1994).

(3)  Social capital[8]
(4)  Trust[9]
(5)  Intrinsic motivation[10]

No attempt is made here to assess exactly the relationships among these various concepts of noncalculative motives; the usefulness of each concept depends anyway on the use to which it is put. For the purpose here, noncalculative motives will be understood to be *intrinsic motivation*, while calculative motives are identified with *extrinsic motivation*. Among all the concepts mentioned, intrinsic and extrinsic motivation is best suited for an individualistic approach as employed here. Consequently, the terms "civic virtue," which will be used in the empirical analysis of the NIMBY problem, and "tax morale," which will be used to analyze tax compliance, are looked at here as particular manifestations of intrinsic motivation.

## 2.2   *Relevance*

Is intrinsic motivation empirically relevant at all? Everyday experience and literary and historical evidence certainly point in that direction. Why did Emily Dickinson write poetry without any inclination to publish a single line? Why did Goethe seal *Faust II* for posthumous publication? Why did Cavendish undertake experiments in his private laboratory without any desire to announce his intentions to the public? Why did the mathematician Galois, facing death in a duel next morning, stay awake all night to write down his major discoveries in higher algebra? (He would certainly have been better off getting a good night's sleep [Simonton 1994, p. 207].)

We economists are, however, rarely satisfied with commonsense observations. Perhaps rightly so, because such "evidence" may be illusionary, but perhaps wrongly so because it makes us overlook important

---

[8]  See Coleman (1990), who takes it to be the norms and network of civic engagement, to which Tocqueville (1835–40) attributed the success of democracy in America. Putnam (1993) explains the differences in the working of regions in Italy. Most recently, efforts have been made to measure social capital over time and across countries; see Putnam (1995).

[9]  Recently, there is a rapidly rising interest in the various forms of trust, particularly in social trust and political trust. In economics see Arrow (1974) and Williamson (1993), in sociology Gambetta (1988), in administrative science Wilson (1993), in political science Mansbridge (1990) or Fukuyama (1995), and in social psychology Kramer and Tyler (1996).

[10] Individuals are intrinsically motivated when they undertake an activity for its own sake, i.e., "when one receives no apparent reward except the activity itself" (Deci 1971, p. 105). In contrast, extrinsic motivation is activated by rewards or punishment from outside the person.

aspects of real life.[11] Fortunately, there is econometric evidence of the importance of intrinsic motivation for human behavior available. It has been well established that tax-paying behavior cannot satisfactorily be explained by the deterrence model à la Allingham and Sandmo (1972), despite great efforts by the scholars involved in tax research. The coefficients related to the probability of apprehension and the size of punishment in well-specified tax functions are far from robust (they are rarely statistically significant) and sometimes bear a "wrong" sign.[12] Moreover, in the United States, one needs to explain why anybody *pays* taxes, and not why some people evade taxes. In view of the very low probability of being caught, and the low punishments normally administered, citizens would have to exhibit an enormous extent of risk aversion (an extent by far not observed in any other activity) to make it individually rational for a utility-maximizing person to pay any taxes (see Alm, McKee, and Beck 1990; Graetz and Wilde 1985). As a consequence, on the basis of an extensive analysis using the American Internal Revenue Service's Taxpayer Compliance Maintenance program, Graetz and Wilde (1985, p. 358) conclude that "the high compliance rate can only be explained either by taxpayers' ... commitment to the responsibilities of citizenship and respect for the law or to lack of opportunity for tax evasion." The same authors (with Reinganum 1986) attribute the falling tax compliance in the United States to the erosion of tax morale.[13]

A whole literature dealing with the more general issue "Why people obey the law?" (Tyler 1990) seems to have been overlooked by economists. On the basis of both carefully designed experiments and surveys of behavior in real life situations, social psychologists have forcefully argued that the deterrence variables (probability of apprehension and size of punishment) are unable to account for various sorts of crime. Noncalculative motives play a large role. It has, in particular, been empirically established that perceived procedural fairness induces individuals to follow the law even if the outcome for them is unfavorable, and even if it would be advantageous not to obey the law (see Lind and Tyler 1988; as well as several contributions in Kramer and Tyler 1996).

---

[11] Krugman (1995, p. 43) remarks, "It is a fact of life that trained economists find it very difficult to see the obvious unless it has been encapsulated in a clear formal model." For a more analytical view of economists' behavior see Mayer (1993), Frey and Eichenberger (1993).

[12] See, e.g., Witte and Woodbury (1985) and the extensive surveys in Roth, Scholz, and Witte (1989); Pyle (1990); and Slemrod (1992).

[13] The same conclusion is drawn, e.g., by Schwartz and Orleans (1967) and Lewis (1982).

## 2.3 *Counterarguments*

It could well be argued that the whole discussion so far is of little relevance. If intrinsic motivation such as tax morale or civic virtue is indeed empirically relevant, it is no problem to introduce it into economic analysis.[14] The marginalist analysis remains completely unchanged if a level effect of an exogenously given intrinsic motivation of one form or other is introduced. In a tax equation, for example, the amount of tax noncompliance is reduced by an empirically estimated constant term which can be associated with tax morale. Or if individuals enjoy work for intrinsic reasons, i.e., have a high work morale, they need ceteris paribus to be paid a lower wage – a phenomenon which is rampant, for instance, in the cultural sector (see Throsby 1994, p. 18, for corresponding quantitative estimates).

As will be argued in the following parts, the problem is not so simple. Intrinsic motivation is not exogenously given but rather determined endogenously. In particular, external policy interventions via pricing instruments or regulations systematically affect intrinsic motivation.

## 3 Crowding-out intrinsic motivation

Social psychologists have analyzed and empirically measured the "hidden cost of reward" (see, e.g., Deci and Ryan 1985; Pittman and Heller 1987) which appears when an external intervention in the form of a reward reduces individuals' intrinsic incentives to act. The hidden cost of reward has, for instance, been observed in asylums where paying the patients to perform certain tasks (such as making the bed or cleaning their room) undermines their motivation to do it on their own (see, e.g., Lepper and Greene 1978). An everyday example would be an invitation for dinner to a friend's home. Nobody would at the end of the evening make an attempt to pay him for the effort because this would destroy his intrinsic motivation (his friendship).

Two psychological processes have been identified to account for the "hidden cost of reward":

(1) When individuals perceive the external intervention to be controlling in the sense of reducing the extent to which they can determine actions by themselves, intrinsic motivation is substituted by extrinsic control. Following Rotter (1966), the locus of

---

[14] Which, of course, has been done. See, for instance Becker's (1991) use of altruism in the family, or North's (1991) use of ideology. More general are Becker (1992) and Denzau and North (1994).

control has shifted from the inside to the outside of the person affected. Individuals who are forced to behave in a specific way by outside intervention would feel "overjustified" if they maintained their intrinsic motivation. Then, they behave rationally when reducing the motivational factor under their control, that is, intrinsic motivation.

(2)    An intervention from the outside undermines the actor's intrinsic motivation if it carries the notion that the actor's intrinsic motivation is not acknowledged. The person affected feels that his or her competence is not appreciated, and that perception leads to an impaired self-esteem,[15] resulting in a reduced effort.

On the basis of these psychological processes, the "hidden cost of reward" can be generalized in two respects:

(1)    *All* outside interventions can affect intrinsic motivation: In addition to *rewards* the same effect can come about by external *regulations* (commands).

(2)    External interventions *crowd-out* intrinsic motivation if they are perceived to be *controlling* and they *crowd-in* intrinsic motivation if they are perceived to be *acknowledging*.

So far, crowding theory only relates to the effect on intrinsic motivation (in which psychologists are particularly interested). In order to make the concept useful for our purpose, it is necessary simultaneously to take into account the disciplining or (generalized) relative price effect normally considered in economics. This is best done in a principal–agent setting.

An (representative) agent adjusts his or her performance considering the benefits $B$ and the cost $C$ induced. Both benefits and costs increase in performance $P$, i.e., $\delta B/\delta P \equiv B_p > 0$, and $\delta C/\delta P \equiv C_p > 0$. Higher performance exhibits diminishing marginal returns ($B_{PP} < 0$) and has increasing marginal cost ($C_{PP} > 0$). Benefits and cost are also influenced by the principal's external intervention $E$

$$B = B(P, E); \qquad B_P > 0, \quad B_{PP} < 0 \tag{1}$$

$$C = C(P, E); \qquad C_P > 0, \quad C_{PP} > 0 \tag{2}$$

A rational agent chooses that level of performance $P^*$ that maximizes net benefits $(B - C)$, which yields the first-order condition

---

[15]    Self-esteem is taken to be of central importance for human beings by many scholars; see, e.g., Rawls (1971, p. 86), who considers it the most valuable of the goods he designates as "primary."

$$B_P = C_P \tag{3}$$

Differentiating this utility-maximizing condition with respect to $E$ shows how the agent's optimal performance $P^*$ is affected when the principal changes the extent of external intervention

$$B_{PE} + B_{PP} \frac{dP^*}{dE} = C_{PE} + C_{PP} \frac{dP^*}{dE}, \quad \text{or}$$

$$\frac{dP^*}{dE} = \frac{B_{PE} - C_{PE}}{C_{PP} - B_{PP}} \lessgtr 0 \tag{4}$$

Following standard principal–agent theory (e.g., Alchian and Demsetz 1972; Fama and Jensen 1983), external intervention raises performance by imposing higher marginal cost on shirking or, equivalently, by lowering the marginal cost of performing, $C_{PE} < 0$. This is the *disciplining effect* of external intervention. As the crowding effect is neglected, i.e., a change in external intervention does not affect the marginal utility of performing ($B_{PE} = 0$), the orthodox economic theory predicts that external intervention raises performance ($dP^*/dE > 0$).

This positive effect is strengthened if the external intervention bolsters intrinsic motivation (*crowding-in effect*, $B_{PE} > 0$). On the other hand, the *crowding-out effect* ($B_{PE} < 0$) and the disciplining effect ($C_{PE} < 0$) of an external intervention work in opposite directions, so that the outcome $dP^*/dE$ depends on the relative (absolute) size of $C_{PE}$ and $B_{PE}$.

The following propositions on the size of the crowding effect can be formulated on the basis of the relevant literature (e.g., Lane 1991; Frey 1993, 1994). The crowding-out effect is the *larger* (i.e., $B_{PE}$ is the more negative)

(1) the more personal the relationship between a principal and his or her agent is
(2) the larger the agent's participation possibilities are
(3) the more uniform the external intervention is, i.e., the less individual differences in intrinsic motivation are acknowledged by the principal
(4) the more the external intervention (in particular the rewards extended) is contingent on specific performance instead of being directed at general behavior

External interventions may moreover have an *indirect* damaging effect on intrinsic motivation. The crowding-out effect may spread to further areas, even into those in which the external intervention has not been applied. If intrinsic motivation is crowded out in areas in which it is a major (or even the only) behavioral incentive, the overall outcome of an external intervention tends to be even more strongly against the principal's interest. There may thus be an indirect *motivational spill-over effect* which has to be added to the direct crowding-out effect. An example is provided by policy instruments such as effluent charges or tradable permits. They work efficiently where they are applied, but an induced substitution of environmental ethics by monetary incentives may well lead people to protect the environment less in areas where no external incentives exist. This undesired spill-over effect takes place not only with monetary incentives but also with rules and regulations.

That intrinsic motivations (in the broadest sense) may be linked across areas has been observed by various economists (though they have not related this linkage to crowding-out). Akerlof (1989, p. 6) notes that "sociologists and anthropologists have asserted that problems of thought concerning one area are duplicated in other seemingly unrelated areas." Sugden (1989, p. 93) stresses that norms can be spread by analogy. If an analogy can be drawn between an area in which a norm is valid and another area where the norm is not yet applied, its validity can expand to the latter area too. Williamson (1975, p. 37) uses the concept of "attitudinal spill-over," while Jensen (1992) focuses on "reputational spillovers." Neurological research suggests that the molecular construction of the brain limits the power to differentiate between varying circumstances, in our case between those areas in which external interventions produce overjustification and those where a similar type of intrinsic motivation applies, but no external intervention takes place. In psychology, this is known as the "spread effect" (Thorndike 1933).

## 4     Empirical evidence on crowding-out

### 4.1     *Experimental and econometric analyses*

Experiments are a useful method of empirically observing the crowding-out effect under controlled conditions. We[16] undertook such an experiment at the University of Zurich in autumn 1994 using the framework of the dictator game (developed by Kahneman et al. 1986). The purpose was to test the extent to which individuals are prepared to share with others, a particular kind of civic virtue. The students ($N = 14$) initially received an endowment of Swiss Francs (CHF) 7.00 and in the first treatment condition were asked to pass on at least CHF 2.50 to an anonymous other person. Under these conditions the median amount given was CHF 3.00. When the same persons thereafter were again

---

[16] Coworkers were Iris Bohnet, Reiner Eichenberger, and Felix Oberholzer-Gee.

endowed with CHF 7.00 but without any minimum sharing rule imposed, the median amount allocated to the second person was CHF 1.80. This reduction in the amount shared is especially surprising as subjects confronted with the sharing decision without any prior enforcement passed on CHF 3.00. The difference between CHF 3.00 (unforced treatment) and CHF 1.80 (forced treatment) is consistent with the crowding-out effect. The same experiment ($N = 14$) was repeated with a mandatory donation of CHF 4.00 to be given. In this situation the median amount passed on was CHF 4.00, and when the rule was lifted it dropped to CHF 2.00, which is again clearly lower than the CHF 3.00 given in the unforced treatment. The experimental result is again consistent with the crowding-out effect: The subjects' "civic virtue" of giving to other persons was undermined when they were *forced* to share.

This result is supported by those of a large number of experiments applied to other settings, undertaken by social psychologists (see, e.g., Deci and Ryan 1985; Pittman and Heller 1987; Lane 1991). Econometric analyses of real life behavior also present evidence in favor of the crowding-out effect. A particularly important study by Barkema (1995) looks at firms in which the intensity of the personal relationship between the principals and agents depends on the form of supervision. For the case of managers as agents of a certain firm, one can distinguish three major types of supervision: (1) The managers are controlled by the parent company. This corresponds to a rather impersonal relationship, so that, following our earlier proposition, a positive influence of monitoring managers' performance is expected, because intrinsic motivation is little or not at all affected. (2) The managers are controlled by their firm's chief executive officer, a personalized relationship. According to our proposition, monitoring in this case tends to reduce the agents' effort, as an external intervention shifts the locus of control away from their intrinsic work motivation, and the agents perceive that their competence is not acknowledged by their superior. (3) The managers' behavior is regulated by the board of directors. The crowding-out effect, according to our hypothesis, is expected to be greater than in case (1) but smaller than in case (2). Barkema's data set refers to 116 managers in medium-sized Dutch firms in 1985. They range from fewer than 100 to more than 30,000 employees and cover a wide variety of industries. The managers' individual effort is, in line with Holmström and Milgrom (1991), operationalized as the number of hours invested. The intensity of regulating is captured by three aspects: the regularity with which the managers' performance is evaluated, the degree of formality of the evaluation procedure, and the degree to which the managers are evaluated by well-defined criteria. A measurement model is used to establish empirically that these variables meaningfully represent the latent variable "regulating." A structural model is then applied to measure the influence of so-defined external intervention on managers' performance. The empirical results are consistent with the theoretical proposition advanced. The econometrically estimated parameters capturing the effect of external intervention on work performance turn out to be positive and statistically significant in case (1) of impersonal control. In case (2) of personalized control, on the other hand, the corresponding parameter is statistically significant and negative; regulating strongly crowds out intrinsic motivation, so that the net effect of control on performance is counterproductive. In the intermediate case (3) of somewhat personalized control, the estimated parameter does not deviate from zero in a statistically significant way.

### 4.2    Crowding-out in NIMBY problems

The undermining effect of the use of the price system – the offer of monetary compensation – on intrinsic motivation – the civic virtue to accept an unwanted project within one's community – has been empirically analyzed for the case of a nuclear waste site in Switzerland.[17]

The Swiss government intends to build a repository to store low-level and midlevel radioactive wastes. It has proved to be extremely difficult to find a site because of strong local opposition. In June 1993, it was proposed to build the repository in Wolfenschiessen, a small village (population 2100) of 640 families located in central Switzerland. Half a year before this announcement was made, we conducted a one-hour personal interview with 305 persons living in Wolfenschiessen. At that time, four communities were still under consideration as possible sites. Many respondents found it likely that Wolfenschiessen would be chosen. In order to test the theory, it seemed ideal to conduct a survey. As at the polls, moral behavior is inexpensive in interviews. The respondent knows that his answers are not binding and that he is unlikely to influence the aggregate outcome. Carefully conducted personal surveys are thus generally thought to represent how people would vote in an actual referendum (Arrow et al. 1993).

We asked all respondents whether they would vote in favor of building the Swiss low-level and midlevel radioactive waste repository in their community if the developer and the federal parliament proposed this. The procedure we described was identical to the one actually employed

---

[17] The study and results are more fully reported (in German) in Oberholzer-Gee et al. (1995). See also Frey and Oberholzer-Gee (1996).

in Switzerland. In order to build a repository, the developer, the federal parliament, and the local town hall meeting all have to agree on the project.

The in-person interviews were conducted on the basis of contingent valuation (CV) questions utilizing the referendum format, which is superior to other frames used in earlier CV studies (Portney 1994; Hanemann 1994). The present study is best thought of as representing how people would vote if they had to decide on siting a nuclear waste repository in their home community. Proponents of the CV approach, as well as some of its critics, all agree that a CV study should be considered "essentially a self-contained referendum" (Arrow et al. 1993, 20). Indeed, careful CV studies have correctly predicted ballot votes (Carson, Hanemann, and Mitchell 1986). The survey contained a detailed description of the siting procedure and the compensation mechanism. Moreover, the survey was undertaken in the week before the respondents had to decide in a referendum on an amendment to the canton constitution regarding the construction of underground facilities. At the time of the survey, the issue had been debated extensively.

A good number of social scientists object to the use of attitudes and opinions elicited in surveys, arguing that they are not relevant to behavior (Braden and Kolstad 1991; Zaller and Feldman 1992; Neill et al. 1994; for a more favorable view of the contingent evaluation method, see Mitchell and Carson 1989). In our case, this point does not seem to be valid for two reasons: Comparisons between the results of contingent valuation studies and research on revealed preferences indicate that most individuals answer questions as if they had to bear the consequential costs of their statements (Cummings, Brookshire, and Schulze 1986; Pommerehne 1988; Jones-Lee 1989). Moreover, in his study of siting decisions for obnoxious facilities, Hamilton (1993) points to the potential for political protest as the key determinant for location choice. Since the Swiss authorities were about to decide where to locate the low-level radioactive waste facility, participants had real incentives to state their preferences in order politically to influence the siting decision correspondingly.

All respondents were asked whether they were willing to permit the construction of a nuclear waste repository for short-lived, low-level and midlevel radioactive waste on the grounds of their community. More than half of the respondents (50.8 percent) agreed to have the nuclear waste repository built in their community, 44.9 percent opposed the siting, and 4.3 percent did not care where the facility was built. Thus, this NIMBY project is widely supported in spite of the fact that a nuclear waste repository is mostly seen as a heavy burden for the residents of the host community. This is shown by the fact that nearly 40 percent of all respondents believed the risk of serious accidents in the facility and groundwater contamination to be considerable; 34 percent were convinced that some local residents would die as a result of any environmental contamination, and close to 80 percent believed that many local residents would suffer long-term effects should any accident occur.

To test the effect of external compensation, the same question was repeated, asking respondents whether they were willing to accept the construction of a nuclear waste repository. This time, however, we added that the Swiss parliament had decided to compensate all residents of the host community. The amount offered varied from CHF 2500 per individual and year ($N = 117$), to CHF 5000 ($N = 102$), and CHF 7500 ($N = 86$).[18] While 50.8 percent of the respondents agreed to accept the nuclear waste repository without compensation, *the level of acceptance drops to 24.6 percent* when compensation is offered. About one-quarter of the respondents seem to reject the facility simply because financial compensation is attached to it. The amount of compensation has no significant effect on the level of acceptance. There is further evidence which suggests that it is not the level of compensation which caused so many individuals to decline the offer. Everyone who rejected the first compensation was made a better offer, thereby raising the amount of compensation from CHF 2500 to 3750, from 5000 to 7500, and from 7500 to 10,000. Despite this marked increase, only a single respondent who declined the first compensation was now prepared to accept the higher offer.

To test the crowding-out effect further, we conducted an identical survey in northeastern Switzerland, namely, in six communes which are designated as potential sites for the second repository the Swiss government intends to build. This is a facility for long-lived highly radioactive wastes. In these communes 206 interviews were conducted.[19] The sampling procedure and survey methodology were identical to the one described. Of these respondents 41 percent stated they would vote for the high level radioactive waste facility, 56.4 percent would vote against it, and 2.6 percent did not care. When they were offered compensation, *the level of acceptance drops to 27.4 percent*. Again, variations of the financial incentives do not result in significant changes of the supportive votes.

---

[18] The compensation offered here is quite substantial. Median household income for our respondents is CHF 5250 per month.

[19] Unfortunately, there was no pending referendum in northeastern Switzerland. Thus, the information level of respondents may not have exactly corresponded to the one right before a referendum. However, seismic measurements conducted by the developer in all six communes before the survey was conducted caused considerable discussion among the residents.

The hypothesis that financial incentives do not necessarily increase stated levels of acceptance is also supported by other research. Siting procedures based on price incentives have rarely been successful in reality. The search for hazardous waste landfills and nuclear waste repositories in the United States provides a good example. Despite the use of hefty compensation, only one small radioactive waste disposal facility and a single hazardous waste landfill (located in – nomen est omen – Last Chance, Colorado) have been sited since the mid-1970s (Gerrard 1994). States that rely on compensation-based siting have experienced no greater success than those using other methods (Portney 1991, pp. 28–29). Kunreuther and Easterling (1990) also find that increased tax rebates do not elicit an increased willingness to accept a nuclear waste facility in Nevada. They explicitly reject the possibility that the rebates offered were simply too small.

While the results correspond to the crowding theory, there are two alternative interpretations of the observations:

(1)  Strategic behavior: Since the observations relate to a real world problem, we cannot rule out that the respondents answered strategically. In order to maximize the amount of compensation received from the central government, the citizens could understate their willingness to accept the repository. This could account for the observed rejection of the compensation offered. This incentive to understate the support should be greatest at zero compensation. But we observe that the stated support was higher when no compensation was offered. This is incompatible with a strategic interpretation of the observed behavior. The rejection of this competing explanation is corroborated by additional questions included in the survey. When asked why they declined the compensation offered, only 4.9 percent of the respondents indicated that the amount was insufficient to win their approval. Therefore, for the majority of the respondents, strategic behavior can be ruled out.

(2)  Signaling: Citizens may take the offer of a generous compensation as an indication that the facility is more hazardous than they previously thought. If this is true, a higher compensation leads to a higher risk evaluation and, ceteris paribus, to a lower level of acceptance. This competing explanation was tested by directly asking the respondents whether they perceived a link between the size of the compensation and the level of risk. Only 6.3 percent agreed with this connection. This clearly refutes the signaling hypothesis.

### 4.3     *Crowding-out in taxation*

The intrinsic motivation to pay one's taxes – or tax morale – depends strongly on the extent of trust the citizens have in the political system. When individuals are alienated from government and do not think that they are treated fairly by the political process, they are more inclined to pursue their selfish interests, i.e., to evade taxes, taking into account only the expected probability of being punished (see Lind and Tyler 1988; Kramer and Tyler 1996). A crucial factor which increases trust in government is the extent to which the citizens can actively participate in the political process (see, e.g., Mansbridge 1994; Barber 1983).

Switzerland presents a suitable test case because the various cantons have different degrees of political participation possibilities. It is hypothesized that the more extended political participation possibilities in the form of citizens' meetings and obligatory and optional referenda and initiatives are, and the broader the respective competencies are, the higher is tax morale and (ceteris paribus) tax compliance. On the basis of these characteristics, about one-third of the 26 Swiss cantons are classified as pure direct democracy $(D)$, another third as pure representative democracies $(R)$; the rest satisfy only some of the characteristics (see, more fully, Frey and Pommerehne 1993). There are at least a dozen methods to estimate the extent of tax fraud (an extensive survey is given in Frey and Pommerehne 1984; see also Pommerehne 1994). In this case, several different methods were combined, including small-scale surveys, results of tax audits, and extensive interviews with tax experts from various cantonal tax offices (see Weck-Hannemann 1983; Schneider 1994). A cross section/time series (for the years 1965, 1970, 1978, i.e., 78 observations) multiple regression explaining the part of income not declared $Y_{nd}$ yields the following results[20] ($t$ values in parentheses):

$$Y_{nd} = 7.17 - 3.52p - 2.42f + 0.79t - 0.36d - 2.72Y(\ln)$$
$$(-1.98)\,(-0.62)\quad(2.10)^*\,(-2.51)^*(-0.30)$$
$$+0.57NY - 1.09A - 7.70D$$
$$(2.98)^{**}\ (-2.53)^*(-3.80)^{**} \tag{5}$$

where $R^2(\text{adj.}) = 0.69$, d.f. $= 41$, $F = 11.08$, and $*$ and $**$ indicate statistical significance at the 95 percent and 99 percent levels, respectively.

---

[20] Because of multicolinearity between $D$ and $R$ ($r = 0.6$) two separate equations including $D$ and $R$ have been estimated.

$$Y_{nd} = 8.98 - 3.22p - 2.32f + 0.59t - 0.42d + 1.03Y(\ln)$$
$$(-1.72)(-0.36) \quad (1.70)(-3.47)^{**}(0.29)$$
$$+ 0.60NY - 0.82A + 4.02R$$
$$(3.07)^{**} \quad (-1.93) \quad (2.23)^* \tag{6}$$

where $R^2$(adj.) = 0.65, d.f. = 41, and $F$ = 9.43.
The explanatory variables are as follows:

$p$ = probability of detection (the number of individual income tax audits per 1000 taxpayers)
$f$ = penalty tax rate
$t$ = mean marginal tax rate
$d$ = income deduction possibilities
$Y(\ln)$ = per capita income (in natural log)
$NY$ = nonwage income
$A$ = old-age taxpayers' share (reflecting experience in tax matters)

The coefficients of the variables indicating the type of democracy ($D$, $R$) – the other variables are used to control for other influences[21] – have the theoretically expected signs. In cantons with a high degree of direct political control ($D$), tax morale is (ceteris paribus) higher. The part of income concealed falls short of the mean of all cantons by 7.7 percentage points, or in absolute terms the average amount of income concealed is about CHF 1600 (per taxpayer) less than the mean income concealed in all cantons. In contrast, in cantons with a low degree of political control ($R$), tax morale is (ceteris paribus) lower. The part of concealed income is 4 percentage points higher than the average income gap, and the mean income undeclared exceeds the mean of all cantons by about CHF 1500. The estimation results are consistent with the hypothesis that greater democratic participation possibilities lead to higher civic virtue as reflected in taxpayer behavior (for corresponding evidence for the United States, see, e.g., Smith 1992; Kinsey 1992).

The empirical evidence collected for Switzerland can be generalized. In a broad sense, two kinds of democratic tax institutions can be distinguished: One is based on the premise that the citizens are responsible persons, and that in principle they are prepared to contribute to the

---

[21] It may be observed that while many coefficients are statistically highly significant and have the theoretically expected signs, the probability of detection $p$ and the size of the fine $f$ are not statistically significant at the conventional levels; i.e., it cannot be presumed that deterrence is effective.

provision of public goods and the redistribution of income by the state, provided this process is reasonably efficient and fair (see, e.g., Smith 1992). The corresponding tax laws allow the citizens to declare their own income and to make generalized deductions. The tax statements are in principle accepted as trustworthy, and the tax authority bears the burden of proof if it doubts the declarations.

The second type of tax institution starts from the assumption that all citizens want to exploit the tax laws to the fullest and cheat whenever they can. The corresponding tax laws deduct the taxes directly from gross income, and the citizens must claim a refund from the government, depending on the deductions granted by the tax authorities. In the whole process the burden of proof always lies with the individual citizen.

## 5     What follows?

In the introduction to this chapter, two questions were raised:

(1)   Are compensations effective to overcome the resistance to accept NIMBY projects?
(2)   Does increased deterrence raise (gross) tax revenue?

As has been pointed out, economic theory based on the relative price effect suggests a resounding yes.

This chapter advises a more careful answer: It *may* be yes, but under relevant and politically important conditions the answer is no. Indeed, we have presented econometric evidence that in industrial, democratic societies the answer has actually been no. The offer of compensation to the citizens of the prospective host community of a NIMBY project in Switzerland has strongly decreased the level of acceptance (from 50.8 percent down to 27.4 percent). Swiss taxpayers do not systematically react to deterrence (probability of being caught and size of fine when cheating on taxes). But they are prepared to comply more fully when their tax morale is high as a result of more developed institutions of direct political participation (popular initiatives and referenda).

The empirical results presented are consistent with the *crowding-out effect* stating that (under identifiable and relevant conditions) external interventions induced by institutions undermine intrinsic motivation in the form of civic virtue or tax morale.

In the context of economics, our theoretical and empirical analysis suggests that the relative price effect on which our arguments are founded presents an important, but not the only relevant link between institutions and human behavior. An effect working in exactly the opposite direction, crowding-out intrinsic motivation, should be taken into account. Crowding-out theory allows the establishment of connections among institutions, ethical values, and human behavior in a well-defined context, amenable to empirical testing.

## REFERENCES

Akerlof, George A. (1989). "The Economics of Illusion," *Economics and Politics* 1 (Spring): 1–15.

Alchian, Armen A. (1977). *Economic Forces at Work*. Indianapolis: Liberty Press.

Alchian, Armen A., and Harold Demsetz (1972). "Production, Information Costs and Economic Organization," *American Economic Review* 62 (December): 777–95.

Allingham, Michael G., and Agnar Sandmo (1972). "Income Tax Evasion: A Theoretical Analysis," *Journal of Public Economics* 1 (November): 323–38.

Alm, James, Gary H. McClelland, and William D. Schulze (1992). "Why Do People Pay Taxes?" *Journal of Public Economics* 48: 21–38.

Alm, James, Michael McKee, and William Beck (1990). "Amazing Grace: Tax Amnesties and Compliance," *National Tax Journal* 43 (March): 23–38.

Arrow, Kenneth J. (1974). *The Limits of Organizations*. New York: Norton.

Arrow, Kenneth J., Robert S. Solow, Edward Leamer, Paul Portney, Ray Radner, and Howard Schuman (1993). "Report of the NOAA-Panel on Contingent Valuation," *Federal Register* 58(10): 4601–14.

Barber, Bernard (1983). *The Logic and Limits of Trust*. New Brunswick, N.J.: Rutgers University Press.

Barkema, Harry G. (1995). "Do Job Executives Work Harder When They Are Monitored?" *Kyklos* 48:19–42.

Becker, Gary S. (1968). "Crime and Punishment: An Economic Approach," *Journal of Political Economy* 76: 169–217.

——— (1976). *The Economic Approach to Human Behavior*. Chicago: Chicago University Press.

——— (1991). *A Treatise on the Family*, enlarged ed. Cambridge, Mass.: Harvard University Press.

——— (1992). "Habits, Addictions, and Traditions," *Kyklos* 45(3): 327–46.

Blau, Peter M. (1964). *Exchange and Power in Social Life*. New York: Wiley.

Braden, John B., and Charles D. Kolstad (1991). *Measuring the Demand for Environmental Quality*. Amsterdam: North Holland.

Budziszewski, J. (1994). "Politics of Virtues, Government of Knaves," *First Things* (June/July): 38–44.

Burtt, Shelley (1993). "The Politics of Virtue Today: A Critique and Proposal." *American Political Science Review* 87 (June): 360–68.

Carson, Richard T., W. Michael Hanemann, and Robert Cameron Mitchell (1986). "The Use of Simulated Political Markets to Value Public Goods." Manuscript, Economics Department, University of California, San Diego.

Coase, Ronald H. (1978). "Economics and Contiguous Disciplines," *Journal of Law, Economics and Organization* 4 (Spring): 33–47.

Coleman, James S. (1990). *Foundations of Social Theory*. Cambridge, Mass.: Belknap.

Cummings, Ronald G., David S. Brookshire, and Willian Schulze (1986). *Valuing Public Goods: An Assessment of the Contingent Valuation Method*. Totowa, N.J.: Rowman & Allanheld.

Deci, Edward L. (1971). "Effects of Externally Mediated Rewards on Intrinsic Motivation," *Journal of Personality and Social Psychology* 18: 105–15.

——— (1975). *Intrinsic Motivation*. New York: Plenum Press.

Deci, Edward L., and Richard M. Ryan (1985). *Intrinsic Motivation and Self-Determination in Human Behavior*. New York: Plenum Press.

Denzau, Arthur T., and Douglass C. North (1994). "Shared Mental Models: Ideologies and Institutions," *Kyklos* 47(1): 3–32.

Easterling, Douglas H., and Howard Kunreuther (1995). *The Dilemma of Siting a High-Level Nuclear Waste Repository*. Boston: Kluwer.

Eggertsson, Thrainn (1990). *Economic Behaviour and Institutions: Principles of Neoinstitutional Economics*. Cambridge: Cambridge University Press.

Fama, Eugene F., and Michael C. Jensen (1983). "Separation of Ownership and Control," *Journal of Law and Economics* 26: 301–51.

Fehr, Ernst, Simon Gächter, and Georg Kirchsteiger (1995). "Reciprocity as a Contract Enforcement Device: Experimental Evidence." Working paper, University of Zurich.

Frey, Bruno S. (1992). *Economics as a Science of Human Behaviour*. Boston and Dordrecht: Kluwer.

——— (1993). "Does Monitoring Increase Work Effort? The Rivalry with Trust and Loyalty," *Economic Inquiry* 31(4): 663–70.

——— (1994). "How Intrinsic Motivation Is Crowded Out and In," *Rationality and Society* 6(3) (July): 334–52.

——— (1997). *Not Just for the Money: An Economic Theory of Personal Motivation*. Cheltenham, England, and Brookfield, Vt.: Edward Elgar.

Frey, Bruno S., and Felix Oberholzer-Gee (1996). "Fair Siting Procedures: An Empirical Analysis of Their Importance and Characteristics," *Journal of Policy Analysis and Management* 15(3): 353–76.

Frey, Bruno S., and Reiner Eichenberger (1993). "American and European Economics and Economists," *Journal of Economic Perspectives* 7(4): 185–93.

Frey, Bruno S., and Werne W. Pommerehne (1984). "The Hidden Economy: State and Prospect for Measurement," *Review of Income and Wealth* 30 (March): 1–23.

Frey, Bruno S., and Werner W. Pommerehne (1993). "On the Fairness of Pricing – an Empirical Survey among the General Population," *Journal of Economic Behavior and Organization* 20: 295–307.

Fukuyama, Francis (1995). *Trust: The Social Virtues and the Creation of Property*. New York: Free Press.

Gambetta, Diego, ed. (1988). *Trust: Making and Breaking Cooperative Relations.* Cambridge: Cambridge University Press.

Gerrard, Michael B. (1994). *Whose Backyard, Whose Risk: Fear and Fairness in Toxic and Nuclear Waste Siting.* Cambridge, Mass.: MIT Press.

Graetz, Michael J., and Louis L. Wilde (1985). "The Economics of Tax Compliance: Facts and Fantasy," *National Tax Journal* 38 (September): 355–63.

Hamilton, James T. (1993). "Politics and Social Costs: Estimating the Impact of Collective Action on Hazardous Waste Facilities," *Rand Journal of Economics* (Spring) 24: 101–25.

Hanemann, W. Michael (1994). "Valuing the Environment through Contingent Valuation," *Journal of Economic Perspectives* 8(4): 19–43.

Holmström, Bengt, and Paul Milgrom (1991). "Multi-Task Principle-Agent Analysis: Incentive Contracts. Asset Ownership and Job Design," *Journal of Law, Economics and Organization* 7: 24–52.

Homans, George C. (1958). "Social Behavior as Exchange," *American Journal of Sociology* 63: 597–606.

Jensen, Richard (1992). "Reputational Spillovers, Innovation, Licensing and Entry," *International Journal of Industrial Organization* 10: 193–212.

Jones-Lee, M. W. (1989). *The Economics of Safety and Physical Risk.* Oxford: Blackwell.

Kahneman, Daniel, Jack Knetsch, and Richard Thaler (1986). "Fairness as Constraint on Profit Seeking: Entitlements in the Market," *American Economic Review* 76 (September): 728–41.

Kelman, Steven (1987). *Making Public Policy.* New York: Basic Books.

Kinsey, Karyl A. (1992). "Deterrence and Alienation Effects of IRS Enforcement: An Analysis of Survey Data," in Joel Slemrod, ed., *Why People Pay Taxes: Tax Compliance and Enforcement.* Ann Arbor: University of Michigan Press.

Kirchgässner, Gebhard (1991). *Homo Oeconomicus: Das ökonomische Modell individuellen Verhaltens und seine Anwendung in den Wirtschafts- und Sozialwissenschaften.* Tübingen: Mohr (Siebeck).

Kramer, Roderick M., and Tom R. Tyler, eds. (1996). *Trust in Organizations.* Thousand Oaks, Calif.: Sage.

Krugman, Paul (1995). "Incidents from My career," in Arnold Heertje, ed., *The Makers of Modern Economics*, Vol. II. Aldershot, England: Edward Elgar.

Kunreuther, Howard, and Douglas Easterling (1990). "Are Risk Benefit Tradeoffs Possible in Siting Hazardous Facilities?" *American Economic Review* 80 (May): 252–56.

Kunreuther, Howard, and Douglas Easterling (1991). "Gaining Acceptance for Noxious Facilities with Economic Incentives," in Daniel W. Bromley and Kathleen Segerson, eds., *The Social Response to Environmental Risk: Policy Formulation in an Age of Uncertainty,* pp. 151–86. Boston: Kluwer.

Kunreuther, Howard, and Paul Portney (1991). "Wheel of Misfortune: A Lottery Auction Mechanism for the Siting of Noxious Facilities," *Journal of Energy Engineering* 117: 125–32.

Kunreuther, Howard, and Paul R. Kleindorfer (1986). "A Sealed-Bid Auction Mechanism for Siting Noxious Facilities," *American Economic Review* Papers and Proceedings 76 (May): 295–99.

Lane, Robert E. (1991). *The Market Experience.* Cambridge: Cambridge University Press.

Lepper, Mark R., and Greene, David, eds. (1978). *The Hidden Costs of Rewards: New Perspectives on the Psychology of Human Motivation.* New York: Erlbaum.

Lewis, Alan (1982). *The Psychology of Taxation.* Oxford: Blackwell.

Lind, E. Allan, and Tom R. Tyler (1988). *The Social Psychology of Procedural Justice.* New York and London: Plenum Press.

Linnerooth-Bayer, Joanne, Benjamin Davy, Andrea Faast, and Kevin Fitzgerald (1994). *Hazardous Waste Cleanup and Facility Siting in Central Europe: The Austrian Case.* Laxenburg, Austria: International Institute for Applied Systems Analysis.

Mansbridge, Jane (ed.) (1990). *Beyond Self-Interest.* Chicago: University of Chicago Press.

——— (1994). "Public Spirit in Political Systems," in Henry Aaron, Thomas E. Mann, and Timothy Taylor, eds., *Values and Public Policy,* pp. 146–72. Washington, D.C.: Brookings.

Mayer, Thomas (1993). *Truth versus Precision in Economics.* Aldershot, England: Edward Elgar.

Michelman, F. I. (1967). "Property, Utility and Fairness: Comments on the Ethical Foundations of 'Just Compensation' Laws," *Harvard Law Review* 80: 1165–1258.

Mitchell, Robert C., and Richard T. Carson (1986). "Property Rights, Protest, and the Siting of Hazardous Waste Facilities," *American Economic Review* (Papers and Proceedings) 76 (May): 285–90.

Mitchell, Robert C., and Richard T. Carson (1989). *Using Surveys to Value Public Goods: The Contingent Valuation Method.* Baltimore: John Hopkins Press.

Neill, Helen R., Ronald Cummings, Philip T. Ganderton, Glenn W. Harrison, and Thomas McGuckin (1994). "Hypothetical Surveys and Real Economic Incentives," *Land Economics* 70: 145–54.

North, Douglass C. (1981). *Structure and Change in Economic History.* New York: Norton.

——— (1991). "Institutions," *Journal of Economic Perspectives* 5: 97–112.

Nozick, Robert (1989). *The Examined Life: Philosophical Meditations.* New York: Simon & Schuster.

Oberholzer-Gee, Felix, Bruno S. Frey, Albert Hart, and Werner W. Pommerehne (1995). "Panik, Protest und Paralyse: Eine empirische Untersuchung über nukleare Endlager in der Schweiz," *Schweizerische Zeitschrift für Volkswirtschaft und Statistik* 131: 147–77.

O'Hare, Michael (1977). "Not on My Block You Don't: Facility Siting and the Strategic Importance of Compensation," *Public Policy* 25: 409–58.

Pittman, Thane S., and Jack F. Heller (1987). "Social Motivation," *Annual Review of Psychology* 38: 461–89.

Pommerehne, Werner W. (1988). "Measuring Environmental Benefits: A Comparison of Hedonic Technique and Contigent Valuation," in Dieter Bös, Manfred Rose, and Christian Seide, eds., *Welfare and Efficiency in Public Economics*. Berlin: Springer.

———, ed. (1994). *Public Finance and Irregular Activities*. Supplement to *Public Finance* 49.

Portney, Kent E. (1991). *Siting Waste Treatment Facilities: The NIMBY-Syndrome*. New York: Auburn House.

Portney, Paul R. (1994). "The Contingent Valuation Debate: Why Economists Should Care," *Journal of Economic Perspectives* 8(4): 3–17.

Putnam, Robert D. (1993). *Making Democracy Work: Civic Traditions in Modern Italy*. Princeton, N.J.: Princeton University Press.

——— (1995). "Tuning In, Tuning Out: The Strange Disappearance of Social Capital in America," *PS: Political Science and Politics* (Dec.): 664–83.

Pyle, D. J. (1990). "The Economics of Taxpayer Compliance," *Journal of Economic Surveys* 5: 163–98.

Rawls, John (1971). *A Theory of Justice*. Cambridge, Mass.: Harvard University Press.

Reinganum, Jennifer E., and Louis L. Wilde (1986). "Equilibrium Verification and Reporting Policies in a Model of Tax Compliance," *International Economic Review* 27(3): 739–60.

Roth, Jeffrey A., John T. Scholz, and Ann Dryden Witte, eds. (1989). *Taxpayer Compliance*. Philadelphia: University of Pennsylvania Press.

Rotter, Julian B. (1966). "Generalized Expectancies for Internal versus External Control of Reinforcement," *Psychological Monographs* 80(1, Whole No. 609).

Schneider, Friedrich (1994). "Can the Shadow Economy Be Reduced through Major Tax Reforms?" in Werner W. Pommerehne, ed., *Public Finance and Irregular Activities*. Supplement to *Public Finance* 49: 137–52.

Schwartz, Richard D., and Sonya Orleans (1967). "On Legal Sanctions," *University of Chicago Law Review* 34: 282–300.

Simonton, Dean K. (1994). *Greatness: Who Makes History and Why*. New York and London: Guilford Press.

Slemrod, Joel, ed. (1992). *Why People Pay Taxes: Tax Compliance and Enforcement*. Ann Arbor: University of Michigan Press.

Smith, Kent W. (1992). "Reciprocity and Fairness: Positive Incentives for Tax Compliance," in Joel Slemrod, ed., *Why People Pay Taxes. Tax Compliance and Enforcement*. Ann Arbor: University of Michigan Press.

Sugden, Robert (1989). "Spontaneous Order," *Journal of Economic Perspectives* 3: 85–98.

Sunstein, Cass R. (1989). "Beyond the Republican Revival," *Yale Law Journal* 97: 1539–90.

460    **Bruno S. Frey**

Thorndike, E. L. (1933). *An Experimental Study of Rewards*. Teachers College Contributions to Education no. 580.

Throsby, David (1994). "The Production and Consumption of the Arts: A View of Cultural Economics," *Journal of Economic Literature* 32 (March): 1–29.

Tocqueville, Alexis de (1945). *Democracy in America*. New York: Vintage.

Tyler, Tom R. (1990). *Why People Obey the Law*. New Haven and London: Yale University Press.

Walzer, Michael (1980). *Radical Principles: Reflections of an Unreconstructed Democrat*. New York: Basic Books.

Weck-Hannemann, Hannelore (1983). *Schattenwirtschaft: Eine Möglichkeit zur Einschränkung der Öffentlichen Verwaltung?* Bern: Lang.

Williamson, Oliver E. (1975). *Markets and Hierarchies: Analysis and Antitrust Implications*. New York: Free Press.

Williamson, Oliver E. (1993). "Calculativeness, Trust and Economic Organization. Organizational Behavior and Industrial Relations," *Journal of Law and Economics* 36 (April): 453–86.

Wilson, James Q. (1993). *The Moral Sense*. New York: Free Press.

Witte, Ann D., and Diane F. Woodbury (1985). "The Effects of Tax Laws and Tax Administration on Tax Compliance: The Case of the U.S. Individual Income Tax," *National Tax Journal* 38 (March): 1–13.

Zaller, John, and Stanley Feldmann (1992). "A Simple Theory of the Survey Response: Answering Questions versus Revealing Preferences," *American Journal of Political Science* 36: 579–616.

CHAPTER 18

# The joyless market economy

*Robert E. Lane*

If we do not live in a happy society, why not? Do markets, indeed, make happy societies? The thesis of this chapter is twofold: First, the one source of happiness that is within the power of markets to give, money, is losing its power to make people happy. And second, the principal sources of happiness and unhappiness are market externalities, things that markets may casually ignore, make better, or make worse without endogenous correction. If markets facilitate choices, why, within our means, do we not choose the things that make us happy? The reason is that markets control the very values that inform these choices; markets create a market culture that guides (I would say misguides) the pursuit of happiness. What made people happy in earlier periods of scarcity, no longer does so.

In this chapter I will first give a portrait of a decline in happiness, marital satisfaction, work satisfaction, financial satisfaction, and satisfaction with one's place of residence in the United States for a quarter or a half century. These infelicitous trends are supported by an account of the rising tide of clinical depression in the United States and in most other advanced and rapidly advancing economies. After giving a brief analysis of what it is that makes people depressed and happy or unhappy, I will turn to the first thesis: the waning power of income to yield utility. In dealing with the second thesis (that the sources of happiness are externalities), I will focus on the labor market, taking up such questions as job insecurity, enhancement of intrinsic work enjoyment, and the market's treatment of those special spheres of felicity: family solidarity, social inclusion, and warm friendships. In brief, it is people, not money, that

I hereby thank Yale's Institution for Social and Policy Studies for a grant to facilitate statistical work, Soo Yeon Kim of the Social Science Statistical Laboratory for invaluable help with the graphs, and Nuffield College, Oxford, for hospitality while I was writing this chapter.

461

make people happy. In these several respects, markets often inhibit, rather than facilitate, the maximization of utility. At the end of this discussion I will ask whether we may interpret these dramatic and apparently persistent hedonic changes as a possible turning point in history.

### Well-being in market democracies

*Recent decline of happiness and satisfaction in the United States*

"Taken all together, how would you say things are these days – would you say that you are very happy, pretty happy, or not too happy?" And "How do you feel about your life as a whole?" They are imperfect measures but quite good indicators of subjective well-being (SWB)[1] and are supported by other measures with different wording. Episodically from 1946 to 1972 and annually from that date on, survey organizations have asked national samples the happiness question, giving us a profile of changing morale and mood in the United States. Does this series support the idea of declining subjective well-being in the United States?

The variations from year to year conceal an underlying trend discovered by fitting a line (Figure 1) to the 1946–90 data.[2] The declining trend charting the "very happy" responses of the roughly one-third of the nation claiming this positive mood does, modestly, support the claim that we are, in this market democracy, an increasingly unhappy people. One

---

[1] These questions and slight variations have been asked many times throughout the world; their correlates are known and fairly common to all settings; their validity is good – though not perfect (happiness changes with the weather!), their reliability fairly well established. The happiness question is taken from the GSS (General Social Survey, National Opinion Research Center [NORC]) surveys; the question on feelings about "life-as-a-whole" is taken from Andrews and Withey (1976). There are at least four literature reviews on various aspects of subjective well-being: Diener (1984), Michalos (1986), Argyle (1993 [1987]), and Veenhoven (1993).

[2] The graph and calculations (for the variables in Figure 1, $p = 0.025$) are courtesy of Ed Diener, whose pre-1972 data come, by way of Ruut Veenhoven's archive at Erasmus University, from AIPO (American Institute of Public Opinion), SRC (Social Research Center), Harris, and NORC (GSS) surveys. After 1972 we both rely on NORC's GSS almost annual surveys. In a personal communication Ruut Veenhoven has noted that the use of the "very happy" responses for the 1972–94 period is misleading since the "not too happy" responses have, for part of this period, disappeared into the middle category, leaving a net happiness figure that, although negative, is not statistically significant. I am grateful for this observation but believe that if the figures for the period 1947–71 were included in this net analysis, there would be a significant net decline in happiness by Veenhoven's measures. For example, the unhappy answers in the late 1940s and the 1950s were far fewer than the unhappy answers in the 1980s and, especially, the 1990s.

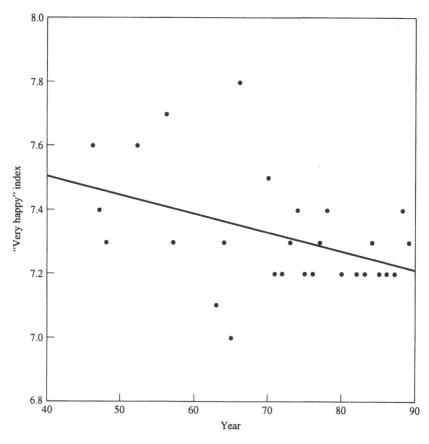

Figure 1. "Very happy" score: 1946–1990. Courtesy of Ed Diener. *Sources*: AIPO, NES, Harris, and GSS

of the most alarming findings of this series is that loss of happiness increasingly strikes the young with disproportionate force. This is a remarkable reversal of early postwar patterns, for then the youngest group (eighteen to twenty-three years) were the happiest.

Other studies of the quality of life have shown that levels of satisfaction in the specific domains of life contribute in a straight linear fashion to whatever measure of overall subjective well-being was used in the various studies. Thus, we would expect that satisfaction with marriage, work, finances, and one's community would move in the same direction as our overall measure of well-being. They do, as may be seen in Figures 2, 3, 4, and 5.

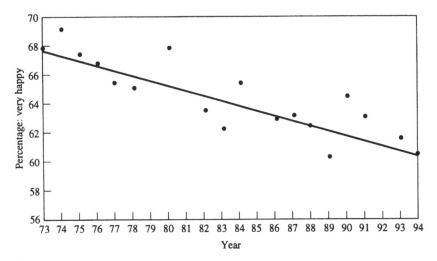

Figure 2. Happiness of marriage: 1973–1994 (fitted line). *Question*: "Taking things all together, how would you describe your marriage? Would you say that your marriage is very happy, pretty happy, or not too happy?" *Source*: General Social Survey (NORC); statistical analysis and fitted line by Soo Yeon Kim of the Yale Social Science Statistical Laboratory, January 1996

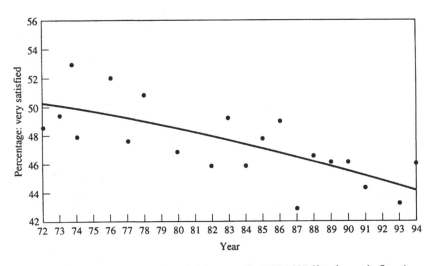

Figure 3. Satisfaction from job/housework: 1972–1994 (fitted curve). *Question*: "On the whole, how satisfied are you with the work that you do – would you say you are very satisfied, moderately satisfied, a little dissatisfied, or very dissatisfied?" (Asked only if currently working, temporarily not at work, or keeping house.) *Source*: General Social Survey (NORC); statistical analysis and fitted curve by Soo Yeon Kim of the Yale Social Science Statistical Laboratory, January 1996

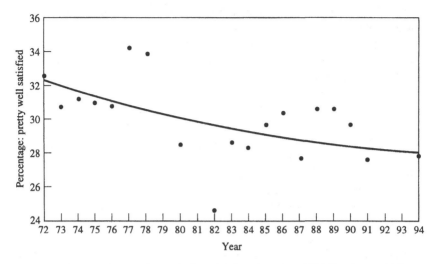

Figure 4. Satisfaction with financial situation: 1972–1994 (fitted curve). *Question*: "We are interested in how people are getting along financially these days. So far as you and your family are concerned, would you say that you are pretty well satisfied with your financial situation, more or less satisfied, or not at all satisfied?" *Source*: General Social Survey (NORC); statistical analysis and fitted curve by Soo Yeon Kim of the Yale Social Science Statistical Laboratory, January 1996

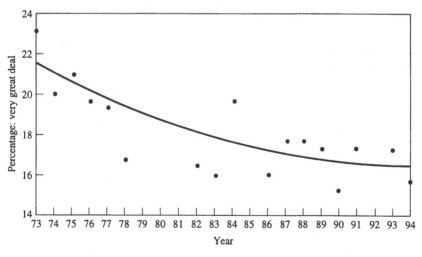

Figure 5. Satisfaction with place of residence: 1973–1994 (fitted curve). *Question*: "For each area of life I am going to name, tell me the choice that shows how much satisfaction you get from that area. . . . The city or place that you live in." [A very great deal. A great deal. Quite a bit. A fair amount. Some. A little. None.] *Source*: General Social Survey (NORC); statistical analysis and fitted curve by Soo Yeon Kim of the Yale Social Science Statistical Laboratory, January 1996

Satisfaction with one's circumstances in the various domains of life should also correlate with these indicators: They do, but in line with my theory that it is people, not money, that makes people happy, a happy marriage (0.47) is by far the best indicator of happiness with life as a whole (e.g., satisfaction with finances: 0.27).

The obvious fact that correlations do not necessarily imply causation leaves open many interpretations. Does overall SWB *cause* people to be more satisfied with, say, their jobs and finances in what is called a "top down" pattern of well-being, or do the satisfactions with particular parts of a person's life *cause* a person to be happier and more satisfied with life (the "bottom up" theory).[3] Or, most probably, are they interactive? Thus, Veenhoven finds that "having a partner" is a strong cause of happiness and that happiness makes having a partner more likely.[4] Finally, does some exogenous factor, such as a personality predisposition, greatly influence both the domain and the overall feeling of well-being? That is also true: Extroverts are happier in most situations but being with others further enhances their happiness. The quality of life studies support all four possibilities: Top down, bottom up, interactive, and exogenous factors.[5]

One other observation on this pattern of correlations of domain satisfaction and general happiness: Satisfaction with one's finances and satisfaction with one's friends have almost exactly the same relationship to happiness (0.29). To me this suggests that both economic answers, favored by economists and most journalists, and human relations answers, which I favor, have similar standing. But the stronger correlation of overall happiness with "happiness with marriage" tilts the scale toward the human relations explanation.

*Depression*

Consider some evidence of a rising tide of depression in economically advanced democracies. "In some [advanced] countries the likelihood that people born after 1955 will suffer a major depression – not just sadness, but a paralyzing listlessness, dejection and self-deprecation, as well as an overwhelming sense of hopelessness – at some point in life is more than three times greater than for their grandparents' generation."[6] A nine nation study under the direction of Myrna Weissman found that

---

[3] Diener (1984, p. 565).
[4] Veenhoven (1984, exhibit 9/1.1, p. 36).
[5] See, for example, Andrews and Withey (1976).
[6] Goleman (1992), p. C3. In this piece Goleman reviews the findings of a number of then recent epidemiological studies of depression.

this epidemic is characteristic of rapidly modernizing countries, like Taiwan, as well as advanced economies like Germany and New Zealand.[7] Since World War II, each succeeding generation in these advanced and rapidly advancing countries is more likely to be depressed, for, said Martin Seligman, "depression has not only been getting more frequent in modern times, but it occurs much earlier in life the first time."[8] A World Health Organization study reports, "Each year at least 100 million people in the world develop clinically recognizable depression and for several reasons the number is likely to increase."[9]

While the United States is not the most depressed country in the world,[10] it may be on its way to that infelicitous rank. On the basis of two earlier (1982, 1985) epidemiological studies in the United States involving a total of about twelve thousand people, a U.S. rate of *increase* much higher than the rates of other countries seems evident: "People born after 1945 were 10 times more likely to suffer from depression than people born 50 years earlier."[11] Myrna Weissman and associates report research covering five sites in the United States with similar results. These authors found "an increasing risk of depression at some point in life for younger Americans. For example, of those Americans born before 1955, only one percent had suffered a major depression by age 75; of those born after 1955 six percent had become depressed by *age 24*."[12] Results of studies of depression among children in both the United States and Great Britain are even more alarming.[13]

Major depression is not just a matter of mood, for among its symptoms are insomnia, loss of energy, "loss of interest or pleasure in usual activities," "feelings of worthlessness, self-reproach, or excessive or inappropriate guilt," and "recurrent thoughts of death, suicidal ideation,

---

[7] The Cross-National Collaborative Group report states, "The results show an overall trend for increasing rates of major depression over time for all sites." The multiple authors of this cross-national study were the first to use a standardized instrument (*Diagnostic Statistical Manual of Mental Disorders* – III [*DSM-III*]) for large-scale cross-national work. See Cross-National Collaborative Group (1992, p. 3102).

[8] James Buie (quoting Martin Seligman) (1988, p. 18).

[9] Sartorius et al. (1983, p. 1).

[10] Weissman et al. (1993) found that compared to samples in Germany, Canada, and New Zealand, U.S. figures were lower for both lifetime rates and one year rates for both men and women.

[11] Seligman in Buie (1988, p. 18).

[12] Weissman et al. (1991). This finding corresponds to an earlier report of a six-year study tracking 956 American men and women: Those below age forty were three times more likely to become severely depressed than were older groups. Goleman (1992, p. C3).

[13] On the United States, see Lewisohn et al. (1993) and Klerman (1989). On Britain, see Lewis (1993); Lewis is quoting June McKerrow, director of the Mental Health Foundation.

wishes to be dead, or suicide." Hopelessness is said by some to be the key variable.[14] The validity, reliability, and significance of the data have sometimes been questioned, but if the details are uncertain, the overall direction is well documented.[15]

How can one blame a rising tide of depression and a falling level of happiness on markets which long antedate these infelicitous events? One cannot explain a variable with a constant. The first answer is to turn to a familiar way of explaining a change in attitude by a constant whose very constancy is the cause of the change: declining marginal utility. The second answer accepts the allegation but claims that exploration of sources of unhappiness in institutions is relevant whether unhappiness is rising or falling. Furthermore, even if one accepts the evidence of declining well-being and morale, one may remain uncertain about whether we are witnessing a blip in history, a part of some larger cycle, or, as I will suggest at the end of this chapter, a genuine climactic change. After only a quarter, or perhaps a half, of a century it is too early to know – but not too early to speculate.

### Causes of happiness and depression

If you ask people why they are unhappy, they often cannot tell you; more often they tell you but borrow their explanations from conventional theories of why a person in their circumstances *ought* to be unhappy. They employ the values of their culture and have little of what the philosophers call "privileged information," information deriving from special knowledge of the sources of their own moods.[16] So let us look at the studies that arrive at their interpretations of the sources of SWB by correlating evaluations of particular features of people's lives with overall measures of happiness or satisfaction with life-as-a-whole. Note that these correlations are not satisfaction scores, but measures of association

---

[14]  Beck, Kovacs, and Weissman (1975).

[15]  A literature review and appraisal by the specialists consulted by the *Harvard Mental Health Letter* (1994, p. 4) report: "Twelve independent studies covering 43,000 people in several countries have found an overall rise in the rate of depression during the twentieth century, both for people born in each successive five- or ten-year period and for the general population in each successive decade. The recent National Comorbidity Survey of more than 8000 people aged 15 to 54 found a lifetime rate of 17% for major depression (21% among women and 13% among men) and a rate of 5% when people were asked whether they had been depressed in the previous month." The authors of this report then take up the various objections raised to these findings and conclude, "Most experts do not believe these potential biases fully explain the findings."

[16]  Lane (1991, chap. 27). The research reported in that chapter comes substantially from Nisbett and Ross (1990).

Table 1. *Beta correlations of domain satisfaction with satisfaction with one's life: six items with high beta scores*

| | |
|---|---|
| Efficacy index | 0.26 |
| Family index | 0.19 |
| Money index | 0.15 |
| Amount of fun | 0.15 |
| House/apartment | 0.12 |
| Things do with family | 0.11 |

*Source*: Andrews and Withey (1976, p. 124). The national samples were around 2000; the date of the survey whose results are reported here was 1972.

Table 2. *Amount of variance ($r^2$) explained by satisfaction in several domains*

| | |
|---|---|
| Nonworking activities (leisure) | 0.29 |
| Family life | 0.28 |
| Standard of living | 0.23 |
| Work | 0.18 |
| Marriage | 0.16 |
| Savings and investments | 0.15 |
| Friendships | 0.13 |

*Source*: Campbell, Converse, and Rodgers (1976, p. 76). The national sample was 2164 and the date of the survey was 1971.

between satisfaction *or dissatisfaction* and an overall measure of well-being. Tables 1 (Andrews and Withey) and 2 (Campbell et al.) show the kinds of evaluations that contribute most to two different measures of subjective well-being. These entries are cryptic without some clue regarding the contents of the indices. Briefly: The *efficacy index* deals with "the way you handle the problems that come up in your life," "what you are accomplishing," and feelings about yourself. The *family index* deals with feelings about one's children, one's spouse, and one's marriage; the *money index* deals with feelings about one's family income and – confounding meanings I would like to keep separate – with feelings

Table 3. *Household events precipitating depression in a London working class sample*

| | |
|---|---|
| Given notice must leave long-term laundry job | Because of housing, must have unwanted abortion |
| Long estranged husband coming home to live | Husband sent to prison |
| | Move to escape difficult neighbors |
| Leaving job in order to look after son | Left alone after move of daughter |
| Arrangement about new flat falling through | Notice to quit flat |
| | Husband released from prison |
| Threatened with eviction by landlord | Overdose by school age daughter |
| Court appearance for not paying rent (husband out of work) | Husband row at work, lost his job |

*Source*: Brown and Harris (1978, p. 160).

on "how secure you are financially." And *amount of fun* deals with "the amount of fun and enjoyment you are having." The other two are self-explanatory.

A second inventory, created by a different survey and analyzed by a different team, gives a partially overlapping list. Economic explanations receive a little more support here, but so do theories of intrinsic work enjoyment and, as in the first study, of the importance of family as well as marriage, and friends.

In turning to depression I do not have so convenient a list of correlates. Instead, let me provide an informative account of the events that precipitated depression in a working-class sample of women in London (leaving out of the account the dispositions that made these events so traumatic). Do these troubles pass through the market? The list shown in Table 3 is helpful because it shows so plainly and painfully the interaction of human dispositions and socioeconomic circumstances. Housing and jobs are frequent problems and, as we shall note later, unemployment is an externality for the market, but who knows why the depressed housewife had to leave her laundry job; was *she* delinquent? But overall *family* problems seem central (husband coming home or released from prison or losing his job because of a row at the plant; must take care of son; daughter takes an overdose). Can the market be blamed for the underlying problems that precipitated these family events? The vulnerability of markets to recession is one source of such blame, for admissions to mental hospitals increase during recessions.[17] Historically,

---

[17] Brenner (1973).

however, market economies have relieved poverty – but poverty in poorer societies is not an important source of depression.[18] Because of these complexities, let us focus on the sources of happiness/unhappiness in the studies of quality of life. I will turn to market externalities in a moment, but first the relationship of income to SWB.

## Money and well-being

Because of the influence of market values, most Americans find economic explanations both natural and cogent. Of these, the failure of the income of the average household to increase in the past two decades is probably the most common, although Figure 1 covers earlier periods of sharply rising income. But how much weight should be given to level of income?

The *economistic fallacy* is the belief that beyond the poverty level higher levels of income increase a sense of well-being. Almost all the evidence from economically advanced countries shows that although more money to the poor decreases their unhappiness and increases their satisfaction with their lives, above the poverty line this relationship between level of income and level of subjective well-being is weak or nonexistent. Thus, the rich are no more satisfied with their lives than the merely comfortable, who, in turn, are only slightly, if at all, more satisfied with their lives than the lower middle classes.[19]

A substantial number of people in rich countries are on a hedonic treadmill where they think if they had just 25 percent more income they would be happy, but if and when they get there, like those who are already there, they find that, well, just one more 25 percent increase would do it. Adam Smith understood this:

> Through the whole of his life [a poor man] pursues the idea of a certain artificial and elegant repose which he may never arrive at, for which he sacrifices a real tranquility that is at all times in his power, and which, if in the extremity of old age he should at last attain, he will find to be in

---

[18] Brown and Harris (1978, pp. 252–53). The authors compare the incidence of depression in their study with that in a crofting village in the Hebrides and find that something about the poverty in London makes the poor more depressed than in the village in the Hebrides. Urbanism, rather than the market economy, is indicted here.

[19] Lane (1991, chap. 26). Jonathan Freedman (1980) says that money matters a lot to those who do not have enough to live on, but otherwise it is unimportant. The rich are rarely happier than people with only middle incomes. Almost all other quality of life studies confirm this general finding.

no respect preferable to that humble security and contentment which he had abandoned for it.[20]

Like these studies of individuals in richer countries, cross-national studies of the effect of increasing income show similar patterns: Although rich societies are happier than poor societies (see Table 7 later in this chapter), the so-called affluence effect,[21] there is little systematic difference in subjective well-being between richer and less rich societies.[22]

In passing, only two of the many policy implications of the economistic fallacy can be mentioned. If, over most of its distribution, income has only minor effects on SWB (which is already much more equally distributed than income), the target of reform policy should be relief of poverty rather than greater income equality.[23] And, as Scitovsky pointed out more than twenty years ago, most sources of pleasure do not go through the market.[24] It is time to look for the major sources of "utility" in work and social life.

As we turn to the second main thesis, the market externality of the main sources of unhappiness, I shall focus on the labor, not the consumer, market. Nevertheless, we must bear in mind that this unhappiness has many origins in the values of the consumer market.

### The sources of happiness are externalities in labor markets

Marx's belief that the circumstances of work are the principal sources of ill- and well-being and Durkheim's belief that insatiable demands for ever more commodities destroy contentment are both right and both support the arguments in this chapter. But, following Marx, here we will focus on work and the labor market. I now wish to draw attention to how certain differences between the consumer market and the labor market influence well-being. The feedback in the consumer market is direct and rapid, giving consumers more control over the sources of their well-being (utility). They may want things that, in aggregate, do not make them

---

[20] Smith (1974 [1759], p. 181).

[21] Lane (1991, pp. 27–28).

[22] Inglehart and Rabier (1986). Note, however, that the differences between, say, Greece and Portugal (but not Ireland), on the one hand, and Germany and Sweden (but not Belgium), on the other, are still substantial.

[23] The worst results of great disparities of income in market democracies are their consequent political inequality and bias toward the rich. If income can be insulated from politics, the case for equality of income is greatly weakened. It is exactly this insulation that Michael Walzer (1983) advocates.

[24] Scitovsky (1977).

happy, but, within their budget constraints, they have a fair chance of getting what they want. In labor markets, workers have far less choice, for their skills are not fungible, as is money; they are often faced with a monopsony, whereas consumers are less often faced with monopoly; exit as a means of control is far more costly to the worker than is exit for the consumer, and many of their "choices" are in internal labor markets under tight control by their employers. Moreover, the choices of rewards in the labor market are more constrained; it often denies employees a choice between, for example, job security and level of pay.[25]

The main point, however, is that labor markets often treat unemployment, work enjoyment, and the need for secure jobs as externalities. There is a deep reason for this partial undervaluation of the psychic income and enjoyment of work: In market accounting work is a cost whereas consumption is a source of benefit. Making workers happier and work more pleasing is likely to be a charge on profits whereas making goods more pleasant and consumption more pleasing is probably a source of profits.[26] The underlying assumption is that people work in order to earn in order to consume; work is a disutility for which income and consumption (and leisure) are the compensating utilities. But even in a market economy, this is often, perhaps usually, not true.[27] In the studies of intrinsic work enjoyment, and in the accounts of the "hidden cost of rewards" to be treated shortly, it is clear that for many people work is not a disutility at all, but rather work and work mastery are the sources of very great pleasure, as most professionals and artisans intuitively know. Finally, competition in the market often detracts from worker welfare: Where competition among firms is limited by market power, firms are more indulgent in relation to such worker benefits as inhouse training, job security, and other worker amenities.

There are two good reasons for thinking of the pleasantness and security of work as externalities, if not always for workers, at least usually for employers: First, worker satisfaction has almost no effect on productivity.[28] And second, although Adam Smith thought that wage differentials would reimburse workers for such unpleasant features of work as hazards and dirtiness, in fact, they are rarely reimbursed by

---

[25] As Juliet Schor points out, employers do not offer their workers a choice between more income or more leisure; except for the roughly 18 percent who are represented by unions, these choices are usually decided unilaterally by the employer (Schor 1991, pp. 1, 3).

[26] Lane (1991, pp. 309, 334).

[27] Lane (1992).

[28] Vroom (1964). But for the exceptions, see Lawler (1982).

the market; they are true externalities.[29] It does not "pay" to devote resources to benefits accruing to workers but not to the firm's net income.

I now turn to more detailed examination of some of these unacknowledged market pains and pleasures.

### Longer hours and greater stress?

Before proceeding further, I want to raise a candidate for explaining unhappiness – in order to dismiss it. Recently, Juliet Schor has presented a forceful argument that the American worker is overworked and severely stressed. She says that although for a hundred years up to 1940 hours of work had declined, from that time forward (a little earlier than the rise of depression and the decline in happiness) hours of work have generally increased.[30] The stress is from the "time squeeze" rather than from what people actually do at work or greater responsibilities thrust upon them.

As to the longer hours, Schor discounts official data and various time studies, but their cumulative weight does not indicate that many people have increased their work hours recently. The matter is technical (and Schor might be right), but two sets of figures suggest caution: U.S. Bureau of Labor statistics show almost no change in average work time over the twenty-eight years from 1960 to 1988 (38.3 vs. 39.1). And, as recently as March 1995, Federal Reserve Board officials said that the "average length of the workweek fell in the preceding quarter by 24 minutes to 34.5 hours."[31]

I am also skeptical about the nature and meaning of work stress. In an impressive ten-year longitudinal study of the effects of work on personality and attitudes, Kohn and Schooler report: "Working longer hours tends, in the long run, to be reassuring. Certainly one cannot conclude that job pressures, as we have measured them, are uniform in their psychological import. . . . Since all . . . job pressures might be regarded as 'stressful,' these findings cast doubt on any interpretation that the effects of stress are necessarily deleterious."[32] Other studies show

---

[29] Brown (1980). Adam Smith (1937 [1776], p. 100) said, "The wages of labor vary with the ease or hardship, the cleanliness or dirtiness, the honourableness or dishonourableness of employment."

[30] Schor (1991). Other studies (whose data Schor challenges) disagree. See Robinson (1985) and U.S. Bureau of the Census (1990, table 639).

[31] "Reserve Board Officials Say the Economy Wasn't Braked Too Heavily," *New York Times*, March 15, 1995, p. 23.

[32] Kohn and Schooler (1983, p. 142).

that there are more people with "time on their hands" than who "always feel rushed," with the former unhappier than the latter.[33]

Granted that Schor shows that "workers' compensation claims related to stress have tripled during the first half of the 1980s,"[34] in light of the fact that from 1960 to 1988 the "workers killed or disabled on the job" have declined from 21 to 9 per 100,000, the increased claims for compensation are very likely to be related to other features of work, especially job insecurity, or to greater health consciousness in the population.[35]

### Unemployment

Because the time sequence of unemployment and inflation bears no close relation to the rising tide of unhappiness and depression, it is hard to blame them for the increase in infelicity. Moreover, following patterns of adaptation familiar in other areas of life, it seems that living in a society with relatively high unemployment does not cause the employed to be more unhappy.[36] Nevertheless, *being* unemployed is excruciating. As Argyle has pointed out, among the unemployed, "depression increases and becomes worse with time ... [and] attempted suicide is 8 times more common, especially during the first months. In several [of the relevant] studies it was possible to demonstrate that unemployment caused the mental ill health rather than vice versa."[37] Unemployment for the breadwinner injures children chiefly through damaging their relations with their parents.[38] On the other hand, inflation seems to have no effect on happiness, either within an American community or across nations.[39]

---

[33] Campbell et al. (1976, pp. 356, 357).

[34] Schor (1991, p. 11).

[35] In a somewhat hyperbolic statement (not accounting for the one hundred capitalist years when hours were shortened or the greater leisuretime in Europe), Schor says: "In the starkest terms, my argument is this: Key incentive structures of capitalist economies contain biases toward long working hours. As a result of these incentives, the development of capitalism led to the growth of what I call 'long hour jobs'" (1991, p. 7). For other theories of the sources and meaning of the trade-off between work and leisure, see Becker (1965) and Linder (1970).

[36] Veenhoven (1984, p. 56). Veenhoven found that unemployment decreases happiness only for those who want to work; that is, the retired, housewives happy in their homemaking role, and the unemployed who have given up are no less happy than working people. But most of those we think of as "the unemployed" do want to work.

[37] Argyle (1993 [1987], p. 264).

[38] The worst effects of the Great Depression on children had little to do with material deprivation and much to do with parental stress. Elder, Nguyen, and Caspi (1985).

[39] Catalano and Dooley (1977); Veenhoven (1993, p. 127).

Making a distinction between *economic* costs (operation of the economy below the production possibility frontier) and *market* costs (costs that invoke homeostatic tendencies to maintain or return to equilibrium), we can say that unemployment incurs high economic costs. "The losses during periods of high unemployment are the greatest documented waste in a modern economy. They are many times larger than the estimated inefficiencies (or 'deadweight losses') from monopoly or of waste induced by tariffs and quotas."[40] But is unemployment a market cost? Apparently not: Under pressure from inflation, and because of the collapse of "natural" tendencies for inflation and unemployment to check each other, what is called "the natural rate of unemployment" has crept up so that what was thought "natural" in the 1950s has grown to a point where it is now quite high enough to inflict on many the misery that Argyle describes. High unemployment seems to be quite compatible with market equilibrium.[41]

### Economic security

While the economistic fallacy deals with *levels of income,* it does not apply at all to the *security* of income or security of one's job, both of which do undermine SWB. The fact that money buys security as well as goods and services obscures many interpretations of people's desire for money.[42] A very simple way of sorting out these meanings is to ask people what money means to them. In a recent poll, people were asked what "money represents . . . to you personally." The percentage of respondents citing the various aspects of money as "very important" is given in Table 4. People's estimates of what is "important" to them are often an unreliable indicator of the contribution of that feature of their lives to their overall sense of well-being, but correlations between levels of concern and some criterial measure of well-being help to correct this

---

[40] Samuelson and Nordhaus (1985, pp. 206–7).

[41] On this matter, Samuelson and Nordhaus observe: "The natural rate of unemployment seems tragically high – far above the rate necessary for frictional migration of young workers searching for jobs. This sober finding must restrain the most enthusiastic defender of mixed capitalism" (1985, p. 258). The European pattern of high wages, high taxes, high welfare provisions – and high unemployment (compared to U.S. standards) – reflects a market equilibrium that distributes well-being in a curiously selective way.

[42] The security offered by money has political consequences, as well. Georg Simmel puts it this way: "The feeling of personal security that the possession of money gives is perhaps the most concentrated and pointed form and manifestation of confidence in the social–political organization and order" (1978 [1907], p. 179). Simmel omits to observe that it is precisely this relationship between politics and money that concerns most people who are not rich.

Table 4. *"Very important" aspects of money*

| | |
|---|---|
| Security | 78% |
| Being able to help your children | 63 |
| Comfort | 62 |
| Freedom | 58 |
| Pleasure | 45 |

*Source*: Roper Starch Worldwide Inc., May 15–22, 1993, reported in *The American Enterprise*, November/December 1994, p. 98.

fault. Reporting on his 1983 study of a Michigan sample, Alex Michalos found that "of the 12 domains, satisfaction with *financial security* has the greatest relative impact on satisfaction with life as a whole." In accounting for this priority, Michalos finds that "fifty four percent of the variance in satisfaction with financial security" can be explained by "the gap between what one has and wants."[43] People tend to want security more than they want more commodities, and, in contrast to level of income, the absence of such security detracts substantially from their well-being.

There can be little doubt that the American public has grown increasingly insecure in the past several years, as the excerpts from interviews and survey reports in *The New York Times* sampled in the footnote indicate.[44] Of course, wages have stagnated for twenty years, but it seems from a variety of surveys and studies, some cited in the footnote, that it is the growth of job insecurity rather than the loss of income that is most

[43] Michalos (1986, p. 75; my emphasis).

[44] "Robert Reich calls salaried people with a growing sense of insecurity, 'the anxious class ... consisting of those Americans who no longer can count on having their jobs next year, or next month, and whose wages have stagnated or lost ground to inflation.' ... 'Over and over people tell us they are concerned about their jobs, that they don't feel secure, that the economy is doing badly. ... For most people, if the economy is not synonymous with jobs, it is at least highly coordinated with jobs.' (From Louis Harris polls) ... The Michigan Consumer Survey and the University of Chicago's NORC 'describe the anxiety and insecurity that emerge from life without this safety net, and even among people with good jobs at good pay.' ... 'For the first time in 50 years, we are recording a decline in people's expectations and their uncertainty and anxiety grows the farther you ask them to look into the future.' ... 'Over the last decade or so, layoffs have spread from Uchitelle blue-collar workers and the less educated across the income and education stratum'" (Richard Curtin, Director of Michigan Consumer Surveys). These excerpts are taken from Uchitelle (1994, sect. 4, pp. 1, 5).

distressing. And how does the market deal with insecurity of jobs and income? Not well, as we saw earlier in the discussion of unemployment.

### Work and leisure satisfaction

Putting together a variety of findings of quality of life studies and studies of work satisfaction, we can suggest the relation between certain features of work in the labor market and overall feelings of well-being. For those *seeking* jobs, pay may be the most important consideration, but for the employed, the intrinsic features of work not easily priced by the market are more important.[45] On the job, lack of close supervision, absence of routine and repetitive work, and substantive complexity in what one does contribute most to work satisfaction.[46] For a large proportion of workers, Herzberg is right: The intrinsic characteristics of work make the most important contributions to satisfaction with one's work, pleasure in what one actually does, probably (the matter is disputed), the congeniality of colleagues, and the sense of making a difference.[47] Although accounts differ, the correlation of work satisfaction with happiness at a modest but respectable +0.29 (GSS [General Social Survey, National Opinion Research Center] data) seems to fit with the majority of studies dealing with the contribution of work satisfaction to SWB.[48]

Look at Figure 3 again. It shows a steady drop in work satisfaction of about 5 percentage points over the 1972 to 1994 period (a decline more marked among women than among men). The decline, dating at least from 1959, is not new.[49] As shown in Table 5, a Gallup poll in 1991 reveals a different aspect of the decline in work satisfaction. As Scitovsky has pointed out, intrinsic work enjoyment, which, again, is not priced by the market, is a major source of well-being: "The difference between liking and disliking one's work," he says, "may well be more important than the differences in economic satisfaction that the disparities in our income lead to."[50] And in a study of what people liked *doing*, not because of

---

[45] Jencks, Perman, and Rainwater (1988, p. 1343).

[46] Kohn and Schooler (1983, pp. 117–18).

[47] Herzberg (1973).

[48] Rice, Hunt, and Near (1980).

[49] A literature review in 1979 found that in the twenty years from 1959 to 1979 there had also been a decline in satisfaction with the intrinsic qualities of work, and in that period no objective change in the nature of the work could account for it. The implication was that people's standards had changed (Mortimer 1979, p. 10). One review of twenty-three studies found that "for more than 90 percent of the cases, the direction of this relationship [between job satisfaction and overall well-being] was positive; none of the scattered negative relationships was statistically reliable" (Rice et al. 1980, p. 37).

[50] Scitovsky (1977, p. 104). In *The Market Experience* (1991, pp. 302–4) I refer to the elite

Table 5. *Declining preferences for work compared to leisure, 1955 and 1991: "Which do you enjoy more, the hours when you are on your job, or the hours when you are not on your job?"*

|                  | 1955 | 1991 |
|------------------|------|------|
| Hours on the job | 38%  | 18%  |
| Hours off the job| 49   | 68   |
| No opinion       | 13   | 14   |
|                  | 100  | 100  |

*Source*: *The Gallup Monthly*, September 1991, p. 2.
*Note*: We cannot attribute this difference between pleasure in work and pleasure in leisure to a relative increase in leisure satisfaction, for the General Social Survey (not shown above) shows that from 1973 to 1994 there was almost no change in leisure satisfaction – even though there was, it is said, a decline of leisuretime over this period.

subsequent benefits like pay but intrinsically and in itself, the authors were amazed to find that, after certain social activities with children and friends, activities at work ranked highest, higher than most consumption activities (eating out, going to movies, and much higher than watching television).[51]

There are two important questions about the market's response to changes in work satisfaction: (1) Has the market inherent tendencies to correct low "utility" from work? And (2) do increases in pay compensate for the lost work "utility"? On the first of these, the answer must be "very little." As is the case with hazards, the market does not usually compensate people for doing things which most people dislike doing or (with the exception of artists, actors, and certain professionals) reduce their pay because they are doing what they enjoy.[52] As mentioned, because work

who received more psychic, rather than monetary, income from their work as "the privileged classes."

[51] F. Thomas Juster (1985, p. 336).

[52] The relative pay of professors may be high or low, according to one's standards, but there is no question about their liking their work: Asked whether they would choose the same career if they had a second chance, 93 percent of urban university professors said

satisfaction is not reflected in productivity, the market is unresponsive to low work satisfaction.

On the second point, does higher pay compensate for lower intrinsic satisfaction, the answer is a curious one. The authors of a book reporting *The Hidden Costs of Rewards* show that if one enjoys what one is doing and is then paid for it, one enjoys the actual work *less*. It seems that being paid by someone reduces the sense that this is *my* work over which *I* have control. There is a constraining condition: For the hidden costs to occur, one must think of pay as control instead of as information, but if one does that, then one believes that if one is paid for the work it is really the payer's work and because one accepts pay for doing it, the work must not be very enjoyable in itself. Under these, admittedly limited, circumstances, pay *reduces* intrinsic work enjoyment[53] and the economistic fallacy is enlisted again.

Work life is not unrelated to the second broad topic I wish to treat as a market externality: the effect of the market on family and friends.[54]

### Market externalities: friends and families

*Friendship*

The number of friends one has (or claims) is a better predictor of subjective well-being than the number of dollars one has (or claims), as may be seen in Table 6. I wish to draw attention to the difference in relationships between *satisfaction* with something (money or friends) and the different response to actually *having* that something. Satisfaction with income is minimally related to actual income and contributes much more to SWB than does actual income.[55] On the other hand, satisfaction with friends contributes only a little more to SWB than does the number of friends one has (or claims to have). From these differences in the relations to well-being of money and friends, I draw two important inferences: As Easterlin has argued,[56] increasing income for everyone has little effect on

---

that they would repeat their choice, more than the members of any other occupation (U.S. Department of Health, Education, and Welfare, Task Force, n.d. [c. 1972], p. 16). Professors were followed in close order by mathematicians, physicists, biologists, and chemists. Then came lawyers (83–85 percent), journalists, and then, at 77 percent, church university professors. White-collar workers (43 percent) were far above blue-collar workers (24 percent).
[53] Lepper and Greene, eds. (1978).
[54] Kanter (1977).
[55] "The product moment correlation between the perception that the pay is good and reported earnings is about 0.30, certainly not very impressive" (Kanter 1977, p. 304).
[56] Easterlin (1974). Recently Easterlin has returned to the argument; see Easterlin (1995).

Table 6. *Prediction of SWB by various resources*

| Resources | Eta coefficients | Beta coefficients #1 | Beta coefficients #2 |
|---|---|---|---|
| Family income | 0.17 | 0.19 | |
| Personal income | 0.07 | 0.04 | |
| Number of friends | 0.27 | | 0.24* |

\* The table deals separately with the contributions of "achieved resources" and "other current resources." The eta coefficients are in an array that includes both of these kinds of resources and such "ascribed resources" as intelligence, health, and attractiveness (age controlled). The amount of variance explained by number of friends, time pressure, and religious faith (13.5%) is more than five times the variance explained by family *and* personal income *and* education (2.5%). Beta weights represent accounts of the variance within an array with all other resources controlled; they may be summed.
*Source*: Campbell et al. (1976, p. 368).

SWB because income satisfaction is not closely related to actual income. But with friendship, because having and liking *are* closely related, increasing friendship would have a substantial effect on SWB. Think of this difference in terms of the hedonic treadmill. In the economic relationship, "*Here,* you see," said the Red Queen, "it takes all the running you can do to stay in the same place." On the other hand, if you take the trouble to gain a friend, you are very likely to find that your new friendship contributes to your life satisfaction. The friendship route is less invidious, less vulnerable to escalation of standards to match any improvement of circumstances, and, therefore, further from that utilitarian hell, the hedonic treadmill.[57]

The reasons why friendship is not a market commodity are so obvious that they will not bear repeating. If you put a price on friendship you change its character.[58] Moreover, as mentioned, if most other forms of satisfaction are not priced, it is unlikely that such person-particular enjoyments as those of friendship should be given price values (the idea of shadow pricing does not work with such intrinsic satisfactions as friendship). As in African markets where you cannot exchange across currencies, say, women for cattle, so the currencies of commodities markets will "buy" friends only at a discount – though trading the other way

[57] Income *satisfaction* (beta 0.29) has a stronger influence on SWB than friendship *satisfaction* (beta 0.20), whereas, as we saw, actual income makes a weaker contribution to SWB than *actual* friendships. Campbell et al. (1976, p. 374).

[58] Lane (1991, chaps. 11–12).

(using friends to increase one's income opportunities) might be temporarily successful.

### Family

In Table 1 the "family index" ranked second and "things you do with the family" ranked sixth in their contributions to SWB, together accounting for twice the variance of the "money index." In Table 2, family life again ranked second and marriage ranked fifth. But these are measures of contribution to SWB and its opposite, not measures of family felicity, which has not prospered of late. Only about half of the marriages now being created are destined to survive. Is this decline in the family attributable to the market?

Here I would like to reinstate the "time squeeze," not because it may affect stress at work, but because it influences family felicity. Strain at work inevitably spills over into strain in family life (work dissatisfaction is closely correlated with marital dissatisfaction). About half of the working population report that they now have less time for their family, and working mothers, surely the most overworked part of the population, report "a lot of" or "extreme" stress from their dual roles.[59] Inevitably, this strain has an influence on the well-being of children, a strain that is not captured in the surveys of adult happiness but, as noted, is revealed in the epidemiological studies of depression, in which children are found to experience a rising tide of depression that is even greater than that of adults.

These familial costs are externalities to the generation of employers whose decisions count, but they are family internalities and may imply actual money costs to a future generation of employers. Thus, to relate this theme of insecurity and lack of work enjoyment to the hypothesis that the breakdown of family (and friendship) relations is a principal cause of the rise of depression and unhappiness, it seems that the labor market's tendency to externalize worker costs is a major source of this dysphoria, not because work is a disutility – often quite the opposite – but because the practices of the market rob workers of time for family life. Family values have no standing in the market, and, therefore, family life is a market externality.

I have suggested that market economies can no longer count on increased income to "maximize utility" and have no endogenous interest in or power to cope with many of the sources of unhappiness, and, in

---

[59] Arlie Hochschild (1989), quoted in Schor (1991, p. 12). Sylvia A. Hewlett (1991, p. 1) reports that "child neglect has become endemic to our society."

Table 7. *Correlations with SWB of economic development*

| Economic modernization | Zero order correlation | Source |
|---|---|---|
| GDP per capita | +0.58** | Diener |
| " " "   "Real national income" | +0.69* | Veenhoven |
| Purchasing power | +0.61** | Diener |
| Equality of income (gini coeff.) | | |
| (low score = more equality) | −0.43† | Diener |

† $p > 0.05$; * $p > 0.01$; ** $p > 0.001$.
*Sources*: Diener, Diener, and Diener (1995, pp. 857, 859); Veenhoven (1993, p. 50).

more extreme cases, of depression. Now I turn to an assessment of the historical meaning of this unexpected and distressing infelicity.

### A turning point in history?

To return to our starting point, few people would say that we have created a happy society. Did we follow for too long some destiny heralded by the Enlightenment, made possible by the industrial revolution, informed by science, and guided by market forces? If we got what market values told us to pursue, did we want the wrong things, things that once seemed freighted with "utility," but in the event, brought unexpected sorrows to match the new satisfactions? To shift to a nautical metaphor, if we were once on the right course, did we hold on course too long?

That course may be characterized as *modernization*; its goal is *modernity*. The evidence suggests that modernization is a felicitous process with gains in subjective well-being at every step but that, on arrival, a fairly dramatic change in values and payoffs takes place. Table 7 shows that as countries go from poverty toward wealth, increases in per capita national income are associated with substantial gains in SWB. Then, as in the advanced countries of Europe, with increased income there are only trivial gains in SWB.[60] Finally, as our data have shown, over the past twenty-five years in the (almost) richest nation in the world, there has been a *decline* in happiness and a rise in depression. SWB has a curvilinear path through history, climbing toward modernity for a long (or

[60] Inglehart and Rabier (1986, pp. 45–46).

sometimes brief) period and then, after a little plateau, turning down for reasons we have explored in this chapter. Apparently the law of diminishing returns applies to money as it does to everything that money buys. Contrasting the happy tone of the cross-cultural studies comparing nations across the spectrum from mostly less to more "advanced" status and the gloomy course of recent history I have charted, one can see the rising portion of this curving trajectory more clearly. On the basis of several cross-national studies of SWB, in Table 7 I summarize these data. Where the affluence effect meets the economistic fallacy, there is a downturn in felicity. Hence the curvilinearity.

A. L. Kroeber employs a useful metaphor for the kind of social change we are addressing. Speaking of the life cycles of great cultures, Kroeber says the death of a culture is not usually encountered by cataclysmic events, not by either a bang or a whimper, but by failure to adapt, a monotonous repetition of what it had done before. "The very selection which at the outset is necessary if a distinctive pattern is to be produced, is almost certain later on to become a limitation."[61] Is that where we are now? This is a very different view of "the end of history" recently said to characterize the triumph of market democracies.[62]

Durkheim asks: "Even from a purely utilitarian point of view, what is the use of increasing abundance, if it does not succeed in calming the desires of the greatest number, but, on the contrary, only serves to increase their impatience. It is forgotten that economic functions are not their own justification. . . . Society has no *raison d'être* if it does not bring men a little peace, peace in their hearts and peace in their mutual relations."[63] Deprived of its original utilitarian raison d'être, does the market society now reflect something like Kroeber's exhaustion of a cultural configuration in which the old, material civilization has exhausted the possibilities of that particular pattern? The offerings of the market no longer satisfy, not because the payoff is not large enough but because it is denominated in the wrong currency.

---

[61] Kroeber (1944, p. 840).     [62] Fukuyama (1989).
[63] Emile Durkheim (1957, p. 16), quoted in Lukes (1973, p. 267).

## REFERENCES

Andrews, Frank M., and Stephen B. Withey (1976). *Social Indicators of Well-Being: Americans' Perceptions of Life Quality*. New York: Plenum.

Argyle, Michael (1993 [1987]). *The Psychology of Happiness*. London: Routledge.

Beck, Aaron T., Maria Kovacs, and Arlene Weissman (1975). "Hopelessness and

Suicidal Behavior: An Overview," *Journal of the American Medical Association* 234 (December): 1146–49.

Becker, Gary (1965). "A Theory of the Allocation of Time," *Economic Journal* 75: 493–517.

Brenner, M. Harvey (1973). *Mental Illness and the Economy.* Cambridge, Mass.: Harvard University Press.

Brown, C. (1980). "Equalizing Differences in the Labor Market," *Quarterly Journal of Economics* 94: 113–34.

Brown, George W., and Tirril Harris (1978). *Social Origins of Depression: A Study of Psychological Disorder in Women.* London and Cambridge: Tavistock/Cambridge University Press.

Buie, James (1988). "'Me' Decades Generate Depression: Individualism Erodes Commitment to Others," *APA Monitor* 19 (October): 18 (quoting Martin Seligman).

Campbell, Angus, Philip E. Converse, and Willard L. Rodgers (1976). *The Quality of American Life: Perceptions, Evaluations, and Satisfactions.* New York: Russell Sage.

Catalano, Ralph, and David C. Dooley (1977). "Economic Predictors of Depressed Mood and Stressful Life Events in a Metropolitan Community," *Journal of Health and Social Behavior* 18: 292–307.

Cross-National Collaborative Group (1992). "The Changing Rate of Depression: Cross-National Comparisons," *Journal of the American Medical Association* 268 (December 2): 3098–3105.

Diener, Ed. (1984). "Subjective Well-Being," *Psychological Bulletin* 95: 542–75.

Diener, Ed, Marissa Diener, and Carol Diener (1995). "Factors Predicting the Subjective Well-Being of Nations," *Journal of Personality and Social Psychology* 69: 851–64.

Durkheim, Emile (1957). *Professional Ethics and Civic Morals.* Trans. C. Brookfield. London: Routledge and Kegan Paul.

Easterlin, Richard A. (1974). "Does Economic Growth Improve the Human Lot?" in Paul A. David and Melvin W. Reder, eds., *Nations and Households in Economic Growth: Essays in Honor of Moses Abramovitz.* Stanford, Calif.: Stanford University Press.

Easterlin, Richard A. (1995). "Will Raising the Incomes of All Increase the Happiness of All?" *Journal of Economic Behavior and Organization* 27: 35–47.

Elder, Glen H., Tri Van Nguyen, and Avshalom Caspi (1985). "Linking Family Hardship to Children's Lives," *Child Development* 85: 361–75.

Freedman, Jonathan (1980). *Happy People.* New York: Harcourt, Brace.

Fukuyama, Francis (1989). "The End of History?" *The National Interest* (Summer): 3–30.

Goleman, Daniel (1992). "A Rising Cost of Modernity: Depression," *New York Times*, December 8, p. C3.

*Harvard Mental Health Letter* (1994). "Update on Mood Disorders – Part I." 11 (December): 1–4.

Herzberg, Frederick (1973). *Work and the Nature of Man*. New York: Mentor/ New American Libray.

Hewlett, Sylvia A. (1991). *When the Bough Breaks: The Cost of Neglecting Our Children*. New York: Basic Books.

Hochschild, Arlie (1989). *The Second Shift: Working Parents and the Revolution at Home*. New York: Viking Penguin.

Inglehart, Ronald, and Jacques-René Rabier (1986). "Aspirations Adapt to Situations – But Why Are the Belgians So Much Happier Than the French: A Cross-Cultural Analysis of the Subjective Quality of Life," in Frank M. Andrews, ed., *Research on the Quality of Life*. Ann Arbor, Mich.: Institute for Social Research.

Jencks, Christopher, Lauri Perman, and Lee Rainwater (1988). "What Is a Good Job? A New Measure of Labor-Market Success," *American Journal of Sociology* 93: 1322–57.

Juster, F. Thomas (1985). "Preferences for Work and Leisure," in Juster and Frank P. Stafford, eds., *Time, Goods, and Well-Being*. Ann Arbor, Mich.: Institute for Social Research.

Juster, F. Thomas, and Frank P. Stafford, eds. (1985). *Time, Goods, and Well-Being*. Ann Arbor, Mich.: Institute for Social Research.

Kanter, Rosabeth Moss (1977). *Work and Family in the United States*. New York: Russell Sage.

Klerman, Gerald L. (1989). "The Current Age of Youthful Melancholia: Evidence for Increase in Depression among Adolescents and Young Adults," in *Annual Progress in Child Psychiatry & Child Development*, pp. 333–54. New York: Brunner/Mazel.

Kohn, Melvin L., and Carmi Schooler (1983). *Work and Personality: An Inquiry into the Impact of Social Stratification*. Norwood, N.J.: Ablex.

Kroeber, A. L. (1994). *Configurations of Culture Growth*. Berkeley, Calif.: University of California Press.

Lane, Robert E. (1991). *The Market Experience*. New York: Cambridge University Press.

Lane, Robert E. (1992). "Work as 'Disutility' and Money as 'Happiness': Cultural Origins of a Basic Market Error," *Journal of Socio-Economics* 21: 43–64.

Lawler, Edward E., III (1982). "Strategies for Improving the Quality of Work Life," *American Psychologist* 37: 486–93.

Lepper, Mark R., and David Greene, eds. (1978). *The Hidden Costs of Rewards: New Perspectives on the Psychology of Human Motivation*. Hillsdale, N.J.: Erlbaum.

Lewis, Paul (1993). "'Quarter of Children' Mentally Ill," (London) *Observer*, September 19.

Lewisohn, Peter M., Paul Rohde, John R. Seeley, and Scott A. Fischer (1993). "Age-Cohort Changes in the Lifetime Occurrence of Depression and Other Mental Disorders," *Journal of Abnormal Psychology* 102: 110–20.

Linder, Steffan (1970). *The Harried Leisure Class*. New York: Columbia University Press.

Lukes, Steven (1973). *Emile Durkheim: His Life and Work*. London: Allen Lane/ Penguin.

Michalos, Alex C. (1986). "Job Satisfaction, Marital Satisfaction, and the Quality of Life: A Review and a Preview," in Frank M. Andrews, ed., *Research on the Quality of Life*. Ann Arbor, Mich.: Institute for Social Research.

Mortimer, Jeylan T. (1979). *Changing Attitudes toward Work: Highlights of the Literature*. New York: Pergamon for American Institute Studies in Productivity.

Nisbett, Richard, and Lee Ross (1990). *Human Inference: Strategies and Shortcomings of Social Judgment*. Englewood Cliffs, N.J.: Prentice-Hall.

Rice, R. E., R. G. Hunt, and J. P. Near (1980). "The Job-Satisfaction/Life-Satisfaction Relationship: A Review of Empirical Research," *Basic and Applied Social Psychology* 1: 37–64.

Robinson, John P. (1985). "Changes in Time Use: An Historical Overview," in F. Thomas Juster and Frank P. Stafford, eds., *Time, Goods, and Well-Being*, pp. 288–312. Ann Arbor, Mich.: Institute for Social Research.

Samuelson, Paul A., and William D. Nordhaus (1985). *Economics*, 12th ed. New York: McGraw-Hill.

Sartorius, Norman, H. Davidian, G. Ernberg, F. R. Fenton, I. Fujii, et al. (1983). *Depressive Disorders in Different Cultures*. Report of the World Health Organization Collaborative Study in Standardized Assessment of Depressive Disorders. Geneva: World Health Organization.

Schor, Juliet B. (1991). *The Overworked American: The Unexpected Decline of Leisure*. New York: Basic Books.

Scitovsky, Tibor (1977). *The Joyless Economy*. New York: Oxford University Press.

Simmel, Georg (1978 [1907]). *The Philosophy of Money*. Trans. T. Bottomore and D. Frisby. London: Routledge & Kegan Paul.

Smith, Adam (1937 [1776]). *The Wealth of Nations*. Ed. Edwin Cannan. New York: Random House.

Smith, Adam (1974 [1759]). *The Theory of Moral Sentiments*. Ed. D. D. Raphael and A. L. Macfie. Indianapolis: Liberty Press.

Uchitelle, Louis (1994). "The Rise of the Losing Class," *New York Times*, November 20, sect. 4, pp. 1, 5.

U.S. Bureau of the Census (1990). *Statistical Abstract of the United States, 1990*. Washington, D.C.

U.S. Department of Health, Education, and Welfare, Task Force (n.d. [c. 1972]). *Work in America*. Cambridge, Mass.: MIT Press.

Veenhoven, Ruut (1984). *Conditions of Happiness: Summary Print*. Dordrecht, Holland: Reidel.

Veenhoven, Ruut (1993). *Happiness in Nations: Subjective Appreciation of Life in 56 Nations, 1946–1992*. Rotterdam: Erasmus University, RISBO.

Vroom, Victor H. (1964). *Work and Motivation*. New York: Wiley.

Walzer, Michael (1983). *Spheres of Justice*. Oxford: Robertson.

Weissman, Myrna M., Roger Bland, Peter R. Joyce, Stephen Newman, et al. (1993). "Sex Differences in Rates of Depression: Cross-National Perspectives. Special Issue: Toward a New Psychobiology of Depression in Women," *Journal of Affective Disorders* 29: 77–84.

Weissman, Myrna M., Martha Livingston Bruce, Philip J. Leaf, Louise Florio, and Charles Holzer, III (1991). "Affective Disorders," in Lee N. Robins and Darrel A. Regier, eds., *Psychiatric Disorders in America: The Epidemiological Catchment Area Study*. New York: Free Press.

# EPILOGUE

CHAPTER 19

# Where have we been and where are we going?

*Douglass C. North*

## 1    Introduction

Increasing our knowledge of the nature of economic change requires that we utilize the only laboratory we have – the past. But to understand the past we must impose order on the myriad facts that have survived to explain what has happened, and doing so requires theory. The theories we develop to understand where we have been are from the social sciences. There is a constant give and take between the theories we develop and their application to explain the past. Do they improve our understanding – is the resultant explanation broadly consistent with the surviving historical evidence? The first issue that concerns us in this essay is, just how good is our understanding of the past?

The second issue is, just how useful is a good understanding of the past for solving present and future problems? Can the gradual accretion of "sound" explanations of the past help in understanding where we are going? That depends on the degree to which there are lessons from history. If there are lessons they are not those that are the bread and butter of politicians, statesmen, and soothsayers. Rather, they would be the persistent features of the human landscape that are the underlying interrelationships between the rules of the game that humans devise to structure human interaction and the way those rules evolve in the interaction between humans and their environment, an environment which changes as a result not only of external natural forces, but also of changes induced by the players themselves. It is the interactions among the evolving beliefs and preferences of the players, the consequent institutions they create to structure human interaction, and the way those

I am indebted to Avner Greif for providing helpful comments on an earlier version of this essay and to Elisabeth Case for editing the essay.

institutions shape economic performance that are an enduring feature of the human landscape and the subject of this essay.

I want first to assess what we have learned from the past and the usefulness of the tools at hand – i.e., the rationality assumption and growth theory we employ in economics. I then shall attempt to develop better tools in order to gain an understanding of what have been permanent features of the human landscape. These should provide some clues as to where we are going – or at least an agenda for research on the subject.

## 2    Societal evolution

The overall process of evolution involves three stages: (1) the physical and chemical evolution of the stars and planets, (2) the biological evolution starting with DNA (deoxyribonucleic acid) and development of living species, and (3) the societal evolution starting with *Homo sapiens* (see Boulding 1991). Stage one is a given in our analysis. Stage two, concerned with the evolving genetic structure of humans, particularly the way the mind has evolved and the development of language, plays a major role in the third stage, societal evolution.

The first great discontinuity in societal evolution was the development of agriculture, which took place almost four million years after human beings became separate from other primates – that is, only ten thousand years ago. It probably evolved independently in different parts of the world at different times and may have resulted from some combination of constriction of the environment and local population pressure (North and Thomas 1977). Whatever the source, agriculture provided the conditions for civilization both by expanding the productive potential of humans and by establishing the sedentary conditions that made possible the growth of specialization and division of labor.

In the ensuing ten thousand years the rate of change appears to have been very slow for at least the first half of that period, although the surviving archaeological evidence has been scarce. In the second half, change has been episodic for most of the time; periods of what appear to have been economic growth in particular geographic regions have been interrupted by stagnation and decline, and sometimes those geographic areas have failed to recover. Athens in the fifth century B.C., Rhodes in the third century B.C., and Rome in the early empire are examples of growth followed by decline and failure to recover for centuries. Following the demise of Rome in the West there was a long hiatus until the beginning of revival in the tenth century. With Mohammed came expansion of the Muslim world in North Africa and beyond. And in the Far

East Chinese dynasties produced enormously rich cultures, although it remained for the relatively backward area of Western Europe to be the incubator of modern growth.

If modern economic growth had its genesis in the tenth century revival of Western Europe, sustained growth appears to have begun perhaps four hundred years ago but been confined to a small part of the earth for most of that time – Western Europe and the overseas settlements of England. Widespread growth is a recent phenomenon mostly dating since World War II. Even today large parts of the world either are not experiencing growth (e.g., the republics of the former Soviet Union and sub-Saharan Africa) or are experiencing growth that continues to be episodic (e.g., Latin America).

## 3 Rethinking the process of economic change

How useful are our tools of analysis? The rational choice paradigm assumes that people know what is in their self-interest and act accordingly, or at the very least that competition will weed out those who make incorrect choices and reward those who make correct choices. But it is impossible to reconcile this argument with the historical and contemporary record briefly outlined here.

Growth theory as it has evolved from neoclassical theory is equally unhelpful in explaining this historical and contemporary record. Convergence of the growth paths of economies (Baumol 1986) has tended to occur only among the developed countries. Persistent divergence, as argued among some of the new growth theory variants of the Solow model, cannot explain the rise of the "Asian Tigers" or China. In fact, to put it bluntly, the growth theory stemming from neoclassical economics, old or new, suggests not only ignorance of the empirical evidence, historical or contemporary, but failure to recognize that incentives matter – surely a remarkable position for economists whose theory is built around incentives.

It has to be the incentive structure imbedded in the institutional/organizational structure of economies that is a key to unraveling the puzzle of uneven and erratic growth. But that entails a still deeper puzzle. Why don't economies that have institutional frameworks that are inhospitable to economic growth simply adopt the frameworks of the successful economies? They do, or at least they try to: The rush to create market economies is a ubiquitous characteristic of third world and transition economies. But look at the results. They vary enormously, from China and the Czech Republic, which *so far* are successful; to the republics of the ex Soviet Union, which *so far* show few signs of success; to sub-Saharan Africa, which remains a basket case. In our search for better analytical tools, therefore, we must be concerned not only with the fundamental structure of successful economies but also with "how to get there."

To make sense out of the historical and contemporary evidence, we must rethink the whole process of economic change. Current theory stems from the development of national income and growth accounting literature and explores the superficial aspects of economic growth – technology or human or physical capital. It ignores the structure of incentives and disincentives that make up the institutional framework of the economy, the polity, and the society (and our compass must include much more than purely economic variables). If we consider these incentives and why they vary, we are driven to examine the various belief systems that determine the institutional framework.

We are far from being able to understand the whole process of change, but I can suggest some explanations which offer the promise of improving our understanding of where we have been. Specifically I shall support three arguments that are at wide variance with the received wisdom. The first is that contrary to both the economic history literature and the economic growth literature, old and new, the primary source of economic growth is the institutional/organizational structure that determines incentives. Until we focus on that subject we shall not advance knowledge of economic growth. Economies are poor when institutions are structured in such a way as to produce high costs of transacting in political and economic markets. Efficient economic and political markets, once in place, will then provide the context within which the new growth theory has relevance. The second is that it is necessary to create impersonal political and economic markets for sustained economic growth. The third is that the belief systems of societies and the way they evolve are the underlying determinants of institutions and their evolution. In the rest of this essay I shall support these arguments.

## 4    Institutional change

Curiously enough, institutions are front and center in all current explanations of growth or lack of it in third world or transition economies, but the explanations lack both analytical content and an understanding of the nature of institutions or the way they evolve. The implication of standard economic analysis is that institutions can be created at will or that they are a dependent variable to getting the prices right. But recent experience provides convincing evidence that neither can they be taken for granted nor do they automatically evolve from getting the prices right. And historical experience makes clear that efficient economic institutions are the exception. To proceed we must understand what institutions are and how they evolve.

Institutions provide the structure that humans impose on human interaction in order to reduce uncertainty. There is nothing about that structure that implies that institutions are efficient in the sense of inducing economic growth. Sometimes they are created to facilitate exchange, encourage technological change, and induce human capital formation and in consequence reduce transaction and/or transformation costs; at other times they are created to support monopoly, prevent technological change, thwart human capital development, and generally raise the costs of transaction and/or transformation. In fact the inefficient has been the far more common pattern throughout history. To provide an understanding of why, I shall state six propositions that, I believe, underlie institutional change, but first let me dispel any confusion between institutions and organizations. Institutions are the rules of the game – both formal rules and informal constraints (conventions, norms of behavior, and self-imposed codes of conduct) – and their enforcement characteristics. Together they define the way the game is played. Organizations are the players. They are groups of individuals held together by some common objectives. Economic organizations are firms, trade unions, cooperatives, etc.; political organizations are political parties, legislatures, regulatory bodies; educational organizations are universities, schools, vocational training centers. The immediate objective of organizations may be maximizing profit (for firms) or improving reelection prospects (for political parties), but the ultimate objective is survival because all organizations live in a world of scarcity and hence competition.

Now to the six propositions:

1. The continuous interaction between institutions and organizations in the economic setting of scarcity and hence competition is the key to institutional change.
2. Competition forces organizations continually to invest in new skills and knowledge to survive. The kind of skills and knowledge individuals and their organizations acquire will shape evolving perceptions about opportunities and hence choices that will incrementally alter institutions.
3. The institutional framework provides the incentive structure that dictates the kinds of skills and knowledge perceived to have the maximum payoff.
4. Perceptions are derived from the mental constructs of the players.

5. The economies of scope, complementarities, and network externalities of an institutional matrix make institutional change
overwhelmingly incremental and path dependent.

6. Institutional change threatens existing order because it typically
involves a conflict between the organizations (read interest
groups) that were dominant in the old institutional order and
those of the new institutional order.

Having already dealt with proposition 1, let me expand on propositions 2 through 6.

2. New or altered opportunities may be perceived to be a result of
exogenous changes in the external environment that alter relative prices
to organizations or a consequence of endogenous competition among the
organizations of the polity and the economy. In either case the ubiquity
of competition in the overall economic setting of scarcity induces entrepreneurs and members of their organizations to invest in skills and
knowledge. Whether through learning by doing on the job or acquiring
formal knowledge, improving the efficiency of the organization relative
to that of rivals is the key to survival.

While idle curiosity surely is an innate source of human beings' desire
for knowledge, the rate of accumulating knowledge is clearly tied to the
payoffs. Secure monopolies, be they organizations in the polity or in the
economy, simply do not have to improve to survive. But firms, political
parties, or even institutions of higher learning faced with rival organizations must strive to improve their efficiency. When competition is muted
(for whatever reasons) organizations will have less incentive to invest in
new knowledge and in consequence will not induce rapid institutional
change. Stable institutional structures will be the result. Vigorous
organizational competition will accelerate the process of institutional
change.

3. There is *no implication* in proposition 2 of evolutionary progress
or economic growth – only of change. The institutional matrix defines the
opportunity set, be it one that makes income redistribution the highest
payoff in an economy or one that provides the highest payoffs to productive activity. While every economy provides a mixed set of incentives for
both types of activity, the relative weights (as between redistributive and
productive incentives) are crucial factors in the performance of economies. The organizations that come into existence will reflect the payoff
structure. More than that, the direction of their investment in skills and
knowledge will equally reflect the underlying incentive structure. If the
highest rate of return in an economy comes from piracy we can expect
that the organizations will invest in skills and knowledge that will make

them better pirates. Similarly, if there are high returns to productive activities we will expect organizations to devote resources to investing in skills and knowledge that will increase productivity (the new growth economics literature becomes relevant at this point).

The immediate investment by economic organizations in vocational and on the job training obviously will depend on the perceived benefits. But an even more fundamental influence on the future of the economy is the extent to which societies will invest in formal education, schooling, dissemination of knowledge, and both applied and pure research, which will mirror the perceptions of the entrepreneurs in political and economic organizations.

4. The key to the choices that individuals make is their perceptions, which are a function of the way the mind interprets the information it receives. The mental constructs individuals form to explain and interpret the world around them are a result partly of the genetic evolution of the mind, partly of their cultural heritage, partly of the local everyday problems they confront and must solve, and partly of nonlocal learning.[1] The cultural heritage not only embodies learning from the experiences of past generations, but carries over the values from past generations, and the resultant perceptions are a blend of beliefs and preferences.

The mix among these sources in interpreting one's environment obviously varies as between, for example, a Papuan tribesman, on the one hand, and an economist in the United States, on the other hand (although there is no implication that the latter's perceptions are independent of his or her cultural heritage).

The implication of the foregoing paragraph is that individuals from different backgrounds will interpret the same evidence differently; they may, in consequence, make different choices. If the information feedback of the consequences of choices were complete, then individuals with the same utility function would gradually correct their perceptions and over time converge to a common equilibrium; but as Frank Hahn has succinctly put it, "There is a continuum of theories that agents can hold and act upon without ever encountering events which lead them to change their theories" (Hahn 1987, 324). The result is that multiple equilibria are possible as a result of different choices by agents with identical tastes.

5. The viability, profitability, and indeed survival of the organizations of a society typically depend on the existing institutional matrix. That institutional structure has brought them into existence, and their

---

[1] This argument is elaborated in a cognitive science approach to the development of learning and belief systems in Denzau and North (1994).

complex web of interdependent contracts and other relationships has been constructed on it. Two implications follow: (a) institutional change is typically incremental and (b) it is path dependent.

Why can't economies reverse their direction overnight? This would surely be a puzzle in a world that operates as neoclassical theory would have us believe. That is, in a neoclassical world abrupt, radical change in institutions and organizations should immediately result from a radical change in relative prices or performance. Now it is true that on occasion accumulated pressures do produce an abrupt change in institutions akin to the punctuated equilibrium models in evolutionary theory. But it is simply a fact that the overwhelming majority of change is incremental and gradual. It is incremental because large-scale change would harm large numbers of existing organizations and therefore is stoutly opposed by them.

Path dependence could mean nothing more than that yesterday's choices are the initial starting point for today's. But path dependence appears to be a much more fundamental determinant of long-run change than that.[2] The difficulty of fundamentally altering paths is evident and suggests that the learning process by which we arrive at today's institutions constrains future choices. The institutional structure builds in a set of constraints with respect to downstream changes that biases choices.

6. But nothing in the foregoing discussion conflicts with the point that institutional change is potentially destabilizing because it replaces old dominant organizations with new ones. Indeed, the tension between order/disorder and institutional change is a fundamental influence on the process of economic/political change. Whether the institutional change is peaceful and orderly or leads to a breakdown in order is a central issue of societal evolution.

## 5     Historical success stories

In the historical success stories of institutional adaptation, the belief system of the players filtered the information from current experiences and interpreted it in ways that induced choices that led to the modification, alteration, or adoption of institutions that resolved existing problems or led to improvements in competitive performance.

In early modern Europe[3] the lack of large-scale political and economic order created the environment essential to political/economic development. In that competitive, decentralized environment lots of

---

[2] The concept of path dependence was pioneered by Arthur (1989) and David (1985).
[3] This section on the development of early modern Europe is elaborated at length in North (1995).

alternatives were pursued as each society confronted its own unique external environment. Some worked, as in the cases of the Netherlands and England; some failed, as in the cases of Spain and Portugal; and some, such as France, fell between these two extremes. But the keys to the story are the variety of options pursued and the likelihood (as compared to a single unified policy) that some would turn out to produce political/economic development. Even the relative failures in Western Europe played an essential role in European development and were more successful than other parts of the world because of competitive pressures.

The last point deserves special emphasis. It was the dynamic consequences of the competition among fragmented political bodies that resulted in an especially creative environment. Europe was politically fragmented, but it was integrated in having both an overall belief structure, derived from Christendom, and information and transportation connections that caused scientific, technological, and artistic developments in one part to spread rapidly throughout the others. To treat the Netherlands and England as success stories in isolation from the stimulus received from the rest of Europe (and to a lesser degree Islam and China) is to miss a vital part of the explanation. Italian city states, Portugal, and Germanic states all fell behind the Netherlands and England, but banking, artistic development, improvements in navigation, and printing were just a few of the obvious contributions that the former states made to European advancement.

Throughout Western Europe, competition among the evolving nation states was a deep underlying source of change and equally a constraint on the options available to them. Competition forced crowns to trade rights and privileges – including protection of property rights – for revenue, including most fundamentally the granting to representative bodies – variously Parliament, States General, Cortes – control over tax rates and/or certain privileges in return for revenue. But it was the evolving bargaining strength of rulers vis-à-vis constituents that was the decisive feature of subsequent economic development. Three considerations were at stake: (1) the size of the potential gains the constituents could realize by the state taking over protection of the constituents' property; (2) the closeness of substitutes for the existing ruler – that is, the ability of rivals (both within and outside the political unit) to the existing ruler to take over and provide the same, or more, services; (3) the structure of the economy which determined the benefits and costs to the ruler of various sources of revenue. Let me briefly describe the background conditions of the Netherlands and England that led to the external environments shaping their belief systems.

To understand the success of the Netherlands one must cast a backward glance at the evolution of the prosperous towns of the Low Countries such as Bruges, Ghent, and Liege; their internal conflicts; and their relationship to Burgundian and Habsburg rule. The prosperity of the towns, whether based on the wool cloth trade or on the metals trade, early on made for an urban-centered, market-oriented area unique at a time of overwhelmingly rural societies. Their internal conflicts reflected ongoing tensions between patricians and craftsmen and persistent conflicts over ongoing efforts to create local monopolies which, when successful, led to a drying up of the very sources of productivity which had been the mainspring of their growth. Burgundian (and later Habsburg) rule discouraged restrictive practices such as those that developed in the cloth towns of Bruges and Ghent; it also encouraged the growth of new centers of industry that sprang up in response to the favorable incentives embodied in the rules and property rights. In 1463 Philip the Good created a representative body, the States General, which enacted laws and had the authority to vote taxes for the ruler. The tax revenue generated by their level of prosperity made the Low Countries the jewel in the Habsburg Empire.

England evolved along a route different from those of Continental polities. As an island generally invulnerable to external conquest, it had no standing army. The exception to its invulnerability was, of course, the Norman conquest, and here William succeeded in imposing a feudal structure that was more centralized than any on the Continent. The political institutions, in consequence, were exceptional in several respects. There was a single parliament for the entire country rather than regional estates as in France, Spain, and the Netherlands. There were also no divisions into towns, clergy, and nobility. But the more centralized feudal structure did not ensure that the crown would not overstep the traditional liberties of the barons, as the Magna Carta attests.

We can now examine the evolving bargaining strength of ruler versus constituent that shaped the belief structure and the path of each polity. In the Netherlands the productive town economies stood to gain substantially by the political order and protection of property rights provided by the Burgundians and then by Charles V. The structure of the economy built around export trades provided the means for easy-to-collect taxes on trade but not at a level to affect the comparative advantage of those export trades adversely. The liberty to come and go, to buy and sell, led to the evolution of efficient economic markets. But when Philip II altered the "contractual agreement" the Seven Provinces became convinced that they could prosper only with independence. The resistance was initiated by the States General, which in 1581 issued the

Act of Abjuration of allegiance to Philip II and claimed sovereignty for the provinces themselves. The powers of the newly independent country resided with each province (which voted as a unit), and a unanimity rule meant that the States General could act only with the unanimous approval of the Seven Provinces. Cumbersome as that process was, this political structure survived. The polity devolved the elements of political representation and democratic decision rules, and additionally supported religious toleration. The belief structure that had evolved to shape the independent polity was more pragmatic than intellectual, a consequence of the incremental evolution of the bargaining strength of constituents and rulers.

As with the Netherlands, it was England's external trade that provided an increasing share of crown revenue with taxes on wine, general merchandise, and wool cloth; but it was the wool export trade that was the backbone of the augmented revenue. Eileen Powers' classic story of the wool trade (1941) describes the exchange among the three groups involved in that trade: the wool growers as represented in Parliament, the merchants of the staple, and the crown. The merchants achieved a monopoly of the export trade and a depot in Calais; Parliament received the right to set the tax; and the crown received the revenue. Stubbs (1896, vol. 3, p. 599) summarizes the exchange as follows: "The admission of the right of parliament to legislate, to inquire into abuses, and to share in the guidance of national policy, was practically purchased by the money granted to Edward I and Edward III."

With the Tudors the English crown was at the zenith of its power, but it never achieved the unilateral control over taxing power that the crowns of France and Spain achieved. The confiscation of monastery lands and possessions by Henry VIII alienated many peers and much of the clergy, and as a consequence "Henry had need of the House of Commons and he cultivated it with sedulous care" (Elton 1953, p. 4). The Stuarts inherited what the Tudors had sown, and the evolving controversy between the crown and Parliament is a well known tale. Two aspects of this controversy are noteworthy for this analysis. One was the evolving perception of the common law as the supreme law of the land – a position notably championed by Sir Edward Coke – and the other was the connection made between monopoly and a denial of liberty as embodied in the crown grants of monopoly privileges.

## 6    The efficiency of political markets

England and the Netherlands represent historical success stories in which evolving belief systems shaped by external events induced institutional evolution to provide the beginning of modern economic growth. Key institutional/organizational changes were those that permitted the growth of impersonal exchange – both economic and political. By permitted I mean that, to use game theory terminology, they altered the payoff between defection and cooperation to favor the latter in both political and economic markets. That is, personal exchange provides settings in which it typically pays to cooperate. Impersonal exchange is just the antithesis and necessitates the development of institutions to alter payoffs in favor of cooperative activity.

In the case of economic markets, recent historical research has provided analytical accounts of the evolution of the institutions that undergirded long-distance trade in the Middle Ages (Greif 1993); that led to the development of merchant codes of conduct that became the foundation of commercial law (Milgrom, North, and Weingast 1990); that converted uncertainty to risk, leading to the development of marine insurance (deRoover 1945); and that provided the foundation of an impersonal capital market with the development of the bill of exchange and the growth of early banking organization. By the end of the sixteenth century these and other institutional/organizational innovations had created the first modern economy in Amsterdam and the Seven Provinces that formed the Netherlands.[4]

But the creation of efficient economic markets is only half, and the less puzzling half, of the story. It is much more difficult to account for and explain the growth of "efficient" political markets that are a necessary precondition to the development of efficient economic institutions. It is the polity that specifies and enforces the economic rules of the game, and our knowledge of the essential conditions for the creation of such political institutions has not progressed much beyond the insightful observations of James Madison in the *Federalist Papers*.

However, the historical evidence cited provides essential clues to the evolutionary process in early modern Europe. A growing need for revenue in the face of the rising costs of warfare forced monarchs to create "representative bodies" – Parliament, Estates General, Cortes – and cede them certain rights in return for revenue. But at this point the stories diverge between the Netherlands and England, on the one hand, and much of the rest of Europe, on the other. In the former, the three considerations cited in section 5 led to the growth of representative government; in the latter they led to the persistence or revival of absolutist regimes with centralized decision making over the economy.

---

[4] See North (1990) and Greif (1993) for a summary of the game-theoretic and other analytical literature.

The contrasting subsequent history of the New World bears striking testimony to the significance of path dependence. In the case of North America, the English colonies were formed in the century when the struggle between Parliament and the crown was coming to a head. Religious and political diversity in the mother country was paralleled in the colonies. The general development in the direction of local political control and the growth of assemblies was unambiguous. Similarly the colonies carried over free and common socage tenure of land (fee simple, unrestricted ownership rights) and secure property rights in other factor and product markets. Independence did not cause a fundamental change in the dominant organizations and therefore was accomplished with a minimum of disorder.

The Spanish Indies conquest occurred at the precise time that the influence of the Castilian Cortes was declining and the monarchy of Castile, which was the seat of power in Spain, was firmly establishing centralized bureaucratic control over Spain and the Indies. The conquerors imposed a uniform religion and bureaucratic administration on already existing agricultural societies. When revolution led to colonial independence from Spain in the early nineteenth century wealth maximizing behavior by organizations and their entrepreneurs (political and economic) entailed getting control of, or influence over, the bureaucratic machinery; a struggle for power was the inevitable result. The result was ongoing internal disorder, which plagued Latin America throughout much of the nineteenth century as conflicting interest groups struggled for supremacy. One cannot make sense out of the contrasting subsequent history of the Americas north and south of the Rio Grande River without taking into account this historical background.[5]

## 7    An agenda for future research

Whatever lessons history provides arise from the fundamentals of human interaction over time. Let me draw some specific implications from the previous two sections that can form an agenda for future research.

We can deal briefly with economies that have failed to develop. These are cases in which the belief system, reflecting the historical experiences of that economy, failed to create institutions, economic and political, that will permit impersonal exchange. Markets remain local and/or poorly developed. As these economies became exposed to the larger world economy the institutional matrix typically spawned the development of

---

[5] The downstream consequences in the New World are discussed in more detail in North (1990, chap. 12). Robert Putnam tells a similar story of the contrasting development of different regions in Italy from the twelfth century onward in Putnam (1993).

organizations whose profitable opportunities predominantly favored redistributive activities.[6] Political organizations in such cases will appear similar to those postulated by the classic Virginia school of political economy, in which the state is little more than a theft machine. We do not have to look very far to see instances of such polities in Africa or, with some modification, in Latin America.

The obverse, the success stories, have been briefly described in the outlines of the Netherlands and England, where external experiences reinforced evolving belief systems in the direction of productive activities by the economic organizations. Political organizations in these cases have developed strong informal constraints – norms of behavior – that have constrained the behavior of the political actors. This point deserves special emphasis. The gradual development of informal norms of behavior that become deeply embedded in the society provides the stable underpinning to the adaptive efficiency characterizing the Western economies with a long history of growth. Adaptive efficiency refers to a process of institutional change that accompanies alterations in the dominant organizations and yet maintains order and stability.

This last point can serve as an opening wedge to explore some fundamentals of human interaction. What underlies the formation and evolution of institutions? It is the ubiquitous human drive to reduce uncertainty – to create order from disorder – that leads humans to scaffold both the mental models they possess, i.e., belief systems, and the external environment, i.e., institutions. But the very structure of the scaffolding is the key to whether this process of change can be orderly and in the case of economic growth can produce productivity growth as well.

Part of the scaffolding is an evolutionary consequence of successful mutations and is therefore a part of the genetic architecture of humans; part is a consequence of cultural evolution. Just what the mix is between the genetic architecture and the cultural heritage is in dispute. Evolutionary psychologists have stressed the genetic architecture in the scaffolding process at the expense of the role of the cultural heritage.[7] Others such

---

[6] The second economic revolution, the wedding of science to technology which began in the last half of the nineteenth century, is the source of modern economic growth and entails enormous specialization, division of labor, urban societies, and global markets. The organizational restructuring – economic, political, and social – necessary to capture the gains from trade with this technology has necessitated fundamental changes in societies. The institutional adjustments are difficult enough for developed economies and much more difficult for transition and third world economies. See North (1981, chap. 13) for further discussion.

[7] *The Adapted Mind* (Barkow, Cosmides, and Tooby 1992) is an excellent statement of this perspective.

as Stephen J. Gould have suggested that there is a lot of slack in the genetic architecture, which gives greater scope to cultural evolution. Certainly many of our personal preferences – hunger, thirst, sex – and perhaps some of our beliefs are genetically determined, but some preferences and most beliefs surely must be acquired.

Ken Binmore (1996) maintains that our genes probably do not insist that we prefer or believe certain things but that they do organize our cognitive processes in terms of preferences and beliefs. He maintains that we come equipped with algorithms that not only interpret the behavioral patterns we observe in ourselves and others in terms of preference-belief systems, but actively build such models into our own operating systems. The evolutionary advantage of such an inductive process is that new behaviors are tested against past experience in our internal laboratory. Humans enjoy the benefits of having the potential to learn a second best strategy in any game. Interactive learning is a two-stage affair in which we first receive a social signal that tells us how to behave, and then test the behavior against our preferences to see whether we wish to follow its recommendation.

An issue then is the extent to which the "mind is adapted" by several million years of genetic encoding versus cultural evolution; another, obviously related issue is just how the mind works. Both are central to answering the questions posed at the beginning of this essay, and we are far from settling them in either evolutionary psychology or cognitive science. Therefore what follows is tentative – more the intuitions of an economist in reading in both of these fields than any settled conclusions.

It is easier to be convinced of the genetic aptitude of human beings for language – a subject in which there is a lot of interesting research – than to be similarly convinced of the genetic aptitude for cooperation. No, that is too strong. There is evidence of the innate drive for cooperation. Recent research in experimental economics has reinforced the findings of evolutionary psychologists that human beings are preprogrammed to achieve cooperative outcomes in social exchange environments. Cooperation increases with communication, observability, opportunities to punish cheaters even at one's own expense, and ability to signal intentions without direct communication. In a recent paper, Elizabeth Hoffman, Kevin McCabe, and Vernon Smith summarize a large number of experimental game results:

> People invoke reward/punishment strategies in a wide variety of small group interactive contexts. These strategies are generally inconsistent with, but more profitable than, the non cooperative strategies predicted by game theory. There is, however, consistency with the game theoretic folk theorem which asserts that repetition favors cooperation, although

we observe a substantial use of reward/punishment strategies and some achievement of cooperative outcomes even in single play games.

Non cooperative outcomes are favored, however, where it is very costly to coordinate a cooperative outcome, in larger groups, and even in smaller groups under private information. In large groups interacting through markets using property rights and a medium of exchange, and with dispersed private information, non cooperative interaction supports the achievement of socially desirable outcomes. Experimental studies have long supported this fundamental theorem of markets. This theorem does not generally fail, however, in small group interactions because people modify their strict self-interest behavior, using reward/ punishment strategies that enable some approximation of surplus maximizing outcomes. Seen in the light of evolutionary psychology, such behavior is not a puzzle, but a natural product of our mental evolution and social adaptation.

But the immense variation in the forms it takes and its varying degrees of success make the cultural component of cooperative behavior an important part of the story. The problems of impersonal exchange suggest that whatever drives exist for innate cooperation must be supplemented by cultural factors in successful impersonal political and economic markets. Creating cooperative frameworks of economic and political impersonal exchange is at the heart of solving problems of societal, political, and economic performance.[8] While formal rules can help in creating such frameworks it is the informal constraints embodied in norms of behavior, conventions, and internally imposed codes of conduct that are critical.

How does the mind work? It is easy to be impressed by the immense strides of cognitive science in recent years. It is also clear that there is immense disagreement among cognitive scientists.[9] Is connectionism a promising research agenda? Is there a commonsense problem? Can we explain consciousness? On a far more mundane level but one we can build on, what is the relationship between rationality and intelligence, and is rationality deductive in nature, proceeding from the general to the specific? We are concerned to understand the way in which humans develop the fundamental equipment to put knowledge to work. "On the one hand, there is a large body of research that documents striking failures of naive humans when confronting relatively simple tasks in probability theory, decision making, and elementary logic. On the other hand, there is the continuing belief of psychologists and computer scientists that by understanding human problem solving performance we will

---

[8] See North (1990, chap. 2) for a discussion of the problems of cooperation in impersonal exchange.

[9] See Baumgartner and Payr (1995).

be better able to build machines that are truly intelligent."[10] The most promising approach to improving our understanding of how the mind works is one that suggests humans have a quite different kind of intelligence than is implied by the rationality postulate and its deductive corollary. Indeed the pattern-based reasoning of connectionist models is congenial to my understanding of the way belief systems evolve.

Here is the way a leading study on cognition characterizes the inductive process by which rule-based mental models are formed and revised in an ongoing process:

> The (cognitive) system is continually engaged in pursuing its goals, in the course of which problem elements are constantly being recategorized and predictions are constantly being generated. As part of this process, various triggering conditions initiate inductive changes in the systems rules. Unexpected outcomes provide problems that the system solves by creating new rules as hypotheses. Concepts with shared properties are activated, thus providing analogies for use in problem solving and rule generation. . . . the major task of the system may be described as reducing uncertainty about the environment. (Holland et al. 1986, 69)

## 8    Conclusion

This essay is little more than an agenda for research. How do we achieve economic growth, order, and a creative and democratic society? The issues go far beyond the customary agenda of economists and entail the cooperative interaction of social scientists in the elusive pursuit of understanding the process of societal change. That is a big enough challenge for all of us.

---

[10] Lopes and Oden (1991).

REFERENCES

Arthur, Brian (1989). "Competing Technologies, Increasing Returns, and Lock-In by Historical Events," *Economic Journal* 99(394): 116–31.

Barkow, Jerome H., Leda Cosmides, and John Tooby, eds. (1992). *The Adapted Mind: Evolutionary Psychology and the Generation of Culture.* New York: Oxford University Press.

Baumgartner, Peter, and Sabine Payr, eds. (1995). *Speaking Minds: Interviews with Twenty Eminent Cognitive Scientists.* Princeton, N.J.: Princeton University Press.

Baumol, William J. (1986). "Productivity Growth, Convergence, and Welfare: What the Long-Run Data Show," *American Economic Review* 76(5): 1072–85.

Binmore, Ken (1996). "Game Theory and the Social Contract." Draft manuscript.

Boulding, K. E. (1991). "What Is Evolutionary Economics?" *Journal of Evolutionary Economics* 1(1): 9–17.

David, Paul A. (1985). "Clio and the Economics of QWERTY," *American Economic Review* 75(2): 332–37.

Denzau, Arthur, and Douglass North (1994). "Shared Mental Models: Ideologies and Institutions," *Kyklos* 47(1): 3–31.

De Roover, Florence (1945). "Early Examples of Marine Insurance," *Journal of Economic History* 5: 172–200.

Elton, Geoffrey (1976). *The Tudor Revolution in Government*. Cambridge: Cambridge University Press.

Greif, Avner (1993). "Cultural Beliefs and the Organization of Society: A Historical and Theoretical Reflection on Collectivist and Individualist Societies," *Journal of Political Economy* 102(5): 912–50.

Hahn, Frank (1987). "Information, Dynamics and Equilibrium," *Scottish Journal of Political Economy* 34(4): 321–34.

Hoffman, Elizabeth, Kevin McCabe, and Vernon Smith. (1995). "Behavioral Foundations of Reciprocity: Experimental Economics and Evolutionary Psychology." Working paper, University of Arizona.

Holland, John H., Keith J. Holyoak, Richard E. Nisbett, and Paul R. Thagard (1986). *Induction: Processes of Inference, Learning, and Discovery*. Cambridge, Mass.: MIT Press.

Lopes, Lola, and Gregg C. Oden (1991). "The Rationality of Intelligence," in E. Eells and T. Murazewski, eds., *Probability and Rationality*, p. 200. Amsterdam: Rodopi.

Milgrom, Paul, Douglass North, and Barry Weingast (1990). "The Role of Institutions in the Revival of Trade: Law Merchants, Private Judges, and the Champagne Fairs," *Economics and Politics* 2(1): 1–24.

North, Douglass (1981). *Structure and Change in Economic History*. New York: W.W. Norton.

———(1990). *Institutions, Institutional Change, and Economic Performance*. Cambridge: Cambridge University Press.

———(1995). "The Paradox of the West," in Richard R. Davis, ed., *The Origins of Modern Freedom in the West*. Stanford, Calif.: Stanford University Press.

North, Douglass, and Robert Paul Thomas (1977). "The First Economic Revolution," *Economic History Review*, Second series, 30(2): 229–41.

Powers, Eileen (1991). *The Wool Trade in English Medieval History*. London: Clarendon Press.

Putnam, Robert (1993). *Making Democracy Work: Civic Traditions in Modern Italy*. Princeton, N.J.: Princeton University Press.

Stubbs, William (1896). *The Constitutional History of England*. Oxford: Clarendon Press.

# Index

509